A FIELD GUIDE TO
WESTERN
BUTTERFLIES

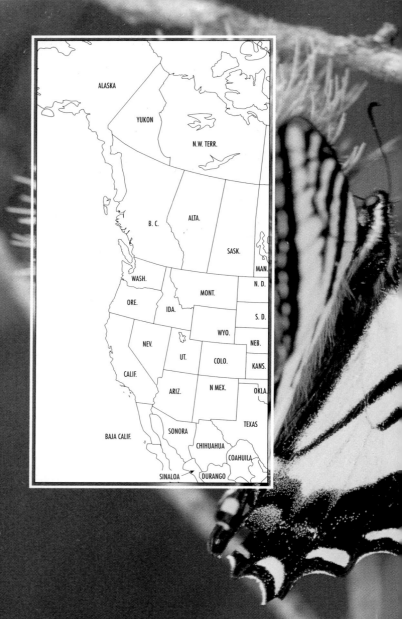

THE PETERSON FIELD GUIDE SERIES®

A FIELD GUIDE TO

WESTERN BUTTERFLIES

SECOND EDITION

PAUL OPLER

Illustrated by
AMY BARTLETT WRIGHT

SPONSORED BY THE NATIONAL AUDUBON SOCIETY,
THE NATIONAL WILDLIFE FEDERATION, AND
THE ROGER TORY PETERSON INSTITUTE

HOUGHTON MIFFLIN COMPANY
BOSTON   NEW YORK   1999

For information about permission to reproduce selections from this
book, write to Permissions, Houghton Mifflin Company,
215 Park Avenue South, New York, New York 10003.

PETERSON FIELD GUIDES and PETERSON FIELD GUIDE SERIES
are registered trademarks of Houghton Mifflin Company.

LIBRARY OF CONGRESS CATALOGING-IN-PUBLICATION DATA

Opler, Paul A.
A field guide to western butterflies / Paul Opler ;
illustrated by Amy Bartlett Wright. — 2nd ed.
p. cm. — (Peterson field guide series)
Rev. ed. of: Field guide to western butterflies / James W. Tilden
and Arthur Clayton Smith. 1986.
Includes bibliographic references (p.   ) and indexes.
ISBN 0-395-79152-9 (cloth). — ISBN 0-395-79151-0 (pbk.)
1. Butterflies—West (U.S.)—Identification. I. Tilden, James W.
(James Wilson), 1904– Field guide to western butterflies.
II. Title. III. Title: Western butterflies. IV. Series.
QL551.W3065   1998
595.78'9'0978 — dc21   98-43204

Drawings on pages 5, 6, 7, and 10 by Paul A. Opler. From A Field Guide
to Eastern Butterflies. Copyright © 1992 by Paul A. Opler.
Photographs by Paul Opler except where noted.

Book design by Anne Chalmers
Typeface: Linotype-Hell Fairfield; Futura Condensed (Adobe)

PRINTED IN THE UNITED STATES OF AMERICA
RMT 10 9 8 7 6 5 4 3 2 1

I dedicate this book to those persons who pioneered the study of western butterflies and to the authors of the first western butterfly guide, J. W. Tilden, my former mentor, and Arthur C. Smith. Their extensive years of toil, often under difficult conditions, prepared the table on which this book is served.

—P. O.

I dedicate this book to my young sons, John and Peter. May they continue to be fascinated by the intricacies of nature. And to all those who are now children, it is my hope that the fragility of our Earth is protected in order that there be many lifetimes of appreciation and learning.

—A. B. W.

The legacy of America's great naturalist, Roger Tory Peterson, is preserved through the programs and work of the Roger Tory Peterson Institute of Natural History. The RTPI mission is to create passion for and knowledge of the natural world in the hearts and minds of children by inspiring and guiding the study of nature in our schools and communities. You can become a part of this worthy effort by joining RTPI. Just call RTPI's membership department at 1-800-758-6841, fax 716-665-3794, or e-mail (webmaster@rtpi.org) for a free one-year membership with the purchase of this Field Guide.

EDITOR'S NOTE

Butterflies, the bright wings of summer, give beauty and movement to gardens, roadsides, and woodland trails. Like the birds, they are a litmus of the environment, sending out signals when things are out of kilter. They are an early warning system; thus the butterfly watcher inevitably becomes an environmentalist.

In North America, north of the Mexican border, there are more than 760 species of butterflies. The number of butterfly species west of the 100th meridian is greater than the number found to the east. This is because the West is more complex in its terrain, with a variety of habitats — the higher mountains, lower valleys, humid regions, arid deserts.

It is with alarm that we note that in the western states there are more butterflies on the endangered list than in the East. Several species have already become extinct and a number of others are endangered, most of them in California — the western state that has been subject to the greatest human pressures. One of the extinct species, the Xerces Blue, has been chosen as the symbol of the Xerces Society, a group invertebrate biologists and supporters who are concerned with conservation.

Gardening is a wonderful way to enhance your enjoyment of butterflies without harming them or their habitats. Some flower lovers plant their gardens not only with traditional favorites such as roses and tulips but also with zinnias, buddleias, and other plants whose nectar is attractive to passing butterflies. Inviting butterflies into your garden is an excellent way to observe them.

Whether you watch butterflies in your own garden or in fields and woodlands far from home, these beautiful creatures can help to further insights about our natural world.

ROGER TORY PETERSON

ACKNOWLEDGMENTS

The artist and I begin by expressing our love and thanks to our spouses John Wright and Evi Buckner, respectively, for their patience with our sometimes single-minded devotion to preparation of the illustrations and text for this Field Guide.

Critical to the quality of such publications are the comments, suggestions, and corrections of draft text provided by reviewers. I thank Richard Bailowitz, James Brock, Kenelm Philip, Ray Stanford, and Andrew D. Warren for critical review of selected portions of the text. Additional persons provided comments on the list of included species; these include John Emmel, Tom Emmel, Jeffrey Glassberg, J. Donald Lafontaine, Robert Pyle, Robert Robbins, and Kilian Roever.

Gordon Pratt wrote extensively about species problems and relationships in the *Euphilotes* blues and the *Apodemia mormo* group. Robert Robbins provided advice and information on several systematics problems involving North American and Neotropical hairstreaks. Jeffrey Glassberg advised on common name usage for western butterflies.

I thank the following for providing photographs of butterflies and early stages used as models for the color paintings on the plates or as text photographs: John Acron, Greg Ballmer, Jim Brock, Evi Buckner, Steve Cary, Whitney Cranshaw, James Ebner, C. D. Ferris, Jeffrey Glassberg, Frank Hedges, George Krizek, Jack Levy, David Nunnallee, James Troubridge, Idie Ulsh, and Ernest Williams.

For providing specimens used as models for paintings on the plates I am indebted to the American Museum of Natural History — James Miller, curator; Colorado State University — Boris Kondratieff, curator; Richard Holland; Gordon Pratt; Smithsonian Institution — John M. Burns, curator; Ray E. Stanford; University of Colorado — Virginia Scott, curator; and Andrew D. Warren.

I owe a debt of gratitude to J. Donald Lafontaine who worked with me to coordinate the scientific and common names of butterflies used in this book. Dr. Lafontaine also provided extensive discussion related to the systematics and biology of many Canadian butterflies that was invaluable in deciding how to treat certain northern species. I also thank Drs. Tom Emmel and John Emmel for allowing me to use material from their manuscript *Systematics of Western North American Butterflies.*

The range maps and range statements in the text are based on distribution records provided by hundreds of lepidopterists, museums, and literature references. My close friend Ray Stanford played the critical role by acting as compiler for all of this information gleaned from many sources, including his own extensive fieldwork. In each state there are usually one or two coordinators who keep track of the records provided by individual lepidopterists and butterfliers. At the risk of omitting some persons who made valuable contributions, I will list the compilers for each of the western states: Kenelm Philip, Alaska; Rich Bailowitz, Arizona; John Emmel, Robert Langston, and Sterling Mattoon, California; Ray Stanford, Colorado, Utah, and Wyoming; B. P. Bishop Museum, Hawaii; Nelson Curtis, Idaho; Charles Ely, Kansas; Steven Koehler, Montana; Neil Dankert and Steven Spomer, Nebraska; George Austin, Nevada; Steve Cary and Richard Holland, New Mexico; Ron Royer, North Dakota; Chuck Harp and John Nelson, Oklahoma; John Hinchliff, Oregon and Washington; Gary Marrone, South Dakota; and Roy Kendall, Texas. Special thanks to Sandy Upson who showed me unique specimens documenting new Arizona records. The names of most collectors who contributed may be seen in the acknowledgments to *Atlas of Western USA Butterflies* by Stanford and Opler.

Librarians at the Mid-continent Ecological Science Center, U.S. Geological Survey; and the Morgan Library, Colorado State University, both in Fort Collins, graciously assisted in searching for and providing reference materials vital to the writing of the text.

I wish to thank the editorial, design, production, and publicity departments at Houghton Mifflin in Boston for their invaluable help in initiating and completing this project. Ms. Lisa White led the effort for Houghton Mifflin and prevented many gaffes by the author.

PAUL A. OPLER

PREFACE

My interest in butterflies was kindled in 1948 when my friend Peter Robinson and I admired the butterflies enameled onto the lid of his mother's jewelry box. We set out with nets made of discarded nylon stockings (with runs) and wire coat hangers. Our only book was a small nature guide with crude paintings of 20 or so butterfly species — primarily eastern. Since we lived in California, of course almost none of the butterflies we encountered were in this book. Later I acquired W. J. Holland's *Butterfly Book* by mowing our lawn all summer to earn the $10 purchase price. My parents presented me with a copy of J. A. Comstock's *Butterflies of California* for my eleventh birthday. By the time I entered high school, I was already a long-time member of the Lepidopterists' Society and attended some of the first meetings of the Pacific Slope Section. I had many mentors, including a dealer, Robert G. Wind; the author of this guide's previous edition, J. W. Tilden, who later became my academic advisor at San Jose State University, and many others.

My interest in western butterflies and the field of entomology was further encouraged by my parents and teachers. My fifth-grade teacher, Mrs. McKeon, arranged for my friend and me to tour the entomology collection at the University of California at Berkeley. Similar kinds of encouragement continued through grammar school and high school, so that by the time I entered college at U.C. Berkeley (of course!), my path was already set.

I grew up with western butterflies and now live with my wife Evi in Colorado, so I have had extensive experience with western butterflies. As I grew up, on several occasions I took spring field trips to California's Mojave and Colorado Deserts. I also became quite familiar with the fauna of the coast ranges, central valley, and Sierra Nevada. In later years, I have studied, observed, and photographed butterflies in every state covered in this guide except Kansas and Washington. I have little personal experience in western Canada and have relied on the excellent recent books on butterflies of Canada, including Alberta and Manitoba.

I have included all species documented to occur in the West and have tried to provide the most important kinds of information for each species: What are the identifying marks? Where is its range and habitat? When does it fly? Unfortunately, there are so many named subspecies of western butterflies that space does not permit even their listing, let alone their description. A few notable subspecies are mentioned in the text where it seemed appropriate.

Chapters on butterfly biology, butterfly study, butterfly gardening, butterfly conservation, western habitats, and speciation and variation of western butterflies should make this book especially useful to the growing army of butterfly observers and photographers. Collectors will find it useful as well, but though collection is necessary to identify some difficult skipper species, most butterflies can be identified without being killed. The collection of specimens is still important in some instances, but I feel strongly that individuals should be collected only for useful purposes and should not merely be stockpiled.

CONTENTS

Map of Area Covered ii
Editor's Note vii
Acknowledgments viii
Preface x

1. How to Use This Book 1
2. About Butterflies 4
   Their structure, life history, and behavior
3. How to Study Butterflies 14
   Watching, photographing, and collecting
4. Butterfly Gardening 20
5. Conservation of Butterflies 24
6. Butterfly Distribution 27
7. Speciation and Variation of Western Butterflies 30

PLATES (See list on page xiii) 33

SPECIES ACCOUNTS

TRUE BUTTERFLIES: SUPERFAMILY PAPILIONOIDEA
8. Parnassians and Swallowtails: Papilionidae 125
9. Whites and Sulphurs: Pieridae 144
10. Harvester, Coppers, Hairstreaks, and Blues:
    Lycaenidae 185

11. Metalmarks: Riodinidae   255
12. Brushfoots: Nymphalidae   266

SKIPPERS: SUPERFAMILY HESPERIOIDEA
13. Skippers: Hesperiidae   372

  Life List of Western Butterflies   481
  Glossary   497
  References   503
  Index to Host and Nectar Plants   508
  Index to Butterflies   515

LIST OF ILLUSTRATIONS

Map of Area Covered   ii
Fig. 1. Parts of the butterfly   5
Fig. 2. Parts of butterfly wing areas and margins   6
Fig. 3. Butterfly wing veins   7
Fig. 4. The four life stages of the Monarch butterfly   10
Fig. 5. Some federally endangered and threatened butterflies   26
Fig. 6. Biomes and habitats of western North America   29

Range maps and photographs distributed throughout the book

LIST OF PLATES

1. Parnassians   34
2. Swallowtails   36
3. Swallowtails   38
4. Swallowtails   40
5. Swallowtails   42
6. Swallowtails   44
7. Whites   46
8. Whites and Marbles   48
9. Marbles and Orangetips   50

10. Sulphurs   52
11. Sulphurs   54
12. Sulphurs   56
13. Sulphurs and Yellows   58
14. Harvesters and Coppers   60
15. Coppers and Hairstreaks   62
16. Hairstreaks   64
17. Hairstreaks   66
18. Hairstreaks   68
19. Blues   70
20. Blues   72
21. Blues   74
22. Metalmarks and Snout   76
23. Heliconians, including Fritillaries   78
24. Fritillaries   80
25. Lesser Fritillaries   82
26. Checkerspots and Patches   84
27. Checkerspots, Crescents, and Elf   86
28. Crescents and Checkerspots   88
29. Anglewings, Tortoiseshells, and Ladies   90
30. Brushfoots and Admirals   92
31. Admirals, Leafwings, and Emperors   94
32. Morpho and Satyrs   96
33. Satyrs   98
34. Arctics and Royalty   100
35. Dull Firetip and Spread-wing Skippers   102
36. Spread-wing Skippers   104
37. Spread-wing Skippers   106
38. Spread-wing Skippers   108
39. Spread-wing Skippers   110
40. Skipperlings and Grass Skippers   112
41. Grass Skippers   114
42. Grass Skippers   116
43. Grass Skippers   118
44. Giant-Skippers   120

A FIELD GUIDE TO

WESTERN
BUTTERFLIES

How to Use This Book

This book replaces J. W. Tilden and A. C. Smith's 1983 Field Guide to Western Butterflies in the Peterson Field Guide Series. Now, although only 16 years have passed since its publication, discovery of additional butterfly species, many changes in nomenclature, expanded knowledge of species' life histories, and extensive new information on butterfly distribution have necessitated the preparation of this completely new Field Guide.

The sequence of species follows the 1981 Miller and Brown checklist and catalog of North American butterflies, except that the true butterflies (superfamily Papilionoidea) appear before the skippers (superfamily Hesperioidea). The choice of Latin generic and species names is conservative and generally follows those that appear in the North American Butterfly Association's list of common (and scientific) names for North American butterflies and other recent publications. Common name usage follows the North American Butterfly Association's list as closely as possible.

IDENTIFICATION

SPECIES INCLUDED: The number of butterflies west of the 100th meridian is greater than that to the east of it. Although I reported 524 butterfly species in my 1992 eastern butterfly guide, and only 512 western butterflies were treated in Tilden and Smith's 1983 western guide, there are more than 590 butterflies treated in the present work. This is because of new colonists and strays from Mexico being found in western Texas, southern New Mexico, and southern Arizona. The ranges of eastern butterflies not previously known west of the 100th meridian have been found in our territory. Additionally, several new species and butterflies of far eastern Russia have been found in Alaska and northern Canada. Detailed morphological and genetic studies of western butterflies have resulted in the splitting of several single species into groups of reproductively isolated "sibling species" (see Speciation and Variation of Western Butterflies, p. 31).

AREA COVERED: The area covered in this book is North America west of the 100th meridian and north of the Mexico-U.S. border: the western United States, including Hawaii, and western Canada, including the western Canadian arctic archipelago (see map opposite title page).

ILLUSTRATIONS: Most species are illustrated by color paintings executed by Amy Bartlett Wright. Virtually all resident butterfly species in the area covered, as well as most nonresidents (strays and temporary colonists), are illustrated. The color paintings are supplemented by 110 color photographs of butterflies that appear with the species accounts. A few butterflies are illustrated only by such photographs. We have selected the most diagnostic views to illustrate the species. In a first for a major North American field guide, the butterflies have been painted in natural postures. These paintings were based on color photographs of living butterflies taken in nature. When such photographs were not available or when we wished to show views not available in living postures, specimens from museums or private collections were used as models. In these cases the upperside is indicated by the portrayal of the left-hand wings and the body, the underside by wings pointed to the right without the body. In most cases we have tried to show that portion of the butterfly that can be used for identification without capture, but we have shown the upper surfaces of some butterflies that never perch with open wings. For example, most hairstreaks perch with the wings closed above the body. In some instances, however, the critical characteristics are on portions of the butterfly that can be seen only if the insect is netted. This will help collectors and those who wish to confirm a butterfly's identity with a specimen.

In addition to adult butterflies, paintings of the caterpillars and chrysalids of many species have been included on the plates. Those of many common butterflies are included, and enough of other species are shown that one should be able to place an unknown caterpillar or chrysalid at least to subfamily.

MEASUREMENTS: Size of each butterfly is given in both inches and millimeters, the latter in parentheses. In most cases these are based on actual measurements. These are intended to give the normal expanse of the butterfly from one wingtip to the other. In many butterflies, one sex is normally larger than the other. These differences are not mentioned in the species accounts unless they are extreme, but general tendencies are mentioned in the family or generic statements.

EARLY STAGES: Only the last instar of the caterpillars (larvae) is described, and that only in very general terms, since the book is intended as an identification guide to adult butterflies. The plants used as food by the caterpillars are listed. Common names for most plants are given in the text. Scientific names are given in the text only for unfamiliar or rare plants. The flight dates for the adult insects are given, and if the species ranges widely in the West, some indication of flight period differences in several areas is given. For butterflies found rarely as strays along the Mexican boundary, the months of occurrence are given, but the dates when the butterflies are known in their permanent range to the south in Latin America are also given. This will give a better idea of when the butterfly might be expected north of the Mexican border. When the number of distinct adult flights is known, this is given in parentheses following the flight period.

RANGE: The entire range of the butterfly is given, with greatest emphasis on its occurrence in western North America. If the butterfly also occurs in Eurasia, this fact is indicated by the word Holarctic. The occurrence in the West and the range in Latin America, including the butterfly's southern limit, is given in general terms. In addition to the text description, range maps are included for most species. These are placed with or near the species account. Distributional atlases and literature sources were used for distributional information to construct the range statements and maps. Major contributors and state compilers are listed in the acknowledgments. On the maps, magenta shading indicates the region where each butterfly is resident, while blue shading, if any, indicates places that the butterfly might appear as a stray or may colonize and become a temporary resident. Single dots indicate the extralimital appearance of strays where the species is not expected to appear on a regular basis.

HABITAT: The key to finding butterflies in nature often depends on a knowledge of their habitats. This knowledge is also an important aid to identification. For example, the very similar Western Tiger Swallowtail and Pale Swallowtail are found in very different habitats — the former in cities, gardens, or along streamcourses, the latter on hilltops or hillsides in the mountains. Knowledge of the habitats of tropical butterflies is often scanty, but I have made a good attempt to describe the habitats of these extralimital species. Strays often may be found in habitats not typical of their resident territory.

2

ABOUT BUTTERFLIES

WHAT ARE BUTTERFLIES?

Whenever I give a talk on butterflies, I am invariably asked, "What is the difference between butterflies and moths?" This question once had the facile answer, "Butterflies fly in the day, are brightly colored, have clubbed antennae, and lack the wing-coupling mechanism, the frenulum, possessed by most moths." Recently, a group of tropical American "moths" has been shown to possess the detailed structure of butterflies rather than that of geometrid moths, to which they had been assigned. These butterflies, then, are the Hedyliidae and are most closely related to the true butterflies (superfamily Papilionoidea). They are nocturnal and lack the clubbed antennae of most other butterflies.

Now when I am asked the butterfly versus moth question, I respond that "butterflies" are a related group of the order Lepidoptera. They *tend* to be primarily diurnal, and have clubbed antennae; but butterflies are really just part of the vast evolutionary variation in the order. Another way to put it is to say that butterflies are just "fancy moths." Butterflies have become popular partly because they are conspicuous and because there are neither too few nor too many species to pique our interest.

STRUCTURE

Butterflies share many traits with other related insects. The adults have compound eyes, antennae, three main body divisions (head, thorax, and abdomen), three pairs of legs, and a hard, chitinous exoskeleton (Fig. 1). They share with other higher Lepidoptera their two pairs of scale-covered wings, suctorial tubelike proboscis, and long filamentous antennae.

HEAD: Looking in greater detail, we find the antennae are made up of

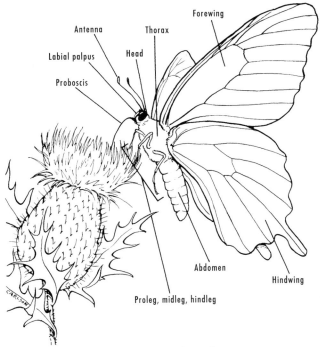

Figure 1. Parts of the butterfly

separate segments. The underside of the terminal club is the *nudum*. The antennal clubs of true butterflies are rounded, but in most skippers there is an extension, the *apiculus*. The adult's compound eyes are composed of a variable number of separate visual elements, the *ommatidia*. It has been shown that most insects, including butterflies, can see better in the ultraviolet wavelengths, including those not detectable by human sight. On the underside of the head, the coiled *proboscis* lies between the 2 three-segmented *labial palpi*. The antennae contain sensory organs and cells to help with balance, motion, and smell. The proboscis is used to take in fluids such as moisture from wet sand or mud, nectar from flowers, and fluids from ripe fruit, sap flows, carrion, or dung. The length of the proboscis is a good indication of the adult food habits. It is relatively long in nectar-feeding species, especially skippers, and is relatively short in butterflies that feed on sap flows or rotting fruit. The palpi serve as "book-ends" for the proboscis. They may be long and directed forward as in the Snout Butterfly or curved upward as in most gossamer wings.

THORAX: The thorax is composed of three segments: the *prothorax, mesothorax,* and *metathorax.* A pair of legs is attached to each thoracic segment, and the wings are attached to the mesothorax and metathorax. Each leg consists of several segments. Beginning at the leg's origin next to the body, these segments are the *coxa, trochanter, femur, tibia,* and five-segmented *tarsus.* At the end of each leg is a *tarsal claw* surrounded by a pad or *pulvillus.* The front legs (*prolegs*) of butterflies in some families are strongly reduced and are not used for walking. The best known of these are the brushfoots or Nymphalidae, but snouts, metalmarks, and gossamer wings have reduced front legs in at least one sex. Internally, the thorax is largely muscular, containing the muscles that move the wings and legs. The thoracic muscles in some butterflies may aid in warming the body through shivering.

ABDOMEN: The elongated abdomen contains the majority of the digestive, excretory, and reproductive organs. It also contains the most

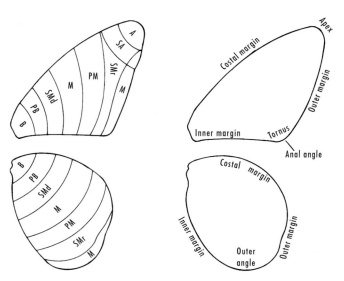

Figure 2. Parts of butterfly wing areas and margins

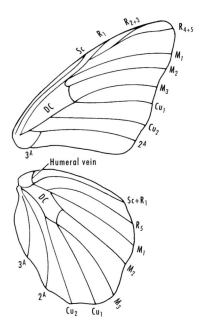

Figure 3. Butterfly wing veins

important energy storage structures, the *fat body*. At the end of the abdomen are the external genitalia. These structures have been shown to be of importance in the separation of butterfly species by taxonomists. Some species, especially certain tropical skippers, can be identified with certainty only by killing them and dissecting their genitalia. These species are mentioned in the book, but the associated genitalia features are not described.

WINGS: Adult butterflies have two pairs of wings, the *forewings* and the *hindwings*. The wings are used by butterflies not only for flight; they also play an important role in courtship, regulating body temperature, and avoiding predators. The colors and patterns on both surfaces of the wings are among the most obvious features of these insects, and they play an important role in the identification of species.

Each wing is made of two chitinous sheets that are pressed together and enclose a system of lengthwise veins, with a few strengthening cross structures. Both surfaces of the wings are covered with overlapping rows of tiny scales. The scales are usually finely ribbed and may be pigmented. *Androconia* are scales that appear to be modified dispensers of sex attractants—the *pheromones*. Androconia, or modified sex scales, occur on the wings, legs, or bodies of adults, usually males. On the wings they may be scattered or appear in specialized patches or "brands." The scales may be in folds of the forewings (some skippers) or hindwings (some swallowtails). Identifying field marks are usually located by referring to specific areas of the wings or specific veins or *cells*, or spaces enclosed by specific veins. Each of these areas, veins, and cells has a name; all are labeled in Figs. 2 and 3.

The areas and margins of the wings are shown on Fig. 3. Proceeding from the base toward the outer edge, these areas are *basal, postbasal, submedian, median, postmedian, submarginal,* and *marginal*. The margins are the *costal* for the leading margin, the *outer* for the outer edge, and the *inner* for the trailing edge. The tip of the forewing is termed the *apex,* while just in from the apex are the *apical* and *subapical* areas. The junction of the hindwing's outer and inner margins is the *tornus.*

The veins have had both letter and number systems devised by different workers. Current specialists prefer the letter system (Fig. 3). In a clockwise sequence (on right-hand wings) these veins or vein systems are lettered *Sc* (subcostal), *R* (radial), *M* (medial) *Cu* (cubital), *A* (anal). All but the subcostal have more than one branch, and these are numbered with subscripts proceeding from the most forward branch, e.g., R_1, R_2 R_5. As mentioned above, the areas between veins are the cells, and the most basal of these is termed either the *cell* or *discal cell*. The other cells are named for the vein or vein branch in front of them.

LIFE HISTORY

The life cycle of butterflies is termed complete, because there are four different stages: the *egg, larva* (caterpillar), *pupa* (chrysalis), and *adult* (Fig. 4). The complete life cycle is shared by other advanced insects such as beetles, flies, caddis flies, and wasps (*Holometabola*), but less advanced groups such as grasshoppers and true bugs (*Hemimetabola*) have only three stages: the egg, nymph, and adult. In butterflies, each life stage may proceed directly through its development. If there is no resting stage, the entire life cycle, from deposition of the egg to emergence of the adult, requires about a month for most butterflies. The egg hatches in about five days; the caterpillar stage, which involves four or five instars with a molt after each one, takes about 15 days; the adult emerges about 10 days after formation of the chrysalis. The summer generations of butterflies with more than one flight period each year develop directly in the manner described above.

Most species of butterflies have a resting stage at one or two points in their life cycle. If the rest is merely a slowing down of metabolism due to cold temperature, it is termed *hibernation*, but if it's a physiological arrest, usually triggered by a seasonal change in day length, it is called *diapause*. Diapause is a way that insects have evolved to space out their stages so that the adults emerge when weather is likely to be favorable and so that caterpillars hatch when there is food to eat. Hibernation or diapause occurs at distinctive times in the cycle of different species or higher groups. Some species, usually those of arid western habitats, can spend several years in diapause, usually in the pupal stage.

EGGS: Females lay eggs singly or in groups. They are usually laid directly on the host plant, but in some species, such as fritillaries (*Speyeria*), they may be dropped on the ground near dried violets, or they may be attached to other plants or objects next to the host. The female detects the proper host plant using sensory cells on her prolegs or antennae. Inside the egg, the development of the insect embryo takes place. If development proceeds directly, the egg will hatch in a period ranging from a few days to about a week.

LARVAE: The young caterpillar's first solid food may be its eggshell. Depending on the species, the caterpillar either begins to eat immediately after hatching, or it enters diapause, as do most fritillaries (*Speyeria*). Young caterpillars usually eat more tender materials (young leaves or flower buds) than they do in their later instars. Since the skin of the caterpillar does not grow or stretch, it must be exchanged for a new one several times during larval development. As the caterpillar grows, the new skin is developing underneath the old one. When its skin becomes relatively taut, molting is stimulated; the old skin splits, and the larva emerges with a new skin and head capsule. Caterpillars usually pass through four or five instars, and the color patterns and sizes and distribution of *setae* (the "hairs" of the caterpillar) usually differ with each instar. Some species may undergo diapause or hibernation in the caterpillar stage. Caterpillars of Cabbage Whites (*Pieris rapae*) and sulphurs (*Colias*) usually hibernate, while those of many woodnymphs and satyrs (subfamily Satyrinae) undergo diapause.

Most caterpillars live solitarily, but those of several species, usually those whose eggs are laid in groups, feed communally, at least for the first few instars. Examples of such species are com-

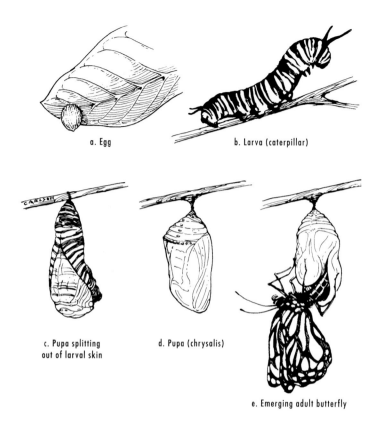

a. Egg

b. Larva (caterpillar)

c. Pupa splitting
out of larval skin

d. Pupa (chrysalis)

e. Emerging adult butterfly

Figure 4. The four life stages of the Monarch butterfly

mon in the brushfoots, for example, checkerspots, patches, crescentspots, tortoiseshells (including the Mourning Cloak), and emperors. In other families, communal feeding is rare; among our residents only the Golden-Banded Skipper *(Autochton cellus)* is known to have such behavior.

Relatively few butterflies have caterpillars that feed in the open during broad daylight. Most live in folded or bunched leaf shelters or hide during the day under loose bark or in leaf litter. Caterpillars found feeding in the open are either distasteful or possess physical deterrents, such as spines, that discourage would-be predators. The searching ability of insect parasites, usually tiny wasps or flies, is so highly developed that they usually discover and parasitize most butterfly eggs and caterpillars. Remember that, on average, only two of the hundreds of eggs laid by each female butterfly must complete their development and reproduce to ensure the next generation.

CHRYSALIDS: When the caterpillar completes its feeding, it usually leaves the host plant and wanders to find a sheltered spot where it will form its chrysalis. The chrysalis is an immobile (except for giant-skippers), nutritious object that would make a welcome meal for many a predator. Different species pupate in different sorts of situations. For example, many gossamer wings form their pupae in leaf litter or loose soil under their host plant, while swallowtails often pupate on tree trunks. The caterpillars of most butterflies make a silk mat into which the cremaster, a hook at the distal end of the chrysalis, is set. This is done in one deft movement as the skin of the last caterpillar instar is discarded. Inside the chrysalis, the structures of the caterpillar are broken down and the adult structures are formed.

ADULTS: Upon emergence from the chrysalis, the adult butterfly must expand its wings by pumping its body fluid (called hemolymph — insects do not have blood in the usual sense) through its still-soft veins. After expanding, the adult usually rests for an hour or more before the wings can support flight.

Each butterfly species has a different adult life span, and different generations of the same species may have very different life expectancies. Some butterflies have a life expectancy of only a few days upon emergence. The Barred Yellow (*Eurema daira*) and several blues are examples of such short-lived species. In most situations a life span of a week or two is normal, and much longer life spans are exceptional. Butterflies that have delayed egg development, such as some fritillaries (*Speyeria*) and wood-nymphs (*Cercyonis*), or that overwinter as adults may have much longer life spans. The winter (dry-season) generation of many tropical butterflies, such as might be found in southeastern Arizona or west Texas, must survive for at least three or four months to lay eggs at the beginning of the next growing season. The generation of the Monarch (*Danaus plexippus*) that migrates to the California coast or central Mexico for the winter lives six or seven months, whereas the adults of the summer generations live only a few weeks. Female Zebras (*Heliconius charithonius*) develop their eggs slowly and may lay only one or two eggs a day over a period of several months. The northern butterflies that overwinter as adults, tortoiseshells (*Nymphalis milberti* and *N. vaualbum*) and anglewings or commas (*Polygonia*), may live for six months. The

Mourning Cloak (*Nymphalis antiopa*), which usually has only a single generation each year, is the butterfly longevity champion at 10 to 11 months. You can determine the life span of butterflies near where you live by capturing them, putting distinctive marks on their wings with square-tipped marking pens, and then watching for them on subsequent days and weeks.

FINDING A MATE: The adult butterfly spends its time searching for mates, mating, laying eggs, and in maintenance activity (feeding and resting). Each butterfly species has one of two primary mate-locating strategies. The males of *patrolling* species fly through likely habitats in search of receptive females, while the males of *perching* species select a perch on top of a leaf, twig, or rock, and fly out to investigate passing insects in hopes that they may be receptive females. If the passing insect is a receptive female, the male forces her to the ground and the steps leading to mating take place. If the passing insect is another male, who might also have a nearby perch, the two will often engage in an upward spiraling flight, after which one male, usually the resident, will return to his perch or another one nearby. If the passing insect is another species (or if the butterfly encounters an inanimate object) the male will almost immediately return to his perch after only a perfunctory investigation. This behavior of perching males has been termed territoriality by some and aggressiveness by others. But only in a few butterflies does it seem that the males actually *defend* an established territory, although the spiral flight of interacting males does seem to spread the males more evenly through the environment. In mountainous areas, especially in western North America, perching males will select hilltops as their perching sites, and unmated females will orient toward hilltops. The perching mate-location method seems to work best for species that are relatively rare in the environment.

FEEDING: Adults have only a suctorial proboscis and cannot chew solid foods. As a result, they feed on sugar-rich or proteinaceous fluids to renew their energy reserves. Many butterflies feed on the nectar of flowers, and many others, especially brushfoots, feed on sap flows, rotting fruit, bird droppings, or dung. Freshly emerged butterflies, usually males of patrolling species, gather in groups on wet sand or mud to imbibe water that is rich in salts. It is thought that this salt intake may have a role in temperature regulation, especially cooling.

KEEPING WARM: Butterflies are cold-blooded; that is, they have no internal mechanism that keeps their body temperature at a constant level. In order to become active and engage in flight and other daily activities, butterflies must warm their bodies to a certain level. This is usually done by basking in full sun. Some butterflies are *lateral* *baskers;* these species sit with their wings closed, holding them perpendicular to the sun. These species may have black or otherwise darkened scales under their wings, especially where they overlap the abdomen. *Dorsal baskers* perch with their wings opened to take full advantage of the sun. In cool or cloudy weather, butterflies may not fly at all, or they may have to alight frequently to bask.

An adult butterfly has a schedule that it adheres to each day. Flight usually does not begin until after eight o'clock (daylight-saving time), although some tropical skippers may become active before sunrise. During the day, males may restrict their courtship activities to particular hours or may seek mates all day. In any event, mating pairs are usually seen only during a characteristic part of the day, and egg laying (oviposition) is usually limited to a few hours. For example, sulphurs *(Colias)* usually lay eggs only around midday.

ROOSTING: Each species of butterfly has a characteristic roosting posture and location that it assumes during inclement weather and overnight. Most butterflies perch with their wings closed, with their head directly downward, and their antennae straight ahead. Many tropical butterflies that roost under large leaves do so with their wings open, and duskywings *(Erynnis)* roost with their wings wrapped around a small twig. Some species roost under leaves, some on tree trunks, and some in low, dense vegetation. A few tropical species roost in caves or under cliff hangings. Most butterflies roost alone, but some form communal roosts. Most notable are the roosts that heliconians, including the Zebra, return to night after night.

HOW TO STUDY BUTTERFLIES

Butterfly awareness and appreciation among the public has increased appreciably in recent years. The fact that large animals are not readily accessible to city-dwellers and suburbanites has increased interest in bird watching and appreciation of invertebrates. Birders who seek new challenges are another element in the growing army of butterfliers. Most users of this book will probably be those interested in observing and photographing butterflies, while those interested in starting or continuing a collection will be in the minority. Concern about conservation and the prevention of inhumane treatment to all animals is in part behind these trends.

BUTTERFLY WATCHING

Butterfly watching or "butterflying" can be carried out casually, with little or no equipment. On the other hand, you may get involved in scientific study through observation, or you may wish to take trips to remote locations to see butterflies not found near your normal haunts.

WHAT TO TAKE: Obviously, you should have a copy of this Field Guide. Binoculars or opera glasses are very helpful. The binoculars should be capable of focusing at close distances (5 or 6 feet). They should have low magnification (6–8×) and good light-gathering capability. Bring a small pocket notebook to record your observations. Write down the date and time of each observation. If you wish to capture specimens in order to make a more accurate identification or so that a small group may observe a common species more closely, you should have an insect net. You should have a pair of forceps; the tongs used for handling postage stamps are excellent. Be sure that you handle any butterfly gently by the forewing costal margin. You may want small glassine envelopes or small transparent containers in which to hold butterflies briefly so that they can be passed around in a small group and then released.

WHEN TO WATCH: In southern California and southern Arizona, adult butterflies may be observed throughout the year on any day warm enough for butterfly activity—generally above 60°F (15°C). As you move northward or to higher elevations, the butterfly season will be increasingly brief. In the tundra or above the timberline, the butterfly season lasts about two months, mid-June to mid-August. At middle latitudes in the West, look for butterflies beginning in April. You may expect to find them until there have been nights with temperatures below freezing.

The best conditions are found on clear, calm, warm days. Normally butterflies begin their daily activity about nine o'clock and continue until about four o'clock, but in mid-summer, when it is warmest, some butterflies become active shortly after sunrise and some remain active until after six o'clock. If you're interested in photographing butterflies, go out early when they are just becoming active or on overcast days when they're not fully active.

You should look for butterflies at various times during the season, as different species have different flight periods. Some have just a single flight in the spring; some have a single flight in the summer or fall; many have two or more flights during the year.

In early spring, as buds are just beginning to open, over much of the East you can find Pacific Orangetips, the first whites, Spring Azures, Silvery Blues, elfins, duskywings, overwintered adults of Mourning Cloaks, tortoiseshells, and commas. Most swallowtails, brushfoots, and true skippers don't begin their flights until late spring or early summer, while mid- to late summer is a time when you should expect hairstreaks, fritillaries, some skippers, and immigrants from farther south. Go butterfly watching at different times during the year and keep detailed notes so that you can make your own local butterfly calendar. In Canada, on the Great Plains, and in the Southwest, the timing may be different. In the arctic and subarctic regions, you can find almost all of the species over a period of several weeks in June and July; on the plains, the butterfly fauna is limited, and the early spring species may be absent; while in the most southern areas, the best seasons may vary. In southern California, March to June seems best, while in southeastern Arizona, most residents and butterfly colonists from Mexico are present during July to October.

WHERE TO FIND BUTTERFLIES: Butterflies can be found in any habitat where suitable plants are found, even in cities and suburbs. Many habitats have species found only there, and many species are limited geographically. To find all of the butterflies near your home, you will have to visit each habitat. After becoming familiar with all of the local butterflies, you may wish to travel to more exotic hunting grounds.

To find the different habitats in your area, carefully study the chapter on butterfly distribution and decide which habitats are likely to be found in your vicinity. There are many butterfly habitats in the area covered by this book, but most can be broadly characterized as forests, grasslands, or wetlands. There are many forms of each type, especially when you consider latitude, soil type, and topography. Investigate all of the possible local habitat types that are found on land with public access. There are many well-known sites in the West where special butterflies may be found. You can get an idea about some of these from the states listed for each species in the species accounts.

BUTTERFLY PHOTOGRAPHY

Photographing butterflies is an excellent way to build a collection of the common species in your area, or to document rare species or different kinds of behavior. (Remember that some butterflies, especially certain skippers, cannot be identified without dissection.) Photographing a butterfly is much more difficult than catching one in a net.

EQUIPMENT: You should have a good 35mm single lens reflex camera (SLR) with a lens that can focus at close range and provide a relatively large image of the butterfly on film. A macro lens is best, but extension rings on a normal portrait lens is a less expensive and workable, albeit awkward, substitute. The focusing distance is indicated by the length of the lens. I use a 105mm macro lens and find it much better than a 55mm macro. Others use telephoto macro lenses, with or without zoom capability. You may find that you have focusing problems if you try to use a telephoto lens without a tripod.

Most high-quality cameras and films allow you to take excellent photographs without the use of artificial flash. Such photographs have the benefit of natural light and show natural backgrounds instead of the annoying unnatural colors and black background that one often gets with the use of flash. If you decide to use electronic flash you should obtain a unit that is capable of adjusting its strength based on the distance from the camera to the subject. Many cameras now have a built-in fill flash that is more than adequate. Some professionals use ring light flashes or two flashes mounted on brackets on either side of the camera.

If you specialize in photographing the life stages of butterflies, you should use a tripod. A tripod steadies the camera, allowing you to more easily photograph the life stages. If you specialize in taking photos of free-living butterflies, you will want a bellows that lets you take close-ups of tiny objects, such as butterfly eggs and young caterpillars.

HOW TO PHOTOGRAPH: You should first be familiar with your camera. I usually have my camera set on the smallest aperture possible, f22, or f32. Use film with the slowest speed possible for your setup. I usually use ASA 64 or 100. Take a trial roll or two at various settings duplicating the conditions you expect to encounter.

Approach butterflies in nature slowly. Keep as low as possible, and avoid letting your shadow fall on your subject. Be patient, as you may need to approach a butterfly several times before you can take a picture. Often you may have to inch forward on your knees, kneel on hard rocky surfaces (kneepads may help), or even lie flat on the ground. You may have to wade in water or kneel in mud if you want your photo badly enough. When you do find a cooperative subject, you should take several pictures at different exposures and poses. I usually take pictures at several settings and take vertical as well as horizontal frames.

WHEN TO PHOTOGRAPH: Early in the morning or late in the afternoon are good times to find butterflies that are not too active. Partly cloudy days with somewhat lower than seasonal temperatures will provide good subject cooperation. Learn to recognize the situations in which butterflies are more likely to be successfully approached. Don't try to photograph butterflies in midair! Butterflies taking nectar at flowers or imbibing fluids are usually approachable, as are mating pairs. Basking butterflies and perching males can be photographed with relative ease. Females that are ovipositing or courting pairs usually move too often to be photographed.

RAISING BUTTERFLIES

Raising butterflies is an excellent way to obtain photographs of all the life stages of a butterfly, and it is also the best way to obtain perfect specimens for your collection.

You can raise butterflies either by obtaining eggs or by searching for caterpillars. The former ensures that you observe the entire life cycle, but it involves a much greater effort than if you start with partly grown caterpillars.

Butterfly eggs may be obtained either by following egg-laying female butterflies or by caging mated females. To find butterfly eggs, watch for females engaged in their characteristic egg-laying behavior. Such a female will be found fluttering slowly near plants, periodically touching down and "tasting" plants with the tarsi on her front legs. If the plant is the correct species and is acceptable, the female will deposit one or more eggs, depending on whether she belongs to a species that lays its eggs in batches, and then flutter off in search of the next spot to place an egg. You may follow along behind and collect the number of eggs that you need. Collect each egg on a small piece of the host plant to which it is attached.

Familiarity with the host plants of local butterflies and the time of day that each prefers to lay eggs will make your egg-gathering efforts easier.

Since the females of many species are difficult to follow in nature, you may want to try to obtain eggs from captive females. Different butterflies require different approaches. The best method for most species is to confine females in fine wire mesh cages; these should be large enough so that the butterflies can flutter around freely. You should provide fresh bouquets for larval food and nectar sources. Several bright lamps should be focused on the cage so that the female butterflies cannot find dark corners; if they do so they will not lay eggs. Search the larval host plant each day for eggs and remove them for special handling.

Some butterflies will lay eggs only under special conditions. The best way to obtain eggs from fritillaries (genus *Speyeria*) is to confine gravid females in inflated paper bags.

Keep the eggs in small vials or petri dishes with small pieces of damp paper toweling or filter paper. When the caterpillars hatch out, place them in separate small containers with small amounts of fresh food plant. Never place too many caterpillars in a single container, as overcrowding will often result in disease or cannibalism. Keep damp paper towels or filter paper in the container. Do not let the insides of the containers become either too wet or too dry.

You may also find caterpillars in nature by searching their host plants at the proper season. You should know what part of the plants the caterpillars feed on, and you should be aware that many species construct shelters within which they hide during rest periods — usually during the day.

Remember that butterfly eggs, caterpillars, and chrysalids collected in nature are likely to already have been found by tiny parasitic wasps and flies, and that often half or more of the caterpillars that you find will produce adult parasites instead of adult butterflies.

Whenever you collect caterpillars, make sure that you have an adequate fresh food plant growing nearby or a supply kept in a refrigerator. Growing a variety of local caterpillar plants in your yard is a good idea if you plan to do much rearing. Remember not to use pesticides on or near plants you plan to feed to your "livestock."

You may use a variety of containers to raise your caterpillars. Plastic sandwich boxes or Tupperware may work for small caterpillars, but caterpillars that will eventually produce chrysalids that need to hang should be kept in containers such as small cages or large wide-mouthed jars. Control the moisture in your rearing containers carefully, and provide clean paper toweling every day or so. Remove the caterpillar droppings (frass) if they become too messy or moldy.

As the caterpillars near full size, make sure that they have suitable sites on which to hang or form their chrysalids. Provide sticks or pieces of bark. The chrysalids, once formed, may be kept in a drier environment than that of the caterpillars. The chrysalids of single-brooded species may need to overwinter before they will hatch. You may keep chrysalids in your refrigerator until the following spring.

The chrysalids of some swallowtails, orangetips, and marbles may enter a state of physiological arrest (diapause) and not produce adult butterflies for two or three years. The chrysalids of these species should be kept under natural light and temperature conditions. Sometimes placing water droplets on swallowtail chrysalids each day will help them hatch more readily.

Watch your rearing containers at least daily for signs that the chrysalids are getting ready to produce an adult. Such chrysalids will usually turn dark, and within 24 hours of emergence, you will be able to see the adult's wing pattern (in miniature) through the now transparent shell of the chrysalid. When the adult butterflies hatch, make sure that they have enough room to hang and let their wings spread, expand, and dry. After their wings have hardened, you may photograph them in your garden and then release them, or you may want to keep them for your collection.

BUTTERFLY GARDENING

Planting butterfly nectar plants and caterpillar food plants is an excellent way to increase the number and variety of butterflies in your yard. Whether you live in a garden apartment, in a separate residence, or on a farm, there are ways to increase your enjoyment of butterflies.

Today, we have a better understanding of how caterpillars and adult butterflies use food resources, and this understanding has considerably improved our ability to attract butterflies and fulfill their needs.

When you plan your butterfly garden, you should be aware of several principles. First, of course, you should be familiar with general gardening techniques. You should also know the common butterfly species in your vicinity and include both their adult nectar plants and caterpillar food plants to the extent that this is practical. If your yard lacks caterpillar food plants, you will attract only a few butterflies that happen to wander by. Similarly, if your yard lacks nectar plants, the butterflies that your yard produces will fly elsewhere in search of "greener pastures."

Place your nectar plants (Table 1) in patches, and include a variety of species that flower in different seasons so that your garden will be continually attractive from spring through fall. Patches of plants that flower at the same time are much more attractive to butterflies than a single plant with only a few flowers.

If you live on a farm that already has flowery fields or meadows, you may not need to plant a separate garden. If you have limited space, you can still plant a few attractive plants in flower boxes or other containers.

If you have the space, a separate garden planted especially for butterflies will be most successful. Gardening principles may dictate that trees, shrubs, and some other perennials be planted to the garden's back or sides. Remember that most butterflies love sun and shun shade, so plan the garden's exposure accordingly. If your garden is too shady, open it up by severely pruning or cutting back selected trees or tall shrubs.

You can vary the diversity of your garden by adding large rocks, small hills, and different soils. Take advantage of your yard's special features. For example, if you have a hilltop or a small stream, you might plan your garden to blend with these natural features.

Butterflies are encouraged by weediness. If you can leave a few weeds and let your lawn include some dandelions and clovers, you will see more butterflies. Avoid or minimize the use of pesticides, either insecticides or herbicides, on your property. Plan your vegetable garden so that you include sufficient cabbage family plants (cabbage, turnips, broccoli, kale, etc.) and carrot family plants (carrots, dill, parsley) to account for the needs of both your family and butterflies.

Which plants to include in your butterfly garden will depend on your location as well as the kinds of butterflies found in your region. Some plants that do very well in one site may be failures in others. I have listed nectar plants that will do well in much of our area together with others that do best in a few regions in Table 1.

COMMON NAME	LATIN NAME
abelia	*Abelia* species
bee balm	*Monarda didyma*
bougainvillea	*Bougainvillea* species
butterflybush	*Buddleia* species
butterfly milkweed	*Asclepias tuberosa*
common lilac	*Syringa vulgaris*
dame's-rocket	*Hesperis matronalis*
French lavender	*Lavandula dentata*
French marigold	*Tagetes patula*
lantana	*Lantana camara*
rabbitbrush	*Chrysothamnus nauseosus*
seepwillow	*Baccharis glutinosa*
verbena	*Verbena* species
wild buckwheat	*Eriogonum* species
wild lilacs, buckbrush	*Ceanothus* species
zinnia	*Zinnia* species

Table 1. Nectar plants for western butterfly gardens

There are many other kinds of flowers visited by butterflies. You can find out which ones are most successful in your area by visiting other yards, gardens, or nearby fields.

There is a greater variety of caterpillar food plants than nectar plants. This information is included in the species accounts. A few caterpillar plants that are successful over much of the West are listed in Table 2.

Caterpillar food plants may also include shrubs and trees in your yard as well as grasses in your lawn. I have already mentioned your vegetable garden, and you may encourage a few weeds such as mallows (*Malva*), asters, and lamb's-quarters (*Chenopodium album*). If you live in a rural area, you should ask your county extension agent whether the culture of some plants such as thistles and milkweeds is prohibited.

Some butterflies do not visit flowers, and you may wish to enhance your property for these species as well. Most commas, leafwings, emperors, and wood-nymphs seldom visit flowers, but feed on rotting fruit, sap flows, dung, bird droppings, or carrion instead. Although you will probably not wish to scatter carcasses or fresh dung about your yard, you can place overripe fruit or sugar mixtures in shady areas where these forest dwellers might find them.

Male butterflies, primarily species that patrol for mates, visit

COMMON NAME	LATIN NAME
alfalfa	*Medicago sativa*
beardtongues	*Penstemon* species
Bermuda grass	*Cynodon dactylon*
cabbage, broccoli	*Brassica* species
carrot, dill, parsley	Apiaceae
cassias	*Cassia* species
fennel	*Foeniculum vulgare*
hackberry	*Celtis* species
hollyhock	*Alcea rosea*
lupines	*Lupinus* species
oaks	*Quercus* species
passionvines	*Passiflora* species
pipevines	*Aristolochia* species
willows	*Salix* species

Table 2. Caterpillar host plants for western butterfly gardens

moist sand or mud where they imbibe fluids rich in salts. This behavior is not completely understood, but you might experiment by keeping a wet sand patch or wet sand barrel in a sunny spot in or adjacent to your garden.

Over time you may want to adjust the composition of your garden by adding or substituting different varieties and species. Remember that you should not remove native plants from the wild. You can obtain plants or seeds of native species from specialty nurseries. Seeds or plants of weedy exotics may be removed from vacant lots or fields, but you should first seek permission from the landowner.

5

CONSERVATION OF BUTTERFLIES

Butterflies, as well as other insects, have finally begun to be considered "wildlife," living organisms worthy of conservation attention and concern. The United States Endangered Species Act of 1973, as well as many state and provincial laws, provide the means to recognize, protect, and manage declining butterfly populations. Moreover, private conservation organizations and local jurisdictions may also take actions to protect habitats of endangered species.

Since at least the arrival of European colonists, habitat change and loss due to residential, agricultural, and commercial development has resulted in profound changes in the composition of western butterfly communities. Some species have become rarer, others have become more abundant and widespread, and exotic species from Europe and tropical America have been introduced here. A new host of European weeds have formed plant communities in disturbed areas to which many of our native butterflies have adapted.

Declining species may require intervention at several levels. At the first, local populations may decline or disappear, while at the second, a species may decline throughout much of its range. In the first instance, local citizens should call these changes to the attention of community leaders and conservation groups; while rangewide changes should be of national, state, or provincial concern. Species or subspecies with naturally small ranges or narrow habitat preferences should be watched especially closely.

A number of western butterflies, mostly highly localized subspecies, are protected by federal law as endangered or threatened species under provisions of the U.S. Endangered Species Act (Table 3). Other species and subspecies may be recognized as of special concern or sensitive by individual states and provinces. In the West, a number of habitats have declined since the arrival of European colonists, and the butterflies in these habitats are generally much rarer as a result. Some seriously declining habitats include native unplowed prairies, many wetlands, old-growth forests, streamside vegetation, spring-fed meadows and seeps, and unique coastal habitats, such as salt-spray meadows, dunes, and serpentine grassland. Aggressive introduced exotic weeds are competing with and replacing native plants throughout the West. Among the more serious are leafy spurge, Canada Thistle, Whitetop, Wild Oats, Smooth Brome, knapweeds, and sweet clovers. In much of California and Hawaii, exotic plants dominate most habitats below 2,000 feet in elevation.

FUTURE OF CONSERVATION

Those of us who collect and study butterflies should treat our rich heritage with care and responsibility. We should not collect specimens from small local colonies that are threatened with extinction, and we should not collect huge numbers from any population for whimsical purposes. The Lepidopterists' Society has formulated a policy with regard to collection of specimens, and this has been adopted by several other organizations. Anyone who collects these insects should study its provisions and recommendations.

COMMON NAME	LATIN NAME	STATES
* San Bruno Elfin	*Callophrys mossii bayensis*	Calif.
Smith's Blue	*Euphilotes enoptes smithi*	Calif.
* El Segundo Blue	*Euphilotes battoides allyni*	Calif.
Palos Verdes Blue	*Glaucopsyche lygdamus palosverdesensis*	Calif.
Lotis Blue	*Lycaeides idas lotis*	Calif.
* Mission Blue	*Icaricia icarioides missionensis*	Calif.
Lange's Metalmark	*Apodemia mormo langei*	Calif.
* Callippe Silverspot	*Speyeria callippe callippe*	Calif.
Behren's Silverspot	*Speyeria zerene behrensii*	Calif.
Myrtle's Silverspot	*Speyeria zerene myrtleae*	Calif.
* Oregon Silverspot	*Speyeria zerene hippolyta*	Calif., Ore., Wash.
* Uncompahgre Fritillary	*Boloria improba acrocnema*	Colo.
* Bay Checkerspot	*Euphydryas editha bayensis*	Calif.
* Quino Checkerspot	*Euphydryas editha quino*	Calif.
Laguna Mountain Skipper	*Pyrgus ruralis lagunae*	Calif.
Pawnee Montane Skipper	*Hesperia leonardus montana*	Colo.

Table 3. Federally endangered and threatened western butterflies.
* Pictured in Fig. 5, p. 26.

San Bruno Elfin (*Incisalia mossii bayensis*).
Endangered. San Bruno Mts. (Jim Ebner)

El Segundo Blue (*Euphilotes battoides allyni*).
Endangered. Redondo Beach, Calif. (Jim Ebner)

Mission Blue (*Icaricia icarioides missionensis*).
Endangered. San Bruno Mts., Calif. (Jim Ebner)

Uncompahgre Fritillary (*Boloria improba acrocnema*).
Endangered. San Juan Mts., Colo. (Paul Opler)

Oregon Silverspot (*Speyeria zerene hippolyta*).
Threatened. Oregon coast. (Paul Opler)

Callippe Fritillary (*Speyeria callippe callippe*).
Endangered. San Bruno Mts., Calif. (Jim Ebner)

Quino Checkerspot (*Euphydryas editha quino*).
Endangered. Riverside Co., Calif. (Jim Ebner)

Bay Checkerspot (*Euphydryas editha bayensis*).
Endangered. Santa Clara Co., Calif. (Paul Opler)

BUTTERFLY DISTRIBUTION

The distribution of western butterflies is dynamic, even without the influence of humanity's effects on the biosphere. Each species has a unique distribution that changes from year to year, as some populations contract or die out while others expand or are formed anew by colonists and migrants.

Ecologists and biogeographers have devised many schemes that help us understand the general, broad-scale patterns of animal and plant distributions. I prefer to briefly discuss regions, some of which are termed biomes, that seem to possess a number of unique or geographically limited butterflies (Fig. 5).

1. **CHIHUAHUAN DESERTS AND RANGES.** Extending from extreme southeast Arizona, southern New Mexico, and west Texas north to southeastern Colorado. Some butterflies limited to this region include the Sandia Hairstreak, Poling's Hairstreak, Chisos Metalmark, Definite Patch, and Mary's Giant-Skipper.

2. **MADREAN FORESTS.** This region barely reaches the U.S. in southeastern Arizona and southwestern New Mexico. These include the oak and pine forests of the isolated ranges ("sky islands") near the Mexican boundary that reach south into the Sierra Madre Occidentale of Mexico. Some butterflies more or less limited to this realm include the Chiricahua White, Arizona Hairstreak, Black Checkerspot, Nabokov's Satyr, Red-bordered Satyr, and many skippers.

3. **SONORAN DESERTS.** This area extends from the eastern base of California's transverse and peninsular ranges through low-lying areas of southern California, southern Nevada, southwestern Utah, and Arizona extending south into Baja California and Sonora, Mexico. Included are the Mojave, Colorado, and Sonoran Deserts. Some butterflies limited to the hot, dry region include some races of the Indra Swallowtail, Desert Orangetip, Howarth's White, Leda

Ministreak, Mojave Dotted-Blue, San Emigdio Blue, Wright's Metalmark, Palmers' Metalmark, California Patch, and several skippers.

4. GREAT PLAINS. The vast grasslands extending from the eastern edge of our territory to the eastern base of the Rocky Mountain front and north into the Canadian prairie provinces. These include the short-grass prairie, the midgrass prairie, and river corridors crossing the plains. A number of eastern butterflies follow river courses westward, and some western species extend eastward along such valleys as the Niobrara, Platte, Arkansas, Canadian, and Red rivers. Butterflies of the grasslands, some of which also occur in biomes farther west, include Gray Copper, Bronze Copper, Gorgone Checkerspot, Question Mark, Ridings' Satyr, Ottoe Skipper, Rhesus Skipper, Dusted Skipper, and Strecker's Giant-Skipper.

5. INTERMOUNTAIN WEST AND GREAT BASIN. Includes the dry north-south oriented mountain ranges and valleys extending from the northern limit of the Sonoran Desert and Colorado Plateau north between the Rocky Mountains and Pacific mountains in some forms to southern Yukon and Alaska. Lowlands are dominated by sagebrush and other shrubs, and higher elevations have pinyon-juniper woodlands. Only a few ranges are moist and high enough to have other pines or spruce-fir forests. This region is an important region for butterfly endemics, which include Becker's White, Southwestern Orangetip, Desert Marble, Nokomis Fritillary, Desert Green Hairstreak, Pallid Dotted-Blue, and Bauer's Dotted-Blue.

6. ROCKY MOUNTAINS. Extending from Yukon Territory more or less continuously to northern Utah and northern New Mexico and then discontinuously to southern New Mexico and central Arizona, this is the main mountain archipelago of the West. Typical species include the Rocky Mountain Parnassian, Mead's Sulphur, Canadian Sulphur, Scudder's Sulphur, Queen Alexandra's Sulphur, Northwestern Fritillary, Alberta Fritillary, Gillette's Checkerspot, Weidemeyer's Admiral, Colorado Alpine, Uhler's Arctic, Mead's Wood-Nymph, Russet Skipperling, Taxiles Skipper, and others.

7. CALIFORNIA. The richest area for unique western butterflies lies westward from the crest of the Cascades, Sierra Nevada, and southern California mountains. Montane butterflies include Sierra Nevada Parnassian, Sierra Sulphur, Sierra Nevada Blue, California Crescent, and Sierra Skipper. Foothill butterflies are rich and include the Gray Marble, California Marble, Gorgon Copper, Great Copper, Hedgerow Hairstreak, Gold-hunter's Hairstreak, Muir's Hairstreak, Unsilvered Fritillary, Rural Skipper, Columbian Skipper, and Lindsey's Skipper. A few limited to coastal southern

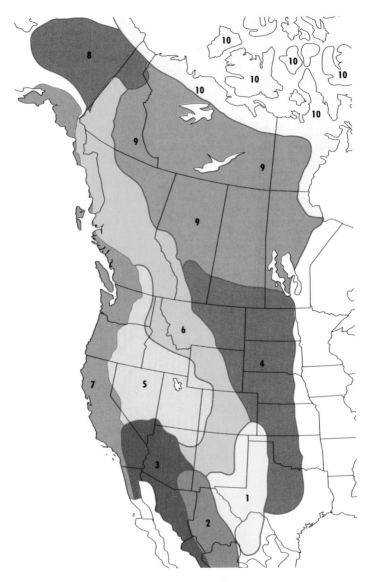

Fig. 6. *Biomes and habitats of western North America.*

California include Harford's Sulphur, Hermes Copper, Avalon Hairstreak, Bernardino Dotted-Blue, and Behr's Metalmark.

8. **ALASKA AND YUKON RANGES.** The mountains in Alaska and Yukon harbor a number of unique butterflies found in bog, taiga, fell-field (rock slides or scree), and tundra habitats. These include the Phoebus Parnassian, Eversmann's Parnassian, Arctic White, Green Marble, Booth's Sulphur, Beringian Fritillary, and several satyrs.

9. **TAIGA.** This zone is characterized by low-lying willow and black spruce bogs and lakes. Occasionally, the low-lying expanse is broken by limited uplifted terrain. The taiga is not very rich in butterflies.

10. **TUNDRA AND ARCTIC ISLANDS.** These are low-lying areas along the coast of the Arctic Ocean and islands. Most areas are flat with scattered low herbaceous vegetation and marshes or ponds, but associated small hills, or "drumlins," are sometimes found just inland. The coastal tundra is fairly rich in butterflies, but few are found on the arctic islands.

HABITATS

A butterfly species will be found where there are the correct climate and habitat, the proper caterpillar hosts, adult food sources, and historical opportunity for colonization. Other factors include competition between species and the presence of parasites and predators. In western North America, our disruption of natural environments and the creation of habitats dominated by crops, ornamental plants, and introduced weeds have altered the abundance and distribution of many of the original butterfly communities—whatever they may have been.

The actual ecological communities found in any region are determined not only by which biome they are in, but by the amount of precipitation in the area, soil, topography, susceptibility to fire, and history of human disturbance. There are a vast number of ecological communities in western North America.

The area covered by this book reaches from the subtropical deserts of southern California and southern Arizona north to the tundra of the Arctic coast, the Aleutian Islands, and the Canadian Archipelago, and from Hawaii and the Pacific Coast east to the short-grass and midgrass prairies of the Great Plains. Within this vast area there are countless land forms and vegetation types. Caterpillars of most butterflies feed on only a few plants, so you will be better able to find butterflies if you know where to look.

Habitats where butterflies are found can be defined by the dominant plant type and by their relative wetness. I find the most convenient categories are forests, treeless regions, and wetlands. Within these major habitat divisions one may subdivide as finely as one wishes.

SPECIATION AND VARIATION
OF WESTERN BUTTERFLIES

In the East, for the most part distinctions between species are clear and variation within species is minimal. By contrast, variation in many species of western butterflies has run rampant, and species distinctions in many groups are not clear-cut.

The number and complexity of western mountain ranges, their role as geographic barriers, drastic changes in climate over short distances, striking differences in plant communities, and the complexity of soil types are the major factors responsible for extreme geographic variation and speciation in the West.

Lepidopterists who have studied western butterflies are often taken with the dramatic differences in the external appearance of the adults from different areas and have made an immense effort to name of these geographic subspecies. As an extreme example, 36 subspecies of the Variable Checkerspot (*Euphydryas chalcedona*) were recognized in a recent checklist. Other species have fewer but comparable magnitudes of described variation.

When butterfly naming of western butterflies began in the 1800s, most new butterflies were named as species, although some were named as forms. Even though Charles Darwin's evolutinary concepts were espoused in the mid-1800s, the understanding of genetics and ecology were not fully formed until the early decades of the 1900s. Thus, although species were described as binomials, a clear understanding of their biological roles did not occur until much later. In the 1930s the existence of geographic variation among species was appreciated, and geographic "races" and subspecies of more widespread species began to be discriminated. In some cases, previously extant names were grouped into species clusters, while in others the description of new subspecies of butterflies took flight. Classic work such as that by Paul Grey took almost 100 species-level names of the genus *Speyeria* and grouped them into 13 more or less widespread species. This sort of work has continued to date.

More recently, thanks to the availability of molecular analysis of the genetic character of organisms through electrophoresis, DNA analysis, and other methods, combined with an understanding of the ecology, behavior, and distribution of western butterflies, some workers have been able to apply the "biological species concept" to western butterflies. This concept is based on reproductive isolation rather than structural or color pattern differences. We now have some cases in which there is evidence that adults of some western butterflies are reproductively isolated but are identical or nearly so. The instance of the *Euphilotes* blues and the recently described *Neominois wyomingo* are concrete examples.

"Good" biological species should not interbreed and produce fertile offspring with other biological species. This standard is not always met in our territory. Some butterflies that were previously considered separate species, but shown to blend over broad geographic areas, are now "lumped" and treated as single species. Examples include *Anthocharis cethura, Callophrys gryneus,* and *Euphydryas anicia.* In the latter example, the butterfly exists in some areas as separate, reproductively isolated populations flying at the same time but with separate host plants, while in others the two forms blend completely together.

There are several examples in this book in which butterflies behave as separate species for most of their ranges but blend or hydridize in narrow zones. I have treated many such examples as separate species, while I've treated others as single species. Such examples include the Lorquin's Admiral *(Limenitis lorquini)* and the Weidemeyer's Admiral *(Limenitis weidemeyerii)* which have a narrow but long hybrid zone. These have traditionally been considered separate species, and they maintain their identities over most of their respective ranges. To keep these species separate or to lump them as one is a subjective decision. Several such decisions were made in this book and there will be those who disagree with many of them. In the text I have tried to point out where such situations exist. There is no doubt that our species concepts for western butterflies will continue to change as new evidence accumulates and as new analytical methods are perfected.

PLATES

PLATE 1   × ⅔

PARNASSIANS

EVERSMANN'S PARNASSIAN *Parnassius eversmanni*   **P. 126**
1⅞–2 in. (48–50 mm). Adults late May–early Aug., possibly biennial. *Wings translucent.* Male yellow, female yellowish-white. Central red spot attached to black mark along inner edge of hindwing. Caterpillar eats bleeding heart.

CLODIUS PARNASSIAN *Parnassius clodius*   **P. 127**
2³⁄₁₆–2¹¹⁄₁₆ in. (55–69 mm). *Wings translucent.* Forewing with 2 *gray* bars near leading edge. Hindwings with 2 *round red spots.* Caterpillar eats bleeding heart.

PHOEBUS PARNASSIAN *Parnassius phoebus*   **P. 127**
1⅞–2¼ in. (47–58 mm). Adults July–Aug. Hairs on abdomen gray-white. *Wings opaque white.* Male usually lacks small black spot on trailing edge of forewing. Broad submarginal *dark band on forewing.* Caterpillar eats stonecrop.

SIERRA NEVADA PARNASSIAN *Parnassius behrii*   **P. 128**
1¹⁵⁄₁₆–2¹⁄₁₆ in. (49–53 mm). Adults July–early Sept. Hairs on abdomen light yellow. *Wings opaque white.* Leading edge of forewing with 2 *round black spots* and 1–3 *small orange* or *yellow spots.* Hindwing has 2 *round yellow* or *orange spots.* Caterpillar probably eats stonecrop.

ROCKY MOUNTAIN PARNASSIAN *Parnassius smintheus*   **P. 128**
1⅝–2³⁄₁₆ in. (42–59 mm). Adults June to Aug. Abdomen with light yellow hairs. Wings opaque white. *At least 2 small red spots near foreward edge of forewing.* At least 2 *round red spots* on hindwing. Female with more extensive red. Male has *narrow black submarginal band* on forewing. Male usually has *median black spot* on trailing edge of forewing. Caterpillar eats stonecrops.

PLATE 1

EVERSMANN'S PARNASSIAN

CLODIUS PARNASSIAN

CLODIUS PARNASSIAN

CLODIUS PARNASSIAN

PHOEBUS PARNASSIAN

SIERRA NEVADA PARNASSIAN

ROCKY MOUNTAIN PARNASSIAN

ROCKY MOUNTAIN PARNASSIAN

PLATE 2   × ⅔

SWALLOWTAILS

WHITE-DOTTED CATTLEHEART *Parides alopius*   **P.129**
   3–3¼ in. (75–82 mm). Adults March–Oct. Black with *sub-marginal row of white and red oblong marks* on hindwing. Hindwing *anal fold tan.* Caterpillar eats pipevines.

PIPEVINE SWALLOWTAIL *Battus philenor*   **P. 130**
   2⅜–4¾ in. (60–120 mm). Adults Feb.–Nov. Upperside black with iridescent blue-green or blue hindwing and submarginal *small white spots.* Below, hindwing has submarginal row of 7 *round orange spots* in an *iridescent blue field.* Subspecies *hirsuta* in Calif. averages smaller, is less iridescent, and is hairier (especially in spring). Caterpillar eats pipevines. Adults are distasteful model for other butterflies, including black female of Eastern Tiger Swallowtail, female of Black Swallowtail, Spicebush Swallowtail, Diana Fritillary, as well as both sexes of Red-spotted Purple.

POLYDAMAS SWALLOWTAIL *Battus polydamas*   **P. 131**
   3⅛–4⅛ (80–104 mm). Adults April–Nov. Tailless. Black. Hindwing *outer margin scalloped.* Both wings with submarginal *yellow band.* Underside of hindwing has marginal row of *red S marks.* Caterpillar eats pipevines.

ZEBRA SWALLOWTAIL *Eurytides marcellus*   **P. 131**
   2½–4 in. (54–94 mm). Adults April–Aug. Wings *green–white* with *black stripes* and *very long tails.* Smaller with shorter tails in spring. Caterpillar eats leaves of pawpaw and related plants.

PLATE 2

WHITE-DOTTED CATTLEHEART

PIPEVINE SWALLOWTAIL

♀

PIPEVINE SWALLOWTAIL

POLYDAMAS SWALLOWTAIL

ZEBRA SWALLOWTAIL

PLATE 3   × ⅔

SWALLOWTAILS

BLACK SWALLOWTAIL *Papilio polyxenes asterias*   **P. 131**
2¹¹⁄₁₆–4¹⁄₁₆ in. (68–102 mm). Adults March–Oct. Primarily black.
Abdomen has lateral row of *yellow dots* along each side. Hindwing
has red-orange eyespot with *centered black pupil* near tail. Below
submarginal *spot rows* with at least some *orange.*

SUBSPECIES *coloro* of desert mountains of w. Ariz., se. Calif., s.
Nev., and n. Baja Calif. has both a normal black form and a predominantly *yellow form* similar to Anise Swallowtail but has *black
tegulae and at least some black dots on abdomen.* Illustrated specimen is from e. San Bernardino Co., Calif.

OLD WORLD SWALLOWTAIL *Papilio machaon*   **P. 132**
2½–2⅜ in. (65–86 mm). Adults June–Sept. Adults usually with
broad yellow median band or uncommon mainly black form. Eyespot at anal angle of hindwing has *black pupil* or *oblong black
patch* that *touches inner edge. Tegulae yellow* and abdomen of yellow forms *mainly yellow.*

SUBSPECIES *aliaska.* Illustrated individual from Eagle Summit,
Alaska. Adults June–July.

SUBSPECIES *pikei.* Illustrated individual from Attachie, B.C.
Adults June–early July.

SUBSPECIES *bairdii.* Illustrated individual is yellow form brucei
from Moffat Co., Colo. Adults May–Sept. (2 flights).

SUBSPECIES *oregonius.* Illustrated individual is male from
Chelan Co., Wash. Adults May–Sept. (2 flights).

ANISE SWALLOWTAIL *Papilio zelicaon*   **P. 134**
2¼–2¹⁵⁄₁₆ in. (58–74 mm). Adults April–mid-July in most areas,
March–Oct. (4 flights) in lowland Calif. and Ore. *Tegulae yellow.*
Abdomen black with *yellow lateral band* along each side (*black
dashes* in rare black form nitra). Broad *yellow median band* on
both wings, *or* black with *narrow submarginal band* (form nitra).
Yellow areas on hindwing have *black veins.* Eyespot on hindwing
has *black pupil centered.*

PLATE 3

BLACK SWALLOWTAIL

♂

♀

aliaska

coloro

♂

OLD WORLD SWALLOWTAIL

pikei

♂

bairdii
form brucei

♂

oregonius

bairdii

♂

ANISE SWALLOWTAIL

♂

PLATE 4   × ²⁄₃

SWALLOWTAILS

INDRA SWALLOWTAIL *Papilio indra*   **P. 135**
   2–2¾ in. (52–71 mm). Adults March–Aug. (1–2 flights). Either
   short or long tails. Abdomen completely *black* or with *short cream
   or pale yellow line* on last half. Upperside black, usually with *narrow pale yellow or cream* submarginal band on both wings. Hindwing eyespot with *centered black pupil*. Caterpillar eats native
   plants in Umbel family.

   SUBSPECIES *indra,* Illustrated male from Platte Co., Wyo.

   SUBSPECIES *minori*. Illustrated female from Mesa Co

   SUBSPECIES *fordi*. Illustrated female from Sheep Hole Mts.,
   San Bernardino Co., Calif.

   SUBSPECIES *martini*. Illustrated female from Providence Mts.,
   San Bernardino Co., Calif.

XUTHUS SWALLOWTAIL *Papilio xuthus*   **P. 135**
   2⅝–3½ in. (66–90 mm). Introduced to Hawaii. Black and cream.
   Heavy black veining and *restricted pale areas*. Caterpillar eats Citrus family plants.

GIANT SWALLOWTAIL *Papilio cresphontes*   **P. 136**
   3½–5⅝ in. (88–144 mm). Black with *diagonal yellow band* of *oval
   spots* on forewing. Tails spoon-shaped, *filled with yellow*. Abdomen of male has *notch* when viewed from above. Caterpillar
   eats plants in Citrus family.

THOAS SWALLOWTAIL *Papilio thoas*   **P. 136**
   3¾–5 in. (95–128 mm). Almost identical to Giant Swallowtail but
   often *paler yellow*. Diagonal band on forewing has *squarish spots,*
   and male abdomen *lacks notch* when viewed from above. Caterpillar eat plants in Citrus and Pepper families.

ORNYTHION SWALLOWTAIL *Papilio ornythion*   **P. 137**
   3¼–5½ in. (82–114 mm). Forewing of male with *narrow pale yellow–cream* diagonal band. Band of *small spots* near edge *do not
   merge*. Female (not shown) similar to male *or* almost entirely
   black. Caterpillar eats Citrus family plants.

BROAD-BANDED SWALLOWTAIL *Papilio astyalus*   **P. 137**
   4⅝–4¾ in. (117–121 mm). Male with *narrow black tails*. Forewing
   with *broad diagonal yellow band* and *small yellow spot* at end of
   cell. Female (not shown) mainly black with short pointed tails.
   Caterpillar eats Citrus family plants.

PLATE 4

indra

minori

fordi

INDRA SWALLOWTAIL

martini

GIANT SWALLOWTAIL

× ½

XUTHUS
SWALLOWTAIL

THOAS
SWALLOWTAIL

× ½

THOAS
SWALLOWTAIL

♂

ORNYTHION
caterpillar

ORNYTHION SWALLOWTAIL

× ½

BROAD-BANDED
SWALLOWTAIL

PLATE 5   × ⅔

SWALLOWTAILS

RUBY-SPOTTED SWALLOWTAIL *Papilio anchisiades*   **P. 137**
  2¾–4 in. (70–102 mm). *Tailless. Black* with *red-purple oval post-median patch* on hindwing. Caterpillar eats Citrus family plants.

EASTERN TIGER SWALLOWTAIL *Papilio glaucus*   **P. 138**
  3–5½ in. (76–144 mm). Male *yellow, tiger-striped.* Hindwing with uppermost *marginal spot orange.* On underside forewing *marginal spot row* is of *continuous spots,* marginal spots on hindwing *strongly suffused* with *orange.* Female has 2 forms: one like male but with more extensive blue on lower half of hindwing and the other mainly *black (black tiger stripes* usually show *vaguely).* Caterpillar eats yellow-poplar, wild cherry, and sweet bay.

CANADIAN TIGER SWALLOWTAIL *Papilio canadensis*   **P. 139**
  2½–3¼ in. (62–82 mm). Adults May–mid-Aug. (1 flight). Yellow with relatively *broad black tiger stripes.* Hindwing with *anal margin black* more than *half distance* to anal vein. Underside of forewing with *marginal spot band continuous. Extensive orange* on underside of hindwing. Black form of female extremely rare. Caterpillar eats leaves of birches, quaking aspen, crab apple, and black cherry. Caterpillars die rather than eat yellow-poplar. Ranges of Eastern and Canadian Tiger meet in places, with very little evidence of hybridization.

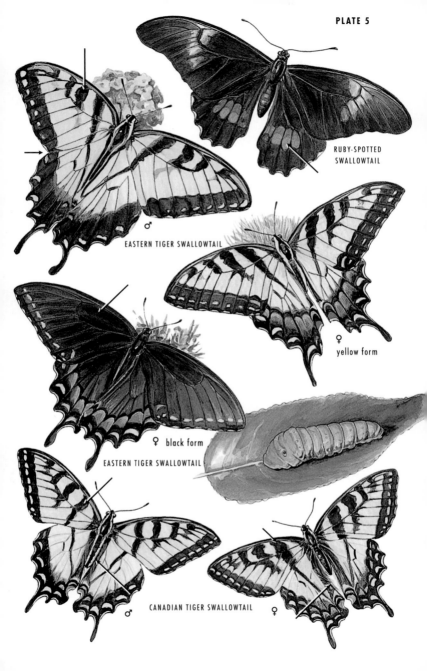

PLATE 5

RUBY-SPOTTED
SWALLOWTAIL

EASTERN TIGER SWALLOWTAIL ♂

♀ yellow form

♀ black form
EASTERN TIGER SWALLOWTAIL

CANADIAN TIGER SWALLOWTAIL ♂ ♀

PLATE 6   × 2/3

SWALLOWTAILS

WESTERN TIGER SWALLOWTAIL *Papilio rutulus*   **P. 139**
2½–3⅜ in. (65–88 mm). Adults June–July in most of West (1 flight), March–Sept. along Pacific Coast (2–3 flights). Adults *black* and *pale yellow tiger-striped*. Hindwing with *uppermost marginal spot yellow* or *absent*. Underside of forewing has marginal row of *separate yellow spots*. Hindwing has *marginal spots narrow* and postmedian area *without orange suffusion*. There is no black female form. Caterpillar eats cottonwoods, quaking aspen, willows, maple, sycamore, hoptree, and plums.

TWO-TAILED SWALLOWTAIL *Papilio multicaudata*   **P. 141**
2¾–5¼ in. (70–122 mm). Adults late May–mid-Aug. in north (1 flight), all year in south (several flights). Male yellow with narrow black tiger stripes. Female with stronger orange hue and extensive iridescent blue on bottom half of hindwing. *Two tails on each hindwing.* Caterpillar eats chokecherry, hoptree, and ashes.

PALE SWALLOWTAIL *Papilio eurymedon*   **P. 140**
2⅝–3½ in. (67–89 mm). Adults May–July in most of west (1 flight), March–Aug. in s. Calif. (2 flights). Very like Western Tiger Swallowtail but *pale cream* and *black tiger-striped*. Caterpillars eat leaves of Rose and Buckthorn families, especially wild plums, wild lilacs, coffeeberry, and buckthorns.

THREE-TAILED SWALLOWTAIL *Papilio pilumnus*   **P. 142**
3⅛–3¾ in. (80–95 mm). Mexico south to El Salvador. Rare stray northward. Adults Jan.–Oct. (several flights). *Forewing yellow with only 2 black tiger stripes. Marginal spots coalesced into a band. Three tails on each hindwing, the longest lined with yellow.* Caterpillar eats laurel.

PALAMEDES SWALLOWTAIL *Papilio palamedes*   **P. 143**
3¾–4½ in. (96–116 mm). Adults March–Dec. (2 flights). Black with *yellow postmedian band*. Tails *filled* with *yellow*. Underside of hindwing with *thin yellow stripe* at base and postmedian row of *orange crescents*.

PLATE 6

WESTERN TIGER SWALLOWTAIL

TWO-TAILED SWALLOWTAIL

TWO-TAILED SWALLOWTAIL

PALE SWALLOWTAIL

THREE-TAILED SWALLOWTAIL

PALAMEDES SWALLOWTAIL

PLATE 7 × ²⁄₃

WHITES

MEXICAN DARTWHITE *Catasticta nimbice* **P. 145**
1½–1¾ in. (40–46 mm). *Wide black borders. Male with white band. Female (not shown) with yellow band. Underside of hindwing mottled with yellow dots.* Caterpillar eats mistletoes.

PINE WHITE *Neophasia menapia* **P. 145**
1¾–1¹⁵⁄₁₆ in. (44–49 mm). *Apex and front edge of forewing lined with black. Veins on hindwing lined with black.* High, floating flight. Caterpillar eats pine needles, Douglas-fir in n. coastal Calif.

CHIRICAHUA WHITE *Neophasia terlootii* **P. 146**
2–2⅜ in. (52–60 mm). *Sexes strikingly dimorphic.* Male white, female orange. *Wide black bar* on front edge of forewing and *wide black outer margin.* Hindwing *veins lined with black below.* Mainly in canopy of pines. Caterpillar eats pine needles.

FLORIDA WHITE *Appias drusilla* **P. 146**
1¾–2½ in. (46–66 in). *Male* mainly *satiny white* with *pointed* forewings. *Female* with *black outer margin* and *yellowish hindwing.* Caterpillar eats plants in Caper family.

BECKER'S WHITE *Pontia beckerii* **P. TKK**
1⅜–1¾ in. (35–45 mm). White with prominent *square black patch* in forewing *cell.* Veins on underside of hindwing with *broad yellow-green bands.* Caterpillar eats plants in Mustard and Caper families, especially prince's plume.

SPRING WHITE *Pontia sisymbrii* **P. 147**
1–1⅜ in. (26–37 mm). Adults white or pale yellow with delicate, almost translucent wings. *Narrow black bar* in forewing cell. *Veins* on hindwing underside have *stippled brown* and *yellow* scaling. Caterpillar eats Mustard family plants, especially rock cresses.

CHECKERED WHITE *Pontia protodice* **P. 148**
1½–2 in. (38–50 mm). White with heavy *brown-black checkered* pattern. Hindwing underside of spring and fall butterflies heavily marbled with green. Caterpillar eats plants in Mustard family, rarely Caper and Reseda families.

PLATE 7

MEXICAN DARTWHITE

PINE WHITE ♀

♂

CHIRICAHUA WHITE ♂

PINE WHITE ♀

CHIRICAHUA WHITE ♀

CHIRICAHUA WHITE ♀

FLORIDA WHITE ♂

♀

FLORIDA WHITE ♀

BECKER'S WHITE ♂

SPRING WHITE ♂

CHECKERED WHITE ♂

CHECKERED WHITE ♂

♀

spring form ♂

CHECKERED WHITE

♀

PLATE 8 × ⅔

WHITES AND MARBLES

WESTERN WHITE *Pontia occidentalis* **P. 149**
1 ⅜–1 ⅝ in. (34–41 mm). Forewing has *marginal chevrons lighter* and contrasting with submarginal band. Below, apex and hind-wing have *veins outlined* with *gray-green.* Spring-fall form has heavy green veining and is very similar to the same form of the Checkered White.

ARCTIC WHITE *Pieris angelika* **P. 150**
1 ¼–1 ⅝ in. (32–42 mm). Male with *black* at *outer margins,* especially at vein endings. Hindwing below is *yellow* with distinct *black-green veining* on both wings.

MARGINED WHITE *Pieris marginalis* **P. 151**
1 ⅜–1 ⅝ in. (36–42 mm). Immaculate white above to dusky with 1 (male) or 2 (female) black spots on forewing. Hindwing underside ranging from *immaculate white* to heavily *veined* with *dusky green.*

MUSTARD WHITE *Pieris oleracea* **P. 151**
1 ½–1 ⅞ (38–48 mm). Completely white above except for *black* on *forewing bases* and *wingtips.* Hindwing underside *pale yellow* with *sharply defined dark veins* (spring) or *weakly veined* or *immaculate* (summer).

CABBAGE WHITE *Pieris rapae* **P. 151**
1 ¼–2 in. (39–50 mm). Mainly white with *black forewing tip and 1 (male) or 2 (female) black spots on forewing. Underside of forewing tip and hindwing yellow-green.*

GREAT SOUTHERN WHITE *Ascia monuste* **P. 153**
2–3 in. (50–76 mm). *Antennal tips bright blue-green. White with zigzag black outer forewing margin. Female also has dusky gray-black form.*

GIANT WHITE *Ganyra josephina* **P. 153**
3 ⅜–3 ⅝ in. (85–93 mm). *Forewing apex bulges outward slightly. Forewing with prominent round black spots in cell and black dashes between veins on outer forewing. Male white, female cream or brownish.*

HOWARTH'S WHITE *Ganyra howarthi* **P. 154**
1 ¾–1 ⅞ in. (43–48 mm). *Both sexes with round black cell spot and black dashes between veins on outer forewing.*

LARGE MARBLE *Euchloe ausonides* **P. 154**
1 ⅛–1 ¾ in. (27–44 mm). *Black patterned forewing apex. Black bar in cell with many included white scales. Underside of hindwing with green marbling.*

PLATE 8

WESTERN WHITE

♂

spring

WESTERN WHITE

♀

spring

ARCTIC WHITE

♂

♀

MARGINED WHITE

♂

♀

MUSTARD WHITE

MARGINED WHITE

♀

MARGINED WHITE

♀

MARGINED WHITE

CABBAGE WHITE

♂

♀

CABBAGE WHITE

♂

♀

dark ♀

GREAT SOUTHERN WHITE

GREAT SOUTHERN WHITE

GIANT WHITE

♂

♂

HOWARTH'S WHITE

♂

LARGE MARBLE

♂

♂

LARGE MARBLE

♀

♀

PLATE 9 × ⅔

MARBLES AND ORANGETIPS

GREEN MARBLE *Euchloe naina* **P. 155**
1¼–1½ in. (31–37 mm). *Small black patches* at *end of veins* above. *Dense gray-green marbling below.*

NORTHERN MARBLE *Euchloe creusa* **P. 155**
1¼–1¾ in. (33–41 mm). *Extensive fractured marbling below.*

SONORAN MARBLE *Euchloe guaymasensis* **P. 156**
1¼–1½ in. (31–37 mm). *Pale yellow* above. *Sparse green marbling.*

OLYMPIA MARBLE *Euchloe olympia* **P. 156**
1⁄16–1⅜ in. (28–35 mm). *Antennae white. Marbling sparse.*

CALIFORNIA MARBLE *Euchloe hyantis* **P. 157**
1⁄16–1½ in. (28–37 mm). *Off-white* with relatively *narrow black* forewing *bar lacking white scales. Green marbling* on underside of hindwing with *yellow cast. Flat white* areas between marbling.

DESERT MARBLE *Euchloe lotta* **P. 157**
1⅛–1⅜ in. (29–36 mm). *Black bar* on forewing *lacks white scales. Dark green marbling* with intervening *pearly white* areas.

DESERT ORANGETIP *Euchloe cethura* **P. 158**
1–1½ in. (26–40 mm). Wings yellow or white, with *orange patch* near apex of forewing between black bar at end of cell and black marks at wingtip. *Heavy green marbling* below.

PACIFIC ORANGETIP *Anthocharis sara* **P. 159**
1⁄16–1½ in. (27–40 mm). Forewing with red-orange apical patch, less red in female. *Black bar* at inner edge is *wide* and, in *male, connected to black stripe* at bottom of apical patch. *Heavy dark green marbling* below.

STELLA ORANGETIP *Anthocharis stella* **P. 160**
1–1⅜ in. (26–36 mm). *Male white* or cream-white, *female pale yellow. Narrow black discal bar,* in male *not connected to black* edging at lower edge of orange patch. *Marbling yellow-green.*

SOUTHERN ROCKY MOUNTAIN ORANGETIP *Anthocharis julia* **P. 159**
1–1¼ in. (25–31 mm). Very similar to Stella Orangetip. *Male* is always *white* above and *marbling* on male is *darker green.*

SOUTHWESTERN ORANGETIP *Anthocharis thoosa* **P. 160**
1–1½ in. (25–37 mm). *Black bar at end of cell wide,* in *male connected with black edging* below orange patch. *Marbling black to green-black* with *prominent white streak* running from base toward outer margin. *Veins lined* with *yellow* or *orange.*

GRAY MARBLE *Anthocharis lanceolata* **P. 161**
1¼–1⅞ in. (33–47 mm). Underside of hindwing *solid gray.*

FALCATE ORANGETIP *Anthocharis midea* **P. 161**
1¼–1½ in. (31–40 mm). Forewing apex *falcate. Dark green highly fractured green marbling.*

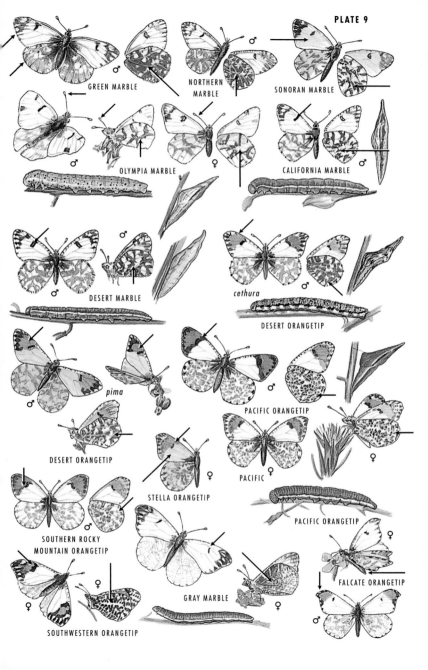

PLATE 9

GREEN MARBLE

NORTHERN MARBLE

SONORAN MARBLE

OLYMPIA MARBLE ♂♀

CALIFORNIA MARBLE ♂

DESERT MARBLE ♂

cethura ♂

DESERT ORANGETIP

pima ♂

DESERT ORANGETIP

PACIFIC ORANGETIP ♂

PACIFIC ♀

STELLA ORANGETIP ♀

PACIFIC ORANGETIP ♀

SOUTHERN ROCKY MOUNTAIN ORANGETIP

FALCATE ORANGETIP

SOUTHWESTERN ORANGETIP ♀

GRAY MARBLE ♀

♂

PLATE 10 $\times$ ⅔

SULPHURS

CLOUDED SULPHUR *Colias philodice* **P. 162**
1 ⅝–2 ¼ in. (42–62 mm). Wing *fringes narrowly pink*. Males and many females *clear yellow* with black outer margins. Underside of forewing with at least some *small black submarginal spots*. *Silver cell spot* on hindwing *pink-rimmed*, almost always *double*.

ORANGE SULPHUR *Colias eurytheme* **P. 163**
1 ½–2 ⅜ in. (39–60 mm). Wing *fringes narrowly pink*. Upperside with at least *some orange* on male and normal female. At least some *small black submarginal marks* on underside of forewing. *Silver cell spot* on underside of hindwing *pink-rimmed*, almost always *double*.

CHRISTINA SULPHUR *Colias christina* **P. 165**
1 ⅜–2 in.(35–52 mm). *Fringes pink*. Male with *two-thirds* or more of forewing *orange* with wing *bases yellow*. Female similar or pale orange, rarely white. Underside of hindwing *olive green* to *dark mossy green* with single *pink-rimmed cell spot*.

WESTERN SULPHUR *Colias occidentalis* **P. 164**
1 ½–2 ¼ in. (45–57 mm). Wings with distinct *pink fringes*. Wings *pale yellow*. White females rare. Black border narrow in males to reduced or absent in females. *Small black cell spot* on forewing. Underside of hindwing yellow to golden with *scattered black scales*. Hindwing *cell spot round* often with *small satellite spot* above.

HARFORD'S SULPHUR *Colias harfordii* **P. 166**
1 ¾–2 in.(45–51 mm). Wing *fringes weakly pink*. *Clear yellow* with narrow black borders in male; normal, reduced, or absent in female. No white female form. Underside of hindwing *yellow* with *narrowly rimmed discal spot* usually with *small satellite spot* above.

QUEEN ALEXANDRA'S SULPHUR *Colias alexandra* **P. 165**
1 ½–2 in. (38–49 mm). *Fringes yellow* or *greenish white*. Wings *clear yellow*. Pale greenish white in rare white female form. Black border reduced in male, normal, reduced or absent in female. Forewing *cell spot usually small* in male, *variable* in female. Underside of hindwing *pale green* with *central white discal spot*, often *rimless* or with weak rim.

MEAD'S SULPHUR *Colias meadii* **P. 166**
1 ¼–1 ⅝ in. (33–41 mm). Wing *fringes pink*. Wings deep *red-orange* with violet sheen. Black *borders wide*. White female form rare. Male has distinct *oblong sex patch* at leading edge of hindwing. Underside of hindwing *green* with *small pink-rimmed discal spot*.

JOHANSEN'S SULPHUR *Colias johanseni* **P. 167**
1 ⅜–1 ½ in. (35–38 mm). Underside of hindwing dark green, *cell spot broadly pink-edged* with *distinct satellite spot*.

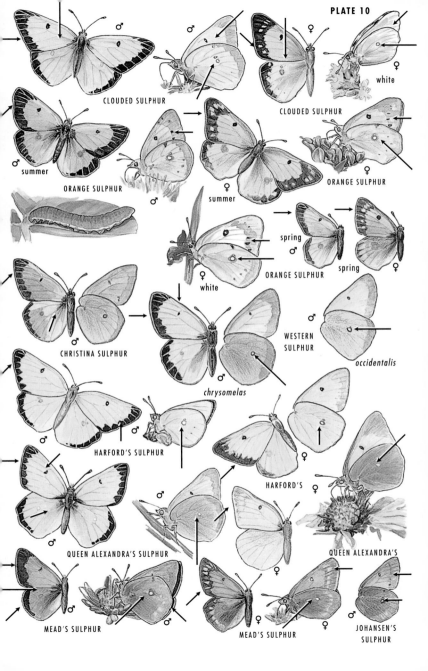

PLATE 10

CLOUDED SULPHUR

♂

♂

♀

CLOUDED SULPHUR

white

♀

summer

♀

ORANGE SULPHUR

summer

♂

ORANGE SULPHUR

♀

spring

♂

ORANGE SULPHUR

white

♀

spring

♀

WESTERN SULPHUR

♂

occidentalis

CHRISTINA SULPHUR

♂

chrysomelas

♂

HARFORD'S SULPHUR

♂

HARFORD'S

♀

QUEEN ALEXANDRA'S SULPHUR

♂

QUEEN ALEXANDRA'S

MEAD'S SULPHUR

♂

MEAD'S SULPHUR

♀

♂

♀

JOHANSEN'S SULPHUR

PLATE 11 × ⅔

SULPHURS

HECLA SULPHUR *Colias hecla* **P. 167**
1⅜–1¾ in. (36–43 mm). Wings *deep orange*. Underside of hindwing *dusky green* with *elongate pink discal spot*.

CANADA SULPHUR *Colias canadensis* **P. 168**
1½–1¾ in. (39–46 mm). Male *yellow-orange*. Female usually *white* with normal black borders. *Yellow* or *white* below with *pink-edged discal spot smeared outwardly*.

LABRADOR SULPHUR *Colias nastes* **P. 169**
1¹⁄₁₆–1¾ in. (28–43 mm). *Dirty white* or *dingy green-yellow* above. Black borders with *enclosed pale spots*. Underside of forewing with a few *submarginal black spots*. Hindwing *green* with *discal cell spot* narrowly *edged* with *pink, sometimes smeared* outwardly.

BOOTH'S SULPHUR *Colias tyche* **P. 168**
1¾–1⅝ in. (35–40 mm). Both sexes with *narrow black borders* edged inwardly by a series of *pale green patches*. *Black scaling* on wing *veins*, especially on female. Underside of forewing with series of *submarginal black spots*. Hindwing *dusky green* with *cell spot's pink edging smeared outwardly*. *Satellite spot* often present.

SCUDDER'S SULPHUR *Colias scudderii* **P. 169**
1¼–1¾ in. (32–43 mm). Male lemon yellow with black borders. Female green-white or yellow-white with hint of black at forewing apex. Underside *greenish yellow*. *Pink-rimmed discal spot single*.

GIANT SULPHUR *Colias gigantea* **P. 170**
1¾–2¼ in. (45–58 mm). Wings yellow. Underside of forewing *lacks submarginal black spots*. Cell spot silver, *brown-rimmed*.

PALAENO SULPHUR *Colias palaeno* **P. 172**
1⅜–1⅝ in. (36–41 mm). Wing *fringes pink*. Male *yellow* with *wide black border*. *Cell spot* on forewing usually *absent*. Underside of hindwing *dusky green* with white *discal spot not rimmed* with *pink*.

PELIDNE SULPHUR *Colias pelidne* **P. 171**
1¼–1¾ in (32–43 mm). Wing *fringes pink*. Forewing has *broad black border*. *Small cell spot below heavily rimmed* with *pink*.

PINK-EDGED SULPHUR *Colias interior* **P. 171**
1½–2 in. (40–52 mm). Prominent *pink wing fringes*. Wings *clear yellow*. Forewing with *small black cell spot*. *Clear yellow* below with single *pink-rimmed silver cell spot*.

SIERRA SULPHUR *Colias behrii* **P. 172**
1⅜–1⅝ in. (35–41 mm). Wings *dusky green* with *black borders*. Underside of hindwing *dark green*.

PLATE 11

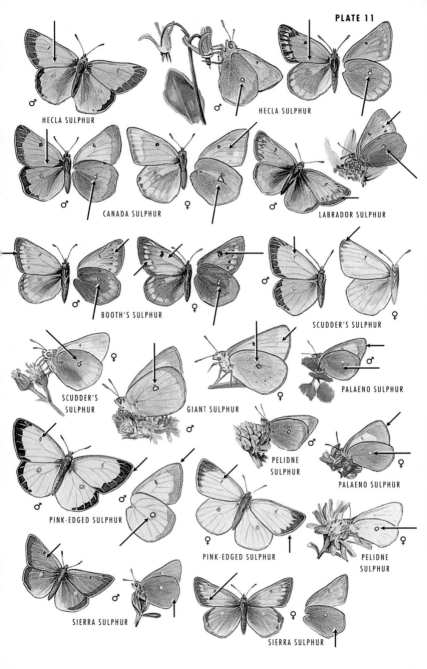

HECLA SULPHUR

HECLA SULPHUR

CANADA SULPHUR

LABRADOR SULPHUR

BOOTH'S SULPHUR

SCUDDER'S SULPHUR

SCUDDER'S SULPHUR

GIANT SULPHUR

PALAENO SULPHUR

PELIDNE SULPHUR

PALAENO SULPHUR

PINK-EDGED SULPHUR

PINK-EDGED SULPHUR

PELIDNE SULPHUR

SIERRA SULPHUR

SIERRA SULPHUR

PLATE 12 × ⅔

SULPHURS

CALIFORNIA DOGFACE *Zerene eurydice* **P. 173**

1⅞–2¼ in. (48–57 mm). *Forewing* tip *pointed*. Male *yellow-orange* with violet *iridescence*. Forewing with black enclosing a *yellow poodlehead*. Female pale yellow with prominent *black discal spot* on forewing. Underside of hindwing yellow (male) or yellow-green (female) with pink-rimmed silver spot. Caterpillar eats California false indigo.

SOUTHERN DOGFACE *Zerene cesonia* **P. 173**

1⅞–2½ in. (48–64 mm). *Forewing* apex slightly *pointed*. Wings *yellow* with black outlining *yellow poodlehead*, diffuse in female. Underside yellow with single *pink-rimmed cell spot*. Caterpillar eats a variety of legumes.

WHITE ANGLED-SULPHUR *Anteos clorinde* **P. 174**

2¾–3½ in. (70–87 mm). *Forewing* tip *hooked*. Hindwing with *short pointed projection*. Wings *pale green* with *yellow-orange bar* on leading edge of forewing. Underside *uniform pale green*. Caterpillar eats leaves of legume trees.

YELLOW ANGLED-SULPHUR *Anteos maerula* **P. 175**

3–3½ in. (76–90 mm). *Forewing* tip *hooked*, hindwing with *short pointed projection*. Male *bright yellow*, female paler. Forewing cell with *black spot*. Underside *pale green*. Caterpillar eats tropical legumes.

CLOUDLESS SULPHUR *Phoebis sennae* **P. 175**

1⅞–2½ in. (48–66 mm). Male *clear lemon yellow* above. Female either yellow or white with black cell spot on forewing and irregular black edgings. *Underside mainly yellow with reddish spots on hindwing*. Caterpillar eats cassias.

ORANGE-BARRED SULPHUR *Phoebis philea* **P. 176**

2¼–3⅜ in. (56–86 mm). Male *orangish yellow* with *red-orange bar* on leading edge of forewing and *red-orange outer margin*. Underside yellow. Female yellow-orange or off-white with *black cell spot* on forewing and a *broken offset* submarginal *line of black smudges*. Yellow form has outer half of hindwing red-orange. Caterpillar eats cassias.

PLATE 12

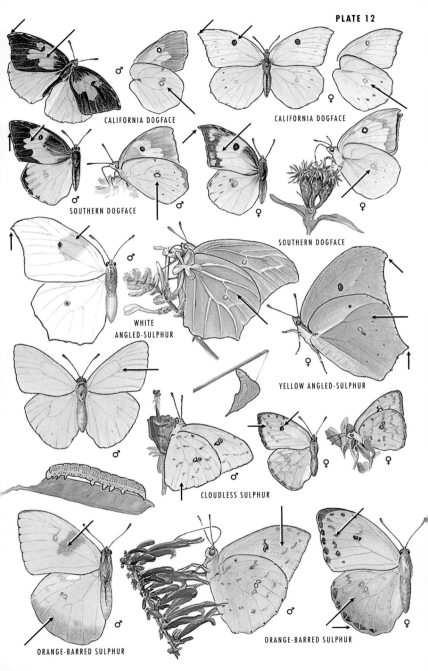

CALIFORNIA DOGFACE ♂

CALIFORNIA DOGFACE ♀

SOUTHERN DOGFACE ♂

SOUTHERN DOGFACE ♀

WHITE ANGLED-SULPHUR ♂

YELLOW ANGLED-SULPHUR ♀

CLOUDLESS SULPHUR ♂ ♀ ♀

ORANGE-BARRED SULPHUR ♂ ♀

ORANGE-BARRED SULPHUR

PLATE 13   × ⅔

SULPHURS AND YELLOWS

LARGE ORANGE SULPHUR *Phoebis agarithe*   **P. 176**
2–3 in. (52–74 mm). Underside of forewing of both sexes with *straight submarginal line.*

LYSIDE SULPHUR *Kricogonia lyside*   **P. 179**
1¼–2 in. (34–51 mm). *Forewing* apex *squared off. Base* of forewing *yellow,* male often with *black bar* on leading edge of forewing. Underside *satiny pale green* with *raised veins.*

STATIRA SULPHUR *Phoebis statira*   **P. 178**
2–2⅜ in. (50–67 mm. Male *pale yellow.* Female with *black cell spot* and *black border* at apex. Underside *pale yellow-green, unmarked.*

BARRED YELLOW *Eurema daira*   **P. 179**
1 1/16–1⅜ in.(28–36 mm). Male forewing with *black bar along trailing edge* and *extensive black at wingtip.* Female with *gray-black* on *wingtip* and *black patch* on outer margin of hindwing.

BOISDUVAL'S YELLOW *Eurema boisduvaliana*   **P. 180**
1 5/16–1½ in.(33–40 mm). Hindwing with *slight projection.* Male *lemon yellow* with weak *dog's head* pattern on forewing. Female with black forewing tip and narrow black margin on hindwing.

MEXICAN YELLOW *Eurema mexicana*   **P. 181**
1¼–2¼ in.(36–55 mm). Hindwing with pronounced *triangular projection.* Wings *pale cream* with *dog's head* more pronounced on male.

TAILED ORANGE *Eurema proterpia*   **P. 181**
1¼–1¾ in. (34–43 mm). *Forewing squared off.* Hindwing of winter form with taillike projection, squarish in summer form. Wings *bright orange* with *black leading edge,* female with *black* at *wingtips.*

MIMOSA YELLOW *Eurema nise*   **P. 182**
1 1/16–1¼ in. (28–33 mm). Pale yellow. Forewing *lacks black cell spot* and has *reduced black marking.* Pale yellow below.

LITTLE YELLOW *Eurema lisa*   **P. 182**
1 1/16–1½ in. (28–37 mm). Forewing with *small black cell spot.* Male with apical third of forewing black. Black border on hindwing.

DINA YELLOW *Eurema dina*   **P. 182**
1½–1⅞ in. (40–48 mm). Yellow or orange-yellow with *black border* on forewing (male) or *black patch* at wingtip (female).

SLEEPY ORANGE *Eurema nicippe*   **P. 183**
1¼–2 in. (32–49 mm). Wings *deep orange* with *broad* slightly irregular *black margins.* Underside of hindwing orange-yellow.

DAINTY SULPHUR *Nathalis iole*   **P. 184**
⅞–1 1/16 in. (22–27 mm). *Wings elongate. Black* and *yellow above.* Underside of hindwing *pale yellow* or *dusky green.*

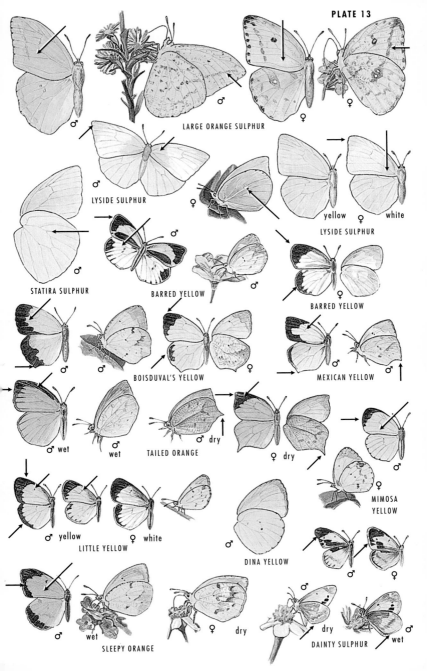

PLATE 13

LARGE ORANGE SULPHUR

♂ ♀

LYSIDE SULPHUR

♂

♀ → ♀ yellow ♀ white

LYSIDE SULPHUR

STATIRA SULPHUR

♂

BARRED YELLOW

♂

♀

BARRED YELLOW

♂

BOISDUVAL'S YELLOW

♂ ♀

MEXICAN YELLOW

♂

♂ wet ♂ wet TAILED ORANGE ♂ dry ♀ dry ♂

♀
MIMOSA YELLOW

♂ yellow ♀ white
LITTLE YELLOW

DINA YELLOW

♂

♂ ♀

♂ wet
SLEEPY ORANGE

♀ dry

♂ dry DAINTY SULPHUR wet

PLATE 14   × ¾

HARVESTER AND COPPERS

HARVESTER *Feniseca tarquinius*   **P. 186**
  1–1¼ in. (25–30 mm). Wings orange-brown with *black areas* and *spots*. Underside of hindwing brown or orange-brown with *faint white scrawls*.

TAILED COPPER *Lycaena arota*   **P. 186**
  1–1¼ in. (26–30 mm). *Single short tail* on hindwing. Underside of hindwing with *black dot* next to tail, series of *black marks*, and *white squiggly submarginal band*.

AMERICAN COPPER *Lycaena phlaeas*   **P. 187**
  ⅞–1¼ in. (22–30 mm). Forewings *iridescent red-orange*. Hindwing gray with red-orange border. Underside of hindwing gray with small black spots and *red-orange zigzag* submarginal line.

LUSTROUS COPPER *Lycaena cupreus*   **P. 187**
  1–1¼ in. (25–30 mm). Wings *iridescent red* or *red-orange* with black border and *scattered black dots*. Underside of hindwing cream to gray with *small black dots* and a thin *red squiggly line* along outer edge.

GREAT COPPER *Lycaena xanthoides*   **P. 188**
  1¼–1¾ in. (33–44 mm). Short taillike projection on hindwing. Wings *gray above* with *yellow-orange border* on hindwing near tail (especially on females). Underside of hindwing *gray with black spots* and *paler band* inside margin.

GRAY COPPER *Lycaena dione*   **P. 189**
  ¹⁵⁄₁₆–1½ in. (24–38 mm). *Dark gray* above. Forewing with 2 *black cell spots*. Hindwing with pale orange and black border on outer margin. Underside of hindwing *pale gray-white* with *small black dots* and *orange-red border* on outer edge.

EDITH'S COPPER *Lycaena editha*   **P. 191**
  ⅞–1¼ in. (22–30 mm). *Minute tail* projects from hindwing. *Dark gray* above. Male may have single black spot on forewing, female may have yellow spotting on forewing. Underside of hindwing *gray* with complex pattern of *black dots, scrawls,* and *paler areas*.

GORGON COPPER *Lycaena gorgon*   **P. 191**
  1¼–1⅝ in. (32–41 mm). *Male iridescent red-purple, female gray with elongate yellow spots*. Underside of hindwing *gray-white* with *many black dots* and row of *separated red dots* on outer margin.

BRONZE COPPER *Lycaena hyllus*   **P. 190**
  1¼–1⅝ in. (32–41 mm). Underside of forewing *orange* with *black spots,* hindwing *off-white* with *black spots* and *wide orange band* on outer margin.

RUDDY COPPER *Lycaena rubidus*   **P. 192**
  1¹⁄₁₆–1⁵⁄₁₆ in. (27–34 mm). *Male iridescent red-orange* above, *female brown* to dull orange-brown. *Gray-white to pale tan* below.

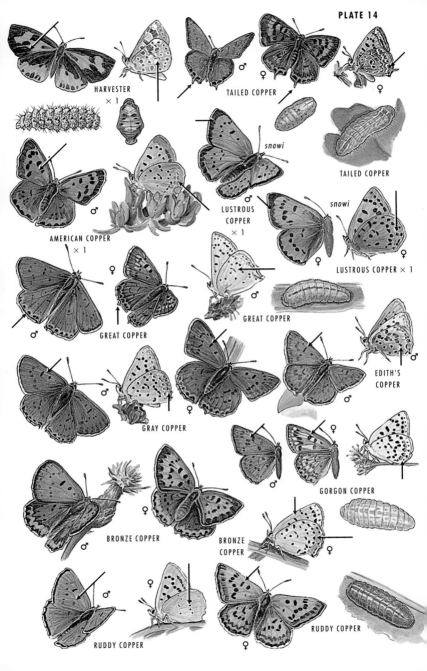

PLATE 14

HARVESTER
× 1

TAILED COPPER

♂

♀

♀

TAILED COPPER

snowi

LUSTROUS
COPPER
× 1

snowi

♀

LUSTROUS COPPER × 1

AMERICAN COPPER
× 1

♀

♂

GREAT COPPER

♂

GREAT COPPER

♂

♀

GRAY COPPER

♂

♂

EDITH'S
COPPER

♂

♀

♂

GORGON COPPER

♀

BRONZE COPPER

BRONZE
COPPER

♀

♂

♀

RUDDY COPPER

♀

RUDDY COPPER

PLATE 15   × 1

COPPERS AND HAIRSTREAKS

BLUE COPPER *Lycaena heteronea*   **P. 193**
1–1⁵⁄₁₆ in. (25–33 mm). *Distinct black border* and *white fringe. Male iridescent blue above, female gray,* sometimes with iridescent blue patches. Underside of hindwing *white or gray-white.*

PURPLISH COPPER *Lycaena helloides*   **P. 194**
¹⁵⁄₁₆–1⁵⁄₁₆ in. (24–33 mm). *Males iridescent purple* above; *female* ranges from *darkish* to having *extensive orange areas* on both wings. Extensive *zigzag red-orange marginal band* on hindwing. Underside of hindwing *orange-brown* with *zigzag band* repeated.

DORCAS COPPER *Lycaena dorcas*   **P. 193**
⅞–1¹⁄₁₆ in. (22–27 mm). Very similar to Purplish Copper but often *smaller* with much *reduced red-orange band* on hindwing, *reduced pale areas* on female, and browner on underside.

LILAC-BORDERED COPPER *Lycaena nivalis*   **P. 195**
¹⁵⁄₁₆–1⁵⁄₁₆ in. (24–33 mm). *Male red-orange above, female brown with variable amounts of yellow. Both sexes with orange and black band* on hindwing outer margin. Underside of hindwing *tan-yellow* with *outer third iridescent pink.*

MARIPOSA COPPER *Lycaena mariposa*   **P. 195**
1¹⁄₁₆–1¼ in. (27–32 mm). Male iridescent dark purple above, female brown with yellow patches on forewing. Underside of hindwing *mottled gray* contrasting with *pale yellow forewing.*

HERMES COPPER *Lycaena hermes*   **P. 195**
⅞–1³⁄₁₆ in. (23–30 mm). Hindwing with *short tail. Yellow* and *brown* above, mainly *yellow below* with *black spotting* on forewing.

COLORADO HAIRSTREAK *Hypaurotis crysalus*   **P. 196**
1³⁄₁₆–1⅜ in. (31–36 mm). Black with *iridescent purple* with a few *orange patches* above. Underside of hindwing *dark gray* to *gray-white* with lighter and darker patches and black-centered *orange patch* near tail.

GOLDEN HAIRSTREAK *Habrodais grunus*   **P. 197**
¹⁵⁄₁₆–1³⁄₁₆ in. (24–31 mm). Tailed. *Brown* with tan patches. Underside is *golden brown* with 2 *rows* of *gold flecks* on hindwing.

GREAT PURPLE HAIRSTREAK *Atlides halesus*   **P. 197**
1–1¾ in. (26–45 mm). *Two long tails* on each hindwing. Abdomen is *iridescent blue* above, *red-orange* below. Wings *iridescent blue* above. Underside is black with *iridescent gold marks* near tails.

SILVER-BANDED HAIRSTREAK *Chlorostrymon simaethis*   **P. 198**
¹³⁄₁₆–1 in. (21–25 mm). Tailed. *Male iridescent purple* above, *female dull gray.* Underside of hindwing *green* with *silver-white postmedian band.*

PLATE 15

BLUE COPPER

♀

BLUE COPPER
♂

BLUE COPPER
♀

DORCAS
COPPER
♀

DORCAS
COPPER
♀

DORCAS
COPPER
♂

PURPLISH COPPER
♂

PURPLISH
COPPER

PURPLISH COPPER
♀

LILAC-BORDERED
COPPER
♀

LILAC-BORDERED COPPER
♂

MARIPOSA COPPER
♂

♀

HERMES
COPPER

HERMES
COPPER
× ¾

COLORADO HAIRSTREAK
× ¾

♂

♀

GOLDEN HAIRSTREAK

GREAT PURPLE HAIRSTREAK
♂   ♀
× ¾

♀

SILVER-BANDED HAIRSTREAK
♀

PLATE 16 ×1

HAIRSTREAKS

SOAPBERRY HAIRSTREAK *Phaeostrymon alcestis*   **P. 203**
¹⁵⁄₁₆–1 ³⁄₁₆ in. (24–31 mm). Band with *sharply jagged VW mark.*

BEHR'S HAIRSTREAK *Satyrium behrii*   **P. 205**
¹⁵⁄₁₆–1 ⅛ in. (24–29 mm). *Tailless. Two rows* of *black spots* and *dashes. Orange-capped black spot* usually near anal angle.

SOOTY HAIRSTREAK *Satyrium fuliginosum*   **P. 205**
⅞–1 ³⁄₁₆ in. (23–30 mm). Postmarginal and submarginal series of *black spots sometimes obscured by white scales.*

ACADIAN HAIRSTREAK *Satyrium acadica*   **P. 206**
1–1 ³⁄₁₆ in. (26–31 mm). *Round black spots. Blue tailspot capped with orange; black bar spot above tailspot often sharply angled.*

CALIFORNIA HAIRSTREAK *Satyrium californica*   **P. 207**
⅞–1 ³⁄₁₆ in. (23–31 mm). *Oval black spots* and extensive *series of orange spots. Blue patch capped* with *orange.*

SYLVAN HAIRSTREAK *Satyrium sylvinus*   **P. 207**
⅞–1 ⅛ in. (23–29 mm). *Small black round spots. Blue tailspot often lacks orange cap.* Small *black triangular mark* above tailspot.

EDWARDS' HAIRSTREAK *Satyrium edwardsii*   **P. 209**
1–1 ¼ in. (26–32 mm). *Separate oval dark brown spots.* Marginal row of *orange spots. Blue tailspot not capped with orange.*

CORAL HAIRSTREAK *Satyrium titus*   **P. 208**
⅞–1 ⁵⁄₁₆ in. (22–33 mm). *Tailless. Row* of *coral red spots* below.

MOUNTAIN-MAHOGANY HAIRSTREAK *Satyrium tetra*   **P. 211**
1–1 ³⁄₁₆ in. (26–30 mm). *Irregular dark median line edged* outwardly with *white* and outer half of wing with *white flush.*

BANDED HAIRSTREAK *Satyrium calanus*   **P. 209**
¹⁵⁄₁₆–1 ³⁄₁₆ in. (24–30 mm). *Dark white-edged dashes. Blue patch* at anal angle *not capped* with *orange.*

STRIPED HAIRSTREAK *Satyrium liparops*   **P. 210**
¹⁵⁄₁₆–1 ³⁄₁₆ in. (24–31 mm). Rows of *widely separated thin white lines. Blue patch* at anal angle *capped with orange.*

GOLD-HUNTER'S HAIRSTREAK *Satyrium auretorum*   **P. 210**
⅞–1 ³⁄₁₆ in. (23–30 mm). Faint dark crescents on outer margin and small *orange tailspot* with *black center.*

HEDGEROW HAIRSTREAK *Satyrium saepium*   **P. 211**
⅞–1 ³⁄₁₆ in. (22–30 mm). Inconspicuous pattern. *Tailspot blue.*

SOUTHERN HAIRSTREAK *Satyrium favonius*   **P. 203**
⅞–1 ¼ in. (22–32 mm). Narrow *orange cap* on *blue tailspot,* postmedian line with *white-edged black W* near inner margin.

ILAVIA HAIRSTREAK *Satyrium ilavia*   **P. 204**
⅞–1 ¹⁄₁₆ in. (22–28 mm). *Faint black* postmedian *line. Blue* patch above tail and *red-orange spot greatly reduced or absent.*

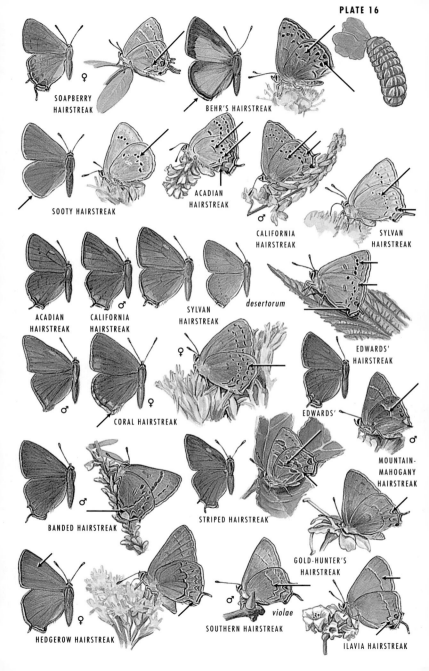

PLATE 16

SOAPBERRY HAIRSTREAK ♀

BEHR'S HAIRSTREAK

SOOTY HAIRSTREAK

ACADIAN HAIRSTREAK

CALIFORNIA HAIRSTREAK ♂

SYLVAN HAIRSTREAK

ACADIAN HAIRSTREAK

CALIFORNIA HAIRSTREAK ♂

SYLVAN HAIRSTREAK

desertorum

EDWARDS' HAIRSTREAK

CORAL HAIRSTREAK ♂ ♀ ♀

EDWARDS' ♂

MOUNTAIN-MAHOGANY HAIRSTREAK

BANDED HAIRSTREAK ♂

STRIPED HAIRSTREAK

GOLD-HUNTER'S HAIRSTREAK

HEDGEROW HAIRSTREAK ♀

SOUTHERN HAIRSTREAK *violae* ♂

ILAVIA HAIRSTREAK

PLATE 17   × 1

HAIRSTREAKS

POLING'S HAIRSTREAK *Satyrium polingi*   **P. 204**
1–1 ³⁄₁₆ in. (25–30 mm). See text.

AMYNTOR GREENSTREAK *Cyanophrys amyntor*   **P. 212**
¹⁵⁄₁₆–1 ¹⁄₁₆ in. (24–28 mm). See text.

LONG-WINGED GREENSTREAK *Cyanophrys longula*   **P. 212**
¹³⁄₁₆–1 ³⁄₁₆ in. (21–30 mm). See text.

Western Green Hairstreak *Callophrys affinis*   **P. 213**
¾–1 ³⁄₁₆ in. (19–30 mm). See text.

Coastal Green Hairstreak *Callophrys dumetorum*   **P. 213**
¹⁵⁄₁₆–1 ⁵⁄₁₆ in. (24–33 mm). See text.

SHERIDAN'S HAIRSTREAK *Callophrys sheridani*   **P. 214**
¹¹⁄₁₆–¹³⁄₁₆ in. (17–21 mm). See text.

DESERT GREEN HAIRSTREAK *Callophrys comstocki*   **P. 214**
¹³⁄₁₆–1 in. (21–25 mm). See text.

THICKET HAIRSTREAK *Callophrys spinetorum*   **P. 215**
⅞–1 ¹⁄₁₆ in. (23–28 mm). See text.

JOHNSON'S HAIRSTREAK *Callophrys johnsoni*   **P. 216**
1 ¹⁄₁₆–1 ⁵⁄₁₆ in. (27–34 mm). See text.

NELSON'S HAIRSTREAK *Callophrys nelsoni*   **P. 217**
⅞–1 ¹⁄₁₆ in. (23–28 mm). See text.

MUIR'S HAIRSTREAK *Callophrys muiri*   **P. 217**
⅞–1 in. (22–25 mm). See text.

JUNIPER HAIRSTREAK *Callophrys gryneus*   **P. 217**
¹⁵⁄₁₆–1 ¹⁄₁₆ in. (24–28 mm). See text.

THORNE'S HAIRSTREAK *Callophrys thornei*   **P. 219**
1–1 ⅛ in. (25–29 mm). See text.

XAMI HAIRSTREAK *Callophrys xami*   **P. 219**
¹⁵⁄₁₆–1 ⅛ in. (24–29 mm). See text.

SANDIA HAIRSTREAK *Callophrys mcfarlandi*   **P. 219**
¾–1 ⅛ in. (20–29 mm). See text.

BROWN ELFIN *Callophrys augustinus*   **P. 220**
¹³⁄₁₆–¹⁵⁄₁₆ in. (21–24 mm). See text.

DESERT ELFIN *Callophrys fotis*   **P. 220**
¾–⅞ in. (19–23 mm). See text.

PLATE 17

POLING'S HAIRSTREAK

♀

AMYNTOR GREENSTREAK

♂

LONG-WINGED GREENSTREAK

perplexa

WESTERN GREEN HAIRSTREAK

homoperplexa

COASTAL GREEN HAIRSTREAK

SHERIDAN'S

DESERT GREEN

THICKET HAIRSTREAK

♀

JOHNSON'S HAIRSTREAK

♂

THICKET

NELSON'S HAIRSTREAK

rosneri

MUIR'S HAIRSTREAK

barryi

JUNIPER HAIRSTREAK

siva

THORNE'S

XAMI HAIRSTREAK

SANDIA HAIRSTREAK

♂

BROWN ELFIN

DESERT ELFIN

PLATE 18   × 1

HAIRSTREAKS

MOSS' ELFIN *Callophrys mossii* See text.	**P. 221**
HOARY ELFIN *Callophrys polios* See text.	**P. 221**
HENRY'S ELFIN *Callophrys henrici* See text.	**P. 222**
WESTERN PINE ELFIN *Callophrys eryphon* See text.	**P. 223**
EASTERN PINE ELFIN *Callophrys niphon* See text.	**P. 222**
WHITE M HAIRSTREAK *Parrhasius m-album* See text.	**P. 198**
LEDA MINISTREAK *Ministrymon leda* See text.	**P. 199**
GRAY MINISTREAK *Ministrymon azia* See text.	**P. 199**
ARIZONA HAIRSTREAK *Erora quaderna* See text.	**P. 200**
SONORAN HAIRSTREAK *Hypostrymon critola* See text.	**P. 200**
RED-BANDED HAIRSTREAK *Calycopis cecrops* See text.	**P. 201**
DUSKY-BLUE HAIRSTREAK *Calycopis isobeon* See text.	**P. 201**
RED-SPOTTED HAIRSTREAK *Tmolus echion* See text.	**P. 199**
CREAMY STRIPE-STREAK *Arawacus jada* See text.	**P. 202**
MARIUS HAIRSTREAK *Rekoa marius* See text.	**P. 202**
GRAY HAIRSTREAK *Strymon melinus* See text.	**P. 223**
AVALON SCRUB-HAIRSTREAK *Strymon avalona* See text.	**P. 224**
RED-LINED SCRUB-HAIRSTREAK *Strymon bebrycia* See text.	**P. 224**
LACEY'S SCRUB-HAIRSTREAK *Strymon alea* See text.	**P. 225**
MALLOW SCRUB-HAIRSTREAK *Strymon istapa* See text.	**P. 225**
TAILLESS SCRUB-HAIRSTREAK *Strymon cestri* See text.	**P. 225**
LANTANA SCRUB-HAIRSTREAK *Strymon bazochii* See text.	**P. 226**
BROMELIAD SCRUB-HAIRSTREAK *Strymon serapio* See text.	**P. 226**

PLATE 18

schryveri
MOSS' ELFIN ♀

MOSS' ELFIN

HOARY ELFIN

HENRY'S ELFIN ♂

WESTERN PINE ELFIN

EASTERN PINE ELFIN

WHITE M
HAIRSTREAK

LEDA MINISTREAK

GRAY MINISTREAK

ARIZONA HAIRSTREAK

SONORAN
HAIRSTREAK

RED-BANDED
HAIRSTREAK

DUSKY-BLUE
HAIRSTREAK

RED-SPOTTED

CREAMY STRIPE-STREAK

MARIUS
HAIRSTREAK

GRAY
HAIRSTREAK ♂

GRAY
HAIRSTREAK

AVALON SCRUB-HAIRSTREAK

RED-LINED SCRUB-HAIRSTREAK

LACEY'S
SCRUB-HAIRSTREAK ♂

MALLOW
SCRUB-HAIRSTREAK

TAILLESS
SCRUB-HAIRSTREAK

× 1¼
LANTANA
SCRUB-HAIRSTREAK

BROMELIAD
SCRUB-HAIRSTREAK ♂

PLATE 19   × 1

BLUES

WESTERN PYGMY-BLUE *Brephidium exilis*   **P. 227**
  ½–¾ in. (13–19 mm). Hindwing *white* at *base* below.

CASSIUS BLUE *Leptotes cassius*   **P. 228**
  ¹¹⁄₁₆–1 ¹⁄₁₆ in. (17–27 mm). *Broken pale lines* on both wings.

MARINE BLUE *Leptotes marina*   **P. 228**
  ¾–1 in. (19–26 mm). Forewing with *continuous pale brown lines* from leading to trailing edge.

PEA BLUE *Lampides boeticus*   **P. 229**
  ⅞–1 ¼ in. (23–32 mm). *Tailed.* Underside *brownish* with *wavy light lines. Black spot* near tail.

CYNA BLUE *Zizula cyna*   **P. 229**
  ⅝–⅞ in. (16–21 mm). *Pale gray* below with *minute black dots.*

CERAUNUS BLUE *Hemiargus ceraunus*   **P. 230**
  ⅝–⅞ in. (16–23 mm). Postmedian row of *dark dashes below. Two small round spots* on hindwing margin.

REAKIRT'S BLUE *Hemiargus isola*   **P. 230**
  ¹¹⁄₁₆–1 in. (17–25 mm). Forewing has 5 *prominent round black spots.*

EASTERN TAILED-BLUE *Everes comyntas*   **P. 231**
  ¹¹⁄₁₆–1 ⅛ in. (18–29 mm). *Two orange spots* near tail.

WESTERN TAILED-BLUE *Everes amyntula*   **P. 232**
  ⅞–1 ³⁄₁₆ (22–31 mm). Only a *single orange spot* near tail.

SPRING AZURE *Celastrina ladon*   **P. 232**
  ⅞–1 ⁵⁄₁₆ in. (22–33 mm). Underside variable. Often gray-white with *faint small black spots, darker gray* with *larger black spots.*

SUMMER AZURE *Celastrina neglecta*   **P. 233**
  ¹⁵⁄₁₆–1 ⅛ in. (24–29 mm). Female with *extensive white areas* on both wings. Underside white or pale gray with *small dark marks* and *zigzag dark line* in submarginal area.

HOPS AZURE *Celastrina humulus*   **P. 234**
  ¹³⁄₁₆–1 ¹⁄₁₆ in. (21–27 mm). Underside of hindwing *white* with pattern of *small black marks* ranging from almost none to heavy.

SONORAN BLUE *Philotes sonorensis*   **P. 235**
  ¹³⁄₁₆–1 in. (21–25 mm). Iridescent blue with *bright red-orange patches* above. *Round black spots* under forewing.

WESTERN SQUARE-DOTTED BLUE *Euphilotes battoides*   **P. 236**
  ¹¹⁄₁₆–¹³⁄₁₆ in. (17–21 mm). Underside gray-white to off-white. *Black spotting* varying from *heavy* and *smudged* to *small.*

PACIFIC DOTTED-BLUE *Euphilotes enoptes*   **P. 239**
  ¾–⅞ in. (19–23 mm). Forewing *spots larger* than on hindwing.

BERNARDINO DOTTED-BLUE *Euphilotes bernardino*   **P. 236**
  ¹¹⁄₁₆–¹³⁄₁₆ in. (17–21 mm). Underside *off-white* with *distinct black spots* and a moderate *orange aurora.*

PLATE 19

WESTERN PYGMY-BLUE

CASSIUS BLUE

♂

MARINE BLUE

♀

PEA BLUE

CYNA BLUE

MARINE BLUE

♂

CERAUNUS BLUE

♂

REAKIRT'S BLUE

♂ ♀

EASTERN TAILED-BLUE

♂ ♀

WESTERN TAILED-BLUE

♂

EASTERN TAILED-BLUE

♀

SPRING AZURE

♂

SUMMER AZURE

♀

SPRING AZURE

♀

SPRING AZURE

HOPS AZURE

♂ ♀

♀

SPRING AZURE

SONORAN BLUE

♂ ♂

glaucon

WESTERN SQUARE-DOTTED BLUE

PACIFIC DOTTED-BLUE

BERNARDINO DOTTED-BLUE

PLATE 20 ×1

BLUES

ELLIS' DOTTED-BLUE *Euphilotes ellisi* **P. 238**
¾–⅞ in. (19–22 mm). Underside with *black spotting*. Submarginal *row* on forewing *smudged. Continuous red-orange aurora.*

BAUER'S DOTTED-BLUE *Euphilotes baueri* **P. 238**
¾–⅞ in. (19–22 mm). Underside *snowy white* with *bold black spotting* and *terminal line.* Hindwing *aurora narrow, pale orange.*

WESTERN SQUARE-DOTTED BLUE *Euphilotes battoides*   See text. **P. 236**

PACIFIC DOTTED-BLUE *Euphilotes enoptes* **P. 239**
¾–⅞ in. (19–23 mm). Forewing *spots larger* than on hindwing.

MOJAVE DOTTED-BLUE *Euphilotes mojave* **P. 240**
¾–⅞ in. (19–23 mm). *Male pale blue* above, *female,* hindwing *aurora absent.* Underside similar to Pacific Dotted-Blue.

ROCKY MOUNTAIN DOTTED-BLUE *Euphilotes ancilla* **P. 240**
⅝–1 in. (16–25 mm). Underside *blue-gray.* Forewing *suffused* with *smoky dark gray.* Hindwing with *prominent black spots.*

PALLID DOTTED-BLUE *Euphilotes pallescens* **P. 241**
⅝–¹³⁄₁₆ in. (16–21 mm). *Fringes not checkered.* Underside *white* with *prominent black spots. Orange aurora* continuous but *narrow.*

RITA DOTTED-BLUE *Euphilotes rita* **P. 241**
¹¹⁄₁₆–⅞ in. (17–22 mm). Underside *off-white* with *distinct black spots,* smudged on forewing. *Orange aurora continuous.*

SPALDING'S DOTTED-BLUE *Euphilotes spaldingi* **P. 242**
¾–¹⁵⁄₁₆ in. (19–24 mm). Underside *gray* with *black spots. Continuous orange aurora* on hindwing. *Orange* extending on forewing.

SMALL DOTTED-BLUE *Philotiella speciosa* **P. 243**
⅝–¾ in. (16–20 mm). Underside *off-white* with *small black dots.*

ARROWHEAD BLUE *Glaucopsyche piasus* **P. 243**
⅞–1¼ in. (22–32 mm). *Black spots* on *gray background* with distinctive patches of *white arrowhead-shaped marks.*

NORTHERN BLUE *Lycaeides idas* **P. 248**
¹³⁄₁₆–1⅛ in. (21–29 mm). Hindwing has *black terminal line broken* into *small spots* at vein endings, *orange spots* usually *reduced.*

SILVERY BLUE *Glaucopsyche lygdamus* **P. 245**
⅞–1³⁄₁₆ in. (22–30 mm). Underside off-white to gray-brown with single submarginal row of *round black white-edged spots.*

GREENISH BLUE *Plebejus saepiolus* **P. 249**
1–1¼ in. (26–32 mm). Underside with rows of *irregular black spots.*

MELISSA BLUE *Lycaeides melissa* **P. 249**
⅞–1¼ in. (22–32 mm). *Red-orange* usually extending to forewing.

SAN EMIGDIO BLUE *Plebulina emigdionis* **P. 249**
¹³⁄₁₆–1¹⁄₁₆ in. (21–27 mm). *Diffuse orange aurora above.* Below forewing with *black spots* larger than on hindwing.

PLATE 20

ELLIS' DOTTED-BLUE

BAUER'S DOTTED-BLUE

WESTERN SQUARE-DOTTED BLUE

PACIFIC DOTTED-BLUE

MOJAVE DOTTED-BLUE

ROCKY MOUNTAIN DOTTED-BLUE

PALLID DOTTED-BLUE

RITA DOTTED-BLUE

SPALDING'S DOTTED-BLUE

SMALL DOTTED-BLUE

ARROWHEAD BLUE

NORTHERN BLUE

SILVERY BLUE

NORTHERN BLUE

GREENISH BLUE

xerces

SILVERY BLUE

blue ♀   brown ♀   GREENISH BLUE

MELISSA BLUE

SAN EMIGDIO BLUE

PLATE 21   × 1

BLUES

BOISDUVAL'S BLUE *Icaricia icarioides*   **P. 250**
¹³/₁₆–1 ⁵/₁₆ in. (21–33 mm). Underside off-white to brown with 2 *rows* of roundish to irregular *black spots* on both wings. Black spots *often obscured by white patches.*

SHASTA BLUE *Icaricia shasta*   **P. 251**
¾–1 in. (19–26 mm). Dull blue or brown above. Below wings with *distinct mottled appearance.* Hindwing with *inconspicuous* submarginal band of *metallic spots.*

ACMON BLUE *Icaricia acmon*   **P. 252**
¾–¹⁵/₁₆ in. (19–24 mm). *Male blue* above, often pale, *female brown* sometimes with blue at base. Below wings *off*-white with pattern of *black spots.* Hindwing with submarginal *orange* and *metallic aurora.*

LUPINE BLUE *Icaricia lupini*   **P. 252**
¹¹/₁₆–1 ⅛ in. (17–29 mm). Similar to Acmon Blue, but male usually not powdery blue, with *distinct black spot in cell* above and *black edging* on inside of orange aurora. Underside like Acmon Blue.

VEINED BLUE *Icaricia neurona*   **P. 253**
¹¹/₁₆–1 in. (17–26 mm). Both sexes *brown above* with *orange veins.* Hindwing with *broad orange aurora.*

ARCTIC BLUE *Agriades glandon*   **P. 246**
⅞–1 in. (22–26 mm). Forewings pointed. Underside of hindwing with postmedian *black spots* surrounded by *white patches* in *dark background* or *completely obscured* with *white.*

HAWAIIAN BLUE *Vaga blackburni*   **P. 245**
⅞–1 in. (22–26 mm). Wings iridescent *violet* above, *bright green* below.

CRANBERRY BLUE *Vacciniina optilete*   **P. 245**
⅞–1 in. (22–25 mm). Underside of both wings with strong postmedian *row of black spots.* Hindwing with 1 *black-edged orange* submarginal *spot* near anal angle.

CASSIOPE BLUE *Agriades cassiope*   **P. 247**
¾–1 in. (21–25 mm). Underside of forewing with submarginal *spots squarish* or *oblong.* *Black discal spot* on hindwing usually present.

SIERRA NEVADA BLUE *Agriades podarce*   **P. 247**
⅞–1 in. (22–26 mm). Underside of forewing with submarginal *spots arrowhead-shaped, pointing inward.* *Discal spot* on hindwing *not black.*

PLATE 21

BOISDUVAL'S BLUE

BOISDUVAL'S BLUE

SHASTA BLUE

ACMON BLUE

LUPINE BLUE

VEINED BLUE

franklinii

ARCTIC franklinii

HAWAIIAN BLUE

CRANBERRY BLUE

franklinii

ARCTIC BLUE

megalo

megalo

ARCTIC BLUE

megalo

rustica

CASSIOPE BLUE

SIERRA NEVADA BLUE

PLATE 22 × 1

METALMARKS AND SNOUT

FATAL METALMARK *Calephelis nemesis* **P. 255**
¾–1 in. (18–26 mm). Both sexes have *dark median band* above.

WRIGHT'S METALMARK *Calephelis wrighti* **P. 256**
¹⁵⁄₁₆–1⅛ in. (24–29 mm). *Forewings pointed. Outer margin* of forewing *wavy*. Upperside uniform reddish brown.

ROUNDED METALMARK *Calephelis nilus* **P. 257**
¹¹⁄₁₆–¹⁵⁄₁₆ in. (17–24 mm). *Male* has *rounded* forewing *apex*. May or may not have *dark median band*. *Fringes indistinctly checkered*.

RAWSON'S "ARIZONA" METALMARK *Calephelis rawsoni arizonensis* **P. 257**
¾–1¹⁄₁₆ in. (19–28 mm). May or may not have *dark median band*.

ZELA METALMARK *Emesis zela* **P. 258**
1¹⁄₁₆–1⁵⁄₁₆ in. (28–33 mm). Wings brown above with *darkened discal cell on forewing and broadly diffuse yellow patch* on hindwing.

ARES METALMARK *Emesis ares* **P. 258**
1⅛–1⁵⁄₁₆ in. (29–34 mm). Forewing has submarginal *dark dashes* and hindwing has *sharply delimited yellow patch* on leading edge.

MEXICAN METALMARK *Apodemia duryi* **P. 262**
1–1⁵⁄₁₆ in. (25–33 mm). *Black outer edges* on forewings above. Remainder of wing *yellow-orange* with *white spots*.

MORMON METALMARK *Apodemia mormo* **P. 260**
1–1³⁄₁₆ in. (25–31 mm). Forewing *black* with *white spots* and *red–orange* to *yellow-orange* at base. Hindwing *black* with *small white spots* or with areas of *red-orange* to *yellow*.

SONORAN METALMARK *Apodemia mejicanus* **P. 261**
⅞–1⁵⁄₁₆ in. (23–33 mm). Forewings above with *white-spotted black* on outer third, *red-orange* to *yellow-orange* with *scattered small white spots* on basal two-thirds.

BEHR'S METALMARK *Apodemia virgulti* **P. 261**
¾–¹⁵⁄₁₆ in. (19–24 mm). Wings above ranging from *black* only at *outer edges* to *entirely black* with *white spots*. *Remainder of* wings *red-orange* to *yellow-orange*.

HEPBURN'S METALMARK *Apodemia hepburni* **P. 262**
¹³⁄₁₆–⅞ in. (21–23 mm). *Brown* above with *tiny white* spots and only *trace of orange scaling* at wing bases.

PALMER'S METALMARK *Apodemia palmeri* **P. 263**
⅝–¹³⁄₁₆ in. (16–21 mm). *Brown* above with *small white spots* and variable amounts of *orange* at margins.

NAIS METALMARK *Apodemia nais* **P. 264**
1–1³⁄₁₆ in. (25–31 mm). *Red-orange* above with *black dots* and *dashes. Small white* dot on leading edge of forewing near wingtip.

AMERICAN SNOUT *Libytheana carinenta* **P. 266**
1⅜–1¹³⁄₁₆ in. (35–46 mm). *Snoutlike palpi*. Wingtip *squared off*.

PLATE 22

FATAL METALMARK

WRIGHT'S METALMARK ♂

ROUNDED METALMARK ♂

RAWSON'S METALMARK *arizonensis*

ZELA METALMARK ♂ ♀

ARES METALMARK ♂

MEXICAN METALMARK ♀

MORMON METALMARK

MORMON METALMARK *langei*

MORMON METALMARK *langei*

SONORAN METALMARK

BEHR'S METALMARK

mejicanus

SONORAN METALMARK *deserti*

BEHR'S METALMARK *dialeuca*

HEPBURN'S METALMARK

PALMER'S METALMARK

NAIS METALMARK ♂

AMERICAN SNOUT

PLATE 23 ×⅓

HELICONIANS, INCLUDING FRITILLARIES

GULF FRITILLARY *Agraulis vanillae* **P. 268**
2¼–3¼ in. (58–82 mm). Bright orange with 3 *white black-rimmed spots*. Underside of hindwing with *elongate metallic silver spots*.

MEXICAN SILVERSPOT *Dione moneta* **P. 268**
3–3¼ in. (76–82 mm). Forewings pointed. *Dull brownish orange* above. Underside with *dense pattern* of *elongate metallic silver*.

JULIA *Dryas julia* **P. 269**
3–3¾ in. (74–82 mm). Forewings pointed. *Bright orange* above with few black marks. Mainly *yellow-orange* below.

ISABELLA'S HELICONIAN *Eueides isabella* **P. 269**
3⅛–3½ in. (78–90 mm). Orange with black tiger stripes.

ZEBRA *Heliconius charithonius* **P. 269**
2½–3⅝ in. (65–92 mm). Wings long, *black* and *yellow zebra-striped*.

VARIEGATED FRITILLARY *Euptoieta claudia* **P. 270**
1⅜–2¾ in. (36–72 mm). *Forewings pointed. Hindwing angled.* Black and orange above. Below hindwing *mottled orange* and *tan*.

MEXICAN FRITILLARY *Euptoieta hegesia* **P. 270**
2⁹⁄₁₆–2¹⁵⁄₁₆ in. (66–74) mm). Like Variegated Fritillary but *less black* above, and *uniform orange-brown* below.

GREAT SPANGLED FRITILLARY *Speyeria cybele* **P. 271**
2⁹⁄₁₆–3⁹⁄₁₆ in. (66–90 mm). Male tawny. Female white or pale with black pattern in western mountains but tawny on Great Plains. Male with *black scaling* along *forewing veins*. Underside of hindwing with *broad pale submarginal band*. Metallic silver spots reduced in size in western mountains.

APHRODITE FRITILLARY *Speyeria aphrodite* **P. 272**
2¼–3 in. (58–76 mm). Similar to Great Spangled Fritillary. Male red-orange above, female paler. Male forewing has *small black spot* below cell and *lacks black scaling* on veins. Underside of hindwing has *pale* submarginal *band pale* or *absent*.

REGAL FRITLLARY *Speyeria idalia* (half size) **P. 273**
2¹¹⁄₁₆–3⅝ in. (68–93 mm). Forewing *red-orange* with *ornate black marks*. Hindwing *black* with postmedian row of *white spots* and submarginal row of *orange (male)* or *white (female) spots*.

NOKOMIS FRITILLARY *Speyeria nokomis* **P. 274**
2½–3¹⁄₁₆ in. (63–78 mm). *Male bright cinnamon-orange* above with black pattern. *Female white* with black pattern. Underside of hindwing with *small metallic silver spots*. Hindwing of male light to dark brown basally with *tan submarginal band*; female hindwing *gray-green* basally with *yellow-green submarginal band*.

PLATE 23

GULF FRITILLARY

GULF FRITILLARY

MEXICAN SILVERSPOT

JULIA

ISABELLA'S HELICONIAN

ZEBRA

VARIEGATED FRITILLARY

MEXICAN FRITILLARY

GREAT SPANGLED FRITILLARY

leto ♂

leto ♀

GREAT SPANGLED FRITILLARY

APHRODITE FRITILLARY

REGAL FRITILLARY

NOKOMIS FRITILLARY

PLATE 24   × ⅔

FRITILLARIES

CORONIS FRITILLARY *Speyeria coronis*   **P. 276**
1¹⁵⁄₁₆–2½ in. (49–65 mm). Hindwing with *silver spots* in marginal row *rounded* on inner edge or *flattened* and *capped* with *pale green* or *greenish brown. Submarginal band pale straw yellow* or *buff*.

EDWARDS' FRITILLARY *Speyeria edwardsii*   **P. 275**
2–2¾ in. (51–70 mm). *Bold black* border on both wings. Underside of hindwing *green* or *gray-green* with *elongate metallic silver marks* and *narrow buff submarginal band*.

ZERENE FRITILLARY *Speyeria zerene*   **P. 276**
1⅞–2⅝ in. (48–67 mm). Variable. Underside ranging from brown-purple to pale yellow-brown. Spots usually silvered but unsilvered in California Coast Range and s. Nev. *Postmedian spots round* to *elongate* with *outward brown extensions. Submarginal spots rounded inwardly* with *brown caps*.

GREAT BASIN FRITILLARY *Speyeria egleis*   **P. 278**
1¾–2¼ in. 44–58 mm). *Basal half* of wings usually *dark*. Below the *basal disk* is *dark*, and *postmedian spots* are *small* and *elongate. Marginal spots* slightly *triangular* or *rounded* with *brown* or *greenish caps*.

CALLIPPE FRITILLARY *Speyeria callippe*   **P. 277**
1⅞–2½ in. (47–65 mm). Pale tan to bright orange above. Underside of hindwing tan, brown, or red-brown with silver or unsilvered spots and *tan submarginal band* (west of Cascade-Sierra Nevada crests) or *green* with or without a *narrow yellow-green submarginal band*.

UNSILVERED FRITILLARY *Speyeria adiaste*   **P. 278**
1¾–2¼ in. (45–57 mm). Wings red-brown above. Underside *reddish orange* to *pale tan* with *spots unsilvered* and *almost obsolete*.

ATLANTIS FRITILLARY *Speyeria atlantis*   **P. 279**
1¹⁵⁄₁₆–2⁷⁄₁₆ in. (49–62 mm). Forewing with *black margin* above. Hindwing with *chocolate* to *purplish brown basal disk* and *narrow pale submarginal band. Spots always silvered*.

NORTHWESTERN FRITILLARY *Speyeria hesperis*   **P. 279**
2–2¾ in. (50–68 mm). *Very similar to Atlantis Fritillary but with red-brown* or *orange-brown basal disk* on underside of hindwing. *Spots* may be *either silvered* or *unsilvered*.

HYDASPE FRITILLARY *Speyeria hydaspe*   **P. 281**
1⅝–2¼ in. (41–58 mm). *Red-orange* with *heavy black pattern.* Underside purplish brown with relatively *round unsilvered spots*.

MORMON FRITILLARY *Speyeria mormonia*   **P. 281**
1⅝–2 in. (41–52 mm). Forewing *without black scaling* on veins. Underside of hindwing with *base sometimes greenish. Spots* relatively *small,* may be either *silvered* or *unsilvered*.

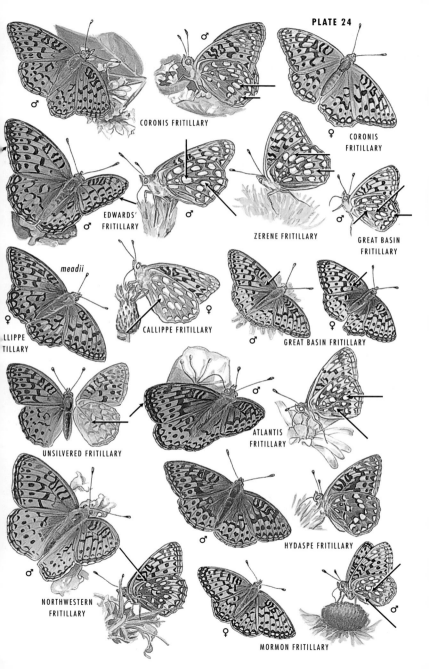

PLATE 24

CORONIS FRITILLARY

♂

CORONIS FRITILLARY

♀

EDWARDS' FRITILLARY

♂

ZERENE FRITILLARY

GREAT BASIN FRITILLARY

♂

meadii

CALLIPPE FRITILLARY

♀

LLIPPE TILLARY

♀

GREAT BASIN FRITILLARY

♂

♀

UNSILVERED FRITILLARY

ATLANTIS FRITILLARY

♂

HYDASPE FRITILLARY

NORTHWESTERN FRITILLARY

♂

MORMON FRITILLARY

♀

♂

PLATE 25 × 1

LESSER FRITILLARIES

MOUNTAIN FRITILLARY *Boloria napaea* **P. 282**
1 5/16–1 9/16 in. (33–40 mm). *Forewings pointed, outer margin* of hindwing *arched*. Underside of hindwing with *faint pattern*.

SILVER-BORDERED FRITILLARY *Boloria selene* **P. 283**
1 3/8–1 7/8 in. (35–47 mm). Hindwing with *metallic silver spots*.

BOG FRITILLARY *Boloria eunomia* **P. 282**
1 5/16–1 5/8 in. (34–42 mm). Hindwing below with *flat white spots*.

MEADOW FRITILLARY *Boloria bellona* **P. 284**
1 5/16–1 3/4 in. (35–45 mm). Forewing *apex angled and cut off*. Below, hindwing *mottled purple-brown*.

FRIGGA FRITILLARY *Boloria frigga* **P. 285**
1 1/2–1 3/4 in. (38–46 mm). Underside of hindwing *purplish* with *small off-white or silvery patch* on leading edge.

DINGY FRITILLARY *Boloria improba* **P. 285**
1 1/8–1 3/8 in. (28–35 mm). Underside of hindwing plain —*basal half pale, outer half orangish* or *gray*.

POLARIS FRITILLARY *Boloria polaris* **P. 287**
1 3/16–1 1/2 in. (31–38 mm). Hindwing *frosted white* with sub-marginal *dark triangles* and *black spots surrounded* with *white*.

RELICT FRITILLARY *Boloria kriemhild* **P. 286**
1 5/16–1 3/4 in. (34–45 mm). Above submarginal *chevrons* on hind-wing *point inward*. Below, hindwing with *black-lined yellow spots*.

PACIFIC FRITILLARY *Boloria epithore* **P. 284**
1 5/16–1 15/16 in. (34–49 mm). Hindwing light purplish below with yellow spot row. Submarginal row of slightly *darkened crescents points outward*.

BERINGIAN FRITILLARY *Boloria natazhati* **P. 287**
1 3/8–1 3/4 in. (36–44 mm). Pattern *blackish* with *long hairs* at wing bases. Below, muted pattern, but includes median *dark zigzag line*.

FREIJA FRITILLARY *Boloria freija* **P. 287**
1 1/4–1 1/2 in. (32–39 mm). Hindwing reddish with median *black zigzag line* and *arrow-shaped white spots* in center and at margin.

ALBERTA FRITILLARY *Boloria alberta* **P. 288**
1 1/2–1 3/4 in. (38–44 mm). Wings with *smudged pattern*. Below or-ange with *smudging* including *dull white bands* on hindwing.

ASTARTE FRITILLARY *Boloria astarte* **P. 288**
1 1/2–1 7/8 in. (38–48 mm). Below, hindwing orange with *black-edged postbasal band*, median row of *white marks*.

ARCTIC FRITILLARY *Boloria chariclea* **P. 289**
1 3/16–1 1/2 in. (31–39 mm). Below, hindwing with thin marginal *white spots capped inwardly with brown*. Median band with *strong black line* outwardly.

PLATE 25

MOUNTAIN FRITILLARY ♂

SILVER-BORDERED FRITILLARY

SILVER-BORDERED FRITILLARY

BOG FRITILLARY ♂

MEADOW FRITILLARY

FRIGGA FRITILLARY

DINGY FRITILLARY

acrocnema

DINGY FRITILLARY

MEADOW FRITILLARY chrysallis

POLARIS FRITILLARY

RELICT FRITILLARY

PACIFIC FRITILLARY ♂

BERINGIAN FRITILLARY

FREIJA FRITILLARY

♀

♂

ALBERTA FRITILLARY

distincta

ASTARTE FRITILLARY

♂

astarte

ARCTIC FRITILLARY ♂

PLATE 26　　　　　　　　　　　　　　　　　　　× 1

CHECKERSPOTS AND PATCHES

DOTTED CHECKERSPOT *Poladryas minuta*　　　　**P. 290**
1 ⅛–1 ½ in. (29–39 mm). Underside of hindwing with *double row* of marginal *white spots* and *median white band* with *doubled row* of *black dots*.

THEONA CHECKERSPOT *Thessalia theona*　　　　**P. 291**
1 ¹⁄₁₆–1 ½ in. (27–39 mm). Underside of hindwing cream with *veins outlined* in *black*, overlain by *red-orange postbasal blotch* and *postmedian band*.

BLACK CHECKERSPOT *Thessalia cyneas*　　　　**P. 292**
1 ⁵⁄₁₆–1 ⁹⁄₁₆ in. (34–40 mm). Wings above *black* with small yellow spots and hindwing with *red-orange marginal band*. Below, hindwing cream with *black* along *veins* and submarginal band with *circular cream spots between veins*.

FULVIA CHECKERSPOT *Thessalia fulvia*　　　　**P. 293**
1–1 ⅜ in. (26–36 mm). Wings above ranging from *blackish* to *orangish*. *Lacks* distinct *marginal* band on hindwing. Underside of hindwing similar to Black Checkerspot's.

LEANIRA CHECKERSPOT *Thessalia leanira*　　　　**P. 293**
1 ⁵⁄₁₆–1 ¹¹⁄₁₆ in. (34–43 mm). Wings *bright orange* to *black* with small yellow spots. Underside of hindwing similar to Black Checkerspot's.

CALIFORNIA PATCH *Chlosyne californica*　　　　**P. 294**
1 ⁵⁄₁₆–1 ¾ in. (34–45 mm). Wings above primarily *orange* with *black* at base. Submarginal black band on both wings with row of *tiny white dots*.

BORDERED PATCH *Chlosyne lacinia*　　　　**P. 295**
1 ⁵⁄₁₆–1 ⅞ in. (34–48 mm). Wings above *black* with variable *transverse* cream, white, or orange *band* on hindwing. Band may be very narrow or absent.

DEFINITE PATCH *Chlosyne definita*　　　　**P. 295**
¹⁵⁄₁₆–1 ⁵⁄₁₆ in. (24–33 mm). Wings above with *checkered pattern* of red–orange, yellow-orange, and dark brown. Underside with submarginal band on hindwing with only *1 included white spot*.

ROSITA PATCH *Chlosyne rosita*　　　　**P. 296**
1 ⁷⁄₁₆–1 ¹¹⁄₁₆ in. (36–42 mm). Hindwing patch *yellow* at base, *red-orange* at outer edge.

BANDED PATCH *Chlosyne endeis*　　　　**P. 295**
1 ⅛–1 ½ in. (29–38 mm). Similar to a large strongly marked Definite Patch. Orange above with *orange-yellow median band* above. Two submarginal *red-orange spots* on hindwing.

CRIMSON PATCH *Chlosyne janais*　　　　**P. 296**
1 ⅞–2 ⁹⁄₁₆ in. (47–65 mm). Wings above black with *large orange-red patch* on basal half of hindwing.

PLATE 26

minuta

DOTTED CHECKERSPOT

♂

DOTTED CHECKERSPOT

♂

arachne

THEONA CHECKERSPOT

BLACK CHECKERSPOT

FULVIA CHECKERSPOT

FULVIA CHECKERSPOT

LEANIRA CHECKERSPOT

alma

cerrita

LEANIRA CHECKERSPOT

THEONA CHECKERSPOT

CALIFORNIA PATCH

BORDERED PATCH

DEFINITE PATCH

ROSITA PATCH

BORDERED PATCH

BANDED PATCH

CRIMSON PATCH

PLATE 27 × 1

CHECKERPOTS, CRESCENTS, AND ELF

GORGONE CHECKERSPOT *Chlosyne gorgone* **P. 296**
1 1/16–1 7/16 in. (28–37 mm). Underside of hindwing has *zigzag pattern* of alternating *brown* and *white bars* and *scallops*.

SILVERY CHECKERSPOT *Chlosyne nycteis* **P. 297**
1 3/16–1 3/4 in. (30–45 mm). Hindwing has at least *1 white submarginal spot* unless obscured by black scaling. Underside of hindwing with median *row* of *black-* or *brown-bordered silvery checks*. Submarginal row may show several silvery crescents.

NORTHERN CHECKERSPOT *Chlosyne palla* **P. 298**
1 3/16–1 3/4 in. (31–44 mm). Underside of hindwing has checkered pattern of *buff-yellow and red-orange*. Some areas *white-cream*.

HARRIS' CHECKERSPOT *Chlosyne harrisii* **P. 297**
1 3/16–1 13/16 in. (30–46 mm). Underside of hindwing has *checkered pattern* with *marginal band* on both wings.

GABB'S CHECKERSPOT *Chlosyne gabbii* **P. 300**
1 3/16–1 3/4 in. (31–44 mm). Underside of hindwing *checkered* with *red-orange* and *pearly white*.

SAGEBRUSH CHECKERSPOT *Chlosyne acastus* **P. 299**
See text.

ROCKSLIDE CHECKERSPOT *Chlosyne whitneyi* **P. 301**
1 3/16–1 1/2 in. (31–39 mm). *Dingy red-orange* and black above. Underside of hindwing checkered *orange* and *dull white*.

HOFFMANN'S CHECKERSPOT *Chlosyne hoffmanni* **P. 301**
1 5/16–1 5/8 in. (34–42 mm). *Basal* portion of lower forewing and basal third of hindwing *mainly black*.

ELF *Microtia elva* **P. 302**
1–1 3/8 in. (26–36 mm). Wings black with *yellow-orange patches*.

TINY CHECKERSPOT *Dymasia dymas* **P. 302**
13/16–1 3/16 in. (21–30 mm). Underside of hindwing with *terminal black line* and *marginal white spots*.

ELADA CHECKERSPOT *Texola elada* **P. 302**
7/8–1 1/8 in. (22–29 mm). Underside of hindwing with *red-orange marginal band*.

TEXAN CRESCENT *Phyciodes texana* **P. 303**
1 3/16–1 9/16 in. (30–40 mm). Outer *margin* of forewing *concave* below wingtip. Upperside black with white spots.

TULCIS CRESCENT *Phyciodes tulcis* **P. 303**
1–1 1/2 in. (26–38 mm). Black with yellow overscaling and *broad cream band* on hindwing.

VESTA CRESCENT *Phyciodes vesta* **P. 304**
1 1/4–1 1/2 in. (31–37 mm). Orange with *fine black lines*. Underside of forewing with *orange circles* amidst black lines.

PLATE 27

drusius

SILVERY CHECKERSPOT

GORGONE CHECKERSPOT

NORTHERN CHECKERSPOT

HARRIS' CHECKERSPOT

GABB'S CHECKERSPOT

SAGEBRUSH CHECKERSPOT *acastus*

ROCKSLIDE CHECKERSPOT

manchada

HOFFMANN'S

HOFFMANN'S CHECKERSPOT *manchada*

ELF

TINY CHECKERSPOT

TINY CHECKERSPOT

ELADA CHECKERSPOT

TEXAN CRESCENT

TULCIS CRESCENT

ELADA CHECKERSPOT

VESTA CRESCENT

PLATE 28   × 1

CRESCENTS AND CHECKERSPOTS

PHAON CRESCENT *Phyciodes phaon*   **P. 304**
 1–1¼ in. (26–32 mm). Forewing with *pale cream median band* above. Hindwing below *cream* with black smudges and lines.

PEARL CRESCENT *Phyciodes tharos*   **P. 305**
 1–1⅜ in. (26–35 mm). Males with areas broken by *fine black marks*. Underside of hindwing has crescent in *dark marginal patch*.

TAWNY CRESCENT *Phyciodes batesii*   **P. 307**
 1¹⁄₁₆–1½ in. (28–38 mm). Males with *pale orange* postmedian patch on forewing contrasting with *darker orange* submarginal band. Underside of forewing with *black patch* on inner margin larger than that on costal margin.

NORTHERN CRESCENT *Phyciodes cocyta*   **P. 306**
 1¼–1¹¹⁄₁₆ in. (32–43 mm). Males often with *open orange areas*. Underside of hindwing usually has *pale tan* marginal *patch*.

FIELD CRESCENT *Phyciodes pratensis*   **P. 308**
 ¹⁵⁄₁₆–1½ in. (24–39 mm). *Antennal knobs brown*. Underside of forewing with *yellow discal bar* and smaller *black patches*.

PAINTED CRESCENT *Phyciodes picta*   **P. 309**
 ⅞–1³⁄₁₆ in. (23–30 mm). *Yellow patch* near wingtip contrasting with *orange* on hindwing. Hindwing *clear yellow-cream below*.

CALIFORNIA CRESCENT *Phyciodes orseis*   **P. 309**
 1³⁄₁₆–1⅝ in. (30–41 mm). See text.

PALE CRESCENT *Phyciodes pallida*   **P. 310**
 1³⁄₁₆–1½ in. (30–39 mm). Underside of forewing with *squarish black patch* in center of trailing margin. Submarginal *spot row* on hindwing *off-white*.

MYLITTA CRESCENT *Phyciodes mylitta*   **P. 311**
 1–1½ in. (26–37 mm). Underside of forewing *plain orange*. Underside of hindwing *lacks submarginal off-white spots*.

GILLETTE'S CHECKERSPOT *Euphydryas gillettii*   **P. 312**
 1⁷⁄₁₆–1¹³⁄₁₆ in. (37–46 mm). Both wings with *broad submarginal red-orange bands*.

VARIABLE CHECKERSPOT *Euphydryas chalcedona*   **P. 313**
 1⅛–2³⁄₁₆ in. (29–55 mm). Variable. Abdomen with *white dots*. Mainly black, red, or orange above. Hindwing with postmedian *red-orange band* clearly *separated* from *median cream band*.

EDITH'S CHECKERSPOT *Euphydryas editha*   **P. 314**
 1–1¹¹⁄₁₆ in. (26–43 mm). Abdomen black often with *red rings*. Underside of forewing with *cream postmedian spot* on trailing edge. Postmedian *red-orange band* on hindwing often *extends into cream median bands*.

PLATE 28

PHAON CRESCENT

PEARL CRESCENT

TAWNY
CRESCENT

anasazi

NORTHERN CRESCENT

TAWNY
CRESCENT

FIELD
CRESCENT

PAINTED
CRESCENT

CALIFORNIA CRESCENT

PALE CRESCENT

MYLITTA CRESCENT

GILLETTE'S
CHECKERSPOT

VARIABLE
CHECKERSPOT
chalcedona

VARIABLE
CHECKERSPOT
chalcedona

GILLETTE'S
CHECKERSPOT

bayensis

EDITH'S CHECKERSPOT

VARIABLE CHECKERSPOT
bernadetta

PLATE 29 × ⅔

ANGLEWINGS, TORTOISESHELLS, AND LADIES

QUESTION MARK *Polygonia interrogationis* **P. 316**
1 ⅞–2½ in. (48–66 mm). Underside with *silvery question mark.*

EASTERN COMMA *Polygonia comma* **P. 316**
1 ⅝–2 ¹⁄₁₆ in. (42–52 mm). Forewing with *single* dark postmedian *spot near trailing edge.* Underside with central silver comma.

GREEN COMMA *Polygonia faunus* **P. 318**
1 ⅜–2 in. (36–52 mm). Wing *outline* exceptionally irregular and *ragged.* Underside of hindwing usually *has submarginal green spots.*

SATYR COMMA *Polygonia satyrus* **P. 317**
1 ¼–2 ¹⁄₁₆ in. (45–53 mm). Forewing usually with 2 *black spots near trailing edge.* Underside usually striated *golden brown.*

HOARY COMMA *Polygonia gracilis zephyrus* **P. 319**
1 ½–1 ⅞ in. (39–47 mm). Underside of hindwing gray-brown; *outer half distinctly paler. Comma* abruptly curved in *fishhook shape.*

GRAY COMMA *Polygonia progne progne* **P. 319**
1 ¼–2 in. (44–52 mm). Hindwing gray, gray-brown, or black with little *contrast* between basal and outer portions.

GRAY COMMA *Polygonia progne oreas* **P. 319**
Underside of hindwing usually *dark brown or black.*

COMPTON TORTOISESHELL *Nymphalis vaualbum* **P. 320**
2 ⁷⁄₁₆–2 ¾ in. (62–72 mm). *Single white spots* on forewing and hindwing *leading margins.* Hindwing with central silver comma below.

CALIFORNIA TORTOISESHELL *Nymphalis californica* **P. 321**
1 ¾–2 ⅛ in. (45–54 mm). Orange with *large black spots.*

KAMEHAMEHA LADY *Vanessa tameamea* **P. 326**
2–2 ¾ in. (52–70 mm). Hindwing *outer margin scalloped.* Forewing with *large red-orange median area* with 2 *black dots.*

MOURNING CLOAK *Nymphalis antiopa* **P. 322**
2 ¹¹⁄₁₆–3 ⁷⁄₁₆ in. (68–87 mm). Unmistakable.

MILBERT'S TORTOISESHELL *Nymphalis milberti* **P. 323**
1 ½–2 in. (38–51 mm). Basal *two-thirds* of both wings *black.* Outer third *orange grading into yellow.*

AMERICAN LADY *Vanessa virginiensis* **P. 325**
1 ¾–2 ¼ in. (44–57 mm). Hindwing below with 2 *large eyespots.*

WEST COAST LADY *Vanessa annabella* **P. 327**
1 ½–1 ⅞ in. (39–47 mm). Forewing tip *squared off.* Forewing *costal bar orange,* not white. Hindwing with 3 *or* 4 *blue spots.*

PAINTED LADY *Vanessa cardui* **P. 325**
1 ¹³⁄₁₆–2 ½ in. (46–64 mm). Hindwing with submarginal row of 5 *black spots,* occasionally with blue scaling.

RED ADMIRAL *Vanessa atalanta* **P. 324**
1 ⅞–2 ½ in. (48–65 mm). Contrasting *red-orange bands* on black.

PLATE 29

QUESTION MARK

× ½

EASTERN COMMA

GREEN COMMA

SATYR COMMA

HOARY COMMA

HOARY COMMA

oreas

GRAY COMMA

COMPTON TORTOISESHELL

× ½

CALIFORNIA TORTOISESHELL

KAMEHAMEHA LADY

MOURNING CLOAK

× ½

MILBERT'S TORTOISESHELL

AMERICAN LADY

RED ADMIRAL

WEST COAST LADY

PAINTED LADY

PLATE 30 × ⅓

BRUSHFOOTS AND ADMIRALS

COMMON BUCKEYE *Junonia coenia* **P. 328**
1⅜–2¼ in. (36–58 mm). At least part of *white* subapical *bar* on forewing is *inside large eyespot*. On hindwing *uppermost eyespot much larger* and with *magenta crescent*.

WHITE PEACOCK *Anartia jatrophae* **P. 330**
1¹³⁄₁₆–2⅜ in. (46–60 mm). *White*. Small *round black spot* on forewing and 2 on slightly *scalloped hindwing*.

TROPICAL BUCKEYE *Junonia genoveva* **P. 329**
1¾–2⅜ in. (44–60 mm). Upperside mostly dark brown. Hindwing with 2 *eyespots* of *equal size*.

BANDED PEACOCK *Anartia fatima* **P. TKK**
2⅜–2⁹⁄₁₆ in. (60–66 mm). Brown above with *median white band*.

MALACHITE *Siproeta stelenes* **P. 330**
2¹³⁄₁₆–3½ in. (72–90 mm). Each hindwing with *pointed tail*. Wings brown–black with translucent *yellow-green patches*.

RUSTY-TIPPED PAGE *Siproeta epaphus* **P. 330**
3–3¼ in. (75–82 mm). Forewing tip extended. Hindwing with pointed *taillike extensions*. Outer half of forewing *orange* separated from *black* basal half by *white band*.

WHITE ADMIRAL (RED-SPOTTED PURPLE) *Limenitis arthemis astyanax* **P. TKK**
2½–3⅝ in. (66–92 mm). *Blue* to *blue-green* above with iridescent highlights. Underside of hindwing has 3 basal red-orange spots and submarginal row of *red-orange spots*.

VICEROY *Limenitis archippus* **P. 332**
2¼–3 in. (58–76 mm). Orange or brown above with *postmedian black line* on hindwing and *single row* of *white spots* in black marginal band. Similar to Monarch or Queen.

WEIDEMEYER'S ADMIRAL *Limenitis weidemeyerii* **P. 333**
2–3¹⁄₁₆ in. (52–78 mm). Black with *striking white median band*.

LORQUIN'S ADMIRAL *Limenitis lorquini* **P. 334**
1⁵⁄₁₆–2½ in. (49–65 mm). Like Weidemeyer's Admiral but with *red-orange tip* to forewing and more *red-orange below*.

DINGY PURPLEWING *Eunica monima* **P. 336**
1⅞–2 in. (48–52 mm). *Faint white spots* near wingtip. Below gray-brown with muted pattern of *wavy lines* and *circles*.

CALIFORNIA SISTER *Adelpha bredowii* **P. 334**
2¼–3 in. (57–77 mm). Black with narrow *median white band* and squarish black-outlined *orange patch* on forewing tip.

FLORIDA PURPLEWING *Eunica tatila* **P. 337**
1¹⁵⁄₁₆–2⅜ in. (49–61 mm). Outer margins sinuous. Iridescent violet-blue above. Forewing tip with 6–7 *distinct white spots*. Underside of hindwing has 6–7 small white-pupilled marginal eyespots.

PLATE 30

COMMON BUCKEYE

WHITE PEACOCK ♂

TROPICAL BUCKEYE

WHITE PEACOCK

RUSTY-TIPPED PAGE

BANDED PEACOCK

MALACHITE

♂ *astyanax*

WHITE ADMIRAL

VICEROY

WEIDEMEYER'S ADMIRAL

LORQUIN'S ADMIRAL ♂

DINGY PURPLEWING

CALIFORNIA SISTER

FLORIDA PURPLEWING

LORQUIN'S ADMIRAL

PLATE 31   × ⅔

ADMIRALS, LEAFWINGS, AND EMPERORS

COMMON MESTRA *Mestra amymone*   **P. 338**
1⅜–1¼ in. (36–43 mm). Base of forewing costal vein swollen. *White* or *gray-white*. *Outer portion* of hindwing *orange*.

RED RIM *Biblis hyperia*   **P. 338**
2–2⁵⁄₁₆ in. (50–59 mm). *Pink-red band* on hindwing.

GRAY CRACKER *Hamadryas februa*   **P. 339**
2¾–3⅜ in. (72–85 mm). At least some *red* in forewing *discal bar*. Hindwing eyespots have *orange scales* outside *black crescent*. Underside of forewing with *black submarginal patch* on lower half.

GLAUCOUS CRACKER *Hamadryas glauconome*   **P. 339**
2¹¹⁄₁₆–3⅛ in. (68–80 mm). Underside of forewing has *black submarginal ring* surrounding *white circle* of trailing half.

BLACK-PATCHED CRACKER *Hamadryas atlantis*   **P. 339**
2¾–3½ in. (72–88 mm). Outer *margin* of hindwing *wavy*. Underside strikingly black and white.

ACHERONTA *Historis acheronta*   **P. 340**
2¾–3⅜ in. (72–85 mm). Underside of forewing has small *white spot* on *leading edge* of forewing near wingtip. Hindwing has a *squiggly black median line*.

MANY-BANDED DAGGERWING *Marpesia chiron*   **P. 341**
2⁷⁄₁₆–2⅝ in. (62–67 mm). *Long thin tail* on each hindwing. Basal third of hindwing below *pale gray* with *faint orange stripes*.

RUDDY DAGGERWING *Marpesia petreus*   **P. 341**
2⁹⁄₁₆–3⅜ in. (66–86 mm). Forewing *apex extended*. Long daggerlike *tail* on each hindwing. *Orange* with thin black lines.

TROPICAL LEAFWING *Anaea troglodyta*   **P. 342**
2¼–2½ in. (57–65 mm). Outer wing *margins slightly uneven*. Short tail on each hindwing. Underside *mottled gray-brown*.

BLOMFILD'S BEAUTY *Smyrna blomfildia*   **P. 340**
3–3½ in. (76–90 mm). Forewing apical area black with 3 *white spots*. Hindwing has many *wavy markings* and 2 *large eyespots*.

GOATWEED LEAFWING *Anaea andria*   **P. 342**
1¾–2¹³⁄₁₆ in. (44–72 mm). Underside *unmarked*, gray-brown.

HACKBERRY EMPEROR *Asterocampa celtis*   **P. 344**
1½–2¼ in. (40–56 mm). Forewing with 1 submarginal *black spot* and 1 *solid black discal bar* together with 2 *separate black spots*.

TAWNY EMPEROR *Asterocampa clyton*   **P. 345**
1⅝–2 in. (42–65 mm). Forewing *lacks white spots* and *black submarginal spots* but has 2 *prominent dark discal bars*.

EMPRESS LEILIA *Asterocampa leilia*   **P. 344**
1½–2 in. (38–50 mm). *Chestnut brown* above. Forewing has 2 *submarginal black spots* and 2 *solid brown discal bars*.

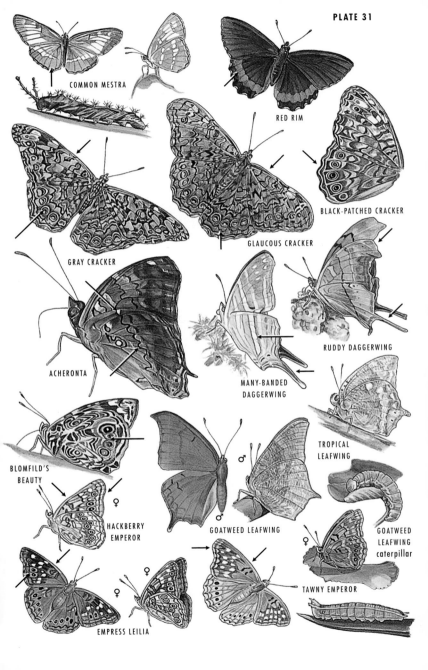

PLATE 31

COMMON MESTRA

RED RIM

GRAY CRACKER

GLAUCOUS CRACKER

BLACK-PATCHED CRACKER

ACHERONTA

MANY-BANDED DAGGERWING

RUDDY DAGGERWING

TROPICAL LEAFWING

BLOMFILD'S BEAUTY

HACKBERRY EMPEROR ♀

GOATWEED LEAFWING ♂

GOATWEED LEAFWING caterpillar ♀

EMPRESS LEILIA ♀

TAWNY EMPEROR

PLATE 32 × 1

MORPHO AND SATYRS

WHITE MORPHO *Morpho polyphemus* **P. 346**
  3¼–5¼ in. (90–123 mm). *Six yellow-rimmed eyespots.*

NORTHERN PEARLY-EYE *Enodia anthedon* **P. 347**
  1¾–2¼ in. (45–58 mm). *Four black yellow-rimmed eyespots.*

EYED BROWN *Satyrodes eurydice* **P. 347**
  1½–2¼ in. (38–55 mm). White-centered *yellow-rimmed eyespots.*

NABOKOV'S SATYR *Cyllopsis pyracmon* **P. 348**
  1½–1¾ in. (38–43 mm). *Postmedian line* goes to leading margin.

CANYONLAND SATYR *Cyllopsis pertepida* **P. 348**
  1¼–1⅝ in. (32–42 mm). *Postmedian line does not reach margin.*

PINE SATYR *Paramacera allyni* **P. 350**
  1⁵⁄₁₆–1¾ in. (34–46 mm). *Six small yellow-rimmed eyespots.*

HAYDEN'S RINGLET *Coenonympha haydenii* **P. 350**
  1⁵⁄₁₆–1¾ in. (33–45 mm). *Six small orange-rimmed eyespots.*

LITTLE WOOD-SATYR *Megisto cymela* **P. 349**
  1⁵⁄₁₆–1¹¹⁄₁₆ in. (34–43 mm). *Two prominent eyespots.*

RED SATYR *Megisto rubricata* **P. 349**
  1⅜–1⅞ in. (34–46 mm). Forewing with *reddish flush.*

COMMON WOOD-NYMPH *Cercyonis pegala* **P. 352**
  1⅞–2¹¹⁄₁₆ in. (48–68 mm). *Two large yellow-rimmed eyespots.*

COMMON RINGLET *Coenonympha tullia* **P. 350**
  1–1⁵⁄₁₆ in. (26–33 mm). Small *black eyespot* near wingtip.

GREAT BASIN WOOD-NYMPH *Cercyonis sthenele* **P. 352**
  1⅜–1¹¹⁄₁₆ in. (35–43 mm). *Upper eyespot* usually *larger* than lower.

SMALL WOOD-NYMPH *Cercyonis oetus* **P. 354**
  1¼–1¾ in. (32–46 mm). *Dark line jutting* strongly *inward.*

MEAD'S WOOD-NYMPH *Cercyonis meadii* **P. 353**
  1½–1¹¹⁄₁₆ in. (39–43 mm). Forewing with *extensive reddish.*

VIDLER'S ALPINE *Erebia vidleri* **P. 355**
  1⅝–1¾ in. (41–46 mm). Yellow-orange submarginal band.

ROSS' ALPINE *Erebia rossii* **P. 355**
  1⅝–1⅞ in. (41–47 mm). *One to three subapical black eyespots.*

DISA ALPINE *Erebia disa* **P. 356**
  1½–1¾ in. (39–43 mm). Conspicuous *small white dash* on hindwing.

TAIGA ALPINE *Erebia mancinus* **P. 356**
  1¾–1⁵⁄₁₆ in. (44–49 mm). *Black spots* in *broader yellow field.*

MAGDALENA ALPINE *Erebia magdalena* **P. 357**
  1¾–2¼ in. (43–57 mm). Almost *completely black.*

MT. McKINLEY ALPINE *Erebia mackinleyensis* **P. 357**
  1¾–2¹⁄₁₆ in. (44–53 mm). *Red-orange flush* on forewing.

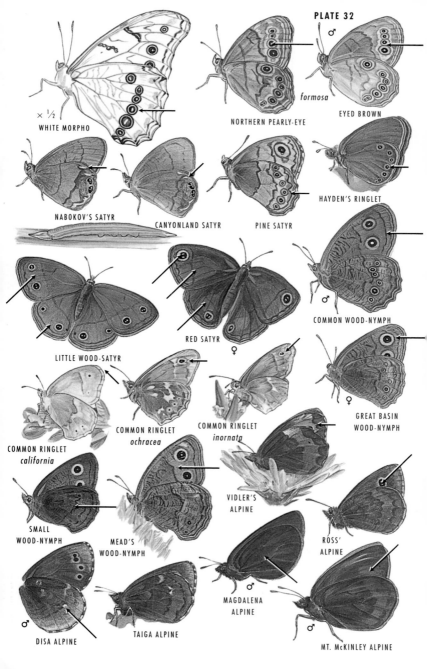

PLATE 32

× ½

WHITE MORPHO

NORTHERN PEARLY-EYE

♂

formosa

EYED BROWN

NABOKOV'S SATYR

CANYONLAND SATYR

PINE SATYR

HAYDEN'S RINGLET

LITTLE WOOD-SATYR

RED SATYR
♀

COMMON WOOD-NYMPH
♂

COMMON RINGLET
ochracea

COMMON RINGLET
inornata

GREAT BASIN
WOOD-NYMPH
♀

COMMON RINGLET
california

VIDLER'S
ALPINE

SMALL
WOOD-NYMPH

MEAD'S
WOOD-NYMPH

ROSS'
ALPINE

DISA ALPINE
♂

TAIGA ALPINE

MAGDALENA
ALPINE
♂

MT. McKINLEY ALPINE
♂

PLATE 33   × 1

SATYRS

BANDED ALPINE *Erebia fasciata*   **P. 358**
  1 ¾–1 ⅞ in. (44–47 mm). *Lacks eyespots*. Underside banded.

RED-DISKED ALPINE *Erebia discoidalis*   **P. 358**
  1 ½–1 ¾ in. (38–45 mm). Forewing with *large chestnut patch*.

THEANO ALPINE *Erebia theano*   **P. 358**
  1 ¼–1 ⅜ in. (32–36 mm). *Red-orange and yellow-cream dashes*.

SCREE ALPINE *Erebia anyuica*   **P. 359**
  1 ⁹⁄₁₆–1 ⅝ in. (40–42 mm). Hindwing with *long gray scales*.

REDDISH ALPINE *Erebia lafontainei*   **P. 360**
  1 ⅝–1 ¾ in. (42–45 mm). Hindwing with long *reddish scales*.

FOUR-DOTTED ALPINE *Erebia youngi*   **P. TKK**
  1 ⁷⁄₁₆–1 ⅝ in. (37–42 mm). Hindwing with long or *red-brown scales*.

COLORADO ALPINE *Erebia callias*   **P. 361**
  1 ³⁄₁₆–1 ½ in. (31–39 mm). Two *black eyespots in reddish field*.

RIDINGS' SATYR *Neominois ridingsii*   **P. 362**
  1 ⅜–2 in. (35–50 mm). *Pale patches* and 2 *black eyespots* on
  forewing.

COMMON ALPINE *Erebia epipsodea*   **P. 361**
  1 ½–1 ⅞ in. (38–48 mm). *Black eyespots on both wings*.

GREAT ARCTIC *Oeneis nevadensis*   **P. 363**
  2–2 ¼ in. (50–55 mm). *Margin of hindwing wavy*. Forewing with
  1–2 *black eyespots* near wingtip; 1 *small black spot* usually at corner of hindwing. Underside of hindwing *cloudy* brown.

MACOUN'S ARCTIC *Oeneis macounii*   **P. 364**
  2 ⅛–2 ½ in. (54–66 mm). Upperside bright orange-brown with
  heavy *black marginal band* on both wings. Underside of hindwing
  cloudy gray-brown with *median band*.

RED-BORDERED SATYR *Gyrocheilus patrobas*   **P. 362**
  2–2 ¼ in. (51–57 mm). Velvety black-brown with submarginal series of *small white dots* on forewing and *purple-red submarginal
  band along* outer edge of hindwing.

CHRYXUS ARCTIC *Oeneis chryxus*   **P. 364**
  1 ⅝–2 ¹⁄₁₆ in. (41–52 mm). Underside of hindwing with *fine black*
  and *white striations*, often a broad *dark median band*. Usually 1–2
  black spots at anal angle of hindwing.

CHRYXUS ARCTIC *Oeneis chryxus ivallda*   **P. 364**
  Normal orange of most populations replaced with *gray-white* to
  match color of granite in California's Sierra Nevada.

UHLER'S ARCTIC *Oeneis uhleri*   **P. 365**
  1 ½–1 ⅞ in. (38–47 mm). Both wings with more than 1, usually
  many, small submarginal *black spots*. Underside of hindwing with
  wavy black striations on white or gray background.

PLATE 33

BANDED ALPINE

RED-DISKED ALPINE

THEANO ALPINE

FOUR-DOTTED ALPINE

SCREE ALPINE

REDDISH ALPINE

COLORADO ALPINE

RIDINGS' SATYR

COMMON ALPINE ♀

COMMON ALPINE ♀

RIDINGS' SATYR

GREAT ARCTIC

MACOUN'S ARCTIC

RED-BORDERED SATYR ♂

CHRYXUS ARCTIC

ivallda

UHLER'S ARCTIC

PLATE 34   × 1

ARCTICS AND ROYALTY

ALBERTA ARCTIC *Oeneis alberta*   **P. 366**
 1 ¼–1 ⅝ in. (31–41 mm). Underside of forewing with postmedian *line bent sharply outward* at end of discal cell. Hindwing with sharply outlined *dark median band*.

WHITE-VEINED ARCTIC *Oeneis bore*   **P. 366**
 1 ⅜–1 ⅞ in. (35–47 mm). Underside of hindwing with strong dark *median band outlined* with *white. Veins* usually *lined* with *white scales.*

JUTTA ARCTIC *Oeneis jutta*   **P. 367**
 1 ¹¹⁄₁₆–2 ¹⁄₁₆ in. (43–53 mm). Both wings with *yellow-orange submarginal band* (usually interrupted) containing *2–4 black spots.*

MELISSA ARCTIC *Oeneis melissa*   **P. 367**
 1 ½–1 ¾ in. (37–45 mm). Underside of hindwing *mottled black* and *white. Median band weak* or *absent,* bordered by white if present.

POLIXENES ARCTIC *Oeneis polixenes*   **P. 368**
 1 ½–1 ¾ in. (38–43 mm). *Wings translucent.* Underside of hindwing with *strong median dark band, edged* with *white.*

SENTINEL ARCTIC *Oeneis alpina*   **P. 369**
 1 ½–1 ¾ in. (39–45 mm). *Forewings* relatively *short.* Underside of hindwing similar to that of Chryxus Arctic but *pattern indistinct.*

PHILIP'S ARCTIC *Oeneis rosovi*   **P. 368**
 1 ¾–2 in. (39–45 mm). *Wings translucent.* Underside of hindwing narrowly *black-edged* with *tiny yellow submarginal points.*

MONARCH *Danaus plexippus*   **P. 369**
 3–4½ in. (76–114 mm). Bright *orange* with *black along veins. Two rows* of *tiny white points* in black border.

QUEEN *Danaus gilippus*   **P. 370**
 2¾–3½ in. (70–88 mm). *Chestnut brown* with marginal black border cotaining *2 rows of tiny white spots.* Underside with *veins outlined* in *black.*

SOLDIER *Danaus eresimus*   **P. 371**
 2½–3½ in. (62–91 mm). Very similar to Queen but *veins marked thinly* with *black* above. Below, hindwing with *postmedian band* of *blotchy pale whitish spots.*

PLATE 34

ALBERTA ARCTIC

WHITE-VEINED ARCTIC

JUTTA ARCTIC

MELISSSA ARCTIC

POLIXENES ARCTIC

SENTINEL ARCTIC

PHILIP'S ARCTIC

MONARCH ♀

MONARCH ♂

× ⅔

MONARCH

QUEEN ♀

QUEEN ♂

× ⅔

SOLDIER ♀

× ⅔

SOLDIER

PLATE 35   × 1

DULL FIRETIP AND SPREAD-WING SKIPPERS

DULL FIRETIP *Pyrrhopyge araxes*   **P. 373**
 1 ¾–2 ⅜ in. (44–61 mm). Upperside with *large square white spots*.
 Underside of hindwing almost completely *yellow*.

SILVER-SPOTTED SKIPPER *Epargyreus clarus*   **P. 374**
 1 ⅝–1 ⅞ in. (41–47 mm). Translucent *gold spots* on forewing.
 Metallic *silver band* in center of hindwing underside.

WIND'S SILVERDROP *Epargyreus windi*   **P. 374**
 See text.

HAMMOCK SKIPPER *Polygonus leo*   **P. 374**
 1 ¾–2 in. (46–52 mm). Upperside black-brown with 3 prominent
 square *white patches*. Underside of hindwing with *violet sheen*
 and small *dark round basal spot*.

WHITE-STRIPED LONGTAIL *Chioides catillus*   **P. 375**
 1 ¾–2 in. (46–52 mm). Exceptionally long *tails* and long *silver
 white stripe* on underside of hindwing.

ZILPA LONGTAIL *Chioides zilpa*   **P. 376**
 1 ⅞–2 ¼ in. (48–58 mm). *Forewing tip squared off*. Hindwing with
 long outcurved *tail* and *white trapezoidal patch* in center of hindwing underside.

GOLD-SPOTTED AGUNA *Aguna asander*   **P. 376**
 1 ⅞–2 3/16 in. (47–56 mm). Top of *head and thorax golden orange*.
 Underside of hindwing with *basal third brown* and outer two-
 thirds with *vague blurred silver patch*.

MEXICAN LONGTAIL *Polythrix mexicana*   **P. 376**
 1 ½–1 ¾ in. (40–46 mm). Tailed. Forewing with *translucent white
 spots* in central band and near wingtip; 2 *dark spots* near trailing
 edge. Underside of hindwing with 2 *darker* postbasal and postmedian *bands*.

SHORT-TAILED SKIPPER *Zestusa dorus*   **P. 377**
 1 ½–1 ⅝ in. (38–42 mm). *Fringes checkered*. *Short tail* on hindwing. Forewing with 4 *translucent squarish white patches*. Hindwing has small *oval translucent white patch*.

ARIZONA SKIPPER *Codatractus arizonensis*   **P. 378**
 1 ⅝–2 5/16 in. (42–59 mm). *Fringes checkered*. Hindwing with *slight
 elongate extension*. Forewing with *transverse row* of large *square
 white patches*. Underside of hindwing *mottled* with darker black
 patches. Vague submarginal *white patch*.

LONG-TAILED SKIPPER *Urbanus proteus*   **P. 379**
 1 ½–2 in. (38–52 mm). Upperside dark brown with *body* and *basal
 portion* of wings *iridescent blue-green*.

WHITE-CRESCENT LONGTAIL *Codatractus alcaeus*   **P. 378**
 See text.

PLATE 35

DULL
FIRETIP
× ¾

SILVER-SPOTTED
SKIPPER

WIND'S
SILVERDROP
♂

WHITE-STRIPED
LONGTAIL

HAMMOCK SKIPPER

ZILPA LONGTAIL

GOLD-SPOTTED AGUNA
♀

MEXICAN LONGTAIL

SHORT-TAILED
SKIPPER

ARIZONA SKIPPER

WHITE-CRESCENT
LONGTAIL
♂

LONG-TAILED SKIPPER

PLATE 36 × 1

SPREAD-WING SKIPPERS

DORANTES LONGTAIL *Urbanus dorantes*   **P. 379**
   1 ⅜–1 ¾ in. (36–46 mm). Tailed. *Fringes checkered.* Forewing with conspicuous transparent spots. *Lacks iridescent blue-green.*

PLAIN LONGTAIL *Urbanus simplicius*   **P. 380**
   1 ½–1 ¹⁵⁄₁₆ in. (37–50 mm). *Dark postbasal band* on underside of hindwing *joined to brown spot* near leading edge.

BROWN LONGTAIL *Urbanus procne*   **P. 380**
   1 ⅝–1 ⅞ in. (42–48 mm). Tailed. Fringes uncheckered. Brown. Forewing of male has costal fold. Underside of hindwing has post-basal *band separated* from *brown spot* near leading edge.

TWO-BARRED FLASHER *Astraptes fulgerator*   **P. 381**
   1 ⅞–2 ⅜ in. (47–60 mm). *Head and thorax golden yellow.* Basal portions of both wings *iridescent blue.*

SONORAN BANDED-SKIPPER *Autochton pseudocellus*   **P. 381**
   1 ¼–1 ⅝ in. (32–42 mm). Each antenna with *white ring* below club. Wing fringes distinctly checkered. Slightly *curved gold band* crosses forewing. Hindwing has 2 *darker bands* below.

GOLDEN-BANDED SKIPPER *Autochton cellus*   **P. 381**
   1 ¼–1 ¾ in. (32–46 mm). Each antenna has *white ring* below club. Upperside is black with *broad yellow band* crossing forewing.

CHISOS BANDED-SKIPPER *Autochton cinctus*   **P. 382**
   1 ⅜–1 ¾ in. (36–44 mm). *Hindwing* fringe white. *Brown-black with* white translucent band *across forewing.*

DESERT CLOUDYWING *Achalarus casica*   **P. 382**
   1 ½–1 ¹⁵⁄₁₆ in. (37–50 mm). Hindwing *fringe white.* Underside of hindwing with 2 *dark bands* and broad *mottled white marginal band.*

SKINNER'S CLOUDYWING *Achalarus albociliatus*   **P. 383**
   1 ¹¹⁄₁₆–1 ¹³⁄₁₆ in. (43–46 mm). Hindwing with *white fringe.* Forewing underside has *pale outer margin* contrasting with darker inner area.

COYOTE CLOUDYWING *Achalarus toxeus*   **P. 383**
   1 ⅝–1 ¹⁵⁄₁₆ in. (40–50 mm). Upperside dark brown with *darker rectangular spots* on forewing. Hindwing usually with *white fringe.*

SOUTHERN CLOUDYWING *Thorybes bathyllus*   **P. 384**
   1 ¼–1 ⅝ in. (32–42 mm). Male *lacks costal fold.* Forewing with *aligned* broad transparent *spot band.* Hindwing *fringe often pale.*

NORTHERN CLOUDYWING *Thorybes pylades*   **P. 383**
   1 ¼–1 ⁹⁄₁₆ in. (31–40 mm). Male has *costal fold.* Forewing has small *nonaligned triangular transparent spots.* Hindwing *fringe dark.*

WESTERN CLOUDYWING *Thorybes diversus*   **P. 384**
   1 ⅛–1 ⅜ in. (29–36 mm). Male *lacks costal fold. Aligned row* of elongate *spots* crosses forewing. Underside of hindwing with base dark brown, *gray* outwardly and 2 *indistinct black bands.*

PLATE 36

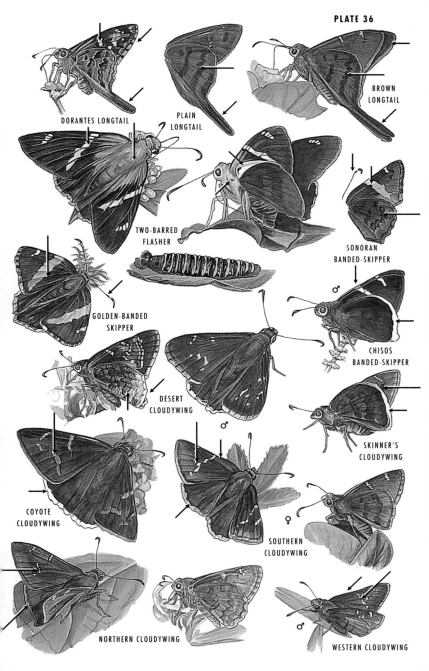

DORANTES LONGTAIL

PLAIN LONGTAIL

BROWN LONGTAIL

TWO-BARRED FLASHER

SONORAN BANDED-SKIPPER

GOLDEN-BANDED SKIPPER

CHISOS BANDED-SKIPPER

♂

DESERT CLOUDYWING

♂

SKINNER'S CLOUDYWING

COYOTE CLOUDYWING

♀

SOUTHERN CLOUDYWING

NORTHERN CLOUDYWING

♂

WESTERN CLOUDYWING

PLATE 37   × 1

SPREAD-WING SKIPPERS

MEXICAN CLOUDYWING *Thorybes mexicanus*   See text.   P. 385

DRUSIUS CLOUDYWING *Thorybes drusius*   See text.   P. 385

DESERT MOTTLED SKIPPER *Codatractus mysie*   See text.   P. 378

OUTIS SKIPPER *Cogia outis*   See text.   P. 388

POTRILLO SKIPPER *Cabares potrillo*   See text.   P. 386

FRITZGAERTNER'S FLAT *Celaenorrhinus fritzgaertneri*   See text.   P. 386

MIMOSA SKIPPER *Cogia calchas*   See text.   P. 387

MOTTLED BOLLA *Bolla clytius*   See text.   P. 389

ACACIA SKIPPER *Cogia hippalus*   See text.   P. 387

MAZANS SCALLOPWING *Staphylus mazans*   See text.   P. 390

CAICUS SKIPPER *Cogia caicus*   See text.   P. 388

WIND'S SKIPPER *Windia windi*   See text.   P. 389

GOLDEN-HEADED SCALLOPWING *Staphylus ceos*   See text.   P. 389

HAYHURST'S SCALLOPWING *Staphylus hayhurstii*   See text.   P. 390

EMORSUS SKIPPER *Antigonus emorsus*   See text.   P. 391

GLASSY-WINGED SKIPPER *Xenophanes tryxus*   See text.   P. 391

TEXAS POWDERED-SKIPPER *Systasea pulverulenta*   See text.   P. 391

HERMIT SKIPPER *Grais stigmatica*   See text.   P. 392

ARIZONA POWDERED-SKIPPER *Systasea zampa*   See text.   P. 392

WHITE-PATCHED SKIPPER *Chiomara georgina*   See text.   P. 393

BROWN-BANDED SKIPPER *Timochares ruptifasciatus*   See text.   P. 393

FALSE DUSKYWING *Gesta invisus*   See text.   P. 394

PLATE 37

MEXICAN CLOUDYWING ♂

DRUSIUS CLOUDYWING

DESERT MOTTLED SKIPPER ♂

OUTIS SKIPPER ♂

POTRILLO SKIPPER

ACACIA SKIPPER ♂

FRITZGAERTNER'S FLAT

MIMOSA SKIPPER ♀

MOTTLED BOLLA ♂

WIND'S SKIPPER

MAZANS SCALLOPWING

CAICUS SKIPPER ♂

GOLDEN-HEADED SCALLOPWING

EMORSUS SKIPPER ♂

HAYHURST'S SCALLOPWING

GLASSY-WINGED SKIPPER

TEXAS POWDERED-SKIPPER

HERMIT SKIPPER ♀

ARIZONA POWDERED-SKIPPER

WHITE-PATCHED SKIPPER ♂

BROWN-BANDED SKIPPER

FALSE DUSKYWING ♂

PLATE 38   × 1

SPREAD-WING SKIPPERS

DREAMY DUSKYWING *Erynnis icelus*   **P. 395**
⅞–1 1/16 in. (24–27 mm). See text.

SLEEPY DUSKYWING *Erynnis brizo*   **P. 395**
1 3/16–1 ⅜ in. (30–35 mm). See text.

JUVENAL'S DUSKYWING *Erynnis juvenalis*   **P. 396**
1 5/16–1 ½ in. (33–38 mm). See text.

ROCKY MOUNTAIN DUSKYWING *Erynnis telemachus*   **P. 397**
1 5/16–1 ⅝ in. (33–41 mm). See text.

PROPERTIUS DUSKYWING *Erynnis propertius*   **P. 397**
1 ⅛–1 ¾ in. (29–44 mm). See text.

MERIDIAN DUSKYWING *Erynnis meridianus*   **P. 397**
1 5/16–1 11/16 in. (33–43 mm). See text.

SCUDDER'S DUSKYWING *Erynnis scudderi*   **P. 398**
1 3/16–1 ½ in. (31–38 mm). See text.

HORACE'S DUSKYWING *Erynnis horatius*   **P. 398**
1 5/16–1 ¾ in. (33–44 mm). See text.

MOURNFUL DUSKYWING *Erynnis tristis*   **P. 399**
1 3/16–1 11/16 in. (30–43 mm). See text.

FUNEREAL DUSKYWING *Erynnis funeralis*   **P. 401**
1 5/16–1 ½ in. (33–38 mm). See text.

PACUVIUS DUSKYWING *Erynnis pacuvius*   **P. 400**
1 1/16–1 5/16 in. (28–33 mm). See text.

MOTTLED DUSKYWING *Erynnis martialis*   **P. 399**
1–1 3/16 in. (25–30 mm). See text.

WILD INDIGO DUSKYWING *Erynnis baptiseae*   **P. 401**
1 3/16–1 9/16 in. (31–40 mm). See text.

AFRANIUS DUSKYWING *Erynnis afranius*   **P. 402**
⅞–1 5/16 in. (23–33 mm). See text.

PERSIUS DUSKYWING *Erynnis persius*   **P. 403**
⅞–1 ⅜ in. (23–36 mm). See text.

GRIZZLED SKIPPER *Pyrgus centaureae*   **P. 403**
⅞–1 3/16 in. (22–31 mm). See text.

TWO-BANDED CHECKERED-SKIPPER *Pyrgus ruralis*   **P. 404**
¾–1 1/16 in. (20–28 mm). See text.

MOUNTAIN CHECKERED-SKIPPER *Pyrgus xanthus*   **P. 404**
¾–1 in. (20–25 mm). See text.

PLATE 38

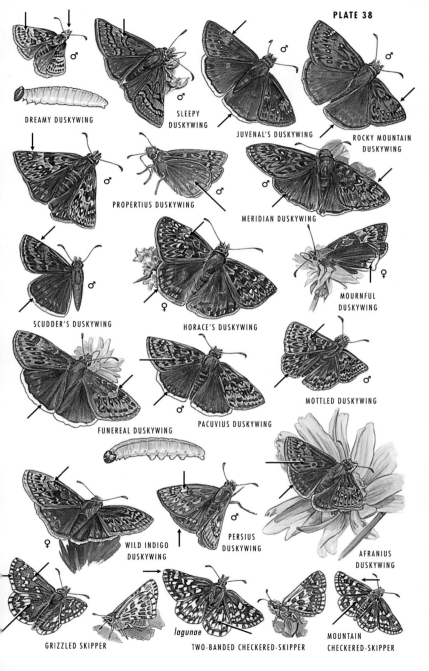

DREAMY DUSKYWING

SLEEPY DUSKYWING

JUVENAL'S DUSKYWING

ROCKY MOUNTAIN DUSKYWING

PROPERTIUS DUSKYWING

MERIDIAN DUSKYWING

SCUDDER'S DUSKYWING

HORACE'S DUSKYWING

MOURNFUL DUSKYWING

FUNEREAL DUSKYWING

PACUVIUS DUSKYWING

MOTTLED DUSKYWING

WILD INDIGO DUSKYWING

PERSIUS DUSKYWING

AFRANIUS DUSKYWING

GRIZZLED SKIPPER

lagunae
TWO-BANDED CHECKERED-SKIPPER

MOUNTAIN CHECKERED-SKIPPER

PLATE 39 × 1

SPREAD-WING SKIPPERS

SMALL CHECKERED-SKIPPER *Pyrgus scriptura* **P. 405**
⅝–⅞ in. (16–22 mm). Black with small white checks. *Square white spot* usually present in center of hindwing.

COMMON CHECKERED-SKIPPER *Pyrgus communis* **P. 406**
⅞–1¼ in. (22–32 mm). Fringes checkered but *black checks often reach only halfway.*

WHITE CHECKERED-SKIPPER *Pyrgus albescens* **P. 407**
1–1³⁄₁₆ in. (25–30 mm). Fringes checkered with *black checks full length,* and male pattern elements *more clear-cut.*

TROPICAL CHECKERED-SKIPPER *Pyrgus oileus* **P. 408**
1–1³⁄₁₆ in. (26–31 mm). Hindwing of both sexes with marginal and submarginal *spots small and equal-sized.*

DESERT CHECKERED-SKIPPER *Pyrgus philetas* **P. 408**
⅞–1¹⁄₁₆ in. (22–28 mm). Hindwing has *minute* marginal and submarginal *spots above. Below hindwing is pale gray with *pattern elements indistinct.*

ERICHSON'S WHITE-SKIPPER *Heliopetes domicella* **P. 409**
1–1⅜ in. (26–34 mm). Upperside with *broad white median band* on both wings. Below hindwing whitish and dull yellow-brown.

NORTHERN WHITE-SKIPPER *Heliopetes ericetorum* **P. 409**
1¹⁄₁₆–1½ in. (27–37 mm). Male white above with *black marginal chevrons.* Female has broad *irregular white band* on both wings.

LAVIANA WHITE-SKIPPER *Heliopetes laviana* **P. 410**
1¼–1⅝ in. (32–41 mm). Forewing *apex squared off.* Underside of hindwing with *outer third olive-brown,* sharply cut off.

COMMON STREAKY-SKIPPER *Celotes nessus* **P. 411**
⅞–1 in. (21–25 mm). Wings with *inward-projecting dark brown streaks* and irregular median series of small transparent spots.

COMMON SOOTYWING *Pholisora catullus* **P. 412**
⅞–1 in. (23–26 mm). *Black with small white spots.*

MEXICAN SOOTYWING *Pholisora mejicana* **P. 412**
⅞–1¹⁄₁₆ in. (22–28 mm). Identical to Common Sootywing except underside of hindwing *iridescent blue-gray* with *black-lined veins.*

MOHAVE SOOTYWING *Hesperopsis libya* **P. 412**
¹⁵⁄₁₆–1¹⁄₁₆ in. (24–33 mm). Upper surface of forewing with *white bar* on leading edge. Below, *forewing apex and hindwing gray.*

SALTBUSH SOOTYWING *Hesperopsis alpheus* **P. 413**
¾–1³⁄₁₆ in. (20–30 mm). Blackish. Forewing above has *series of darker discal dashes* at the base of which are *tiny whitish spots.*

MacNEILL'S SOOTYWING *Hesperopsis gracielae* **P. 414**
¹¹⁄₁₆–¹⁵⁄₁₆ in. (18–24 mm). *Buffy overscaling* on both wings above. Forewing has *shorter discal dashes* than Saltbush Sootywing.

PLATE 39

SMALL CHECKERED-SKIPPER ♀

COMMON CHECKERED-SKIPPER ♂ ♀

WHITE CHECKERED-SKIPPER ♂

TROPICAL CHECKERED-SKIPPER ♀

COMMON CHECKERED SKIPPER ♀

DESERT CHECKERED-SKIPPER

ERICHSON'S WHITE-SKIPPER

LAVIANA WHITE-SKIPPER ♀

NORTHERN WHITE-SKIPPER ♂

COMMON STREAKY-SKIPPER ♂

COMMON SOOTYWING ♀

LAVIANA WHITE-SKIPPER

COMMON SOOTYWING ♀

MEXICAN SOOTYWING ♂

MacNEILL'S SOOTYWING ♂

MOHAVE SOOTYWING ♀

SALTBUSH SOOTYWING

MacNEILL'S SOOTYWING

PLATE 40 × 1

SKIPPERLINGS AND GRASS SKIPPERS

ARCTIC SKIPPER *Carterocephalus palaemon*   **P. 414**
1–1¼ in. (26–31 mm). See text.

RUSSET SKIPPERLING *Piruna pirus*   **P. 415**
⅞–1 in. (22–26 mm). See text.

FOUR-SPOTTED SKIPPERLING *Piruna polingi*   **P. 415**
¾–1 in. (20–26 mm). See text.

MANY-SPOTTED SKIPPERLING *Piruna aea*   **P. 416**
¹³⁄₁₆–⅞ in. (21–23 mm). See text.

CHISOS SKIPPERLING *Piruna haferniki*   **P. 416**
¾–⅞ in. (19–22 mm). See text.

JULIA'S SKIPPER *Nastra julia*   **P. 417**
¹⁵⁄₁₆–1⅛ in. (24–28 mm). See text.

FACETED SKIPPER *Synapte syraces*   **P. 417**
1–1¼ in. (26–32 mm). See text.

CLOUDED SKIPPER *Lerema accius*   **P. 418**
1⅜–1¾ in. (34–44 mm). See text.

COMMON LEAST SKIPPER *Ancyloxipha numitor*   **P. 419**
⅞–1⅛ in. (22–28 mm). See text.

TROPICAL LEAST SKIPPER *Ancyloxipha arene*   **P. 419**
⅞–1¹⁄₁₆ in. (22–27 mm). See text.

GARITA SKIPPERLING *Oarisma garita*   **P. 420**
¾–1³⁄₁₆ in. (20–30 mm). See text.

EDWARDS' SKIPPERLING *Oarisma edwardii*   **P. 420**
⅞–1¹⁄₁₆ in. (22–28 mm). See text.

ORANGE SKIPPERLING *Copaeodes aurantiaca*   **P. 421**
¹⁵⁄₁₆–1⅛ in. (24–29 mm).See text.

SOUTHERN SKIPPERLING *Copaeodes minima*   **P. 421**
⁹⁄₁₆–¾ in. (14–20 mm). See text.

SUNRISE SKIPPER *Adopaeoides prittwitzi*   **P. 422**
⅞–1¹⁄₁₆ in. (22–28 mm). See text.

FIERY SKIPPER *Hylephila phyleus*   **P. 423**
1¼–1½ in. (32–38 mm). See text.

EUROPEAN SKIPPER *Thymelicus lineola*   **P. 422**
1–1⅛ in. (25–29 mm). See text.

ALKALI SKIPPER *Pseudocopaeodes eunus*   **P. 424**
⅞–1⅛ in. (22–28 mm). See text.

MORRISON'S SKIPPER *Stinga morrisoni*   **P. 425**
1–1¼ in. (26–32 mm). See text.

UNCAS SKIPPER *Hesperia uncas*   **P. 426**
1¼–1⅝ in. (32–40 mm). See text.

JUBA SKIPPER *Hesperia juba*   **P. 426**
1–1½ in. (26–38 mm). See text.

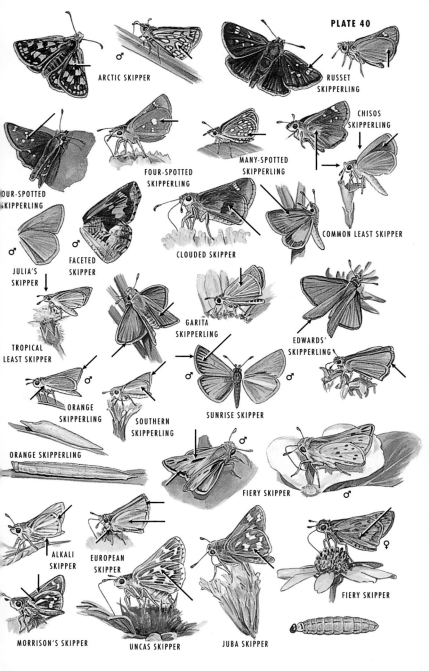

PLATE 40

ARCTIC SKIPPER

RUSSET SKIPPERLING

CHISOS SKIPPERLING

FOUR-SPOTTED SKIPPERLING

MANY-SPOTTED SKIPPERLING

FOUR-SPOTTED SKIPPERLING

COMMON LEAST SKIPPER

JULIA'S SKIPPER

FACETED SKIPPER

CLOUDED SKIPPER

TROPICAL LEAST SKIPPER

GARITA SKIPPERLING

EDWARDS' SKIPPERLING

ORANGE SKIPPERLING

SOUTHERN SKIPPERLING

SUNRISE SKIPPER

ORANGE SKIPPERLING

FIERY SKIPPER

ALKALI SKIPPER

EUROPEAN SKIPPER

FIERY SKIPPER

MORRISON'S SKIPPER

UNCAS SKIPPER

JUBA SKIPPER

PLATE 41   × 1

GRASS SKIPPERS

WESTERN BRANDED SKIPPER *Hesperia colorado*   See text.   **P. 428**

PLAINS SKIPPER *Hesperia assiniboia*   See text.   **P. 427**

COMMON BRANDED SKIPPER *Hesperia comma*   See text.   **P. 427**

APACHE SKIPPER *Hesperia woodgatei*   See text.   **P. 429**

OTTOE SKIPPER *Hesperia ottoe*   See text.   **P. 429**

LEONARD'S SKIPPER *Hesperia leonardus*   See text.   **P. 430**

PAHASKA SKIPPER *Hesperia pahaska*   See text.   **P. 431**

COLUMBIAN SKIPPER *Hesperia columbia*   See text.   **P. 432**

LINDSEY'S SKIPPER *Hesperia lindseyi*   See text.   **P. 434**

GREEN SKIPPER *Hesperia viridis*   See text.   **P. 433**

SIERRA SKIPPER *Hesperia miriamae*   See text.   **P. 434**

NEVADA SKIPPER *Hesperia nevada*   See text.   **P. 437**

RHESUS SKIPPER *Polites rhesus*   See text.   **P. 439**

CARUS SKIPPER *Polites carus*   See text.   **P. 440**

PECK'S SKIPPER *Polites peckius*   See text.   **P. 440**

SANDHILL SKIPPER *Polites sabuleti*   See text.   **P. 441**

MARDON SKIPPER *Polites mardon*   See text.   **P. 441**

DRACO SKIPPER *Polites draco*   See text.   **P. 442**

TAWNY-EDGED SKIPPER *Polites themistocles*   See text.   **P. 442**

WHIRLABOUT *Polites vibex*   See text.   **P. 444**

LONG DASH *Polites mystic*   See text.   **P. 443**

CROSSLINE SKIPPER *Polites origenes*   See text.   **P. 443**

SONORAN SKIPPER *Polites sonora*   See text.   **P. 444**

SOUTHERN BROKEN-DASH *Wallengrenia otho*   See text.   **P. 445**

NORTHERN BROKEN-DASH *Wallengrenia egeremet*   See text.   **P. 445**

LITTLE GLASSYWING *Pompeius verna*   See text.   **P. 446**

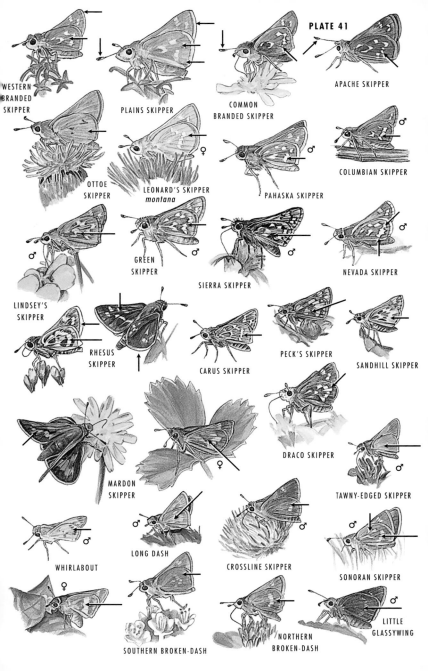

PLATE 41

WESTERN BRANDED SKIPPER

PLAINS SKIPPER

COMMON BRANDED SKIPPER

APACHE SKIPPER

OTTOE SKIPPER

LEONARD'S SKIPPER
montana ♀

PAHASKA SKIPPER

COLUMBIAN SKIPPER

LINDSEY'S SKIPPER ♂

GREEN SKIPPER ♂

SIERRA SKIPPER ♂

NEVADA SKIPPER ♂

RHESUS SKIPPER

CARUS SKIPPER

PECK'S SKIPPER

SANDHILL SKIPPER

MARDON SKIPPER

♀

DRACO SKIPPER

TAWNY-EDGED SKIPPER ♂

WHIRLABOUT ♂

LONG DASH ♂

CROSSLINE SKIPPER ♂

SONORAN SKIPPER ♂

♀

SOUTHERN BROKEN-DASH

NORTHERN BROKEN-DASH

LITTLE GLASSYWING ♂

PLATE 42 × 1

GRASS SKIPPERS

SACHEM *Atalopedes campestris*   **P. 438**
  1 ⅜–1 ⅝ in. (35–41 mm). See text.

DELAWARE SKIPPER *Anatrytone logan*   **P. 447**
  1–1 ⅝ in. (25–42 mm). See text.

AROGOS SKIPPER *Atrytone arogos*   **P. 446**
  1 ⅛–1 ⁷⁄₁₆ in. (28–36 mm). See text.

WOODLAND SKIPPER *Ochlodes sylvanoides*   **P. 447**
  ¾–1 ⅛ in. (20–29 mm). See text.

RURAL SKIPPER *Ochlodes agricola*   **P. 448**
  ¾–1 in. (20–26 mm). See text.

YUMA SKIPPER *Ochlodes yuma*   **P. 449**
  1 ¹⁄₁₆–1 ⅜ in. (28–36 mm). See text.

HOBOMOK SKIPPER *Poanes hobomok*   **P. 449**
  1 ⅜–1 ⅝ in. (34–42 mm). See text.

UMBER SKIPPER *Poanes melane*   **P. 452**
  1 ¹⁄₁₆–1 ⁵⁄₁₆ in. (28–34 mm). See text.

TAXILES SKIPPER *Poanes taxiles*   **P. 451**
  1 ⅜–1 ¹¹⁄₁₆ in. (36–43 mm). See text.

ZABULON SKIPPER *Poanes zabulon*   **P. 450**
  1 ⅜–1 ¹⁵⁄₁₆ in. (34–49 mm). See text.

SNOW'S SKIPPER *Paratrytone snowi*   **P. 453**
  1 ¹⁄₁₆–1 ⅜ in. (28–36 mm). See text.

DUN SKIPPER *Euphyes vestris*   **P. 454**
  1 ¹⁄₁₆–1 ⅜ in. (28–35 mm). See text.

TWO-SPOTTED SKIPPER *Euphyes bimacula*   **P. 453**
  1 ⅜–1 ⅝ in. (35–41 mm). See text.

DUSTED SKIPPER *Atrytonopsis hianna*   **P. 454**
  1 ⅜–1 ⅝ in. (35–42 mm). See text.

MOON-MARKED SKIPPER *Atrytonopsis lunus*   **P. 455**
  1 ⁹⁄₁₆–1 ¾ in. (40–44 mm). See text.

DEVA SKIPPER *Atrytonopsis deva*   **P. 455**
  1 ½–1 ⅝ in. (38–42 mm). See text.

VIERECK'S SKIPPER *Atrytonopsis vierecki*   **P. 456**
  1 ⁵⁄₁₆–1 ½ in. (34–38 mm). See text.

WHITE-BARRED SKIPPER *Atrytonopsis pittacus*   **P. 456**
  1 ¼–1 ⁵⁄₁₆ in. (32–34 mm). See text.

PYTHON SKIPPER *Atrytonopsis python*   **P. 457**
  1 ¼–1 ½ in. (32–38 mm). See text.

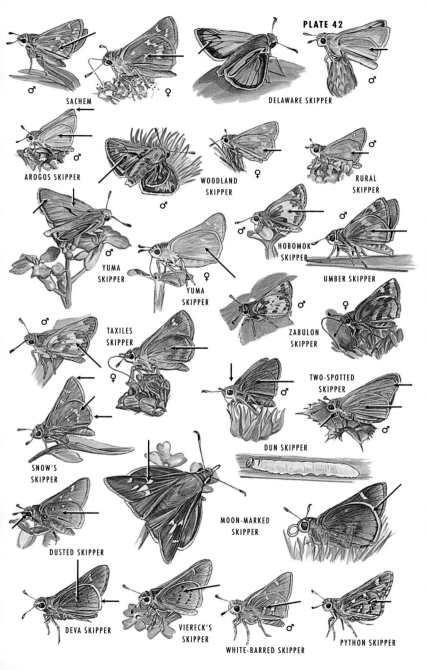

PLATE 42

SACHEM

♂

♀

DELAWARE SKIPPER

♂

AROGOS SKIPPER

♂

WOODLAND SKIPPER

♂

♀

RURAL SKIPPER

♂

YUMA SKIPPER

♂

YUMA SKIPPER

♀

HOBOMOK SKIPPER

♂

UMBER SKIPPER

♂

TAXILES SKIPPER

♂

ZABULON SKIPPER

♂

♀

SNOW'S SKIPPER

♀

TWO-SPOTTED SKIPPER

♂

DUN SKIPPER

♂

MOON-MARKED SKIPPER

DUSTED SKIPPER

PYTHON SKIPPER

DEVA SKIPPER

VIERECK'S SKIPPER

WHITE-BARRED SKIPPER

♂

PLATE 43   × 1

GRASS SKIPPERS

CESTUS SKIPPER *Atrytonopsis cestus*   See text.   **P. 457**

SHEEP SKIPPER *Atrytonopsis edwardsi*   See text.   **P. 458**

SIMIUS ROADSIDE-SKIPPER *"Amblyscirtes" simius*   See text.   **P. 458**

LARGE ROADSIDE-SKIPPER *Amblyscirtes exoteria*   See text.   **P. 459**

CASSUS ROADSIDE-SKIPPER *Amblyscirtes cassus*   See text.   **P. 459**

BRONZE ROADSIDE-SKIPPER *Amblyscirtes aenus*   See text.   **P. 460**

OSLAR'S ROADSIDE-SKIPPER *Amblyscirtes oslari*   See text.   **P. 460**

ELISSA ROADSIDE-SKIPPER *Amblyscirtes elissa*   See text.   **P. 461**

PEPPER AND SALT SKIPPER *Amblyscirtes hegon*   See text.   **P. 461**

TEXAS ROADSIDE-SKIPPER *Amblyscirtes texanae*   See text.   **P. 461**

SLATY ROADSIDE-SKIPPER *Amblyscirtes nereus*   See text.   **P. 462**

TOLTEC ROADSIDE-SKIPPER *Amblyscirtes aea*   See text.   **P. 462**

NYSA ROADSIDE-SKIPPER *Amblyscirtes nysa*   See text.   **P. 463**

DOTTED ROADSIDE-SKIPPER *Amblyscirtes eos*   See text.   **P. 464**

CELIA'S ROADSIDE-SKIPPER *Amblyscirtes celia*   See text.   **P. 465**

COMMON ROADSIDE-SKIPPER *Amblyscirtes vialis*   See text.   **P. 464**

ORANGE-HEADED ROADSIDE-SKIPPER *Amblyscirtes phylace*   See text.   **P. 465**

ORANGE-EDGED ROADSIDE-SKIPPER *Amblyscirtes fimbriata*   See text.   **P. 466**

EUFALA SKIPPER *Lerodea eufala*   See text.   **P. 466**

OLIVE-CLOUDED SKIPPER *Lerodea arabus*   See text.   **P. 467**

BRAZILIAN SKIPPER *Calpodes ethlius*   See text.   **P. 467**

PURPLE-WASHED SKIPPER *Panoquina leucas*   See text.   **P. 469**

WANDERING SKIPPER *Panoquina errans*   See text.   **P. 467**

OCOLA SKIPPER *Panoquina ocola*   See text.   **P. 468**

VIOLET-BANDED SKIPPER *Nyctelius nyctelius*   See text.   **P. 469**

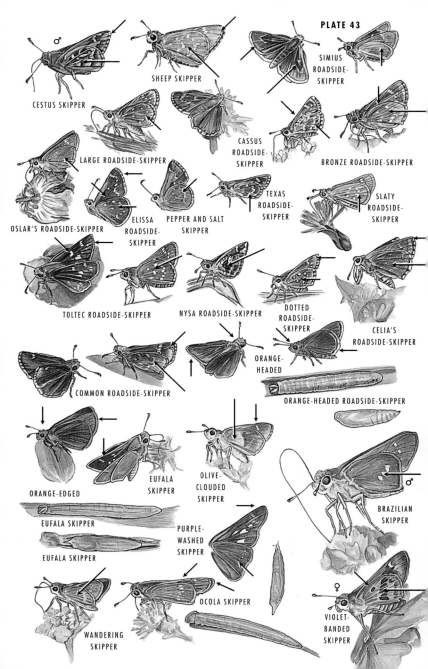

CESTUS SKIPPER

SHEEP SKIPPER

SIMIUS ROADSIDE-SKIPPER

CASSUS ROADSIDE-SKIPPER

BRONZE ROADSIDE-SKIPPER

LARGE ROADSIDE-SKIPPER

OSLAR'S ROADSIDE-SKIPPER

ELISSA ROADSIDE-SKIPPER

PEPPER AND SALT SKIPPER

TEXAS ROADSIDE-SKIPPER

SLATY ROADSIDE-SKIPPER

TOLTEC ROADSIDE-SKIPPER

NYSA ROADSIDE-SKIPPER

DOTTED ROADSIDE-SKIPPER

CELIA'S ROADSIDE-SKIPPER

COMMON ROADSIDE-SKIPPER

ORANGE-HEADED

ORANGE-HEADED ROADSIDE-SKIPPER

ORANGE-EDGED

EUFALA SKIPPER

OLIVE-CLOUDED SKIPPER

BRAZILIAN SKIPPER

EUFALA SKIPPER

EUFALA SKIPPER

PURPLE-WASHED SKIPPER

OCOLA SKIPPER

WANDERING SKIPPER

VIOLET-BANDED SKIPPER

PLATE 44 × 1

GIANT-SKIPPERS

ORANGE GIANT-SKIPPER *Agathymus neumoegeni*　　**P. 470**
　　2–2⅜ in. (50–60 mm). Both wings *suffused extensively with orange*. Wings orange or orange-yellow with *broad black margins*.

ARIZONA GIANT-SKIPPER *Agathymus aryxna*　　**P. 471**
　　2–2⅜ in. (50–61 mm). Both *wings suffused with orange*, especially *basally*. Postmedian band of *yellow-orange spots on both wings*.

HUACHUCA GIANT-SKIPPER *Agathymus evansi*　　**P. 472**
　　1¾–2¼ in. (45–58 mm). *Orange overscaling* only on *basal half* of hindwing. Forewing with *broad band* of orange-yellow spots.

MARY'S GIANT-SKIPPER *Agathymus mariae*　　**P. 472**
　　1¾–2 in. (45–50 mm). Both wings with *narrow orange-yellow* spot *band*, that on hindwing becoming *broader toward abdomen*.

COAHUILA GIANT-SKIPPER *Agathymus remingtoni*　　**P. 473**
　　2–2¼ in. (50–55 mm). Both wings with *very narrow postmedian spot bands,* cream in male, wider and orangish yellow in female. Spot *band* on hindwing becomes *narrower toward abdomen*.

CALIFORNIA GIANT-SKIPPER *Agathymus stephensi*　　**P. 473**
　　2–2³⁄₁₆ in. (51–56 mm). Both wings with *narrow postmedian spot band*, cream in males, slightly yellower in females.

POLING'S GIANT-SKIPPER *Agathymus polingi*　　**P. 474**
　　1⅝–1¾ in. (41–44 mm). Wing bases suffused with orange-yellow. *Wide yellow-orange spot band* on both wings.

MOJAVE GIANT-SKIPPER *Agathymus alliae*　　**P. 475**
　　2³⁄₁₆–2⅜ in. (56–61 mm). Wing bases suffused with orange–yellow. Both wings with *yellow-orange band.*

MANFREDA GIANT-SKIPPER *Stallingsia maculosus*　　**P. 477**
　　1⅞–2 in. (47–50 mm). Brown-black. Upperside with postmedian series of *small oval cream spots* on forewing.

YUCCA GIANT-SKIPPER *Megathymus yuccae*　　**P. 475**
　　1⅞–3⅛ in. (48–79 mm). Forewing with linear submarginal *yellow band, marginal yellow band* on hindwing. Underside of hindwing gray with small white marks on leading edge.

STRECKER'S GIANT-SKIPPER *Megathymus streckeri*　　**P. 476**
　　2½–3³⁄₁₆ in. (64–78 mm). Submarginal *band* on forewing usually *broad and nonaligned*. Underside of hindwing *gray* with several *large postmedian spots*.

URSINE GIANT-SKIPPER *Megathymus ursus*　　**P. 476**
　　2½–3¼ in. (63–83 mm). *Antennae white*. Fringes predominantly *white*. Forewing with *broad yellow or yellow-orange postmedian band*. Hindwing black except for *narrow white strip* along leading edge. Underside primarily gray-white with *small black area* at base and 2 *small white spots on leading edge*.

PLATE 44

ORANGE GIANT-SKIPPER ♂

ARIZONA GIANT-SKIPPER ♂

HUACHUCA GIANT-SKIPPER ♂

MARY'S GIANT-SKIPPER ♂

COAHUILA GIANT-SKIPPER ♂

CALIFORNIA GIANT-SKIPPER ♀

POLING'S GIANT-SKIPPER ♂

MOJAVE GIANT-SKIPPER ♂

MANFREDA GIANT-SKIPPER ♂

YUCCA GIANT-SKIPPER ♂

STRECKER'S GIANT-SKIPPER ♀

URSINE GIANT-SKIPPER ♀

SPECIES ACCOUNTS

TRUE BUTTERFLIES:
SUPERFAMILY PAPILIONOIDEA

The true butterflies have antennae with rounded clubs and are usually more slender-bodied and larger-winged than skippers, the only other North American butterfly superfamily. The swallowtails (Papilionidae), whites and sulphurs (Pieridae), gossamer wings (Lycaenidae), metalmarks (Riodinidae), and brushfoots (Nymphalidae) are the true butterflies. Their wings are often covered with brightly colored scales. Androconia, scales believed to disseminate pheromones used in courtship, may be located in patches on almost any part of the wings, as scale tufts sheathed in the abdomen, or, rarely, on the abdomen itself. These butterflies may have two or three pairs of walking legs; in several families the front legs are modified in structure, reduced in size, and not used for walking.

Eggs may be turban-shaped, globular, or columnar and are usually but not always deposited singly. Caterpillars undergo four to six instars, each of which may have a different color pattern. Caterpillars may be brightly colored, although many are predominantly green or brown, and many are ornamented with groups of bristles or spines. Caterpillars usually feed from the outside, but a few bore into fruits and seeds. Caterpillars lack narrowed neck-like areas. Pupae usually lack cocoons, and those of most families hang from or are slung to objects such as stones, twigs, or bark with a silk girdle and hooks (cremaster) set into a silk mat.

PARNASSIANS AND SWALLOWTAILS:
FAMILY PAPILIONIDAE

The swallowtails are worldwide in distribution and comprise about 560 species. They are richest in the tropics. Many are brilliantly colored and are favorites of butterfly enthusiasts, including watchers, collectors, and photographers. Many species, especially those in the tropics, mimic other butterflies that are distasteful, while others are distasteful themselves and cause birds and other vertebrate predators to regurgitate. Swallowtail adults are medium to large and may or may not have tails (most of ours do), while adults of our parnassians are medium, tailless, and have translucent wings. After mating once, female parnassians develop a prominent white waxy structure, the sphragis, that prevents additional matings. All adult parnassians and swallowtails have three pairs of walking legs. A unique trait is that forewing vein 3 A ends on the inner margin. Adults of all species visit flowers for nectar. Males of most species patrol in search of mates, while males of one group, represented by the Black, Old World, Anise, and Indra Swallowtails in our area, perch on hilltops or ridges instead of patrolling.

Eggs are globular. Older parnassian caterpillars have short hairs, while older swallowtail caterpillars are hairless. Caterpillars have repellent structures, the hornlike osmateria, that can be extruded from behind the head. They vary from yellow to red and are found only in the swallowtail family. The pupae are usually protectively colored (green or brown are the usual colors). Parnassian caterpillars pupate on the ground in loose silken webbing, while swallowtail pupae are attached at the posterior end by a silk button and slung by a silk girdle. Parnassians overwinter as eggs, while swallowtail species overwinter as pupae. In alpine or arctic areas where parnassians may be biennial, older larvae or pupae pass the second winter. Swallowtails may spend more than one year in the pupal stage, and it is thought that in arid areas the Black, Anise, and Indra Swallowtails often display this survival strategy to survive drought years when little caterpillar food is available.

PARNASSIANS: SUBFAMILY PARNASSIINAE

EVERSMANN'S PARNASSIAN *Parnassius eversmanni*   **PL. 1**
1 ⅞–2 in. (48–50 mm). Upperside: Male *yellow;* female yellowish white. Both sexes with 2 round red spots on each hindwing—the *central spot attached to a black mark* extending to anal angle. Underside: More extensive red marks along inner edge of hindwing. **SIMILAR SPECIES:** Clodius Parnassian is white, has shorter dark forewing bars, and is more coastal in northern B.C. where the two might be encountered. **EARLY STAGES:** Caterpillar is black with short black hairs and a lateral row of white or pale yellow spots and dashes. **FOOD:** Bleeding heart and corydalis are eaten in Asia. **FLIGHT:** Late May–early Aug., possibly biennial. **RANGE:** Holarctic. In N. Amer., Alaska and Yukon south to n. B.C. **HABITAT:** Open areas at or below treeline.

EVERSMANN'S PARNASSIAN

CLODIUS PARNASSIAN

extirpated

CLODIUS PARNASSIAN *Parnassius clodius*   **PL. 1**

2³⁄₁₆–2¹¹⁄₁₆ in. (55–69 mm). Upperside: Both sexes with *wings translucent* white showing 2 *round red hindwing spots*. Underside: Similar to upperside but with female showing more red along inner edge of hindwing. **GEOGRAPHIC VARIATION:** Very white at southern end of range in Calif. and darker toward northern range limit. **SIMILAR SPECIES:** (1) Rocky Mountain Parnassian is less translucent and often has some red spots or dark black spots on forewing. (2) Sierra Nevada Parnassian is small and flies only above timberline in Calif., where Clodius is unlikely. **EARLY STAGES:** Caterpillar is grayblack with short hairs and a lateral row of yellow or orange lateral spots. **FOOD:** Bleeding heart. **FLIGHT:** May–July, rarely to Oct. (1 flight). **RANGE:** Nw. B.C. (possibly se. Alaska) east to Alta., cen. Mont., and w. Wyo., thence south to cen. Calif. and cen. Utah. **HABITAT:** Forest meadows and openings.

PHOEBUS PARNASSIAN *Parnassius phoebus*   **PL. 1**

1⅞–2¼ in. (47–58 mm). Antennae with alternating black and white rings. *Hairs on abdomen gray-white*. Front with white hairs centrally, black peripherally. Upperside: Male usually lacking small black median spot near trailing edge of forewing. *Submarginal dark band on forewing broad*. **SIMILAR SPECIES:** Rocky Mountain Parnassian has yellow hairs on abdomen and light yellow hairs on face. Male usually has narrow black submarginal band on forewing and small black median spot near trailing edge of forewing. **EARLY STAGES:** Not reported. **FOOD:** Stonecrop. **FLIGHT:** Late June–late Aug. (1 flight), possibly biennial. **RANGE:** Holarctic. In N. Amer., Alaska (Walker Lake, Seward Pen. and sw. Alaska coast, Alaska Range and south to Kodiak Is.) and Yukon (Ogilvie Mts.). **HABITAT:** Moist tundra, alpine meadows.

SIERRA NEVADA PARNASSIAN *Parnassius behrii*　　**PL. 1**

1 ⁵⁄₁₆–2 ¹⁄₁₆ in. (49–53 mm). Antennae with alternating black and white rings. *Hairs on abdomen light yellow*. Front with light yellow hairs surrounded by black. Upperside: Both sexes extensively white. *Two roundish black spots and 1–3 small orange or yellow spots* along front edge of forewing. Two round *yellow or orange marks on hindwing*. Underside: Similar to upperside but yellow or orange spotting more extensive. **SIMILAR SPECIES:** Clodius Parnassian, found mainly below timberline, has more translucent wings and red spots on hindwing only. **EARLY STAGES:** Not reported. **FOOD:** Stonecrop (*Sedum*). **FLIGHT:** May–early Oct., mainly mid-July–early Sept. (1 flight). **RANGE:** Sierra Nevada in Calif. **HABITAT:** Rocky slopes and meadows at or above timberline.

ROCKY MOUNTAIN PARNASSIAN　　**PL. 1**
Parnassius smintheus

1 ⅝–2 ⁵⁄₁₆ in. (42–59 mm). Antennae with alternating black and white rings. *Abdomen and front of face with light yellow hairs.* Upperside: White. Usually with at least 2 *small red spots* near forward edge of forewing and at least 2 round red spots on hindwing. Red more extensive in females. Male has *narrow black submarginal band* on forewing and usually a *median black spot on rear of forewing.* Underside: Red markings often more extensive than on upper-

Male Rocky Mountain Parnassian nectaring at fleabane in Rocky Mt. National Park, Colo. Pale yellow hairs of face and more pronounced red spots may be seen. Photo by Evi Buckner.

side. **GEOGRAPHIC VARIATION:** Size and extent of dark markings is variable—usually darker in butterflies from alpine and more northern areas. **SIMILAR SPECIES:** Phoebus Parnassian has gray-white hairs on abdomen and white hairs on face. Male has broad black submarginal band on forewing and usually lacks median black spot at rear of forewing. The two species may be found nearby only in n. B.C. **EARLY STAGES:** Caterpillar black with short black hairs and several rows of yellow or white spots. **FOOD:** Stonecrop. **FLIGHT:** Late May–Aug., occasionally Sept. (1 flight), likely biennial in alpine and arctic habitats. **RANGE:** Se. Alaska (panhandle), nw. B.C., and s. Yukon south in Rocky Mts. and hills on high plains to nw. Calif., ne. Nev., se. Utah, and n. N.M. **HABITAT:** Many types including foothill canyons, sagebrush flats, and alpine tundra.

SWALLOWTAILS: SUBFAMILY PAPILIONINAE

WHITE-DOTTED CATTLEHEART *Parides alopius*   PL. 2
3–3¼ in. (75–82 mm). Tailed. Upperside: Black. Hindwing with a *submarginal row of white and red oblong marks* and a postmedian row of white dots. Anal fold is tan. **SIMILAR SPECIES:** Pipevine Swallowtail has no red marks above and has a submarginal row of orange spots on hindwing below. **EARLY STAGES:** Caterpillar black with white cross bands and 4 rows of stout yellow or red tubercles. **FOOD:** Pipevines. **FLIGHT:** March–late Oct. (possibly 2 flights). **RANGE:** S. Mex. (Guerrero) north in the Sierra Madre Occidentale to se. Ariz. (once). **HABITAT:** Pine and oak forests.

Female Pipevine Swallowtail (subspecies hirsuta*) nectaring at blue dicks, Placer Co., Calif. Note reduced blue-green iridescence compared to male.*

PIPEVINE SWALLOWTAIL *Battus philenor*   PL. 2

2⅜–4¾ in. (60–120 mm). Larvae and adults of this common butterfly are distasteful and, when eaten, cause birds to regurgitate. Adult is "model" for several mimics: Black Swallowtail, Old World Swallowtail (black form of subspecies *bairdii*), Indra Swallowtail (possibly subspecies *kaibabensis*), Spicebush Swallowtail (rare stray in our area), female Diana Fritillary (not in our area), and Red-spotted Purple. Upperside: Black with *iridescent blue-green hindwing*, especially in male. Underside: Hindwing has *submarginal row of 7 round orange spots in iridescent blue field*. Flight rapid, wings flutter shallowly. Adults flutter wings when visiting flowers. **GEOGRAPHIC VARIATION:** An isolated breeding population in n. Calif. and extreme s. Ore. (subspecies *hirsuta*) is smaller, has denser hairlike scales, and has short tails. **SIMILAR SPECIES:** (1) Black Swallowtail females have red-orange eyespot at hindwing anal angle. (2) Red-spotted Purple is usually smaller, lacks tails, and has

PIPEVINE SWALLOWTAIL

basal red-orange markings on hindwing below. **EARLY STAGES:** Caterpillar is brown or black with rows of fleshy tubercles—the 2 rows on back orange to red. **FOOD:** Pipevines. **FLIGHT:** Jan.–Nov. (3–4 flights), late March–Oct. in n. Calif. (most fly in spring with stragglers later). **RANGE:** Resident from southern portion of our area and in n. Calif. south to s. Mex.; wanders north to s. Ore.,

n. Colo., e. S.D., and Man. **HABITAT:** Open fields, desert, thorn forest, stream valleys, and foothills.

POLYDAMAS SWALLOWTAIL *Battus polydamas* PL. 2

3⅛–4⅛ in. (80–104 mm). *Lacks tails.* Hindwing has scalloped margin. Upperside: Both wings black with *submarginal yellow band.* Underside: Hindwings has *marginal row of red S-marks.* **SIMILAR SPECIES:** Pipevine Swallowtail is tailed and lacks yellow bands. **EARLY STAGES:** Caterpillar similar to that of Pipevine Swallowtail but has lateral yellow band on thorax. **FOOD:** Various pipevines. **FLIGHT:** April–Nov. (2–3 flights). **RANGE:** Resident from coastal Mex. and pen. Fla. south to Argentina. Rarely strays north to s. Ariz., s. Calif., and s. N.M. **HABITAT:** Overgrown thorn scrub and openings in tropical woods.

ZEBRA SWALLOWTAIL *Eurytides marcellus* PL. 2

2½–4 in. (54–94 mm). Upperside: Wings very *pale green-white* with black stripes and very *long tails.* Spring individuals are smaller and lighter in appearance. **EARLY STAGES:** Caterpillar pea green with alternating yellow and black bands. **FOOD:** Pawpaw and related plants. **FLIGHT:** In north, April–Aug. (2 flights). **RANGE:** Eastern U.S., rare vagrant in cen. Neb. **HABITAT:** Moist woods along rivers and wooded swamps.

BLACK SWALLOWTAIL *Papilio polyxenes* PL. 3

2¹¹⁄₁₆–4¹⁄₁₆ in. (68–102 mm). Upperside: Both sexes primarily black; male with *yellow postmedian band* of variable width; female with sumarginal row of small yellow spots; hindwing with *black pupil centered in red-orange eyespot* at anal angle. Hindwing of female has iridescent blue submarginal patch. Underside: Spot rows on hindwing mainly or at least with some orange. *Abdomen with longitudinal rows of yellow dots.* **GEOGRAPHIC VARIATION:** In deserts of w. Ariz., s. Calif., s. Nev., and n. Baja Calif. butterflies are of either a yellow form (predominates westwardly) or a black form (subspecies *coloro*). Yellow form is similar to Anise Swallowtails that may co-occur but usually has black tegulae and at least some yellow dots on abdomen. **SIMILAR SPECIES:** (1) Black form of female Eastern Tiger Swallowtail is very similar to female but has ghosts of

BLACK SWALLOWTAIL

Male Black Swallow-tail nectaring at thistle, Larimer Co., Colo. Note presence of orange coloration on postmedian bands and yellow spots along abdomen.

darker black tiger stripes and lacks yellow dots on abdomen. (2) Dark form of Anise Swallowtail is similar to male, but yellow band on wings is broader, and there are faint yellow stripes (not yellow dots) on abdomen. **EARLY STAGES:** Caterpillar green with black bands around middle of each segment and 5 longitudinal rows of orange dots coinciding with front edge of each black band. **FOOD:** Leaves of various plants in parsley family, including cultivated carrot, dill, parsley, celery, and many wild species. Caterpillars of subspecies *coloro* eat turpentine broom (Citrus family). **FLIGHT:** Feb.–Nov. (2 flights). **RANGE:** Se. Sask. and sw. Man. south along Rocky Mt. front and Southwest, most of temperate e. N. Amer. then south through Mex. and Cen. Amer. to n. S. Amer. **HABITAT:** Gardens, fields, foothills, deserts. **REMARKS:** In s. Man. butterflies hybridize with Old World Swallowtails. These have been treated by several authors as a subspecies of the Black Swallowtail (subspecies *kahli*).

OLD WORLD SWALLOWTAIL *Papilio machaon*   PL. 3

2¹⁄₂–3³⁄₈ in. (65–86 mm). Variable. Thorax with *tegulae yellow* and *abdomen mostly yellow* in mainly yellow forms, abdomen black with 2 rows of yellow dots along side in predominantly black forms. Upperside: Usually with broad yellow median bands or as uncommon mainly black form. *Eyespot* at anal angle with pupil *not centered* — either off-center touching inner margin of eyespot or as oblong black patch at eyespot's lower margin. Underside: Yellow bands usually with little orange. **SIMILAR SPECIES:** (1) Anise Swallowtail has centered black pupil in hindwing eyespot and largely black abdomen with single lateral yellow stripe. (2) Black Swallowtail has black tegulae, centered black pupil in hindwing eyespot, and yellow spot rows on abdomen. **GEOGRAPHIC VARIATION:** Butterflies are mainly of yellow-banded form in north with some black forms in south (w. Colo. west to s. Calif.) and form of hindwing eyespot varies from Alaska south to Calif. **EARLY STAGES:** Caterpillar similar to that of Black Swallowtail. **FOOD:** Usually wild tarragon or arctic wormwood, rarely sweet coltsfoot or um-

OLD WORLD SWALLOWTAIL

belliferous plants. **FLIGHT:** In north, June–July (1 flight); and in south, April–Sept. (2 flights). **RANGE:** Holarctic. Alaska south through Canada and w. U.S. to Ariz., s. Calif., and s. N.M. Found east of plains to cen. Dakotas, cen. Neb., and nw. Kans. **HABITAT:** Woods, arctic tundra, prairie, arid canyons, river valleys, and hills.

Male Old World Swallowtail (subspecies oregonius) *nectaring on Canada thistle. Note the black bar at the bottom of the eyespot at corner of hindwing. This subspecies is also known as the Oregon Swallowtail, is the official Oregon state butterfly, and has appeared on a U.S. postage stamp. Photo by Jim Ebner.*

Male Anise Swallowtail (form nitra) perching on rock, Larimer Co., Colo. Note increased black on wings and burnt orange tegulae. These forms may indicate past hybridization with Black Swallowtails.

ANISE SWALLOWTAIL *Papilio zelicaon* **PL. 3**

2¼–2¹⁵⁄₁₆ in. (58–74 mm). Tailed. *Tegulae* at edge of thorax *yellow*; abdomen black with *single lateral yellow band,* except mainly black in form nitra. Upperside: Forewing with *yellow band* running length of wing and 2 *yellow bars* along front of wing in black field. Hindwing yellow with black veins except for black marginal and submarginal area. Eyespot at anal angle has *centered black pupil.* Underside: Pattern repeated from upperside but yellow areas cream instead of bright yellow. **GEOGRAPHIC VARIATION:** Along the w. Great Plains and Rocky Mts. there occurs a rare black form (nitra) that is similar to and may represent a low level of hybridization with the Black Swallowtail. In these populations the yellow form remains most abundant. **SIMILAR SPECIES:** Other species are more restricted in occurrence. (1) Yellow forms of Old World Swallowtail have more yellow on abdomen and have hindwing eyespot pupil touching inner edge of wing or as a narrow black bar. (2) Yellow form of Black Swallowtail has black tegulae on thorax, usually some yellow dots on abdomen, and some submarginal orange scaling on submarginal area of hindwing. Black form of Anise Swallowtail has darker tegulae but only rarely has 1 row of yellow dots on abdomen. **EARLY STAGES:** Nearly identical to those of Black Swallowtail. **FOOD:** Many plants in the Parsley family. Most frequent along West Coast is sweet fennel (anise), an introduced weed from Europe, and, in gardens, parsley, dill, and carrots. Cultivated citrus trees are also eaten in California. **FLIGHT:** April–July (1 flight) in most areas, all year (4 flights) in lowland Calif. **RANGE:** W. N. Amer. from cen. N.M., n. Ariz., and n. Baja Calif. north to Sask., n. Alta., and B.C. **HABITAT:** Usually open hilly or mountainous terrain but also valleys, suburbs, and cities.

INDRA SWALLOWTAIL *Papilio indra* PL. 4

2–2¾ in. (52–71 mm). With either normal or short tails. *Abdomen* completely *black* or with *short cream or pale yellow line* on last half. Upperside: Usually black with a *narrow pale yellow or cream band* on both wings. Hindwing has series of postmedian iridescent blue patches, more extensive in female. Hindwing eyespot with *centered black pupil*. Underside: Similar to upperside. **GEOGRAPHIC VARIATION:** Many geographic subspecies, especially in desert ranges and Colo. Plateau. Tail length may range from short to long, and wing coloration varies from completely black (subspecies *kaibabensis*) to having very wide cream bands on both wings (subspecies *fordi*). **SIMILAR SPECIES:** Black Swallowtail, black form of Anise Swallowtail, and black forms of Old World Swallowtail can all be separated by different abdominal markings. **EARLY STAGES:** Caterpillar variable. Usually mainly black with pink, whitish, orange, or yellow marks. **FOOD:** Various wild plants in Parsley family, often *Cymopterus, Lomatium,* and *Pteryxia.* Eats turpentine broom if preferred plants are already eaten. **FLIGHT:** May–early July (1 flight); March–April and sometimes July–Aug. (1–2 flights) in Colo. Plateau and desert areas. **RANGE:** W. mountains from n. Baja Calif. and n. Ariz. north to Mont. and s. B.C. and east to w. S.D. and w. Neb. **HABITAT:** Rocky mountainous areas from canyon bottoms to ridgetops.

XUTHUS SWALLOWTAIL *Papilio xuthus* PL. 4

2⅝–3½ in. (66–90 mm). Tailed. Upperside: *Black- and cream-*colored. Similar pattern to Anise Swallowtail but heavier *black veining* and more restricted pale areas. Underside: Similar to upperside. **EARLY STAGES:** Caterpillar green with blue transverse bands. **FOOD:** Many plants in Citrus family. **FLIGHT:** All year (several flights). **RANGE:** Asia, introduced to Hawaii where it is the only swallowtail. **HABITAT:** Gardens, fields, citrus groves.

Giant Swallowtail nectaring at thistle, Lower Rio Grande Valley National Wildlife Refuge, Texas. Note greater amount of yellow below and largely yellow abdomen.

GIANT SWALLOWTAIL *Papilio cresphontes* PL. 4

3½–5⅝ in. (88–144 mm). Tailed. Large. Upperside: Forewing with diagonal yellow spot band. Hindwing with broad yellow band at base. Tails spoon-shaped, filled with yellow. Underside: Mostly yellow. SIMILAR SPECIES: (1) Thoas Swallowtail has center 2 spots in yellow forewing band more or less square. Tip of male abdomen lacks notch when viewed from above. (2) Ornythion Swallowtail lacks yellow center in tails, and yellow forewing bands do not merge. (3) Broad-banded Swallowtail male has broader yellow band on forewing, small yellow spot in forewing cell, and narrow, all-black tails. EARLY STAGES: Caterpillar ("orange dog") is brown with white mottled middle and rear saddles, closely resembling a fresh bird dropping. FOOD: Various plants in Citrus family including hoptree and cultivated citrus in West. FLIGHT: All year in tropics, March–Nov. in s. Ariz. and s. Calif. (several flights). RANGE: Americas from S. Amer. north to Penn., s. Tex., s. Ariz., and s. Calif. as breeding resident. Strays regularly to e. Colo. and rarely to N.D. and Wyo. HABITAT: Mountains, suburbs, and citrus groves.

GIANT SWALLOWTAIL

THOAS SWALLOWTAIL
Papilio thoas PL. 4
3¾–5 in. (95–128 mm). Tailed. Large. Almost identical to Giant Swallowtail but often *paler yellow.* Tip of male abdomen has *notch* when viewed from

above. Upperside: Forewing with diagonal yellow band with *spots more or less square in a neat row*. SIMILAR SPECIES: Giant Swallowtail upperside with center 2 spots in yellow postmedian row rounded or triangular. Tip of male abdomen has notch when viewed from above. EARLY STAGES: Caterpillar like a large bird dropping—mottled olive green, dull white, brown, and yellow with a whitish thoracic saddle. FOOD: Various plants in Citrus family, also pipers. FLIGHT: All year in tropics. Summer or fall in our area. RANGE: Tropical Amer. from s. Tex. south to Brazil. Rare stray to Colo. and w. Kans. Doubtful in Ariz. HABITAT: Tropical forests and edges in lowlands and mid-elevations.

ORNYTHION SWALLOWTAIL *Papilio ornythion*   PL. 4

3¼–5½ in. (82–114 mm). Tailed. Upperside: Males with forewing with *narrow* median *diagonal pale yellow band* and submarginal band of *smaller spots not merging*. Underside: Extensively yellow with postmedian blue spot row on hindwing. Females are dimorphic, either resembling the male (but with paler yellow markings) or largely black. SIMILAR SPECIES: (1) Giant and Thoas Swallowtails have broader bright yellow diagonal bands and broader tails filled with yellow. (2) Broad-banded Swallowtail male has broader, yellower diagonal band on forewing, while female lacks tails and has submarginal (not postmedian) row of blue spots. EARLY STAGES: Caterpillar similar to that of Thoas Swallowtail but smaller and with more yellow. FOOD: Citrus. FLIGHT: April–Sept. in Mex. (probably 2 flights). RANGE: S. Tex. south to Guatemala. Rarely strays to w. Tex., s. N.M., and w. Neb. HABITAT: Mountains and canyons in Mex., gardens and citrus groves in s. Tex.

BROAD-BANDED SWALLOWTAIL *Papilio astyalus*   PL. 4

4⅝–4¾ in. (117–121 mm). Males tailed. Female with very short tail. Upperside: Male forewing with broad diagonal yellow band; small yellow spot at end of cell. Hindwing with narrow all-black tails. Female largely black with blue submarginal spot band on hindwing. SIMILAR SPECIES: (1) Giant and (2) Thoas Swallowtails have narrower diagonal band on forewing, lack yellow spot in forewing cell, and have tails filled with yellow. EARLY STAGES: Caterpillar similar to that of Thoas Swallowtail. FOOD: Citrus. FLIGHT: April–Oct. (probably 2 flights). RANGE: Mex. and Cen. Amer. south to Argentina, rarely strays to s. Ariz. and s. Tex.. HABITAT: Tropical forests.

RUBY-SPOTTED SWALLOWTAIL *Papilio anchisiades*   PL. 5

2¾–4 in. (70–102 mm). Tailless. Sexes similar. Upperside: Black with postmedian pink patch on hindwing. Female has diffuse

Female Eastern Tiger Swallowtail (black form) nectaring on common milkweed, Bath Co., Va. Note that tiger stripe pattern can still be seen as well as orange submarginal spots on hindwing.

white cell patch on forewing. **SIMILAR SPECIES:** Polydamas Swallowtail is black and lacks tails but is smaller and has yellow submarginal band. **EARLY STAGES:** Caterpillar is green-brown with many cream or white streaks, spots, and flecks. There are also 5 rows of short tubercles—each row with one tubercle on each abdominal segment. **FOOD:** Citrus, *Zanthoxylum*, and *Casimiroa*. **FLIGHT:** May–Oct. (probably 2 flights). **RANGE:** Resident from s. Tex., Mex., and Cen. Amer. to Argentina. Rarely strays to n. and w. Tex., w. Kans., and se. Ariz. **HABITAT:** Lowland tropical forest and nearby second growth, flower gardens.

EASTERN TIGER SWALLOWTAIL *Papilio glaucus*   **PL. 5**

3–5½ in. (76–144 mm). Male yellow, *tiger-striped*. Female dimorphic—one form yellow like male and the other black, although shadows of dark stripes can usually be seen. Upperside: Both female forms have extensive blue iridescent scales on hindwing. Both sexes with uppermost marginal spot orange. Underside: Forewing marginal spot row *discontinuous*—with separate spots. Hindwing has *marginal spots* suffused with orange. **SIMILAR SPECIES:** (1) Canadian Tiger Swallowtail is smaller, has black edging along anal margin, and has continuous spot row on forewing underside; black female form extremely rare. (2) Western Tiger Swallowtail has narrower forewings, upperside hindwing with uppermost submarginal spot yellow instead of orange, underside hindwing submarginal area without orange suffusion. No black female form. (3) Two-tailed Swallowtail has narrower black stripes, has 2 tails on each hindwing. (4) Spicebush Swallowtail can be confused only with black female form, from which it differs in lower, more rapid flight, underside hindwing with postmedian orange spot row, upperside hindwing with round orange spot on costa, and

EASTERN TIGER SWALLOWTAIL

CANADIAN TIGER SWALLOWTAIL

spoon-shaped tails. **EARLY STAGES:** Caterpillar is dark green with 2 large eyespots on swollen thoracic area. **FOOD:** Various trees and shrubs, especially yellow-poplar, wild cherry, and sweet bay. **FLIGHT:** Feb.–Nov. in Deep South (3 flights), April–Sept. in north (2 flights). **RANGE:** E. N. Amer. from s. Ont. south to Gulf Coast, west to c. Colo. and cen. Tex. Rare in Sierra Madre of e. Mex. **HABITAT:** Deciduous broadleaf forests, edges, and river valleys. **REMARKS:** The black form is believed to be an edible mimic of the distasteful Pipevine Swallowtail.

CANADIAN TIGER SWALLOWTAIL   PL. 5
Papilio canadensis

2½–3¼ in. (62–82 mm). Northern. Both sexes tiger-striped. *Small.* Upperside: *Black stripes* relatively *broad*; hindwing with anal margin *black more than half distance to anal vein.* Underside: Forewing with marginal yellow spot band continuous. Hindwing has extensive *orange overscaling.* **EARLY STAGES:** Identical to those of Eastern Tiger Swallowtail. **FOOD:** Birches, Quaking Aspen, crabapple, and Black Cherry. **FLIGHT:** May–mid-Aug. (1 flight). **RANGE:** Subarctic N. Amer. from cen. Alaska, Yukon, and sw. corner of N.W. Terr. south to Wash., Mont., n. Wyo., w. Dakotas, and n. Great Lakes states east to n. New England and the Maritimes. **HABITAT:** Northern deciduous (especially aspen parklands) and mixed evergreen-deciduous forests and associated edges. **REMARKS:** Black female form extremely rare. Canadian Tiger Swallowtails rarely hybridize with Western Tiger Swallowtails. Adult males often congregate at muddy spots on back roads or trails.

WESTERN TIGER SWALLOWTAIL *Papilio rutulus*   PL. 6

2½–3⅜ in. (65–88 mm). Tiger-striped pale yellow and black. Upperside: Hindwing with uppermost *marginal spot yellow or absent.* Underside: Forewing with *continuous yellow marginal band.*

Western Tiger Swallowtail nectaring on lilac, Larimer Co., Colo. Note in comparison to Eastern Tiger Swallowtail. Submarginal yellow spots on forewing are more continuous, those on hindwing less crescent-shaped.

Hindwing has *marginal spots narrow* and postmedian area without orange suffusion. No black female form. **SIMILAR SPECIES:** (1) Eastern Tiger Swallowtail and (2) Canadian Tiger Swallowtail have upperside with marginal yellow spot clearly separate in a black field; uppermost marginal spot on hindwing orange, not yellow; and more orange postmedian suffusion on underside hindwing. (3) Pale Swallowtail marked almost identically but has wider black stripes and ground is white or cream instead of pale yellow. **EARLY STAGES:** Caterpillar similar to that of Eastern Tiger Swallowtail but is usually brighter green. **FOOD:** Cottonwood, willow, quaking aspen, alder, maple, sycamore, hoptree, plum, and ash. **FLIGHT:** June–July (1 flight) in most of West, Feb.–Nov. (2–4 flights) along Pacific Coast, all year in s. Calif. **RANGE:** W. N. Amer. from e. B.C. south to n. Baja Calif. and s. N.M., east to w. S.D. and se. Colo. Rare strays to cen. Neb. **HABITAT:** Woodlands near streams and rivers, wooded suburbs. **REMARKS:** Genetic studies have shown this species, our commonest swallowtail, to be most closely related to the Pale Swallowtail, not to the other yellow-and-black-striped species.

PALE SWALLOWTAIL *Papilio eurymedon* PL. 6

2⅝–3½ in. (67–89 mm). Like Western Tiger Swallowtail but *black and white* tiger-striped. **SIMILAR SPECIES:** Western Tiger Swallowtail, its closest relative, is yellow with narrower black bands. **EARLY STAGES:** Caterpillar is similar to that of Western Tiger Swallowtail but eyespots are narrower. **FOOD:** Many woody plants in Rose and Buckthorn families, especially wild plums, wild lilacs, and buckthorns. **FLIGHT:** Late April–July (1 flight) in most of West, Feb.–Oct. (2–3 flights) in s. Calif. **RANGE:** W. N. Amer. from s. B.C. and sw.

WESTERN TIGER SWALLOWTAIL

PALE SWALLOWTAIL

Alta. south through western mountains and foothills to n. Baja Calif., s. Utah, and n. N.M. **HABITAT:** Oak woodland, chaparral, conifer forests, canyons. **REMARKS:** Males patrol on hilltops and knolls.

TWO-TAILED SWALLOWTAIL *Papilio multicaudatus* PL. 6

2¾–5¼ in. (70–122 mm). Large. *Two tails on each hindwing*. Male with *narrow black stripes* on forewing. Female often deeper yellow or orange with *wider black stripes* and more iridescent blue on hindwing. **SIMILAR SPECIES:** Tiger Swallowtail has only a single tail on each hindwing. Forewing black stripes broader, orange suffusion on hindwing below. **EARLY STAGES:** Caterpillar is green or brown with a pair of green, black-edged oval eyespots on the swollen thorax. Two rows of tiny iridescent blue points run down the body. **FOOD:** Ash, hoptree, and chokecherry. **FLIGHT:** April–Oct. in north (1 ex-

Male Pale Swallowtails (subspecies albanus) at moisture, Mariposa Co., Calif. Note pale off-white color and increased orange on hindwing spots compared to Western Tiger Swallowtail.

Female Two-tailed Swallowtail nectaring at milkweed, Larimer Co., Colo. Note increased amount of blue and deeper yellow-orange color compared to male. Females are larger and more intensely colored to the south in Ariz.

tended flight), most of year in south. **RANGE:** W. N. Amer. from s. B.C. and s. Alta. east to w. Dakotas, cen. Neb., and cen. Tex. and south to s. Mex. **HABITAT:** Foothill canyons and slopes, cities, and suburbs. **REMARKS:** Adults have a high, soaring flight. May be common in western towns and cities where green ash, a favorite host, is often used as a streetside tree.

THREE-TAILED SWALLOWTAIL *Papilio pilumnus*   **PL. 6**
3⅛–3¾ in. (80–95 mm). *Three tails* on each hindwing, the longest *lined with yellow.* Forewing with only 2 *black stripes,* marginal yellow spots coalesced into a solid band. **SIMILAR SPECIES:** Two-tailed Swallowtail has only 2 tails on each hindwing, black forewing stripes much narrower. **EARLY STAGES:** Caterpillar like others in "tiger group," but body green and head brown. **FOOD:** Laurel. **FLIGHT:** Jan.–Oct. **RANGE:** El Salvador north to Mex. Rare stray north to s. Tex. and se. Ariz. **HABITAT:** Not reported. **REMARKS:** Although similar to the tiger swallowtails, its closest U.S. relative is the Spicebush Swallowtail.

TWO-TAILED SWALLOWTAIL

SPICEBUSH SWALLOWTAIL
Papilio troilus   **NOT SHOWN**
3⁷⁄₁₆–4¼ in. (78–108 mm). *Black.* Upperside: Hindwing has *blue iridescence* (female) or *blue-green pigment* (male). Underside: Hindwing has marginal spots *pale green* and

tails *spoon-shaped*, with both marginal and postmedian orange spot rows. **SIMILAR SPECIES:** (1) Black and (2) Joan's Swallowtail males have postmedian row of yellow spots on upperside. Marginal spots yellow above; tails linear, not spoon-shaped. Eyespot with black pupil. (3) Tiger Swallowtail (black female) tails are not spoon-shaped; shadows of black stripes usually visible; hindwing below is without postmedian orange spot row. (4) Pipevine Swallowtail hindwing below has a single submarginal row of large oval red-orange spots, entire hindwing above has highly reflective blue-green iridescence. **EARLY STAGES:** Caterpillar is dark green above and whitish laterally; has 2 large black orange-edged eyespots on swollen thoracic dorsum and 4 longitudinal lines of black-edged blue spots on the abdominal dorsum. **FOOD:** Sassafras and Spicebush. Other reports need confirmation. **FLIGHT:** April–Oct. (2 flights, sometimes a partial third). **RANGE:** E. N. Amer. from s. Ont. and s. New England south to Fla. and Gulf Coast; resident west to Okla. and cen. Tex. (rare stray to N.D. and cen. Colo.). **HABITAT:** Second-growth woods, deciduous woodlands, edges, wooded swamps, and pine barrens. **REMARKS:** Usually flies low, often through shaded woodlands. Flutters wings slowly when visiting flowers. This butterfly is an edible mimic of the distasteful Pipevine Swallowtail.

PALAMEDES SWALLOWTAIL *Papilio palamedes* PL. 6

3¾–4½ in. (96–116 mm). Sexes alike. Upperside: Both wings with *yellow postmedian band*; tails *filled with yellow*. Underside: Hindwing with *thin yellow stripe* at base and postmedian row of *orange crescents*. Flies slowly. **SIMILAR SPECIES:** Black Swallowtail male has spotted abdomen and eyespot with black pupil. **EARLY STAGES:** Caterpillar is pale green with 2 black orange-margined eyespots on swollen thoracic dorsum. **FOOD:** Redbay, possibly sassafras. **FLIGHT:** March–Dec. (2 flights, partial third in south). **RANGE:** Atlantic and Gulf of Mexico coastal plains from s. N.J. (rarely) south to cen. Mex. Strays inland, e.g., cen. Neb., n. N.M. **HABITAT:** Broadleaf evergreen swamp forests and wet woods near rivers.

TRUE BUTTERFLIES:
SUPERFAMILY PAPILIONOIDEA
WHITES AND SULPHURS:
FAMILY PIERIDAE

The whites and sulphurs are worldwide in distribution. Most species are found in the tropics. The majority have medium to small white, yellow, or orange wings with small amounts of black or red. Many have hidden ultraviolet patterns that are used in courtship. Fully developed wing appendages such as tails are absent, although a few species have falcate forewing apexes or short projections from the hindwings. Adults of both sexes have three pairs of walking legs. Most of our species with more than one generation have distinct seasonal variations. The more temperate species have smaller, darker individuals in the spring and fall, while the tropical-affiliated species have distinct dry- (winter) and wet- (summer) season forms. Adults of all species visit flowers for nectar.

Males of our species patrol likely environments in search of receptive mates. Females lay eggs singly on leaves, buds, or stems of the appropriate food plants. Most species are narrow in their choice of caterpillar hosts, usually selecting plants within a single genus, but rarely more than two closely related families. The vast majority of North American whites and sulphurs feed on either legumes or crucifers (plants in the Mustard family). Eggs are columnar. The caterpillars are relatively smooth and are covered with short, fine setae, often clumped onto low tubercles. Like swallowtails, the pupae are attached to a silk mat and are slung in a girdle. Most temperate species overwinter in the pupal or larval stage. Tropical species overwinter as adults in warm, southern areas and then recolonize northward during spring or early summer.

In North America 31 whites, orangetips, and marbles are included. The adults of most species are predominantly white above with some black pattern elements. Below, their hindwings often have a pattern of yellow and black scales (appearing green). The two sexes of most are only slightly dimorphic, although male orangetips have bright orange wingtips. The adults are avid flower visitors, often selecting flowers of their host plants when available. The males of almost all our species patrol open, sunny habitats in search of receptive females, although males of some tropical whites, e.g., Mexican Dartwhite, perch along ravines. Most of our western whites select mustards (family Brassicaceae) as their caterpillar host plants, although the related capers (family Capparidaceae) are used by some, such as Becker's White and Florida White. Pine White and Chiricahua White caterpillars eat pine needles. Eggs are laid singly on host plant leaves or flowering parts. The young caterpillars feed externally and develop directly. Winter is passed by the chrysalis stage. Orangetips and marbles may pass several unfavorable years in the chrysalis stage before hatching.

MEXICAN DARTWHITE *Catasticta nimbice* PL. 7

1 ½–1 ¾ in. (40–46 mm). Upperside: *Wide black borders.* Male with white band; female with yellow band. Underside: Hindwing *mottled* with *yellow dots.* EARLY STAGES: Caterpillar dull red-brown with black granulations and short hairs. FOOD: Tropical mistletoes. FLIGHT: March–May in w. Tex. March–Dec. in Mex. RANGE: Mex. south to Panama. Strays to Chisos Mts., Tex. HABITAT: Moist mountain forests and associated openings. REMARKS: Caterpillars feed in groups. Adults perch in forest openings or along ravines, unlike other family members.

PINE WHITE *Neophasia menapia* PL. 7

1 ¾–1 ¹⁵/₁₆ in. (44–49 mm). White. Upperside: Forewing with *costa lined black from base to cell.* Apical area extensively black. Underside: Hindwing of male has *veins lined narrowly with black,* that of female more heavily marked, margin lined with red, submarginal black stripe. High, floating flight near conifers. SIMILAR SPECIES: (1) Checkered White and (2) Western White lack black costa and have more checkered appearance. Both have low, rapid, erratic flight. EARLY STAGES: Caterpillar is dark green with a broad white lateral band and a narrow white dorsal stripe. FOOD: Usually ponderosa pine, rarely other pines, occasionally Douglas-fir, firs, and other conifers. FLIGHT: Late June–Sept. (1 flight). RANGE: W.

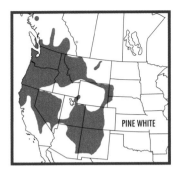 

U.S. and s. Canada from s. B.C. and sw. Alta. East to Black Hills and nw. Neb. thence south to s. Sierra Nevada in Calif., cen. Ariz., and N.M. Rare stray to n. Minn. **HABITAT:** Pine forests in most of range; mixed Douglas-fir forests in n. coastal Calif. **REMARKS:** Occasional outbreaks cause extensive defoliation of Ponderosa Pine forests. Adults come to ground level to visit flowers.

CHIRICAHUA WHITE *Neophasia terlootii* PL. 7

2–2⅜ in. (52–60 mm). Strikingly dimorphic — males white, females orange. Upperside: Both sexes with *wide black bar* on forewing costal margin and *wide black outer margin*. Underside: Hindwing veins outlined in black. **SIMILAR SPECIES:** Male is similar to Pine White, but ranges of the two do not overlap. **EARLY STAGES:** Not reported. **FOOD:** Ponderosa pine and Engelmann spruce. **FLIGHT:** June–Nov. (2 flights). **RANGE:** Se. Ariz. and sw. N.M. s. to Nuevo León and Jalisco, Mex. **HABITAT:** Pine forests, usually above 2,000 m. **REMARKS:** Adults spend most time flying around crowns of conifers but will descend to nectar at flowers or take moisture at mud.

FLORIDA WHITE *Appias drusilla* PL. 7

1¾–2½ in. (46–66 mm). Sexes dimorphic. Male has elongate forewing, white above and below. Upperside: Forewing has *costa and outer margin edged very narrowly with black*. Underside: Hindwing has satiny sheen. Female may be almost completely white (dry-season form) or with black outer margin and yellow-orange upper hindwing, especially at base (wet-season form). Flight is rapid and erratic, often in shade. **SIMILAR SPECIES:** Great Southern White male upperside forewing has black outer margin extended along veins. White female form has black cell spot. **EARLY STAGES:** Caterpillar with head yellow-green with blue-green tubercles; body dark green above and pale gray-green laterally, the two tones divided by a thin white lateral line. **FOOD:** Capers. **FLIGHT:** All year in areas of residence; Oct.–April (dry-season form), May–Sept. (wet-season form). **RANGE:** Resident in tropical Amer. from Brazil north, including the Antilles, as well as s. peninsular Fla. and the Keys. Frequent immigrant to coastal Tex., occasionally to se. Ariz., and rarely north to Colo. and Neb. **HABITAT:** Lowland tropical evergreen or semideciduous forests.

BECKER'S WHITE *Pontia beckerii* PL. 7

1 ⅜–1 ¾ in. (34–45 mm). White. Upperside: Strong *square black patch* in forewing cell. Small black marks on outer third of forewing. Underside: Forewing cell shows strongly. Hindwing with *broad yellow-green bands* along veins. **SIMILAR SPECIES:** (1) Checkered White and (2) Western White have smaller, weaker forewing cell patches and either lighter or darker green veining below. **EARLY STAGES:** Caterpillar is green-white or gray with orange bands on the segments. The body is covered with small black tubercles. **FOOD:** Several plants in the caper family (Bladderpod and Prince's Plume) and mustard family. **FLIGHT:** March–Oct. (2–4 flights), as early as late Dec. in s. Calif. **RANGE:** Arid areas from s. B.C. south through interior West (mainly between Continental Divide and Sierra-Cascade crest to cen. Baja Calif., n. Ariz., and ne. N.M. Expanding range eastward to e. Mont., e. Wyo., and se. Colo. **HABITAT:** Canyons and hills in deserts, sagebrush, and juniper woodland. **REMARKS:** Some have referred to Becker's White as a New World race of the Eurasian Small Bath White (*Pontia chloridice*) to which it is closely allied.

SPRING WHITE *Pontia sisymbrii* PL. 7

1 –1 ⅜ in. (26–37 mm). White or pale yellow. Wings delicate, more translucent than close relatives. Upperside: *Narrow black bar* in forewing cell and both postmedian and marginal series of black

Spring White (subspecies transversa) nectaring, Animas Mts., N.M. This subspecies is very pale but still has the narrow black mark on forewing and the veining pattern below, but yellow scales are absent.

marks on forewing *along veins.* Underside: Hindwing with pattern of *brown-black scaling along veins* with some yellow scales directly on veins. **SIMILAR SPECIES:** Western White has wider forewing cell mark. Its spring form has green along veins, not black-brown. Geographic variation: Pale yellow individuals, usually females, are more prevalent in north. Some population at southern end of range have greatly reduced black markings and have weak gray veining below (subspecies *transversa*). **EARLY STAGES:** Caterpillar is light yellow with 2 black bands on each segment. Head black with tiny white processes, or projections, and streaks. **FOOD:** Mainly native plants in the mustard family including rock cresses, jewelflowers, tansy mustard, and tumble mustard. **FLIGHT:** Feb.–June (1 flight). **RANGE:** S. Yukon and w. N.W. Terr. south through low- to midelevation in mountains to cen. Baja Calif. and nw. Mex., east to w. S.D., Neb., w. Okla., and w. Tex. **HABITAT:** Lower canyons, desert hills, chaparral, pine forests. **REMARKS:** Males usually patrol on hilltops or along ridges.

CHECKERED WHITE *Pontia protodice*   **PL. 7**

1 ¼–2 in. (38–50 mm). White. Upperside: Forewing of male with *black checkered pattern* on outer half, hindwing white; female *heavily checkered* above. Underside: Hindwing of male faintly checkered; female has yellow-tan pattern on hindwing and forewing apex. Short-day (spring, fall) form with underside hindwing veins outlined with gray-green. **SIMILAR SPECIES:** (1) Western White, with which the Checkered White is often found, has more elongate forewing, upperside forewing submarginal band fully connected and underside hindwing veins outlined with gray-green, at least faintly. Spring forms may be difficult to separate.

(2) Becker's White has large black patch on forewing cell; strong yellow-green veining on hindwing below. **EARLY STAGES:** Caterpillar alternately striped yellow and purple-green; body with many small black tubercles. **FOOD:** Flowers and seedpods of many plants in mustard family: peppergrasses, tumble mustard, true mustards, etc.; rarely plants in caper and reseda families. **FLIGHT:** Feb.–Nov. (3 flights), all year in s. Ariz., s. Calif., and Mex. **RANGE:** Resident from cen. Calif. east to se. Colo and s. Neb., thence south into Mex. Regular immigrant and colonist north to e. Wash., se. B.C., s. Alta., s. Sask. and s. Man. and eastward to East Coast. **HABITAT:** Open areas, including meadows, fields, deserts, suburbs, and prairies. **REMARKS:** Flight low and erratic. Males patrol on flats or hilltops when available. Either sex may seek the opposite sex.

WESTERN WHITE *Pontia occidentalis* PL. 8

1 ⅜–1 ⅝ in. (34–41 mm). White. Upperside: Forewing has *marginal chevrons lighter and contrasting* with submarginal band. Underside: Forewing apex and hindwing with *veins outlined with gray-green*. Spring and fall short-day forms more heavily marked. **SIMILAR SPECIES:** Checkered White is the species found throughout most of our territory. It lacks the contrast between the black marginal chevrons and submarginal band. Spring-form individuals may be difficult to distinguish. **EARLY STAGES:** Caterpillar is dull green to dark blue-gray covered with tiny black dots and with alternating dark and light stripes. Head blue-gray with yellow spots near top and some black areas. **FOOD:** Mustard family, native rock cresses, peppergrasses, tansy mustards, tumble mustards, black mustard, etc. **FLIGHT:** Feb.–Nov. (2 flights), only 1 flight (June–July) at high elevations and in Far North. **RANGE:** In boreal N. Amer.

from Alaska, Yukon, and w. N.W. Terr. south to cen. Calif., n. Ariz., and n. N.M., east to cen. Ont. (James Bay), Wisc. (rare), Mich. (rare), n. Minn., S.D., and w. Neb. **HABITAT:** Subarctic and montane slopes and peaks, alpine tundra, meadows, open plains, railyards. **REMARKS:** Males patrol ridges and hilltops. Species spreading eastward across n. plains and s. Canada. A close relative of the Eurasian Peak White *(Pontia callidice).*

ARCTIC WHITE *Pieris angelika*   **PL. 8**

1 ¼–1 ⅝ in. (33–42 mm). Upperside: Males white to dusky gray (on Alaska coast and islands), females pale yellow to dusky yellow. Male with *black at outer edge of wing,* especially at vein endings. Female with 2 blurred black spots on forewing and *black scaling along veins.* Underside: Forewing white, hindwing yellow. *Distinct black-green veining* on both wings. **SIMILAR SPECIES:** (1) Margined White overlaps in nw. B.C. (see below). (2) Mecky's White *(P. meckyae)* has been applied to populations in s. Alaska and B.C. These populations are amidst those of Arctic White, but cannot be distinguished from them except by genetic analysis. Status of this species is unclear. **EARLY STAGES:** Not reported. **FOOD:** Almost certainly plants in Mustard family. **FLIGHT:** Late May–late July (1 flight). **RANGE:** Alaska, Yukon, w. N.W. Terr., and nw. B.C. **HABITAT:** Moist woodlands and edges, alpine tundra. **REMARKS:** Recent genetic studies have shown that what were previously considered North American populations of the Eurasian Green-veined White *(P. napi)* are four separate species—none of which are *napi.* There is additional unexplained complex variation of these butterflies in Alaska.

Arctic White, Eagle Summit, Alaska. Note distinct veining along veins of hindwing. Dark scaling at vein endings cannot be seen from below.

MARGINED WHITE *Pieris marginalis*   PL. 8

1 ⅜–1 ⅝ in. (36–42 mm). White. *Forewing* somewhat *pointed*. Upperside: Ranges from immaculate white to heavily dusted with black. Male may have 1 round black spot in discal cell, while female may have 2 black spots—1 in discal cell and 1 toward trailing edge of wing. Underside: Ranges from nearly *immaculate white* to heavily marked with *dusky green* along hindwing veins. **SIMILAR SPECIES:** (1) Cabbage White has hindwing below solid gray-green or yellow-green—without veining. (2) Arctic White has black markings on outer portion of forewing. **EARLY STAGES:** Caterpillar green to blue-gray covered with tiny black dots and with a white or pale yellow line along each side. **FOOD:** Leaves of plants in mustard family including toothworts, rock cresses, watercress. **FLIGHT:** May–Aug. (1 flight) in most of range, April–Sept. (2 flights) in s. N.M., Feb.–July (2 flights) in Calif. **RANGE:** Alaska panhandle and B.C. south through w. N. Amer. to cen. Calif., e.-cen. Ariz., and N.M. **HABITAT:** Moist woods and meadows, often near streamcourses. **REMARKS:** Adults nectar at a variety of flowers, especially those of their caterpillar hosts.

MUSTARD WHITE
Pieris oleracea   PL. 8

1 ½–1 ⅞ in. (38–48 mm). *Forewings rounded*. Upperside: Almost immaculate white with some *blackish on wing bases* and *forewing tips*. Female may have 2 faint submarginal blackish spots. Underside: Hindwing pale *yellow*. Spring generation butterflies with *sharply*

Mustard White nectaring on dandelion, Alta. Note nearly immaculate wings of summer form and yellow spot at base of hindwing. Photo by John Acorn.

defined dark scaling on hindwing veins. Summer generation butterflies have underside hindwings either immaculate or with less intense dark scaling on veins. **SIMILAR SPECIES:** (1) Cabbage White usually has black forewing apex above and yellow-green hindwing below. (2) Margined White, which co-occurs only in Alta., can have more distinct dark upperside forewing spots or vein endings. Forewings less rounded. **EARLY STAGES:** Caterpillar green with a yellow stripe along each side. **FOOD:** Various Mustard family plants including rock cresses, toothworts, watercress, and mustards. **FLIGHT:** April–Aug. (2 flights). **RANGE:** Se. Yukon and Alta. east across Canada to Lab., also n. Great Plains, Great Lakes states, and New England. **HABITAT:** Open woods and small clearings in conifer forests.

CABBAGE WHITE *Pieris rapae*   **PL. 8**
1½–2 in. (39–50 mm). White. Upperside: *Forewing tip black*, and 1 (male) or 2 (female) submarginal black spots. Underside: Forewing apex and hindwing uniformly *yellow-green or gray-green*. Spring forms weakly marked. Flight floating and fluttery. **SIMILAR SPECIES:** (1) Checkered White has checkered forewing; hindwing underside is either plain white (summer male) or patterned. Flight more direct. (2) Western Veined White and (3) Mustard White have hindwing underside nearly immaculate or with veins evenly outlined with gray-green. **EARLY STAGES:** Caterpillar is green with a thin broken yellow line on each side and a thin yellow dorsal line. **FOOD:** Many Mustard family plants including cabbage, broccoli, mustards, winter Cress, watercress, peppergrass, also rarely Caper family and nasturtium. **FLIGHT:** March–Nov. (3 flights) to all year in south (7–8 flights). **RANGE:** Holarctic. Introduced to

N. Amer. (about 1860) in Que., Canada. Has since spread to se. Alaska, nw. and cen. Canada (nw. B.C., s. Lab., cen. Que., s. N.W. Terr.), throughout the contiguous U.S. except Fla. Keys, extreme s. La., s. Tex., and some offshore islands, south to nw. Mex. **HABITAT:** Many kinds of open, weedy habitats: cities and suburbs, gardens, mountain meadows, streamsides, desert washes, road edges, etc. **REMARKS:** One of our most common and widespread butterflies. Its caterpillars occasionally cause economic damage to kale crops such as cabbage, broccoli, and collards, especially in home gardens.

CABBAGE WHITE

GREAT SOUTHERN WHITE *Ascia monuste*　　　　**PL. 8**

2–3 in. (50–76 mm). Antennal tips bright blue-green. Male white with upperside forewing *zigzag black outer margin*. Female dimorphic. One form (dry season) similar to male with upperside forewing black more extensive on outer margin, also with *small black spot in cell*. Wet-season female almost completely *clouded* above and below with black scaling. **SIMILAR SPECIES:** (1) Cabbage Butterfly is smaller and has tip of forewing black. (2) Florida White male has elongated all-white forewing without zigzag black outer margin. See (3) Giant White. **EARLY STAGES:** Caterpillar's body has 5 longitudinal orange bands or lines separated by areas of mottled gray. Head is tan-yellow with orange front. **FOOD:** Beach cabbage and saltwort along coast, but others such as peppergrasses, cultivated cabbage, and other kale crops used at inland sites. Plants in Caper family also used. **FLIGHT:** All year in peninsular Fla., Gulf Coast, and s. Tex. **RANGE:** Migratory along Southeast coastlines. Resident along s. Atlantic and Gulf Coasts south through much of tropical Amer. Strays north to Kans., ne. Colo, s. N.M., and s. Ariz. **HABITAT:** Primarily coastal salt marshes, dunes, also open sites such as fields and gardens. Migrants appear in a variety of open habitats such as arroyos, well-vegetated deserts, and prairies.

GIANT WHITE *Ganyra josephina*　　　　**PL. 8**

3⅜–3⅝ in. (85–93 mm). *Very large.* Forewing apex bulges outward slightly. Upperside: Forewing of male with prominent *round black cell spot*; in addition to black cell spot, female distinctly cream or brownish; wet-season female has *blurred black postmedian spots* and marginal portions of veins *outlined with black*. Dry-season female marked less prominently. **SIMILAR SPECIES:** (1) Very similar Howarth's White is much smaller but in our area is found only in s. Ariz. where Giant White is unrecorded. (2) Great Southern White is smaller, has zigzag black outer margin, and lacks prominent black forewing cell spot. **EARLY STAGES:** Caterpillar dark green with yellow lateral line; back covered with tiny black tubercles. **FOOD:** Plants in Caper family. **FLIGHT:** All year in lowland tropics, Sept.–Dec. in s. Tex. **RANGE:** Greater Antilles, Cen. Amer., and Mex. Strays regularly to s. Tex., very rarely to N.M. and Kans. **HABITAT:** Forest edges, usually in seasonally dry tropical lowlands.

HOWARTH'S WHITE *Ganyra howarthi* PL. 8

1¾–1⅞ in. (43–48 mm). White. Upperside: Both sexes have *round black dot* in forewing cell and *black dashes between veins* on outer edge of forewing. **SIMILAR SPECIES:** A large species relative to all other whites with which it might be found except (1) Giant White, which is much larger and more heavily marked, and (2) Great Southern White, which lacks black forewing cell spot. **EARLY STAGES:** Caterpillar not reported. **FOOD:** *Atamisquea emarginata* (Caper family). **FLIGHT:** April–May, Aug. in Ariz., all year in Mex. **RANGE:** N.W. mainland Mex. and s. Baja Calif., rarely strays into s. Ariz. **HABITAT:** Thorn scrub. Other habitats as stray. **REMARKS:** Formerly considered a subspecies of Giant White.

LARGE MARBLE *Euchloe ausonides* PL. 8

1¹⁄₁₆–1¾ in. (27–44 mm). Upperside: Forewing with *black-patterned apex*. Upperside: Cream to off-white, females in coastal Calif. may be pale yellow. Black bar in forewing cell with scattered white scales. Underside: Hindwing with *complex green mar-*

bling. **SIMILAR SPECIES:** (1) Along Rocky Mountain front, Olympia Marble is smaller, with marbling less complex and with rose pink highlights (these fade after death) along underside hindwing costa. Forewing upperside with less black. (2) In Calif. west of mountains California Marble is smaller and lacks white scaling in black forewing bar. (3) In w. Canada and Alaska Northern Marble is smaller, has narrower cell bar, has highly fractured green marbling below, and usually flies earlier in year. (4) In Alaska and nw. Canada, Green Marble is smaller, has blunter wingtip and dense, dark green marbling on hindwing below. **EARLY STAGES:** Caterpillar is gray with yellow stripes and white stripes subtended by yellow. **FOOD:** Mustard family plants such as tower mustard, mustards, tansy mustard, etc., and rock cresses. **FLIGHT:** Late April–Aug. (1 flight) in most of range; mid-Feb.–early Sept. in lowland Calif. (2 flights). **RANGE:** Boreal w. N. Amer. south to cen. Calif., cen. Nev., n. Ariz., and n. N.M., east to nw. Neb., Black Hills, and sw. Man. **HABITAT:** Stream bottoms, hillsides, and meadows in a wide variety of settings, usually in mountains or foothills. **REMARKS:** Flight low, direct. Males patrol hillsides or valley bottoms. The introduction of mustards as a new caterpillar host in lowland Calif. enabled the development of a regular second flight.

GREEN MARBLE *Euchloe naina*   **PL. 9**

1 ¼–1 ½ in. (34–37 mm). White, *forewing squared off at tip.* Upperside: *Black at base of both wings. Some small black patches at ends of veins on both wings.* Wings may have dusting of black scales in Alaska populations. Otherwise similar to Large Marble. Underside: Hindwings with *gray-green marbling extensive* and blurred. **SIMILAR SPECIES:** Large Marble has more pointed forewing, less black scaling above, and more restricted, distinct green and yellow marbling on hindwing below. **EARLY STAGES:** Not reported but probably similar to Large Marble. **FOOD:** Probably rock cresses and other mustards. **FLIGHT:** June–July (1 flight). **RANGE:** Far eastern Russia, Alaska, Yukon. **HABITAT:** Scree slopes above timberline, also valley bottoms. **REMARKS:** A poorly known recently described butterfly.

NORTHERN MARBLE *Euchloe creusa*   **PL. 9**

1 ¼–1 ¾ in. (33–41 mm). White. Upperside: Narrow black bar in forewing cell. Black at base of both wings. Underside: Hindwing with *green marbling extensive and highly fractured.* **GEOGRAPHIC VARIATION:** Isolated population near Prince Albert, Sask. has butterflies that lack yellow scales in marbling, giving it a gray appearance. **SIMILAR SPECIES:** (1) Large Marble and (2) Green Marble average larger, have more solid green marbling on underside of hindwing, and fly later in season. **EARLY STAGES:** Not reported, probably similar

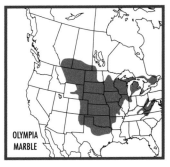

to Large Marble. **FOOD:** *Draba*s and rock cresses. **FLIGHT:** Mid-May–July, rarely to Aug. (1 flight). **RANGE:** Alaska, Yukon, and w. N.W. Terr. south in mountains and taiga to w. Mont. **HABITAT:** Tundra in valleys, subalpine forest, and openings in coniferous forest. **REMARKS:** Butterfly flies exceptionally early in its northern habitat.

SONORAN MARBLE *Euchloe guaymasensis*   PL. 9

1¼–1½ in. (31–37 mm). Forewing *apex relatively round*. Upperside: *Pale yellow* with black bar in discal cell and black on forewing apex. Underside: *Green marbling sparse*. Spaces between marbling not highly reflective. **SIMILAR SPECIES:** (1) Desert Marble, only other marble in area, is white above with pearly ground between marbling on underside of hindwing. (2) Desert Orangetip is deeper yellow above in s. Ariz. and has orange tip on forewing. **EARLY STAGES:** Not reported. **FOOD:** Tansy mustard. **FLIGHT:** Feb.–March (1 flight). **RANGE:** Se. Ariz. (once) south to Sonora, Mex. **HABITAT:** Rocky desert hills and ridges in thorn scrub and oak-juniper zones. Males fly to hilltops in search of likely mates.

OLYMPIA MARBLE *Euchloe olympia*   PL. 9

1¹⁄₁₆–1⅜ in. (28–35 mm). *Antennae all-white*. Wings white. Upperside: *Limited black* on forewing tip, black forewing bar narrow. Underside: *Marbling* on hindwing *limited*. *Rose flush* along *forward edge* of hindwings (disappears after death). **SIMILAR SPECIES:** Large Marble, only other co-occurring marble, is larger and has black and white antennae and more extensive green marbling pattern. **EARLY STAGES:** Caterpillar is virtually identical to that of Large Marble. **FOOD:** Various rock cresses, and occasionally other Mustard family plants. **FLIGHT:** Early April–rarely early July (1 flight). **RANGE:** S. Canada and U.S. from s. Alta., s. Ont., and sw. Que. south through plains and Rocky Mountains east of Continental

Divide to cen. Tex. Also widespread in Midwest with isolated population in Appalachians. **HABITAT:** Various open areas, mainly prairie hills, foothills, and badlands. **REMARKS:** Males patrol hilltops and ridges in search of females.

CALIFORNIA MARBLE *Euchloe hyantis* PL. 9

1 ⅟₁₆–1 ½ in. (28–37 mm). Upperside: Off-white with *black forewing bar lacking white scales*. Underside: Green marbling on hindwing with *yellow cast*, white area between marbling *lacks pearly iridescence*. **GEOGRAPHIC VARIATION:** Every population differs slightly. San Bernardino Mt. population (subspecies *andrewsi*) has large butterflies that most resemble Large Marble. **SIMILAR SPECIES:** Large Marble is usually larger and has scattered white scales in black forewing bar. Desert Marble does not overlap in range. **EARLY STAGES:** Caterpillar green with lateral white or yellow stripe, above which is a purplish band. Head green. **FOOD:** Mainly jewelflower species. **FLIGHT:** March–early July (1 flight). **RANGE:** Sw. Ore. south through w.-cen. Nev. and Calif., usually seaward of Sierra Nevada and Transverse range crests and n. Baja Calif. **HABITAT:** Open mountain and hilly slopes including granitic moraines, serpentine outcrops, and sunny cliffs. **REMARKS:** Previously considered same species as Desert Marble. Male California Marbles patrol areas of host plant, usually hillsides, in search of females. Some areas of intermediacy with Desert Marble have been reported on Kern Plateau, Tulare Co., Calif. Marbles in mountains of se. Ariz. and sw. N.M. may represent this species.

DESERT MARBLE *Euchloe lotta* PL. 9

1 ⅛–1 ⅜ in. (29–36 mm). Upperside: White with *black bar lacking scattered white scales*. Underside: Hindwing with *dark green marbling and intervening white areas with pearly iridescence*. **SIMILAR**

SPECIES: (1) Large Marble is larger, has white scales in black forewing bar, lacks pearly iridescences on hindwing below, and usually flies later in season. (2) California Marble does not overlap in range. **EARLY STAGES:** Caterpillar variable, green or gray-green, usually with white stripe along each side with purple band above. Head green. **FOOD:** Often tansy mustards, but also rock cresses, Prince's Plume, and others. **FLIGHT:** Feb.–June (1 flight). **RANGE:** Se. B.C. south through intermountain West to w. Tex. and nw. Mex. **HABITAT:** Arid open areas, including desert foothills, pinyon-juniper, and sagebrush flats. **REMARKS:** Male Desert Marbles patrol ridges and hilltops in search of females.

DESERT ORANGETIP *Anthocharis cethura*   PL. 9

1–1½ in. (26–40 mm). Upperside: Yellow or white. Forewing usually with *small orange patch* between black bar at end of cell and black marks at tip of wing, which also has *white or yellow marks on margin*. Underside: Hindwing with *heavy green marbling* similar to that of marble butterflies. **GEOGRAPHIC VARIATION:** Ranging from East to West, Desert Orangetips range from all-yellow with little difference between sexes (subspecies *pima*) to all-white with orange tips, but more limited orange in female (subspecies *cethura*), to populations that have varying mixtures of females that completely lack an orange patch. **SIMILAR SPECIES:** (1) Desert Marble and other whites lack orange wing patch. Female Desert Orangetips that lack orange patch are very similar but lack pearly iridescence. (2) Pacific and (3) Southwestern Orangetips have more solid black-green marbling on hindwing below. **EARLY STAGES:** Caterpillar has alternating bands of orange-yellow and green together with a row of segmental white patches along each side. **FOOD:** A variety of mustards including tansy-mustard, jewelflower, and tumble mustards. **FLIGHT:** Early Feb.–April, rarely to June (1

DESERT ORANGETIP

PACIFIC ORANGETIP

flight). **RANGE:** Cen. Calif. south to s. Baja Calif. and nw. mainland Mex. east across Nev., sw. Utah, Ariz., and sw. N.M. to w. Tex. **HABITAT:** Desert hills and ridges. **REMARKS:** The Desert and Pima Orangetips were formerly considered separate species, but the two intergrade across a wide area. Males fly along ridges and hilltops.

PACIFIC ORANGETIP *Anthocharis sara*   PL. 9

1 ⅟₁₆–1 ½ in. (27–40 mm). Upperside: Usually white, with females often pale yellow. Forewing with *red-orange patch*, redder in male with iridescent cast. Male with patch extending completely to black edging at tip. *Black bar at end of cell is wide* and connected to *black stripe* at bottom of red-orange patch. Female has white stripe beyond orange patch that is bordered on inside by an *irregular black line* and on outside by *black dashes* at tip and outer margin. Hindwing often with *small black points* at vein endings. Underside: Hindwing with heavy *dark green marbling*. Sporadic second generation (usually in wetter years), mainly found in Calif. lowlands and Coast Range foothills, is larger with reduced black markings and sparse yellow-green marbling. **SIMILAR SPECIES:** (1) Desert Orangetip has different, more yellow-green marbling. (2) Stella Orangetip always has yellow females, cream males, reduced black markings, and yellow-green marbling. **EARLY STAGES:** Caterpillar is green with lateral white stripe. **FOOD:** Milk maids, rock cresses, tower mustard, introduced mustards. **FLIGHT:** Late Dec. to May, rarely late June (1–2 flights). **RANGE:** Pacific Coast from se. Alaska south to n. Baja Calif. **HABITAT:** Foothill canyons and washes, usually in oak woodland. **REMARKS:** The former Sara Orangetip is treated here as four separate species based on chemical studies. These species are difficult to distinguish. The marbling on the underside of the hindwing is made up of black patches with or without a scattering of pale yellow scales and yellow or orange scaling along the wing veins. Individuals with apparently yellow-green marbling have fairly dense mixtures of yellow scales in the black patches, while those with dark green or black marbling have few to no yellow scales. Male Pacific Orangetips usually patrol along streams and valley bottoms in search of females. Males of other species patrol hillsides or ridges.

SOUTHERN ROCKY MOUNTAIN ORANGETIP   PL. 9
Anthocharis julia

1–1 ¼ in. (25–31 mm). Upperside: Male is white, female pale yellow. As for Pacific Orangetip except that *black bar is narrower* and, in male, is *not connected with black edging* at lower edge of orange patch. *Black margin* outside orange tip at apex *toothed inwardly* in male. Underside: *Marbling green*, darker in male. **SIMILAR**

SPECIES: Southwestern Orangetip flies earlier in different habitat and has heavier black markings above and black marbling below. **EARLY STAGES:** Not reported. **FOOD:** Rock cresses. **FLIGHT:** May–July (1 flight). **RANGE:** Southern Rocky Mts. from cen. Wyo. south to n.-cen. N.M. **HABITAT:** Ponderosa and lodgepole pine forests. **REMARKS:** Males patrol along streams.

STELLA ORANGETIP *Anthocharis stella* PL. 9

1–1⅜ in. (26–36 mm). Upperside: Male varies from white to cream-white; female is *pale yellow*. *Black bar* on forewing *narrow*, in male *not connected* with *black edging* at lower edge of orange patch. Underside: *Marbling yellow-green*. **SIMILAR SPECIES:** Southern Rocky Mountain Orangetip does not co-occur. Females are nearly identical. Males are whiter above and have darker green marbling below. **EARLY STAGES:** Not reported. **FOOD:** Rock cresses. **FLIGHT:** Late March–mid-Aug. (1 flight). **RANGE:** Sw. Canada (s. B.C. and sw. Alta.) south through mountainous West to Sierra Nevada, n. Utah, n. Wyo., and w. S.D. **HABITAT:** Montane forests, sunny slopes, and meadows. **REMARKS:** Males patrol ridges and hillsides.

SOUTHWESTERN ORANGETIP *Anthocharis thoosa* PL. 9

1–1½ in. (25–37 mm). Upperside: White; female may have pale yellow hindwing. *Black bar* at end of cell *wide* and *connected with black edging* below orange patch in males, and sometimes in females. Underside: Forewing has *subapical black line* in both sexes. Hindwing with *marbling green-black to black* with *prominent white streak* running from base toward outer margin. Rarely are small yellow scales found in the black marbling patches. Veins tend to be lined with yellow or orange. **SIMILAR SPECIES:** Southern Rocky Mountain Orangetip has narrower black forewing bar above, and below has yellow marbling and lacks prominent white

streak. **EARLY STAGES:** Caterpillar probably similar to that of Pacific Orangetip. **FOOD:** A variety of mustards, including rock cress, jewelflower, and tansy-mustard. **FLIGHT:** Jan.–May. **RANGE:** N. Nev. (possibly se. Ore.), Utah, cen. Colo. south to se. Calif., Ariz., N.M., w. Tex., and N.M. **HABITAT:** Juniper, pinyon-juniper, and pinyon woodlands. **REMARKS:** Males patrol along hillsides and depressions; occasionally found along canyon bottoms or streams.

GRAY MARBLE *Anthocharis lanceolata*   PL. 9

1 ¼–1 ⅞ in. (33–47 mm). Forewing with slightly hooked tip. Upperside: White Forewing with solid *black dot in cell* and diffused black scaling at tip. Underside: Forewing with gray scaling at apex. *Hindwing* almost *solid gray* with *narrow white dash* below costa. **GEOGRAPHIC VARIATION:** In s. Calif. and n. Baja Calif. the adults are smaller with more limited black scaling above. **EARLY STAGES:** Caterpillar green with white flecks and a broad white band along each side, sometimes with yellow along its upper edge. **FOOD:** Mainly rock cresses, occasionally other mustards. **FLIGHT:** Late Feb.–early July, mainly March–May (1 flight). **RANGE:** S. Ore. south in Calif. and w. cen. Nev. to n. Baja Calif. **HABITAT:** Sunny open slopes in foothills and desert canyons. **REMARKS:** Although its common name is "marble," it is really just an orangetip without orange tips to the wings. Rare hybrids are found with the Pacific Orangetip.

FALCATE ORANGETIP *Anthocharis midea*   PL. 9

1 ¼–1 ½ in. (31–40 mm). *Forewing apex falcate.* Upperside: Forewing of both sexes with *small round black cell spot*; male forewing *apex orange-tipped.* Female lacks orange wingtip. Underside: Hindwing has dark green marbling highly fractured. **SIMILAR SPECIES:** Olympia Marble has rounded forewing apex and sim-

Male Falcate Orangetip nectaring at winter cress, Fairfax Co., Va. Note pointed forewings with small black spot in discal cell and orange tips typical of males.

pler marbling; lacks orange forewing tip. **EARLY STAGES:** Caterpillar blue-green with greenish orange line up middle of back and white stripe along each side. **FOOD:** Various Mustard family plants, including rock cresses, shepherd's purse, and winter cress. **FLIGHT:** Early March–June (1 flight). **RANGE:** Cen. Neb., s. Wisc., Ohio, and s. New England south to s. Tex., Gulf Coast, and n. Fla. **HABITAT:** Wet, open woods along rivers and streams, open swamps; sometimes dry woods and ridge tops. **REMARKS:** This dainty sprite, which barely enters our territory, nectars at low flowers, including winter cress and violets.

SULPHURS: GENUS *Colias* FABRICIUS

This is a predominantly temperate group, with most species found in mountainous or alpine habitats. Among our most familiar butterflies are the Clouded Sulphur and Orange Sulphur, which have greatly benefited from the alfalfa and clover fields planted as fodder for livestock. You can find most species in western mountains and the Arctic. Caterpillars of different species specialize on legumes, heaths, or willows.

CLOUDED SULPHUR *Colias philodice*   PL. 10
1⅝–2½ in. (42–62 mm). A common, widespread butterfly. Wing fringes narrowly pink, mixed with pale scales. Upperside: Male *clear yellow* with solid black outer margins. Underside: Forewing with at least some *small dark submarginal spots*; hindwing with silver *cell spot* pink-rimmed, *almost always double.* Female dimorphic—yellow form with black outer margins uneven with en-

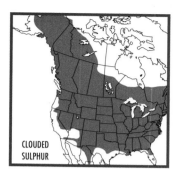

CLOUDED SULPHUR

ORANGE SULPHUR

closed yellow spots. White form (alba) identical but green-white instead of yellow. Spring and fall forms small, less prominently marked. SIMILAR SPECIES: (1) Orange Sulphur has at least some orange above; white female form cannot be reliably separated. (2) Pink-edged Sulphur has upperside forewing black cell spot smaller, and underside hindwing cleaner with silver cell spot single—less prominently pink-rimmed. EARLY STAGES: Caterpillar is dark green, blue-green, or yellow-green with a lateral white stripe subtended by black. Lateral white stripe may contain red spots. FOOD: Various legumes, especially alfalfa, milk vetches, golden banner, white clover, white sweet clover, and other clovers. FLIGHT: May–Oct. (3 flights in north), March–Nov. in south (4–5 flights); occasionally emerges during warm spells in midwinter. RANGE: Alaska, Yukon, and w. N.W. Terr. south through w., cen., and se. Canada; Maritime Provinces; all of contiguous U.S. except much of Fla., s. Tex., and on w. slopes of Calif. mountains. Also occurs in nw. Mex. and has an isolated population in Guatemalan highlands. HABITAT: Many open habitats, mountain meadows, open fields, prairies, alfalfa fields. REMARKS: Rarely hybridizes with Orange Sulphur when both butterflies are abundant, such as in alfalfa or clover fields. This butterfly can survive harsher winters than the Orange Sulphur.

ORANGE SULPHUR *Colias eurytheme*   PL. 10

1½–2⅜ in. (39–60 mm). Highly variable. Wing fringes narrowly pink, mixed with pale. Upperside: At least *some orange* on male and normal female, *black borders often broader*, otherwise as described for Clouded Sulphur. SIMILAR SPECIES: (1) Clouded Sulphur lacks any orange above. White female cannot be reliably separated. (2) Hecla Sulphur does not overlap in range or habitat. Underside hindwing is deep green usually with elongate pink cell spot. (3) Sleepy Orange has black margins more irregular, lacks underside hindwing cell spot. **EARLY STAGES:** Caterpillar is dark green with a white stripe underlined with black along each side. **FOOD:** Various legumes, especially alfalfa, white sweet clover, white clover, and vetches. Others used less frequently. **FLIGHT:** May–Oct. (2–3 flights in north), Feb.–Nov. (occasionally Jan., Dec.; 4–5 flights) in lowland Calif., Ariz., and s. Tex. **RANGE:** Cen. Canada south through contiguous U.S. to cen. Mex. Thought to colonize areas with long, freezing winters. Residency status in northern and more mountainous areas uncertain. **HABITAT:** Wide variety of open habitats, alfalfa fields, lawns, gardens, fields, deserts, prairies, foothills, and mountain meadows. **REMARKS:** One of our commonest butterflies. Occasional pest of alfalfa fields. Male Orange Sulphurs have ultraviolet reflective wings, while those of Clouded Sulphur are ultraviolet absorptive. Females can accept males of the correct species and reject males of the wrong species, thus the species' identities are maintained.

WESTERN SULPHUR *Colias occidentalis*   **PL. 10**

1¾–2¼ in. (45–57 mm). Wings with distinct *pink fringe*. Upperside: Pale yellow. Black border is narrow in males to reduced or absent in females, black *forewing cell spot is small*; white females rare. Underside: Hindwing yellow to golden or white with evenly scattered dusting of black scales; hindwing *cell spot round, often with small satellite* above, *no marginal marks*. **GEOGRAPHIC VARIATION:** Butterflies range from pale yellow above and golden yellow below in nw. Calif. (subspecies *chrysomelas*) to orange in n. Rocky Mts. **SIMILAR SPECIES:** (1) Orange Sulphur has wing bases orange (except white female), underside with tiny marginal black marks. (2)

WESTERN SULPHUR

CHRISTINA SULPHUR

Other sulphurs in range have single cell spot on hindwing below. **EARLY STAGES:** Caterpillar is yellow-green covered with tiny black points and has a white line containing orange dashes along each side. Head yellow-green. **FOOD:** Various legumes, including milk vetches, golden banner, lotis, *Oxytropis*. **FLIGHT:** May–Aug., mainly June–July (1 flight). **RANGE:** W. N. Amer. from s. B.C. south to nw. Calif. and n. Utah. **HABITAT:** Wide variety of open situations including forest openings, prairies, and power-line cuts. **REMARKS:** This treatment includes populations in e. Ore., Idaho, and Utah, with variable amounts of orange on their wings above. These populations may represent intermediates with Christina's Sulphur. More research is required on these difficult insects.

CHRISTINA SULPHUR *Colias christina*   **PL. 10**

1 ⅜–2 in. (35–52 mm). Fringes pink. Upperside: Over two-thirds of male *forewing orange with wing bases yellow*. Female similarly marked or pale orange, rarely white. Underside: Hindwing *olive green to dark mossy green* and has *single pink-rimmed cell spot*. **SIMILAR SPECIES:** Orange Sulphur has orange wing bases above (except white female form) and has double pink-rimmed discal cell spot on underside of hindwing. **EARLY STAGES:** Caterpillar yellow-green covered with tiny black points and a white lateral line containing orange dashes along each side. **FOOD:** Various legumes including sweet-vetch. **FLIGHT:** May–Sept., mainly mid-June–mid-July (1 flight). **RANGE:** E. Alaska east to w. N.W. Terr. south through ne. B.C., Alta., Sask., and Man. to n. Wyo. and w. S.D. **HABITAT:** Forest openings, roadsides, and power-line cuts. **REMARKS:** This butterfly may be the eastern and northern expression of the Western Sulphur but is here treated as a separate species based on the research of C. D. Ferris. Krauth's Sulphur (*Colias krauthii*) is also included here as a subspecies.

QUEEN ALEXANDRA'S SULPHUR *Colias alexandra*   **PL. 10**

1 ½–2 in. (38–49 mm). *Fringes yellow* or greenish white. Upperside: Clear yellow in males and most females. Pale greenish white female form is uncommon. Black border reduced in males; normal, reduced, or absent in females; forewing cell spot usually small in males, variable in females. Underside: *Hindwing pale green with central white discal spot, often rimless or with weak rim*. **SIMILAR SPECIES:** All similar yellow sulphurs have rimmed cell spot and pink fringes. **EARLY STAGES:** Caterpillar light green with a white and pink band along each side. **FOOD:** Various wild legumes including milk vetches, and other vetches, golden banner, and lupines. **FLIGHT:** Mid-May–Sept. (1–2 flights). **RANGE:** S. Alta. and s. Sask. south through intermountain West, and high plains to e. Calif.,

cen. Ariz., and sw. N.M. **HABITAT:** Open situations, including prairies, mountain meadows, and sagebrush flats.

HARFORD'S SULPHUR *Colias harfordii*   PL. 10

1¾–2 in. (45–51 mm). *Wing fringes weakly pink.* Upperside: Clear yellow with even black borders in male; black borders in female normal, often reduced, and occasionally absent. All females are of yellow form. Underside: *Yellow with narrowly rimmed discal spot, usually with small satellite spot above.* Spring individuals have heavy dusting of black scales; summer individuals have clear yellow hindwing. **SIMILAR SPECIES:** Orange Sulphurs always have some orange above and have distinct marginal black marks on underside. **EARLY STAGES:** Caterpillar green with double lateral white line enclosing a narrow red line. **FOOD:** Rattleweed and rarely deerweed. **FLIGHT:** Feb.–Aug., occasionally to Nov. (2 flights). **RANGE:** Cen. Calif. south to n. Baja Calif. **HABITAT:** Dry canyons and hillsides of coast and transverse ranges. **REMARKS:** Sometimes considered a subspecies of Western Sulphur or Alexandra Sulphur. Has an isolated distribution and is genetically distinct.

MEAD'S SULPHUR *Colias meadii*   PL. 10

1¼–1⅝ in. (33–41 mm). Wing fringes pink. Upperside: *Deep redorange* with violet sheen; black borders wide. Male has *distinct oblong sex patch* at upper edge of hindwing. White female form rare. Underside: *Deep green with small pink-rimmed discal spot.* **SIMILAR SPECIES:** Canada Sulphur of Canadian Rockies is paler orange, has distally smeared discal spot below, its males lack sex patch, white females are more prevalent, and it flies at lower elevations. **EARLY STAGES:** Caterpillar is dark yellow-green to grass green with black points and a narrow white line along each side and a pale yellow stripe to each side of back. Head pale green. **FOOD:**

Alpine clover and other clovers. **FLIGHT:** Late June–early Sept., mainly July–Aug. (1 flight), possibly biennial. Caterpillars probably require two summers to complete development, at least in some years. **RANGE:** Rocky Mt. cordillera from n. B.C. and Alta. south to n. N.M. **HABITAT:** Alpine tundra. **REMARKS:** This is an Ice-Age relict with a close relative at the edge of the Arctic Ocean (Johansen's Sulphur).

JOHANSEN'S SULPHUR *Colias johanseni*   **PL. 10**

1⅜–1½ in. (35–38 mm). *Wing fringes* of male *pale*, those of female pink. Upperside: *Deep orange*. Black borders as in most related sulphurs. *Black overscaling* extensive on hindwing, especially female. Male with *bare sex patch on forward edge of hindwing* near base. Underside: Dark green. Hindwing *cell spot broadly pink-edged with distinct satellite spot*. **SIMILAR SPECIES:** Hecla Sulphur male lacks sex patch in male, is deeper orange, and lacks satellite spot on underside of hindwing. **EARLY STAGES:** Unknown. **FOOD:** Unknown. **FLIGHT:** July (1 flight). **RANGE:** Known only from Barnard Harbour, N.W. Terr. **HABITAT:** Hilly tundra (drumlins) near coast. **REMARKS:** Related to Mead's Sulphur and another sulphur in Far East of Russia.

HECLA SULPHUR *Colias hecla*   **PL. 11**

1⅜–1¾ in. (36–43 mm). *Wing fringes pink*. Upperside: *Deep orange*. Underside: Hindwing *dusky green* usually with elongate *pink discal spot*. **SIMILAR SPECIES:** (1) Orange Sulphur and (2) Western Sulphur have hindwing underside yellow, not green, and are not found in alpine or arctic habitats; (3) Canadian Sulphur is pale orange and is yellow below, not green; (4) Johansen's Sulphur is found only at Bernard Harbor, N.W. Terr. and has male sex patch. **EARLY STAGES:** Caterpillar green with tiny black points and light line along each side. **FOOD:** Alpine milk vetch. **FLIGHT:** Late June–mid-Aug. (1 flight). **RANGE:** Holarctic. Greenland coast, Canadian Arctic Archipelago, Alaska, Yukon, and N.W. Terr. south to n. Que. Isolated occurrence on Nfld. **HABITAT:** Arctic tundra. **REMARKS:** Male Booth's Sulphurs were previously thought to be hybrids between Hecla Sulphurs and Labrador Sulphurs.

CANADA SULPHUR *Colias canadensis*   **PL. 11**

1 ½–1 ¾ in. (39–46 mm). Wing fringes narrowly pink. Upperside: Male yellow-orange with narrow black borders and *minute black discal spot*. Female usually white, but sometimes orange or yellow with normal black borders. Underside: Hindwings yellow or white with *pink-edged discal spot smeared outwardly. A smaller satellite spot usually lies above*. **SIMILAR SPECIES:** (1) Hecla and (2) Mead's Sulphurs have wider black borders and are deeper orange above with hindwings green below. Western Sulphurs in the range of this species are orange but have yellow at base of wings and lack smearing of discal spot below. **EARLY STAGES:** Unknown. **FOOD:** Unknown. **FLIGHT:** Early May–Aug., mainly May–June at low elevation, July at higher elevation (1 flight). **RANGE:** E. Alaska and n. B.C. w. to west N.W. Terr. and south to cen. Alta. **HABITAT:** Mixed forest in mountain valleys and alpine tundra. **REMARKS:** A recently distinguished species, previously confused with Hecla Sulphur.

BOOTH'S SULPHUR *Colias tyche*   **PL. 11**

1 ⅜–1 ⅝ in. (35–40 mm). *Wing fringes pink.* Upperside: Male yellow-orange to greenish or white. Female greenish yellow to white. Both sexes with *narrow black borders edged inwardly by a series of pale green patches. Black scaling on wing veins,* especially so on female. Underside: Forewing with a series on *submarginal black spots*. Hindwing *dusky green with cell spot's pink edging smeared outwardly. Satellite spot often present.* Outer edge paler. **SIMILAR SPECIES:** (1) Male Hecla Sulphurs are deeper orange, have wider

black borders, and lack black spots below. (2) Labrador Sulphurs may be confused with female Booth's Sulphurs, but black border is wider and they have less prominent black spotting under forewing. **EARLY STAGES:** Unknown. **FOOD:** Unknown. **FLIGHT:** July–early Aug. (1 flight). **RANGE:** Holarctic. N. Alaska, n. Yukon, n. N.W. Terr., and Canadian Arctic archipelago. **HABITAT:** Arctic tundra. **REMARKS:** These butterflies were previously though to be hybrids between Hecla Sulphurs and Labrador Sulphurs or were confused with Labrador Sulphurs. In N. Amer., the species has been called *Colias boothii.*

LABRADOR SULPHUR *Colias nastes* PL. 11

1¼–1¾ in. (28–43 mm). Small, variable. Wing *fringes barely tinged with pink.* Upperside: Both sexes *dirty white or dingy green-yellow.* Black borders with *enclosed white or green-yellow spots.* Underside: Forewings with a few submarginal black spots. Hindwing green; *discal cell spot narrowly edged with pink, sometimes smeared outwardly.* **SIMILAR SPECIES:** Female Booth's Sulphurs very similar but black border is narrower not enclosing paler spots. Black spotting under forewing is more prominent. **EARLY STAGES:** Caterpillar dark green with lateral pink-edged stripe. **FOOD:** Legumes, including showy locoweed. **FLIGHT:** Mid-June–mid-Sept. (1 flight). **RANGE:** Holarctic. Arctic America from n. Alaska, Yukon, N.W. Terr., and Canadian Arctic Archipelago south in Rocky Mts. to n.-cen. Wash., nw. Mont., n. Que., and coastal Lab. **HABITAT:** Arctic and alpine tundra. **REMARKS:** This small dark green sulphur is difficult to observe. It flies rapidly and erratically over tundra and suddenly drops between rocks to hide.

SCUDDER'S SULPHUR *Colias scudderii* PL. 11

1¼–1¾ in. (32–43 mm). *Wing fringes of male yellow,* tinged with pink, those of female pink. Upperside: Males clear lemon yellow with relatively wide black borders. Females greenish white or yel-

LABRADOR SULPHUR

SCUDDER'S SULPHUR

lowish white with only *hint of black at forewing apex.* Underside: *Greenish yellow with dusting of black scales; discal spot on hindwing large and pink-rimmed.* **SIMILAR SPECIES:** Clouded Sulphurs have the hindwings below yellow with a double discal spot and submarginal black marks. **EARLY STAGES:** Caterpillar grass green with white and yellow band along each side, and faint yellow-green line just below back on each side. Head gray-green. **FOOD:** Dwarf bilberry and small scrub willows. **FLIGHT:** July–early Sept. (1 flight). **RANGE:** Rocky Mt. cordillera from s. Wyo. and ne. Utah south through Colo. to n. N.M. **HABITAT:** Montane willow bogs and adjacent meadows.

GIANT SULPHUR *Colias gigantea* PL. 11

1¾–2¼ in. (45–58 mm). Wing fringes yellow in male, tinged with pink. All-pink in female. Upperside: Male yellow with *narrow black borders*; lower edge of forewing straight. Underside: Forewing *lacks* submarginal black spots. Hindwing with *large pink-rimmed cell spot.* Females dimorphic—yellow form common in Riding Mts., Man., while white form commoner to the north at Churchill, Man. *Black border often absent.* **SIMILAR SPECIES:** (1) Clouded Sulphur has submarginal black spot row on forewing underside. Female has broad black border on both wings. (2) Pink-edged Sulphur is smaller, with upperside forewing black, cell spot small, and lower edge of forewing bowed slightly downward. Female with broad black upperside forewing apical area. (3) Palaeno Sulphur with upper black border wide, upperside forewing cell spot missing, underside hindwing green with silver spot not pink-rimmed. (4) Pelidne Sulphur has small black upperside forewing cell spot, underside hindwing heavily marked with black. **EARLY STAGES:** Not reported. **FOOD:** Willows. **FLIGHT:** Early June–early Aug. (1 brood). **RANGE:** Arctic and subarctic N. Amer. from Alaska

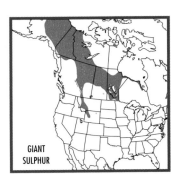

GIANT SULPHUR

PELIDNE SULPHUR

east to w. N.W. Terr., south along Rockies to Idaho and n. Wyo., east to Man. Isolated population in n. Ont. along Hudson Bay. **HABITAT:** Tundra and willow bogs in taiga. **REMARKS:** Some consider this butterfly to be a subspecies of Scudder's Sulphur.

PELIDNE SULPHUR *Colias pelidne*   **PL. 11**

1¼–1¾ in. (32–43 mm). *Fringes pink.* Upperside: Forewing has *broad black border* and *small black cell spot.* Small hindwing cell spot *heavily rimmed with dark pink.* Underside: Hindwing with *heavy black scaling.* White females commoner than yellow forms. **SIMILAR SPECIES:** (1) Palaeno Sulphur upperside often has wider black borders, is usually missing upperside forewing cell spot, and has underside hindwing white cell spot not rimmed with pink. (2) Pink-edged Sulphur has underside hindwing plain yellow without heavy black scaling. (3) Giant Sulphur has narrower black borders, plain yellow underside hindwing. **EARLY STAGES:** Not reported. **FOOD:** Blueberry and *Gaultheria.* **FLIGHT:** Late June–early Sept., mainly July (1 brood). **RANGE:** Several disjunct populations: (1) N. Rocky Mts. from B.C. and w.-cen. Alta. south to nw. Wyo.; (2) coastal areas of extreme s. Hudson and James Bays; (3) w. Nfld., Lab., and ne. Que. Isolated records in w. Arctic (Yukon). **HABITAT:** Subalpine or arctic forest openings and arctic tundra. **REMARKS:** Adults will fly through shade in open forest, whereas most other sulphurs avoid flying through shade.

PINK-EDGED SULPHUR *Colias interior*   **PL. 11**

1½–2 in. (40–52 mm). *Prominent pink wing fringes.* Upperside: Forewing with small black cell spot. Female apical area black; hindwing without black. Hindwing with discal spot orange. Underside: Hindwing *clear yellow with single, pink-rimmed silver cell spot.* White females very rare. **SIMILAR SPECIES:** (1) Clouded Sulphur underside hindwing has submarginal black spot row. (2) Giant Sulphur is larger, males very similar, females with black borders often absent. (3) Pelidne Sulphurs have narrower black borders and yellow (not orange) discal spot on upper hindwing. White females are the rule not the exception. **EARLY STAGES:** Caterpillar is yellow-green with merged white and red longitudinal line along each side. **FOOD:** Various blueberries and bilberries. **FLIGHT:**

PINK-EDGED SULPHUR

Mid-June–late Aug. (1 flight). **RANGE:** N. Amer. from B.C. and cen. Ore. east across subarctic Canada through Great Lakes area to Maritime Provinces and n. New England. Isolated population in cen. Appalachians of ne. Pa., w. Md., e. W. Va., and nw. Va. **HABITAT:** Boggy or scrubby areas dominated by blueberries and other heaths. Often in recovering burns or logged sites.

PALAENO SULPHUR *Colias palaeno* PL. 11

1 ⅜–1 ⅝ in. (36–41 mm). Wing fringes pink. Upperside: Male with *wide black border;* forewing black cell spot usually *missing.* Underside: Hindwing *dusky green* with white spot not rimmed with *pink.* White females predominate and have upperside forewing apical area black. **SIMILAR SPECIES:** (1) Pelidne Sulphur males have narrower black borders, and both sexes usually have small black upperside forewing cell spot and have underside hindwing silver discal spot rimmed with pink. (2) Male Booth's Sulphur usually shows some orange and has narrower black border. **EARLY STAGES:** In Europe, caterpillars are green with a yellow lateral band. **FOOD:** Arctic Bilberry. **FLIGHT:** Mid-June–early Aug. (1 brood). **RANGE:** Holarctic. Arctic America from Alaska east to e. N.W. Terr., n. Alta., and n. Ont.; s. Baffin Is. and isolated records on Victoria and Southampton Is. **HABITAT:** Subarctic bogs, taiga openings, and arctic tundra.

SIERRA SULPHUR *Colias behrii* PL. 11

1 ⅜–1 ⅝ in. (35–41 mm). Wing fringes of male yellow, those of female pink. Upperside: *Green with black borders.* Some females paler green. Underside: *Dark green* with hindwing cell spot not pink-edged—white in male, yellow in female. **EARLY STAGES:** Caterpillar green with black-edged pinkish white dorsal line and white lateral line along each side edged above with black dashes. **FOOD:** Shrub willow or low blueberry. **FLIGHT:** July–Aug. (1 flight). **RANGE:**

SIERRA SULPHUR

PALAENO SULPHUR

Cen. Sierra Nevada of Calif. **HABITAT:** Subalpine and alpine meadows. **REMARKS:** A unique Calif. endemic, most closely related to the blueberry-feeding sulphurs: Palaeno, Pelidne, and Pink-edged.

CALIFORNIA DOGFACE *Zerene eurydice*   **PL. 12**

1⅞–2¼ in. (48–57 mm). *Forewing tip pointed.* Upperside: Male with black forewing enclosed in an iridescent pink overlain *yellow "poodlehead."* Hindwing yellow-orange, sometimes with black border. Female pale yellow with prominent round black discal spot on forewing. Females rarely have traces of black. Underside: Yellow. **SIMILAR SPECIES:** Southern Dogface, more likely in low deserts, shows dog's head in both sexes, though most distinct on male. Male always has black hindwing border on yellow hindwing. **EARLY STAGES:** Caterpillar dull green with white lateral line edged below with orange or red and above with black spot and whitish cross band on each segment. **FOOD:** California false indigo, occasionally other legumes. **FLIGHT:** April–early June, late July–Sept., occasionally as early as Jan. or as late as Nov. (2 flights). **RANGE:** N. Calif. south to n. Baja Calif. **HABITAT:** Openings in chaparral, oak woodland, or conifer forest, usually in foothills or mountains. **REMARKS:** Also known as the "Flying Pansy," this is the official state insect of Calif.

SOUTHERN DOGFACE *Zerene cesonia*   **PL. 12**

1⅞–2½ in. (48–64 mm). Forewing *apex slightly pointed,* not rounded. Upperside: Forewing of both sexes usually shows central *yellow dog's head surrounded by black.* Male forewing with distinct pink iridescence overlying yellow. Female with black areas diffuse. Two seasonal forms. Underside: Summer form has hindwing yellow, that of winter form has dark and pink mottling. **SIMILAR SPECIES:** (1) California Dogface male has pink iridescence and yellow-orange hindwing, usually lacks a black border; female

CALIFORNIA DOGFACE

SOUTHERN DOGFACE

Southern Dogface caterpillar feeding on Calliandra, Sonora state, Mex. Note striking yellow-cream bands and red spots along side. California Dogface caterpillar is similar. Photo by Evi Buckner.

usually lacks any hint of dog's head markings. (2) Alfalfa Butterfly has at least some orange on upperside forewing; has black borders but never in shape of dog's head; (3) Mexican Yellow has dog's head pattern on upperside forewing but ground color is cream, not yellow. **EARLY STAGES:** Caterpillars variable, usually green and covered with black hairy bumps—body unmarked or with yellow and black longitudinal lines or cross bands. **FOOD:** Many legumes, including leadplant, indigo-bush, prairie-clovers, false indigo, and others. **FLIGHT:** All months in Deep South and s. Tex., 2 flights during May–Aug. and overwintering adults (Aug.–April). Colonists to north either do not reproduce or bring off only 1 adult generation before winter. **RANGE:** Resident from S. Amer. north through Cen. Amer. and s. U.S. (s. Tex. and peninsular Fla.). Irregular colonist and temporary resident northward, occasionally reaching Alb., n. Calif., Nev., Utah, se. Wyo., s. Man., s. Ont., and N.J. **HABITAT:** Various open places; thorn scrub, deserts, brushy hills, prairie hills, and weedy pastures. **REMARKS:** Occurs with California Dogface in Sierra Juarez of Baja Calif. without evidence of hybrids.

WHITE ANGLED-SULPHUR *Anteos clorinde*   PL. 12

2¾–3½ in. (70–87 mm). *Large.* Forewing *tip hooked;* hindwing with short marginal projection. Ground *pale green*, turning white with age, with *yellow-orange bar* across forewing cell. Flies high and swiftly. **SIMILAR SPECIES:** (1) Yellow Angled-Sulphur has pale yellow ground and lacks yellow-orange bar. (2) Giant White lacks hindwing projections. **EARLY STAGES:** Caterpillar is yellow-green, with interrupted yellow lateral line above the spiracles and a wide whitish green line below the spiracles. **FOOD:** *Cassia spectabilis.* **FLIGHT:** May, July–Dec. in s. Ariz., all year in tropics. **RANGE:** Resident in mainland tropical Amer. from Argentina north to Mex., regular fall vagrant to s. Ariz., N.M., and w. Tex. during monsoons. Rarely to Neb., ne. Colo., and n. Utah. **HABITAT:** Open, sunny areas in a variety of tropical plant formations. Migrants almost anywhere. **REMARKS:** Both Angled-Sulphurs often fly high above the ground with deep wingbeats.

YELLOW ANGLED-SULPHUR *Anteos maerula*   PL. 12

3–3¼ in. (76–90 mm). Large. Forewing *tip hooked*; hindwing with short marginal projection. Male *bright yellow* above, female slightly paler. Upperside: Forewing cell with black spot. Flies high and swiftly. **SIMILAR SPECIES:** (1) White Angled-Sulphur ground color is pale green or white, upperside forewing has yellow-orange bar across cell. (2) Cloudless Sulphur is smaller and has regular wing shape. **EARLY STAGES:** Caterpillar is olive green, with a broad yellow-buff lateral stripe and 2 irregular rows of subdorsal blotches. **FOOD:** *Cassia.* **FLIGHT:** Mid-Aug.–Nov. in extreme s. Ariz. and sw. N.M.; all year in tropics. **RANGE:** Resident in tropical Amer. from Peru north to Mex., irregular rare vagrant in Fla., Miss., s. and w. Tex., se. Ariz., sw. N.M., and e. Neb. **HABITAT:** Open, sunny places in a variety of tropical plant formations. Migrants almost anywhere.

CLOUDLESS SULPHUR *Phoebis sennae*   PL. 12

1⅞–2½ in. (48–66 mm). This is by far the commonest giant sulphur. Upperside: Male is *clear lemon yellow;* female dimorphic, yellow or white. Forewing of female with *hollow black cell spot,* outer margins of both wings edged irregularly with black. Underside: Both sexes have hindwing with 2 *centered pink-rimmed silver spots.* **SIMILAR SPECIES:** (1) Large Orange Sulphur male has upperside bright orange. Female has upperside forewing with interrupted diagonal row of black smudges. (2) Orange-barred Sulphur is larger, male has upperside forewing with red-orange costal bar and hindwing red-orange outer margin. Female upperside forewing with broken line of diagonal smudges. Yellow female form has outer half of upperside hindwing red-pink. (3) Statira Sulphur male has upperside forewing with outer portions paler yellow. Female has only upperside forewing edged in black, and black cell spot is smaller, not hollow. **EARLY STAGES:** Caterpillar is yellow or green with tiny black tubercles and a yellow longitudinal stripe with small blue dots along each side. **FOOD:** *Cassias.*

CLOUDLESS SULPHUR

FLIGHT: March–Jan. in s. Ariz. and w. Tex., usually summer and fall to north. All year in tropics. **RANGE:** Permanent resident in tropical Amer. from Argentina north through Cen. Amer. and the Caribbean to s. Tex. and the Deep South. Regular vagrant and temporary breeding resident in the Southwest and much of the e. U.S. Frequent vagrant north to s. Ore., Calif., s. Mont., N.D., and s. Ont. **HABITAT:** Wide variety of open, weedy tropical and subtropical situations. May appear anywhere during northward incursions, e.g., Ariz. mountains, timberline in Colo., etc. **REMARKS:** This is commonest all-yellow large tropical sulphur seen north of the Mexican border.

ORANGE-BARRED SULPHUR *Phoebis philea* PL. 12

2¼–3⅜ in. (56–86 mm). Upperside: Male forewing with *red-orange bar* and hindwing with *red-orange outer margin*. Female much larger than male, dimorphic: one form yellow-orange, the other off-white. Both female forms have forewing with solid black cell spot and a broken, offset, submarginal line of black smudges. Yellow form with outer half of hindwing red-orange. Flies high and swiftly. **SIMILAR SPECIES:** (1) Large Orange Sulphur is smaller, male bright orange above; female upperside forewing with continuous diagonal row of black smudges. (2) Cloudless Sulphur is smaller, male bright yellow above, female upperside forewing without row of black smudges. **EARLY STAGES:** Caterpillar is yellow-green with black tubercles and lateral black and yellow bands, the latter with included white-ringed reddish black spots. **FOOD:** *Cassias.* **FLIGHT:** Vagrants from late July–early Oct. in s. Ariz.; all year in tropics. **RANGE:** Resident in much of lowland tropical Amer. south to Brazil, and in peninsular Fla. and the Keys (since around 1928). Irregular vagrant to se. Ariz. (occasionally breeds), s. Calif., s. N.M., and s. Tex., extremely rare vagrant northward to Colo., Nev., Kans., and Neb. **HABITAT:** Foothill canyons, forest edges, city gardens. Thorn scrub, rural gardens, and forests in tropics.

LARGE ORANGE
SULPHUR

LARGE ORANGE SULPHUR

Phoebis agarithe PL. 13

2–3 in. (52–74 mm). Upperside: Male *bright orange*. Female dimorphic, yellow-orange or pink-white. Underside: Forewing of both sexes with *straight submarginal line*, not offset as in all other *Phoebis*.

Female Large Orange Sulphur (white form) nectaring at fleabane, Hidalgo Co., Texas. Most female sulphurs have a white form. The abundance of the two forms relative to each other varies widely.

SIMILAR SPECIES: (1) Apricot Sulphur (very rare in U.S.) underside has submarginal line on forewing broken and offset. (2) Cloudless Sulphur male is pure yellow above; female upperside forewing lacks submarginal smudges. (3) Orange-barred Sulphur is larger; male has upperside with red-orange bar on forewing and red-orange outer margin on hindwing. Female has upperside submarginal spot line on forewing interrupted and offset. **EARLY STAGES:** Caterpillar is green with lateral yellow line edged with black below. **FOOD:** Woody plants in Mimosa family—*Pithecellobium* and *Inga* are known host genera. **FLIGHT:** All year in s. Fla. and s. Tex., strays north in mid- to late summer. Has recognizable seasonal forms. **RANGE:** Resident in much of lowland tropical Amer. from Peru north to peninsular Fla. and s. Tex. Vagrant and sometimes temporary resident north to s. Calif., Ariz., N.M., Colo., S.D., Wisc., and N.J. **HABITAT:** Many open, lowland tropical situations including forest edges, pastures, and city gardens.

APRICOT SULPHUR *Phoebis argante* **NOT SHOWN**

2¼–2½ in. (57–66 mm). Upperside: Male *bright orange*. Female dimorphic. Underside: Both sexes with forewing *submarginal line broken and offset*. **SIMILAR SPECIES:** Large Orange Sulphur has underside forewing submarginal line straight, not offset. **EARLY STAGES:** Caterpillar is green or yellow-green with many small creamy granulations and a white or yellow stripe along each side; back with short reddish hairs. **FOOD:** Woody plants in Mimosa family, including *Pentaclethra* and *Inga*. **FLIGHT:** All year in tropics. Strays to Tex. June–Oct. **RANGE:** Paraguay north to Mex. Extremely rare vagrant (3 times) to Tex. **HABITAT:** Tropical forest clearings, roadsides, gardens, pastures.

2–2⅝ in. (50–67 mm). Upperside: Male *two-toned* with ridged scale line down middle of both wings. Outer portion beyond scale ridge is pale yellow-cream, inner portion lemon yellow. Female with even black borders on apex and outer margin of forewing. Cell spot solid black. **SIMILAR SPECIES:** Cloudless Sulphur is solid yellow, lacks scale ridge. Female with apex and outer margin unevenly edged with black, forewing cell spot hollow, filled with yellow or white. **EARLY STAGES:** Caterpillar pale orange with green tinge; blue-black band along each side. **FOOD:** Legumes from all three families—*Dalbergia* and *Cassia* in Fla. **FLIGHT:** June–early Feb. (summer flight and overwintering adults). **RANGE:** Resident in lowland tropical Amer. north to peninsular Fla. Vagrant in Tex., N.M., and Kans. **HABITAT:** Second-growth or scrub habitats in tropical lowlands. Vacates seasonally dry habitats, and large migrations have been seen in the tropics.

TAILED SULPHUR *Phoebis neocypris* **SEE PHOTO**

2⅜–2¾ in. (60–72 mm). Hindwings with *distinct taillike projections.* Upperside: Male yellow with tiny black dots at vein endings. Female usually white with round black dot in discal cell; with or without red margin on hindwing. Underside: Yellow with *reddish mottlings.* **SIMILAR SPECIES:** The smaller Cloudless Sulphur and larger Yellow Angled-sulphur lack the distinct taillike projections. **EARLY STAGES:** Caterpillar yellow-green covered with many yellow and blue raised spots. **FOOD:** Tree cassias. **FLIGHT:** All year in tropics. June in se. Ariz. **RANGE:** S. Amer. north to Mex. Strays rarely to se. Ariz. and s. Tex. **HABITAT:** Mainly premontane and montane forests and associated openings in Mex. and Cen. Amer.

Male Tailed Sulphur nectaring, Durango state, Mex. Note triangular extension on hindwing. Females are smaller and mainly of the white form, but have the same wing shape.

LYSIDE SULPHUR
Kricogonia lyside   **PL. 13**

LYSIDE SULPHUR

1¼–2 in. (34–51 mm). Extremely variable. Forewing apex abruptly *squared off*. Upperside: Base *of forewing yellow;* male often with black bar on hindwing costa. Underside: Hindwing with satiny sheen and raised veins. Female dimorphic, with both yellow and white forms. **SIMILAR SPECIES:** (1) Cabbage White upperside forewing has 1 (male) or 2 (female) black spots. (2) Great Southern White upperside forewing has black outer margin in both sexes. (3) Cloudless Sulphur has normal wing shape, male upperside is uniformly yellow, while female upperside forewing has black outer margin and black cell spot. **EARLY STAGES:** Caterpillar dull green with dorsal and lateral gray or silver lines, the dorsal line bordered on both sides by chocolate brown and the sides with variegated brown and golden yellow. **FOOD:** Lignumvitae in much of range, *Porliera* in Tex. **FLIGHT:** All year in s. Tex. and tropics, July–Dec. in s. Ariz. **RANGE:** Resident in lowland tropical Amer. from Antilles and Venezuela north to s. peninsular Fla. (rare) and s. Tex. (abundant). Migrates and found regularly north to Calif., s. Ariz., Colo., and Neb. **HABITAT:** Lowland scrub and seasonally dry forest edges. Various open habitats during emigrations. **REMARKS:** Synchronous mass flights have been noted in s. Arizona and elsewhere.

BARRED YELLOW *Eurema daira*   **PL. 13**

1 1⁄16–1 3⁄8 in. (28–36 mm). Sexually dimorphic and with 2 seasonal forms. Summer (wet season) form smaller. Upperside: Male forewing with *black bar* along inner margin and extensive black on apical area. Female forewing with *gray-black on apex* as in male and black patch on hindwing outer margin. *Hindwing white.* Summer (wet-season) form with black more extensive. Underside: Hindwing satiny white (summer form), or brick red or tan with 2 black spots in cell (winter form). **SIMILAR SPECIES:** (1) Dainty Sulphur is smaller, has elongated forewing; upperside black bar along hindwing costal margin; underside hindwing more patterned. (2) Little Sulphur upperside has small black forewing cell spot, lacks black bar on forewing inner margin. **EARLY STAGES:** Caterpillar light green above and translucent green below with pale stripe on each side. **FOOD:** Joint vetch, also pencil flower and other legumes. **FLIGHT:** Aug.–Oct. in se. Ariz. All year in tropics and se.

BOISDUVAL'S YELLOW

MEXICAN YELLOW

U.S. RANGE: Widespread resident and migrant from Argentina north through Caribbean, Cen. Amer., and Mex. Resident in Deep South. Vagrant north to s. Tex., s. Ariz., s. N.M., and S.D. **HABITAT:** Pastures, dunes, forest edges in subtropical and tropical zones. Mid-elevations in southwestern mountains.

BOISDUVAL'S YELLOW *Eurema boisduvaliana* PL. 13

1 5/16–1 1/2 in. (33–40 mm). Sexes dimorphic. Upperside: *Lemon yellow* with *black borders* and *slight projection* on each hindwing. Male with weakly expressed *dog's-head* pattern on forewing; hindwing with black border projecting into yellow ground. Female forewing with black apical area, narrow black margin on hindwing. **SIMILAR SPECIES:** (1) Mexican Yellow has ground pale cream, dog's snout more pronounced, and hindwing projections more accentuated. (2) Dina Yellow is deeper yellow, upperside forewing

Cluster of male Boisduval's Yellows at moisture, Sinaloa state, Mex. The upperside pattern can be seen with transmitted light. This was taken in early dry season, and these must be of the dry-season form.

lacks dog's-head pattern. No taillike projections on hindwing. **EARLY STAGES:** Not known. **FOOD:** *Cassia leptocarpa.* **FLIGHT:** All year in tropics, March–Nov. in s. Ariz. and s. Tex. **RANGE:** Resident from Costa Rica north to Mex. and the Antilles. Regular vagrant north to se. Ariz. (occasional breeder), sw. N.M., and s. Tex., rarely to s. Calif., s. Nev. and s. Fla. **HABITAT:** Thorn scrub, dry woodland, pastures, and roadsides.

MEXICAN YELLOW *Eurema mexicana* PL. 13

1¼–2¼ in. (36–55 mm). Sexes dimorphic. Upperside: Ground *pale cream;* forewing of both sexes with *dog's-head* pattern, which is more accentuated in male. Triangular *taillike projections* from hindwing outer margin. **SIMILAR SPECIES:** Boisduval's Yellow has ground yellow with less pronounced taillike projections. **EARLY STAGES:** Caterpillar is variable pale green to dark green. **FOOD:** *Acacia angustissima* and *Diphysia;* reports of *Cassia* are probably in error. **FLIGHT:** All year in tropics, midsummer to fall as vagrant. **RANGE:** Resident in n. S. Amer. north to s. Ariz., s. N.M., and s. Tex. A common vagrant in the Southwest (incl. Calif.), intermountain West, and Great Plains, rarely north to s. Man. and s. Ont., east to Miss. and Ill. **HABITAT:** Mountain canyons and dry open hillsides, thorn scrub, prairies. **REMARKS:** The Mexican Yellow occurs far to the north (1,000+ miles), sometimes commonly, of its nearest potential breeding areas.

TAILED ORANGE *Eurema proterpia* PL. 13

1¼–1¾ in. (34–43 mm). Sexually dimorphic and with 2 seasonal forms. Summer (wet-season) form without tails. Winter (dry-season) form with distinct triangular projection on hindwing. Upperside: *Orange* with black edges. Forewing apex *squared off.* Male with forewing costa black; female with arced black forewing costa, apex, and outer margin. Underside: Hindwing *unpatterned.* **SIMILAR SPECIES:** Sleepy Orange has rounded forewing apex; upperside forewing has small black cell spot, underside hindwing with faintly mottled pattern. **EARLY STAGES:** Caterpillar is grass green. **FOOD:** Beggar's-ticks and Mesquite. **FLIGHT:** All year in tropics; March, July–Jan. in se. Ariz. **RANGE:** Resident in the Greater Antilles, S. Amer. from Peru north through lowland Cen. Amer. and Mex., espe-

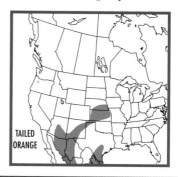

TAILED ORANGE

cially dry-season zones; strays regularly north to cen. Ariz. (breeds but does not survive winters), sw. N.M. and s. Tex., very rarely to Kans. and Neb. **HABITAT:** Seasonally dry scrub, forest edges, pastures. **REMARKS:** As recently as 1951, the strikingly different appearing seasonal forms were still considered separate species.

LITTLE YELLOW *Eurema lisa* — PL. 13

1 1/16–1 1/2 in. (28–37 mm). Sexually dimorphic. Upperside: Forewing of both sexes with *small black cell spot*. Male yellow with broad black forewing apex. Hindwing with *black border*. Female also dimorphic—yellow form much more common than white form. Underside: Hindwing yellow with 2 *tiny black dots in center*. **SIMILAR SPECIES:** (1) Nise Yellow lacks forewing cell spot; forewing black apical area less extensive on male. Female and winter male upperside usually with black border on hindwing. Tiny black dots absent from underside of hindwing. (2) Dina Yellow is larger, with narrower black borders on forewing upperside, usually none on hindwing. (3) Dainty Sulphur is smaller with more complex pattern above and below. Both sexes with black bar along upperside forewing inner margin. **EARLY STAGES:** Caterpillar is grass green with 1 or 2 lateral white lines. **FOOD:** *Cassias*. **FLIGHT:** All year in Deep South, s. Tex., and tropics (4–5 broods); April–May, July–Oct. in se. Ariz., late spring to early fall farther north in plains states. **RANGE:** Resident in lowland tropical Amer. and s. U.S. from Tex. eastward; seasonally colonizes and may breed in se. Ariz.; common stray in eastern plains, but rare stray on high plains and elsewhere in West. **HABITAT:** Dry sandy fields, roadsides, old fields, power-line cuts.

MIMOSA YELLOW *Eurema nise* — PL. 13

1 1/16–1 1/4 in. (28–33 mm). Sexually dimorphic. Ground yellow in both sexes—no white female form. Upperside: Forewing *lacks* black cell spot and has *narrow black outer margins*. Hindwing black margin lacking in female, infrequent in male. **SIMILAR SPECIES:** Little Sulphur upperside has forewing black cell spot and broader black margins on both wings. **EARLY STAGES:** Caterpillar is green with short white setae and a white lateral line. **FOOD:** Sensitive-plant. **FLIGHT:** All year in tropics and s. Tex.; April–June, Aug.–Nov. in se. Ariz. **RANGE:** Resident in lowland tropical Amer. south to Argentina, irregular stray northward to se. Ariz., cen. Tex., and s. Fla., rarely s. Calif., s. Nev., s. Utah, s. Colo., Kans., s. N.M., and s. Nev. **HABITAT:** Brushy edges and openings in woods, rarely pastures.

DINA YELLOW *Eurema dina* — PL. 13

1 1/2–1 7/8 in. (40–48 mm). Sexually dimorphic. Upperside: Male or-

Male Dina Yellow (dry-season form) resting, Sinaloa state, Mex. Dry-season form individuals of tropical yellows spend much time resting in the shade and are often marked more cryptically.

ange-yellow with very *narrow black* on forewing costa and outer margin, hint of black outer hindwing margin on summer form. Female with black forewing apex. Underside: Hindwing has 3 *black spots* on underside hindwing. **SIMILAR SPECIES:** (1) Boisduval's Yellow has irregular black borders. (2) Other similar yellows can be immediately separated by their much smaller size. **EARLY STAGES:** Caterpillar is light green with dark green lateral line. **FOOD:** Woody members of Simarouba family, Mexican Alvaradoa in Fla., *Picramnia* in Costa Rica. **FLIGHT:** May, Aug.–Sept. in se. Ariz. All year in tropics. **RANGE:** Resident in Cen. Amer., Mex., and Caribbean north to peninsular Fla. (since 1962). Irregular vagrant to s. Tex. and se. Ariz. **HABITAT:** Edges of brushy fields and forest.

SLEEPY ORANGE *Eurema nicippe* PL. 13

1¼–2 in. (32–49 mm). Sexually dimorphic. Dry and wet seasonal forms. Upperside: Both wings *orange* with *irregular black borders* on costal and outer margins. Orange-yellow form rare. Male with black border sharply defined, female with black border edge diffuse. Forewing with *small black cell spot*. Underside: Hindwing of summer form orange-yellow, that of winter form brick red, brown, or tan. **SIMILAR SPECIES:** Orange Sulphur male has more regular black borders on outer margin. Female has pale yellow spots enclosed within black border. Both sexes have at least a small amount of yellow above. Hindwing underside with silver cell spots. **EARLY STAGES:** Caterpillar green with lateral white and yellow stripe edged by black along lower edge. **FOOD:** Various *Cassias*. **FLIGHT:** All year in tropics, s. Calif., s. Ariz., and s. Tex. (4–5 flights, including 1 of overwintering adults). Mid- to late summer farther north. **RANGE:** Resident in the West Indies, Mex., and s. U.S. Regular vagrant

and temporary colonist north to central states, rarely strays to Nev., Utah, Colo., Wyo., and S.D. **HABITAT:** Low areas in lower austral and subtropical zones, including dry washes, pine forests, open fields, roadsides, and many other habitats. **REMARKS:** Misnamed, the Sleepy Sulphur is a rapid flier at most times, except when visiting flowers or resting during its winter period of inactivity.

DAINTY SULPHUR *Nathalis iole*   PL. 13

⅞–1 1/16 in. (22–27 mm). Forewings elongated. Sexes and seasonal forms differ. Upperside: Black and yellow. Forewing with *black bar along inner margin*. Female with more extensive black. Hindwing with some orange infusion. White form rare. Underside: Forewing showing *orange or yellow basal patch* with *black spots* on outer edge. Hindwing of summer form pale yellow, that of winter form dusky green. **SIMILAR SPECIES:** (1) Barred Yellow is larger and lacks black cell spot on forewing upperside. (2) Little Sulphur is larger and lacks black bar along inner margin of upperside forewing. **EARLY STAGES:** Caterpillar is dark green with purple dorsal stripe and fused black and yellow line along each side. **FOOD:** Low plants in aster family, especially Fetid Marigold and Bur Marigold. **FLIGHT:** All year in s. Calif., s. Ariz., and s. Tex. (number of flights indefinite). No more than 6 months in colonized areas to north. **RANGE:** Resident from Guatemala and the West Indies north to peninsular Fla. and the Southwest. Regular vagrant and colonist north to se. Wash., se. and sw. Idaho, Mont., N.D., cen. Man., Minn., and s. Ont. **HABITAT:** Dry open areas, including desert, thorn scrub, weedy fields, prairies, road edges, and hillsides. **REMARKS:** Dainty Sulphur is unique among our sulphurs in several structural features, so much so that some feel it belongs in a separate subfamily.

True Butterflies:
Superfamily Papilionoidea
Harvester, Coppers, Hairstreaks, and Blues: Family Lycaenidae

Butterflies of this family are worldwide in distribution, with about 4,700 species, but the proportions of species differ in different regions. Coppers are especially dominant in north temperate regions, blues are richest in the Old World tropics and north temperate zone, and hairstreaks are particularly abundant and diverse in the New World tropics. The adults are usually small to tiny and are often brilliantly colored. Iridescent blues, bright reds, and oranges are common colors on the upper surfaces. Front legs of most males lack a pretarsus and their tarsomeres are fused into one segment, but their legs are still used for walking. Females have three pairs of normal walking legs. Adults of most of our species visit flowers for nectar, but adults of harvesters feed on woolly aphid honeydew, and adults of some hairstreaks never visit flowers but probably feed on aphid honeydew or bird droppings.

Eggs are usually laid singly on host leaves or flower buds. Most of our species are relatively specific in their caterpillar host choice, usually limited to plants of the same family, but many species of tropical affinities are catholic in their choice of hosts. In fact, the Gray Hairstreak has one of the broadest host ranges of any butterfly. The eggs of most species are sea urchin shaped. Most caterpillars are slug-shaped with retracted heads; their bodies are covered with short, fine setae. The caterpillars of many species depend on ants for protection. These caterpillars have abdominal glands that produce sugary secretions collected by the ants. The early stages of some species are actually maintained inside ant nests.

The pupae are stout and may be attached to the surface by a fine girdle. Pupae of some species have a mechanism for producing sounds that are probably related to protection from predators by ants. Overwintering is accomplished in either the egg or pupal stage.

HARVESTER *Feniseca tarquinius* PL. 14

1–1¼ in. (25–30 mm). Adults unique. Upperside: *Orange-brown* with *black areas and spots*. Underside: Hindwing brown or orange-brown with *faint white scrawls*. **EARLY STAGES:** Caterpillar is greenish brown with faint lines along the sides; long white hairs originate from between the segments. **FOOD:** Woolly aphids, especially on alders. **FLIGHT:** Mid-May–mid-Aug. in north (2 flights); Feb. or March–Sept. in south (3 broods). **RANGE:** E. N. Amer. from s. Canada south to Fla. and Gulf Coast west to cen. Neb. and w. Kans. **HABITAT:** Woodlands, usually deciduous, near slow-moving or swampy streams.

COPPERS: SUBFAMILY LYCAENINAE

Most coppers are found in sunny, open habitats throughout the temperate zone, with 50 species found in Eurasia and North America. One isolated species, *Lycaena pyrrhias*, lives on volcanos in Guatemala. A few species occur in New Guinea, New Zealand, and northern Africa. The upper wing surfaces are iridescent purple or red-orange in most species, but some of ours are blue, brown, or gray. Our species may bask with open wings. Males perch and interact, seemingly aggressively, with other males, while they await receptive females. No species are known migrants, but several are good colonists at least on a local basis. Most species are single-brooded, but the Purplish Copper and Bronze Copper may have two or three broods. They overwinter as eggs or as first instar caterpillars within the egg. The caterpillars feed on leaves of the host plants, which in our area are docks, knotweeds, buckwheats, cinquefoils, gooseberries, currants, or redberry.

TAILED COPPER *Lycaena arota* PL. 14

1–1¼ in. (26–30 mm). *Single short tail* on each hindwing. Upperside: Male iridescent purple, female orange-yellow with black margin, and black spots. Underside: Hindwing with a black dot next to tail and with series of black marks and squiggly white submarginal band on gray background. **SIMILAR SPECIES:** Hedgerow Hairstreak is red-orange above but hindwing is uniformly colored below. **EARLY STAGES:** Caterpillar is green with 2 closely placed lines on back and 1 pale yellow line along each side. **FOOD:** Wild currants and gooseberries. **FLIGHT:** Late May (Calif.)–Sept. (1 flight). **RANGE:** W. Ore. south to n. Baja Calif. and east to Colo. and n. N.M. **HABITAT:** Foothill woodlands and canyons. **REMARKS:** Its small

TAILED COPPER

AMERICAN COPPER

tail gives the misleading impression of a hairstreak. Tailed coppers readily sip nectar from flowers, especially those of asters and yellow composites.

AMERICAN COPPER *Lycaena phlaeas* PL. 14

⅞–1¼ in. (22–30 mm). Small. Sexes similar. Upperside: Forewing *iridescent fiery red-orange*; hindwing gray with *red-orange border* on outer edge. Underside: Hindwing gray with small black spots and zigzag red-orange submarginal line. **SIMILAR SPECIES:** (1) Ruddy and (2) Lustrous Coppers are similar in color but lack gray hindwing and marginal orange band. **EARLY STAGES:** Caterpillar varies from green to rose red; some have red stripe up middle of back. **FOOD:** Sheep sorrel, rarely curled dock, on plains east of Rockies; alpine sorrel in western mountains and Arctic. **FLIGHT:** May–Sept. (2 flights) on plains; July–Aug. (1 flight) in West and Arctic. **RANGE:** Holarctic. In N. Amer. probably introduced from Europe to eastern half of continent. Native populations in Arctic and western alpine habitats from Alaska, Yukon, and arctic islands south discontinuously to cen. Calif., ne. Ore., Idaho-Mont. border, cen. Utah, and nw. Wyo. **HABITAT:** Introduced populations in waste lots and hayfields; native western populations on tundra and rocky alpine slopes. **REMARKS:** American Copper is a misnomer for the introduced eastern populations of this butterfly, but it is a traditional name of long standing.

LUSTROUS COPPER *Lycaena cupreus* PL. 14

1–1¼ in. (25–30 mm). Upperside: Both wings *iridescent red or red-orange* with black border and scattered *small black dots*. Underside: Hindwing cream to gray with small black dots and a *thin red squiggly line* along outer edge. **SIMILAR SPECIES:** Male Ruddy Copper is most similar but the two butterflies usually occupy different

Male Lustrous Copper (subspecies cupreus) *perching on white flower, Plumas Co., Calif. Note general similarity but difference in wing shape and red color compared to subspecies* snowi *shown on plate.*

habitats. Ruddy Coppers lack black border above and are uniformly pale-colored below. **EARLY STAGES:** Caterpillar light green to reddish with red side stripe and red dashes on back. **FOOD:** Alpine Sorrel in Rocky Mt. alpine habitats; various docks elsewhere. **FLIGHT:** Mid-June–mid-Aug., sometimes as early as May and as late as Sept. (1 flight). **RANGE:** Cen. B.C. and Alta. south to cen. Calif. and n. N.M. **HABITAT:** Montane meadows (Calif. and Ore.), sagebrush flats, and alpine rock slides (Rocky Mts.). **REMARKS:** The two groups of populations (Calif., Ore.) and Rocky Mts. have distinctly different forewing shapes and habitats.

GREAT COPPER *Lycaena xanthoides* PL. 14

1¼–1¾ in. (33–44 mm). Very *short taillike projection* on hindwing. Upperside: *Gray,* male with black spot (sometimes indistinct) in forewing cell and with or without small amount of yellow-orange at lower edge of hindwing. Female with yellow-orange on lower

LUSTROUS COPPER

GREAT COPPER

Female Great Copper, Calif. Shows intense coloration of individuals in more coastal populations. Note short taillike extension and pale submarginal band on hindwing. Photo by Greg Ballmer.

outer margin of forewing and complete orange and black band on outer margin of hindwing. Variable amounts of yellow on both wings. Underside: *Gray with black spots and paler band* inside margin. **SIMILAR SPECIES:** (1) Edith's Copper is smaller, has more complex pattern of pale and black marks on underside of hindwing, and is found in mountains. (2) Female Gorgon Coppers are similar to Great Copper females but have more elongate yellow marks above and small red marks on outer edge of hindwing below. **EARLY STAGES:** Caterpillar green, yellow-green, or red-orange with magenta marks. Cervical shield green bisected by narrow white line. Chrysalis pink-brown, spotted with black. **FOOD:** Several docks. **FLIGHT:** Mid-May–July, rarely Aug. (1 flight). **RANGE:** W. Ore. south through valleys and foothills of Calif. to n. Baja Calif. **HABITAT:** Open fields, valleys, and slopes. **REMARKS:** Hybrids with Edith's Copper are found in limited areas. Caterpillar spins a light cocoon to surround chrysalis.

GRAY COPPER *Lycaena dione* PL. 14

1 5/16–1 1/2 in. (24–38 mm). Upperside: *Dark gray.* Forewing has 2 black cell spots; hindwing has pale *orange and black border* on outer edge. Underside: *Pale gray-white with pattern of small black dots* and repetition of *hindwing border* but with *orange-red.* **SIMILAR SPECIES:** Great Copper is very similar but the two species are widely separated geographically. **EARLY STAGES:** Caterpillar is green with darker green or red stripe up middle of back. **FOOD:** Several docks, including broad dock. **FLIGHT:** Mid-June–July, occasionally Aug. (1 flight). **RANGE:** N. Idaho, Mont., Wyo., e. Colo., s. Man., Sask., and Alta. south to cen. Ill., cen. Mo., n. Tex., and ne. N.M. **HABITAT:** Weedy fields, pastures, open grassy areas along ditches and

Female Gorgon Copper nectaring on fasciculate buckwheat, Orange Co., Calif. Note lack of yellow on hindwing compared to individual on Plate 14. Many populations are being invaded by weeds. Photo by Jack N. Levy.

streams. **REMARKS:** Adults nectar at flowers such as orange milkweed, Canada thistle, and dogbane.

BRONZE COPPER *Lycaena hyllus* **PL. 14**

1¼–1⅝ in. (32–41 mm). Large. Sexes differ strikingly above. Upperside: Male iridescent brown-purple; female forewing yellow-orange with black spots. Underside: Both sexes have orange forewing with *black spots*; hindwing is *off-white with black spots* and *wide orange outer margin*. **SIMILAR SPECIES:** Purplish Copper often shares same habitat but is smaller, has narrower orange submarginal band on hindwing, and is orange-brown on underside of hindwing. **EARLY STAGES:** Caterpillar is yellow-green with blackish stripe up middle of back. **FOOD:** Water dock, curled dock, and smartweeds. **FLIGHT:** Mid-June–early Oct. (2 flights). **RANGE:** Cen. N. Amer. from cen. Man., Mont., and e. Idaho south to s. Utah, s. Colo., ne. N.M., and Okla., thence east in a band through Mid-

GORGON COPPER

BRONZE COPPER

west to Atlantic Coast. **HABITAT:** Open areas with low vegetation in or near marshes, bogs, wet meadows, and seeps. **REMARKS:** Bronze Copper may be spreading west of Continental Divide in agricultural areas and wetlands.

EDITH'S COPPER *Lycaena editha*   PL. 14
⅞–1¼ in. (22–30 mm). *Minute tail* projects from lower edge of hindwing. Upperside: *Dark gray.* Male uniform—sometimes with single black spot on forewing, female with variable yellow spotting. Underside: *Gray with complex pattern of black dots and scrawls* as well as paler areas. **SIMILAR SPECIES:** Great Copper is larger, has less complex pattern on hindwing below, and usually lacks yellow-orange below. The two species co-occur only in limited areas of Calif. **EARLY STAGES:** Not reported. **FOOD:** Various docks and knotweed. **FLIGHT:** Late June–Aug., rarely Sept. (1 flight). **RANGE:** Sw. Wash., Idaho, n. Nev., and w. Mont. south to cen. Calif., n. Utah, and n. Colo. **HABITAT:** Mountain meadows, streamsides, and sagebrush flats. **REMARKS:** Color variable, sometimes light gray; size of black spots varies.

GORGON COPPER *Lycaena gorgon*   PL. 14
1¼–1⅝ in. (32–41 mm). Upperside: Male iridescent red-purple, female gray with elongate yellow spots. Underside: *Gray-white with many black spots* and *row of separated red dots* on hindwing outer margin. **SIMILAR SPECIES:** Female Great Copper is less distinctly spotted below and lacks row of red spots. **EARLY STAGES:** Caterpillar pale green with dense white hairs. **FOOD:** Nude and elongate buckwheats. **FLIGHT:** Late March–mid-July (1 flight). **RANGE:** S. Ore. through much of Calif. to n. Baja Calif. **HABITAT:** Grassy slopes and chaparral in foothills. **REMARKS:** Colonies are closely tied to host plants.

RUDDY COPPER *Lycaena rubidus* PL. 14

1 ¹⁄₁₆–1 ⁵⁄₁₆ in. (27–34 mm). Sexes differ strikingly. Upperside: Male *fiery red-orange*; female brown to dull orange-brown. Underside: Both sexes *gray-white or pale tan-white*; hindwing with only *tiny black spots*. **SIMILAR SPECIES:** Female Blue Copper may be confused with female Ruddy Copper, but on the hindwing underside the former never shows cream or tan and often has larger black spots. **EARLY STAGES:** Caterpillar is brown with dark red strip up middle of back. **FOOD:** Various docks, knotweeds, and alpine sorrel. **FLIGHT:** Late May–early Sept. (1 flight). **RANGE:** Plains and intermountain West from s. Alta. and sw. Sask. south to n. N.M., s. Utah, and s. Calif. east to cen. N.D. and Neb. **HABITAT:** Well-drained sandy or gravelly flats or gently sloping meadows, usually near streambed or alluvial washes. **REMARKS:** Males perch prominently and chase other males or similar-sized insects while awaiting receptive females. Ferris' Copper (*Lycaena ferrisi*) is nearly identical but is likely a reproductive isolate found during July and August in the White Mts. along the Ariz.-N.M. boundary.

Female Ferris' Copper nectaring on yellow composite, White Mts., Ariz. This butterfly is closely related to the Ruddy Copper but is geographically isolated. Photo by Jim Brock.

Female Blue Copper nectaring at sulphur-flower, Laramie Co., Wyo. Note extensive blue scaling compared to individual shown on Plate 15. Most females of subspecies clara in southern Calif. have extensive blue.

BLUE COPPER *Lycaena heteronea* PL. 15

1–1 ⁵⁄₁₆ in. (25–33 mm). Upperside: Both sexes *with distinct black border* and *white fringe*. Male *blue*, female *gray*, sometimes with extensive blue. Underside: *White or gray-white* with or without black spots. **SIMILAR SPECIES:** Boisduval's Blue, often found with Blue Copper, has duller blue above and more contrasting pattern below. Blues fly much more slowly than the swift Blue Copper. **EARLY STAGES:** Caterpillar gray-green with white hairs, dark band up middle of back and 3 yellow green dashes below midline on each segment. A weak yellow green line along each side. **FOOD:** Wild buckwheats. **FLIGHT:** June–Aug. in most of range (1 flight), May–Sept. in Calif. **RANGE:** S. B.C. east to Alta., Mont., Wyo., and Colo. then south to s. Calif., n. Ariz., and n. N.M. **HABITAT:** Open fields, flats, and slopes, usually in mountains or intervening valleys. **REMARKS:** Males of the only "blue copper" often patrol as do male blues in search of females, in contrast to males of most other coppers, who take up perches while awaiting females.

DORCAS COPPER
Lycaena dorcas PL. 15

⅞–1 ¹⁄₁₆ in. (22–27 mm). Sexes differ in color and markings. Upperside: Male has blue-purple iridescence; female brown with *limited light areas*. Red-orange border on hindwing outer margin limited to a *few spots near anal angle*. Underside: Orange-brown. **SIMILAR SPECIES:** Purplish Copper is

DORCAS COPPER

slightly larger; upperside of male lighter, that of female usually with extensive light areas. Orange border at edge of hindwing usually extends over much of outer margin. **EARLY STAGES:** Caterpillar is pale green with faint white oblique dashes, dark green line up middle of back, and diamond-shaped shield behind head. **FOOD:** Various cinquefoils. **FLIGHT:** Mid-June to late Sept. (1 flight). **RANGE:** Boreal Alaska and Canada south and east to e. Ont. and n. Great Lakes states. **HABITAT:** Brushy old-fields, moist meadows, fringes of bogs, and open areas near streams. **REMARKS:** The Dorcas Copper and Purplish Copper probably hybridize in some areas and remain separate in others. Populations in U.S. Rocky Mts. previously referred to this species are known to cross freely with Purplish Coppers and are arbitrarily referred to that species.

PURPLISH COPPER *Lycaena helloides*   PL. 15

1 ⁵⁄₁₆–1 ⁵⁄₁₆ in. (24–33 mm). Sexes differ in color and markings. Upperside: Males has purplish iridescence on both wings; female usually has *extensive orange areas* on both wings. Marginal *zigzag orange hindwing band* on hindwing of both sexes *usually extensive*. **SIMILAR SPECIES:** Dorcas Copper overlaps in Canada and may be told by more restricted orange hindwing band and by restricted light areas on females. **EARLY STAGES:** Caterpillar is green with many oblique yellow lines; body covered with short white hairs. **FOOD:** Various docks, knotweeds, smartweeds, and cinquefoils. **FLIGHT:** March–Nov. in lowlands and plains (2–3 flights); June–Aug. in mountains (1 flight). **RANGE:** Alaska south to n. Baja Calif. and n. Ariz. east in narrowing zone including Rocky Mts. and Great Plains to s. Ont. and w. N.Y. **HABITAT:** Wet fields and meadows, streamcourses, and roadsides. **REMARKS:** Butterflies in moderate to high elevations in several areas of Rocky Mts. are extremely variable, ranging from butterflies that look like typical Purplish Coppers to those that resemble Dorcas Coppers.

PURPLISH COPPER

LILAC-BORDERED COPPER

LILAC-BORDERED COPPER *Lycaena nivalis* **PL. 15**

¹⁵⁄₁₆–1 ⁵⁄₁₆ in. (24–33 mm). Upperside: Male *red-orange* with iridescent *purplish blue highlights*, female brown with variable amounts of yellow. Both sexes with *orange and black band* on hindwing outer margin. Underside: *Tan-yellow with outer third of hindwing iridescent pink*, becoming less distinct with age. **SIMILAR SPECIES:** Purplish Copper is same size but is duller above and lacks iridescent outer hindwing below. **EARLY STAGES:** Caterpillar green with red line up middle of back. **FOOD:** Knotweeds, possibly docks. **FLIGHT:** June–Sept., occasionally Oct. (1 flight). **RANGE:** S. B.C. south in mountains to cen. Calif. (Sierra Nevada), s. Utah, and s. Colo. **HABITAT:** Mountain meadows, moist slopes, and terraces near streams. **REMARKS:** Amount of black spotting below is quite variable.

MARIPOSA COPPER *Lycaena mariposa* **PL. 15**

1 ¹⁄₁₆–1 ¼ in. (27–32 mm). Fringes black and white checked. Upperside: Males *iridescent dark purple*, female brown with yellow patches on forewing. Underside: *Hindwing mottled gray contrasting with pale yellow forewing*. **SIMILAR SPECIES:** No other coppers have mottled gray hindwing below. **EARLY STAGES:** Not reported. **FOOD:** Low blueberries. **FLIGHT:** July–Sept. (1 flight). **RANGE:** Se. Alaska and Yukon south to cen. Calif., Idaho, and w. Wyo. **HABITAT:** Moist openings and bogs, usually in lodgepole pine forests. **REMARKS:** Some populations have individuals with forewings gray below. In Alta., adults are reported from June through Sept.

HERMES COPPER *Lycaena hermes* **PL. 15**

⅞–1 ³⁄₁₆ in. (23–30 mm). Unique. *Tailed*. Upperside: *Yellow and brown*. Underside: Mainly *yellow with black spotting* on forewing. **EARLY STAGES:** Caterpillar green with darker green band up middle of back. **FOOD:** Redberry (*Rhamnus crocea*). **FLIGHT:** Mid-May–mid-July

MARIPOSA COPPER

HERMES COPPER

(1 flight). **RANGE:** W. San Diego Co., Calif. south to n. Baja Calif. **HABITAT:** Openings in chaparral. **REMARKS:** This butterfly has a very limited range and is the only copper whose caterpillars eat a plant in the Blackthorn family.

HAIRSTREAKS: SUBFAMILY THECLINAE

Hairstreaks are richest in tropical habitats throughout the world, but they are especially numerous in the Americas, with about 1,000 species. We have a number of tropical species that barely reach the southern limits of our area. In tropical species, the upperside of the small to medium-sized adults is often iridescent blue. The iridescent colors are due to reflected light from the physical structure of the wing scales and are not pigmental. Few of our species are so colored; most of ours are brown above. Males perch with their wings closed over their back, and most perch to await the appearance of receptive females. Males of a few species (Golden Hairstreak, Colorado Hairstreak, Creamy Stripe-Streak, Scrub-Hairstreaks, Arizona Hairstreak) will perch with wings open at about a 45° angle. Most species are local in their occurrence, and migration is rare, even though a few species, for example the Gray Hairstreak, are good long-distance colonists, and a mass movement of Hedgerow Hairstreaks was once reported. Eggs are usually laid singly. Caterpillars feed on leaves or reproductive structures of a wide variety of plants, usually woody trees or shrubs. Those of *Calycopis* are exceptional in their consumption of recently dead leaves. The chrysalids of several species can produce sounds between their abdominal segments—likely related to interactions with ants. The butterflies overwinter in either the egg or pupal stage.

COLORADO HAIRSTREAK *Hypaurotis crysalus* PL. 15
1 3/16–1 3/8 in. (31–36 mm). Tailed. Upperside: Black and *iridescent purple* with a *few orange patches* on edge of forewing and hindwing. Underside: Dark gray to gray-white with both white and darker streaks and patches, orange patch on margin of forewing and *black-centered orange spot* on hindwing near tail. **SIMILAR SPECIES:** Great Purple Hairstreak is similar in size but is iridescent blue above and primarily black below. **EARLY STAGES:** Not reported. **FOOD:** Gambel oak. **FLIGHT:** Late June–Aug., rarely mid. Oct. (1 flight). **RANGE:** E.-cen. Wyo., Utah, and s. Wyo. south to n. Mex. and w. Tex. **HABITAT:** Groves of Gambel oak. **REMARKS:** The beautiful butterfly is the official state insect of Colo. The adults do not visit flowers but feed on tree sap and exudates from insect galls.

GOLDEN HAIRSTREAK *Habrodais grunus* PL. 15

¹⁵⁄₁₆–1 ³⁄₁₆ in. (24–31 mm). Tailed. Upperside: Brown with patches of tan. Underside: *Golden brown with 2 rows of metallic gold flecks* on hindwing. **SIMILAR SPECIES:** Gold-hunter's Hairstreak, usually darker below, has longer tail and small orange spot near tail. **EARLY STAGES:** Caterpillar is gray-green with brown hairs. **FOOD:** Canyon live oak, huckleberry oak, tan oak, and chinquapin. **FLIGHT:** Late June–early Sept. (1 flight). **RANGE:** Sw. Wash. and w. Ore. south through Calif. and w. Nev. Isolated populations on Mogollon Rim in Ariz. **HABITAT:** Groves of host trees in foothills and mountains. **REMARKS:** Adult butterflies never visit flowers and are active on sunlit host trees in the afternoon.

GREAT PURPLE HAIRSTREAK *Atlides halesus* PL. 15

1–1 ¾ in. (26–45 mm). *Two long tails* on each hindwing. Abdomen is black or iridescent blue above, *red-orange below*. Upperside: *Iridescent blue* (not purple!). Underside: *Black with iridescent gold marks* near tails. **SIMILAR SPECIES:** Colorado Hairstreak is iridescent purple, not blue. **EARLY STAGES:** Caterpillar is green and covered with short green or yellow-orange hairs. **FOOD:** Mistletoes on oaks, walnuts, and other trees. **FLIGHT:** Late Jan.–late Nov. (3 or more flights). **RANGE:** W. Ore., Nev., Utah, sw. Colo. and cen. Kans. east to Md. and south to Guatemala. **HABITAT:** Wooded areas including suburbs, oak woods, deserts, pinyon-juniper

forest. **REMARKS:** The brilliant butterfly belongs to a tropical group and is an avid flower visitor.

SILVER-BANDED HAIRSTREAK PL. 15
Chlorostrymon simaethis
¹³⁄₁₆–1 in. (21–25 mm). Sexually dimorphic. Upperside: Male suffused with iridescent purple; female dull gray. Underside: Green with silver-white postmedian band on both wings. **SIMILAR SPECIES:** Usually not found in same habitat with Juniper Hairstreak, which can be separated by its orange-brown color above and differing pattern below. **EARLY STAGES:** Caterpillar is light green to light brown, covered with fine short black hairs, with an irregular wavy black stripe along each side and a green-black stripe up middle of back; head same color as body with 2 black eyespots. Caterpillars feed inside pods of host. **FOOD:** Balloon vine. **FLIGHT:** March–June, Oct.–Nov. (2 flights). **RANGE:** U.S. from sw. Utah, s. Calif., s. Nev., Ariz., s. Tex., s. Fla and Keys, south through West Indies, Mex., Cen. Amer., and S. Amer. to Argentina. **HABITAT:** Open areas or edges in or near deserts, seasonally dry tropical forest, or scrub.

WHITE M HAIRSTREAK *Parrhasius m-album* PL. 18
1 ¹⁄₁₆–1 ³⁄₈ in. (27–36 mm). Upperside: *Iridescent blue*. Underside: Gray-brown; hindwing with white, black-edged postmedian line forming a *white M* (or W) near anal angle; *small white spot on costa near base*. **SIMILAR SPECIES:** (1) Great Purple Hairstreak is black below, abdomen red-orange. Tails double and long. (2) Southern Hairstreak upperside is brown, not blue, and has extensive submarginal orange patch on hindwing underside. **EARLY STAGES:** Caterpillar is green with dark stripe up middle of back and dark green oblique stripes on sides. **FOOD:** Oaks. **FLIGHT:** Feb.–Oct. in south (3 flights, 4 in Fla.). **RANGE:** Se. U.S. Rare vagrant north to n. Colo., s. Ont., Mich., and Wisc. Related butterflies occur in the moun-

SILVER-BANDED HAIRSTREAK

RED-SPOTTED HAIRSTREAK

tains of Cen. Amer. and S. Amer. **HABITAT:** Various woods with broad-leafed trees.

RED-SPOTTED HAIRSTREAK [Hawaii]   **PL. 18**
Tmolus echion

¹⁵⁄₁₆–1⅛ in. (24–29 mm). Tailed. Upperside: Male iridescent blue, female blue-gray. Underside: *Pale gray; hindwing has irregular postbasal and postmedian rows of orange spots.* **SIMILAR SPECIES:** None in Hawaii. **EARLY STAGES:** Not reported. **FOOD:** Wide variety of tropical plants, including lantana. **FLIGHT:** Year-round in tropics, including Hawaii. **RANGE:** S. Tex. (rare vagrant) south through tropical lowlands to Brazil. Introduced in Hawaiian Is. in 1902 for control of lantana; found on all major islands. **HABITAT:** Open scrub, woodland edges. **REMARKS:** One of the few butterflies intentionally introduced as a biological control agent. The success of the introduction is unknown.

LEDA MINISTREAK *Ministrymon leda*   **PL. 18**

¹¹⁄₁₆–⅞ in. (17–22 mm). Tiny. Upperside: *Gray* with variable amount of *blue at base of both wings.* Underside: Forewing with black cell line and postmedian line. Hindwing gray with *irregular white-edged orange postmedian line* and *orange spot* near tail. Dry-season form ines is darker gray and has orange much reduced. **SIMILAR SPECIES:** Gray Hairstreak is much larger, lacks blue above, and has black included in postmedian line on hindwing underside. **EARLY STAGES:** Caterpillar is green with short diagonal yellow-white lines along back. **FOOD:** Mesquite. **FLIGHT:** April–December (2 flights). **RANGE:** Sw. U.S. from s. Calif., Nev., sw. Utah, Ariz., N.M., and w. Tex. south into Baja Calif. and nw. mainland Mex. **HABITAT:** Low desert valleys, dry washes, alluvial fans, and lower canyons. **REMARKS:** Like Sonoran Hairstreak this butterfly has two very different seasonal forms. Fall-winter form is probably a dry-season form homologous to that of many tropical butterflies that live in seasonal thorn scrub and dry forest.

LEDA MINISTREAK

GRAY MINISTREAK
Ministrymon azia   **PL. 18**

⅝–¾ in. (16–19 mm). Tailed. Tiny. Underside: Gray. Hindwing with *narrow orange white-edged postmedian line.* **SIMILAR SPECIES:** Leda Ministreak can be separated by its more complex pattern below. **EARLY STAGES:** Not reported. **FOOD:** Plants in Mimosa family, *Mimosa malacophylla* in lower Rio Grande Valley. **FLIGHT:** March–Sept.; flies all year in most of the tropics; flights not determined. **RANGE:** W. and s. Tex., s. Fla. and Keys, south through West Indies, Mex., and Cen. Amer. to s. Brazil. Rare strays found in Colo. and Kans. **HABITAT:** Subtropical thorn scrub.

ARIZONA HAIRSTREAK *Erora quaderna* PL. 18

¹³⁄₁₆–1 ¹⁄₁₆ in. (21–27 mm). *Tailless.* Upperside: Dark gray, variable amounts of *dark iridescent blue*, especially on females. *Fringe orange*, especially in females. Underside: *Soft blue-green with scattered tiny red spots.* **SIMILAR SPECIES:** Western Green Hairstreak has short projection from hindwing and lacks red spots on underside of green (not blue-green) hindwing. **EARLY STAGES:** Caterpillar pale green covered with tan hairs. A pair of yellow-brown spots on thorax and other dark spots and patches on back. **FOOD:** Oaks and wild lilacs. **FLIGHT:** March–April and June–Aug. (2 flights) with other scattered records. **RANGE:** Cen. Ariz., cen. N.M., and w. Tex. south into Mex. **HABITAT:** Heavily wooded oak belt in more heavily wooded lower canyons. **REMARKS:** Males perch on trees on hilltops. Some consider this a subspecies of the eastern Early Hairstreak, but evidence is not conclusive.

SONORAN HAIRSTREAK *Hypostrymon critola* PL. 18

¾–1 in. (21–25 mm). Two distinct seasonal forms. Upperside: *Iridescent purple-blue with large dark sex patch on male* forewing. Underside: Gray. Wet-season form with *postmedian line and large orange spot* near tail. Dry-season form with *solid pattern* of *short dark dashes* and *reduced orange spot.* **SIMILAR SPECIES:** No similar species in U.S. portion of range. **EARLY STAGES:** Not reported. **FOOD:** Possibly *Maytenus phyllanthoides* in Mex. **FLIGHT:** May and Sept. in

ARIZONA HAIRSTREAK

SONORAN HAIRSTREAK

Arizona (2 flights), all year in Mex. **RANGE:** Se. Ariz. (rare stray), especially near Patagonia, south along east coast of Baja Calif. and west coast of mainland Mex. **HABITAT:** Thorn scrub (with *Maytenus*) in valleys, estuaries, and coastal hills. **REMARKS:** The butterflies visit flowers avidly. The only other hairstreak in our territory with distinct seasonal forms is the Leda Ministreak.

RED-BANDED HAIRSTREAK *Calycopis cecrops* PL. 18

¾–1 in. (19–26 mm). Tailed. Upperside: Black with *variable amounts of iridescent blue* at wing bases. Underside: Both wings are *gray-brown with postmedian line edged inwardly with red-orange.* **SIMILAR SPECIES:** Dusky Blue Hairstreak has thinner red-orange edging and has large red cap on black eyespot between tails. **EARLY STAGES:** Caterpillar is identical to that of Dusky Blue Hairstreak and develops very slowly. **FOOD:** Fallen leaves of sumacs, wax myrtle, and oaks. **FLIGHT:** April–early Oct. (2 flights), all year in peninsular Fla. **RANGE:** Se. U.S. from Long Is. west to Mo., se. Kans., and e. Neb. rarely to e. Colo. and n. Tex. south through entire area to s. Tex. Strays north to Mich. and e. Neb. **HABITAT:** Overgrown fields, coastal hammocks, edges.

DUSKY-BLUE GROUNDSTREAK *Calycopis isobeon* PL. 18

⅞–1 ⅟₁₆ in. (22–33 mm). Tailed. Underside: Both wings gray-brown with *postmedian line edged narrowly on inner edge with red-orange. Eyespot* at anal angle of hindwing with *orange equal to black.* **SIMILAR SPECIES:** Red-banded Hairstreak is larger, has broader red-orange edging on postmedian line below, and eyespot at anal angle has more black than orange. **EARLY STAGES:** Caterpillar is dark brown; has 2 black dorsal lines and long dark brown hairs. **FOOD:** Dead leaves, fruits, and detritus on ground, especially under trees in Anacardium family. **FLIGHT:** Jan.–April, June–July, Sept. in Tex.,

Creamy Stripe-Streak perching. Note powdery blue at base and black on outer half. Some hairstreaks never perch with their wings open, but others such as this species will do so with varying degrees of frequency.

at least as late as late Nov. in Mex. **RANGE:** W. (rarely), cen. and s. Tex. south along coastal lowlands of Mex. and Cen. Amer. to n. S. Amer. (Venezuela). Strays east to Miss. and north to Kans. **HABITAT:** Lowland forest edges, valley bottoms. **REMARKS:** Some individuals in s. Tex. appear to be intergrades between this species and the Red-banded Hairstreak, suggesting that they are the same species. Adults are often seen in small sunlit patches perching on the ground or low vegetation. Adults court in late afternoon.

CREAMY STRIPE-STREAK *Arawacus jada*   **PL. 18**

1–1 ¹⁄₁₆ in. (25–27 mm). Hindwing elongate. Upperside: *Powdery blue* with outer half of forewing black. Underside: *Yellow-cream* with slightly *darker stripes*. **SIMILAR SPECIES:** No other butterfly has a similarly marked hindwing below. **EARLY STAGES:** Not reported. **FOOD:** *Solanum umbellatum* in Mex. **FLIGHT:** All year in Mex., mid-March–early Nov. in se. Arizona (possibly 3 flights). **RANGE:** Se.

CREAMY STRIPE-STREAK

Ariz. south through lowlands of mainland Mex. to Cen. Amer. **HABITAT:** Open weedy areas in low canyons or waste places along streams. **REMARKS:** This rare butterfly is believed to be at least a temporary resident in se. Ariz.

MARIUS HAIRSTREAK
Rekoa marius   **PL. 18**

⅞–1 ¼ in. (22–32 mm). Upperside: Sexually dimorphic. Male

iridescent dark blue; female gray. Orange eyespot near tail. Underside: Foreward edge of forewing *edged* narrowly with *orange at base*. Hindwing: Gray with *postmedian white line edged inwardly with black dashes. Orange patch* near tail *with small black spot.* **SIMILAR SPECIES:** Gray Hairstreak averages smaller, lacks orange edging of costa, and has some orange in postmedian band on hindwing below. **EARLY STAGES:** Not reported. **FOOD:** Many plants in several families, especially legumes and malpighias. **FLIGHT:** May (1 record) in se. Ariz., all year in tropics. **RANGE:** Tropical lowlands from Sonora, Mex. south through Cen. Amer. to s. Brazil and Paraguay. **HABITAT:** Open fields, scrub, and forest edges in lowlands.

SOAPBERRY HAIRSTREAK *Phaeostrymon alcestis*   **PL. 16**

¹⁵⁄₁₆–1 ⁵⁄₁₆ in. (24–31 mm). Sexes similar. Upperside; Plain brown; hindwing without orange anal spot. Underside: Forewing and hindwing cells have *narrow white bars bounded by black*. Postmedian band has a *sharply jagged VW mark*. **SIMILAR SPECIES:** Banded Hairstreak underside has lines thicker; lacks VW on hindwing postmedian band. **EARLY STAGES:** Not reported. **FOOD:** Western soapberry. **FLIGHT:** April–late July (1 flight). **RANGE:** S. Midwest from sw. Mo., s. Kans., se. Colo., and cen. Ariz. south to n. Mex. **HABITAT:** Mixed oak scrub, prairie valleys, hedgerows. **REMARKS:** Always found in close association with soapberry, its caterpillar foodplant.

SOUTHERN HAIRSTREAK *Fixsenia favonius*   **PL. 16**

⅞–1 ¼ in. (22–32 mm). Highly variable over geographic range, especially in amount of orange above and below. Tailed. Underside: Hindwing is gray-brown with *narrow orange cap on blue tail-spot*, and *postmedian line with white-edged black W* near inner margin. **SIMILAR SPECIES:** (1) Gray Hairstreak has hindwing underside grayer, blue tail-spot indistinct, lacks W in postmedian line. (2) White M

Hairstreak upperside is iridescent blue, and underside of hindwing has prominent white spot on costal margin and white M mark near tail. **EARLY STAGES:** Caterpillar is pale green with narrow dark green median stripe, lateral oblique green stripes, and yellow stripe along each side. **FOOD:** Various oaks. **FLIGHT:** Mid-March–early July (1 flight). **RANGE:** S. New England and Atlantic Coast west to cen. Ill., se. Colo., and cen. N.M., south to peninsular Fla., the Gulf Coast, and s. Tex. **HABITAT:** Variety of woods, oak brush, or edges with evergreen or deciduous oak, often with hilly terrain. **REMARKS:** Southeastern populations were previously considered a species separate from more northern and western butterflies, which were called *Fixsenia ontario,* the Northern Hairstreak.

ILAVIA HAIRSTREAK *Fixsenia ilavia*   PL. 16

⅞–1 ¹⁄₁₆ in. (22–28 mm). Tailed. Upperside: Dark brown with *large oval to squarish orange patch* on outer portion of each wing. Underside: *Pale brownish tan. Postmedian black line faint to almost absent. Blue patch above tail and red-orange spot greatly reduced or absent.* **SIMILAR SPECIES:** Golden Hairstreak flies later in year and lacks orange patches on upper wing surfaces. **EARLY STAGES:** Not reported. **FOOD:** Scrub oak. **FLIGHT:** May–July (1 flight). **RANGE:** Cen and se. Ariz., sw. N.M. **HABITAT:** Scrub-oak thickets, sometimes mixed with junipers, cacti, and other shrubs. **REMARKS:** Closely related to the Southern Hairstreak. Adults visit flowers such as dogbane and horehound.

POLING'S HAIRSTREAK *Fixsenia polingi*   PL. 17

1–1 ³⁄₁₆ in. (25–30 mm). Tailed. Upperside: *Dark brown with orange and black spot* near tail. Underside: Dark brown with *black-edged white postmedian line having W-shape* near inner edge of hindwing. Small *orange and black spot* as well as *blue patch* near

tail. **SIMILAR SPECIES:** Southern Hairstreak does not overlap in range, lacks orange patches above, and is paler below. **EARLY STAGES:** Not reported. **FOOD:** Gray oak and Emory oak. **FLIGHT:** May–June and Aug.–Sept. (2 flights). **RANGE:** S. N.M. and w. Tex. south to n. Mex. **HABITAT:** Oak woodland. **REMARKS:** The Chisos Mts. of Big Bend National Park is the best place to observe this species.

BEHR'S HAIRSTREAK *Satyrium behrii* PL. 16

¹⁵⁄₁₆–1⅛ in. (24–29 mm). *Tailless.* Upperside: *Orange with black on leading and outer edges* of forewing. Underside: Gray to brown with *postmedian and submarginal rows of black spots and dashes.* Hindwing usually with *orange-capped black spot* near anal angle; sometimes orange spot may be absent or there may be 2 other smaller orange spots. **SIMILAR SPECIES:** Hedgerow Hairstreak has tail and is unicolored below. **EARLY STAGES:** Caterpillar green with white line up middle of back; yellow, white, and green diagonal lines; and a dark green stripe edged in yellow along each side. **FOOD:** Deerbrush and mountain-mahogany. **FLIGHT:** May–Aug. (1 flight). **RANGE:** Montane and intermountain West from s. B.C. and cen. Wash. south and east to s. Calif., cen. Ariz., cen. N.M., w. Okla., and n. Tex. **HABITAT:** Arid foothills, slopes, and scrubby flats. **REMARKS:** The males perch and interact on tops of shrubs and small trees on hilltops and ridges.

SOOTY HAIRSTREAK *Satyrium fuliginosum* PL. 16

⅞–1³⁄₁₆ in. (23–30 mm). *Tailless.* Forewing rounded, *fringes light gray to light tan.* Upperside: Brownish black to warm brown. Unmarked. Underside: Hindwing ranges from *dark brown to sooty gray*, depending on geographic location. All populations have an irregular *postmedian series of small black spots circled with white and often obscured* by it as well as an even submarginal series

BEHR'S HAIRSTREAK

SOOTY HAIRSTREAK

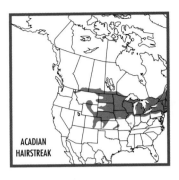

ACADIAN
HAIRSTREAK

CALIFORNIA
HAIRSTREAK

which is more often obscured. There is a *small bar* in the discal cell that is *often obscured by white.* **SIMILAR SPECIES:** Female Boisduval's Blue is most similar but has white fringes, and individuals that are darkest above have at least some blue scaling at base of wings. Underneath Boisduval's Blue forewing has black spot in discal cell and hindwing is almost always lighter with more distinct spot pattern. **EARLY STAGES:** Not reported. **FOOD:** Lupines. **FLIGHT:** Mid-June–early Aug. (1 flight). **RANGE:** Extreme s. B.C. and sw. Alta. south in mountains to cen. Calif., cen. Nev., cen. Utah, and nw. Colo. **HABITAT:** Open sagebrush with intervening herbaceous growth usually in hilly terrain, often on ridges. **REMARKS:** Males patrol lupine patches in search of receptive mates. Adults nectar at wild buckwheats, yellow composites, and others.

ACADIAN HAIRSTREAK *Satyrium acadica* PL. 16
1–1 ³⁄₁₆ in. (26–31 mm). Tailed. Underside: Gray with row of *orange submarginal spots capped with black.* Hindwing has postmedian row of more or *less uniform round black spots* and blue *tail-spot capped with orange. Black bar* above tail-spot often *sharply angled.* **SIMILAR SPECIES:** Edwards' Hairstreak is usually found in different habitat. Hindwing underside much less gray, with blue tail-spot not capped with orange and postmedian spots dark brown, not black. **EARLY STAGES:** Caterpillar has brown head and green body with paired longitudinal yellow stripes along each side. **FOOD:** Willows, especially sandbar willow on plains. **FLIGHT:** June–Aug. (1 flight). **RANGE:** Se. B.C., n. Idaho, w. Mont., Wyo., and e. Colo. west across n. plains, n. Midwest, and Great Lakes region to Maritimes and south to N.J. and Md. **HABITAT:** On or near willows along streamcourses and in marshes. **REMARKS:** Females lay eggs with a transparent glue in tiny holes or crevices on host twigs.

CALIFORNIA HAIRSTREAK *Satyrium californica* **PL. 16**

⅞–1 3⁄16 in. (23–31 mm). Tailed. Upperside: Gray-brown with *smeared orange marks* on hindwing. Underside: Brown to gray, usually gray-brown with *round or oval black postmedian spots* and an extensive *series of submarginal orange spots. Blue patch* by tail *capped with orange. Black bar* above tail-spot *only slightly angled.* **SIMILAR SPECIES:** (1) Range does not overlap very similar Acadian Hairstreak. (2) Similar Sylvan Hairstreak has less orange on hindwing above — often limited to a single orange spot near tail, and is usually grayer below with smaller black spots. **EARLY STAGES:** Caterpillar is gray-brown with lighter gray patches on back and narrow white diagonal lines along sides. **FOOD:** Oaks, mountain mahoganies, plums, deerbrush, juneberries, and willows. **FLIGHT:** June–early Aug. (1 flight). **RANGE:** S. B.C. south to n. Baja Calif., sw Utah, and s. Colo. **HABITAT:** Usually hilly terrain with variable vegetation, often oak woodland, chaparral, or scrub. **REMARKS:** The fact that the California Hairstreak uses only oaks as its caterpillar plants in lowland Calif. and s. Ore. and has a wider array of hosts elsewhere suggests a group of several sibling species.

SYLVAN HAIRSTREAK *Satyrium sylvinus* **PL. 16**

⅞–1⅛ in. (23–29 mm). Tailed or tailless. Upperside: Pale gray to brown-gray, with a *bluish sheen* when recently emerged. Underside: Gray to brown-gray with *row of small round black postmedian spots. Blue tail-spot* often *lacks orange cap, small black triangular mark* (part of postmedian row) lies above tail-spot. Small *orange marginal patch* lies just outside tail-spot. **SIMILAR SPECIES:** California Hairstreak lacks blue sheen and has more extensive orange above; below it is browner and has much more extensive orange marginal spots. **EARLY STAGES:** Caterpillar light green with paired white lines up middle of back and 2 diagonal white lines on each segment. **FOOD:** Willows. **FLIGHT:** Mid-May–mid-Aug. (1 flight), flies earlier and later in lowland Calif. **RANGE:** S. B.C. and w. Mont. south to n. Baja Calif., s. Ariz., and cen. N.M. **HABITAT:** Streamsides or marshes in foothills, canyons, or valleys. **REMARKS:** This butterfly has extreme geographic variation in presence of tails, extent of orange above, and background cast of underside. In lowland Calif. tailless populations of the south Coast Ranges (subspecies *dryope*) blend to tailed forms in s. Calif. and the Sierra Nevada. Fully

SYLVAN
HAIRSTREAK

Male Coral Hairstreak nectaring at spreading dogbane, Laramie Co., Colo. Males have more pointed forewings than female (see Plate 16). Individuals in the West may have small black marks below.

tailed butterflies come within a few miles of tailless butterflies north of San Francisco Bay. The butterflies favor milkweeds for nectar.

CORAL HAIRSTREAK *Satyrium titus* **PL. 16**

⅞–1 5/16 in. (22–33 mm). Tailless. Underside: Hindwing brown with marginal *row of coral red spots* capped inwardly with a white-edged black line, as well as a postmedian *row of 8 black spots and dashes circled with white.* **SIMILAR SPECIES:** (1) California and (2) Sylvan Hairstreaks lack tails and lack the submarginal row of neat red-orange spots. **EARLY STAGES:** Caterpillar has black head and dull green body tinted with rose or yellow toward the front. During the day, full-grown caterpillars hide in litter at base of small sprouts or saplings of host. **FOOD:** Wild cherry, wild plum, and chokecherry. **FLIGHT:** Mid-May–late Aug. (1 flight), flies earlier in more southern latitudes. **RANGE:** Canada and U.S. from Alta. and B.C. east to s. Que. and s. Ont., south to ne. Calif., s. Nev., s. N.M., cen. Tex., n.

CORAL HAIRSTREAK

EDWARDS' HAIRSTREAK

Ark., and cen. Ga. **HABITAT:** Open brushy foothills and rolling terrain with or without scattered trees.

EDWARDS' HAIRSTREAK *Satyrium edwardsii* PL. 16

1–1¼ in. (26–32 mm). Tailed. Underside: Hindwing pale brown, *postmedian row of separate oval dark brown spots, marginal orange spots on hindwing, blue tail-spot not capped with orange.* **SIMILAR SPECIES:** (1) Banded Hairstreak underside hindwing has postmedian row of short white-edged darkened dashes, not spots. (2) Acadian Hairstreak underside is pale gray with round postmedian spots, and blue tail-spot is capped with orange. **EARLY STAGES:** Caterpillar has black head and brown body with pale yellow brown marks. During the day the nearly full-grown caterpillars hide in ant nests at base of host trees. **FOOD:** Scrub oak, occasionally northern black oak. **FLIGHT:** Late June–late July in north; mid-May–early July in south (1 flight). **RANGE:** Extreme se. Sask. east through s. Ont. to s. Me. thence south through w.-cen. N.D. to e. Tex., cen. Mo., and n. Ga. **HABITAT:** On or near scrub oaks in sand barrens, shale barrens, limestone ridges, and similar open areas.

BANDED HAIRSTREAK *Satyrium calanus* PL. 16

¹⁵⁄₁₆–1³⁄₁₆ in. (24–30 mm). Tailed. Underside: Hindwing brown with *postmedian line of dark, white-edged dashes. Blue tail-spot not capped with orange.* **SIMILAR SPECIES:** (1) Striped Hairstreak has series of parallel lines—not dashes—below. (2) Edwards' Hairstreak (overlaps only on plains) has underside paler and postmedian row of dark oval spots, not dashes. **EARLY STAGES:** Caterpillar is green with white oblique lines. **FOOD:** Gambel oak and bur oak in West. **FLIGHT:** June–early Aug. (1 flight). **RANGE:** S. Rocky Mts, e. U.S., and s. Canada; s. N.S. and Me. west to se. Sask. and ne.

Banded Hairstreak (subspecies albidus) nectaring at goldenrod, Rio Blanco Co., Colo. Note whitish maculation compared to more widespread dark brown individuals of other subspecies.

Wyo., south to s.-cen. Tex., Gulf States, and cen. Fla, and then isolated s. Rocky Mt. population from s.-cen. Wyo. and Colo. south to se. Utah, and cen. N.M. **HABITAT:** Gambel oak brush, and bur oak groves along plains rivers. **REMARKS:** A widespread, common eastern butterfly that is relatively uncommon in West. Banded Hairstreaks in s. Wyo. and w. Colo. are whitish gray below.

STRIPED HAIRSTREAK *Satyrium liparops*   **PL. 16**

¹⁵⁄₁₆–1 ³⁄₁₆ in. (24–31 mm). Tailed. Upperside: Brown, sometimes with orange patches. Underside: Both wings have *median and postmedian rows of widely separated thin white lines* (stripes); hindwing underside with *blue tail-spot capped with red-orange* and outer edge of *wing indented above second short tail.* **SIMILAR SPECIES:** Banded Hairstreak has series of dark dashes on underside of wings and lacks red-orange cap to blue tail-spot. Usually on oaks, not on wild plum. **EARLY STAGES:** Caterpillar is dark green with oblique yellow lines on each abdominal segment. **FOOD:** American plum, chokecherry, possibly hawthorns. **FLIGHT:** Mid-June–Aug. (1 flight). **RANGE:** Cen. Alta. east to N.S. and Me. south to s. Colo., ne. N.M., n. Kans., e. Tex., and cen. Fla. **HABITAT:** Brushy areas with host plants near watercourses, usually in foothills. Also found on host planted in rows as windbreaks in farmland. **REMARKS:** In West, Striped Hairstreaks are most easily found by tapping branches of host trees or searching nearby nectar sources such as dogbane or snowberry.

GOLD-HUNTER'S HAIRSTREAK   **PL. 16**
Satyrium auretorum

⅞–1 ³⁄₁₆ in. (23 - 30 mm). Tailed (short on male). Upperside: Tan to dark brown. Underside: Golden brown to tan with *faint dark crescents* on outer margin and *small orange tail-spot with black center.*

SIMILAR SPECIES: (1) Hedgerow Hairstreak is also obscurely marked below but is red-orange above; and (2) Mountain-mahogany Hairstreak is dark gray below with white fringe. **EARLY STAGES:** Caterpillar bright green or pale orange with white points and white lateral band. **FOOD:** Oaks. **FLIGHT:** Mid-May–early Aug. (1 flight). **RANGE:** S Ore. south through much of Calif. west of Sierran divide to n. Baja Calif. **HABITAT:** Oak woodland and chaparral with oaks. **REMARKS:** Rarely seen, but often common when found at flowers near hosts. Adults favor California buckeye, dogbane, wild buckwheat, horehound, and others.

MOUNTAIN-MAHOGANY HAIRSTREAK   PL. 16
Satyrium tetra

1–1 3/16 in. (26–30 mm). Tailed (short on male). Upperside: *Gray.* Underside: Light to dark gray with *irregular dark median line* on hindwing *lined outwardly with white and a white flush* on outer half of wing. *Small orange spot capped with black. Tail-spot blue.* Fringes white. **SIMILAR SPECIES:** (1) Gold-hunter's Hairstreak (see above); (2) Hedgerow Hairstreak is red-orange above and lacks distinct median line and white flush on lower surface of hindwing. **EARLY STAGES:** Caterpillar is pale green covered with orange hairs; white band up middle of back and 4 pale blue-white marks on side of each segment. **FOOD:** Mountain-mahoganies. **FLIGHT:** Late May–early Aug. (1 flight). **RANGE:** S. Ore. south through extreme w. Nev. and Calif. to n. Baja Calif. **HABITAT:** Chaparral and brush in foothills. **REMARKS:** Adults may be found on host or flowers—often with other hairstreaks.

HEDGEROW HAIRSTREAK *Satyrium saepium*   PL. 16
7/8–1 3/16 in. (22–30 mm). Tailed (short on male). Upperside: *Orange to dark red-orange.* Underside: Tan to dark red-brown with

green iridescent sheen when recently emerged. *Dark pattern lines inconspicuous. Tail-spot blue.* **SIMILAR SPECIES:** (1) Gold-hunter's Hairstreak and (2) Mountain-mahogany Hairstreak (see above). **EARLY STAGES:** Caterpillar green with white points, faint yellow-green diagonal stripes on abdominal segments, and white or yellow lateral line along each side. **FOOD:** Various wild lilacs and buckbrush. **FLIGHT:** Mid-May–Aug. (1 flight). **RANGE:** S. B.C. south and east through western mountains to n. Baja Calif., cen. Ariz., and n. N.M. **HABITAT:** Brushy areas and forests in foothills and mountains. **REMARKS:** Hedgerow Hairstreaks fly as early as late April on Santa Cruz Is., off s. Calif. coast. Most often seen on flowers of hosts and other plants such as wild buckwheats, dogbane, and horehound.

AMYNTOR GREENSTREAK *Cyanophrys amyntor*   **PL. 17**
    $^{15}/_{16}$–1 $^1/_{16}$ in. (24–28 mm). *Face green.* Tailed. Upperside: Male deep iridescent blue. Female dull blue, black outwardly. Underside: Forewing with *forward two-thirds apple green,* trailing one-third gray. Apple green with *orange spot above tail* and *white dash above orange spot.* Black tip extending from inner angle. **SIMILAR SPECIES:** Long-winged Greenstreak has brown face. Other species with green face must be captured and examined closely for definite identification. **EARLY STAGES:** Not reported. **FOOD:** Many plants including Elm and Verbena families. **FLIGHT:** July–Jan. in Mex. (possibly 2 flights). **RANGE:** Lowland tropics from Mex. south to Brazil. **HABITAT:** Lowland tropical scrub. **REMARKS:** Known in the U.S. from a single specimen collected in Big Bend National Park.

LONG-WINGED GREENSTREAK   **PL. 17**
Cyanophrys longula
    $^{13}/_{16}$–1 $^3/_{16}$ in. (21–30 mm). *Face brown. Hindwing extended at trailing edge,* somewhat triangular. Tailed with *brown pad at anal angle.* Hindwing with *black tufts at vein endings.* Upperside: Male light iridescent blue with narrow black margins. Female dark iridescent blue, broadly black along front edge of forewing and margins of both wings. Underside: Apple green. Hindwing with discontinuous *postmedian band of white dashes and brown margins.* **SIMILAR SPECIES:** *Cyanophrys agricola* of Mex. is similar. **EARLY STAGES:**

Not reported. **FOOD:** Several plants, including those in Aster and Verbena families. **FLIGHT:** March–May, Aug.–Dec. in Mex. (2 flights). **RANGE:** Mex. south in mountains to s. Mex. Strays to se. Ariz. **HABITAT:** Oak-pine and deciduous forests.

WESTERN GREEN HAIRSTREAK *Callophrys affinis*   PL. 17

¾–1 ³⁄₁₆ in. (19–30 mm). Upperside: Usually gray, but orange-brown in some areas. Underside: *Green with varying amounts of white spots in a sinuous median line* — ranging from none to an almost solid line. **SIMILAR SPECIES:** Coastal Hairstreak is blue-green below, has a strong pattern of white spots on hindwing, and has a marked white fringe. Sheridan's Hairstreak is smaller, is often found in higher mountainous terrain, and has an earlier flight. **EARLY STAGES:** Caterpillar yellow-green, green, or red, usually with 2 white lines up back and white line along each side. **FOOD:** Leaves of wild buckwheats in most of range, but feeds on legumes in many Pacific Coast sites and Fendler's buckbrush in Colo. **FLIGHT:** Feb. (s. Calif.)–July, usually May–June (1 flight). **RANGE:** S. B.C. and n. Mont. south through most of w. U.S. (except low deserts and high boreal mountains) to Baja Calif. and Sierra Madre of w. Mex. **HABITAT:** Open, sunny slopes with low vegetation in many land forms and ecosystems, including sand dunes, chaparral, brush, and pine forest openings. **REMARKS:** Previously divided into several nonoverlapping western species; these included *Callophrys apama* and *C. perplexa*.

COASTAL GREEN HAIRSTREAK   PL. 17
Callophrys dumetorum

¹⁵⁄₁₆–1 ⁵⁄₁₆ in. (24–33 mm). Tailless, *fringes white*. Antennal shaft mainly white below. Upperside: *Usually dark gray*, occasionally with small brownish areas. Underside: *Blue-green with sinuous*

WESTERN GREEN HAIRSTREAK

COASTAL GREEN HAIRSTREAK

median row of white spots. **SIMILAR SPECIES:** See Western Green Hairstreak. **EARLY STAGES:** Caterpillar variable: whitish, green to pink or red, often with lighter lines and oblique dashes. **FOOD:** Wild buckwheats and deerweed. **FLIGHT:** Feb.–June (1 flight). **RANGE:** Oregon Coast Range and immediate coast of Calif. from Mendocino Co. to San Luis Obispo Co., also a few inland sites. **HABITAT:** Coastal scrub on rocky hills, serpentine soils, or sand dunes, also oak woodland at inland sites. **REMARKS:** The range of this species and the Western Green Hairstreak overlap slightly, but the two species maintain separate caterpillar host plants and rarely hybridize. Formerly referred to as *Callophrys viridis.*

DESERT GREEN HAIRSTREAK   **PL. 17**
Callophrys comstocki
¹³⁄₁₆–1 in. (21–25 mm). Tailless. Upperside: Gray. Underside: *Gray-green with a sinuous median row of white spots.* **SIMILAR SPECIES:** Not usually found with other green hairstreaks, but usually smaller size and early spring flight help identification. **EARLY STAGES:** Caterpillar green or pale pink-green with 2 cream lines up back, 1 along each side, and oblique dashes on ridges along each side. **FOOD:** Wild buckwheats, including Wright's buckwheat and racemose buckwheat. **FLIGHT:** March–September (2 flights), fall flight with few butterflies. **RANGE:** N. Nev., e.-cen., and se. Calif. east across Great Basin to s. Utah and w. Colo. **HABITAT:** Dry, sunny slopes and ravines with host-plant colonies. **REMARKS:** The intermountain high desert range indicates the species is separate from Sheridan's Green Hairstreak, whose range follows the western mountain cordillera, although some intermediates are found in cen. Nev.

SHERIDAN'S HAIRSTREAK *Callophrys sheridanii*   **PL. 17**
¹¹⁄₁₆–¹³⁄₁₆ in. (17–21 mm). Upperside: Gray. Underside: *Apple green with solid median white line, discontinuous white spots, or none,*

DESERT GREEN HAIRSTREAK

SHERIDAN'S HAIRSTREAK

Male Sheridan's Hairstreak perching on ground. Jefferson Co., Colo. One of the earliest spring-emerging species. Note strong white line that is usually lacking in Pacific coastal state populations.

usually not quite as sinuous as in other green hairstreaks. **SIMILAR SPECIES:** (1) Western Green Hairstreak is larger and usually flies later in year where the two overlap. (2) Desert Green Hairstreak does not overlap in range. **EARLY STAGES:** Caterpillar variable: green, blue-green, or pink, usually with white or cream lines up back and along each side. **FOOD:** Various species of wild buckwheats, often sulphur-flower. **FLIGHT:** March–July, rarely as early as Feb. (1 flight). **RANGE:** S. B.C., Alta., and w. N.D. south through western mountain archipelago and high plains to cen. Calif., s. Utah, and s. N.M. **HABITAT:** Open, sunny slopes ranging from brushy ravines to rocky slopes above timberline. **REMARKS:** In the Sierra Nevada and Cascades the adults have much reduced white spotting, but those in the Rocky Mt. front range have a solid white line.

THICKET HAIRSTREAK *Callophrys spinetorum*   PL. 17

⅞–1 1/16 in. (23–28 mm). Tailed. Fringes white. Upperside: *Steel blue* with faint iridescent sheen. Underside: Reddish brown with strong *white postmedian line edged inwardly with black*, usually with a *W* along lower portion. Series of 5 or 6 small black submarginal points. **SIMILAR SPECIES:** Johnson's Hairstreak is nearly identical below but is orange-brown above. **EARLY STAGES:** Caterpillar green or reddish with pale band up middle of back and oblique orange-brown white-edged ridges on each segment. **FOOD:** Conifer

THICKET HAIRSTREAK

Thicket Hairstreak at moisture, Larimer Co., Colo. Note red-brown color and strong postmedian line with W along trailing portion of hindwing. The caterpillars eat conifer mistletoes.

mistletoe (genus *Arceuthobium*). **FLIGHT:** March–Oct. (1–2 flights), only 1 in north, usually June. **RANGE:** S. B.C. and Alta. south through most of the West to n. Baja Calif. and the Sierra Madre of w. Mex. **HABITAT:** Mountainous or hilly habitats with pines, firs, or larches. **REMARKS:** Thicket Hairstreaks spend most of their time in the crowns of conifers, but they often come low to sip flower nectar or visit wet spots along streams.

JOHNSON'S HAIRSTREAK *Callophrys johnsoni* PL. 17

1 ¹⁄₁₆–1 ⁵⁄₁₆ in. (27–34 mm). Tailed. Upperside: *Orange-brown* in females, *dark brown* in males. Underside: *Reddish brown with strong white postmedian line without W.* Series of about 3 black submarginal points. **SIMILAR SPECIES:** Thicket Hairstreak is almost identical below, but is steel blue above. Johnson's Hairstreak lacks black edging of postmedian white line and has fewer postmarginal black points. **EARLY STAGES:** Not reported. **FOOD:** Conifer

JOHNSON'S HAIRSTREAK

NELSON'S HAIRSTREAK

mistletoe (genus *Arceuthobium*). **FLIGHT:** Feb.–Aug. (1 flight). **RANGE:** S. B.C. south through e. and w. Wash., Ore., and w. Idaho to cen. Calif. **HABITAT:** Conifer forests, often old growth. digger pine, true fir, and others have been reported. **REMARKS:** This species is usually rare, possibly because it spends much time in the canopy of tall conifers.

NELSON'S HAIRSTREAK *Callophrys nelsoni* PL. 17

⅞–1 ¹⁄₁₆ in. (23–28 mm). Tailed. Upperside: Brown to orange-brown. Underside: Variable. *Orange-brown with or without partial median white line*. Newly emerged individuals often have purplish sheen. **SIMILAR SPECIES:** Muir's Hairstreak is usually mahogany brown below with greenish sheen and lacks orangish cast. **EARLY STAGES:** Not reported. **FOOD:** Incense-cedar and western redcedar, rarely juniper. **FLIGHT:** May–July, rarely April (1 flight). **RANGE:** S. B.C. south through w. slope of Cascades, n. Coast Ranges, and west slope of Sierra Nevada to s. Calif. **HABITAT:** Mixed conifer forests with incense-cedar or western redcedar. **REMARKS:** Rosner's Hairstreak *(Callophrys nelsoni rosneri)* from cen. Ore. northward and Byrne's Hairstreak *(Callophrys nelsoni byrnei)* from n. Idaho and nw. Mont. are here considered subspecies of Nelson's Hairstreak.

MUIR'S HAIRSTREAK *Callophrys muiri* PL. 17

⅞–1 in. (22–25 mm). Tailed. Underside: *Dark purplish brown* with *iridescent greenish sheen* that fades after death. *Postmedian line irregular, dark inwardly and white outwardly.* **SIMILAR SPECIES:** Juniper Hairstreaks found in inner Coast Range of cen. Calif. are brown below, but lack green sheen of Muir's Hairstreak and are found on junipers. **EARLY STAGES:** Not reported. **FOOD:** Sargeant's cypress. **FLIGHT:** Late March–June (1 flight). **RANGE:** N. and cen. Calif. outer Coast Ranges. **HABITAT:** Sargeant's cypress groves on serpentine rock outcrops. **REMARKS:** In Lake Co., Calif., Muir's Hairstreak is found within a few miles of Nelson's Hairstreak—each maintaining its own appearance and each found on its own host.

MUIR'S HAIRSTREAK

JUNIPER HAIRSTREAK
Callophrys gryneus PL. 17

¹⁵⁄₁₆–1 ¹⁄₁₆ in. (24–28 mm). Tailed. Underside: Forewing postmedian white spot row aligned. Hindwing apple green (eastern) to yellow-green (western) with 2 *white anteme-*

Juniper Hairstreak (subspecies barryi) nectaring in e. Ore. Note the lack of green and weak white median line. These populations are found in juniper groves. All juniper-associated populations are assumed to be Juniper Hairstreaks.

dian spots, and outer margin with *white trim* (eastern) or *with irregular* postmedian white line edged inwardly with red-brown (western). Populations with underside hindwings brown occur in Calif.'s inner Coast Range, Great Basin, and the Northwest. **SIMILAR SPECIES:** Xami Hairstreak is very rare and has the postmedian line strongly indented in a W-shape. **EARLY STAGES:** Caterpillar green with subdorsal oblique white or yellow bars along each side. **FOOD:** Eastern red cedar, junipers. **FLIGHT:** May–Aug. in north, Mar.–July in West, Feb.–Nov. (mainly April–Aug.) in Southwest (2 flights). **RANGE:** S. B.C. south to s. Calif., and nw. Mex. east including most of U.S. to New England and s. Ont., south to n. peninsular Fla. and cen. La. **HABITAT:** Pinyon-juniper woodland, juniper forests, and planted windbreaks in hilly or mountainous situations in a wide variety of ecosystems. **REMARKS:** Formerly considered a species separate from the Juniper Hairstreak (*Callophrys siva*). The oc-

JUNIPER HAIRSTREAK

THORNE'S HAIRSTREAK

currence of intermediate populations in w. Tex. and s. N.M. indicates that *gryneus* and *siva* should be treated as a single, widespread, variable species. Usually found by tapping eastern redcedars or junipers with a net handle or pole. Several variable subspecies including *barryi* and *loki* are included with the Juniper Hairstreak.

THORNE'S HAIRSTREAK *Callophrys thornei* **PL. 17**

1–1⅛ in. (25–29 mm). Tailed. Upperside: Brown. Underside: *Base of hindwing gray-green, brown median band indented near wing base*. Outer edge shaded with shiny gray-green. **SIMILAR SPECIES:** (1) Juniper Hairstreak (subspecies *loki*) has underside of hindwing with brown median band less indented at base. **EARLY STAGES:** Not reported. **FOOD:** Tecate cypress. **FLIGHT:** Late Feb.–early June (1 flight). **RANGE:** Restricted to San Isidro Mts., San Diego Co., Calif. **HABITAT:** Cypress grove in woody chaparral slopes. **REMARKS:** This isolated species lives an uncertain existence in a fire-prone habitat.

XAMI HAIRSTREAK *Callophrys xami* **PL. 17**

1⁵⁄₁₆–1⅛ in. (24–29 mm). Tailed. Underside: Hindwing is *yellow-green*, with *postmedian white line formed into a W* toward tails. **SIMILAR SPECIES:** (1) Juniper Hairstreak lacks sharp W mark in postmedian white band; (2) Silver-Banded Hairstreak hindwing underside has broad silver-white postmedian line and hoary patch on outer margin. **EARLY STAGES:** Caterpillar is yellow-green with rose markings. **FOOD:** Succulents including *Echeveria*. **FLIGHT:** March–Dec. (2 or more flights). **RANGE:** Cen. Tex., sw. N.M., and se. Ariz. south to Guatemala. **HABITAT:** Sunny areas along shady rocky slopes and canyonsides in mountain coniferous or oak-pine forests. **REMARKS:** Males perch and patrol back and forth near host plants.

SANDIA HAIRSTREAK
Callophrys mcfarlandi **PL. 17**

¾–1⅛ in. (20–29 mm). Tailless, fringes white. Upperside: Brown to orange-brown. Underside: Golden green with strong white postmedian line edged inwardly with black. **SIMILAR SPECIES:** Juniper Hairstreak has tails and is found near junipers. **EARLY STAGES:** Caterpillar pink to maroon. **FOOD:** Texas nolina. **FLIGHT:** Mid-Feb.–late June (1 flight), sometimes late July

XAMI HAIRSTREAK

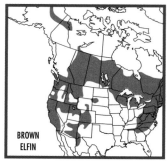

—mid-Aug. (rare second flight). **RANGE:** Se. Colo. south through e. N.M. and w. Tex. to ne. Mex. **HABITAT:** Steep, dry, south-facing slopes with stands of caterpillar host plant. **REMARKS:** This distinctive butterfly rarely strays from its host plant, and its flights are timed to the flowering of the nolina, which in turn flowers in response to snow or rainfall.

BROWN ELFIN *Callophrys augustinus*   **PL. 17**
¹³⁄₁₆–¹⁵⁄₁₆ in. (21–24 mm). Tailless. Sexes similar. Underside: *Chestnut to reddish brown* (fades to gray-brown with age) *with irregular dark postmedian line.* Hindwing darker at base. **SIMILAR SPECIES:** Moss' Elfin is very local, and hindwing has white fringe and wavy margin. Hindwing underside markings usually more complex. **EARLY STAGES:** Caterpillar is bright green with yellow-green dorsal stripe and oblique lateral stripes and dashes. **FOOD:** Primarily plants in Heath family (Rocky Mts.) or wide variety of plants in many families (Pacific Coast). **FLIGHT:** April–July in north; mid-March–early June in south (1 flight). **RANGE:** Much of boreal N. Amer. from Alaska, s. Yukon, and w. N.W. Terr. south through Canadian prairie provinces and western mountain archipelago to Chihuahua and n. Baja Calif., thence east to Lab., Nfld., and e. U.S. **HABITAT:** Hills and mountains in a wide variety of habitats. **REMARKS:** Although the adults are nearly identical in appearance, caterpillars of eastern and Rocky Mt. populations eat only plants of Heath family while those along the Pacific Coast feed on plants in many families.

DESERT ELFIN *Callophrys fotis*   **PL. 17**
¾–⅞ in. (19–23 mm). Tailless. Fringes pale but dark at wingtips. Upperside: Male gray, female browner. Underside: *Hindwing base dark gray or brownish*, outer area beyond *irregular median dark line is pale gray.* **SIMILAR SPECIES:** No similar species in its habitat.

EARLY STAGES: Not reported. **FOOD:** Cliff rose. **FLIGHT:** March–May (1 flight). **RANGE:** Western intermountain U.S. from se. Calif. east to w. Colo. and nw. N.M. **HABITAT:** Rocky canyons and flats in arid intermountain West and foothills.

MOSS' ELFIN *Callophrys mossii*   **PL. 18**

¾–¹⁵⁄₁₆ in. (20–24 mm). Tailless. Fringes white and outer margin of hindwing wavy. Upperside: Male gray-brown, female light brown, variable. Underside: *Usually reddish brown*, but varies. Base darker, area beyond *irregular pale median line much lighter*. **SIMILAR SPECIES:** Brown Elfin (see above). **EARLY STAGES:** Caterpillar yellow or red. Feeds in flower heads of host. **FOOD:** Stonecrop. **FLIGHT:** Late Feb.–May (1 flight). **RANGE:** Western mountain archipelago from s. B.C. and Alta. to s. Calif. and s. Colo. Absent from intermountain areas. **HABITAT:** Moist slopes and canyons in foothills or mountains. **REMARKS:** San Bruno Elfin (*Callophrys mossii bayensis*) is an endangered subspecies found in the San Bruno Mts. south of San Francisco.

HOARY ELFIN *Callophrys polios*   **PL. 18**

¹¹⁄₁₆–⁷⁄₈ in. (18–23 mm). Tailless. Sexes similar. Underside: Forewing has irregular white postmedian line and white "frosted" outer margin. Hindwing has *outer half frosted light gray*. **SIMILAR SPECIES:** (1) Brown Elfin, often found on same host, does not have a 2-toned hindwing below; (2) Moss' Elfin is slightly larger, has wavy hindwing outer margin, and is brownish (not gray-white) on outer edge of hindwing below. **EARLY STAGES:** Caterpillar is green. **FOOD:** Bearberry, probably also trailing arbutus. **FLIGHT:** April–May, occasionally to early July (1 flight). **RANGE:** Much of boreal North America. Yukon and Alaska south through Canadian prairie provinces and Rockies to n. Utah, n. N.M. and along Pacific Coast to n. Calif. Also Maritimes, ne. U.S., and cen. Appalachi-

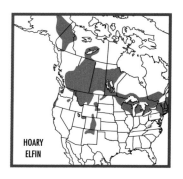

ans. **HABITAT:** Sunny glades along forest edges, rocky ridges, barrens, and dunes. **REMARKS:** Butterflies usually perch directly on host plants, where males carry out their search for mates.

HENRY'S ELFIN *Callophrys henrici* PL. 18

⅞–1 in. (22–26 mm). *Tailed.* Sexes similar. Upperside: Male is the only elfin to *lack forewing stigma.* Underside: Forewing has *postmedian line relatively straight*; hindwing with *strong white dash in postmedian line at costal margin.* **SIMILAR SPECIES:** No similar species where found in our area. **EARLY STAGES:** Caterpillar is light green or red-brown with lighter lateral bars and stripes. **FOOD:** *Ungnadia* (Heath family). **FLIGHT:** March–April (1 flight). **RANGE:** Se. N.M. and w. Tex. Also e. N. Amer. from N.S. and Me. west through s. Que. and cen. Ont. to se. Man. south to cen. peninsular Fla., the Gulf Coast, and e. and cen. Tex. **HABITAT:** Ravines and streamsides in woody scrub.

EASTERN PINE ELFIN *Callophrys niphon* PL. 18

¹⁵⁄₁₆–1⅛ in. (24–29 mm). Tailless. Sexes similar. Underside: Forewing has *extra dark bar in discal cell.* Hindwing has *submarginal gray band just inside of blunt black inverted crescents.* **SIMILAR SPECIES:** Western Pine Elfin lacks extra bar in discal cell of forewing underside, lacks gray postmarginal band, and has sharply pointed submarginal black crescents. **EARLY STAGES:** Caterpillar is pale green with 2 cream stripes along each side and a white patch on the prothorax. **FOOD:** Pines, including Jack pine. **FLIGHT:** May–June (1 flight). **RANGE:** N. Alta. east across s. Canada and south to Gulf Coast (not in w. U.S.). **HABITAT:** Stands of Jack Pine with young trees. **REMARKS:** Occurs with Western Pine Elfin at only a few sites in n. Alta. where some hybridization may take place.

EASTERN PINE ELFIN

WESTERN PINE ELFIN

WESTERN PINE ELFIN *Callophrys eryphon* **PL. 18**

⅞–1 1/16 in. (22–27 mm). Tailless. Sexes similar. Underside: Forewing often *lacks dark bar in discal cell. Hindwing has sharply pointed submarginal dark crescents.* **SIMILAR SPECIES:** Eastern Pine Elfin (see above). **EARLY STAGES:** Caterpillar is very similar to that of the Eastern Pine Elfin. **FOOD:** Young leaves of hard pines, such as Ponderosa pine, lodgepole pine, Bishop pine, and Monterey pine. **FLIGHT:** Early April–mid July, rarely as late as early Sept. (1 flight). **RANGE:** W. N. Amer. from cen. B.C. and cen. Alta. south to s. Calif., s. Ariz., and s. N.M.; also east to cen. Neb., cen. Ont., n. Mich., and Me. Isolated population in N.W. Terr. **HABITAT:** Pine forests, especially with young trees. **REMARKS:** The butterfly has apparently colonized stands of cultivated Monterey Pine in central coastal Calif.

GRAY HAIRSTREAK *Strymon melinus* **PL. 18**

⅞–1 3/16 in. (23–30 mm). Our most widespread hairstreak. Tailed. Upperside: Navy gray with orange spot near tail. Underside: Paler gray (except for dark spring-fall form). Hindwing *postmedian line often edged inwardly with orange, usually relatively straight.* **SIMILAR SPECIES:** (1) Southern Hairstreak has upperside of both wings with orange patches. Underside browner, usually with more submarginal orange. (2) Redlined Scrub-Hairstreak underside hindwing has postmedian line orange and white without

GRAY HAIRSTREAK

black, and whitish submarginal dashes. **EARLY STAGES:** Caterpillar extremely variable, ranging from green to yellow to red-brown with oblique marks of various colors. **FOOD:** Flowers and fruits of an almost infinite variety of plants, most often from Pea and Mallow families. **FLIGHT:** March–Nov. (2–3 flights), all year in Calif. and Ariz. **RANGE:** U.S. and s. Canada south through Mex. and Cen. Amer. to S. Amer. **HABITAT:** Wide variety of open, sunny situations with suitable host plants.

AVALON SCRUB-HAIRSTREAK *Strymon avalona*   PL. 18

¾–⅞ in. (19–23 mm). Upperside: Navy gray with or without small orange spot near tail. Underside: *Gray, darker hindwing base separated from pale outer portion by irregular dark postmedian line.* **SIMILAR SPECIES:** Gray Hairstreak has black orange-edged postmedian line. **EARLY STAGES:** Caterpillar pale green or pale pink. **FOOD:** Wild buckwheats and lotis. **FLIGHT:** Feb.–Dec. (several flights). **RANGE:** Santa Catalina Is., Calif. **HABITAT:** Grassy areas and chaparral. **REMARKS:** Gray Hairstreak has colonized Santa Catalina Is. and has reportedly hybridized with Avalon Scrub-Hairstreak. This could pose a threat to the continued existence of the latter.

RED-LINED SCRUB-HAIRSTREAK   PL. 18
Strymon bebrycia

1–1 3/16 in. (25–30 mm). Underside: Hindwing gray with *white submarginal spots and postmedian line red-orange lined outwardly with white.* **SIMILAR SPECIES:** Gray Hairstreak hindwing underside postmedian line usually has some black and relatively little orange. **EARLY STAGES:** Not reported. **FOOD:** Balloon vine (*Cardiospermum*). **FLIGHT:** May–June in s. Ariz., most of year in Mex. (several flights). **RANGE:** Mex. from Sonora and Nuevo León south through Cen. Amer. to nw. Costa Rica. Rare vagrant to s. Ariz., w. and s. Tex. **HABITAT:** Subtropical thorn scrub.

YOJOA SCRUB-HAIRSTREAK *Strymon yojoa*   **NOT SHOWN**

⅞–1¼ in. (22–31 mm). Tailed. Upperside: Gray. Underside: Hindwing *gray with faint irregular postmedian line bounding submarginal gray-white band.* **SIMILAR SPECIES:** Gray Hairstreak hindwing underside has strong postmedian line and lacks submarginal gray-white band. **EARLY STAGES:** Not reported. **FOOD:** Hibiscus and other mallows. **FLIGHT:** Late Oct.–mid-Dec. in s. Tex., most of year in Mex. (several flights). **RANGE:** Mex. south through Cen. Amer. to s. Brazil. Rare vagrant to se. Ariz. and s. Tex. **HABITAT:** Scrub, lightly disturbed pastures.

LACEY'S SCRUB-HAIRSTREAK   **PL. 18**
Strymon alea (Grote & Robinson)

¾–1⅛ in. (21–28 mm). Small. Underside: Hindwing is *gray with complex pattern: postbasal blotches, irregular brown postmedian line, submarginal band of small brown triangular spots.* **SIMILAR SPECIES:** Mallow Scrub-Hairstreak hindwing underside has small round black basal spot and postmedian line of separate black spots. **EARLY STAGES:** Not reported. **FOOD:** *Bernardia.* **FLIGHT:** April–Dec. (possibly 4 flights). **RANGE:** Cen. and s. Tex. (1 report west of 100th meridian) south through Mex. to nw. Costa Rica. **HABITAT:** Subtropical thorn scrub.

MALLOW SCRUB-HAIRSTREAK *Strymon istapa*   **PL. 18**

¹¹⁄₁₆–1 in. (18–26 mm). Small. *Tails short.* Underside: Hindwing is gray with 2 *round black spots on costa; postmedian line of small black spots.* **SIMILAR SPECIES:** Leda Ministreak lacks black spots on costa of hindwing below and usually perches on catclaw acacia. **EARLY STAGES:** Caterpillar is green with darker dorsal line and dirty white patch near head. **FOOD:** Mallows. **FLIGHT:** All year; number of flights not determined. **RANGE:** Peninsular Fla., s. Tex., s. N.M., s. Ariz., s. Nev., and s. Calif. south through Mex. and Cen. Amer. to S. Amer. **HABITAT:** Desert thorn scrub, open waste areas. **REMARKS:** This species was formerly referred to as *Strymon columella.*

MALLOW SCRUB-HAIRSTREAK

TAILLESS SCRUB-HAIRSTREAK
Strymon cestri   **PL. 18**

⅞–1⅛ in. (22–29 mm). *Tailless.* Forewing *apex squared off.* Underside: Hindwing is *marbled gray and white, with black submarginal spot on outer margin.* **SIMILAR SPECIES:** Lantana Scrub-Hairstreak has forewing more

Tailless Scrub-Hairstreak visiting moist sandy area, Sonora state, Mex. Note pattern compared to Lantana Scrub-Hairstreak, another tailless species on Plate 18.

pointed; hindwing underside lacks submarginal black spot. **FOOD:** Unknown. **EARLY STAGES:** Not reported. **FLIGHT:** Aug. in s. Ariz. **RANGE:** Se. Ariz. (1 record) and s. Tex. south through Mex. to Guanacaste Province, Costa Rica. **HABITAT:** Seasonal mid-elevation tropical forests and edges.

LANTANA SCRUB-HAIRSTREAK *Strymon bazochii*   **PL. 18**

⅞–1⅛ in. (23–28 mm). Tailless. Forewing pointed. Underside of hindwing has prominent *postbasal black spot* on leading edge, as well as *dark basal* and *apical patches*. **SIMILAR SPECIES:** Tailless Scrub-Hairstreak has squared-off forewing apex. Underside of hindwing is marbled gray and white and has submarginal black spot. **EARLY STAGES:** Caterpillar is dull green. **FOOD:** Flowering parts of lantana, lippias, and several mints. **FLIGHT:** May–Dec. (2–3 flights). **RANGE:** Hawaii (all larger islands). Native to s. Tex., Mex. south through tropical Amer., including West Indies, to Paraguay. **HABITAT:** Scrubby tropical vegetation. **REMARKS:** This butterfly was intentionally introduced to Hawaii to control lantana, a noxious weed there.

LANTANA SCRUB-HAIRSTREAK

BROMELIAD SCRUB-HAIRSTREAK
Strymon serapio
(Godman & Salvin)   **PL. 18**
¹¹⁄₁₆–1³⁄₁₆ in. (18–30 mm). Tailed. Upperside: Male black. Forewing with *quadrangular*

sex patch in discal cell and 2 *iridescent dark blue bars on lower half.* Hindwing diffuse iridescent dark blue with black tail spot. Female gray, may or may not be invaded with powder blue scales. Black tail spot capped with orange. Underside: Gray. Forewing with postmedian dark lines. Hindwing with *irregular postmedian line of squarish segments. A right-angle inward bend near tail. Submarginal area clouded gray and white. Orange spot with black center near tail.* **EARLY STAGES:** Not reported. **FOOD:** Spanish moss (*Tillandsia*) and related plants. **FLIGHT:** July–Aug., Nov.–Dec. in Mex. (2 flights). **RANGE:** Mex. south through tropics to s. Brazil. Once found in the Big Bend region of w. Tex. **HABITAT:** Arid situations. **REMARKS:** Adults perch and interact in early morning.

BLUES: SUBFAMILY POLYOMMATINAE

Blues are tiny to small butterflies found throughout the world, but they are most diverse in Southeast Asia, tropical Africa, and northern temperate regions. Almost 50 species of blues are found in North America, and most of these are western. Adult males are predominantly blue above, while females and males of a few species are predominantly brown. The blue of the males is due to reflected light rather than pigmentation. Below, the wings are usually gray-white with black spots or streaks. Adults in some genera (*Euphilotes, Lycaeides, Plebulina,* and *Icaricia*) have more or less prominent orange submarginal bands on their hindwings. These are termed the "aurora." The black line at the end of the wings just in from the fringe is called the "terminal line." Adults are usually found near their host plants, and they do not fly long distances. Our tropical and subtropical species (*Brephidium, Hemiargus,* and *Leptotes*) are exceptional, since their species may undertake long migrations and are often long-distance colonists. Adult males are frequent visitors to moist sand or mud, and the adults avidly visit flowers for nectar. Eggs are laid singly on host plant leaves or flowers. The caterpillars usually feed on external plant parts, but those of some species bore into succulent host plants. Caterpillars have glands that secrete sugary secretions that attract ants. Caterpillars of some species are raised in ant nests. Host plants occur in many plant families, but legumes and wild buckwheats are frequent choices in the West. Winter is usually passed by the pupal stage, but for tropical species development may be continuous, with adults overwintering.

WESTERN PYGMY-BLUE *Brephidium exile*   PL. 19
¼–¾ in. (13–19 mm). *Tiny.* Upperside: Both wings with *blue only on basal areas.* Underside: Hindwing is *white at base*, fringe mostly

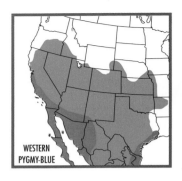

WESTERN PYGMY-BLUE

MARINE BLUE

white. **SIMILAR SPECIES:** None in most of the West, but smaller Ceraunus Blue may approach the Pygmy-Blue in size. Ceraunus Blue is gray below and has 1 or 2 prominent black spots on outer margin of hindwing. **EARLY STAGES:** Caterpillar is yellow-green with many small brown tubercles. **FOOD:** Saltbushes, Russian-thistle, salicornia, pigweeds, and others. **FLIGHT:** All year where resident, June–Nov. northward (several flights). **RANGE:** Resident from cen. Calif., s. Ariz., s. N.M., and s. Tex. south to w. cen. Mex. Immigrates and colonizes northward to Ore., Idaho, Wyo., Neb., and Mo. **HABITAT:** Waste areas, deserts, coastal salt marshes. **REMARKS:** One of the smallest butterflies in the world. Males patrol host plants. Easily overlooked.

CASSIUS BLUE *Leptotes cassius*   **PL. 19**

¹¹⁄₁₆–1 ¹⁄₁₆ in. (17–27 mm). Upperside: Males pale blue; females with much white. Underside: *Both wings have pale lines broken; forewing with blank areas along inner margin.* **SIMILAR SPECIES:** Marine Blue is larger; uppersides of both wings have violet-blue overcast. Undersides of both wings have pale brown lines that are continuous. **EARLY STAGES:** Caterpillar is green with a russet overtone. **FOOD:** Ornamental leadwort, hairy milk pea, lima bean, rattlebox. **FLIGHT:** All year in s. Fla. and s. Tex., broods not determined. **RANGE:** Fla., including Keys, and Tex. south through West Indies, Mex., and Cen. Amer. to S. Amer. Strays north to w. Tex., Okla., Kans., S.C., and Mo. **HABITAT:** Thorn scrub, weedy fields, and residential areas. **REMARKS:** A very rare stray in our area.

MARINE BLUE *Leptotes marina*   **PL. 19**

¾–1 in. (19–26 mm). Upperside: Both wings of male have violet overcast; females lack white. Underside: Forewing has most *pale brown lines continuous* from costa to inner margin. **SIMILAR SPECIES:**

Reakirt's Blue lacks striations on underside and has prominent round black submarginal spots on underside of forewing. **EARLY STAGES:** Caterpillar is green or brownish with dark brown oblique stripes and spots. **FOOD:** Blue jasmine, leadwort, and legumes including milk vetch, clover, and alfalfa. **FLIGHT:** All year in s. Ariz. and s. Calif., April–Oct. northward (several flights). **RANGE:** Resident in Southwest from s. Calif, s. Ariz., s. N.M., and w. Tex. south through Mex. to Guatemala. Emigrates northward (and may colonize) to cen. Ore., n. Calif., n. Nev., Utah, s. Wyo., S.D., Man., Wisc., and Ind. **HABITAT:** Mesquite thorn scrub, town gardens, alfalfa fields, and waste areas. **REMARKS:** May be abundant in residential areas in s. Calif. and s. Ariz.

PEA BLUE *Lampides boeticus* [Hawaii] PL. 19

⅞–1¼ in. (23–32 mm). *Tailed.* Upperside: Brownish with lavender-blue reflection. Black spot on hindwing margin near tail. Underside: *Brownish with wavy light lines. Black spot near tail.* **SIMILAR SPECIES:** None in Hawaii. **EARLY STAGES:** Caterpillar yellow-green with dark stripe up middle of back. **FOOD:** Many legumes, including both cultivated and native plants. **FLIGHT:** Most of year. **RANGE:** Mediterranean area, Africa, Asia, Australia, Hawaii. **HABITAT:** Wide variety of open, sunny situations including fields, dunes, residential areas, and brushlands. **REMARKS:** Accidentally introduced into Hawaiian Is. more than 100 years ago.

CYNA BLUE *Zizula cyna* PL. 19

⅝–⅞ in. (16–21 mm). *Tiny. Wings rounded.* Upperside: Pale violet-blue with broad black borders. Underside: *Hindwing pale gray with minute black dots.* **SIMILAR SPECIES:** Ceraunus Blue has 1 or 2 submarginal eyespots on underside of hindwing. **EARLY STAGES:** Not reported. **FOOD:** Flower buds of *Acanthaceae.* **FLIGHT:** March–early

Nov., broods not determined. **RANGE:** Resident from w. and s. Tex. south through Mex., Cen. Amer., and S. Amer. to Argentina. Strays north to Kans. and n. Tex., N.M., and se. Ariz. **HABITAT:** Open scrub in desert and subtropics. **REMARKS:** Apparently not an accidental introduction from Africa, as was previously reported.

CERAUNUS BLUE *Hemiargus ceraunus*   **PL. 19**

⅝–⅞ in. (16–23 mm). Underside: Both wings have *postmedian row of dark dashes. Two small round black spots* on margin of hindwing. **SIMILAR SPECIES:** Reakirt's Blue has forewing underside with postmedian chain of prominent round black spots. **EARLY STAGES:** Caterpillars vary from green to yellow to red, with short silverwhite hairs. **FOOD:** Flower buds of woody legumes from all 3 families: pea, mimosa, and cesalpinia. **FLIGHT:** All year in Tex. and se. Ariz., March–Oct. in s. Calif., late summer elsewhere. **RANGE:** Resident from s. Calif., s. Ariz., w. and s. Tex., and Fla. south through Mex., West Indies, and Cen. Amer. to S. Amer. Vagrants north to Nev., sw. Utah, w. Colo., Kans., Mo., and N.C. **HABITAT:** Deserts, thorn scrub, beach dunes, second growth, pastures, etc.

REAKIRT'S BLUE *Hemiargus isola*   **PL. 19**

¹¹⁄₁₆–1 in. (17–25 mm). Forewing apex *sharply cut off.* Underside: Forewing with *postmedian row of 5 prominent round black spots.* **SIMILAR SPECIES:** (1) Ceraunus Blue has forewing apex rounded, as in most blues, and forewing below has a submarginal row of black dashes instead of rounded black spots. (2) Marine Blue has striations on both wings below. **EARLY STAGES:** Caterpillar white-green with red marks. **FOOD:** Many plants in Pea and Mimosa families. **FLIGHT:** March–Nov. (3 broods), all year in s. Tex. **RANGE:** Resident in Southwest from s. Calif., s. Ariz., s. N.M., and s. Tex. south through Mex. and Cen. Amer. to Costa Rica. Vagrant and warmseason colonist north and east to n. Calif., cen. Wash., cen.

Male Reakirt's Blue backing with open wings, Larimer Co., Colo. These blues cannot survive freezing winters in any stage and must reinvade their more northern habitats each year from farther south.

Idaho, Wyo., se. Sask., s. Man., Wisc., Ohio, and Miss. Remarkably, one individual was found in Alaska. **HABITAT:** Open weedy areas, deserts, thorn scrub, pastures, fields. **REMARKS:** A regular summer and fall emigrant and colonist on the Great Plains.

EASTERN TAILED-BLUE *Everes comyntas*   PL. 19

¹¹⁄₁₆–1 ⅛ in. (18–29 mm). *Tailed.* Upperside: Male iridescent blue, female brown but with much blue at wing base in spring individuals. Underside: Hindwing pale gray with distinct black spots, *black bar at end of cell, 2 small orange spots* on outer margin, one at tail. **SIMILAR SPECIES:** Western Tailed-Blue often larger; hindwing underside often has black spots lacking or indistinct; lacks bar at end of cell; only single reduced marginal orange spot by tail. **EARLY STAGES:** Caterpillar is dark green with dark dorsal stripe and faint

Female Eastern Tailed-Blue nectaring at wild strawberry, Fairfax Co., Va. Spring females often have some blue at base of wings above. This female is from one of the summer flights.

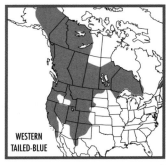

oblique lateral stripes. **FOOD:** Flowers and young seeds of a wide variety of herbaceous legumes including alfalfa, clovers, and lotises. **FLIGHT:** March–Dec. (several flights). **RANGE:** E. U.S. and se. Canada (where widespread and common) extending west to s. Man., w. N.D., cen. Colo., and cen. Tex. Isolated populations in cen. Calif. north through n. and w. Idaho, w. Ore., e. Wash. to sw. B.C., probably introduced. Also w. Tex., w. N.M., and se. Ariz. south through Mex. and Cen. Amer. to Costa Rica. **HABITAT:** Open, sunny, weedy environments.

WESTERN TAILED-BLUE *Everes amyntula*   PL. 19

⅞–1 ³⁄₁₆ (22–31 mm). *Tailed*. Variable. Underside: Hindwing *black spots lacking or indistinct*, and only a *single reduced orange spot near tail*. **SIMILAR SPECIES:** Eastern Tailed-Blue is usually (but not always) smaller; there are 2 orange spots on outer margin, including 1 near tail; black spots beneath are usually present. **EARLY STAGES:** Caterpillars vary from green to yellow-green to straw; they may have pink or maroon marks. **FOOD:** Flowers and young seeds of various legumes, usually those with inflated pods, especially vetches and milk vetches. **FLIGHT:** May–June (1 flight), May–Oct. in s. N.M. and Calif. (2 flights). **RANGE:** W. N. Amer., n. Alaska south to n. Baja Calif., in all western mountains, extends east across prairie provinces to n. Mich. and Ont. Isolated population on Gasp Peninsula, Que. **HABITAT:** Open areas with low shrubs; found in native situations much more often than Eastern Tailed-Blue. **REMARKS:** Caterpillars may feed inside inflated pods of some legumes.

SPRING AZURE *Celastrina ladon*   PL. 19

⅞–1 ⁵⁄₁₆ in. (22–33 mm). Variable. Sexually dimorphic. Upperside: Males blue; females with at least some black on outer portion of forewing. Underside: Hindwing *gray-white with faint small black*

Male Spring Azure (subspecies echo) *at moisture, Monterey Co., Calif. An abundant subspecies in Pacific coastal states, it is unusual among azures in having a second generation. Photo by Evi Buckner.*

spots, darker gray with larger black spots, or with black-gray margins and blotches in center. **SIMILAR SPECIES:** (1) Hops Azure, found along Colorado Front Range foothills, has hindwing underside white with only a few small black spots. (2) Summer Azures, found mainly on Great Plains in our area, often have white patches on upper surface of both fore- and hindwings. **EARLY STAGES:** Caterpillars vary from yellow-green to pink with a dark dorsal stripe and oblique lateral stripes. **FOOD:** Flowering parts of dogwoods, waxflower, California buckeye (Calif.), many other woody plants, and occasionally some herbaceous plants such as Chinese houses (*Collinsia*). **FLIGHT:** Late Jan.–early July depending on latitude and elevation; all year in se. Ariz. (1 flight; 2 flights in Calif.; several flights in s. Ariz.). **RANGE:** Most of Alaska, Canada, and the contiguous U.S. south of the tundra except peninsular Fla., southern plains, and s. Tex. coast; extends south in mountains to Colombia. **HABITAT:** Deciduous woods and nearby openings or edges. **REMARKS:** Often the first spring butterfly to emerge from its chrysalis. Species relationships remain unclear. There may be as many as 3 or more western species included in our current concepts.

SUMMER AZURE
Celastrina neglecta   **PL. 19**
 ¹⁵⁄₁₆–1⅛ in. (24–29 mm). Sexually dimorphic. Upperside: Male powdery blue, often with *white patch on hindwing.* Female pale blue with black

SPRING AZURE

along costal band outer portions of forewing. *Extensive white areas* on both forewing and hindwing. Underside: *White or pale gray* with small blackish marks and a *zigzag dark line* in submarginal area. **SIMILAR SPECIES:** Spring Azure lacks white patches above and is darker below. **EARLY STAGES:** Not specifically reported. **FOOD:** Osier dogwood, New Jersey tea, and other woody plants. **FLIGHT:** June–Oct. (1 main midsummer flight with late stragglers). **RANGE:** Eastern base of Rocky Mt. front from cen. Mont. and s. Sask. south to cen. Colo. and extending eastward to N.S. and southward to at least Va. **HABITAT:** Open woodland, power-line cuts, cultivated gardens, and other habitats. **REMARKS:** The Summer Azure has been shown to be a separate species from the Spring Azure.

HOPS AZURE *Celastrina humulus* PL. 19

¹³⁄₁₆–1 ¹⁄₁₆ in. (21–27 mm). Variable. Sexually dimorphic. Upperside: Male powdery blue; female usually with extensive black on costal and outer portions of forewing and costal portion of hindwing. Other areas light iridescent blue invaded with variable amounts of white from extensive to almost none. Underside: *White with pattern of small black marks* varying from almost absent, especially in females, to somewhat heavily marked in some males. **SIMILAR SPECIES:** Spring Azures in range of Hops Azure fly earlier and are grayer below with more black markings. **EARLY STAGES:** Caterpillar yellow-green, green, blue-green, to reddish with variable dark band up back and many white to cream marks below back. Usually a paler line along each side. **FOOD:** Hops and *Lupinus argenteus*. **FLIGHT:** Late May–July, usually June (1 flight). **RANGE:** Eastern foothills of Rocky Mts. in Colo. and possibly s. Wyo. **HABITAT:** Moist canyon bottoms and gulches. **REMARKS:** The flight of this species immediately follows and slightly overlaps that of the Spring Azure. It is similar to the Appalachian Azure but lays eggs only on wild hops vines. Hops Azure adults visit flowers such as

waxflower, sumac, and dog-bane for nectar.

SONORAN BLUE
Philotes sonorensis   **PL. 19**

SONORAN
BLUE

¹³⁄₁₆–1 in. (21–25 mm). Unmistakable! Upperside: *Iridescent blue* with *bright red-orange patches.* Males are almost neon blue in flight, and females have more extensive red-orange markings. Underside: *Mottled dark and light gray* with round submarginal black dots on forewing. **SIMILAR SPECIES:** Silvery Blue is larger, lacks orange patches above, and has pale gray underside with black dots on hindwing. **EARLY STAGES:** Caterpillar pale green to mottled rose. **FOOD:** *Dudleya*s. **FLIGHT:** Jan.–June (1 flight). **RANGE:** Central Calif. west of Sierra Nevada s. to cen. Baja Calif., including Cedros Is. **HABITAT:** Sunny, open or lightly forested slopes and flats, often in canyons. **REMARKS:** Unique butterfly with no close relatives. Caterpillars bore inside the leaves of host plants. Common name derives from the old name for the California gold rush area where it was first found, not for Sonora, Mex., where it does not occur.

DOTTED-BLUES—GENUS *Euphilotes* MATTONI

The dotted-blues is another of the complex groups of western butterflies. The adults are closely associated with their wild buckwheat caterpillar hosts where they nectar, mate, and lay eggs. The caterpillars feed on flowers and developing seeds. When feeding is complete the caterpillars burrow into soil at the base of the host, where they await to emerge at the host's next blooming period—usually once a year.

Although some have distinct wing-pattern differences, the species are best separated on the basis of adult genitalia, host plants, geographic occurrence, and flight seasons. The Rita Group which includes the Rita Dotted-Blue, Pallid Dotted-Blue, and Spalding's Dotted-Blue, is most distinct, whereas the Battoides Group of five species and the Enoptes Group of three species are more closely related. Species within each group sometimes co-occur but are separated seasonally and/or by association with separate hosts. There are clear-cut differences in the male genitalia among the three species groups and among species in the Rita Group.

WESTERN SQUARE-DOTTED BLUE   PL. 19
Euphilotes battoides

¹¹⁄₁₆–¹³⁄₁₆ in. (17–16 mm). Wings relatively broad and rounded. Upperside: Males blue with black outer margin and with or without trace of orange aurora on hindwing outer margin; females brown often with orange aurora. Underside: Ground varies from gray-white to off-white, black spotting varies from heavy and smudged (typical subspecies) to small. *Best distinguished by host, locality, and season.* **SIMILAR SPECIES:** Best distinguished from the butterflies in the Enoptes Group by its relatively broad, rounded wings and by distinctive genitalia. **EARLY STAGES:** Caterpillar variable green, dirty yellow, pink, or brown, with dark brown lines along sides and middle of back. **FOOD:** Coastal buckwheat, sulphur-flower, and other buckwheats. **FLIGHT:** Mid-April–early Aug., usually a few weeks for any given population that depends on host bloom period (1 flight). **RANGE:** S. B.C. south to s. Calif. and inland to w. Mont., sw. Idaho, sw. Colo., and w. N.M. **HABITAT:** Usually open, sunny areas with host buckwheat, ranging from slightly above sea level to more than 11,000-ft. elevations, including coastal dunes, alpine fellfields, hills in sagebrush desert, desert canyons, etc. **REMARKS:** There are no constant wing characters that can distinguish this geographically variable species from other species in the Battoides or Enoptes groups.

BERNARDINO DOTTED-BLUE *Euphilotes bernardino*   PL. 19

¹¹⁄₁₆–¹³⁄₁₆ in. (17–21 mm). Wings relatively *elongate and narrow*, especially in female. Upperside: Male blue with narrow black outer

Mating pair of Western Square-Dotted Blues resting on sulphur-flower, Mono Co., Calif. This is the host plant where eggs are laid and the resultant caterpillars will feed.

margin; female brown with orange aurora on hindwing. Underside: *Off-white with distinct black spots and a moderate orange aurora*. **SIMILAR SPECIES:** Among other early summer dotted blues in s. Calif., this is the only butterfly whose caterpillars eat fasciculate buckwheat. The similar El Segundo Blue, an endangered subspecies of the Square-dotted Blue of s. Calif., feeds on coastal buckwheat. **EARLY STAGES:** Caterpillar variable pale blue-green, green with chocolate markings, lemon yellow with chocolate, or plain pink. All forms with fine, short silvery white hairs. **FOOD:** Fasciculate buckwheat, cinereous buckwheat, and Shockley buckwheat. **FLIGHT:** Feb.–late Aug. (1 flight). **RANGE:** Cen. and s. Calif. south to cen. Baja Calif. (including Cedros Is.) and east to s. Nev. and w. Ariz. **HABITAT:** Chaparral, rocky desert slopes, and dry lake bed. **REMARKS:** Each population has a single flight. The long range of recorded dates may indicate that the cinereous and fasciculate buckwheat populations represent distinct species with separate flight periods.

Female Bernardino Dotted-Blue nectaring at fasciculate buckwheat, southern Calif. This photo shows the orange aurora often found on the hindwing of this species and close relatives. Photo by Greg Ballmer.

ELLIS' DOTTED-BLUE *Euphilotes ellisi*   **PL. 20**

¾–⅞ in. (19–22 mm). Forewing fringe with 2 *black checks.* Hindwing uncheckered. Upperside: Male blue with narrow black margins and restricted pale pink aurora on hindwing; female brown or with extensive blue. Orange aurora narrow to broad. Underside: Off-white with moderate black spotting, *submarginal spot row on forewing smudged. Red-orange aurora on outer margin of hindwing continuous* but variable in width. **SIMILAR SPECIES:** (1) Rocky Mountain Dotted-Blue flies earlier. (2) Spalding's Dotted-Blue (see p. 242). **EARLY STAGES:** Caterpillar white with brown markings (on Heerman buckwheat) or yellow with brown markings (on Corymbose buckwheat). **FOOD:** Corymbose and Heerman buckwheats. **FLIGHT:** Mid-July–early Sept. (1 flight). **RANGE:** Utah and w. Colo. south to n. Ariz. and nw. N.M., west to e. Calif. and w. Nev. **HABITAT:** Dry rocky or gravelly brushy slopes or flats. **REMARKS:** Mormon Metalmarks (black hindwing form) are also found on the hosts at the same time.

BAUER'S DOTTED-BLUE *Euphilotes baueri*   **PL. 20**

¾–⅞ in. (19–22 mm). *Checkering of fringes reduced.* Upperside: Male pale blue *without aurora;* female with *variable amount of blue* from extensive to almost none. Orange aurora on hindwing ranging from medium to almost none. Underside: *Snowy white with bold black terminal line, black spotting bold; aurora on hindwing narrow, pale orange.* **SIMILAR SPECIES:** Western Square-dotted Blue, which may occur nearby, flies a bit later and is found on varieties of sulphur-flower. It often has less blue in both sexes. **EARLY STAGES:** Caterpillar white with pink stripes (on Kennedy buckwheat) or yellow with pink stripes (on strict buckwheat). **FOOD:** Kennedy, strict, and oval-leafed buckwheats. **FLIGHT:** Mid-April–late June (1 flight). **RANGE:** E. and ne. Calif. east of Sierra

Nevada, Nev., and n. Ariz. **HABI-TAT:** Dry slopes and flats with scattered short brush. **REMARKS:** Flies at some of the same localities as Ellis' Blue but three months earlier.

PACIFIC DOTTED-BLUE

INTERMEDIATE DOTTED-BLUE
Euphilotes intermedia   **NOT SHOWN**
¾ in. (19–20 mm). Fringes white, may be dark-checked at vein endings, less so on hindwing. Upperside: Male blue with *broad black outer margins and restricted orange aurora at hindwing anal angle*. Female brown with orange hindwing aurora. Underside: Black *terminal line not strong*. Forewing dark, smudged with white-edged black spots. Black-spotted hindwing less prominent; *aurora orange, often broken.* **SIMILAR SPECIES:** Pacific Dotted-Blue may overlap with Intermediate Blue but is found on other buckwheat species and has smaller spots and a more restricted aurora on the hindwing below. **EARLY STAGES:** Caterpillar often yellow with red-orange bands. **FOOD:** Late sulphur-flower and Lobb's buckwheat. **FLIGHT:** Late June–mid-Aug. (1 flight). **RANGE:** W. Ore. south to n. Calif. Isolated population in cen. Ariz. **HABITAT:** Rocky plateaus and slopes.

ENOPTES GROUP

PACIFIC DOTTED-BLUE *Euphilotes enoptes*   **PL. 20**
¾–⅞ in. (18–23 mm). Upperside: Male blue with variable black outer borders, female brown with indistinctly edged orange aurora. Underside: Off-white with black spotting. *Forewing spots larger and more squarish* than those on hindwing. Orange *aurora usually broken into separate spots.* **SIMILAR SPECIES:** Western Square-dotted Blue usually has larger spots below and is found on different wild buckwheats. **EARLY STAGES:** Caterpillar white with touches of pink, marked with pink-brown stripe up middle of back and diagonal brown slashes. May be darker or lighter. **FOOD:** Nude buckwheat, inflated buckwheat, Wright's buckwheat, and others. **FLIGHT:** Mid-May–early Oct. (1 flight). **RANGE:** Wash. south through Ore. and Calif. to cen. Ariz. and n. Baja Calif. **HABITAT:** Sun-exposed rocky slopes and flats in foothills, mountains, and deserts. **REMARKS:** The fall-flying desert subspecies *dammersi* may be considered a full species after more thorough study.

MOJAVE DOTTED-BLUE *Euphilotes mojave* PL. 20

¾–⅞ in. (19–23 mm). Upperside: Male pale blue with narrow black border, female blackish brown often with extensive blue but sometimes restricted at base. *Hindwing aurora absent or restricted to a few orange scales.* Underside: Similar to Pacific Dotted-Blue. **SIMILAR SPECIES:** Bernardino Blue co-occurs with the Mojave Dotted-Blue only in the e. Mojave Desert, where it is found on fasciculate buckwheat. Above female is browner with a more prominent orange aurora, and below hindwing is more prominently spotted with a continuous orange aurora. **EARLY STAGES:** Caterpillar yellow with bars, dashes, and spots of deep rose. **FOOD:** Low, wild buckwheats (*Eriogonum pusillum* and *E. reniforme*). **FLIGHT:** Mid-March–June (1 flight). **RANGE:** Mojave and Colorado Deserts and nearby mountain foothills of s. Calif., s. Nev., and sw. Utah, possibly s. to nw. Ariz. and n. Baja Calif. **HABITAT:** Dry desert washes and slopes. **REMARKS:** Other members of the Enoptes group fly in midsummer or fall and use different buckwheats as host plants.

ROCKY MOUNTAIN DOTTED-BLUE PL. 20
Euphilotes ancilla

⅝–1 in. (16–25 mm). Fringe white, *weakly checkered.* Upperside: Male deep blue (rarely pale blue) with medium black border. Hindwing *aurora usually absent,* sometimes present. Female brown with orange aurora varying wide to thin to absent. Terminal line thin. Underside: Light *blue-gray.* Forewing often, but not always, *suffused with smoky dark gray.* Hindwing with prominent black spots. **SIMILAR SPECIES:** In w. Ore., Nev., and s. Idaho, can be reliably separated in the field from subspecies *glaucon* of Western Square-dotted Blue only by collection and dissection of genitalia. Both butterflies use sulphur-flower as their caterpillar host and have overlapping flight periods. **EARLY STAGES:** Not reported. **FOOD:**

MOJAVE
DOTTED-BLUE

ROCKY MOUNTAIN
DOTTED-BLUE

Several wild buckwheats, especially sulphur-flower. **FLIGHT:** Late April–early Aug. (1 flight). **RANGE:** E. Ore. and w. Nev. east to Mont., se. Wyo., and cen. Colo. **HABITAT:** Sun-exposed rocky slopes and flats with host-plant colonies.

RITA GROUP

PALLID DOTTED-BLUE *Euphilotes pallescens*   **PL. 20**
⅝–1³⁄₁₆ in. (16–21 mm). Upperside: Male pale blue often without aurora. Female brown, often with white scaling at base, especially forewing. Underside: *Almost white with distinct black spotting. Distinct black terminal line* at margins. Fringes usually not checkered. *Aurora continuous but narrow.* **SIMILAR SPECIES:** No other similar blues in this habitat at same time of year. **EARLY STAGES:** Caterpillar ivory white with slight green tinge. Also a discontinuous brown-pink line up back and diagonal brown-pink dashes on each segment. **FOOD:** Several wild buckwheats, including Kearney's buckwheat and plumate buckwheat. **FLIGHT:** Early July–Sept. (1 flight). **RANGE:** Ne. Calif., n. Nev., and cen. Utah south to s. Calif. and n. Ariz. **HABITAT:** Desert flats with host-plant colonies. **REMARKS:** Has distinctive genitalia, but reported to blend with Rita Dotted-Blue at eastern edge of its range.

RITA DOTTED-BLUE *Euphilotes rita*   **PL. 20**
¹¹⁄₁₆–⅞ in. (17–22 mm). Fringes weakly checkered. Upperside: Male lilac blue with silvery sheen; *orange aurora at corner of hindwing*—sometimes barely present. Female brown usually with broad orange aurora. Underside: *Off-white with distinct black spotting*, sometimes smudged on forewing. *Orange aurora continuous, usually fairly broad.* Black terminal line at margins. **SIMILAR SPECIES:** Lupine Blue has scintillant scales on edge of hindwing below. **EARLY**

PALLID
DOTTED-BLUE

RITA
DOTTED-BLUE

Male Rita Dotted-Blue (subspecies *rita*) nectaring at seep-willow, Cochise Co., Ariz. Compare with subspecies *coloradensis* shown on Plate 20. Note weakly checkered fringes, black spotting, and continuous orange aurora.

STAGES: Caterpillar not described. **FOOD:** Wild buckwheats including Wright's buckwheat (subspecies *rita*), effuse buckwheat (subspecies *coloradensis*), and others. **FLIGHT:** July–late Sept. (1 flight). **RANGE:** S. Wyo. and sw. Neb. south through Colo., e. Ariz., and w. N.M. to w. Tex. **HABITAT:** Low desert foothills and rolling prairie with host-plant colonies. **REMARKS:** Rita Dotted-Blue is almost never found with other dotted-blues, but Lupine Blues are often present.

SPALDING'S DOTTED-BLUE *Euphilotes spaldingi*   **PL. 20**
¾–¹⁵⁄₁₆ in. (19–24 mm). Fringes weakly checked below. Upperside: Male lilac blue with pink aurora on hindwing. Female brown with orange hindwing aurora and orange submarginal band on forewing. Underside: Gray with black spotting. *Continuous orange aurora on hindwing, and submarginal orange on forewing. Terminal line weak.* **SIMILAR SPECIES:** Below, the somewhat larger

SPALDING'S DOTTED-BLUE

SMALL DOTTED-BLUE

Mating pair of Small Dotted-Blues, Calif. These butterflies and their relatives do most of their feeding and mating on the same plant species used by their caterpillars. Note the lack of an orange aurora. Photo by Jim Brock.

Melissa Blue has scintillant scales on hindwing margin and is paler with more defined orange banding on forewing; male lacks orange on lower forewing surface and lacks aurora on upper hindwing. **EARLY STAGES:** Caterpillar not described. **FOOD:** Racemose buckwheat. **FLIGHT:** Late June–mid Aug. (1 flight). **RANGE:** E. Nev., cen. Utah, and s. Colo. south to cen. Ariz. and cen. N.M. **HABITAT:** Sun-exposed hills and rocky outcrops at interface of pinyon-juniper and Ponderosa pine-gambel oak woodlands. **REMARKS:** Unlike other two Rita group species, Spalding's Dotted-Blue caterpillars are not attended by ants, but instead build a nest in the host's flower heads.

SMALL DOTTED-BLUE *Philotiella speciosa*   PL. 20

⅝–¾ in. (16–20 mm). Fringes checkered. Upperside: Male pale blue with narrow black margins. Female brown. Underside: *Off-white with pattern of small black spots.* **SIMILAR SPECIES:** (1) Mojave Dotted-Blue has orange aurora on hindwing below. (2) Western Pygmy-Blue usually flies later in year and has different plant association. **EARLY STAGES:** Caterpillar apple green often with rose band up middle of back. **FOOD:** *Oxytheca*s and Reniforme buckwheat. **FLIGHT:** Mid-March–May, rarely June (1 flight), July–Aug. (possible second flight in some years). **RANGE:** S. Ore., cen. Calif., n. Nev., and sw. Utah south through w. Ariz. and s. Calif. to n. Baja Calif. **HABITAT:** Desert flats and dry washes. **REMARKS:** One of our smallest butterflies, it rivals the Western Pygmy-Blue and Cyna Blue in its small size.

ARROWHEAD BLUE *Glaucopsyche piasus*   PL. 20

⅞–1¼ in. (22–32 mm). Fringes white, checkered black at vein

Female Arrowhead Blue nectaring at stonecrop, Lander Co., Nev. The amount of blue on this female is extensive but is often more restricted in other populations. Look for them near vast stands of lupines.

endings. Upperside: Both sexes dull blue with irregular black margins. Female often with variable amounts of orange on margins of both wings. Underside: *Pattern of black spots on gray background with distinctive basal and postmedian patches of white arrowhead-shaped marks.* **SIMILAR SPECIES:** Boisduval's Blue, with which the Arrowhead often flies in close association, is a paler, more iridescent blue above and lacks white patches below. **EARLY STAGES:** Caterpillar variable greenish white, yellow-brown, or blue-green minutely speckled with white or red. Darker bands run up middle of back and along sides. **FOOD:** Usually various lupines, but occasional milk vetch. **FLIGHT:** March–early July (1 flight), rarely Aug.–Sept. (second flight) in Colo. **RANGE:** Sw. Canada south through western mountain ranges to n. Baja Calif., n. Ariz., and nw. N.M. **HABITAT:** Open meadows, gentle slopes, and sagebrush flats with stands of lupines.

ARROWHEAD
BLUE

SILVERY
BLUE

SILVERY BLUE *Glaucopsyche lygdamus* PL. 20

⅞–1 ³⁄₁₆ in. (22–30 mm). Upperside: Both wings have pronounced *black margin with white fringe*. Male with bright iridescent silver-blue; female dark blackish brown with or without blue basally. Underside: Both wings are off-white to gray-brown with *single submarginal row of round black white-edged spots*. **SIMILAR SPECIES:** (1) Boisduval's Blue and (2) Greenish Blue are not as iridescent above and have more irregularly shaped spots on hindwing below. **EARLY STAGES:** Caterpillars vary from green to purplish with a dark dorsal stripe and white oblique lateral lines. Caterpillars are tended by ants. **FOOD:** Lupines, lotis, vetches, milk vetches, and other legumes. **FLIGHT:** Feb. (Calif.)–Aug. (high elevations), usually April–June (1 flight). **RANGE:** Most of boreal N. Amer. Alaska south to n. Baja Calif. and cen. N.M., east across Canada and Great Lakes region to Que., Nfld., and N.S. Isolated populations in Southeast and southern plains states. **HABITAT:** Open areas including tundra, mountain meadows, foothills, grasslands, prairie hills, bogs. **REMARKS:** The Xerces Blue, a subspecies *(xerces)* with the black spots below replaced by small white patches, is extinct. Its sand dune habitat in San Francisco is now covered with houses or ornamental plantings. The Xerces Society, an invertebrate conservation organization, takes its name after this butterfly.

CRANBERRY BLUE *Vacciniina optilete* PL. 21

⅞–1 in. (22–25 mm). Sexually dimorphic. Upperside: Violet-blue; female marked with dark scales. Underside: Both wings with strong *black postmedian spot rows; hindwing with 1 black-edged orange submarginal spot* near anal angle. **SIMILAR SPECIES:** Silvery Blue is iridescent silver-blue on upperside and has round black white-edged postmedian spots on underside. **EARLY STAGES:** Not reported. **FOOD:** Cranberries and low blueberries. **FLIGHT:** Mid-June–mid Aug. (1 flight). **RANGE:** Holarctic. In N. Amer. from Alaska east to cen. N.W. Terr. and nw. Man. **HABITAT:** Spruce bogs in taiga, wet coniferous woods, and tundra.

CRANBERRY BLUE

HAWAIIAN BLUE
Vaga blackburni PL. 21

⅞–1 in. (22–26 mm). Upperside: *Iridescent violet.* Underside: *Hindwing bright green;* upper half of forewing green, lower half gray. **SIMILAR SPECIES:** None in Hawaii. **EARLY STAGES:**

HAWAIIAN BLUE

ARCTIC BLUE

Caterpillar mostly green to yellow-green. **FOOD:** Koa—a native Hawaiian acacia, and several introduced woody legumes. **FLIGHT:** Much of year (several flights). **RANGE:** All of the main Hawaiian Is. **HABITAT:** Forested foothills and mountains. **REMARKS:** Hawaiian Blue is one of only two butterflies native to Hawaii. The other is the Kameamea Lady (*Vanessa tameamea*).

ARCTIC BLUE *Agriades aquilo*   PL. 21

⅞–1 in. (22–26 mm). Geographically variable. Sexually dimorphic. *Forewings pointed.* Upperside: Male gray-blue; female orange-brown. Underside: Hindwing has *postmedian black spots obsolete or surrounded by white patches in darker background.* **SIMILAR SPECIES:** Boisduval's Blue co-occurs in part of range and sometimes has white or white-circled black spots on underside of hindwing, but is usually much larger, duller blue above, and closely tied to

Male Arctic Blue nectaring at cinquefoil, Gilpin Co., Colo. The geographic variation of this species is extensive and confusing. The butterflies are usually close to the ground and visit many kinds of flowers.

stands of lupine. **EARLY STAGES:** Not reported. **FOOD:** Rock-primroses. **FLIGHT:** Early May–late Sept. (1 flight). **RANGE:** Holarctic. Much of boreal N. Amer., including tundra and Arctic Archipelago east to Lab., Nfld., and Greenland, thence south to Wash., e. Ariz. and cen. N.M. **HABITAT:** Gravelly hills, domes, low ridges, alpine tundra, mountain meadows, prairies. **REMARKS:** It is not known whether our North American butterflies are the same species as any Eurasian species. It is also unclear whether various host races exist within the range of *aquilo*. This butterfly is referred to as *Agriades* (or *Plebejus*) *glandon* or *franklinii* in other butterfly books.

SIERRA NEVADA BLUE *Agriades podarce*   **PL. 21**

⅞–1 in. (22–26 mm). Upperside: Male gray-blue. Female red-brown. Underside: Forewing with *sumarginal spots arrowhead-shaped, pointing inward. Discal spot on hindwing not black.* **SIMILAR SPECIES:** Cassiope Blue has forewings more pointed. Ground color below is darker, submarginal spots on forewing below squarish or oblong, discal spot on hindwing usually black. **EARLY STAGES:** Green with blue-black band up back; band bordered by straw yellow. **FOOD:** Shooting stars. **FLIGHT:** Early June–Sept. (1 flight). **RANGE:** Sw. Ore. south through the Sierra Nevada of Calif. and extreme w. Nev. **HABITAT:** Wet mountain meadows. **REMARKS:** Adults are very local and do not wander beyond their meadow habitat.

CASSIOPE BLUE *Agriades cassiope*   **PL. 21**

¾–1 in. (21–25 mm). Upperside: Male metallic, pale gray-blue; female dull dark brown. Submarginal hindwing spots bordered by dark brown or black. Underside: Ground dark brown with pattern of black spots in white field. *Submarginal spots on forewing squar-*

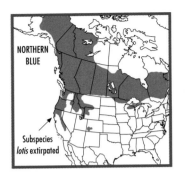

ish or oblong. Black discal spot on hindwing usually present. **SIMILAR SPECIES:** Sierra Nevada Blue is lighter below with submarginal spots on forewing below arrow-shaped and pointed inward. Discal spot on hindwing below usually not black. **EARLY STAGES:** Caterpillar green with row of black spots along side and a colorful band of blue-black, magenta, and yellow. **FOOD:** *Cassiope mertensiana.* **FLIGHT:** Mid-July–early Sept. (1 flight). **RANGE:** Calif.: Trinity Alps and crest of Sierra Nevada. **HABITAT:** Lush subalpine slopes.

NORTHERN BLUE *Lycaeides idas* PL. 20

¹³⁄₁₆–1 ⅛ in. (21–29 mm). Geographically variable. Sexually dimorphic. Upperside: Male blue, female brown with submarginal orange or brown spots. Underside: *Hindwing has black terminal line broken into small spots at vein endings, submarginal orange spots reduced.* **SIMILAR SPECIES:** Melissa Blue has continuous black subterminal line on underside of both wings. In our area, the two species are usually not found in the same locality. Northern Blue is usually found at higher elevations. **EARLY STAGES:** Not reported. **FOOD:** Several plants in pea family in West, including lupine, vetches, milk vetches, and lotis. **FLIGHT:** June–early Oct. (1 flight). **RANGE:** Holarctic. W. N. Amer. from Alaska south to cen. Calif., s. Idaho, n. Utah, and sw. Colo., east across s. Canada to the n. Great Lakes region and ne. Ont. Isolated group of populations in se. Lab., Nfld., s. Que., and N.S. **HABITAT:** Alpine tundra, dry hills and flats, subalpine meadows, bog edges. **REMARKS:** Lotis Blue (subspecies *lotis*), formerly of coastal Mendocino and Sonoma Cos., Calif., is listed as endangered by the U.S. Fish and Wildlife Service. Species relationships are poorly understood, and there may be more than one North American species in this group.

MELISSA BLUE *Lycaeides melissa* **PL. 20**

⅞–1¼ in. (22–32 mm). Sexes dimorphic. Upperside: Male blue, female brown with submarginal orange trim on both wings. Underside: Both wings have a *continuous black subterminal line. Red-orange submarginal row usually extending to forewings* in both sexes. **SIMILAR SPECIES:** Below, Acmon Blue has submarginal band restricted to hindwing. Above, male has orange submarginal band on hindwing and female has orange band restricted to hindwing. **EARLY STAGES:** Caterpillar is green with short pale lines. Caterpillars are tended by ants. **FOOD:** Wide variety of legumes, including alfalfa, sweet clover, and lupines. **FLIGHT:** April–Nov. (3 flights). **RANGE:** S. B.C., s. prairie provinces south through w. U.S. (mainly intermountain and plains) to n. Baja Calif., n. Mex., and w. Tex. In upper Midwest and Northeast as endangered Karner Blue (subspecies *samuelis*). **HABITAT:** A variety of open situations including native prairies, dry meadows, alfalfa fields, and waste areas. **REMARKS:** This is the commonest blue is much of the intermountain West.

GREENISH BLUE *Plebejus saepiolus* **PL. 20**

1–1¼ in. (26–32 mm). Sexes dimorphic. Upperside: Male blue, sometimes green-blue; female orange-brown to brown, sometimes with blue at base. Underside: *Gray-white or brown with postbasal and submarginal rows of irregular black spots.* **SIMILAR SPECIES:** (1) Boisduval's Blue is larger and usually has white or white-encircled black spots on underside of hindwing. (2) Silvery Blue is more iridescent above and has more regular row of round black spots on underside of hindwing. **EARLY STAGES:** Caterpillars green or red. **FOOD:** Flowering parts of various clovers and milk vetches. **FLIGHT:** Mid-May–mid-Aug. (1 flight). **RANGE:** Boreal w. N. Amer. from Alaska south in mountains to s. Calif., cen. Ariz., and cen. N.M., east across s. Canada and the n. Great Lakes region to N.B., s. N.S., and n. Me. **HABITAT:** Stream edges, bogs, roadsides, open meadows. **REMARKS:** Expanded range eastward into se. Canada and n. New England after 1912.

SAN EMIGDIO BLUE
Plebulina emigdionis **PL. 20**

¹³⁄₁₆–1¹⁄₁₆ in. (21–27 mm). Upperside: Males mainly dark blue, females with blue at base. Outer portion of wings black—dif-

SAN EMIGDIO
BLUE

BOISDUVAL'S
BLUE

fusely blending with the blue. Both sexes with *diffuse orange aurora on hindwing*. Underside: Forewing with black spots more pronounced than on hindwing. *Submarginal band of metallic spots on hindwing devoid of orange scaling.* **SIMILAR SPECIES:** Acmon Blue is more precisely marked, has orange aurora on underside of hindwing. **EARLY STAGES:** Variable, green to brown, spotted and blotched with black. Body covered with short white hairs. **FOOD:** Saltbush. **FLIGHT:** Early April–late Sept. (3 flights). **RANGE:** S. Calif. (north of Los Angeles). **HABITAT:** Desert washes and drainages.

BOISDUVAL'S BLUE *Icaricia icarioides*   **PL. 21**

¹³⁄₁₆–1 ⁵⁄₁₆ in. (21–33 mm). A widely ranging variable butterfly. Upperside: Male is *dull blue* with a relatively broad *black submarginal area* on both wings. Female is extremely variable from solid brown to primarily blue with diffuse blackish wing edges. Females in some areas, e.g., s. Calif. (subspecies *evius*), have submarginal orange marks on hindwing. Underside: Ground varies from dark brown to off-white usually with 2 *rows of roundish to irregular black spots on both wings*—the postmedian band of which is most prominent, especially on forewing. Black spots on hindwing are often *replaced with white areas* in several populations. **SIMILAR SPECIES:** (1) Silvery Blue males are more metallic blue above, and both sexes have only a single row of uniform rounded spots on underside of hindwing. (2) Greenish Blues are smaller, greener in males, oranger in females, with more complete spot pattern. **EARLY STAGES:** Green with white diagonal bars on each segment. **FOOD:** Lupines—females usually select species with hairiest leaves at any site. **FLIGHT:** April–mid-Aug. (1 flight), early March–mid-Sept. on Colo. plains and s. Calif. (2 flights). **RANGE:** Sw. Canada south through mountainous West and high plains to n. Baja Calif., s. N.M., and n. Chihuahua. **HABITAT:** Meadows, sage-

Shasta Blue resting on soil, Cottonwood Pass, Chaffee Co., Colo. Note increased dark scaling of individuals in alpine zone. Close relatives lack the mottled appearance below.

brush flats, grassy hillsides, prairies. **REMARKS:** Mission Blue (subspecies *missionensis*) is an endangered subspecies found on the hills of San Francisco and adjacent San Mateo Co., Calif.

SHASTA BLUE *Icaricia shasta* PL. 21

¾–1 in. (19–26 mm). Upperside: Males dull to dark iridescent blue; female brown with some blue basally. Discal black spot in forewing and row of submarginal black spots on hindwing. Underside: Gray with pattern of black spots, brown blotches, and pale wing veins gives a *distinct mottled appearance*. Hindwing with an inconspicuous *band of submarginal metallic spots*. **SIMILAR SPECIES:** (1) Acmon Blue and (2) Lupine Blue have orange aurora on hindwing above and lack mottled appearance below. **EARLY STAGES:** Caterpillar brown, white, or green, with band along each side and darker oblique bars. **FOOD:** Various legumes, including milk vetches, locoweed, lupines, and clover. **FLIGHT:** June–Sept., rarely to Nov. (1 flight). **RANGE:** Ore., s. Alta. and Sask. south in mountains and intermountain West to cen. Calif., s. Nev., s. Utah, and s. Colo. **HABITAT:** Alpine and subalpine rocky slopes, blowouts, sagebrush flats, and prairie hills. **REMARKS:** Usually found in barren, windswept habitats with "cushion" plants. Adults usually fly no more than a few inches above the ground.

SHASTA BLUE

ACMON BLUE *Icaricia acmon*   PL. 21

¾–¹⁵⁄₁₆ in. (19–24 mm). Sexually dimorphic. Upperside: Male blue, often pale powdery; female brown, sometimes with extensive blue at base (spring brood in Calif.); both sexes with orange (often pinkish) aurora on hindwing. Underside: *Off-white with pattern of black spots and hindwing with submarginal orange and metallic aurora.* **SIMILAR SPECIES:** (1) Lupine Blue is often somewhat larger, is duller blue, has black discal spot and black marginal border on forewing, and often black scaling interior to hindwing orange aurora. (2) Melissa Blues have males without orange on upperside; females have submarginal orange on both wings above. (3) Euphilotes Blues, often found with Acmon on wild buckwheats, are usually smaller and lack metallic spots in submarginal hindwing band. **EARLY STAGES:** Caterpillar is pale green with coalesced pink and white stripes along each side. **FOOD:** Flowers and developing seeds of buckwheats, lupines, lotises, and milk vetches. **FLIGHT:** Feb.–Oct. in n. and cen. Calif. (several flights), Jan.–Nov. in s. Calif. **RANGE:** Cen. Ore. (west of Cascades) south through Calif. (west of Sierra Nevada crest) to n. Baja Calif. **REMARKS:** Taken together with the Lupine Blue, this an extremely difficult group.

LUPINE BLUE *Icaricia lupini*   PL. 21

¹¹⁄₁₆–1⅛ in. (17–29 mm). Upperside: Male deep blue to greenish blue; female brown, sometimes with orange along veins, to predominantly blue-green. Usually a *black spot present in forewing disk* and *black scaling interior to orange aurora* on hindwing. Underside: Variable, but similar to Acmon Blue. **SIMILAR SPECIES:** In Calif., spring form of Acmon Blue has many features of the Lupine Blue. Acmon Blue is usually smaller, at least in Calif., paler blue, lacks black discal spot and black marginal border on

Male Lupine Blue basking with open wings, Badlands National Park, S. Dak. Recent studies have shown most populations in noncoastal states are not Acmon Blues. Note black margins and black discal dot on forewing.

forewing; lacks black scaling interior to orange aurora on hindwing. **EARLY STAGES:** Caterpillar gray-green with cream bands. **FOOD:** Wild buckwheats, occasionally legumes such as *Lotis* (Sonora, Mex.). **FLIGHT:** Mar.–Sept., sometimes Nov. (1–2 flights). **RANGE:** W. N. Amer. from sw. Canada through all of the w. U.S., usually in mountainous areas or foothills, to nw. Mex. east to cen. Great Plains, strays to se. Minn. **HABITAT:** Oak woodland, desert chaparral, canyons, alpine tundra, rocky slopes and flats, prairie hills, weedy areas, roadsides. **REMARKS:** Lupine Blues in much of the West were previously considered subspecies of the Acmon Blue. The new view by J. A. Scott of a more restricted Acmon Blue and more widespread Lupine Blue as a variable species that may include two or more sibling species is supported by this author and other western students of the group.

VEINED BLUE *Icaricia neurona*

PL. 21

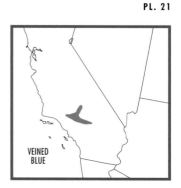

VEINED BLUE

$^{11}\!/_{16}$–1 in. (17–26 mm). Upperside: Both sexes *brown with extensive orange scaling along veins,* although females sometimes lack orange scaling along veins. Forewing *costa orange,* and hindwing with *distinct broad orange aurora.* Underside: Similar to Acmon Blue. **SIMILAR SPECIES:** Acmon Blue females lack extensive orange scaling on veins. Similar Veined Blue females without orange veins should be identified by associated males. **EARLY STAGES:** Caterpillar apple green with abundant white hairs lending a gray overcast. **FOOD:** Wright's Buckwheat. **FLIGHT:** May–mid-Aug. (2 flights); one low-elevation population has only a single flight. **RANGE:** Limited to high elevations of several mountain ranges in s. Calif. **HABITAT:** Barren flats with colonies of host plant. **REMARKS:** Adults fly close to ground over host plants, which grow in low mats.

11

TRUE BUTTERFLIES:
SUPERFAMILY PAPILIONOIDEA
METALMARKS: FAMILY RIODINIDAE

With a few exceptions, the metalmarks are denizens of tropical latitudes, especially those of the Americas. About 1,300 species are known. Our species are small to medium butterflies. The butterflies vary widely in their patterns, postures, and behavior. The front legs of males are reduced in size and are not used for walking, and females have 3 pairs of walking legs. The adults usually perch with their wings spread open or cocked slightly. The adults of many tropical species habitually perch upside down on the lower surface of large leaves. Males locate their mates by perching in likely sites rather than by patrolling. Adults of our species obtain sustenance by imbibing flower nectar. Eggs are widely variable but are generally sea urchin–shaped. Caterpillars of our species are slug-shaped and have dense tufts of long fine setae. Pupae are usually stout and without silk. Overwintering is in either the larval or pupal stage.

FATAL METALMARK *Calephelis nemesis*   **PL. 22**
¾–1 in. (18–26 mm). Male has *pointed forewing*. Fringes *checkered*. Upperside: Both sexes usually have *dark brown median band*, wings paler beyond band to give it more contrast. **SIMILAR SPECIES:** (1) Rounded Metalmark has indistinctly checkered fringes; male has rounded forewing. (2) Rawson's Metalmark is relatively large, has absent or weak expression or dark median band on upperside. Male has pointed forewing. **EARLY STAGES:**

FATAL METALMARK

Fatal Metalmark nectaring at Tridax, Bill Williams River, Ariz. The most widespread and abundant Calephelis *metalmark in most of our area. Photo by Jack N. Levy.*

Caterpillar is dark gray with silvery tubercles and long buff and gray-white hairs. **FOOD:** Seepwillow (*Baccharis*), *Encelia*, possibly *Clematis*. **FLIGHT:** Most of year as temperatures permit (several flights). **RANGE:** Southwest (s. Calif., s. Nev., sw. Utah, Ariz., s. N.M., w. and s. Tex. south to s. Mex.). **HABITAT:** Weedy or brushy areas along streams, washes, ditches, or roadsides. **REMARKS:** Males perch during the afternoon in small sunlit patches along streams or washes.

WRIGHT'S METALMARK *Calephelis wrighti* **PL. 22**
$^{15}/_{16}$–1 ⅛ in. (24–29 mm). Forewings *pointed, outer margin sinuous.* Fringes checkered. Upperside: *Dark reddish brown, little contrast.* Underside: Unicolored yellow-orange. **SIMILAR SPECIES:** Fatal Metalmark is smaller, more rounder-winged, and usually has dark median bands on the upper wing surfaces. **EARLY STAGES:** Caterpillar gray-white with long white hairs. **FOOD:** Sweet bush (*Bebbea*

WRIGHT'S METALMARK

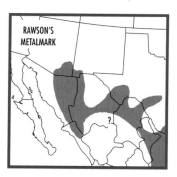

RAWSON'S METALMARK

Male Wright's Metalmark in characteristic perching posture, Anza-Borrego State Park, Calif. Note the pointed forewings and diagnostic sinuous outer wing margins. Photo by Jack N. Levy.

juncea). **FLIGHT:** All year (3 flights). **RANGE:** S. Calif., s. Nev., and w. Ariz. south to Baja Calif. **HABITAT:** Rocky flats, alluvial fans, and associated washes (dry gullies). **REMARKS:** This butterfly is easily identified compared to related species.

ROUNDED METALMARK
Calephelis nilus   **PL. 22**

¹¹⁄₁₆–¹⁵⁄₁₆ (17–24 mm). Male has *rounded forewing apex.* Upperside: May have dark median band and *indistinctly checkered fringes.* **SIMILAR SPECIES:** (1) Fatal Metalmark has distinctly checkered wing fringes, and (2) Rawson's Metalmark is relatively large, brighter, and usually lacks dark median band on upperside. **EARLY STAGES:** Not reported. **FOOD:** Boneset (*Eupatorium odoratum*). **FLIGHT:** All year in s. Tex. (several flights). **RANGE:** Cen. Tex. south to cen. Mex. **HABITAT:** Thorn scrub, fencerows, roadsides. **REMARKS:** This species just barely enters our area along the Rio Grande River. It was formerly referred to as the Lost Metalmark (*Calephelis perditalis*).

RAWSON'S METALMARK *Calephelis rawsoni*   **PL. 22**

¾–1¹⁄₁₆ in. (19–28 mm). Large. Male forewing relatively pointed. Upperside: *Median band weak or absent, fringes checkered.* **SIMILAR SPECIES:** (1) Fatal Metalmark has pointed forewing (in male), dark median band above, and checkered wing fringes. **EARLY STAGES:** Not reported. **FOOD:** Several bonesets (*Eupatorium havanense and E. greggii*) in Tex., possibly Bidens in s. Ariz. **FLIGHT:** All year (several flights). **RANGE:** S. Ariz., sw. N.M., s. and w. Tex. south to cen. Mex. **HABITAT:** Thorn scrub desert along rivers, foothills, moist areas on shaded limestone outcrops, openings in oak forests. **REMARKS:** The Arizona Metalmark (subspecies *arizonensis*) and Freeman's

Rawson's Metalmark (subspecies arizonensis) nectaring at wild morning glory, San Pedro River Preserve, Cochise Co., Ariz. Believed by some to be a separate species. Photo by Jack N. Levy.

Metalmark (subspecies *freemani*) are here considered subspecies of Rawson's Metalmark based on similarities in genitalia.

ZELA METALMARK *Emesis zela*   **PL. 22**

1 ¹⁄₁₆–1 ⁵⁄₁₆ in. (28–33 mm). Male with pointed forewing showing irregular outer margin, female with rounded forewing. Upperside: *Brown with darkened discal cell on forewing and broadly diffuse yellow patch on hindwing.* Underside: Yellow-brown with minute black spots. **SIMILAR SPECIES:** Ares metalmark lacks black cell mark, has black submarginal spots on forewing, and a more sharply defined yellow patch on hindwing. **EARLY STAGES:** Not reported. **FOOD:** Probably oak. **FLIGHT:** Late Feb.–early Sept. (2 flights). **RANGE:** Ariz. and sw. N.M. south along the Sierra Madre Occidentale to cen. Mex. **HABITAT:** Tree-lined canyons and small streams in mountains or foothills. **REMARKS:** This and the next species are often confused and not clearly distinguished unless carefully studied.

ARES METALMARK *Emesis ares*   **PL. 22**

1 ⅛–1 ⁵⁄₁₆ in. (29–34 mm). Male with pointed forewing showing irregular outer margin, female with rounded forewing. Upperside: Forewing *dark brown with submarginal black dashes.* Hindwing reddish brown with a *sharply delimited yellow patch* on forward portion. Underside: Yellow-brown with scattered minute black spots. **SIMILAR SPECIES:** Zela Metalmark has black cell mark, lacks black submarginal spots on forewing, and has more diffuse yellow patch on hindwing. **EARLY STAGES:** Not reported. **FOOD:** Oblong-leafed oak and Emory oak. **FLIGHT:** Aug.–mid-Sept. (1 flight). **RANGE:** Se. Ariz. and sw. N.M. south into the Sierra Madre Occidentale of w. Mex. **HABITAT:** Tree-lined streams and canyons in foothills and

mountains. **REMARKS:** The Zela and Ares Metalmarks may be found together nectaring on seepwillow or milkweed flower patches in late summer.

MARIA'S METALMARK *Lasaia maria* **SEE PHOTOGRAPH**

¹⁵/₁₆–1 ⅛ in. (24–29 mm). Forewing pointed. *Outer margin* of both wings with *slight concavities.* Upperside: Male *dull iridescent blue* with a few dark spots. Female orange-brown or gray-brown suffused with steely blue (can be almost as blue as male). **FOOD:** Unknown. **EARLY STAGES:** Not reported. **FLIGHT:** March–early Dec. (several flights). **RANGE:** Nw. Mex. (Sonora) south along w. Mex. to cen. Guatemala. Found once in se. Ariz. **HABITAT:** Canyons with tropical dry forest or thorn scrub. **REMARKS:** Most often seen on wet gravelly or sandy spots along streams.

Male Maria's Metalmark at moisture, Sinaloa state, Mex. Recently reported for se. Ariz. Note dull blue appearance above. These extremely fast-flying butterflies may be seen along small streams.

Mormon Metalmark (subspecies mormo) nectaring at corymbose buckwheat, Colorado National Monument, Colo. Adults are most often seen nectaring on their buckwheat hosts, but also favor yellow compsite flowers.

MORMON METALMARK *Apodemia mormo* PL. 22

1–1 ³⁄₁₆ in. (25–31 mm). Sexes similar. Fringes white with black checks at vein endings. Upperside: *Forewing black with white spots, red-orange to yellow-orange at base.* White spot in cell sometimes covered with red-orange scaling (subspecies *langei*). Hindwing *black with small white spots* (subspecies *mormo* and *langei*) or with areas of *red-orange or orange* (subspecies *cythera*) or yellow to yellow-orange (subspecies *tuolumnensis*). **SIMILAR SPECIES:** Behr's Metalmarks fly in spring or early summer, while similar forms of the Mormon Metalmark (subspecies *cythera*) fly in late summer or fall. Some forms of the Sonoran Metalmark (subspecies *deserti*) appear like black hindwing forms of the Mormon but have a gray cast to their hindwings and are found in association with Inflated Buckwheat in s. Calif. In se. Ariz. black hindwing forms of the Mormon are found near some locations where the red-orange hindwing forms of the Sonoran Metalmark occur

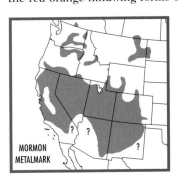

MORMON METALMARK

BEHR'S METALMARK

and may even be found in the same season. **EARLY STAGES:** Caterpillar dark violet with 4 rows of long spines emerging from black bases. **FOOD:** Several species of wild buckwheats. **FLIGHT:** April–Oct. (usually 1 summer or fall flight). **RANGE:** S. B.C. and s. Sask. through much of w. U.S. to s. Calif., s. Ariz, and nw. Mex. **HABITAT:** Arid, open, sunny habitats including rocky slopes, sand dunes, and sagebrush flats. **REMARKS:** The Mormon Metalmark and its relatives form a group of butterflies with varying appearances and adaptations to different plants, usually wild buckwheats. On the basis of populations with very different-appearing adults occurring close to each other or at the same location in different seasons, the group must be comprised of more than a single species. On the recommendation of Gordon Pratt, I divide most of the group into 3 species that differ in their morphology, seasonality, development rates, and adaptation to different hosts. A fourth species, *A. duryi*, is considered on the recommendations of Greg Forbes and Richard Holland. Further research will no doubt modify this treatment. Lange's Metalmark (subspecies *langei*), restricted to the Antioch National Wildlife Refuges in cen. Calif., is found on about 50 acres of sand dunes and is endangered.

BEHR'S METALMARK *Apodemia virgulti*   PL. 22

¾–1⁵⁄₁₆ in. (19–24 mm). Upperside: Wings ranging from black at outer edges to entirely black, *remainder of wings red-orange to yellow-orange with white spots, some black-edged.* **SIMILAR SPECIES:** Some populations of Mormon Metalmark resemble Behr's Metalmarks but the adults fly in late summer or fall—not spring or early summer. **EARLY STAGES:** Caterpillar not reported. **FOOD:** Usually fasciculate buckwheat but Wright's buckwheat for subspecies *dialeuca*. **FLIGHT:** March–Sept. (1 flight, rarely 2), all year in coastal San Diego Co. (3–4 flights). **RANGE:** Cen. Calif. south to cen. Baja Calif. **HABITAT:** Chaparral (brushland) with dense low shrubbery to scattered low shrubs in sand dunes or rocky slopes.

SONORAN METALMARK *Apodemia mejicanus*   PL. 22

⅞–1¹⁄₁₆ in. (23–33 mm). Upperside: Forewing with *outer portion black with white spots. Basal two-thirds red-orange to yellow-orange with scattered white spots—some black-edged.* Hindwing varies from dark gray with white spots (subspecies *deserti*) to red-orange or yellow-orange with black areas and white spots (subspecies *mejicanus*). **SIMILAR SPECIES:** Mormon Metalmark has upper surface of hindwing completely black with small white spots; and flies in late summer or fall. Some Sonoran Metalmark populations have butterflies with gray-black hindwings. **EARLY STAGES:** Caterpillar purplish blue with clumps of short black spines. Head

black. **FOOD:** Inflated Buckwheat, Wright's Buckwheat, other buckwheats, and possibly *Kramerias*. **FLIGHT:** Mid-Feb.–mid-Nov. (2 or more flights). **RANGE:** Se. Calif. and s. Ariz. south to s. Baja Calif. and nw. Mex. **HABITAT:** Desert alluvial fans and flats, oak grasslands. **REMARKS:** The type location is purported to be in the mountains of Sinaloa, Mex. It is unclear if these butterflies match the concept presented here. Very large individuals are found in coastal Sonora, Mex., and the Cape region of s. Baja Calif. (subspecies *maxima*).

MEXICAN METALMARK *Apodemia duryi*   PL. 22

1–1 ⁵⁄₁₆ in. (25–33 mm). Upperside: *Yellow-orange with white spots (some black-edged) and black outer areas.* **SIMILAR SPECIES:** Sonoran Metalmarks are usually darker orange or red-orange, not yellow. **EARLY STAGES:** Not reported. **FOOD:** *Kramerias*. **FLIGHT:** Late April–early Oct. (2–3 flights). **RANGE:** S. N.M. and w. Tex. south into n. Mex. **HABITAT:** Dry, rocky, arid slopes and ridges. **REMARKS:** Much remains to be learned about this species and its relationships to other members of the group.

HEPBURN'S METALMARK *Apodemia hepburni*   PL. 22

¹³⁄₁₆–⁷⁄₈ in. (21–23 mm). Upperside: *Brown with tiny white spots* on both wings and *trace of orange scaling* at wing bases. Lacks white marginal spots. **SIMILAR SPECIES:** Palmer's Metalmark has orange on outer margins, has marginal row of white spots, and more orange on basal area. **FOOD:** Unknown. **EARLY STAGES:** Not reported. **FLIGHT:** Mar.–Nov. (several flights) in Mex. **RANGE:** Se. Ariz. and w. Tex. (rare stray) south into Mex. **HABITAT:** Dry deserts, thorn scrub, and dry forest. **REMARKS:** Adults nectar at flowers of yellow composites.

Hepburn's Metalmark nectaring at yellow composite, Sonora state, Mex. Note pattern on underside is very similar to that of Palmer's Metalmark.

PALMER'S METALMARK *Apodemia palmeri* **PL. 22**

⅝–¹³⁄₁₆ in. (16–21 mm). Upperside: *Brown* with variable amount of *orange at margins*, white spot pattern, and orange on basal half. Underside: *Pale orange with white spots and postmedian band.* **SIMILAR SPECIES:** Mexican Metalmark and Mormon Metalmark are larger, have larger white spots, and are not brown above. They also do not associate with thorny legumes. **EARLY STAGES:** Caterpillar pale blue-green with rows of short white hair tufts and with lemon yellow line up back and along sides. **FOOD:** Honey mesquite. **FLIGHT:** Late March–Nov. (3 flights). **RANGE:** S. Calif., s. Nev., sw. Utah, Ariz., s. N.M., and w. Tex. south into n. Mex. **HABITAT:** Low deserts, especially dry watercourses, with thorn scrub, often dense. **REMARKS:** Adults often perch on host plant, but may nectar at other plants such as seepwillow.

CRESCENT METALMARK **SEE PHOTOGRAPH**
Apodemia phyciodoides

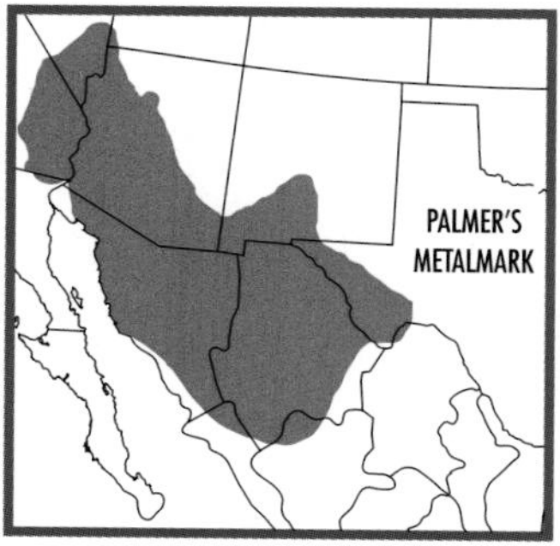

⅞ in. (22–23 mm). Upperside: Front edge of forewing with 2 small white spots just below apex. Remainder of *wings orange-red with black-lined veins and bars* resulting in checkerspot or crescentlike pattern. Underside: Similar to that of Palmer's Metalmark with *tan hindwing having white postbasal and postmedian bands.* **SIMILAR SPECIES:** Nais Metalmark

Male Crescent Metalmark perching on ground, Sonora state, Mex. Adults probably use dry streambeds as their usually perching and mate-location sites. Below they resemble Palmer's Metalmarks.

is larger, has row of submarginal black spots on both wings, and has underside of hindwing largely white with a few red-orange marks. **EARLY STAGES:** Not reported. **FOOD:** *Clematis.* **FLIGHT:** March–Oct. (3 or more flights). **RANGE:** Se. Ariz. south to mountains of e. Sonora and w. Chihuahua, Mex. **HABITAT:** Streambeds or rocky roads in steep mountains near lower edge of oak zone. **REMARKS:** Described from the Chiricahua Mts. of se. Ariz. but not seen there for many years. The species may still occur in Ariz.

NAIS METALMARK *Apodemia nais* PL. 22

1–1 ³⁄₆ in. (25–31 mm). Upperside: *Red-orange* with pattern of black dots and dashes. *Small white mark* on forewing costa near tip. Underside: Forewing orange with black dots, apex white. Hindwing *white with black dots and orange submarginal band.* **SIMILAR SPECIES:** Chisos Metalmark is similar but is not found in range of Nais Metalmark. **EARLY STAGES:** Caterpillar pale pink above with clusters of short black hairs and dark line up back. **FOOD:** Mountain snowbush. **FLIGHT:** Mid-June–mid-Aug. (1 flight). **RANGE:** N. Colo. south through Ariz., and N.M. and to nw. Mex. **HABITAT:** Sunny flats and slope in mountains. **REMARKS:** Adults spend much time at flowers such as dogbane, mountain snowbush, and orange milkweed.

NAIS METALMARK

CHISOS METALMARK

Chisos Metalmark, native to Big Bend National Park, Texas. Compare with illustration of Nais Metalmark (Plate 22). Note hindwing has complete submarginal row of black dots and arrowhead-like dashes. Photo by C. D. Ferris.

CHISOS METALMARK *Apodemia chisosensis*   **SEE PHOTOGRAPH**
1 ⅟₁₆–1 ¼ in. (27–32 mm). Upperside: Similar to Nais Metalmark but lacks suffusion of dark scaling above. Female sometimes has white submarginal band on forewing. Underside: Forewing with white patch at tip. Hindwing with *complete submarginal row of distinct black spots and arrowhead-like dashes.* **SIMILAR SPECIES:** Nais Metalmark has black suffusion above, has only small white patch amid orange on forewing tip below, and underside of hindwing has only partial postmedian band of small, more regular black spots. **EARLY STAGES:** Not reported. **FOOD:** Havard's plum. **FLIGHT:** May and Aug. (2 flights). **RANGE:** Chisos Mts., Big Bend National Park, Tex. **HABITAT:** Slopes and ridges with host plant. **REMARKS:** This butterfly is an isolated relict in the Chisos Mts. of Texas' Big Bend region.

12

TRUE BUTTERFLIES:
SUPERFAMILY PAPILIONOIDEA
BRUSHFOOTS: FAMILY NYMPHALIDAE

Butterflies of this highly variable family are found worldwide, but they are especially rich in the tropics; there are more species in this family than in any other. Some prefer to split this family into several smaller ones, but this book follows the conservative approach of recognizing the major groups as subfamilies. The adults vary from small to large. The front pair of legs is reduced and not used for walking—hence the family name. Wing shape is highly variable: some species have irregular margins (anglewings and commas), and others have long taillike projections (daggerwings). Browns, oranges, yellows, and blacks are frequent colors, while iridescent structural colors such as blues and purples are rare. Both perching and patrolling mate-location strategies occur. Adults of some groups feed primarily on flower nectar, while those of others do not visit flowers at all, but instead feed on sap flows, rotting fruit, dung, or animal carcasses. Adults of the long-wings (genus *Heliconius*) are unusual in their habitat of collecting pollen and then absorbing proteins through the proboscis. Adults of some groups are the longest-lived butterflies, surviving 6 11 months. Eggs are laid in clusters, in columns, or singly, sometimes not directly on the host plant. The caterpillars of some are communal, feeding in groups during their early instars. Caterpillars of many species have rows of bristly tubercles, while others have only scattered short setae. Pupae of most species hang from a silk mat. Overwintering may be as larvae or adults.

SNOUTS: SUBFAMILY LIBYTHEINAE

This small family has one to a few medium-sized species in each of the world's temperate and tropical regions. The family contains only about 1 0 species. In North America there is only one species. The male front legs are reduced and are not used for walking. Pe-

riodically, adults migrate in
massive numbers. The adults
often perch head down on
twigs or small branches, where
they mimic dead leaves—a behavior that is enhanced by the
long proboscis, which might
appear as the leaf petiole.
Males patrol host plants in
search of females. Eggs are laid
in small groups on host leaves.
Winter is passed by adults.
Adults visit flowers for nectar.

AMERICAN
SNOUT

Our species may undergo vast emigrations, especially in Tex. and
Arizona. Here I consider that our North American snouts all represent a single species.

AMERICAN SNOUT *Libytheana carinenta* PL. 22

1 ⅜–1 ¹³⁄₁₆ in. (35–46 mm). Sexes are similar. *Forewing tips squared
off*, extended at apex; *beaklike labial palps ("nose")*. Upperside:
Forewing with white spots on apical third and *orange patches
along inner margin and base*. Underside: Hindwing either *mottled
or uniformly violet-gray*. The species sometimes engages in huge
migrations. Previously, our species was referred to as *L. bachmanii*, but it has been shown that our butterfly is the same as that
in the American tropics. **EARLY STAGES:** Caterpillar is dark green with
lateral and middorsal yellow stripes. Front swollen, with 2 black
tubercles; last segment tapered abruptly. **FOOD:** Hackberries and
Sugarberry. **FLIGHT:** Two broods annually; adults overwinter in
south, including our Southwest, and in tropics. First flight mid-
May–June, second brood emerges early Aug. **RANGE:** Resident from
s. Ariz., s. N.M., and w. Tex. and Southeast south into Mex. and
through the lowland tropics to Argentina. Also in the West Indies.
Periodic migrant and colonist north to cen. Calif., Nev., Utah, se.
Wyo., N.D., e. U.S., and s. Ont. **HABITAT:** Thorn scrub, river woods,
desert mountains, and fields. **REMARKS:** When resting on twigs,
adults resemble dead leaves. The snout (palpi) looks like a leaf
petiole. Adults nectar at lantana, rabbitbrush, seepwillow, and
many other plants.

LONGWINGS: SUBFAMILY HELICONIINAE

This group is richest in the American tropics, but several genera
are prominent in the Northern Hemisphere, including the fritillaries or silverspots (genus *Speyeria*) and lesser fritillaries (genus

GULF
FRITILLARY

Boloria). The adults of some are long-lived, and several are distasteful. Many other species mimic the distasteful butterflies of this group. Males patrol in search of recently emerged females or chrysalids that are about to produce an adult. Life span is long, as long as six months in some instances. The adults of *Heliconius* are unique in that they intentionally collect pollen in their proboscis. The proteins in the pollen are absorbed through the wall of the proboscis.

GULF FRITILLARY *Agraulis vanillae*   PL. 23

2¼–3¼ in. (58–82 mm). Flies steadily with shallow wingbeats. Forewings pointed. Upperside: *Bright orange* with black marks and 3 white black-rimmed spots. Underside: Hindwing and apex with *elongated, iridescent silver spots*. **SIMILAR SPECIES:** Mexican Silverspot is more brown above and has denser iridescent silver patches below. **EARLY STAGES:** Caterpillar glossy black with red-orange lateral and dorsal stripes; 4 longitudinal rows of long complex spines. **FOOD:** Several passion-vine species. In much of our area on ornamental vines in towns. **FLIGHT:** All year in s. Calif. and s. Ariz; number of broods not determined. Found northward Jan. to early Nov. **RANGE:** Resident in Southwest, s. U.S., Mex., Cen. Amer., West Indies, and S. Amer. Regular vagrant north to cen. U.S., rare farther north. Only 1 record for Canada (sw. Man.). Also introduced to Hawaii. **HABITAT:** Deserts, woodland edges, brushy fields, city gardens.

MEXICAN SILVERSPOT *Dione moneta*   PL. 23

3–3¼ in. (76–82 mm). Upperside *dull orange*, darker at wing base; veins lined with black. Underside: Forewing *basal half with cloudy black marks*. Hindwing with dense pattern of *elongate iridescent silver spots*. **SIMILAR SPECIES:** Gulf Fritillary is bright orange. Underside of forewing with more extensive orange, hindwing with fewer silver spots. **EARLY STAGES:** Caterpillar is dark brown with orange and gray spots; body with 4 rows of spines. **FOOD:** Passion-vines. **FLIGHT:** All year in tropics; April–Dec. in Tex. **RANGE:** Periodic stray to cen. and w. Tex., s. N.M., and s. Calif., occasionally reproduces in s. Tex.; resident throughout highlands in mainland tropical Amer. **HABITAT:** Openings and edges of mid-elevation evergreen forests in tropics; known from several habitats in Tex.

JULIA *Dryas julia* PL. 23

3–3¼ in. (74–82 mm). Forewings pointed. Male *bright orange above and below*. Upperside: *Narrow black border on outer margin of hindwing*. Female duller, with more extensive black markings above. **EARLY STAGES:** Caterpillar is dark brown with fine, transverse black lines and spots. Head white with black marks and 2 black tubercles. **FOOD:** Passionvines (*Passiflora lutea* in s. Tex.). **FLIGHT:** All year in s. Fla. and s. Tex.; strays north in summer (several flights). **RANGE:** Resident in s. Tex. and peninsular Fla., West Indies, Mex., and Cen. Amer. south to Brazil. Rare stray in our area north to e. Colo., w. Kans., and e. Neb. **HABITAT:** Openings and edges of subtropical hammocks; often found in nearby fields.

ISABELLA'S HELICONIAN *Eueides isabella* PL. 23

3¹⁄₁₆–3½ in. (78–90 mm). Forewing elongated but with apex rounded. Wings similar above and below. Apical half of forewing *black with yellow patches*. Black stripe through orange area along inner margin. Hindwing orange with *2 black stripes across median area and black white-dotted outer margin*. **SIMILAR SPECIES:** Unrelated Tiger Mimic-Queen, one of a large group of similar distasteful mimics, has a nearly identical pattern, but the 2 hindwing stripes are connected outwardly. **EARLY STAGES:** Caterpillar with upper body black with narrow white transverse bands on back and yellow lateral stripes; orange patch on segments 8 and 9. Head black, spotted white with 2 black tubercles. **FOOD:** Passionvines. **FLIGHT:** All year in tropics; April–July in U.S. **RANGE:** Mex. and West Indies south to Brazil. Rare stray to se. Ariz., N.M., Kans., and w. Tex. More regular to e. Tex. **HABITAT:** Subtropical scrub, woodland edges, and brushy fields.

ZEBRA *Heliconius charithonius* PL. 23

2½–3⅝ in. (65–92 mm). Unique. Wings long and narrow; *black with narrow pale yellow stripes*. **EARLY STAGES:** Caterpillar is creamy white with many fine transverse bands and 6 rows of branched black spines. Head pale yellow. **FOOD:** Passionvines. **FLIGHT:** Year-round resident in s. Fla. and s. Tex. (several flights), found farther north in warmer months. **RANGE:** In our area, an uncommon stray to s. Calif., s. Ariz., N.M., w. Tex., and w. plains states. Resident from peninsular Fla. and s. Tex. through West Indies,

Mex., and Cen. Amer. to S. Amer. **HABITAT:** Tropical hammocks, river forests, edges. **REMARKS:** Where resident in the tropics, it roosts in small to large clusters. The adults return to the same roost night after night.

VARIEGATED FRITILLARY *Euptoieta claudia* **PL. 23**

1 ⅜–2¾ in. (36–72 mm). Flies low with shallow wing beats. Often flutters wings when at flowers. Orange with black markings. Forewing pointed, hindwing *apex and outer margin with angles.* Upperside: Black marginal spots between veins. Underside: Hindwing *mottled without silver spots.* **SIMILAR SPECIES:** (1) Mexican Fritillary is brighter, more uniform orange, and has fewer black markings. (2) Many *Speyeria* fritillaries have pattern of iridescent silver marks on underside of hindwing. **EARLY STAGES:** Caterpillar red-orange with dorsal and lateral stripes of alternating black and white patches and 6 rows of black spines. **FOOD:** Violets, wild flax, and a wide variety of plants in other families. **FLIGHT:** All year in s. Ariz., s. N.M., and w. Tex. (several flights), stray northward, and regular colonist on Great Plains (1 or 2 flights). **RANGE:** Resident from s. U.S. south through higher elevations in tropical Amer. to Argentina. Also highlands of Cuba, Puerto Rico, and Jamaica. Regular colonist north through most of U.S. (except Pacific Northwest) to s. Canada. **HABITAT:** Wide variety of open, sunny areas —waste fields, prairies, pastures, etc. **REMARKS:** Although this is a tropical butterfly that cannot survive freezing winters, it is a highly successful wanderer and colonist on the Great Plains, where it is often abundant.

MEXICAN FRITILLARY *Euptoieta hegesia* **PL. 23**

2 9/16–2 15/16 in. (66–74 mm). Hindwing margins *without strong angles.* Upperside: Bright orange. Wings lack contrast between basal

and outer portions. *Basal half is plain orange, unpatterned.* Underside: Hindwing *orange-brown with muted pattern.* **SIMILAR SPECIES:** Variegated Fritillary has angled fore- and hindwings, more complex and contrasting pattern above, and less uniform pattern below. **EARLY STAGES:** Caterpillar with head and body shining red, dorsal and lateral black-edged silver lines, 6 rows of black spines, head with 2 black clubbed horns. **FOOD:** *Turneras*, passionvines, and morning glories. **FLIGHT:** All year in tropics and s. Tex., April–Nov. in se. Ariz. **RANGE:** Resident in Mex., Cen. Amer., and West Indies. Vagrant to s. Calif., s. Ariz., sw. N.M., w. and cen. Tex. **HABITAT:** Fields, openings, edges in tropical lowlands and foothills.

SILVERED FRITILLARIES: GENUS *Speyeria* SCUDDER

This New World group comprises 16 species. All of these fritillaries are very similar, and in parts of the West, several species that occur together may be difficult even for experts to identify. The iridescent silver spots on the underside of the hindwings owe their metallic appearance to reflected light rather than to pigment. Some western species—Unsilvered and Hydaspe Fritillaries—always lack silver spots, and others—Northwestern, Callippe, Great Basin, Zerene, and Mormon Fritillaries—sometimes lack them. The adults are often found at flowers, especially those of milkweeds, mints, rabbitbrush, and thistles. All species are single-brooded. Females of some species display delayed maturation of their eggs so that they may be laid at the end of the summer. Males patrol suitable habitats in search of females. The females drop their eggs in the vicinity of dried-up violets, foretelling the presence of fresh foliage the following spring. The eggs hatch in the fall, and the young first-instar caterpillars overwinter without feeding. In the spring when the violets leaf out, the caterpillars complete their development, feeding primarily at night.

GREAT SPANGLED FRITILLARY *Speyeria cybele*   **PL. 23**
2⅜–3⅜ in. (66–90 mm). Large. Upperside: Male tawny. *Female white or pale* with black pattern in much of the West (leto group), but tawny on Great Plains. Male *with black scaling on forewing veins.* Underside: *Broad pale submarginal band on hindwing.* **SIMILAR SPECIES:** In most of the West, the most similar species that might be found with the Great Spangled is the (1) Aphrodite Fritillary, which has a narrower pale submarginal band on the underside of the hindwing. (2) Nokomis Fritillary is slightly larger, has brighter cinnamon males, and usually flies later. **EARLY STAGES:** Caterpillar is velvety above and chocolate brown below, black

Great-spangled Fritillary (subspecies char-lottei) nectaring on thistle, Converse Co., Wyo. Very similar to subspecies leto, this is the most frequent appearance of western males. Note small size of silver spots.

spines are red-yellow at base. Dorsal double row of gray dots. **FOOD:** Violets. **FLIGHT:** Mid-June–Sept., occasionally early Oct. (1 brood). **RANGE:** Cen. Canada south to cen. Calif., cen. Nev., s. Utah, n. N.M., and Okla. In East south to n. Ga. and cen. Ark. **HABITAT:** Open meadows, aspen-lined streams or glades, and valleys. Fields, meadows, and power-line cuts in East. **REMARKS:** The eastern and western populations look like separate species, but they blend in Mont. and Alta. The Great Spangled may be a declining species in the West because of long-term habitat changes, particularly loss of meadow habitats and aspen groves.

APHRODITE FRITILLARY *Speyeria aphrodite*   PL. 23

2¼–3 in. (58–76mm). Geographically variable. Upperside: Male red-orange forewing with *small black spot below cell and without heavy black scaling on veins.* Underside: Hindwing with *pale submarginal band narrow or lacking.* **SIMILAR SPECIES:** (1) Great Span-

Male Aphrodite Fritillary nectaring at sunflower, Larimer Co., Colo. Note bright red-orange color and weakly expressed black along veins.

gled Fritillary is larger, has broader submarginal band on underside hindwing. (2) Atlantis Fritillary is smaller, has narrow black margins above, with a darker hindwing disk and narrower pale submarginal band on hindwing underside. **EARLY STAGES:** Caterpillar brown-black with a dorsal black line, spines ocher or brown. **FOOD:** Violets. **FLIGHT:** Mid-May–late Oct. (1 flight). **RANGE:** S. Canada south to n. N.M., with an isolated population in White Mts. of e. Ariz. In East from N.S. and Prince Edward Is. south in Appalachians to n. Ga. **HABITAT:** Moist prairies, foothills, mountain meadows. **REMARKS:** Adults nectar avidly at *Monarda*, thistles, and rabbitbrush.

REGAL FRITILLARY *Speyeria idalia* PL. 23

2¹¹⁄₁₆–3⅝ in. (68–93 mm). Unique. Large. Upperside: *Forewing red-orange with ornate black marks.* Hindwing *black with postmedian row of white spots and submarginal row of orange (male) or white (female) spots.* **EARLY STAGES:** Caterpillar velvety black with ocher-yellow or dull orange mottlings. Dorsal spines black-tipped silver-white. **FOOD:** Violets. **FLIGHT:** Mid-June–mid-Aug., occasionally to mid-Oct. (1 brood). **RANGE:** Formerly from Man. south through plains to cen. Colo., Kans., ne. Okla, Mo., and in East from N.B. south to nw. N.C. Rapidly declining, now rare or absent

REGAL FRITILLARY

Female Regal Fritillary basking, Orange Co., Va. Note the ornate appearance and primarily black hindwing. Females have 2 rows of white spots on the hindwings, while males have 1 white row and 1 orange row. Photo by George Krizek.

from areas east of the Mississippi R. Still common only in midgrass and tall-grass prairie, mainly in preserves to east. **HABITAT:** Wet fields, marshes, midgrass and tall-grass prairie. **REMARKS:** Disappearing or declining in abundance over most of its range. Adults may wander long distances, and many records represent observations of single wandering individuals.

NOKOMIS FRITILLARY *Speyeria nokomis* **PL. 23**

2⅖–3¹⁄₁₆ in. (63–78 mm.) Upperside: *Male cinnamon-orange with* black pattern. *Female white with black pattern, especially strong at base.* Underside: Hindwing *with relatively small silver spots.* Hindwing *"disk" on male light to dark brown, submarginal band tan; on female "disk" gray-green with submarginal band yellow-green.* **SIMILAR SPECIES:** Great Spangled Fritillary is smaller, not as bright, and flies earlier. **EARLY STAGES:** Caterpillar yellow-orange with

NOKOMIS FRITILLARY

Local colonies. Several extirpated or declining.

EDWARDS' FRITILLARY

Female Nokomis Fritillary basking on thistle, N.M. Note pale hindwing band. Adults strongly favor thistles as nectar plants but also visit a few others. Photo by Steve Cary.

rows of yellow-orange spines. Black patches surround spines on back and side. Two black cross stripes at rear of each segment. **FOOD:** Violets. **FLIGHT:** Mid-July–late Sept. (1 flight). **RANGE:** E. Calif., Nev., Utah, and w. Colo. south through e. Ariz. and N.M. to n. Mex. **HABITAT:** Spring seeps and associated marshes with flowing water. **REMARKS:** Many populations have disappeared because of capping of springs, lowering of water tables by pumping, and habitat modification. Adults nectar avidly at thistles.

EDWARDS' FRITILLARY *Speyeria edwardsii*   **PL. 24**

2–2¾ in. (51–70 mm). Large. *Forewings pointed.* Upperside: *Postmedian and marginal spots distinctly paler than surrounding orange ground color. Bold black border* on outer margins of both wings. Underside: *Green or gray-green with elongate metallic silver marks and narrow buff submarginal band.* **SIMILAR SPECIES:** (1) Callippe Fritillary is usually smaller, lacks black border above, and underside hindwing ground is blue-green where it co-occurs. (2) Coronis Fritillary is usually smaller, has rounder forewings, broader pale submarginal band below, and little hint of green. **EARLY STAGES:** Caterpillar dark yellow above, gray along sides with a black dorsal line. **FOOD:** Violets. **FLIGHT:** Mid-May–late Oct. (1 flight). **RANGE:** Short-grass prairie and w. portions of Rockies from s. Alta. east to the cen. Dakotas and w. Neb., south to w. Okla. and n. N.M. **HABITAT:** Short-grass prairie, foothills, meadows, and valleys. **REMARKS:** Most common on short-grass prairies, this butterfly seems to migrate into the mountains during midsummer with females moving back to prairies during late summer when they lay their eggs.

CORONIS FRITILLARY *Speyeria coronis* PL. 24

1 ⁵⁄₁₆–2½ in. (49–65 mm). Upperside: Orange to pale orange, sometimes with postmedian and marginal spots paler that surrounding ground. Underside: Hindwing with *silver spots in marginal row rounded inward or flattened and capped with pale green or greenish brown. Submarginal band pale straw yellow or pale buff.* SIMILAR SPECIES: (1) Zerene Fritillary (east of Calif.) has postmedian spots more elongate, marginal silver spots rounded or slightly triangular and capped with brown. Submarginal band is duller buff. (2) Aphrodite Fritillary has hindwing below with silver spots more elongate and marginal silver spots more triangular and capped with brown or purplish brown. EARLY STAGES: Caterpillar mottled brown and black; lateral spine row orange, others black. FOOD: Violets. FLIGHT: Late May–Oct. (1 flight). RANGE: Pacific Coast from n. Wash. south to nw. Baja Calif. Norte east through Great Basin and cen. Rockies to high plains of e. Mont, w. S.D., w. Neb., and s.-cen. Colo. HABITAT: Many, including oak woodlands, brushy foothills, mixed conifer forests, meadows, and sagebrush flats. REMARKS: Most closely related to Zerene Fritillary and sometimes almost impossible to separate in field. Carol's Fritillary (*Speyeria carolae*) of southern Nevada's Clark Mts. is an isolated intermediate between the two and has recently been judged a separate species.

ZERENE FRITILLARY *Speyeria zerene* PL. 24

1 ⅞–2⅝ in. (48–67 mm.) Upperside: Variable. Ranging from red-orange through brown to tan. Black pattern variable. Some populations with extensive black at base. Intermountain populations paler with less black. Underside: Ground color ranging from brown-purple (Sierra Nevada of Calif.) to pale yellow-brown (Nev., Utah). Spot pattern usually silvered, but is unsilvered in n.

Coast Range and Sierra Nevada of Calif. *Postmedian spots round to elongate with outward brown extensions. Submarginal spots rounded with brown caps.* **SIMILAR SPECIES:** (1) Coronis Fritillary is never reddish above, has rounder postmedian silver spots, and has green or greenish brown caps to submarginal somewhat flattened silver spots below. (2) In Sierra Nevada of Calif., Hydaspe Fritillary has rounder spots on hindwing below, submarginal spots are more triangular. **EARLY STAGES:** Caterpillar orangish to gray-tan with brown-black marking near base of gray-based spines. **FOOD:** Violets. **FLIGHT:** Late May–early Sept. (1 flight). **RANGE:** Se. Alaska and sw. Canada south through most of w. U.S. to cen. Calif., Utah, and sw. Colo. **HABITAT:** Several, including coastal salt-spray meadows, open montane conifer forests, and sagebrush flats. **REMARKS:** Several subspecies: Oregon Silverspot (subspecies *hippolyta*), Behren's Silverspot (subspecies *behrensii*), and Myrtle's Silverspot (subspecies *myrtleae*) are listed as threatened or endangered species by the U.S. Fish and Wildlife Service.

CALLIPPE FRITILLARY *Speyeria callippe* PL. 24

1 ⅞–2½ in. (47–65 mm). Upperside: Variable, pale tan to bright orange, sometimes with heavy black scaling. *Postmedian and marginal spots on hindwing paler than surrounding ground color.* Underside: Populations west of the Cascade-Sierra Nevada crests have tan, brown, or red-brown ground with either silver or unsilvered spots and a *tan submarginal band.* To the east the butterflies vary from pale green to deep blue-green either *without a submarginal band or only a narrow yellow-green band.* **SIMILAR SPECIES:** (1) Edwards' Fritillary is larger, has pointed forewings, and is more gray-green below. (2) West of the Cascade-Sierra Nevada crests, the Coronis Fritillary is usually larger with more rounded marginal silver spots below. **EARLY STAGES:** Caterpillar mottled brown and black with black dorsal line. **FOOD:** Violets. **FLIGHT:** April–Sept. (1 brood). **RANGE:** Pacific Coast from se. B.C. south to nw. Baja Calif. Norte west through Great Basin and Rockies to s. Man., w. S.D., w. Neb., and cen. Colo. **HABITAT:** Many, including grasslands, oak woodland, valleys, brushy hillsides, and prairie ridges. **REMARKS:** In most areas males patrol hilltops awaiting females; while in Calif. males may patrol grasslands or slopes and avoid hill-

CALLIPPE FRITILLARY

tops. Males of most other *Speyeria* species patrol flats or slopes. Coastal n. Calif. population (subspecies *callippe*) is listed as endangered by the U.S. Fish and Wildlife Service.

GREAT BASIN FRITILLARY *Speyeria egleis*　　　PL. 24

1 ¾–2 ¼ in. (44–58 mm). Upperside: Orange to brown with *paler postmedian and marginal spots. Most individuals have dark scaling on basal half of wings.* Underside: The "disk" is red-brown, brown, tan, or greenish, and the *postmedian spots are smaller than most other Speyeria species and relatively elongate.* The spots may be silvered or unsilvered. The *marginal spots are slightly triangular to rounded with brown or greenish caps.* **SIMILAR SPECIES:** Coronis and Zerene Fritillaries are usually larger and have paler wing bases above and larger, more rounded postmedian spots below. **EARLY STAGES:** Caterpillar gray-brown with dark stripe inside yellow band up middle of back. White-edged black streaks around black-tipped spines on back. **FOOD:** Violets. **FLIGHT:** Early June–early Oct. (1 flight). **RANGE:** Se. B.C., w. Ore., Idaho, and w. Mont. south to s. Calif., cen. Utah, and nw. Colo. **HABITAT:** Mixed woodlands, open rocky slopes, meadows, and streambanks.

UNSILVERED FRITILLARY *Speyeria adiaste*　　　PL. 24

1 ¾–2 ¼ in. (45–57 mm). Upperside: Red brown to pale brown. Underside: Reddish orange to pale tan. *Spot pattern unsilvered and almost obsolete.* **SIMILAR SPECIES:** None. Other fritillaries in its range have silvered spots. **EARLY STAGES:** Caterpillar similar to that of Callippe Fritillary. **FOOD:** Violets. **FLIGHT:** June–early Sept. (1 flight). **RANGE:** Coast and Transverse Ranges of coastal cen. and formerly s. Calif. **HABITAT:** Grassy slopes, mixed chaparral and oak woodland, openings in redwood forests. **REMARKS:** The pale southern subspecies *atossa* has been extinct since 1959. Adults of surviving populations nectar at California Buckeye and thistles.

GREAT BASIN FRITILLARY

UNSILVERED FRITILLARY

extirpated

Male Unsilvered Fritillary nectaring on thistle, Monterey Co., Calif. Adults will also nectar at California buckeye flowers. Males will fly to ridgetops to seek females. This is a rare and declining species.

ATLANTIS FRITILLARY *Speyeria atlantis*   PL. 24

1 ⁵⁄₁₆–2⁷⁄₁₆ in. (49–62 mm). Upperside: Forewing has *black outer margin* and male has *black scaling on veins*. Underside: Hindwing has *chocolate or purplish brown disk with narrow pale submarginal band. Spots are always silvered.* **SIMILAR SPECIES:** (1) Aphrodite Fritillary has pale outer margins, males do not have darkened veins, and the hindwing disk below is not darkened. (2) Northwestern Fritillary sometimes lacks black marginal band on upperside; red-brown or orangish disk on underside of hindwing. Spot on underside of hindwing often unsilvered, but some populations may have silvered spots. **EARLY STAGES:** Caterpillar mottled black and brown with black-tipped orange-tan spines and 2 creamy lines up middle of back. **FOOD:** Violets. **FLIGHT:** Mid-June–Sept. (1 flight). **RANGE:** Widespread in w. N. American mountain archipelago from Yukon south to n. Idaho, w. Mont., and cen. Colo. Maritime Provinces and ne. U.S. (south to W. Va.) west across Great Lakes region and s. Canada. **HABITAT:** Cool stream and river valleys, openings in coniferous woods, and bogs.

ATLANTIS FRITILLARY

NORTHWESTERN FRITIL-LARY *Speyeria hesperis*   PL. 24

2–2¾ in. (50–68 mm.) Forewing pointed in some populations. Upperside: Forewing with *margin black or only weakly so*. Underside: Hindwing with *red-brown to orange-*

Male Northwestern Fritillary (subspecies nausicaa) nectaring at yellow composite, White Mts., Ariz. Adults in different populations are quite variable above, but can be identified by color of hindwing disk (see Plate 24).

brown basal disk, spots either silvered or unsilvered. **SIMILAR SPECIES:** Atlantis Fritillary has dark brown disk at base of hindwing below. Spots are always silvered. **EARLY STAGES:** Caterpillar almost solid black with black-tipped orange spines and 2 brown lines up middle of back. **FOOD:** Violets. **FLIGHT:** Early June–late Oct. (1 flight). **RANGE:** Alaska and cen. Yukon and sw. N.W. Terr. south through Canada (east to w. Man.) and w. U.S. to cen. Calif., cen. Ariz., and cen. N.M. **HABITAT:** Moist meadows, gulches, cool slopes. **REMARKS:** Recently distinguished as a species separate from Atlantis Fritillary. They occur together or in close proximity in large areas of the West, and care must be taken in their identification. Adults are fond of flowers such as yellow composites and mints.

NORTHWESTERN FRITILLARY

HYDASPE FRITILLARY

HYDASPE FRITILLARY *Speyeria hydaspe* PL. 24

1⅜–2¼ in. (41–58 mm.) Antennal *clubs relatively large and rounded.* Upperside: Red-orange with *heavy black pattern.* Underside: *Purplish brown with pattern of relatively round unsilvered spots.* **SIMILAR SPECIES:** Zerene Fritillary in Calif. Sierra Nevada is larger and has smaller, more elongate spots on underside of hindwing. **EARLY STAGES:** Caterpillar mostly black with yellow-orange spines along sides, others black. **FOOD:** Violets. **FLIGHT:** June–Sept. (1 flight). **RANGE:** Cen. B.C. and sw. Alta. south through mountain cordillera to s. Sierra Nevada (Calif.), n. Utah, and n. Colo. Earlier reports from n. N.M. are erroneous. **HABITAT:** Openings in moist montane coniferous forests. **REMARKS:** This fritillary is relatively uniform and occupies similar habitats throughout its range. It nectars on low plants such as Pussypaws and asters.

MORMON FRITILLARY *Speyeria mormonia* PL. 24

1⅜–2 in. (41–52 mm). Small. *Antennal clubs relatively large, rounded. Forewing apex rounded.* Upperside: Forewing *without black scaling on veins.* Underside: Hindwing disk sometimes greenish, but not as bright or as solid as on Callippe fritillary. *Spots on hindwing relatively small, either silvered or unsilvered.* **SIMILAR SPECIES:** Great Basin Fritillary has smaller antennal clubs, less contrasty submarginal pale spots above, and larger silver or unsilvered spots on underside of hindwing. **EARLY STAGES:** Caterpillar variable yellow to orange with black blotches and lines. **FOOD:** Violets. **FLIGHT:** Early June–late Oct. (1 flight). **RANGE:** Western mountain archipelago from s.-cen. Alaska south to cen. Calif. and e.-cen. Ariz., extends east to sw. Man. and the Dakotas. **HABITAT:** Mountain meadows, moist prairie valleys. **REMARKS:** Smallest of the

Male Mormon Fritillary (subspecies luski*) resting, White Mts., Ariz. These adults are most unusual among the species in having white unsilvered spots; most other unsilvered populations have spots filled with brown.*

MORMON FRITILLARY

MOUNTAIN FRITILLARY

genus and the one most likely in high mountain habitats. The isolated subspecies *luski* of Ariz.'s White Mts. is most unlike other Mormon Fritillaries in appearance (p. 281) and may be sufficiently isolated to comprise a distinct species.

MOUNTAIN FRITILLARY *Boloria napaea*   PL. 25
1 5/16–1 9/16 in. (33–40 mm). *Forewing is pointed, outer margin of hindwing arched.* Upperside: *Male delicately marked orange; female with heavy black pattern.* Underside: *Hindwing with faint pattern.* **SIMILAR SPECIES:** Arctic Fritillary has rounded forewing apex and hindwing outer margin, more definite pattern on hindwing below. **EARLY STAGES:** Not reported. **FOOD:** Bistorts (*Polygonum bistortoides* and *P. viviparum*). **FLIGHT:** Late June–early Aug. (1 flight). **RANGE:** Holarctic. Alaska and w. Yukon, Victoria Is., tundra of N.W. Terr. east to Distr. of Keewatin south in Canadian Rockies to e.-cen. B.C. and w.-cen. Alta. An isolated population is found in Wyo.'s Wind River Mts. **HABITAT:** Moist tundra, subalpine meadows in valley bottoms. **REMARKS:** Flight is fast.

BOG FRITILLARY *Boloria eunomia*   PL. 25
1 5/16–1 5/8 in. (34–42 mm). Upperside: Dull orange with dark scaling at wing bases. Underside: Hindwing with *nonmetallic white or iridescent silver pattern; submarginal row of white black-outlined spots, and marginal row of triangular white or silver spots.* **SIMILAR SPECIES:** Silver-bordered Fritillary is bright orange above, lacks basal duskiness, and has iridescent silver markings below. There is black basal spot below, and submarginal black spots are not filled with white. **EARLY STAGES:** Caterpillar black with white and blue dots (Alta.). **FOOD:** Scrubby willows, bistorts, and violets. Other plants such as meadow rue, bilberries and others are occasional hosts. **FLIGHT:** Late May–early Sept., mainly June and July (1

Mating pair of Bog Fritillaries, Rocky Mt. National Park, Colo. Note flat white pattern on both individuals' hindwings and submarginal row of white spots.

flight). **RANGE:** Throughout most of Canada (except s. prairie provinces) and Alaska south in Rocky Mts as discontinuous isolated populations south to Colo. Also in n. Great Lakes region and n. Me. **HABITAT:** Wetlands, including acid bogs and dwarf willow seeps.

SILVER-BORDERED FRITILLARY *Boloria selene*   PL. 25

1 ⅜–1 ⅞ in. (35–47 mm). Upperside: *Clear orange with sparse pattern of black marks.* Underside: Hindwing with *basal black spot in silver field.* Median and *marginal rows of metallic silver spots on hindwing*; submarginal spots are black. **SIMILAR SPECIES:** Bog Fritillary has upperside clearer orange without basal black scaling, underside of hindwing with nonmetallic white or rarely metallic silver pattern, and submarginal spots white-centered, not black. **EARLY STAGES:** Caterpillar mottled dark gray with pale yellow spines, except front thoracic pair black. **FOOD:** Violets. **FLIGHT:** Late May–

BOG FRITILLARY

SILVER-BORDERED FRITILLARY

mid-Sept. (1 flight in mountains, 2–3 on plains and eastward.) **RANGE:** Holarctic. Cen. Alaska east across most of Canada (except tundra) south into U.S. In West south to e. Ore., n. Utah, n. N.M., and Neb. **HABITAT:** Wet meadows, marshes, and bogs. **REMARKS:** The Silver-bordered has a lazy flight, perches often, and visits yellow flowers readily. Most likely it is not the same species as the one found in Eurasia.

MEADOW FRITILLARY *Boloria bellona* PL. 25

1 ⁵⁄₁₆–1 ¾ in. (34–45 mm). Forewing *apex angled and cutoff (truncate)*. Upperside: Yellow-orange with heavy black pattern. Underside: *Hindwing mottled purple-brown.* **SIMILAR SPECIES:** Frigga Fritillary has rounded forewing apex, has basal half of hindwing black above, and an off-white basal patch on costal margin of deeper purplish hindwing below. **EARLY STAGES:** Caterpillar dull blackish gray with many black and white marks and lines. Head black with white mark on top. **FOOD:** Violets. **FLIGHT:** Early May–early Sept. (1 or 2 flights; only 1 at higher latitudes and elevations). **RANGE:** N. B.C. east across subarctic and temperate Canada to the Maritimes. South in the West to ne. Ore., sw. Colo., and e. Neb. In East south to Ga. **HABITAT:** Moist meadows, aspen parklands, and prairies. **REMARKS:** In West restricted to native habitats, although in East expanding south and east in pastures, hay meadows, and roadsides.

PACIFIC FRITILLARY *Boloria epithore* PL. 25

1 ⁵⁄₁₆–1 ¹⁵⁄₁₆ in. (34–49 mm.) *Forewing apex and hindwing margin rounded.* Upperside: Orange with black pattern. Underside: *Hindwing mottled light purplish brown with postbasal spot row yellow. A submarginal row of slightly darkened crescents points outward* (inward in most other lesser fritillaries. **SIMILAR SPECIES:** Where

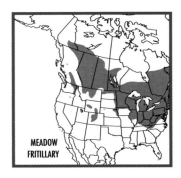

MEADOW
FRITILLARY

PACIFIC
FRITILLARY

the two species co-occur in sw. Canada, the Meadow Fritillary is yellower above, has a truncate forewing apex, and is darker below with a less well defined postbasal yellow spot band. **EARLY STAGES:** Caterpillar Gray with black head and red-brown stripe along each side. **FOOD:** Violets. **FLIGHT:** April–early Aug. (1 flight). **RANGE:** Cen. B.C. and w.-cen. Alta. south to s. Sierra Nevada (Calif.), cen. Idaho, and w. Mont. **HABITAT:** Meadows, mountainsides, and forest openings. **REMARKS:** Nectars at buckbrush, yellow composites, and other flowers.

FRIGGA FRITILLARY *Boloria frigga*   PL. 25

1 ½–1 ¾ in. (38–46 mm). Forewing *apex rounded not angled*. Upperside: Yellow-orange. *Basal half of wings mostly black with heavy overscaling*. Underside: *Hindwing deep purplish with small basal off-white or silvery patch along costal margin*. **SIMILAR SPECIES:** Meadow Fritillary has pointed forewing apex, lacks solid black basal overscaling above, and below is lighter and lacks off-white or silver patch on hindwing costal margin. **EARLY STAGES:** Caterpillar body and spines black with pale purplish lateral line. **FOOD:** Shrub willows, possibly other plants on occasion. **FLIGHT:** Mid-May (Wisc.)–early Aug., mainly June–mid-July (1 flight). **RANGE:** Holarctic. Most of Canada, s. Arctic Archipelago, and Alaska, south, as isolated populations, to ne. Idaho, Wyo. and s.-cen. Colo. Also n. Great Lakes states in East. **HABITAT:** Sphagnum bogs, sedge bogs. **REMARKS:** Adults nectar rarely, but will visit flowers of Labrador tea. In Colo., the species is partly dependent on old beaver dams, where females lay eggs on young willow seedlings.

DINGY FRITILLARY *Boloria improba*   PL. 25

1 ⅛–1 ⅜ in. (28–35 mm). Upperside: Dingy. Basal half yellowish, outer half orangish. Pattern muted in north, brighter in s. Rock-

FRIGGA
FRITILLARY

DINGY
FRITILLARY

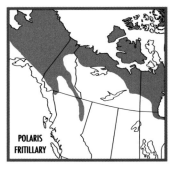

ies. Underside: *Hindwing pattern fairly plain. Basal half pale, outer half orange or gray.* **SIMILAR SPECIES:** No other lesser fritillary or checkerspot has such a lack of pattern elements below. **EARLY STAGES:** Caterpillar mottled dark brown with red-brown spines; head black. **FOOD:** Dwarf willows, including snow willow. **FLIGHT:** Late June–mid-Aug. (1 flight). Probably biennial but flies every year. **RANGE:** Holarctic. Arctic tundra of N.W. Terr. east to Distr. of Keewatin as well as Banks, Melville, and s. Victoria Is.; Yukon and Alaska; isolated populations in cen. Canadian Rockies, nw. Wyo., and sw. Colo. **HABITAT:** Wet tundra and rocky slopes with dwarf willows. **REMARKS:** The endangered Uncompahgre Fritillary (*Boloria improba acrocnema*) is here considered a subspecies of the Dingy Fritillary. Butterflies in the Wind River Mts. of Wyo. (subspecies *harryi*) are essentially identical.

RELICT FRITILLARY *Boloria kriemhild* PL. 25

1 ⁵⁄₁₆–1 ¾ in. (34–45 mm). Forewing *apex rounded.* Upperside: Orange with black pattern. *Submarginal chevrons on hindwing point inward.* Underside: *Hindwing reddish basally with postbasal row of black-outlined yellow spots. Faint submarginal chevrons point outward.* **SIMILAR SPECIES:** Arctic Fritillary has inward-pointing submarginal chevrons on hindwing and lacks postbasal yellow band. **EARLY STAGES:** Not reported. **FOOD:** Violets. **FLIGHT:** Mid-June–early Aug. (1 flight). **RANGE:** Sw. Mont. south through w. Wyo. and e. Idaho to ne. Utah. **HABITAT:** Alpine willow bogs and lush meadows in conifer forests. **REMARKS:** This geographically restricted butterfly shares about the same range with the Gillette's Checkerspot and Hayden's Ringlet. All three are relictual in that their closest relatives live in Eurasia. Adults nectar at flowers of asters and yellow composites.

POLARIS FRITILLARY *Boloria polaris* PL. 25

1 ³⁄₁₆–1 ½ in. (31–38 mm). Distinctive. Upperside: Orange-brown *heavily marked with black*. Underside: Forewing with narrow marginal lines. *Hindwing with frosted white appearance. White marginal slashes extending outward from submarginal dark triangles, and postmedian black spots surrounded with white.* **SIMILAR SPECIES:** (1) Freija and (2) Arctic Fritillaries lack the frosted appearance on hindwing and have black submarginal hindwing spots not surrounded by white. **EARLY STAGES:** Not reported. **FOOD:** Mountain Avens, probably also blueberry (*Vaccinium uliginosum*). **FLIGHT:** Biennial, late June–July in most of range, to mid-Aug. in Lab. Odd-numbered years at a few locales, even-numbered years at many places, and every year in some locales. **RANGE:** Holarctic. Tundra of Alaska, n. Canada (including Arctic Archipelago) extending south to n. B.C. and ne. Greenland. **HABITAT:** Tundra ridges or flat areas below summits.

FREIJA FRITILLARY *Boloria freija* PL. 25

1 ¼–1 ½ in. (32–39 mm). Underside: Hindwing with diagnostic *median zigzag black line, arrowhead-shaped white spots in center of wing and at margin.* Arctic populations darker. **SIMILAR SPECIES:** (1) Arctic Fritillary has irregular not-toothed black median line on hindwing below. (2) Polaris Fritillary (see above). **EARLY STAGES:** Caterpillar dark brown with black spines and a black head. **FOOD:** Various Heath family plants, including bilberries. **FLIGHT:** Late April–early Aug., primarily May (1 flight). **RANGE:** Holarctic. Most of Canada and Alaska; south in Rockies to n. N.M. Also in n. Great Lakes states. **HABITAT:** Subalpine willow bogs and most alpine tundra slopes.

BERINGIAN FRITILLARY *Boloria natazhati* PL. 25

1 ⅜–1 ¾ in. (36–44 mm). *Forewing apex pointed.* Upperside: Wings have "greasy" appearance with *bluish sheen.* Pattern elements similar to Freija Fritillary but most populations have most of wings *blackish with long hairs basally.* Underside: *Ocher background with somewhat muted pattern, but includes median dark zigzag line on hindwing.* **SIMILAR SPECIES:** Freija Fritillary lacks pointed forewing, greasy appearance above, and is reddish rather ocher-

FREIJA FRITILLARY

colored below. **EARLY STAGES:** Not reported. **FOOD:** Possibly Mountain Avens. **FLIGHT:** Mid-June–July (1 flight), probably biennial. **RANGE:** Victoria Is., N.W. Terr. west to n. Yukon and e. Alaska south to n. B.C. **HABITAT:** Rocky ridges, scree slopes, and cobble beaches. **REMARKS:** This species is often found close to populations of the Freija Fritillary, but it flies in a different habitat, usually higher elevations, and later in the season. Adults nectar at flowers of phlox and saxifrages.

ALBERTA FRITILLARY *Boloria alberta*   PL. 25

1½–1¾ in. (38–44 mm.) *Wings rounded.* Upperside: Dull orange with black *pattern smudged and extensive dark, diffuse overscaling.* Underside: Dull orange with extensive dark smudging and overscaling. Hindwing has *smudged dull white postbasal band and submarginal dull white band.* **SIMILAR SPECIES:** Astarte Fritillary, which often flies in the same areas, is bright orange above with a sharp distinct pattern of black marks. Below it has a clear white blacked-edged postbasal band. **EARLY STAGES:** Not reported. **FOOD:** Probably Mountain Avens. **FLIGHT:** Late June–late Aug., peak mid-July (1 flight), probably biennial. **RANGE:** Far East of Russia and Rocky Mts. of w. Alta. and s. B.C. south to Glacier National Park, Mont. **HABITAT:** Rocky alpine slopes and ridges. **REMARKS:** Adults nectar at flowers of Moss Campion and Mountain Avens.

ASTARTE FRITILLARY *Boloria astarte*   PL. 25

1½–1⅞ in. (38–48 mm.) Upperside: Orange to pale orange with a distinct pattern of black marks and pronounced black margins. Underside: Hindwing *orange with clear-cut black-edged white postbasal band, median row of white marks, and a submarginal black line edged on both sides with small indistinct white marks* (subspecies *astarte*). In subspecies *distincta, ground variable dull orange to greenish. Pattern indistinct with postmedian band in-*

Male Astarte Fritillary (subspecies distincta), *Dempster Highway, Yukon Terr. Despite the subspecies' name the adults have indistinct postmedian bands and other muted pattern elements. Photo by Jim Ebner.*

vaded by ground and discontinuously outlined narrowly with black. Postmedian row of white present, but adjacent spots dull, not black. Submarginal black line absent. **SIMILAR SPECIES:** (1) Alberta Fritillary, often found in same habitat with subspecies *astarte*, has a smudged pattern and dark overscaling. (2) In range of subspecies *distincta*, Polaris Fritillary is smaller, marked more heavily with black, and does not inhabit scree slopes and rock slides. **EARLY STAGES:** Not reported. **FOOD:** Spotted Saxifrage. **FLIGHT:** Mid-June–mid. Aug., peak July (1 flight), biennial. **RANGE:** Russian Far East. Alaska, Yukon, w. N.W. Terr., and nw. B.C. south along mountains in w. Alta. and B.C. to n. Wash. and n. Mont. (Glacier National Park). **HABITAT:** Alpine scree slopes and ridges—usually south facing.

ARCTIC FRITILLARY *Boloria chariclea*   **PL. 25**
1 ³⁄₁₆–1 ½ in. (31–39 mm). Extremely variable. Upperside: Bright red-orange to dull red-brown with black markings slight to exten-

ASTARTE
FRITILLARY

ARCTIC
FRITILLARY

sive. Underside: *Hindwing with thin marginal white spots capped inwardly with brown. Median band with variable amount of white or cream, but often invaded by ground color. Median band often outlined outwardly with strong black line.* **SIMILAR SPECIES:** (1) Freija Fritillary flies earlier and has jagged toothed black median line on underside of hindwing. (2) On underside Relict Fritillary has submarginal black marks on forewing pointing inward and cream-yellow median band on hindwing. **EARLY STAGES:** Caterpillar gray with black stripes and orange spines; head black. **FOOD:** Scrub willows, violets, and possibly blueberries. **FLIGHT:** Late June–Sept. (1 flight). Likely biennial, at least in alpine and arctic habitats. **RANGE:** Alaska and most of Canada south to Wash. and in Rockies to n. N.M., and in n. Cascades. N.H. (White Mts.) and n. Minn. in East. **HABITAT:** Damp subalpine streamsides, acid bogs, taiga. **REMARKS:** The Purple Fritillary *(Boloria titania),* previously thought to occur in N. Amer., is limited to Eurasia. In Alaska, two different-appearing butterflies referable to the Arctic Fritillary fly in some localities at different seasons in differing habitats.

BRUSHFOOTS: SUBFAMILY NYMPHALINAE

This subfamily is the most prevalent in the family and is found throughout the world. It is a diverse group and contains several tribes, each with somewhat different structural and biological features. Adults of our species are predominantly orange, brown, and black, and wing shape is variable. Mating systems are variable; patrolling is predominant in the checkerspots and crescentspots, while perching or perching and patrolling is the rule for the remainder. Some of the strongest migrants are found among the lady butterflies, tortoiseshells, and anglewings, but most of the other species are local in their occurrence. Hosts plants span a wide variety of families, but most species limit their choice to plants of a single family. Among butterflies, the Painted Lady, in contrast, has one of the widest host palettes. Eggs may be laid singly but are often clustered in groups, sometimes near the host or on an adjacent plant. Caterpillars feed singly or communally, often at night or in folded leaf shelters. Winter is passed by young caterpillars or by hibernating adults.

DOTTED CHECKERSPOT *Poladryas minuta*   **PL. 26**
1 ⅛–1 ¼ in. (29–39 mm). Upperside: Red-orange or bicolored red-orange and yellow orange with black marks. Underside: Hindwing with *double row of marginal white spots; and median white band containing double row of black dots.* **SIMILAR SPECIES:** Northern Checkerspot is usually larger, has extended forewing outer mar-

DOTTED CHECKERSPOT

THEONA CHECKERSPOT

gin, and lacks median band with black dots below. **EARLY STAGES:** : Caterpillar white with longitudinal black bands; head orange-brown (subspecies *arachne*); orange (subspecies *minuta*). **FOOD:** Beardtongues. **FLIGHT:** Jan.–Nov. (Tex.), June–early Sept., very rarely Nov. in Rockies (2 flights). **RANGE:** Southwest from se. Wyo. and extreme nw. Neb. south to s.-cen. Tex., Chihuahua, and n. Sonora west to e.-cen. Calif. **HABITAT:** Mesquite woodland, oak-pinyon scrub, open Ponderosa pine woodland. **REMARKS:** Males establish perches on low vegetation on ridgetop clearings. Adults nectar at flowers of asters, black-eyed susans, and yellow composites.

THEONA CHECKERSPOT *Thessalia theona*   **PL. 26**
1 ⅟₁₆–1 ½ in. (27–39 mm). Upperside: Checkered pattern with yellow-orange antemedian band and orange postmedian band.

Theona Checkerspot nectaring at yellow composite, Cochise Co., Ariz. Note distinctive pattern on underside of hindwing. Adult males are often found on hill summits or ridgetops.

Amount of black variable. Underside: *Hindwing cream with veins outlined in black, overlain by a red-orange postbasal blotch and postmedian band.* Some populations lack postmedian band (subspecies *chinatiensis*). **SIMILAR SPECIES:** Definite Patch is smaller and has black lines between postbasal orange blotch and postmedian band. **EARLY STAGES:** Caterpillar velvety brown-black with small cream dots and a yellow lateral band; head orange. **FOOD:** Ceniza Blanca, paintbrush, verbena, and others. **FLIGHT:** All year in tropics. April–Oct. in Southwest (several broods). **RANGE:** Cen. Ariz. east to e.-cen. Tex. and thence south through Mex. and Cen. Amer. to Colombia. **HABITAT:** Subtropical scrub, desert foothills, limestone ridges. **REMARKS:** Adults seek nectar at flowers of yellow composites and seepwillow.

BLACK CHECKERSPOT *Thessalia cyneas*   **PL. 26**

1 5⁄16–1 9⁄16 in. (34–40 mm.) Upperside: *Black with small yellow spots and red-orange marginal band on hindwing.* Underside: *Hindwing cream with black along veins and submarginal band with circular cream spots between veins.* **SIMILAR SPECIES:** Fulvia Checkerspot occurs adjacent to populations of Black Checkerspots in se. Ariz. Here, the Fulvia Checkerspot has more extensive yellow and red-orange markings and has more pronounced markings below. **EARLY STAGES:** Not reported. **FOOD:** Paintbrush. **FLIGHT:** Late March–early

Nov. (several flights). **RANGE:** Se. Ariz. south to s. Mex. **HABITAT:** See Fulvia Checkerspot (p. 293). **REMARKS:** This butterfly and the next two species show some intergrades with each other at the edges of their ranges and may comprise one wide-ranging variable species. Adult Black Checkerspots nectar at buckbrush and seepwillow.

Male Black Checkerspot nectaring at fleabane, Huachuca Mts., Cochise Co., Ariz. Very similar to the Fulvia and Leanira Checkerspots (p. 293); adults are mainly black above.

FULVIA CHECKERSPOT *Thessalia fulvia* **PL. 26**

1–1⅜ in. (26–36 mm). Variable within and between populations. Upperside: Ranging from mainly blackish to mainly orange. Underside: *Hindwing with combination of black-lined veins on cream background and black submarginal band enclosing series of cream dots.* **SIMILAR SPECIES:** Usually none, but in se. Ariz. Black Checkerspot is blacker above with more distinct red-orange submarginal band on hindwing. **EARLY STAGES:** Caterpillar ocher-yellow with longitudinal black lines and bands; head red-brown. **FOOD:** Paintbrush. **FLIGHT:** April–Oct. (3 broods). **RANGE:** Southwest from n. Neb., cen. Kans., and cen. Tex. west through Colo., Ariz., s. Utah, and N.M. south to n. Mex. **HABITAT:** Prairie hills, foothills, rocky ridgetops.

LEANIRA CHECKERSPOT *Thessalia leanira* **PL. 26**

1⁵⁄₁₆–1¹¹⁄₁₆ in. (34–43 mm). Upperside: Variable from primarily black to bright orange with pattern of small yellow spots. Underside: Hindwing *cream with black veins and postmedian black band with round cream spots between veins. Some individuals with black marks on basal area of hindwing.* **SIMILAR SPECIES:** Distinct hindwing pattern underneath separates Leanira Checkerspot from all other species in its range. **EARLY STAGES:** Caterpillar black with rows of black bristly spines and pairs of orange stripes along each side and up back. **FOOD:** Paintbrushes. **FLIGHT:** Mar.–June (1

flight), rare fall flight to Oct. in response to rare rains. **RANGE:** S. Ore., Nev., Utah, and sw. Colo. south to n. Baja. Calif. and nw. Ariz. **HABITAT:** Oak woodland, chaparral, and juniper woodland. Adults nectar at flowers of yellow composites. **REMARKS:** Males of this and the previous two species perch on ridges or hilltops, where they await receptive females.

PATCHES: GENUS *Chlosyne* BUTLER

This large, wholly New World genus comprises both the patches (more southern) and small checkerspots (more northern). Most species occur in the tropics, where many species mimic distasteful butterflies. Eggs are laid in clusters under host plant leaves, and young caterpillars feed in groups. Caterpillars crawl under rocks to pupate. Usual hosts belong to the Sunflower and Acanthus families.

CALIFORNIA PATCH *Chlosyne californica*   **PL. 26**

1 5/16–1 3/4 in. (34–45 mm). Upperside: Predominantly *orange with black on basal portion of both wings*. Submarginal *black bands with a row of tiny white dots* on both wings. Underside: Similar to upperside. **SIMILAR SPECIES:** Desert form *(alma)* of Leanira Checkerspot is more red-orange above with very different pattern below. **EARLY STAGES:** Caterpillar usually black with rows of black spines and vertical rows on tiny white dots, but occasional orange or yellow strip, and mainly orange forms are found. **FOOD:** Desert sunflower *(Viguera deltoidea).* **FLIGHT:** Mid-Feb.–Nov. (3 flights), appearance and abundance depends on amount and timing of rains. **RANGE:** S. Calif., s. Nev., and sw. Utah south through w. Ariz. to Baja Calif. Sur and Sonora. **HABITAT:** Dry, rocky desert scrub, including hills

CALIFORNIA PATCH

BORDERED PATCH

and washes. **REMARKS.** Males perch on hilltops to await females. Forms of the Bordered Patch in parts of Mex. resemble the California Patch and are rarely found in se. Ariz.

BORDERED PATCH *Chlosyne lacinia* PL. 26

1 ⁵/₁₆–1 ⅞ in. (34–48 mm). Highly variable geographically. Upperside: *Black with variable transverse cream, white, or orange band on hindwing. Band is occasionally very narrow or even absent.* **EARLY STAGES:** Caterpillar polymorphic—black to orange with black spines; head black. **FOOD:** Sunflower, ragweed, crown-beard and other Sunflower family plants. **FLIGHT:** Late Jan.–mid-Nov. in se. Ariz.; Mar.–Oct. in se. Calif. (many flights), commonest in late summer and fall. Butterfly seen as stray only during warm months to the north. **RANGE:** Resident from se. Calif. and s. Ariz. east to s. Tex. south through Mex., Cen. Amer., and S. Amer. to Argentina. Vagrant and temporary colonist north to s. Nev., s. Utah, and Neb. **HABITAT:** Desert washes, low ridges, openings in moist thorn scrub.

DEFINITE PATCH *Chlosyne definita* PL. 26

¹⁵/₁₆–1 ⁵/₁₆ in. (24–33 mm). Small. Upperside: Checkered pattern of red-orange, yellow-orange, and dark brown checks and bands. Underside: *Hindwing submarginal orange band with 1 included white spot.* **SIMILAR SPECIES:** (1) Tiny and (2) Elada Checkerspots are much smaller and have more regular pattern of smaller checks on hindwing below. **EARLY STAGES:** Not reported. **FOOD:** *Stenandrium barbatum* in Acanthus family. **FLIGHT:** Mid-March–Oct. (several broods). **RANGE:** Resident from s. N.M. and s. Tex. south to s. Mex. **HABITAT:** Openings in subtropical thorn scrub.

BANDED PATCH *Chlosyne endeis* NOT SHOWN

1 ⅛–1 ½ in. (29–38 mm). Underside: Forewing has *outer half black with cream white spots.* Hindwing is cream white with postbasal and submarginal *red- orange bands separated by two black irregular lines.* **SIMILAR SPECIES:** Definite Patch has is smaller, underside of forewing is predominantly orange. **FOOD:** Unknown but likley one or more plants in Acanthus family. **EARLY STAGES:** Not reported. **FLIGHT:** March– Nov. (several broods). **RANGE:** S. Tex. to s. Mex., rare stray to cen. Tex. **HABITAT:** Subtropical thorn forest.

DEFINITE PATCH

RED-SPOTTED PATCH *Chlosyne marina* PL. 26

1 %6–1 ¾ in. (40–45 mm). *Black with yellow band on forewing. Underside of hindwing has broad yellow median band and submarginal series of red spots.* **FOOD:** Unknown. **EARLY STAGES:** Not reported. **FLIGHT:** All year in Mex. **RANGE:** Resident in Mex. Rare stray to s. Tex. and s. Ariz. **HABITAT:** Openings in subtropical thorn scrub.

CRIMSON PATCH *Chlosyne janais* PL. 26

1 ⅞–2 %6 in. (47–65 mm). Upperside: Forewing black with small white spots. Hindwing *black with large orange-red patch on basal half.* **EARLY STAGES:** Caterpillar gray-green with complex black markings and black spines; head red-orange. **FOOD:** Scrubby Acanthus family plants. **FLIGHT:** All year in tropics, July–Nov. in s. Tex. (several broods). **RANGE:** Resident from s. Tex. south through e. Mex. and Cen. Amer. to Colombia. Strays north to se. N.M. and n. Tex. **HABITAT:** Weedy fields and edges in lowland tropical forests.

ROSITA PATCH *Chlosyne rosita* PL. 26

1 ⅜–1 ⅝ in. (36–42 mm). Forewing *apex extended.* Upperside: *Hindwing patch yellow at base, red-orange near edge.* Underside: Hindwing pattern simpler than that of Crimson Patch. **SIMILAR SPECIES:** Crimson Patch is larger, patch on hindwing is entirely red-orange—lacks yellow at base. **EARLY STAGES:** Not reported. **FOOD:** Several low Acanthus family plants. **FLIGHT:** Late Aug.–early Oct. in se. Ariz. as strays. Most of year in s. Tex. and southward (possibly 4 broods). **RANGE:** Mex. south to El Salvador, periodic colonist in s. Tex. (lower Rio Grande Valley). Rare stray to n. Tex. and se. Ariz. **HABITAT:** Openings in subtropical forest in tropics.

GORGONE CHECKERSPOT *Chlosyne gorgone* PL. 27

1 ¼6–1 %6 in. (28–37 mm). Underside: *Hindwing with zigzag pattern of alternating brown and white bars and scallops.* **SIMILAR SPECIES:** Pearl Crescent, Northern Crescent, and Silvery Checkerspot are similar above, but all have much plainer patterns below. **EARLY STAGES:** Caterpillar yellow with longitudinal black stripes; black head and spines. Feed in groups. **FOOD:** Sunflowers, crosswort, and other Sunflower family plants. **FLIGHT:** Late April–mid-July in north (1 flight), to mid-Oct. farther south (2 flights). **RANGE:** Resident in s. Canada from cen. Alta. east to sw. Man. and s. Ont. south through most of cen. U.S. and in West south through cen. Idaho, Mont., n. Utah, Wyo. to cen. N.M. and cen. Tex. Butterfly has disappeared from former haunts in Utah and Idaho. **HABITAT:** Prairies, open ridges, edges of agricultural areas, and ditches. **REMARKS:** Males perch and patrol hilltops to await females. This species and the following *Chlosynes* were formerly included in *Charidryas,* but unified by similar genitalia.

GORGONE CHECKERSPOT

SILVERY CHECKERSPOT

SILVERY CHECKERSPOT *Chlosyne nycteis*   PL. 27

1 ³⁄₁₆–1 ³⁄₄ in. (30–45 mm). Upperside: Variable, ranging from predominantly black in Rockies (subspecies *drusius*) to primarily orange in plains and East, to nearly immaculate orange in parts of the Rockies. Hindwing with *at least one white submarginal spot unless obscured by black scaling.* Underside: Hindwing checkered with strong median row of *black- or brown-bordered silvery checks. Submarginal row on hindwing may show one to several silvery marginal crescents.* SIMILAR SPECIES: (1) Pearl Crescent and (2) Northern Crescent are smaller; have small black spots in submarginal row on upperside of hindwing; and have relatively plain, uncheckered hindwing patterns below. EARLY STAGES: Caterpillar black with rows of shiny black spines and with orange stripes and white dots along side. FOOD: Goldenglow (in genus *Rudbeckia*) is only host in Rockies. Asters, sunflowers, black-eyed Susans, and crown-beard are eaten in East. FLIGHT: June–July (1 flight) in Rockies, May–Sept. (2 flights) farther east on plains, possibly 3–4 flights east of our area in Deep South and Tex. RANGE: Se Sask. and Man. south to e.-cen. Ariz. (White Mts.), s. N.M., and se. Tex. In East from N.B. and s. Que. south to Fla. panhandle (rarely). HABITAT: Openings near streamcourses, second-growth scrub, and mixed woods with clearings.

HARRIS' CHECKERSPOT *Chlosyne harrisii*   PL. 27

1 ³⁄₁₆–1 ¹³⁄₁₆ in. (30–46 mm). Upperside: Black with median and postmedian orange rows. Amount of black variable. Underside: Hindwing has a *white, orange, and black checkered pattern with marginal orange band on both wings.* SIMILAR SPECIES: (1) Gorgone Checkerspot and (2) Silvery Checkerspot differ in their underside hindwing patterns. EARLY STAGES: Caterpillar deep red-orange with dorsal black stripe; cross stripes on each segment. FOOD: Flat-

topped White Aster. **FLIGHT:** June–July (1 flight). **RANGE:** In our area only in se. Sask., sw. Man., and n.-cen. S.D. Also east across s. Canada to Prince Edward Is. south to s. W. Va., s. Ohio, and ne. Ill. **HABITAT:** Moist pastures, fens, marshes, bog edges, damp meadows.

NORTHERN CHECKERSPOT *Chlosyne palla* PL. 27

1 3/16–1 3/4 in. (31–44 mm.). Variable geographically. Fringe checkered black and white. Upperside: Checkered. Males always *red-orange*, sometimes with redder band in forewing cell and postmedian row on hindwing. Females range from very similar to males but *with a light yellow median row and darker postmedian spot row to mainly black with a yellow spot pattern* (Calif. Coast Range). Underside: *Checkered pattern of buff-yellow and red-orange basal complex, postmedian row, and marginal band.* Pacific Northwest specimens (subspecies *sterope*) are duskier above with a white-cream ground color on the hindwing below. **SIMILAR SPECIES:** (1) Rockslide Checkerspot is found in the alpine zone where Northern does not occur. (2) Sagebrush Checkerspot is more unicolored above and has off-white or iridescent silver ground on hindwing below. (3) Gabb's Checkerspot has bright white ground below. **EARLY STAGES:** Caterpillar black with small white spots and rows of black bristly spines. There are 2 rows of orange spots along each side. **FOOD:** Asters, rabbitbrushes, fleabane, goldenrod, and other Sunflower family plants. **FLIGHT:** Mid-March–early Aug. (1 flight), earlier along lowland Pacific Coast, later in mountains. **RANGE:** Sw. Canada from s. B.C. and s. Alta. south (avoiding most of Great Basin) to s. Calif., cen. Utah, and s. Colo. **HABITAT:** Streamcourses and associated flats and slopes in a wide variety of habitats, including sagebrush, oak woodland, chaparral, and mixed coniferous woods. **REMARKS:** Adults nectar at yellow composite flowers. This species, together with the Sagebrush, Rockslide,

Male Sagebrush Checkerspot (subspecies neumoegeni) *resting, Maricopa Co., Ariz. Note pearly color of hindwing spots. Males often perch and patrol along streambeds. Photo by Evi Buckner.*

and Gabb's Checkerspots, are a closely related group. The constituent species occasionally show hybrids or blending, and some populations are difficult to assign to species.

SAGEBRUSH CHECKERSPOT   PL. 27
Chlosyne acastus

1 ³⁄₁₆–1 ½ in. (31–39 mm). Upperside: Checkered dull orange to bright orange with black lines and smudges. Postmedian bands on fore- and hindwings sometimes red-orange. Underside: Hindwing white spots in checkered pattern *have a flat white or pearly white* (subspecies *acastus*) *or pearly sheen* (subspecies *neumoegeni*). **SIMILAR SPECIES:** Northern Checkerspot occasionally co-occurs, is more red-orange above, and has yellow or cream ground on underside of hindwing. **EARLY STAGES:** Caterpillar black with bristly black spines, with or without gray or orange stripes along sides. **FOOD:** Aster (*Machaeranthera*) and rabbitbrush. **FLIGHT:** Early Feb.–Nov. (1–3 flights). **RANGE:** S. Alta. and s. Sask. south through the cen. Dakotas to cen. N.M. and se. Calif. **HABITAT:** Streambeds, dry washes in sagebrush-juniper woodland, sometimes oak or mixed-conifer woodland. **REMARKS:** Neumoegen's Checkerspot, previously considered a separate species by most authors, is combined with the Sagebrush Checkerspot.

SAGEBRUSH
CHECKERSPOT

Male Gabb's Check-erspot basking, Riverside Co., Calif. Adults may be separated from the similar Northern or Sagebrush Checkerspots primarily by the pattern and color of the hindwing underside. Photo by Jack N. Levy.

GABB'S CHECKERSPOT *Chlosyne gabbii*   **PL. 27**

1 ³⁄₁₆–1 ¾ in. (31–44 mm.). Upperside: Both sexes with contrasting checkered patterns of yellow-orange, orange, and red-orange separated by black lines and smudges. Female has more contrasting pattern. Underside: *Hindwing with checkered red-orange and pearly white with red-orange basal complex, postmedian band, and marginal band.* **SIMILAR SPECIES:** Northern Checkerspot narrowly overlaps in mountains of s. Calif. where it may be told by flat creamy ground on hindwing below. **EARLY STAGES:** Caterpillar black with rows of black branching spines. Velvety black stripe up back has adjacent orange and dirty white spots. **FOOD:** *Corethrogyne, Heterotheca,* and possibly other Sunflower family plants. **FLIGHT:** March–June, rarely to Sept. (1 flight), occasional small second flight. **RANGE:** Pacific Coast and adjacent mountains from cen. Calif. south to n. Baja Calif. **HABITAT:** Coastal dunes, streambeds in oak woodland and chaparral.

GABB'S CHECKERSPOT

ROCKSLIDE CHECKERSPOT

Male Rockslide Checkerspot resting, Long's Peak, Rocky Mt. National Park, Colo. Note dull white on hindwing. This is the only Chlosyne *likely to be found on rock slides above timberline.*

ROCKSLIDE CHECKERSPOT *Chlosyne whitneyi*   PL. 27

1 ³⁄₁₆–1 ½ in. (31–39 mm.). Upperside: *Checkered dingy red-orange and black with bluish sheen.* Females with more contrast. Underside: *Checkered orange and dull white.* SIMILAR SPECIES: Usually the only small orange checkerspot in its habitat. EARLY STAGES: Caterpillar black with black spines, cream dots, black line up middle of back with an orange band to each side. Head black. FOOD: Fleabane. FLIGHT: Late June–Aug. (1 flight), requires two or more years to complete development, i.e., multiannual. RANGE: W.-cen. Alta. south in Rockies to s. Colo. A separate isolated population in the Calif. Sierra Nevada. HABITAT: Alpine rockslides and scree slopes. REMARKS: Adults nectar above and below rock slides. Species was previously known under names *damoetas* and *malcolmi.*

HOFFMANN'S CHECKERSPOT *Chlosyne hoffmanni*   PL. 27

1 ⁵⁄₁₆–1 ⅝ in. (34–42 mm). Upperside: *Basal portion of lower forewing and basal third of hindwing mainly black.* On forewing *median orange-yellow band blends into postmedian orange band* (most pronounced in Calif. populations). On hindwing spots in postmedian row relatively rectangular. Underside: *Ground yellow-cream. Marginal red-orange band relatively even and smooth.* SIMILAR SPECIES: Northern Checkerspot lacks black basal area on hindwing, lacks blended appearance of median and postmedian bands on forewing, and has more scalloped underside marginal band. EARLY STAGES: Caterpillar black with rows of bristly black spines. Body speckled with white, a cream line along each side, and white circles around spiracles. FOOD: Asters and *Chrysopsis.* FLIGHT: June–July (1 flight). RANGE: S. B.C. south through Cascades, Klamath Mts., and Sierra Nevada to cen. Calif. HABITAT: Openings in

Canadian zone forests. **REMARKS:** Adults nectar at yellow composites and pussytoes. Freshly emerged males congregate at wet spots adjacent to streams and lakes.

ELF *Microtia elva* **PL. 27**

1–1⅜ in. (26–36 mm). Rounded forewings. Upperside: Both wings *black with 1 or 2 large yellow-orange patches.* Flutters weakly near ground. **EARLY STAGES:** Not reported. **FOOD:** Unknown. **FLIGHT:** All year in tropics, late Aug.–late Oct. in se. Ariz. **RANGE:** Resident from Mex. south through Cen. Amer. to Venezuela. Rare stray to s. Ariz., s. Tex., and Mo. **HABITAT:** Open, weedy fields and brush in seasonal lowland tropics.

TINY CHECKERSPOT *Dymasia dymas* **PL. 27**

¹³⁄₁₆–1³⁄₁₆ in. (21–30 mm). Small. Upperside: Orange with black pattern. Similar to Elada Checkerspot. Underside: Hindwing with *terminal black line and marginal white spots.* **SIMILAR SPECIES:** Elada Checkerspot has outermost band red-orange, not white. **EARLY STAGES:** Caterpillar gray with black and white mottling, dorsal black line and white bands. **FOOD:** Tube-tongue, *Beloperone, Tetramerium.* **FLIGHT:** Jan.–Dec., mainly spring and summer in s. Ariz. (several flights). **RANGE:** Resident from se. Calif., west to s. Tex. south to cen. Mex. **HABITAT:** Desert and subtropical scrub, especially adjacent to washes and valleys. **REMARKS:** Often extremely abundant. Adults nectar at flowers of seepwillow, yellow composites, and other plants. Adults have a weak, fluttery flight.

ELADA CHECKERSPOT *Texola elada* **PL. 27**

⅞–1⅛ in. (22–29 mm). Small. Upperside: Orange and black checkered pattern. Underside: Hindwing *checkered black and white with red-orange marginal band.* **SIMILAR SPECIES:** Female Dymas Checkerspot is larger. Dymas has relatively more narrow

forewing with small white spot on costa; hindwing underside is less checkered and has terminal black line. **EARLY STAGES:** Not reported. **FOOD:** Plants in Acanthus family. **FLIGHT:** Early March–early Dec. (several flights), most common after summer rains. **RANGE:** Resident from cen. Tex. west to cen. Ariz. and south to s. Mex. **HABITAT:** Subtropical scrub and thorn forest.

TEXAN CRESCENT *Phyciodes texana*   **PL. 27**
    1 ³⁄₁₆–1 ⁹⁄₁₆ in. (30–40 mm). *Forewing outer margin concave* below apex. Upperside: *Black with white spots, and at least some red-brown near base.* **EARLY STAGES:** Not reported. **FOOD:** Low Acanthus family plants. **FLIGHT:** All year in tropics, se. Ariz., and s. Tex. (several flights). **RANGE:** Resident from se. Ariz. and s. Tex. east across s. U.S. to S.C., Ga., and n. Fla., thence south through Mex., incl. Baja Calif. to Guatemala; strays north to s. Calif., cen. Nev., sw. Utah, e. Colo., Neb., and S.D. **HABITAT:** Streamcourses, dry gulches, city parks. **REMARKS:** Adults nectar at many low plants including yellow composites, seepwillow, and others.

TULCIS CRESCENT *Phyciodes tulcis*   **PL. 27**
    1–1 ½ in. (26–38 mm). Forewing *outer margin slightly concave.* Upperside: Black with cream-yellow spots and yellow overscaling on basal half. Hindwing has *broad postmedian cream band.* **SIMILAR SPECIES:** Texan Crescent is slightly larger, its forewing has more strongly concave outer margin, has red on basal area of wings, and has a narrow postmedian band on hindwing. **EARLY STAGES:** Not reported. **FOOD:** Found in close association with low Acanthus family plants. **FLIGHT:** All year in lowland tropics, May–Nov. in s. Tex. (several flights). **RANGE:** Resident in s. Tex. south through mainland tropical Amer. to Argentina, strays to w. Tex. and s. Ariz. **HABITAT:** Open fields, shaded forest edges, and second growth in tropical and subtropical lowlands.

VESTA CRESCENT *Phyciodes vesta* PL. 27

1¼–1½ in. (31–37 mm). Upperside: Orange *finely marked with black lines*. Underside: Forewing with postmedian and submarginal *series of orange circles amidst black lines*. **SIMILAR SPECIES:** (1) Pearl and (2) Painted Crescents have their uppersides much less divided by network of fine black lines, and lack yellow-orange submarginal black-outlined circles on underside of forewing. **EARLY STAGES:** Not reported. **FOOD:** Hairy tube-tongue and *Dyschoriste* in Acanthus family. **FLIGHT:** All year in lowland Mex., most of year in s. N.M. and Tex., summer only to north. **RANGE:** Resident from se. Ariz. east to s. Tex., thence south to Guatemala. Strays and temporary colonist north to Colo., Neb., and Ark. **HABITAT:** Mesquite and thorn woodland, roadside verges, streambeds. **REMARKS:** Adults nectar at flowers of low plants, including fog fruit. Several crescents, including Vesta, have a "short-day" form marcia found in early spring and fall. This form is characterized especially on the underside by the hindwing's light median band and darker outer half. The Phaon, Pearl, and (rarely) Northern Crescents have marcia form as well.

PHAON CRESCENT *Phyciodes phaon* PL. 28

1–1¼ in. (26–32 mm). Upperside: Forewing with *pale cream median band. Black markings more extensive* than on similar southern crescents. Underside: *Hindwing cream with black smudges and lines*. Spring and fall individuals have gray hindwing (short-day form). **SIMILAR SPECIES:** (1) Pearl and (2) Vesta Crescents lack distinct cream-yellow median band on upper forewing, and (3) Painted Crescent has relatively uniform cream-yellow hindwing below. **EARLY STAGES:** Caterpillar variable: olive green to olive-brown with both white and darker bands. **FOOD:** Fog fruit and mat grass. **FLIGHT:** All year in tropics, s. Tex., and s. Fla.; more restricted at

Mating pair of Phaon Crescents, Gainesville, Alachua Co., Fla. Note the predominantly cream hindwing with black smudges and lines. The pattern is highly contrasting compared to Pearl or Vesta Crescents with which it may be found.

northern stations. **RANGE:** Resident from s. Calif., s. Ariz., s. N.M., and w. Tex. east to coastal S.C. south to Cuba and through Mex. to Guatemala. Strays and occasionally colonizes as far north as e. Colo., Neb., and Mo. **HABITAT:** Open areas with closely cropped vegetation, pastures, dunes, road verges. **REMARKS:** Adults most often nectar on fog fruit flowers—its caterpillar host—but also on others such as shepherd's needle.

PEARL CRESCENT *Phyciodes tharos* PL. 28

1–1⅜ in. (26–35 mm). Geographically and seasonally variable. Upperside: Male with *postmedian and submarginal orange areas broken by fine black marks.* Underside: *Hindwing with crescent in dark marginal patch.* Spring- and fall-brood individuals have gray mottled hindwing underside (marcia form). **SIMILAR SPECIES:** Northern Crescent may be difficult to separate in areas where the two could co-occur, but is often larger, has more open distinct yellow-orange areas above, and thin orange lines and paler crescent patch on hindwing below. Usually flies between first and second flights of Pearl Crescent. **EARLY STAGES:** Caterpillar is dark chocolate brown; spines brown. Head with white patches. **FOOD:** Asters. **FLIGHT:** All year in Deep South and Mex. (many broods), April or May–Oct. or Nov. farther north (2–4 broods). **RANGE:** Extreme s. Canada from se. Alta. east to s. Ont, south through e. two-thirds of the U.S. (east of Continental Divide) and Southwest to n. Baja Calif. and s. Mex. (Oaxaca). **HABITAT:** Prairies, intermittent stream-courses, wooded marshes, open weedy areas, pastures, vacant lots, roadsides. **REMARKS:** The Pearl and Northern Crescents co-occur in several areas without hybridizing freely; in a few other areas the species are difficult to separate and may hybridize. Adults

Male Pearl Crescent nectaring at white clover, Larimer Co., Colo. Occasionally overlaps with the more montane or higher latitude Northern Crescent from which it may be told with careful study.

nectar at many low flowers, including asters, fleabanes, and yellow composites. One of our commonest, most widespread temperate butterflies.

NORTHERN CRESCENT *Phyciodes cocyta*   PL. 28

1 ¼–1 ¹¹/₁₆ in. (32–43 mm). Upperside: Males have relatively *large open orange postmedian and submarginal areas.* Underside: Hindwing usually with *pale tan marginal crescent patch and pale orange wormlike markings.* Females darker but often inseparable from those of Pearl and Tawny Crescents. Short-day form exceedingly rare. **SIMILAR SPECIES:** Pearl Crescent is usually smaller and has orange areas above broken by black lines; underside of hindwing has ground with fine black marks, and crescent is usually within a dark or blackish field. **EARLY STAGES:** Caterpillar is similar to that of Pearl Crescent, but body is pinkish and spines are pinkish gray.

PEARL
CRESCENT

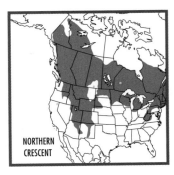

NORTHERN
CRESCENT

FOOD: Asters with large stem-clasping leaves. **FLIGHT:** June–July, rarely as early as mid-May or as late as Aug. (1 flight), possibly 2 flights in s. Canada. **RANGE:** From the Yukon and MacKenzie Delta southeast across Canada and south through the western mountain archipelago to ne. Ore., ne. Nev., cen. Ariz. and s. N.M. In the East from Lab. and Nfld. south to n. Great Lakes states, and nw. N.J. In the Appalachians south to N.C. and W. Va. **HABITAT:** Aspen groves, meadows, openings in woods near streams. **REMARKS:** Very similar to Pearl Crescent but known to be a separate species since the two overlap in range without hybridizing. Western populations are extremely variable, and Northern Crescent may include some unnamed isolated sibling species.

TAWNY CRESCENT *Phyciodes batesii*   PL. 28

1 ⅟₁₆–1½ in. (28–38 mm). *Antennal knobs black* (orange in some Southwest populations). Upperside: *Male dark with forewing postmedian band pale orange, contrasting with orange submarginal band.* Female variable. Adults in Southwest (subspecies *anasazi*) may be very orange above. Underside: *Forewing black patch on inner margin larger than subapical patch on costa.* **SIMILAR SPECIES:** (1) Pearl Crescent usually has black antennal knobs, lacks open yellow-orange areas above, and has small or large black median spot on trailing edge of forewing below. (2) Male Northern Crescents usually have tan or orange crescent in crescent patch on underside of hindwing. Females may be inseparable. Flies after Tawny Crescent in most areas. **EARLY STAGES:** Caterpillar brown with pinkish tinge, covered with tiny cream dots and pale, broad dorsal stripe and reddish or orange spines along side. Head black with cream stripe. **FOOD:** Large smooth-leaved asters. **FLIGHT:** May–July (1 flight). **RANGE:** Ne. B.C. and Cen. Alta.

Two male Tawny Crescents at moisture, Jackson Co., Wisc. Note dark forewing and pale postmedian band. Recently described more westerly subspecies may be oranger above. Photo by Jim Ebner.

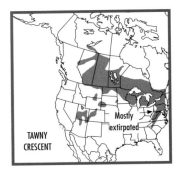
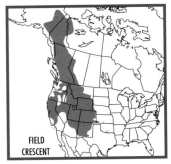

TAWNY CRESCENT

FIELD CRESCENT

south to n. Ariz., w. Colo., and w. Neb. thence east to cen. Ont. and sw. Que., south in to n. Ga. (in mountains), Mich., and Wisc. Many older records are based on misidentifications. **HABITAT:** Moist slopes, steep ravines, pastures, dry rocky ridges. **REMARKS:** Species has disappeared from most of its former haunts in East, but remains locally common in West.

FIELD CRESCENT *Phyciodes pratensis*   **PL. 28**

¹⁵⁄₁₆–1½ in. (24–39 mm). *Antennal knobs brown.* Forewing outer margin not angled. Upperside: *Dark,* very similar to Tawny Crescent. Underside: *Forewing with yellow discal bar and smaller black patches.* Hindwing more heavily patterned. **SIMILAR SPECIES:** (1) In a few areas where they overlap, the Painted Crescent may be identified by its uniformly cream hindwing undersurface and the presence of a cream-yellow postmedian band on the forewing above.

Male Field Crescent nectaring at gumweed, Larimer Co., Colo. This is the commonest crescent is western mountains and intermountain valleys. Note brown antennal knobs and yellow discal bar.

(2) California Crescent has angled forewing outer margins and orange antennal knobs (Field Crescent has smooth outer margin and brown antennal knobs). **EARLY STAGES:** Caterpillar brown-black covered with tiny cream dots and with faint dorsal stripes; head black. **FOOD:** Asters, tansy asters, fleabanes. **FLIGHT:** Feb.–Dec. in cen. Calif. (3 flights), May–Sept. in much of range (2 flights), only

PAINTED CRESCENT

1 flight in Canada and some U.S. mountain ranges, e.g., Sierra Nevada (subspecies *montana*). **RANGE:** Boreal w. N. Amer. from Alaska, Yukon, and sw. N.W. Terr. south to s. Calif., cen. Ariz. and s. N.M., east to sw. Man. **HABITAT:** Open areas and glades in mountains and foothills — often near streamcourses. Also taiga, prairie flats, and marshes. **REMARKS:** Populations in Sierra Nevada of Calif. (subspecies *montana*) are mainly orange above with a distinct even black margin on both wings.

PAINTED CRESCENT *Phyciodes picta*   PL. 28

⅞–1 ³⁄₁₆ in. (23–30 mm). Small. Upperside: Dark forewing with *yellow patch near apex contrasting with often primarily orange hindwing crossed by distinct median cream-yellow band.* Underside: Forewing *apex and hindwing clear yellow-cream.* **SIMILAR SPECIES:** Phaon Crescent is similar but its range overlaps in a few southern areas, where it may be separated by its orange areas on forewing and brighter orange hindwings that lack median cream-yellow band. **EARLY STAGES:** Caterpillar yellow-brown covered with tiny cream dots and with faint dorsal lines; head brown and cream. **FOOD:** Hairy tube-tongue, bindweed, and possibly asters. **FLIGHT:** Late Feb.–late Oct. (2–3 flights). **RANGE:** W. Neb., e. Colo., and cen. Kans. south to s. Ariz., N.M., and w. Tex. south into n. Mex. **HABITAT:** Marsh and stream edges in short-grass prairie, open disturbed areas, road edges. **REMARKS:** This butterfly has switched from its original native host to feed mainly on bindweed, an exotic weed introduced from Europe. Adults nectar at fog fruit and other flowers.

CALIFORNIA CRESCENT *Phyciodes orseis*   PL. 28

1 ³⁄₁₆–1 ⅝ in. (30–41 mm). *Outer margin of forewing angled. Antennal knobs mostly orange.* Upperside: Mainly black in n. Calif. and s. Ore. (subspecies *orseis*), mainly orange in Sierra Nevada of

Female California Crescent (subspecies herlani) *nectaring at aster, Sierra Nevada, Calif. Tip of antennal knob is orange. Adult is mainly orange above. Males perch along gullies. Photo by Greg Ballmer.*

Calif. and Nev. (subspecies *herlani*). Underside: *Hindwing mottled* in subspecies *orseis, yellow* with *fine brown lines* in subspecies *herlani*. **SIMILAR SPECIES:** In range of subspecies *orseis*, Field Crescent may be identified by its brown antennal knobs and unangled forewing outer margin. In subspecies *herlani*'s range, Field Crescent may be told by its angled forewing outer margin and brown antennal knobs, while Mylitta Crescent is somewhat smaller and is often in different habitats. **EARLY STAGES:** Caterpillar maroon-black above, brownish below. Band along sides orange in subspecies *orseis*, ocher brown in subspecies *herlani*. **FOOD:** Thistles (genus *Cirsium*). **FLIGHT:** Mid-May–June for subspecies *orseis*, late June–mid-Aug. for subspecies *herlani* (1 flight). **RANGE:** Klamath Range of s. Ore. south to cen. Sierra Nevada (Calif.). **HABITAT:** Gulches and creeks in mountains. **REMARKS:** Males of California Crescent perch along stream and gully bottoms while males of similar Mylitta and Field Crescents patrol open habitats. Populations may have once occurred in San Francisco and a few counties to the north, but, if so, are now extirpated.

PALE CRESCENT *Phyciodes pallida*   **PL. 28**

1 ³⁄₁₆–1 ½ in. (30–39 mm). Forewing *outer margin angled*. Antennal knobs orange. Upperside: Orange with irregular pattern of black marks and spots. Female with median yellow-orange band. Underside: Forewing *with squarish black patch in center of rear margin next to hindwing* (difficult to see in nature). Hindwing with *submarginal spot row off-white, especially in females*. **SIMILAR SPECIES:** Mylitta Crescent similar but smaller and lacks black patch along trailing edge of forewing below and never has submarginal white spot row on underside of hindwing. **EARLY STAGES:** Caterpillar ocher

CALIFORNIA CRESCENT

extirpated

PALE CRESCENT

with brown line up back and brown band along each side. Head black with cream marks. **FOOD:** Thistles *(Cirsium)*. **FLIGHT:** Late April–early July, Aug.–Oct. (2 flights). **RANGE:** S. B.C. south in mountains to n. Ore., s. Nev., cen. Ariz., Utah, and sw. Colo. and east to cen. Mont. and w. S.D. and w. Neb. **HABITAT:** Sunny gullies and streamcourses in foothills and mountains, occasional hillsides and ridges. **REMARKS:** Adults nectar at yellow composites. Males perch prominently on branches or rocks along gully bottoms or streamcourses.

MYLITTA CRESCENT *Phyciodes mylitta*   **PL. 28**

1–1½ in. (26–37 mm). Forewing outer margin angled. Antennal knobs orange. Upperside: Orange with black lines and spots. Female with yellow-orange median band. Underside: *Forewing plain orange, occasionally with submarginal black streak. Hindwing or-*

Female Mylitta Crescent resting, Solano Co., Calif. This is the commonest crescent in lowland Calif. and much of Ariz. Note orange antennal knobs and yellow-orange median band. Often found along streams or in weedy fields.

MYLITTA
CRESCENT

GILLETTE'S
CHECKERSPOT

ange-brown sometimes with whitish median band and white sub-marginal crescent. **SIMILAR SPECIES:** (1) Pallid Crescent is very similar, and ranges overlap without hybridization. (2) Mylitta Crescents in N.M. and Ariz. seem intermediate between the 2 species in several aspects. **EARLY STAGES:** Caterpillar black to maroon with many pale dots. Spines black or orange-brown (along sides). Paired cream lines along back and sides. Head black with cream marks. **FOOD:** Several thistles (*Cirsium, Carduus,* and *Silybium*). **FLIGHT:** Feb.–Nov. in Ariz. and Calif., April–Oct. to north (several flights). **RANGE:** S. B.C. and cen. Mont. south through much of our area mainly west of Continental Divide but east of it in Colo., Kans., and N.M. south to n. Baja Calif. and s. Mex. **HABITAT:** Streamcourses in foothills and mountains, open meadows or disturbed fields in valleys. **REMARKS:** Adults nectar at a wide variety of flowers, including fogfruit, yellow star-thistle, wild buckwheats, asters, and yellow composites.

GILLETTE'S CHECKERSPOT *Euphydryas gillettii*   PL. 28

1 7/16–1 13/16 in. (37–46 mm). Unique appearance. Upperside: Both wings with *broad submarginal red-orange band and thin black marginal area. Two red-orange bars on black forewing and a row of yellow spots on each wing.* Underside: Both wings with black veins, orange marginal line, narrow yellow submarginal band, and broad red-orange postmedian band. **SIMILAR SPECIES:** No other checkerspot has distinctive red-orange bands. **EARLY STAGES:** Caterpillar black with yellow strip up back and white stripe along each side. Spines on back are yellow, those along sides are black. Head black. **FOOD:** Twinberry, speedwell, and others. **FLIGHT:** Late June–mid-Aug. (1 flight). **RANGE:** Rockies of s. Alta. south through Idaho and w. Mont. to w. Wyo. **HABITAT:** Openings and meadows in moist valleys in conifer forests. **REMARKS:** Resembles some checkerspots found in Eurasia. Habitats are destroyed in periodic fires,

Male Variable Checkerspot (subspecies hermosa) *resting, Sierra Co., N.M. Populations vary from black to red to pale orange. This individual is from one of the palest populations.*

and butterflies recolonize very slowly. Adults nectar at flowers, including yellow composites.

VARIABLE CHECKERSPOT *Euphydryas chalcedona* **PL. 28**

1 ⅛–2 ³⁄₁₆ in. (29–55 mm). Extremely variable geographically. Many named subspecies. *Forewing relatively pointed.* Abdomen often with *white dots along sides.* Upperside: Ranges from almost entirely black with a few yellow checks through checkered red-orange, black, and yellow to primarily yellow-orange. Forewing usually with 2 *red-orange bars on forward margin often bounded by yellow or yellow-cream.* Underside: *Hindwing with postmedian and marginal red-orange bands, separated by median and submarginal cream bands.* **SIMILAR SPECIES:** Edith's Checkerspot abdomen lacks lateral cream spots, has more rounded forewings, has cream postmedian spot along lower edge of forewing underside with more black edging basally, and postmedian red-orange band on underside of hindwing invading median band. **EARLY STAGES:** Caterpillar black with variable amounts of white; rows of variably colored bristly tubercles. **FOOD:** *Besseya,* Indian paintbrushes, beeplant, sticky monkey-flower, penstemons, snowberries, and others. **FLIGHT:** Feb.–early Aug., often Oct. (1 flight). **RANGE:** Resident in much of w. N. Amer. from cen. Alaska and cen. Yukon south through mountainous West, including some prairie hills, to n. Baja Calif. and nw. Mex.; stray to nw. Minn. **HABITAT:** Many kinds of open situations, including oak woodland, streamcourses, pinyon-juniper woodland, sagebrush flats and hills, and high prairie with mixed conifers. **REMARKS:** The Anicia, Colon, and Chalcedon Checkerspots are now considered to be one species, but do not fit well into either a single species or several separate species. The butterfly populations grade into one another from north to

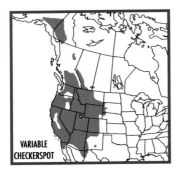

south. But some populations of the Anicia Checkerspot and the Colon Checkerspot occur in the same areas without intergradation.

EDITH'S CHECKERSPOT *Euphydryas editha*   **PL. 28**

1–1 ¹¹⁄₁₆ in. (26–43 mm). *Forewing usually rounded. Abdomen black, usually with red rings.* Upperside: Combination of red, black, and cream bands and checkers. Underside: *Underside of forewing has postmedian cream spot along its lower edge with heavier black scaling basally. Postmedian red-orange band on hindwing often extends into median cream band.* Male genitalia with diagnostic features. **SIMILAR SPECIES:** Variable Checkerspot averages larger and usually has lateral row of cream spots on abdomen and more pointed forewing. **EARLY STAGES:** Caterpillar black, often with white or orange spots or stripes. Black spines often with orange at

Female Edith's Checkerspot nectaring on fleabane, Paiute Co., Utah. Above this butterfly can be identified by rounded wings and black abdomen with narrow red-orange rings.

base. **FOOD:** A variety of plants in the figwort, valerian, plantago, and honeysuckle families. Caterpillars often switch to a different plant after hibernation or estivation. **FLIGHT:** Late Feb.–late Aug. (1 flight), earlier at low elevations. Usually flies earlier than Variable Checkerspot at any given locality. **RANGE:** W. N. Amer. from B.C. and Alta. south through mountains to n. Baja Calif., s. Utah, and sw. Colo. **HABITAT:** Areas with low vegetation or openings including grasslands, sagebrush, montane meadows, and alpine tundra. **REMARKS:** Two subspecies, the Bay Checkerspot (ssp. *bayensis*) and Quino Checkerspot (ssp. *quino*), both from Calif., are listed as endangered by the U.S. Fish and Wildlife Service. This is perhaps our best-studied butterfly, as Dr. Paul Ehrlich and his students at Stanford University have studied its population fluctuations and natural history for four decades.

BALTIMORE CHECKERSPOT SEE PHOTOGRAPH
Euphydryas phaeton

1⅜–2½ in. (36–62 mm). Upperside: *Black with several rows of cream white spots on outer half of both wings. Outer margin of both wings with red-orange crescents.* **EARLY STAGES:** Caterpillar orange-red striped with black; spines black. **FOOD:** Turtlehead, beard-tongues, false foxglove, and English plantain before hibernation, variety of other plants afterward. **FLIGHT:** Late June–mid-Aug. in north, mid-May–late June in south (1 flight). **RANGE:** Nw. Neb., se. Man. east to Maritimes south to e. Tex., n. Ark., and n. portions of Gulf States. **HABITAT:** Usually marshes and wet meadows, but also sandy oak barrens, streamsides, and open or wooded hillsides. **REMARKS:** State butterfly of Maryland.

Male Baltimore Checkerspot perching, Pendleton Co., W. Va. A distinctive eastern species that enters our area in Neb. Note the 3 rows of cream spots on outer portion of wings and the more basal red-orange spots.

QUESTION MARK *Polygonia interrogationis*   **PL. 29**

1 ⅞–2 ½ in. (48–66 mm). Large. Upperside: Hindwing of summer form largely black with short taillike projections, while that of winter form is orange and black with *longer violet-tipped tails*. Forewing with *"extra" black dash not present in similar Eastern Comma*. Underside: *Pearly silver question mark* on hindwing is diagnostic. Sexes are similar, but there are 2 seasonal forms. **SIMILAR SPECIES:** Eastern Comma has similar seasonal forms but is smaller, has shorter hindwing tails, lacks extra black dash on forewing above, and has comma on underside of hindwing. **EARLY STAGES:** Caterpillar variable, body and spines black to yellow; back with 8 metallic silver spots. **FOOD:** Nettle, false nettle, Japanese hops, elms, and hackberry. **FLIGHT:** Two broods: late fall to early spring (winter form), late spring to fall (summer form). Winter form adults overwinter. **RANGE:** E. Alta. (once) east to N.S. and s. N.B. thence south to Colo., se. Ariz., and e. U.S. to cen. Mex. Immigrant and seasonal colonist to northern and western portions of range. **HABITAT:** River woods, wooded swamps, city parks, and other wooded situations. Migrants may be found in virtually any location.

EASTERN COMMA *Polygonia comma*   **PL. 29**

1 ⅝–2 1/16 in. (42–52 mm). Small with *stubby taillike projections on hindwing*. Upperside: Forewing has a *single dark postmedian spot near bottom edge*. Dark border on hindwing encloses pale spots and is broader than forewing border. Hindwing is either primarily black (summer form) or orange with black spots (winter form). Underside: Hindwing has a *central silver or white comma mark* that is swollen at both ends. **SIMILAR SPECIES:** (1) Question Mark is larger, has long violet-tipped taillike projections from hindwing, and has a question mark in center of hindwing below. (2) Satyr

Male Eastern Comma (winter form) resting on vegetation, Fairfax Co., Va. Note single black postmedian spot near trailing edge of hindwing (Question Mark has 2).

Comma has more extensive orange, has 2 dark postmedian spots near bottom edge of forewing above, and has hindwing below golden brown with a relatively straight median line. **EARLY STAGES:** Caterpillar variable, black to green-brown and white, spines black to white, rising from yellow tubercles. **FOOD:** Nettle, false nettle, elms, and hops. **FLIGHT:** Two broods. Sept.–May (winter form), late May–August (summer form). **RANGE:** Se. Sask. and s. Man. east across s. Canada to N.B., thence south to nw. Colo., e.-cen. Tex., and throughout eastern half of U.S. to Gulf Coast. **HABITAT:** Woods near rivers, swamps, marshes, moist woods, etc.

SATYR COMMA *Polygonia satyrus*   **PL. 29**

1¾–2¹⁄₁₆ in. (45–53 mm). Upperside: Forewing usually has 2 *black postmedian spots near bottom edge*. Hindwing with *marginal dark border only as broad as forewing outer margin; has black spot in center*. Underside: *Golden brown with median line relatively straight*. **SIMILAR SPECIES:** Eastern Comma's upperside usually has only 1 dark postmedian spot along bottom edge of forewing; median line on hindwing underside not as straight. **EARLY STAGES:** Caterpillar with green-white dorsal band and lateral lines; spines black (laterals) or green-white (dorsal and subdorsal). Lives in folded leaf shelter. **FOOD:** Nettles. **FLIGHT:** Adults emerge from chrysalis

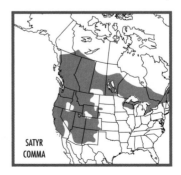

SATYR COMMA

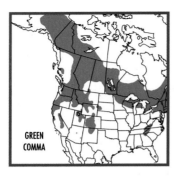

in summer and overwinter to spring (1 long flight). **RANGE:** Alaska panhandle and s. Yukon and sw. N.W. Terr. east across boreal and s. Canada to n. Great Lakes, N.S. and n. New England, thence south through most of w. N. Amer. to s. Calif., s. Ariz., and N.M. **HABITAT:** Openings in river woods and conifer forests, marshes, orchards, nearby fields and edges, wooded ravines in prairies. **REMARKS:** Commonest Comma along lowland Pacific Coast.

GREEN COMMA *Polygonia faunus*   PL. 29

1⅜–2 in. (36–52 mm). Wing *outline exceptionally irregular and ragged.* Upperside: Forewing with *inner 2 costal black spots fused or almost so.* Hindwing with *submarginal light spots in dark field.* Underside: Variable from heavily mottled to uniform gray, often with *submarginal green spots.* **SIMILAR SPECIES:** (1) Hoary and (2) Gray Commas have less irregular wings outlines, have 2 costal black spots on forewing usually separate, and never have any hint

Male Green Comma (subspecies hylas) at moisture, Rocky Mt. National Park, Colo. Note irregular wing outline and pale submarginal spots in darker field on hindwing.

of green below. **EARLY STAGES:** Caterpillars yellow-brown to brick red with the back white; broken double orange lateral bands, and transverse black and yellow bands or spots; most spines white; head black with white W on front. **FOOD:** Willows, aspens, birches, alders, rhododendrons, gooseberries, blueberries. **FLIGHT:** Adults emerge in mid- to late summer, overwinter, and reproduce the following spring. Adults live 9–10 months (1 long flight). **RANGE:** Alaska south through much of boreal and mountainous w. N. Amer. to cen. Calif., e.-cen. Ariz., and cen. N.M. and eastward across most of Canada south of the tundra to the n. Great Lakes region, the Maritimes and New England. A separate isolated population in s. Appalachians. **HABITAT:** Openings in Canadian zone coniferous or mixed woods, often along or near streams. **REMARKS:** *Polygonia hylas* and *P. silvius,* once considered separate species, are included here. Adult Green Commas visit flowers on rare occasions but usually feed on sap flows or dung.

HOARY COMMA *Polygonia gracilis* PL. 29

1 ½–1 ⅞ in. (39–47 mm). Upperside: *Hindwing with light submarginal spots in dark band.* Underside: Wing surfaces gray-brown, *outer half distinctly pale, often hoary white or silver-gray. Comma mark is abruptly curved in fishhook shape.* **SIMILAR SPECIES:** Some individuals of Gray Comma in Colo. (subspecies *nigrozephyrus*) may be nearly identical above, but are mainly black below. **EARLY STAGES:** Caterpillar black with upper part of rear half of abdomen white. **FOOD:** Currants. **FLIGHT:** Adults emerge in July, fly until Sept., overwinter, and fly until May or June of the following spring. **RANGE:** Alaska east across most of Canada south of the tundra to Lab., N.S. and n. New England. In the West through most mountainous areas south to s. Calif., se. Ariz., and s. N.M. Strays to Kans. and Neb. **HABITAT:** Coniferous or mixed woods often near streams. Wanders to many other habitats, including alpine tundra, towns, plains river woods, and prairies. **REMARKS:** Our western populations once called the Zephyr are now considered a subspecies (*P. g. zephyrus*). This species seems to visit flowers more readily than other commas.

GRAY COMMA *Polygonia progne* PL. 29

1 ¾–2 in. (44–52 mm). Upperside: Hindwing with *outer portion black enclosing submarginal yellow-orange spots.* Underside: *Hindwing gray to gray-brown or black with or without fine striations.* Hindwing *has little or no contrast between basal and outer portions. Comma is tapered at both ends.* **EARLY STAGES:** Caterpillar dark brown, yellow-brown, and pale yellow with complex pattern of darker V-marks, rings, and blotches; spines orange or black

Male Gray Comma (subspecies oreas). The Oreas Anglewing is treated as a separate species by some. Males perch in gullies and just above small streams. Photo by Greg Ballmer.

with pale bases. Head black with orange W on front and surmounted by 2 black spiny horns. **FOOD:** Gooseberries and currants; rarely azalea or birch. **FLIGHT:** June or July, overwintering then active April to early June of following year (1 flight). **RANGE:** Sw. N.W. Terr. and n. B.C. across Canada south of taiga to Nfld. and N.S. then south to cen. Calif., n. Utah, Colo., e. Okla., and south in Appalachians to N.C. **HABITAT:** Wooded streams in coniferous or mixed forests, aspen parklands. **REMARKS:** The Oreas Comma (*P. p. oreas*) is included here on the basis of studies by J. Scott. Whether the western (*oreas*) and eastern (*progne*) populations should be considered a single species is still unclear.

COMPTON TORTOISESHELL *Nymphalis vaualbum* **PL. 29**
2⁷⁄₁₆–2¾ in. (62–72 mm). Distinct. Upperside: *Single white spots on forewing and hindwing costal margins.* Vaguely reminiscent of

GRAY COMMA

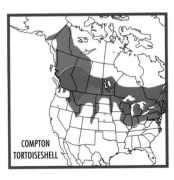

COMPTON TORTOISESHELL

anglewings *(Polygonia)* in that it has somewhat irregular wing outlines, although inner margin of forewing is *straight, not curved,* as in anglewings. Underside: Hindwing striated gray or brown with *central silver comma mark.* **SIMILAR SPECIES:** No other butterfly has similar uppersides, but the commas all have comma marks below but have much more irregular wing shapes. **EARLY STAGES:** Caterpillar light green with black spines. **FOOD:** Aspen, birches, and willows; rarely elm. **FLIGHT:** Adults emerge in July, fly until Oct. or Nov., overwinter, and fly until the following June (1 flight). **RANGE:** Holarctic. In N. Amer. breeding resident from Alaska panhandle, n. B.C., and sw. N.W. Terr. south to nw. Wash. and w. Mont. east in band to N.S., N.B., New England, and N.Y. Wanders north of breeding range to Yukon and Lab. and south to s. Ore., n. Nev., n. Utah, Wyo., Colo., and Neb. in West. **HABITAT:** Upland boreal forests, especially deciduous.

CALIFORNIA TORTOISESHELL

CALIFORNIA TORTOISESHELL   PL. 29
Nymphalis californica

1 ¾–2 ⅛ in. (45–54 mm). Distinct. Upperside: *Orange with large black spots.* **SIMILAR SPECIES:** Milbert's Tortoiseshell is smaller and has black basal and orange outer portions of forewing above sharply divided. **EARLY STAGES:** Caterpillar velvety black with white

Male California Tortoiseshell perching, Jefferson Co., Colo. Underside is lighter and more irregularly marked than the related but dissimilar Milbert's Tortoiseshell.

Mourning Cloak nectaring at common milkweed, Sioux Co., Iowa. On the underside, the butterfly is more cryptically marked to avoid notice, but the same basic pattern may be seen.

dots; spines black except for a yellow dorsal row. **FOOD:** Wild lilacs (*Ceanothus*). **FLIGHT:** Adults emerge in late June, fly until fall, overwinter, and fly until the following April or May (1 flight). **RANGE:** Pacific Coast from s. B.C. south to s. Calif.; east to cen. Alta., cen. Colo., and e. N.M. in most boreal western ranges. Migrants rarely found east to Mich., Pa., N.Y., and Vt. **HABITAT:** Ridgetops (males), open brushy areas, and open woods. **REMARKS:** Undergoes periodic massive population outbreaks and emigrations in the Far West. During outbreak years adults can be so abundant that cars in n. Calif. have been reported to skid on highways from the massive numbers of dead butterflies.

MOURNING CLOAK *Nymphalis antiopa*   **PL. 29**

2¹¹⁄₁₆–3⁷⁄₁₆ in. (68–87 mm). One of our most familiar, readily identified butterflies. Outer margins irregular, with a short taillike projection on hindwing. Upperside: *Purplish brown with a broad, bright yellow marginal border on both wings* (fading to white with age) and a row of iridescent blue spots just inside border. **EARLY STAGES:** Caterpillar black with minute white flecks; a dorsal row of dull red spots; red-orange prolegs; and black spines. Caterpillars feed gregariously. **FOOD:** Willows, birch, cottonwood, elm, hackberry. **FLIGHT:** Adults emerge in June or July, estivate until fall, overwinter, and then fly until the following May or June (1 flight, rarely 2). **RANGE:** Holarctic. Throughout N. Amer. including arctic tundra (except peninsular Fla., s. La., and s. Tex.); extends irregularly south to cen. Mex. **HABITAT:** Streamcourses, woodland glades, city parks, arroyos. Migrants are seen in a wide variety of habitats. **REMARKS:** Mourning Cloak may be our longest-lived butterfly — adults live 10–12 months. Most adults overwinter; apparently,

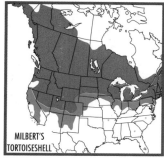

MOURNING CLOAK

MILBERT'S TORTOISESHELL

some of the population migrates south each fall. In the West, where development timing varies with altitude and altitudinal movements occur, in late June or early July one may find worn individuals from the previous year and freshly emerged adults on the same day.

MILBERT'S TORTOISESHELL *Nymphalis milberti*   PL. 29

1¼–2 in. (38–51 mm). Outer margins are irregular with a *short taillike projection* on hindwing. Upperside: Basal two-thirds of both wings black (except for 2 costal orange marks on forewing). *Outer third of both wings orange grading to yellow-orange at inner edge.* A *narrow black marginal border on both wings sometimes includes blue points* on hindwing. **SIMILAR SPECIES:** California Tortoiseshell is usually larger, has more irregular pattern above, and is browner below. **EARLY STAGES:** Caterpillar usually black with minute

Milbert's Tortoiseshell basking, Laramie Co., Colo. This recently emerged individual shows a bright distinctive-patterned black basal area and yellow and orange submarginal area with neat black margins.

Red Admiral nectaring at Rabbitbrush, Larimer Co., Co. The black butterfly with red-orange forewing band and hindwing outer margin cannot be confused with any other butterfly. Photo by Evi Buckner.

white flecks and a broken lateral green-yellow stripe. Caterpillars feed gregariously. **FOOD:** Nettles. **FLIGHT:** Adults emerge in July, overwinter as adults and fly as late as June of following year (1 flight); occasional partial second brood. **RANGE:** Boreal N. Amer. from cen. Alaska, s. Yukon, sw. N.W. Terr. south and east through Canada, n. U.S. and south in the western mountains. Occasionally migrating south of breeding range to s. Calif., s. N.M., s. Ind., and Pa. — rarely to Mo., Ga., S.C., and N.C. **HABITAT:** Moist streamsides, wet meadows, springs, taiga. Found in a wide variety of situations where not resident, such as alpine tundra, towns, gardens, prairie streams, oak woodland, etc. **REMARKS:** Local and altitudinal movements are not well understood. Males establish perches on hilltops where available. Adults visit flowers readily.

RED ADMIRAL *Vanessa atalanta* **PL. 29**

1⅞–2¼ in. (48–65 mm). Common and widespread. Upperside: Black. Forewing with *white apical spots* and *red-orange median band;* hindwing with *red-orange marginal band.* **EARLY STAGES:** Caterpillars variable black to yellow-green with black and yellow lateral stripes. **FOOD:** Nettles, false nettle, wood nettle, pellitory, possibly hops. **FLIGHT:** March or April to Sept. or Oct. in north (2 flights), possibly more in south. Overwinters as adult along immediate Pacific Coast, se. Ariz., and possibly elsewhere to south. **RANGE:** Holarctic. N. Amer. south of the taiga and south through Mexican highlands to Guatemala. Resident on Hawaii. Migrant and temporary colonist in northern part of range. **HABITAT:** Openings in or near streamcourses, marshes, seeps, moist fields, city parks, ridgetops (males). May be found in a wide variety of habitats during migration and overwintering. **REMARKS:** A regular migrant that

RED ADMIRAL

AMERICAN LADY

probably cannot survive the coldest winters and must recolonize more northern and inland areas.

AMERICAN LADY *Vanessa virginiensis*   **PL. 29**

1¾–2¼ in. (44–57 mm). Formerly called the Hunter's Butterfly or Virginia Lady. Upperside: Forewing with *a white dot in orange field just below black apical patch.* Underside: Hindwing with 2 *large submarginal eyespots.* **SIMILAR SPECIES:** (1) Painted and (2) West Coast Ladies both lack submarginal small white spot in orange area near outer edge of forewing outer margin. Neither has the pair of large submarginal eyespots on the hindwing below. **EARLY STAGES:** Caterpillar has a complex pattern—black with transverse white bands; a pair of subdorsal silver-white spots on rear half; 4 rows of black spines, each arising from a broad red base. **FOOD:** Everlastings, pussytoes, rarely other Compositae and other families. **FLIGHT:** April–Nov. (3–4 broods), all year in coastal Calif., se. Ariz., and possibly other areas. **RANGE:** Resident along immediate Pacific coast (Calif.), s. Ariz., s. U.S., Mex., and highlands of Cen. Amer. south to Colombia. Possibly found elsewhere where winter freezing temperatures are rare. Migrant and sometimes temporary colonist to s. Canada, West Indies, Hawaii, and Europe. Strays periodically to Nfld. and once to Lab. **HABITAT:** Open areas with low vegetation, openings in forests, meadows, dunes, gardens, vacant lots. **REMARKS:** Adults probably cannot survive extended cold winters, and it is necessary for migrants to colonize most of the U.S. and se. Canada each year.

PAINTED LADY *Vanessa cardui*   **PL. 29**

1¹³⁄₁₆–2½ in. (46–64 mm). Forewing pointed. Upperside: Orange with pinkish overtone when freshly emerged. Forewing has black apical area with *included white spots.* Hindwing has *submarginal*

Painted Lady nectaring on rabbitbrush, Larimer Co., Colo. Note the small black submarginal spots on hindwing. Compare with the similar West Coast Lady on next page.

row of 5 *small black spots*, occasionally with some blue scaling. Underside: *Mottled gray, brown, and black with 4 small submarginal eyespots.* **SIMILAR SPECIES:** (1) American Painted Lady has small white spot in orange field below black apical forewing patch and always has some blue in upper hindwing submarginal spots. Hindwing below has 2 very large submarginal eyespots (2) West Coast Lady has 4 equal-sized blue-filled submarginal eyespots on upper hindwing. **EARLY STAGES:** Caterpillar variable; lilac to yellow-green with black mottlings and black head. **FOOD:** More than 100 plants, especially thistles, mallows, and legumes. **FLIGHT:** Feb.–Nov. in most of West (1–3 flights) as colonist, periodic year-round resident in se. Ariz., coastal s. Calif., and n. Mex. **RANGE:** Occurs on all continents except Antarctica and Australia. Resident in Mexican plateau, migrant and temporary colonist throughout U.S. (commoner in West) and Canada north to Alaska, s. Yukon, sw. N.W. Terr., n. Que., and Lab. **HABITAT:** Many open situations: fields, marshes, forests, suburbs, prairies, dunes, thorn scrub, gardens. **REMARKS:** Also called Thistle Butterfly because of its preference for thistles and the Cosmopolitan for its virtually worldwide occurrence. Next to the Monarch, this is our most conspicuous migrant. Painted Ladies cannot survive freezing temperatures and must colonize most of our area each year, either as scattered migrants or by spectacular mass emigrations that come out of northern Mex.

KAMEHAMEHA LADY *Vanessa tameamea*   **PL. 29**
2–2¾ in. (52–70 mm). Distinctive. Forewing apex squared off; *hindwing outer margin scalloped.* Upperside: Both wings with extensive dull orange at base. Forewing with *large median red-or-*

PAINTED
LADY

KAMEHAMEHA LADY

ange area containing 2 black spots. Apical area black. Hindwing with *red-orange marginal area contains row of black dots.* **EARLY STAGES:** Caterpillar green with cream stripe along side, purplish with a yellow lateral stripe, or multicolored. Many red black-tipped branching spines. **FOOD:** Several plants in Nettle family, including *Pipterus* and *Boehmeria*. **FLIGHT:** All year (several flights). **RANGE:** Hawaii. All main islands. **HABITAT:** Openings in subtropical forests. **REMARKS:** This is one of Hawaii's two native butterflies. The other is the Hawaiian Blue.

WEST COAST LADY *Vanessa annabella*   PL. 29

1 ½–1 ⅞ in. (39–47 mm). Forewing *apex squared off.* Upperside: Forewing *costal bar is orange*—not white as in our other ladies. Hindwing with *3 or 4 blue submarginal spots.* Underside: Hindwing with *submarginal eyespots obscured.* **SIMILAR SPECIES:** (1) Ameri-

West Coast Lady nectaring on rabbitbrush, Larimer Co., Colo. Note squared-off wingtip, orange bar in apical black area of forewing, and round, blue-filled spots on submargin of hindwing.

WEST COAST LADY

COMMON BUCKEYE

can and (2) Painted Ladies have white costal bars on forewing above and usually do not have 4–5 blue-centered submarginal spots on hindwing. **EARLY STAGES:** Caterpillars variable, tan to black with large orange blotches. **FOOD:** Mallows, hollyhock, occasionally nettles. **FLIGHT:** All year in lowland Calif. and s. Ariz. (several flights), temporary colonist elsewhere in West (1–2 flights). **RANGE:** Resident in lowland Calif., s. Ariz., and nw. Mex., regular or irregular emigrant and colonist to most of w. U.S. north to cen. B.C., s. Alta., s. Sask., and sw. Man. Vagrants occur east to n. and w. Tex., w. Okla., cen. Kans., e. N.D., and s. Ont. **HABITAT:** Open valley flats, open woodland, meadows, weedy areas, roadsides, gardens, prairies. **REMARKS:** A closely related species, *Vanessa caryae,* occurs in S. Amer. West Coast Lady is one of the most regular butterflies in lowland Calif.

COMMON BUCKEYE *Junonia coenia*   **PL. 30**

1 ⅜–2 ¼ in. (36–58 mm). Upperside: Forewing with at least *part of white subapical bar inside the large eyespot. Uppermost of 2 hindwing eyespots is much larger and has a magenta crescent.* Underside: Hindwing tan-brown or rose-red (short-day form). **SIMILAR SPECIES:** Tropical Buckeye, including Dark Buckeye, usually has orange or dark brown costal bar on forewing and small more or less equal-sized eyespots on hindwing. **EARLY STAGES:** Caterpillar black with dorsal and lateral broken yellow lines; 4 rows of iridescent blue-black spines; head orange and black with 2 fleshy orange projections. **FOOD:** Snapdragon, plantain, owl's clover, monkeyflower, toadflax, false foxglove, and others. **FLIGHT:** April–Oct. (2–3 broods), all year in coastal lowland Calif., s. Ariz., s. Tex., and the Deep South. **RANGE:** Resident in s. U.S. and north along the coasts to cen. Calif. and N.C.; south to s. Mex., Bermuda, Cuba, and Isle of Pines; migrant and temporary colonist north to

Tropical "Dark" Buckeye (subspecies nigrosuffusa) *at moisture, Sonora state, Mex. This buckeye, found most commonly in se. Ariz. and s. N.M., has more extensive dark areas that the form shown on Plate 30.*

Ore., se. Idaho, se. Wyo., N.D., s. Man., s. Ont., and s. Me. **HABITAT:** Open, sunny locales: open fields, arroyos, dunes, roadsides, thorn scrub.

TROPICAL BUCKEYE *Junonia genoveva*   **PL. 30**

1¾–2⅜ in. (44–60 mm). Upperside: Upper surface mainly *dark brown*. Hindwing with 2 *eyespots of approximately equal size.* **SIMILAR SPECIES:** Common Buckeye has forewing band white. Upper eyespot on hindwing much larger than lower eyespot. **EARLY STAGES:** Caterpillar black with faint dorsal and lateral rows of cream dots; spines black with blue bases; head black with 2 short fleshy projections. **FOOD:** Speedwell and monkeyflower in s. Ariz., *Lippia*, porterweed, ruellia, stemodia in s. Tex. **FLIGHT:** Mid-March–early Jan. in se. Ariz. (3–4 flights). Most abundant in late summer and fall. **RANGE:** Resident in s. Ariz., s. N.M., s. Tex., s. Fla., south through the West Indies, Mex., and Cen. Amer. to Argentina. Rare vagrant to se. Calif., se. Colo. **HABITAT:** Foothill canyons, mesquite grasslands, and dry arroyos. **REMARKS:** The Dark Buckeye (*J. genoveva nigrosuffusa*) of the Southwest differs from related buckeyes of the tropical lowlands, but is similar to buckeyes found south in the Sierra Madre, at least to Durango and Sinaloa.

TROPICAL BUCKEYE

WHITE PEACOCK *Anartia jatrophae* PL. 30

1 ³⁄₁₆–2⅜ in. (46–60 mm). *Mostly white.* Upperside: *Small round black submarginal spot on forewing and 2 on slightly scalloped hindwing.* **EARLY STAGES:** Caterpillar dark brown to black, yellow-brown below; a transverse row of small silver spots on each segment; spines black with orange bases; head black with 2 long clublike projections. **FOOD:** *Bacopa,* lippia, water hyssop. **FLIGHT:** All year in s. Tex. and Deep South (several flights). **RANGE:** Resident from s. Tex. and s. Fla. (including Keys) south through the West Indies, Mex., and Cen. Amer. to Argentina. Migrant and temporary colonist to coastal S.C. and cen. Tex. Rare vagrant to Utah, N.M., w. Tex., Kans., Neb., Mo., and N.C. **HABITAT:** Moist weedy fields, swamp edges, parks.

BANDED PEACOCK *Anartia fatima* PL. 30

2⅜–2⁹⁄₁₆ in. (60–66 mm). Forewing apex squared off. Hindwing slightly scalloped. *Brown with cream or white median band on forewing, cream or white submarginal band, and median row of small red spots on hindwing.* **EARLY STAGES:** Caterpillar black with rows of light dots; spines red-brown to black-brown. Head purple-black. **FOOD:** Low plants in Acanthus family, such as *Blechum* and *Ruellia.* **FLIGHT:** All year in tropics where native (several flights). **RANGE:** Mex. and Cen. Amer. Strays to and occasionally reproduces in Tex. **HABITAT:** Open weedy areas, orchards, fields, beaches.

MALACHITE *Siproeta stelenes* PL. 30

2¹³⁄₁₆–3½ in. (72–90 mm). This is our only largely green nymphalid. Forewing apex extended; hindwing has pointed tail-like projection. Upperside: *Brown-black with translucent yellow-green or white-green marks.* Underside: Gray with green window-like marks. Has slow, floating flight. **EARLY STAGES:** Caterpillar is velvety black with dark red divisions between segments; prolegs pink; 2 large spined horns on head. **FOOD:** Usually cafetin, but *Ruellia* is also likely. **FLIGHT:** All year — 2 or 3 flights during the summer; 1 brood of the dry-season form overwinters. **RANGE:** Resident from s. Tex. and s. Fla. south through West Indies and mainland tropical Amer. to Brazil. Rare vagrant to se. Ariz., w. Tex., and Kans. **HABITAT:** Clearings in river forest, overgrown orchards, weedy areas near houses.

RUSTY-TIPPED PAGE *Siproeta epaphus* PL. 30

3–3¼ in. (75–82 mm). Forewing tip extended. Hindwing *margin with small pointed extensions and single longer taillike extension.* Upperside: *Outer half of forewing orange, divided from black basal half by white band. Hindwing black with submarginal white band*

and small blue dashes near anal angle. **EARLY STAGES:** Caterpillar velvety maroon with 3 pairs of yellow-orange spines on each segment. Head shiny black with 2 curved knobby projections from top of head. **FOOD:** Acanthus family plants. **FLIGHT:** All year in tropics (several flights). **RANGE:** Ne. Mex. south to Peru. A stray was collected in se. N.M. **HABITAT:** Tropical evergreen forests, forest edges, and river courses. **REMARKS:** Adults visit a variety of flowers for nectar.

ADMIRALS AND RELATIVES: SUBFAMILY LIMENITIDINAE

These butterflies are found on most continents. The adults of most genera are characterized by their flap-and-glide flight. The butterflies share common traits of caterpillar and chrysalis structure.

WHITE ADMIRAL *Limenitis arthemis* PL. 30

2¹⁄₂–3⁵⁄₈ in. (66–92 mm). Our two very different forms were once considered separate species. Red-spotted Purple: Upperside: *Blue to blue-green* with outer portion of hindwing more iridescent. Underside: Forewing has 2 *costal red-orange bars,* and hindwing has 3 basal red-orange spots and a *submarginal row of red-orange spots.* White Admiral: Upperside: Both wings black. Forewing has outwardly curved *broad white band* and a few white spots on apex. Hindwing with postmedian white band, *submarginal series of red spots,* and a marginal row of blue *dashes.* Underside: White bands are repeated. Hindwing has *reddish brown background.* The Banded Purple, form proserpina, is like the White Admiral with a

White Admiral (subspecies arthemis) *perching, Goreham, N.H. Note the bold white band on both wings and submarginal red-orange spots on hindwing. This butterfly shows some features of form* prosepina. *Photo by Jeffrey Glassberg.*

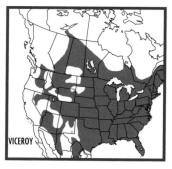

submarginal blue band above. The more northern White Admiral (*L. arthemis arthemis*) freely hybridizes with the more southern Red-spotted Purple (*L. arthemis astyanax*) in a broad belt across New England, s. Ontario, the Great Lakes states, and northern plains (see map). Rarely, individual butterflies appearing to be White Admirals are found far to the south amid Red-spotted Purple populations. **SIMILAR SPECIES:** Weidemeyer's Admiral has white or orange submarginal spots in black field on hindwing upperside. Underside lacks red-brown background. **EARLY STAGES:** Caterpillar cryptic gray-brown and white; humped at thorax. **FOOD:** Leaves of trees and shrubs: wild cherry, poplar, aspens, black oaks, and others. **FLIGHT:** April or May–Oct. (2 flights). **RANGE:** Boreal and temperate N. Amer. from Alaska and subarctic Canada south and east to most of e. U.S. Isolated populations of Red-spotted Purple (subspecies *arizonensis*) occur in Ariz., N.M., and w. Tex. south into n. Mex. **HABITAT:** Deciduous broadleaf forest, evergreen oak-pine forest, mixed evergreen forest, associated edges, and clearings. **RE-MARKS:** The Red-spotted Purple form is a mimic of the distasteful Pipevine Swallowtail and occurs within the permanent or temporary range of that species. The White Admiral form is found to the north of the Pipevine Swallowtail. Hybrids of both Red-spotted Purple forms with the dissimilar-appearing Viceroy are sometimes found in nature. Based on laboratory studies, these hybrids are sterile and cannot reproduce. Adults rarely visit white flowers such as viburnum, privet, sweet pepperbush, and Hercules' club.

VICEROY *Limenitis archippus*   **PL. 30**

2¼–3 in. (58–76 mm). Upperside: Orange, burnt orange, or chocolate brown with *postmedian black line on hindwing* and a *single row of white spots* in the black marginal band. Underside: In

Male Viceroy perching, Weld Co., Colo. Note similarity to Monarch, but black postmedian band is present. Submarginal spots on both wings can be seen, making it appear as if there is more than one white spot row.

Southwest, where resident Monarchs are rare, Viceroys (*L. a. obsoleta*) are brown and mimic the distasteful Queen (*Danaus gilippus*), a close relative of the Monarch. **SIMILAR SPECIES:** Monarch and Queen both lack hindwing postmedian black line and have 2 rows of white spots in their black marginal bands. **EARLY STAGES:** Caterpillar olive green with white dorsal blotch, white sides and a few black spots, antenna-like projections from second thoracic segment. **FOOD:** Leaves of various willows. **FLIGHT:** April–Oct. (2–3 flights in most of range). March–Nov. in Southwest. **RANGE:** N.W. Terr. (rare) south through s. Canada and most of U.S. west of Sierra-Cascade crest to cen. Mex. Not found in high mountains or aridlands away from water. **HABITAT:** River and stream forests and open swamps, lake edges. **REMARKS:** This well-known mimic of the Monarch, and less well known, but still remarkable, mimic of the Queen, may not be completely palatable to birds. Adults visit flowers more frequently than other admirals; especially favored are composites such as goldenrod, Joe-pye weed, Canada thistles, asters, and others.

WEIDEMEYER'S ADMIRAL *Limenitis weidemeyerii*   **PL. 30**
2–3¹⁄₁₆ in. (52–78 mm). Upperside: Black with striking *median white band*. Underside: Hindwing has gray-white marginal spots. Basal area is gray-white with dark lines. **SIMILAR SPECIES:** White Admiral has submarginal red spots on hindwing above. Background of hindwing below is red-brown. **EARLY STAGES:** Caterpillar humpbacked, yellow-green or gray with lighter mottling and bristly antenna-like spines of second thoracic segment. **FOOD:** Willows, aspen, cottonwood, ocean spray, chokecherry, and serviceberry. **FLIGHT:** June–Sept. (1–2 flights), to Nov. in wet years (3 flights).

RANGE: W. N. Amer. from se. Alta. south to se. Ariz. and s. N.M. east to Neb. and w. to e.-cen. Calif. **HABITAT:** Streamsides, mountain aspen groves, river forests, small towns, and suburbs. **REMARKS:** Weidemeyer's Admiral and Lorquin's Admiral hybridize along a narrow band extending from e-cen. Calif. near Mono Lake north to Idaho and w. Mont. Because the hybrid zone is so narrow, they are considered separate species. Adults occasionally visit flowers such as snowberry, cow-parsnip, and rabbitbrush.

LORQUIN'S ADMIRAL *Limenitis lorquini* PL. 30

1 ⁵⁄₁₆–2 ½ in. (49–65 mm). Upperside: Black with *red-orange tip* on forewing and *median white band*. **SIMILAR SPECIES:** California Sister has paler orange and more rounded patch at forewing apex. White band is narrower. **EARLY STAGES:** Caterpillar olive-brown with olive-yellow mottling and white patches. Two antenna-like projections from second thoracic segment. **FOOD:** Usually willows, occasionally quaking aspen or plums. **FLIGHT:** Mar.–Nov. (2 flights), all year in s. Ariz. **RANGE:** Sw. Alta. and cen. B.C. south to w. Mont., Idaho, nw. Nev. and Pacific Coast states to n. Baja Calif. **HABITAT:** Streamsides, marshes, wooded suburbs. **REMARKS:** Hybridizes with both Weidemeyer's Admiral and White Admiral. Adults occasionally visit flowers such as California buckeye, yerba santa, and privet.

CALIFORNIA SISTER *Adelpha bredowii* PL. 30

2¼–3 in. (57–77 mm). Upperside: Black with *narrow median white band* and squarish *black-outlined orange patch* on forewing tip. **SIMILAR SPECIES:** Lorquin's Admiral has smaller more red-orange patch at tip of forewing, and a very different underside. **EARLY STAGES:** Caterpillar is dark green above, lighter below. Six pairs of fleshy green tubercles arrayed along back. **FOOD:** Evergreen oaks

*California Sister (*subspecies* californica) perching by stream, Contra Costa Co., Calif. Orange patch at tip of forewing and white band still show, but rest of underside pattern is complex.*

such as coast live oak, canyon live oak, Arizona oak, and Emory oak. Deciduous Gambel oak utilized in Rockies, and tan oak and chinquapin are likely in Ore. and Wash. **FLIGHT:** April–Sept. (2 flights), occasionally as late as early Dec. in s. Ariz. **RANGE:** Sw. Wash., se. Idaho, Utah, cen. Colo., and sw. Kans. south to n. Baja Calif. and Honduras. **HABITAT:** Foothills and mountains, usually associated with oaks, but frequently moist areas along streams. May wander considerable distances to towns and suburbs. **REMARKS:** Lorquin's Admiral closely resembles California Sister, and the two butterflies may mimic each other. Adults are usually found near oaks or moist spots along streams and rarely visit flowers. On such occasions California buckeye, seepwillow, or rabbitbrush may be utilized.

MEXICAN BLUEWING *Myscelia ethusa*   **SEE PHOTOGRAPH**
2¼–3 in. (64–76 mm). Forewing apex appears cut off. Hindwing outer margin scalloped. Sexes similar. Upperside: *Black with transverse violet bands.* Outer half of forewing with irregular white spots. **EARLY STAGES:** Not reported. **FOOD:** Unknown. **FLIGHT:** All year in s. Tex. and Mex. (several flights). **RANGE:** Mex. south through Cen. Amer. to Guatemala. Periodic stray in Big Bend and temporary resident in lower Rio Grande Valley, Tex. **HABITAT:** Stream valleys

CALIFORNIA SISTER

Mexican Bluewing resting, Santa Ana National Wildlife Refuge, Texas. Note blue bands as well as white spots in black apical area on forewing.

with thorn scrub or scattered forest. **REMARKS:** Adults feed on rotting fruit.

BLACKENED BLUEWING *Myscelia cyananthe*   **NOT SHOWN**
2⅛–3 in. (55–75 mm). Forewing apex appears cut off. Hindwing outer margin scalloped. Sexes have slightly different patterns. Upperside: *Black with short blue-purple band at base of forewing.* Male with 2 small blurred blue spots on forewing costa just in from apex. Female with several white spots at apex and outer margin. Male has two blue-purple bands and narrow blue-purple margin on hindwing while female has one broad band and 2 narrow lines. **SIMILAR SPECIES:** Mexican Bluewing has more extensive pattern above and is less likely to appear in Ariz. or Calif. **EARLY STAGES:** Not reported. **FOOD:** Plants in Euphorbia family, including noseburn. **FLIGHT:** All year in Mex., July–Nov. in s. Ariz. (several flights). **RANGE:** Resident from Baja Calif. Sur and Sonora, Mex. south to s. Mex. Periodic stray to se. Calif. (rare) and s. Ariz. **HABITAT:** Thorn scrub, seasonal dry forest.

DINGY PURPLEWING *Eunica monima*   **PL. 30**
1⅞–2 in. (48–52 mm). Purplewings perch with wings closed and rarely open them. Upperside: Brown-black with slight purplish gloss. Forewing with *dingy, smeared white spots at apex*. Underside: Forewing with central black patch with white spots (not easily seen). Hindwing *gray-brown with muted pattern of wavy lines and circles*. **SIMILAR SPECIES:** Florida Purplewing is larger, with wing margins irregular, and has distinct white spots on outer half of forewing. **EARLY STAGES:** Caterpillar olive green with black and yellow stripes along sides; head black and orange with 2 short stout

horns on top of head. **FOOD:** Gumbo Limbo. **FLIGHT:** All year in Mex. and Cen. Amer. (several flights), late July–late Sept. in s. Ariz. **RANGE:** Mex. and West Indies south through Cen. Amer. to n. S. Amer. (Venezuela). Periodic stray to s. Ariz., sw. N.M., w. and s. Tex., and s. Fla. **HABITAT:** River forests in seasonally dry tropics. **REMARKS:** May be temporary resident in Fla. Usually perches on tree trunks and occasionally found at most spots along streams. Rarely visits flowers.

FLORIDA PURPLEWING *Eunica tatila* PL. 30

1 $^{15}\!/_{16}$–2 $^{3}\!/_{8}$ in. (49–61 mm). Forewing apex somewhat pointed. Outer wing *margins irregularly sinuous*. Upperside: Base of both wings with violet-blue iridescence. Outer portion of forewing with 6–7 *distinct white spots*. Underside: *Hindwing with 6 or 7 small white-pupiled marginal eyespots.* **SIMILAR SPECIES:** Dingy Purplewing (see above). **EARLY STAGES:** Caterpillar description not reported. **FOOD:** Jasmine. **FLIGHT:** All year where resident in s. Fla. and tropics (several flight). **RANGE:** Fla. Keys, West Indies, Mex., and mainland tropical Amer. south to Argentina. Rare stray north to w. and s. Tex. and e. Kans. **HABITAT:** Hardwood hammocks in Fla., river forests in lowland tropics. **REMARKS:** Usually seen perched head down on tree trunks with wings closed. Adults usually feed on rotting fruit but occasionally visit flowers such as lantana and cordias.

TITHIAN SAILOR *Dynamine tithia* NOT SHOWN

1 $^{1}\!/_{8}$–1 $^{5}\!/_{16}$ in. (29–33 mm). Male forewing pointed. Upperside: Both sexes have outer forewing black with postmedian row of 3 white spots. Male iridescent greenish blue. Female blue-green with white patch near lower corner of forewing, ill-defined white median patch and submarginal black stripe on hindwing. Underside:

COMMON
MESTRA

Forewing outer margin rimmed with dark red-brown, complex black and white pattern and a few iridescent blue spots. *Hindwing with postbasal, postmedian, and marginal red-brown lines. Remainder satiny white.* **EARLY STAGES:** Not reported. **FOOD:** *Dalechampia*s (Euphorbia family). **FLIGHT:** Probably most of year in several flights. **RANGE:** Colombia and Venezuela south to Argentina and Paraguay. Strayed once to w. Tex. **HABITAT:** Tropical forest edges near rivers and streams, occasionally dry desertlike situations. **REMARKS:** An unlikely stray from S. Amer.

ANNA'S EIGHTY-EIGHT *Diaethria anna*　　**NOT SHOWN**
1 ½–1 ⅝ in. (38–41 mm). Upperside: Velvet black with iridescent blue-green band across forewing and narrow marginal blue-green line on hindwing. Underside: Forewing with basal half bright red and outer half white and black. Hindwing with *white "88" mark in center with encircling black lines.* **EARLY STAGES:** Not reported. **FOOD:** Probably Sapindaceae. **FLIGHT:** Most of year in Cen. Amer. (several flights). **RANGE:** Mex. south to Costa Rica. One stray found in Big Bend, Tex. **HABITAT:** Tropical forests.

COMMON MESTRA *Mestra amymone*　　**PL. 31**
1 ⅜–1 ¾ (36–43 mm). Sexes similar. Base of forewing costal vein swollen—a feature shared with the unrelated satyr butterflies. Upperside: White or gray-white. Hindwing with *median row of white spots and orange outer portion.* **SIMILAR SPECIES:** Because of its white color some might confuse it with a white (Pieridae) but its flight habits and structure reveal its true identity. **EARLY STAGES:** Caterpillar brown with green diamonds on back; 8 rows of spines; head red with black on crown; 2 prominent head spines, each terminating in a knob. **FOOD:** Noseburn. **FLIGHT:** All year where resident, especially June–Nov. **RANGE:** Resident from s. Tex. and Mex. south through Cen. Amer. to Costa Rica. Strays and occasionally breeds as far north as Ariz., Colo., Neb., and S.D. (rare). **HABITAT:** Weedy fields, roadsides, wood edges. **REMARKS:** This unusual white brushfoot has a slow, sailing flight. Seldom visits flowers.

RED RIM *Biblis hyperia*　　**PL. 31**
2–2 ⁵⁄₁₆ in. (50–59 mm). Upperside: Brown-black; forewing with paler outer area; *hindwing with submarginal pink-red band and*

scalloped outer margin. **EARLY STAGES:** Caterpillar with fine brown, black, and gray lines; many finely branched spines terminating in rosettes; head gray with 2 prominent recurved horns. **FOOD:** Noseburn. **FLIGHT:** Feb., July–Nov. in Tex.; March–Nov. in Mex. and Cen. Amer. **RANGE:** Periodic resident in lower Rio Grande Valley, Tex., and south through West Indies, Mex., and mainland tropical Amer. to Paraguay. Periodic stray to w. and cen. Tex. **HABITAT:** Open, subtropical and tropical forests, streamside forests, and second growth. **REMARKS:** Flies low and slow with shallow wingbeats. Perches with wings open. In the tropics this butterfly mimics several black swallowtails with red-pink markings. It is likely distasteful.

GRAY CRACKER *Hamadryas februa*   **PL. 31**

2¾–3⅜ in. (72–85 mm). Upperside: Forewing discal cell bar with at least some red; hindwing eyespots have orange scales outside black crescent. Underside: Forewing with a *black submarginal patch* on lower half. Hindwing white with submarginal eyespots, each a *brown ring surrounding a black crescent in a white center.* **SIMILAR SPECIES:** Glaucous Cracker lacks any red scales in forewing discal bar above. Black ring surrounds white circle on submarginal area of forewing near trailing edge. **EARLY STAGES:** Caterpillar black with light green spines and 6 longitudinal lines; head red brown with 2 long recurved knobbed spines. **FOOD:** *Dalechampia* and *Tragia.* **FLIGHT:** All year in tropics; Aug.–Oct. in s. Tex. **RANGE:** Resident from s. Tex. (periodic resident in lower Rio Grande Valley) south through Mex. and mainland tropical Amer. to Argentina. Rare stray to sw. N.M. **HABITAT:** Tropical seasonally dry forest, river forest, and associated edges. **REMARKS:** This is the commonest cracker along the west coast of Mex. and may be expected in s. Ariz.

BLACK-PATCHED CRACKER *Hamadryas atlantis*   **PL. 31**

2¾–3½ in. (72–88 mm). *Outer margin* of hindwing *wavy.* Upperside: Blue-gray with dark pupils in hindwing submarginal eyespots. Underside: *Strikingly black and white.* Apical half of male forewing almost entirely black. **EARLY STAGES:** Not reported. **FOOD:** Unknown. **FLIGHT:** Mid-Aug. in se. Ariz. March–Nov. in Mex. **RANGE:** Mex. (mainly western) south to Honduras. Rare stray to se. Ariz. **HABITAT:** Stream valleys in lowland dry forest. **REMARKS:** Males do not make the snapping noise of other crackers. They perch on tree trunks or rocks.

GLAUCOUS CRACKER *Hamadryas glauconome*   **PL. 31**

2¹¹⁄₁₆–3⅛ in. (68–80 mm). Upperside: Forewing discal cell bar without red; hindwing eyespots have orange scales outside black crescent. Underside: Forewing with a *black submarginal ring sur-rounding white circle on lower half* (second intervein space from bottom). Hindwing white with *submarginal eyespots, each a brown ring surrounding a black crescent.* SIMILAR SPECIES: Gray Cracker (see p. 339). EARLY STAGES: Not reported. FOOD: *Dalechampia scandens.* FLIGHT: March–Nov. in w. Mex. Late Sept. in s. Ariz. RANGE: Mex. south to Costa Rica. Rare stray to s. Ariz. HABITAT: Forests in low-land tropical Amer. REMARKS: This species is easily confused with the Gray Cracker. Like most other crackers, males make clicking noises, especially when encountering other males.

BLOMFILD'S BEAUTY *Smyrna blomfildia* PL. 31

3–3½ in. (76–90 mm). Upperside: Male rich orange, female brown. Forewing apex black with 3 white spots. Underside: Hind-wing with *many wavy markings and 2 large submarginal eyespots.* EARLY STAGES: Caterpillar black with white branched spines; head orange with 2 stout recurved horns. FOOD: *Urera* in nettle family. FLIGHT: All year in tropics. RANGE: Resident from Mex. south through mainly tropical Amer. to Peru. HABITAT: Periodic vagrant to w. and s. Tex. REMARKS: Adults feed at fermenting fruit and tree sap. They never visit flowers. Old records for Karwinski's Beauty *(Smyrna karwinskii)* likely refer to this butterfly.

ACHERONTA *Historis acheronta* PL. 31

2¾–3⅜ in. (72–85 mm). Forewing has apex extended outward. Hindwing has short pointed projection from outer margin. Up-perside: Forewing with base orange-brown, outer portion black with several small white spots near apex. Hindwing mainly black-ish brown. Underside: Dark brown with purplish or greenish highlights. Small *white spot on forewing costa* in from wingtip. Hindwing has a *squiggly median black line.* EARLY STAGES: Caterpillar black dotted with blue. Back with 3 orange patches and white spines. Head black with 2 rosetted horns. FOOD: Cecropia. FLIGHT: Most of year in tropics (several flights). RANGE: Resident from cen. Mex. and the West Indies south through Cen. Amer. to Brazil. Rare stray to w. Tex. HABITAT: Tropical lowland forests. REMARKS: Usually seen flying high through forest. May be attracted to fer-menting fruit baits.

WAITER *Marpesia zerynthia* NOT SHOWN

2¾–3⅛ in. (71–80 mm.). Each hindwing with *a long thin dagger-like tail.* Upperside: Brown-black. *Basal half of both wings white, outer half dark brown.* EARLY STAGES: Not reported. FOOD: Unknown. FLIGHT: July, Oct. in Tex., May–Nov. in Mex. (2 or more flights). RANGE: Resident from e.-cen. Mex. south through tropical Amer. to Brazil. Rare stray to Tex. HABITAT: Tropical forests.

MANY-BANDED DAGGER-WING *Marpesia chiron*   PL. 31

RUDDY DAGGERWING

2 7/16–2 5/8 in. (62–67 mm). Each hindwing with a *long thin daggerlike tail*. Upperside: Dark brown with 3 paler strips and 3 faint dots on forewing apex. Underside: *Basal third of hindwing pale gray with faint orange stripes.* EARLY STAGES: Caterpillar yellow-orange above with reddish streaks and 2 black lines; sides yellow; black spines on back. Head yellow-green with 2 black spots at base of paired horns. FOOD: Figs and related tropical trees. FLIGHT: All year in Cen. Amer., May–Dec. in Mex., late Aug. as rare stray in s. Ariz. RANGE: Resident from West Indies and Mex. south through mainland tropical Amer. to Argentina. Stray to s. Ariz., w. and s. Tex., and Kans. HABITAT: Lowland tropical forests, especially river valleys. REMARKS: Usually feeds on animal wastes and tree sap but occasionally nectars at flowers such as boneset and cordia. This species is migratory.

RUDDY DAGGERWING *Marpesia petreus*   PL. 31

2 9/16–3 3/8 in. (66–86 mm). Forewing apex highly extended. Each hindwing with a *long daggerlike tail*. Upperside: Orange with thin black lines. Underside: Pattern somewhat *cryptic, leaflike.* EARLY STAGES: Caterpillar purplish above, white below; abdominal segments yellow above. Weak upright threadlike paired appendages on 4 abdominal segments. FOOD: Leaves of fig trees. FLIGHT: Most of year in Fla., all year in tropics, early Aug.–mid. Oct. in s. Ariz. RANGE: Resident from s. Fla., West Indies, Mex., and mainland tropical Amer. south to Brazil. Stray north to s. Ariz (rare temporary resident), N.M., Colo., Tex., Kans., and Neb. HABITAT: Tropical forests, associated edges, and second growth. REMARKS: Normally feeds on tree sap, rotting fruit, and dung, but also visits flowers such as seepwillow, cordias, and others. Adults perch upside down under leaves when inactive.

LEAFWINGS AND RELATIVES: SUBFAMILY CHARAXINAE

This is a primarily tropical group of medium to large-sized, robust, fast-flying butterflies. Our species are limited to the leafwings (*Anaea* and *Memphis*).

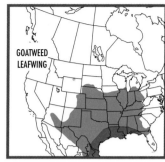

TROPICAL LEAFWING *Anaea troglodyta*   PL. 31

2¼–2½ in. (57–65 mm). Outer *wing margins slightly uneven. Short taillike projection from each hindwing.* Dry-season (winter) form has sickle-shaped forewing apex. Upperside: Dusky orange-red. Marginal areas darkened with black scaling; hindwing with small faint yellow marginal points. Underside: *Mottled gray-brown.* SIMILAR SPECIES: Goatweed Leafwing is larger, has broader taillike projections, and smooth outer wing margins. It has a simple wing pattern on the upper surface. EARLY STAGES: Caterpillar yellow-green with yellow stripes along each side and many white points; a black crescent and round patch are on back near end. Head pale green with 2 short black horns. FOOD: Crotons. FLIGHT: Sept.–April (dry-season form), April–Sept. (wet-season form). Mid-March–mid-Dec. in s. Ariz. RANGE: Mex. south to Cen. Amer. (nw. Costa Rica) with occasional strays to s. Ariz., s. N.M., Kans., and Tex. HABITAT: Wood edges, forest trails, trees near water courses. REMARKS: Adults rarely visit flowers. This butterfly was formerly called *Anaea aidea; aidea* is now a subspecies.

GOATWEED LEAFWING *Anaea andria*   PL. 31

1¾–2¹³⁄₁₆ in. (44–72 mm). The most likely leafwing to be encountered in our area except perhaps in s. Ariz. Like in other leafwings, the sexes and seasonal forms differ. Winter form has sickle-shaped forewing apex. *Hindwing with short pointed tail.* Upperside: Red-orange. Summer males with only faint markings. Females with a broad, irregular submarginal band. Underside: *Unmarked. Faintly mottled gray-brown.* SIMILAR SPECIES: Tropical Leafwing is smaller, redder, has heavier dark markings above, and slightly irregular outer margins. EARLY STAGES: Caterpillar gray-green, covered with small tubercles; orange tubercles on head. FOOD: Goatweed, Texas croton, prairie tea. FLIGHT: Aug.–May. (win-

Angled Leafwing resting, Sinaloa state, Mex. Note angled edges to wings. Upperside is orange with black band on forewing. This butterfly was documented once in southeastern Ariz.

ter form), July–Aug. (summer form; 2 flights). **RANGE:** Resident in s.-cen. and se. U.S., frequent wanderer to n. Mex., west to cen. Ariz., north to Colo. and Wyo. (rare) and S.D. In East to Mich., S.C., and w. Va. **HABITAT:** Open deciduous woods and scrub, especially along streams and in open fields. **REMARKS:** Adults never visit flowers but prefer sap flows on trees, rotting fruit, and other nonfloral rewards.

ANGLED LEAFWING *Memphis glycerium*   **SEE PHOTOGRAPH**
2⅜–3 in. (60–74 mm). Forewing of dry-season form (Nov.–May) falcate. *Outer edge* of forewing *highly irregular* in outline. Outer edge of hindwing *concave between vein endings*. Upperside: Orange. Dark bar on forewing just in from apex. Underside: Orange-brown. *Dark diagonal line dividing hindwing.* **SIMILAR SPECIES:** Tropical Leafwing lacks same irregular outline of outer edge, lacks black bar above and black line of underside of hindwing. **EARLY STAGES:** Caterpillar green with pale stripes, white band, and reddish patches. Head green with 2 black stubby horns. **FOOD:** Crotons. **FLIGHT:** All year in tropics, June–Nov. (wet-season form), Oct.–May (dry-season form; 2 or more flights). **RANGE:** Mex. south through Cen. Amer. to n. S. Amer. Strays to se. Ariz. and s. Tex. **HABITAT:** Lowland dry forest and tropical thorn scrub.

EMPERORS: SUBFAMILY APATURINAE

This is a group of closely related butterflies found worldwide. The adults are brightly colored and stout-bodied. As shown by their early stages, they are most closely related to the Charaxinae and Satyrinae. Our species are limited to the emperors (*Asterocampa*).

Male Hackberry Emperor (subspecies antonia) *perching on vegetation, Lower Rio Grande Valley, Hidalgo Co., Texas. Note single submarginal eyespot on forewing and complex of dark bar and 2 spots near leading margin.*

HACKBERRY EMPEROR *Asterocampa celtis* PL. 31

1 ½–2 ¼ in. (40–56 mm). Our commonest, most widespread emperor, especially on Great Plains and in Southwest. Variable geographically. **Upperside:** Forewing with postmedian row of white spots, *only 1 submarginal black spot and 1 solid black discal bar with 2 separate black spots.* **SIMILAR SPECIES:** (1) Empress Leilia has 2 submarginal black spots and 2 solid brown discal bars; (2) Tawny Emperor lacks submarginal black spots and has 2 solid black discal bars. **EARLY STAGES:** Caterpillar yellow-green; yellow spots along middle of back; 3 yellow lines along each side. **FOOD:** Netleaf hackberry, sugarberry, hackberry. **FLIGHT:** Late April–Oct. (2 flights). **RANGE:** Sw. mountains, n. and cen. Mex., cen. Plains, most of e. U.S. and extreme s. Ont. Stray to s. Man. **HABITAT:** Foothill canyons, wooded streams, forest glades, towns, plantings on prairie. **REMARKS:** Adult males court in late afternoon. At other times they may be found resting on leaves or tree trunks, often high in trees.

EMPRESS LEILIA *Asterocampa leilia* PL. 31

1 ½–2 in. (38–50 mm). **Upperside:** Chestnut brown. Forewing has *2 submarginal black spots and 2 solid brown discal bars.* **SIMILAR SPECIES:** Hackberry Emperor has upperside of forewing with only 1 submarginal black spot and 1 black discal bar. **EARLY STAGES:** Caterpillar green with tiny yellow dots and a yellow stripe along each side. **FOOD:** Spiny hackberry. **FLIGHT:** Late Feb.–early Dec., least abundant early in year (several flights). **RANGE:** Resident from s. Ariz. east to s. Tex. and south to cen. Mex. **HABITAT:** River forests, ravines, washes, and thorn scrub. **REMARKS:** Adult males perch on ground near hackberries or on branches. Adults rarely visit flowers such as desert broom.

TAWNY EMPEROR *Asterocampa clyton*   PL. 31

1⅜–2½ in. (42–65 mm). Geographically quite variable. Upperside: Forewing *lacks white spots and black submarginal spots but has 2 prominent dark discal bars.* Underside: Characters from upper forewing may be seen on underside as well. **SIMILAR SPECIES:** See Hackberry Emperor and Empress Leilia. **EARLY STAGES:** Caterpillar yellow-green with a narrow dark or indigo blue stripe up middle of back. Head white or black or a combination of the two. **FOOD:** Netleaf hackberry, hackberry. **FLIGHT:** Late April–late Oct., most common late spring and late summer (2–3 flights). **RANGE:** Se. Ariz. and sw. N.M. as isolated population (subspecies *texana*), thence on plains from e. S.D., w. Neb, se. N.M., w. Tex., and n. Mex. eastward. **HABITAT:** Mountain canyons in Southwest, elsewhere dense river woods, dry woods, cities. **REMARKS:** Occasionally seen at flowers such as milkweeds and rabbitbrush.

DUSKY EMPEROR *Asterocampa idyja*   NOT SHOWN

2–2¼ in. (52–57 mm). Similar in wing shape to other emperors. Upperside: Brown with *strong median white band* across forewing and darker apical area with *2 small white dots.* Irregular row of black submarginal dots on hindwing. Underside: Similar to upperside but lacks dark apical region and irregular submarginal row of small eyespots. **EARLY STAGES:** Caterpillar with longitudinal yellow and olive green bands, black line up middle of back, and short paired black forks at end. Head black with paired horns, hairy, white

patches on lower face. **FOOD:** Hackberries. **FLIGHT:** Early Oct. in se. Ariz. **RANGE:** West Indies and Mex. south to Costa Rica. Rare stray to se. Ariz. (once). **HABITAT:** Tropical forests.

MORPHOS AND RELATIVES: SUBFAMILY MORPHINAE

WHITE MORPHO *Morpho polyphemus*   **PL. 32**
3¼–5¼ in. (90–123 mm). Very large, looks like flying handkerchief. Forewing tip extended. Outer margin of hindwing with shallow lobes. Upperside: Satiny white with submarginal small black crescents. Underside: *Satiny white* with faint pale pinkish pattern. Forewing with 2 yellow-rimmed eyespots. Hindwing with *postmedian row of 6 yellow-rimmed eyespots.* **EARLY STAGES:** Caterpillar pale brown with pale green patches on back. **FOOD:** *Paullinia* (Sapindaceae family) and *Inga* (Legume family). **FLIGHT:** May–Dec. (several flights). **RANGE:** Cen. Mex. south to n. Costa Rica. Rare stray to se. Ariz. **HABITAT:** Evergreen and deciduous tropical forests. **REMARKS:** Males fly high in the air along streamcourses or over the forest canopy. Adults visit moist spots along streams or rotting fruit to feed.

SATYRS AND WOOD-NYMPHS: SUBFAMILY SATYRINAE

The satyrs are a worldwide group of medium-sized butterflies. They are most often brown with one or more marginal eyespots. One unifying structural feature is the swollen base of the costal vein, although a few other brushfoots share this feature. The males often have visible patches of specialized scales on the fore- or hindwings. Almost all species feed on grasses and grasslike plants, including bamboos, rushes, and sedges, but some tropical species feed on club mosses. The adults have short proboscises and rarely visit flowers, but feed on rotting fruit, animal droppings, or sap flows instead. The adults usually perch with their wings closed but open them wide when basking early in the morning or during cloudy weather. Arctic species perch tilted over, with their closed wings perpendicular to the sun. Males patrol in a characteristic slow, skipping flight. Most species have local colonies and are not migratory. Eggs are laid singly on the host leaves or stems, and caterpillars feed within shelters of several leaves sewn together with silk. Development from egg to adult often takes two years in arctic and alpine species. This biennial life cycle may be synchronized for all individuals in some species; thus the adult butterflies are found only in odd- or even-numbered years. For example the Chryxus Arctic populations in California's Sierra Nevada fly only in odd-numbered years, while

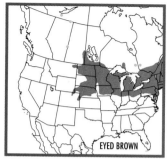

Chryxus Arctics along Colorado's Rocky Mountain front fly only in even-numbered years. Winter is usually passed by partially grown caterpillars.

NORTHERN PEARLY-EYE *Enodia anthedon*   PL. 32

1¾–2¼ in. (45–58 mm). Antennal clubs are black. Forewing apex is somewhat extended and hindwing outer margin is slightly scalloped. Upperside: Dark gray-brown with 3 black spots on forewing and 5 on hindwing. Underside: Brown with purplish sheen. Forewing has *straight row of 4 black yellow-rimmed eyespots* in submarginal area. SIMILAR SPECIES: Eyed brown has rounded forewing apex and hindwing. Eyespots are smaller and more regular. EARLY STAGES: Caterpillar is yellow-green with green and yellow longitudinal stripes. There is a pair of red-tipped horns on top of head and at rear end. FOOD: Grasses including whitegrass, broadleaved uniola, and bottlebrush. FLIGHT: Mid-June–early Aug. (1 flight). RANGE: E.-cen. Alta., w. N.D., cen. Neb., and e. Tex. east to N.S. and south to cen. Ala. and Miss. HABITAT: Damp deciduous woods, usually near streams or marshes; mixed transition-zone woodlands. REMARKS: Adults often fly in shade and characteristically perch head down on tree trunks. Adults feed at sap flows, bird droppings, and carrion.

EYED BROWN *Satyrodes eurydice*   PL. 32

1¼–2¼ in. (38–55 mm). Wings rounded. Upperside: Yellow-brown to dark brown with *4–5 submarginal eyespots on forewing* and 6 on hindwing. Underside: Eyespots from above are repeated but are all white-centered and yellow-rimmed. *Postmedian dark line on hindwing is distinctly zigzag.* SIMILAR SPECIES: Northern Pearly-eye is larger, has larger eyespots, and is usually found in woodlands. EARLY STAGES: Caterpillar green with paler and darker stripes and bands. There may be a red stripe along each side. Head green

with red horns on top. **FOOD:** Several grasses and sedges. **FLIGHT:** Late June–early Sept. (1 flight). **RANGE:** Se. Alta. (rare), ne. Mont., se. Wyo., and ne. Colo. east across s. Canada and n. U.S. to Atlantic Coast from N.S. south to Del. **HABITAT:** Freshwater marshes, sedge meadows, slow-moving streams or ditches. **REMARKS:** Colonies are very local. Adults perch and patrol in late afternoon.

NABOKOV'S SATYR *Cyllopsis pyracmon*   **PL. 32**
   1½–1¾ in. (38–43 mm). Upperside: Light brown to reddish brown with 2 black marginal spots on hindwing. Male has patch of dark scales on forewing. Underside: Reddish brown with 2 marginal patches of iridescent black scales on hindwing surrounded by oval patch of blue scales. *Postmedian line on hindwing goes straight to costal margin* and doesn't touch scale patch. **SIMILAR SPECIES:** On underside of hindwing Canyonland Satyr has postmedian line curved around upper edge of blue scale patch. **EARLY STAGES:** Not reported. **FOOD:** Grasses including *Muhlenbergia*. **FLIGHT:** Early April–late Oct. (2 flights). **RANGE:** Se Ariz. and sw. N.M. south to Guatemala. **HABITAT:** Oak and pine-oak woodlands. **REMARKS:** The butterflies fly in broken shade and land on leaf litter or on the ground, where they are well camouflaged. Henshaw's Satyr is a seasonal form of this species.

CANYONLAND SATYR *Cyllopsis pertepida* (Dyar)   **PL. 32**
   1¼–1⅝ in. (32–42 mm). Upperside: Similar to Nabokov's Satyr. Underside: Similar to Nabokov's Satyr but *postmedian line on hindwing curves around blue scale patch and does not reach forward edge of wing.* **SIMILAR SPECIES:** Nabokov's Satyr (see above). **EARLY STAGES:** Pale yellow-tan with brown band along each side and many fine brown lines. Head pale yellow-tan with paired horns having a brown stripe that reaches each horn tip. **FOOD:** Grasses. **FLIGHT:** Late

LITTLE WOOD-SATYR

RED SATYR

June–July at northern limit (1 flight); April–late Oct. (2 flights) elsewhere. **RANGE:** S. Nev., cen. Utah, n. Colo., and w. Okla. south through lower elevations of western mountains to s. Mex. **HABITAT:** Brushy ravines and canyon bottoms, wooded hillsides. **REMARKS:** Adults do not visit flowers. Males patrol along ravines and gulches.

LITTLE WOOD-SATYR *Megisto cymela*   PL. 32

1 5⁄16–1 11⁄16 in. (34–43 mm). Forewing with 2 *prominent yellow-rimmed eyespots* above and below. Hindwing with 2 *major eyespots*, but smaller eyespots may be present below. **SIMILAR SPECIES:** Red Satyr has only 1 eyespot and a strong reddish patch on each wing above and below. In our area the two species are never found together. **EARLY STAGES:** Caterpillar pale brown tinged with green and black stripe up middle of back. Head and paired horns at rear dirty white. **FOOD:** Grasses. **FLIGHT:** Late May–July (1 flight). **RANGE:** Se. Sask., Dakotas, Neb., ne. Colo., and cen. Tex. east across s. Canada and most of e. U.S. to Atlantic Coast. **HABITAT:** Woods, brushy fields, wooded rivercourses.

RED SATYR *Megisto rubricata*   PL. 32

1 3⁄8–1 7⁄8 in. (35–48 mm). Upperside: Dark brown. Each wing has only 1 eyespot and an adjacent reddish area. Underside: Light brown. Forewing with *reddish flush* and only 1 *eyespot near apex. hindwing with 2 eyespots.* **SIMILAR SPECIES:** (1) Little Wood-Satyr (see above) does not co-occur in our area. (2) Canyonland and Nabokov's Satyrs sometimes co-occur but lack eyespots. **EARLY STAGES:** Caterpillar tan with darker and lighter stripes, the uppermost stripe along each side with white dots. Head light mottled tan. **FOOD:** Grasses. **FLIGHT:** Late April–early Nov., mainly early summer (1 flight, partial second). **RANGE:** Ariz., N.M., cen. Okla.,

Red Satyr sitting on leaf litter, Big Bend National Park, Texas. Note red flush on forewing and light brown hindwing with 2 dark crossing lines and marginal eyespots.

s.-cen. Kans., and w. Tex. south through Mex. to Guatemala. **HABITAT:** Oak woodland, oak-juniper woodland, mesquite, ravines. **REMARKS:** Adults do not nectar and are often found on hillsides or along ravines in or near shade.

PINE SATYR *Paramacera allyni* PL. 32

1 5/16–1 3/4 in. (34–46 mm). Underside: Forewing with *one large yellow-rimmed eyespot at apex*. Hindwing with row of 6 *smaller yellow-rimmed eyespots* along submargin and *irregularly outlined pale band* through center. **SIMILAR SPECIES:** Red Satyr is found at lower elevations and has reddish flush and fewer eyespots. **EARLY STAGES:** Not reported. **FOOD:** Grasses are likely. **FLIGHT:** Late May–mid-Aug., mainly early summer (1 flight). **RANGE:** Se. Ariz. (mainly Chiricahua Mts.) south into Mex. **HABITAT:** Oak-conifer forests above 6,000 ft. **REMARKS:** Adults do not nectar. They have a bouncy flight and may be seen from ground level up into the trees.

HAYDEN'S RINGLET *Coenonympha haydenii* PL. 32

1 5/16–1 3/4 in. (33–45 mm). Pale brown to dark brown. Underside: Submargin of hindwing has 6 *small orange-rimmed eyespots*. **SIMILAR SPECIES:** Common Alpine is larger, darker, and has eyespots both above and below. **EARLY STAGES:** Caterpillar yellow-green with white stripes. **FOOD:** Grasses. **FLIGHT:** Late June–mid-Aug. (1 flight). **RANGE:** Small area of sw. Mont., e. Idaho, and w. Wyo. **HABITAT:** Mountain meadows, clearings, and bogs. **REMARKS:** Most closely related to ringlets of Europe and Asia such as the False Ringlet (*Coenonympha oedippus*). Adults are frequent flower visitors.

COMMON RINGLET *Coenonympha tullia* PL. 32

1–1 5/16 in. (26–33 mm). Highly variable geographically. Upperside:

PINE SATYR

HAYDEN'S RINGLET

Ranges from cream white (Calif.) through yellow-cream and yellow-orange (Rocky Mts.) to orange-brown (prairies). Underside: Ground color variable as on upperside, but often has darker cast, especially where spring flights occur. Forewing often has *pale-rimmed black eyespot at apex*. Hindwing usually has pale irregular median band (often discontinuous), and may or may not have series of submarginal black eyespots or pale spots. **SIMILAR SPECIES:** Most other western satyrs are darker colored. Despite great variability there are no similar species. **EARLY STAGES:** Caterpillar dark green or brown with paler stripes. Head green or brown. Short paired tails at rear. **FOOD:** Grasses. **FLIGHT:** Feb.–Nov. in lowland Calif. (3 flights), May–Sept. in Pacific Northwest and w. Nev. (2 flights), mid-May–Aug. (1 flight elsewhere in West). **RANGE:** Holarctic. In N. Amer. from n. Alaska and n. Canada south to n. Baja Calif., e. Ariz., cen. N.M., east across s. Canada and n. U.S. to Maritimes and New England. Extending range southward along Atlantic Coast (s. N.Y. and N.J.). Not found in deserts, s. Ariz., s. N.M., Tex., or prairies south of S.D. **HABITAT:** Open grassy areas in an incredibly wide array of habitats and biomes. **REMARKS:** Sometimes considered as several species, this butterfly has been demonstrated to gradually change appearance across broad geographic areas. Recent genetic studies have confirmed the exchange of genetic material between "species." Adults are most often seen flying low through sunny grassy areas, but they periodically stop to nectar at flowers, especially in hot, arid habitats.

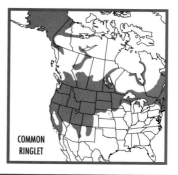

COMMON RINGLET

Female Common Wood-Nymph sitting, Larimer Co., Colo. Note 2 large more or less equal blue-filled eyespots. Outer portion of both wings is distinctly paler in females.

COMMON WOOD-NYMPH *Cercyonis pegala* **PL. 32**

1⅞–2¹¹⁄₁₆ in. (48–68 mm). Widespread and geographically variable. Sexes often differ in color and pattern. Upperside: Forewing with 2 *large yellow-rimmed eyespots.* Females paler and usually have an eyespot at anal angle of hindwing. On southern plains females often have the eyespots in a pale yellow field. Underside: Forewing with eyespots as above, but often with blue centers, especially on females. Hindwing dark to pale brown (invaded by white in adults of some alkaline and sandy habitats) with darker striations. Number of submarginal eyespots ranging from none to 6. **SIMILAR SPECIES:** Great Basin Wood-Nymph is usually smaller. Females have less yellow suffusion on forewing. Males have upper eyespot larger than lower (the reverse or of same size in *pegala*) and male dark stigma on forewing is smaller. This species is found in drier, more densely wooded or brushy habitats. **EARLY STAGES:** Caterpillar yellow-green with darker stripe up middle of back; paler stripes along sides. Short reddish forks at rear. Head green. **FOOD:** Grasses. **FLIGHT:** Late May–mid Sept. in most of West, April–Oct. in Calif. (1 flight). **RANGE:** S. B.C. south to cen. Calif. east across s. Canada and across U.S. (except arid lowland Southwest) to Atlantic Coast. **HABITAT:** Relatively moist grasslands and hillsides, sometimes mixed with shrubs or along woodland edges. **REMARKS:** Adults sip nectar from flowers such as wild geranium, thistles, and yellow composites in the West, although they rarely do so in the East, where the climate is generally more humid.

GREAT BASIN WOOD-NYMPH *Cercyonis sthenele* **PL. 32**

1⅜–1¹¹⁄₁₆ in. (35–43 mm). Upperside: *Upper eyespot usually larger than lower,* occasionally same size in females. Underside: Outer

COMMON WOOD-NYMPH

GREAT BASIN WOOD-NYMPH

portion of hindwing often with white scaling. Submarginal eye-spot row usually present, but often absent in lowland Calif. (sub-species *silvestris*). **SIMILAR SPECIES:** (1) Mead's Wood-Nymph is nearly identical but has red-orange patch on outer half of forewing both above and below. The 2 species have complementary ranges but co-occur in s. Utah. (2) Common Wood-Nymph (see p. 352). **EARLY STAGES:** Caterpillar is grass green with darker stripe up middle of back and yellow or white stripe along each side. Short reddish forks at rear. Head pale green. **FOOD:** Grasses. **FLIGHT:** May–Sept (1 flight). **RANGE:** S. B.C. south to n. Baja Calif., n. Ariz., and nw. N.M., thence east to w. Mont., w. Wyo., and w. Colo. **HABITAT:** Most often juniper or pinyon-juniper woodlands, but oak woodland and chaparral in lowland Calif. **REMARKS:** The Great Basin Wood-Nymph and Mead's Wood-Nymph (see below) are close relatives and are essentially identical except for the red-orange patch of the latter. Although they seem to hybridize in some local areas, in other areas they remain separate. I follow most previous authors in keeping them as separate species. Adults nectar at flowers such as California buckeye, white sweet-clover, and others.

MEAD'S WOOD-NYMPH *Cercyonis meadii*   **PL. 32**

1½–1 ¹¹/₁₆ in. (39–43 mm). Upperside: Forewing with *red-orange flush surrounding eyespots. Upper submarginal eyespot usually larger than lower* (eyespots equal in some females). Dark patch of sex scales on male forewing small. Underside: Red-orange color-ing more extensive under forewing. Postmedian eyespot series usually not extensively developed. **SIMILAR SPECIES:** Great Basin Wood-Nymph (see above). **EARLY STAGES:** Caterpillar yellow-green covered with fine white hair. Dark yellow-edged stripe up middle of back and 2 pale stripes along each side. Short red forks at rear. Head green, covered with short white hair. **FOOD:** Grasses. **FLIGHT:** Late July–early Sept., rarely Oct. (1 flight). **RANGE:** Three discon-

tinuous population areas (1) from cen. Mont. and w. N.D. south to e. Wyo.; (2) e.-cen. Colo.; and (3) s. Utah, sw. Colo. south to Chihuahua, Sonora, and w. Tex. **HABITAT:** Canyons, pine woodlands, sagebrush flats. **REMARKS:** Mead's Wood-Nymphs often nectar at flowers such as rabbitbrush and other yellow composites.

SMALL WOOD-NYMPH *Cercyonis oetus*   PL. 32

1¼–1¾ in. (32–46 mm). Dark brown. Upperside: Forewing with *lower eyespot closer to outer margin than upper eyespot.* Male with extensive dark sex patch on forewing and only the upper eyespot usually present. Underside: Forewing usually without postmedian dark line. Hindwing with *postmedian dark line strongly jutting inward in center.* Postmedian eyespots usually absent or weakly developed. **SIMILAR SPECIES:** (1) Great Basin Wood-Nymph is larger, has forewing eyespots equidistant from outer margin, and does not have angled inward juttings to postmedian line on underside of hindwing. (2) Small Wood-Nymph is usually found in more open habitats, often those dominated by sagebrush or similar shrubs. **EARLY STAGES:** Caterpillar yellow to white-green with short white hairs. Dark green yellow-edged stripe up middle of back and 2 paler stripes along each side. Head green. **FOOD:** Grasses. **FLIGHT:** Early June–Oct. (1 flight). **RANGE:** Much of intermountain West and Rocky Mountain front east of Pacific mountain divide from s. B.C. south to cen. Calif. and east to s. Sask., w. Dakotas, nw. Neb., e. Colo., and cen. N.M. **HABITAT:** Open arid brushlands, often sagebrush flats and slopes, from low foothills to high plains and subalpine habitats. Even found above timberline in a few sites, such as cen. Calif. **REMARKS:** Adults often visit flowers such as yellow composites, buckwheats, and others.

Vidler's Alpine basking, Clallam Co., Wash. Note checkered forewing fringe and few eyespots on hindwing. Photo by David Nunnallee.

VIDLER'S ALPINE *Erebia vidleri* PL. 32

1⅝–1¾ in. (41–46 mm). Fringes distinctly checkered white and dark. Wings brown-black with *yellow-orange submarginal band on forewing containing 2 or 3 white-centered black eyespots.* **SIMILAR SPECIES:** Common Alpine has red-orange eyespots on both wings. **EARLY STAGES:** Not reported. **FOOD:** Possibly grasses. **FLIGHT:** July–late Aug. (1 flight). **RANGE:** Sw. B.C. and Wash. **HABITAT:** Alpine and subalpine meadows and flowery rock slides. **REMARKS:** One of very few butterflies that are more or less limited to the Pacific Northwest. Adults visit flowers for nectar.

ROSS' ALPINE *Erebia rossii* PL. 32

1⅝–1⅞ in. (41–47 mm). Upperside: *Forewing with 1 to 3 subapical black white-centered eyespots* all surrounded by a red-orange

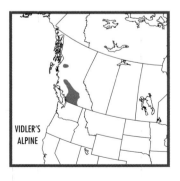

VIDLER'S
ALPINE

ROSS'
ALPINE

ring. Underside: Hindwing with a pale postmedian band. **SIMILAR SPECIES:** No other satyr in its range has combination of large forewing eyespots and bands on underside of hindwing. **EARLY STAGES:** Not reported. **FOOD:** Sedges. **FLIGHT:** Mid-June–mid-July, rarely Aug. in Far North (1 flight). **RANGE:** Holarctic. In N. Amer. from Alaska east along Arctic tundra and mountain archipelago to n. Man., Southhampton Is., and s. Baffin Is. Isolated population in n. B.C. **HABITAT:** Wet tundra and rock slides.

DISA ALPINE *Erebia disa* PL. 32

1½–1¾ in. (39–43 mm). Fringe checkered. Underside: Forewing dark brown with submarginal row of 4 to 5 black spots *surrounded narrowly by yellow-orange*. Hindwing with *dark brown postbasal band* separating small gray basal and broad gray outer half—sometimes divided by thin black line; *conspicuous small white dash* extending from center of wing into outer half. **SIMILAR SPECIES:** Taiga Alpine has strong orange-brown flush on forewing; hindwing lacks distinct median band and gray outer half. Only a tiny inconspicuous white spot. **EARLY STAGES:** Not reported. **FOOD:** Unknown. **FLIGHT:** Late June–early July (1 flight), biennial. **RANGE:** Holarctic. In N. Amer., n. Alaska east to w. N.W. Terr. **HABITAT:** Moist tundra. **REMARKS:** Previously considered with Taiga Alpine as a single species.

TAIGA ALPINE *Erebia mancinus* PL. 32

1¾–1¹⁵⁄₁₆ in. (44–49 mm). Fringe checkered. Underside: Forewing with 4 to 5 black submarginal spots in *yellow-orange field*. Forewing with orange-brown flush. Hindwing dark brown with scattered gray scales on outer half. *Indistinct postmedian band with tiny patch of white scales*. **SIMILAR SPECIES:** Disa Alpine (see

MAGDALENA ALPINE

MT. MCKINLEY ALPINE

above). **EARLY STAGES:** Not reported. **FOOD:** Probably grasses or sedges. **FLIGHT:** Late May–late July (1 flight). **RANGE:** Interior Alaska and s. Yukon south to s. Alta., s. Man., and n. Minn. and east to Labrador. **HABITAT:** Black spruce or tamarack bogs, occasionally lodgepole pine forests.

MAGDALENA ALPINE *Erebia magdalena* PL. 32

1 ¾–2 ¼ in. (43–57 mm). Almost *completely black or dark brown on both surfaces*. Occasional individuals have a reddish flush on the forewing, and there is sometimes a scattering of white scales below. **SIMILAR SPECIES:** Melissa Arctics may be found in the same habitat and time but are rounder winged and are distinctly gray below. **EARLY STAGES:** Incompletely known. **FOOD:** Alpine grasses. **FLIGHT:** Late June–Sept. (1 flight), biennial. **RANGE:** Canadian Rockies of cen. B.C. and cen. Alta. south through Rockies in isolated population in sw. Mont., n. Wyo., n. Utah, Colo., and n. N.M. **HABITAT:** Steep alpine rock slides and high rocky ridges with large lichen-covered rocks. **REMARKS:** Adults nectar at flowers such as alpine forget-me-nots and phlox. Females lay eggs on rocks, and caterpillars must then find the host plant.

MT. MCKINLEY ALPINE *Erebia mackinleyensis* PL. 32

1 ¾–2 ¹⁄₁₆ in. (44–53 mm). Black or brown-black with *red-orange flush on forewing*. **SIMILAR SPECIES:** Red-disked Alpine is smaller and found in bogs rather than on rock slides or scree slopes. **EARLY STAGES:** Not reported. **FOOD:** Unknown. **FLIGHT:** Late June–July (1 flight), biennial. **RANGE:** Holarctic. Far East of Russia, Alaska, Yukon, and w. N.W. Terr. **HABITAT:** Rock slides and rocky ridges. **REMARKS:** Sometimes considered the same species as the Magdalena Alpine.

BANDED ALPINE

RED-DISKED ALPINE

BANDED ALPINE *Erebia fasciata*　　　　　　　　　PL. 33

1 ¾–1 ⅞ in. (44–47 mm). Lacks eyespots. Underside: *Pale gray basal and postmedian bands on hindwing.* **SIMILAR SPECIES:** No other arctic satyr has a combination of no eyespots and distinct pale postmedian band on underside of hindwing. **EARLY STAGES:** Not reported. **FOOD:** Possibly cottongrass—actually a sedge. **FLIGHT:** Mid-June–mid-July (1 flight). **RANGE:** Far East of Russia and arctic America from Alaska east to w. edge of Hudson Bay, including Banks and Victoria Is. **HABITAT:** Moist swales on tundra.

RED-DISKED ALPINE *Erebia discoidalis*　　　　　　PL. 33

1 ½–1 ¾ in. (38–45 mm). Brown-black. Lacks eyespots. Underside: Forewing with *large chestnut red patch*; hindwing gray-brown with more gray outwardly. **SIMILAR SPECIES:** Mt. McKinley Alpine is larger and found on rock slides or scree slopes. **EARLY STAGES:** Caterpillar cream with a dark diagonal stripe on most segments. **FOOD:** Bluegrasses *(Poa)* and possibly sedges. **FLIGHT:** Usually early May–mid-June, but also early April–mid-August (1 flight). **RANGE:** In taiga from Alaska south to nw. Mont., east across Canada to n. Great Lakes region and Que. **HABITAT:** Taiga, open grasslands, fens, and open sphagnum bogs.

THEANO ALPINE *Erebia theano*　　　　　　　　　PL. 33

1 ¼–1 ⅜ in. (32–36 mm). Small and dark brown. Underside: Forewing with postmedian band of *elongated red-orange dashes;* hindwing with 1 blurred cell spot and *a postmedian series, all yellow-cream.* **SIMILAR SPECIES:** All other arctic and alpine satyrs have black-centered spots, if any, and have forewing and hindwing spots of the same color. **EARLY STAGES:** Caterpillar tan with dark brown stripes. **FOOD:** Not reported, but probably grasses or sedges. **FLIGHT:** Early July–late Aug. (1 flight), biennial. **RANGE:** Holarctic. In

THEANO ALPINE

FOUR-DOTTED ALPINE

N. Amer. from Alaska and Yukon south to Colo. and along w. edge of Hudson Bay to n. Man. **HABITAT:** Grassy areas in and above wet tundra. **REMARKS:** Occurs as isolated populations in s. Rockies.

FOUR-DOTTED ALPINE *Erebia youngi*   PL. 33

1 7/16–1 5/8 in. (37–42 mm). Fringes sometimes dark and light checked. Underside: Forewing with *submarginal row of 3 or 4 tiny black dots in orange field paralleled on both sides by sharply cut-off darker fields*. Hindwing with irregular dark median band, lighter on both sides. Hindwing covered with scattered *long thin brown or red-brown hairlike scales* (best seen through a lens). **SIMILAR SPECIES:** Eskimo and Reddish Alpines (see below). **EARLY STAGES:** Not reported. **FOOD:** Unknown. **FLIGHT:** Mid-June–late July (1 flight), probably biennial. **RANGE:** Alaska, Yukon, and w. N.W. Terr. **HABITAT:** Dry alpine or arctic tundra, occasionally rocky scree. **REMARKS:** Sometimes considered a subspecies of *Erebia dabanensis* of Russian Far East. The three closely related butterflies are only reliably separated by habitat preferences and features of the genitalia and antennal clubs.

SCREE ALPINE *Erebia anyuica*   PL. 33

1 9/16–1 5/8 in. (40–42 mm). Male dark brown, female warmer light brown. Fringes dark. Underside: Forewing with row of *red-orange or yellow-orange dots with tiny black points*. Hindwing pattern indistinct without median band (except in Alaska Range). Hindwing covered with *long gray or gray-brown hairlike scales* (best seen through a lens). **SIMILAR SPECIES:** Four-dotted and Reddish Alpines. **EARLY STAGES:** Not reported. **FOOD:** Unknown. **FLIGHT:** Late June–mid-July (1 flight), probably biennial. **RANGE:** Holarctic. In N. Amer. restricted to Alaska and n. Yukon. **HABITAT:** Dry rocky sites in arctic or alpine environments. **REMARKS:** Other characteristics of genitalia

Scree Alpine basking with open wings, Richardson Mts., Yukon Terr. Note uncheckered fringes and 4 small yellow-orange spots on forewing. Photo by Jim T. Troubridge.

and antennal clubs help separate this species from its similar-appearing relatives.

REDDISH ALPINE *Erebia lafontainei*   **PL. 33**

1 ⅝–1 ¾ in. (42–45 mm). Dark brown with dark fringes. Underside: Forewing with submarginal row of 3–4 *black dots surrounded by orange*. Hindwing with median brown band and irregular wide gray postmedian band. Hindwing covered with *fairly dense long reddish hairlike scales*. **SIMILAR SPECIES:** Four-dotted and Scree Alpines. **EARLY STAGES:** Not reported. **FOOD:** Unknown. **FLIGHT:** Mid-June–mid-July (1 flight), probably biennial. **RANGE:** Alaska (mainly n.) and w. Yukon. **HABITAT:** Shrubby arctic or alpine tundra with patches of sedges. **REMARKS:** Sometimes considered a subspecies of the Russian Far Eastern Reddish Four-dotted Alpine (*Erebia kozhantshikovi*).

SCREE ALPINE

REDDISH ALPINE

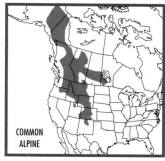

COLORADO ALPINE *Erebia callias*   **PL. 33**

1 ³⁄₁₆–1 ½ in. (31–39 mm). Upperside: Brown-black with 2 *black white-centered submarginal eyespots in reddish field* near apex. Underside: Forewing with eyespots evident. Hindwing *light gray with a few indistinct wavy lines.* **SIMILAR SPECIES:** Common Alpine has more spots on forewing and hindwing spots as well. Underside of hindwing is dark, not gray. **EARLY STAGES:** Midstage caterpillar brown with blue-green tinge on top of thorax, with longitudinal black, tan, and dark brown lines and bands. Head black. **FOOD:** Probably grasses or sedges. **FLIGHT:** July–Sept. (1 flight), probably biennial. **RANGE:** Sw. Mont. south to Colo. in isolated clusters of populations. **HABITAT:** Grassy tundra, especially knolls or ridgetops. **REMARKS:** Fond of flowers such as fleabanes. Closest relatives live in Europe.

COMMON ALPINE *Erebia epipsodea*   **PL. 33**

1 ½–1 ⅞ in. (38–48 mm). The commonest, most widespread alpine. Only species with eyespots on both wings. Dark brown. Upperside: *Black white-centered submarginal eyespot rows surrounded by yellow-orange.* Underside: Hindwing *submarginal black eyespots on gray background.* **SIMILAR SPECIES:** Taiga and Disa Alpines are smaller and lack eyespots on hindwings. **EARLY STAGES:** Caterpillar yellow-brown with both darker and yellowish stripes or green with darker green stripes; head yellow-brown. **FOOD:** Possibly bluegrasses; caterpillars eat grasses and sedges in captivity. **FLIGHT:** Early May–early Oct., usually June–early July (1 flight). **RANGE:** N.-cen. Alaska and Yukon south through Rocky Mts. to n. N.M. and west across prairie provinces to sw. Man. **HABITAT:** Open grassy areas from small openings to large meadows, sometimes wet with sedges and rank grasses. **REMARKS:** Marking studies of Common Alpines have found that individual butterflies move freely and travel long distances—up to 15 km!

RED-BORDERED SATYR *Gyrocheilus patrobas* **PL. 33**

2–2¼ in. (51–57 mm). Trailing edge of hindwing shallowly lobed. Upperside: Velvety blackish brown with *submarginal series of small white dots* on forewing and *broad purple-red submarginal band* along outer edge of hindwing. Underside: Upperside pattern repeated but hindwing band overlain by dark wavy lines. **EARLY STAGES:** Not reported. **FOOD:** *Muhlenbergia* grass. **FLIGHT:** Mid-Aug.–Oct., mainly Sept. (1 flight). **RANGE:** Ariz. (except w. and n.) and sw. N.M. south to s. Mex. **HABITAT:** Mountain forests. **REMARKS:** Adults visit flowers avidly. Males patrol suitable habitat with a bouncy flight.

RIDINGS' SATYR *Neominois ridingsii* **PL. 33**

1⅜–2 in. (35–50 mm). Gray or yellow background with *pale patches and 2 black eyespots* on forewing. **SIMILAR SPECIES:** Swale Satyr is identical but flies in Aug. and Sept., and the males perch in swales instead of on hilltops. **EARLY STAGES:** Caterpillar reddish tan covered with short white hairs and body with variously colored stripes; head yellow-brown with pale brown vertical stripes. **FOOD:** Blue grama and possibly other grasses. **FLIGHT:** Late May–early Aug. (1 flight), biennial at elevation in e.-cen. Calif. (only even-numbered years). **RANGE:** Native prairie and intermountain areas from s. Alta., s. Sask., and sw. Man. south to cen. Ariz. and cen. N.M., west to s. Ore., e. Calif., and Nev. **HABITAT:** Short-grass prairie or similar grasslands, sagebrush, and woodlands. **REMARKS:** May be passed by since its behavior is similar to a grasshopper's—flies low, then quickly lands with closed wings. Adults perch and patrol on hilltops and ridges in search of receptive mates.

Male Swale Satyr basking, Laramie Co., Wyo. This newly described butterfly is identical to the earlier-flying Ridings' Satyr. Males patrol swales instead of ridgetops.

SWALE SATYR *Neominois wyomingo* **SEE PHOTOGRAPH**

1½–1¾ in. (37–43 mm). Variation of the Swale Satyr's wing pattern falls within that of Ridings' Satyr (see above). **SIMILAR SPECIES:** Ridings' Satyr can be separated only by *flight season* and *habitat*. **EARLY STAGES:** Not reported. **FOOD:** Wheatgrasses, possibly other grasses. **FLIGHT:** Mid-Aug.–late Sept. (1 flight). **RANGE:** S.-cen Mont. south to cen. Utah, Wyoming, and ne. Colo. **HABITAT:** Valley bottoms, flats, and gentle slopes in short-grass prairie, grasslands in sagebrush. **REMARKS:** This is the commonest butterfly in Wyo. during its late-season flight period. Rabbit brush is one observed nectar source.

GREAT ARCTIC *Oeneis nevadensis* **PL. 33**

2–2¼ in. (50–55 mm). Hindwing outer margin wavy. Fringes checkered. Upperside: Wings orange to pale orange with *1 or 2*

 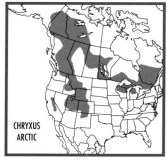

submarginal eyespots on forewing. Usually 1 *small black spot* on lower corner of hindwing. Both wings with black outer border. Male has dark diagonal sex patch on forewing. Underside: *Cloudy brown or gray-brown*. **SIMILAR SPECIES:** Other arctics not usually in same habitats. **EARLY STAGES:** Caterpillar with black, tan, greenish, and gray longitudinal stripes. **FOOD:** Unknown but probably a grass or sedge. **FLIGHT:** Mid-May–mid-Aug. (1 flight). Biennial, primarily in even-numbered years. **RANGE:** Vancouver Is., B.C. south through w. Wash. and w. Ore. to n. Calif. **HABITAT:** Forest glades and hills. **REMARKS:** Adults perch on logs or ground.

MACOUN'S ARCTIC *Oeneis macounii*   PL. 33

2⅛–2½ in. (54–66 mm). Large. Upperside: Bright orange-brown. Heavy black marginal band on both wings. Forewing with 2 submarginal eyespots. Hindwing with eyespot near anal angle. Male forewing lacks specialized scale patch of many other arctics. Underside: Hindwing *cloudy gray-brown with median band*. **SIMILAR SPECIES:** Range of Great Arctic does not overlap. **EARLY STAGES:** Caterpillar is striped pale black, light brown, and gray-green; head is yellow-green. Caterpillars require two years to complete development, and biennial cycle is synchronized for either odd- or even-numbered years. **FOOD:** Grasses and sedges in captivity. **FLIGHT:** Early June–early July (1 flight); adults of western populations fly only in odd-numbered years. **RANGE:** S. Canada from n. B.C. and the Caribou Mts. of Alta. across prairie provinces to cen. Ont., n. Minn., and n. Mich. **HABITAT:** Clearings in open Jack pine forest, rocky ridges in spruce forest.

CHRYXUS ARCTIC *Oeneis chryxus*   PL. 33

1⅝–2¹⁄₁₆ in. (41–52 mm). Upperside: Orange or cream white (subspecies *ivallda* of Calif. Sierra Nevada) usually with 2 (1–3) widely spaced black spots on forewing. Forewing of male with darkened patch of specialized scales. Underside: Hindwing with fine black and white striations; veins scaled white; often with *a broad darker median band; usually 1 (sometimes 2) black spot at anal angle.* **SIMILAR SPECIES:** (1) Uhler's Arctic flies earlier, has more submarginal spots on both wings above and below, lacks median

dark band on hindwing below. (2) Alberta Arctic is smaller, yellow-gray above, and below has forewing with postmedian line bent sharply outward at end of cell. Both similar species fly every year and are not biennial. **EARLY STAGES:** Caterpillar tan with brown stripes; head dark brown. **FOOD:** Sedges, *Danthonia spicata,* and other grasses. **FLIGHT:** Early May–late Aug. (1 flight). Flies every other year in some regions, every year in others, for example, mainly even-numbered years in Colorado Rockies, odd-numbered years in Sierra Nevada, every year in Alta. **RANGE:** W. N. Amer. mountains from e. Alaska south to cen. Calif., s. Utah, and s. N.M. and west across boreal Canada to n. Great Lakes states and the Maritimes. **HABITAT:** Open conifer forests, alpine slopes, especially along ridges. **REMARKS:** In the s. Rockies this is one of few biennial butterflies to occur as low as 6,500 ft. elevation, where almost all other butterflies have at least annual flights. Adults nectar at yellow flowers. Adults are well camouflaged and almost invisible when perched.

UHLER'S ARCTIC *Oeneis uhleri*   **PL. 33**
1½–1⅞ in. (38–47 mm). Upperside: Dull orange-brown. Underside: Both wings with more than 1, usually *many, small submarginal black spots.* Hindwing with *wavy black striations on white or gray background.* **SIMILAR SPECIES:** Chryxus Arctic and Alberta Arctic have fewer submarginal spots below and may have distinct darker median band on hindwing. Alberta Arctic is smaller, grayer, and usually flies earlier. **EARLY STAGES:** Caterpillar green or tan with dark brown stripes; head green yellow with pale vertical stripes. **FOOD:** Grasses and sedges. **FLIGHT:** Usually early June–early July, but extremes from mid-April–late August (1 flight). **RANGE:** Ne. Alaska (North Slope), Yukon, and extreme N.W. Terr., e. Canadian prairie provinces and Rocky Mt. region south to s. Utah, n. N.M., w. Neb. and east to w. Minn. **HABITAT:** Slopes

ALBERTA ARCTIC

WHITE-VEINED ARCTIC

and summits of hills in dry virgin prairie, foothills, subalpine areas, and tundra. **REMARKS:** Adults have a slower, "lazier" flight than the Chryxus Arctic, with which it is sometimes found.

ALBERTA ARCTIC *Oeneis alberta* PL. 34

1 ¼–1 ⅝ in. (31–41 mm). The smallest arctic. Variable. Upperside: Warm yellow-gray. Underside: Forewing with postmedian *line sharply bent outward* at end of cell; hindwing with *sharply outlined dark median band.* **SIMILAR SPECIES:** Uhler's Arctic flies later, is orange-brown above, has many submarginal black spots, and lacks dark median band on hindwing below. Hindwing veins usually lined with white scales. **EARLY STAGES:** Caterpillar dark brown with various-colored stripes. Head dark brown. **FOOD:** Bunchgrass, possibly fescue. **FLIGHT:** Mid-April–early July, usually late May–June (1 flight, possibly partial second in rare circumstances). **RANGE:** Canadian prairie provinces east to s. Man. and isolated Rocky Mt. populations in Mont., Colo., N.M., and Ariz. **HABITAT:** Virgin prairies, montane grasslands. **REMARKS:** Males patrol and perch on ridges and low hills.

WHITE-VEINED ARCTIC *Oeneis bore* PL. 34

1 ⅜–1 ⅞ in. (35–47 mm). Wings translucent. Upperside: Gray brown, without eyespots. Underside: Forewing with faint brown partial postmedian bar extending down from costa; hindwing with *strong median dark band outlined with white. Veins usually lined with white scales.* **SIMILAR SPECIES:** (1) Melissa Arctic may have faint eyespot on forewing near apex; hindwing below is mottled white and black sometimes with dark median band but lacks white scaling on veins. (2) Polixenes Arctic has even more translucent wings, a pronounced median band on hindwing below, and lacks white scaling along veins. **EARLY STAGES:** Caterpillar not reported. **FOOD:** Sedges or grasses. **FLIGHT:** Mid-June–late Aug., usually late

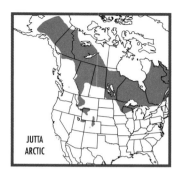

June–July (1 flight). **RANGE:** Holarctic. In N. Amer., high arctic from Alaska east to Lab., including Victoria Is., isolated Rocky Mt. alpine populations south to sw. Colo. Isolated population on Mt. Albert, Que. **HABITAT:** Grassy alpine slopes, tundra, taiga, and subarctic bogs. **REMARKS:** This species is sometimes referred to as *Oeneis taygete*.

JUTTA ARCTIC *Oeneis jutta* PL. 34

1 ¹¹⁄₁₆–2 ¹⁄₁₆ in. (43–53 mm). Upperside: Brown. Both wings with *yellow-orange submarginal band (usually interrupted) containing 2 to 4 black spots* on each wing. Underside: Hindwing with variably contrasting dark median band. **SIMILAR SPECIES:** No other brown arctic has submarginal row of yellow or yellow-orange black-centered spots. **EARLY STAGES:** Caterpillar pale green with darker stripes and a brown spot on each segment along back. **FOOD:** Sedges, including cottongrass. **FLIGHT:** Late June–early Aug. (1 flight), biennial. Found either every year or only odd or only even years in different localities. **RANGE:** Holarctic. In N. Amer. from Alaska south to ne. Utah and cen. Colo. and east across much of Canada and n. Great Lakes states to Maritimes and Me. **HABITAT:** Spruce bogs, wet tundra, dry lodgepole pine forest. **REMARKS:** Adults perch on tree trunks or logs where their hindwing colors help them blend well.

MELISSA ARCTIC *Oeneis melissa* PL. 34

1 ½–1 ¾ in. (37–45 mm). Wings slightly translucent. Wing fringes often checkered. Upperside: Gray-brown. Eyespots often absent, faint if present. Underside: Hindwing *mottled black and white, median band absent or weak, bordered by white*. **SIMILAR SPECIES:** (1) White-veined Arctic (see above). (2) Polixenes Arctic (see below). **EARLY STAGES:** Caterpillar variable with black and dark green stripes. Head yellow-green or green-brown with black bands or spots.

POLIXENES ARCTIC

PHILIP'S ARCTIC

FOOD: Sedges. **FLIGHT:** Mid-June–early Aug. (1 flight), rarely late Aug. in Far North, biennial. **RANGE:** Holarctic. Russian Far East and N. Amer. Arctic from Alaska south in Rockies discontinuously to n. N.M. and east across n. Canada (including Banks and Victoria Is.) to Baffin Is. and Lab., isolated population on Mt. Katahdin, Me. **HABITAT:** Open tundra, rocky summits, saddles, and talus slopes. **REMARKS:** Males often perch along alpine ridges or rock slides.

POLIXENES ARCTIC *Oeneis polixenes* PL. 34

1½–1¾ in. (38–43 mm). Wings relatively *translucent*. Upperside: Gray-brown. Underside: *Median band on hindwing usually strongly expressed, edged with white*. **SIMILAR SPECIES:** (1) Melissa Arctic wings less translucent and lacks strongly expressed medial band. (2) White-veined Arctic is browner, has white-lined veins on hindwing below. **EARLY STAGES:** Caterpillar light brown with darker stripes; head brown. **FOOD:** Sedges and grasses. **FLIGHT:** Early June–late Aug. (1 flight), probably biennial, at least in Arctic. **RANGE:** N. Amer. Arctic from Alaska south along Rockies discontinuously to n. N.M. east across n. Canada to Baffin Is., Lab., e. Que., and cen. Me. **HABITAT:** Open moist tundra. **REMARKS:** Adults land in open gravelly patches amidst grassy slopes or flats in wet areas.

PHILIP'S ARCTIC *Oeneis rosovi* PL. 34

1¾–2 in. (46–50 mm). Wings translucent. Fringe off-white, black at vein endings. Male forewing pointed, that of female more rounded. Upperside: Hindwing *narrowly black-edged and with tiny yellow submarginal points*. Underside: Hindwing *narrowly black-edged* as above. **SIMILAR SPECIES:** Polixenes Arctic is very similar but flies in tundra, not in spruce bogs. **EARLY STAGES:** Caterpillar not described. **FOOD:** Cotton-grass. **FLIGHT:** Mid-June–mid-July, only in odd-numbered years. **RANGE:** Holarctic. Russian Far East, cen. Alaska east to w. Yukon Terr. and south to n. B.C. **HABITAT:** Spruce bogs. **REMARKS:** Previously know as *Oeneis philipi* but found to be the same species as *O. rosovi*.

SENTINEL ARCTIC
Oeneis alpina **PL. 34**

1½–1¾ in. (39–45 mm). *Forewing short*, does not extend beyond hindwing. Fringe checkered. Upperside: Hindwing with 2 indistinct eyespots on inner corner of wing. Male with basal two-thirds of hindwing brown. Underside: Similar to Chryxus Arctic, but *pattern indistinct*. **SIMILAR SPECIES:** Chryxus Arctic is more orange, usually has only one eyespot on corner of hindwing. Ranges overlap only narrowly in Yukon and w. N.W. Terr. **EARLY STAGES:** Not reported. **FOOD:** Unknown. **FLIGHT:** Late June–mid-July (1 flight). Biennial. **RANGE:** Holarctic. Russian Far East, n. Alaska, n. Yukon, and nw. N.W. Terr. **HABITAT:** Rock slides and hills on tundra. **REMARKS:** Males perch on hilltops to court receptive females.

MILKWEED BUTTERFLIES: SUBFAMILY DANAINAE

MONARCH *Danaus plexippus* **PL. 34**

3–4½ in. (76–114 mm). Our most familiar butterfly. Male is *bright orange* and has black scent patch in middle of hindwing above; female is dull orange or brown with more thickly scaled black veins. Black border has 2 *rows of tiny white spots*. **SIMILAR SPECIES:** Viceroy has a strong postmedian black line on upperside of both wings and has only a single marginal row of white spots in the black border. **EARLY STAGES:** Caterpillar transversely ringed with yellow, black, and off-white on each segment; head capsule white and black striped; 3 pairs of black fleshy tubercles on back of segments 2, 5, and 11. **FOOD:** Milkweeds and milkweed vines, rarely dogbane. **FLIGHT:** During warm part of year in w. North America, 1–3 broods in north, 4–6 in south, may breed all year in se. Calif. and s. Ariz. Overwinters in coastal Calif., cen. Mex., and sparingly along west coast of Mex. **RANGE:** Summer resident in s. Canada and entire continental U.S. In West, individuals overwinter along Calif. coast in large aggregations, and east of Continental Divide adults migrate to and overwinter in cen. Mex. Resident in most of tropical Amer. lowlands. Colonized and resident on many oceanic islands (including Hawaii) and Australia. **HABITAT:** Native prairies,

foothills, open weedy areas, roadsides, pastures, prairies, marshes, and similar situations. **REMARKS:** The Monarch undergoes dramatic migrations and forms large overwintering colonies in cen. Mex. and coastal Calif. The Mexican wintering sites, where our eastern, and presumably Great Plains, Monarchs are found, number in the millions of butterflies. During the summer, males patrol open fields or similar areas in search of females. The adults store cardiac glycosides, poisonous chemicals derived from their caterpillars' milkweed hosts, and as a result are both distasteful and emetic to most birds who would attempt to eat them. The Viceroy is a relatively palatable mimic of the Monarch in most of our area, but it mimics the Queen in peninsular Fla. and the Southwest. The adults visit flowers for nectar; these are often those of their milkweed hosts, but also include those of many other plants, especially in the Composite family.

QUEEN *Danaus gilippus* PL. 34

2¾–3½ in. (70–88 mm). Upperside: *Chestnut brown* with marginal black border. Forewing has scattered white spots on apical third. Underside: Hindwing has veins outlined in black; black marginal border has *double row of white spots.* **SIMILAR SPECIES:** (1) Viceroy (Southwest population, *L. a. obsoleta*) is smaller, has black postmedian line across hindwing and only a single row of white spots in black border. (2) Soldier is lighter, has black scaling on veins above, and a patch of off-white spots in center of hindwing below. **EARLY STAGES:** Caterpillar brown-white with yellow and brown transverse rings on each segment in addition to a yellow-green lateral stripe on each side; 3 pairs of black fleshy tubercles on back of segments 2, 5, and 11. **FOOD:** Milkweeds and milkweed vines. **FLIGHT:** All year in Fla. and s. Tex., usually July–Aug. to north, i.e., April–Oct. in Colo. **RANGE:** Resident in extreme s. U.S. and throughout tropical Amer. lowlands. Regular stray (and occasional colonist) north to cen. Calif., Nev., Utah, se. Wyo. and Neb., rarely N.D. **HABITAT:** Open fields, dry washes, thorn scrub, pastures, rivercourses, and other open areas. **REMARKS:** A poisonous and emetic model for Viceroys in the Southwest and Fla. The Monarch is a relatively uncommon breeder in these areas; hence the switch to the Queen as a more advantageous model.

SOLDIER

SOLDIER *Danaus eresimus*   **PL. 34**

2¼–3½ in. (62–91 mm). Upperside: Both wings have *veins* marked *thinly with black.* Forewing with fewer white spots. Underside: Hindwing with postmedian *band* of *blotchy pale whitish spots.* **SIMILAR SPECIES:** Queen lacks black scaling on veins above, is darker, and lacks patch of off-white spots in center of hindwing below. **EARLY STAGES:** Caterpillar yellow-green with fine black transverse rings; 8 pairs of black diamonds on upperside; 3 pairs black fleshy tubercles; head capsule black with yellow stripes. **FOOD:** Milkweeds and milkweed vines. **FLIGHT:** All year in tropics and where resident in s. Fla. and s. Tex., rare strays in se. Ariz. and s. N.M. from late Aug. to early Nov. **RANGE:** Resident from s. Fla. and s. Tex. south through lowland Amer. tropics (including West Indies) to Brazil. Rarely strays to s. Ariz. and s. N.M. **HABITAT:** Open pastures and edges of seasonally dry tropical forests.

LARGE TIGER *Lycorea cleobaea*   **NOT SHOWN**

2¾–3¾ in. (72–94 mm.). Orange with horizontal black stripes. *Black stripes* on hindwing *joined outwardly to form loop.* Male has black hair pencils (scent brushes) at tip of abdomen. **SIMILAR SPECIES:** Isabella's Heliconian is smaller, has more rounded forewing tip, and black stripes on hindwing are unconnected. **EARLY STAGES:** Caterpillar white with narrow black cross rings, one pair of tubercles behind head. **FOOD:** Papaya, jacaratia, fig, bloodflower. **FLIGHT:** April, July, Oct. in Tex. All year in tropics (several flights). **RANGE:** West Indies and cen. Mex. south to Peru. **HABITAT:** Tropical forests. **REMARKS:** Rare stray to Big Bend, Tex.

13

Skippers:
Superfamily Hesperioidea
Skippers: Family Hesperiidae

The skippers are worldwide in distribution. They are poorly represented in the arctic and subarctic, but have many species in the tropics. More than 3,500 species are described, with 276 in North America, many of them tropical species found only in southern Arizona or Texas. Most are small to medium, relatively dull-colored with orange, brown, black, white, and gray being frequent wing colors, but a few have iridescent colors. Their antennal clubs are often hooked and have an extension called an apiculus. Males have scent scales found in modified forewing patches, called "brands," within folds of the forewing costal margin or on their legs. All three pairs of legs are fully developed. Skippers' eyes are large, their antennae are usually short, and the bodies are stout. Flight is often rapid with the wing movement blurred. Males of most species locate mates by perching—especially in the grass and giant-skipper groups, but a few patrol, especially in the open-winged skipper group. Adults of most species have long proboscises ("tongues") and feed on floral nectar, but some also take up nutrients from bird droppings. Globular eggs are laid singly.

Within the family are five North American skipper subfamilies: firetips (Pyrrhopyginae), open-winged skippers (Pyrginae), skipperlings (Heteropterinae), grass skippers (Hesperiinae), and giant-skippers (Megathyminae).

Firetips: Subfamily Pyrrhopyginae

Only the Dull Firetip is found north of the Mexican boundary. Although the underside of its hindwing is bright yellow, it is relatively dull compared to the many colorful species found farther south in the American tropics. Caterpillars live in folded leaf shelters. Adults visit flowers and fly in a direct line with their wings beating with shallow-amplitude—a characteristic fairly slow buzzing flight.

DULL FIRETIP

Pyrrhopyge araxes **PL. 35**

1¾–2⅜ in. (44–61 mm). Antennae with clubs bent at right angles to shaft. Wing fringes white, checkered with black on hindwing. Upperside: Brown-black with *large squarish translucent white spots* on outer half of forewing. Underside: *Hindwing largely yellow.* **SIMILAR SPECIES:** No other skipper in our area has a largely yellow hindwing underside. **EARLY STAGES:** Caterpillar red-brown with narrow yellow cross bands and long white hairs. Head black with long white hairs. **FOOD:** Several oaks, including Arizona oak and Emory oak. **FLIGHT:** Early July–early Oct., mostly Aug.–Sept. (1 flight). **RANGE:** Se. Ariz. and extreme sw. N.M. south through Mexican highlands to Oaxaca. **HABITAT:** Oak woodland, glades along streams. **REMARKS:** The adults are strongly attracted to flowers and rest with their wings completely flat.

SPREAD-WING SKIPPERS (PYRGINES): SUBFAMILY PYRGINAE

Primarily tropical American, the open-winged skippers have 80 species in our area. Most genera are mainly tropical, but two, the duskywings *(Erynnis)* and checkered-skippers *(Pyrgus),* are mainly temperate and also occur in Eurasia. Adults of many species land with their wings open, although some perch with their wings closed or half open. Males of many species imbibe moisture from moist sand or mud. As far as is known, all of our species take nectar from flowers. Some species also feed on bird droppings. Many of our more tropical representatives rest under leaves when not otherwise active. Females lay their eggs singly, directly on host-plant leaves; some species put their eggs on plants or other objects adjacent to their true host. Almost all species use broad-leafed plants as their caterpillar hosts—oaks, mallows, and legumes are hosts for most of our species. Caterpillars live in rolled-leaf or webbed-leaf shelters.

MERCURIAL SKIPPER *Proteides mercurius* **NOT SHOWN**

2¼–2¾ in. (57–71 mm). *Head and thorax golden orange* above. Forewing long, extended. Upperside: Basal portion of both wings golden orange. Underside: Chestnut brown with *white frosting on outer margins. Hindwing with obscure white mark in center.* **EARLY**

STAGES: Caterpillar green- or golden yellow mottled with dark brown; red lateral stripes; head red-brown with red eyespots. **FOOD:** Legume trees and vines. **FLIGHT:** Most of year in native habitats (several flights). **RANGE:** American tropics from Mex. and West Indies south to Argentina, strays north to se. Ariz., s. Tex., Fla., and La. **HABITAT:** Near streams in moist, lowland tropical forests, especially associated edges and openings. In our area most likely in se. Ariz. canyons or gardens. **REMARKS:** Found as rare stray. Adults visit large flowers in tropical Mex.

SILVER-SPOTTED SKIPPER *Epargyreus clarus* PL. 35

1 ⅝–1 ⅞ in. (41–47 mm). Brown-black. The combination of *translucent gold forewing spots* and the *metallic silver band* on the hindwing beneath make it unmistakable. **SIMILAR SPECIES:** None in most of our area. Rare tropical strays along Mexican boundary may be similar. **EARLY STAGES:** Caterpillar yellow with fine black cross lines; head red-brown with 2 large round red-orange spots low on front. **FOOD:** Locusts, wild licorice, wisteria, and many other legumes. **FLIGHT:** Late May–July (1 flight), occasionally as early as April or as late as Sept. in southern portion of our area. **RANGE:** Resident in extreme s. Canada, most of continental U.S. (except w. Tex. and Great Basin), and nw. Mex. **HABITAT:** Foothill canyons, stream edges in prairie, gardens, less likely in disturbed areas in West. **REMARKS:** The most conspicuous skipper in most of our area. Males perch on the ground or low vegetation, usually along streams. Females may lay eggs on objects adjacent to their caterpillar host plants.

WIND'S SILVERDROP *Epargyreus windi* PL. 35

1 ¹⁵⁄₁₆–2 ⁷⁄₁₆ in. (49–62 mm). *Thorax and top of head golden orange. Lower half of face white.* Hindwing with slight pointed extension at rear. Forewing elongate with small separate pale amber translucent spots across center. Underside: Outer half of forewing frosted white. Hindwing with *oval metallic silver patch* in center; otherwise dark brown *frosted white on outer portion.* **EARLY STAGES:** Not reported. **FOOD:** Probably legumes. **FLIGHT:** May–Nov. in Mex. **RANGE:** Resident along west coast of Mex. Unreliably reported from se. Ariz. and s. Calif. **HABITAT:** Tropical woods or scrub and associated edges. **REMARKS:** One of a confusing group of tropical skippers, our records formerly were referred to Exadeus Silverdrop, but most likely are this species—the most frequently observed in nw. Mex.

HAMMOCK SKIPPER *Polygonus leo* PL. 35

1 ¾–2 in. (46–52 mm). Hindwing with slight extension at rear. Upperside: Black-brown; forewing with 3 *prominent square white*

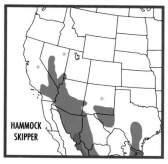

patches. Underside: Hindwing with *violet sheen and small dark, round basal spot.* **SIMILAR SPECIES:** Manuel's Skipper (a potential but unreported stray in our area) is smaller, has bluish gloss at base of forewing and red-brown pale areas on underside of hindwing. **EARLY STAGES:** Caterpillar translucent green with 2 yellow stripes along each side; head green with 2 black spots on upper front. **FOOD:** Jamaican dogwood and karum tree. **FLIGHT:** All year in areas of residence such as s. Fla., lowland Mex. and Cen. Amer. Strays found from July–Oct. in s. Ariz. and may be quite common at times. **RANGE:** S. Fla., West Indies, and Mex. south to Argentina. Strays north to southern portion of our area (s. Calif., Nev., s. Ariz., sw. Utah, s. N.M., and s. Tex.). **HABITAT:** Tropical woodland and scrub in Mex.; hardwood hammocks in s. Fla. Strays may be found in a wide variety of habitats. **REMARKS:** Adults are fond of flowers such as bougainvillea and bonesets. When perched or visiting flowers wings may be open or closed, often upside down.

WHITE-STRIPED LONGTAIL *Chioides catillus*   **PL. 35**

1¾–2 in. (46–52 mm). Our only skipper with exceptionally *long tails and a long silver stripe* on hindwing below. **SIMILAR SPECIES:** Zilpa Longtail (also a rare stray) has a central white trapezoidal patch on hindwing below. **EARLY STAGES:** Caterpillar pale green-yellow with yellow lateral lines and many tiny black dots; prothorax red with a black patch behind head; head red with a

black Y on front. **FOOD:** Viny legumes. **FLIGHT:** All year in s. Tex. and lowland tropics. **RANGE:** Resident from se. Ariz., s. Tex., and West Indies south through tropical Amer. to Argentina. Periodic stray to w. Tex. and sw. N.M. **HABITAT:** Hot, dry canyons in Southwest, lowland tropical scrub elsewhere. **REMARKS:** Adults are fond of nectar of low flowers and perch with wings tightly closed.

ZILPA LONGTAIL *Chioides zilpa* PL. 35

⅞–1¼ in. (48–58 mm). Similar to White-striped Longtail, but *forewing tip squared off* and tails slightly outcurved. Upperside: Forewing with golden yellow translucent marks extensive. Underside: Hindwing mottled and has *a central trapezoidal white patch.* **SIMILAR SPECIES:** (1) White-striped Longtail has rounded forewing tip and long white stripe on underside of hindwing. (2) White-crescent Longtail also has rounded forewing tip and has more irregular submarginal white patch on underside of hindwing. **EARLY STAGES:** Not reported. **FOOD:** Unknown. **FLIGHT:** Flies all year in lowland Mex. and Cen. Amer. Late summer and fall (late Aug.–late Oct.) in se. Ariz. **RANGE:** Resident from Mex. south through tropical Amer. to Colombia. Strays regularly to se. Ariz. and s. Tex., rarely cen. Tex. **HABITAT:** Tropical scrub and associated edges. Can be found in several habitats as stray. **REMARKS:** Perches with wings tightly closed. Nectars at flowers such as thistles, waltheria, and boneset.

GOLD-SPOTTED AGUNA *Aguna asander* PL. 35

1⅞–2³⁄₁₆ in. (47–56 mm). *Top of head and thorax golden orange; lower half of face white.* Fringes uncheckered. Short taillike lobe at rear of hindwing. Upperside: Forewing with row of approximately equal translucent golden yellow spots. Underside: Hindwing with inner third of hindwing brown and outer two-thirds with *vague blurred silver white patch.* **SIMILAR SPECIES:** Silver-spotted Skipper has brighter golden patch on forewing. Silver patch on underside of hindwing is sharper in outline. **EARLY STAGES:** Not reported. **FOOD:** Probably legumes. **FLIGHT:** Most of year in Mex. (several flights), Oct. in Ariz. **RANGE:** Resident from West Indies and Mex. south through tropical Amer. to Argentina. Rare stray to se. Ariz. and periodic stray north to lower Rio Grande Valley, Tex. **HABITAT:** Tropical scrub and associated openings and edges.

MEXICAN LONGTAIL *Polythrix mexicanus* PL. 35

1½–1¾ in. (40–46 mm). Long outcurved tails. Fringes not checkered. Upperside: Mottled dark brown. Forewing: Translucent *white spots in central transverse band* and near apex. *Two dark spots* along trailing edge. Male has costal fold. Hindwing: Two

darker postbasal and postmedian bands. **SIMILAR SPECIES:** (1) Dorantes Skipper has checkered fringe, lacks bands on upper surface of hindwing, and perches with wings closed or slightly opened. (2) Other species of *Polythrix* can be reliably identified only by dissection of genitalia. **EARLY STAGES:** Not reported. **FOOD:** Legume trees, including *Amerimnon* and *Ictyomenthia.* **FLIGHT:** April–Dec. in Mex. (several flights), Oct. in se. Ariz. **RANGE:** Resident in lowland Mex. to Oaxaca, rare stray to se. Ariz. and s. Tex. **HABITAT:** Streams and shady areas within seasonal tropical forest or scrub. **REMARKS:** Adults perch with wings completely open. Found at flowers in early morning and late afternoon. Males are also found at stream edges sipping moisture. Perches upside down under leaves at other times.

SHORT-TAILED SKIPPER *Zestusa dorus*   **PL. 35**

1 ½–1 ⅝ in. (38–42 mm). Antennal clubs curved outwardly in arc. *Short tail* at rear of each hindwing. Fringes checkered. Upperside: Forewing with *4 translucent squarish white patches.* Outer 2 sometimes merged as one. Hindwing with *small oval translucent white patch.* Underside: *Mottled brownish with gray scaling outwardly.* **SIMILAR SPECIES:** No other skipper has combination of short tails on hindwing and white patches on both wings. **EARLY STAGES:** Caterpillar pale yellow-green with lighter stripes up middle of back and along each side; head orange-brown. **FOOD:** Oaks including Arizona oak, Emory oak, and Gambel oak. **FLIGHT:** April–May, early July–early Sept. in s. Ariz. (1 with partial second flight). **RANGE:** Sw. Colo., Ariz., N.M., and w. Tex. south into the oaks zones to central Mex. **HABITAT:** Dense oak forest and thickets. **REMARKS:** Males may congregate on hilltops to locate receptive females. Adults seldom visit flowers but may be found at moist spots along streams taking moisture.

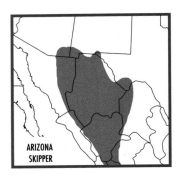

ARIZONA SKIPPER *Codatractus arizonensis*   **PL. 35**
1 ⅝–2 ¾₆ in. (42–59 mm). Fringes checkered. Hindwing extended slightly at rear to give elongate appearance. Upperside: Brownish black with transverse row of large square white patches on forewing. Underside: *Hindwing mottled with darker black patches. Vaguely defined submarginal patch of white scales.* **SIMILAR SPECIES:** Hammock Skipper has narrower forewing, iridescent sheen, and 3 white spots in triangle relation—not bar. Underside has distinct dark bars. **EARLY STAGES:** Not reported. **FOOD:** *Eysenhardtia orthocarpa,* a legume. **FLIGHT:** Late March–mid-Oct., most common in midsummer (1 flight with some individuals appearing at odd times). **RANGE:** Se. Ariz., sw. N.M., and w. Tex. south in Sierra Madre Occidentale to Oaxaca, Mex. **HABITAT:** Foothill canyons and arroyos. **REMARKS:** Males perch on bare branches near steep cliffs.

WHITE-CRESCENT LONGTAIL   **PL. 35**
Codatractus alcaeus
1 ¾–2 ¼₆ in. (46–53 mm). *Tailed.* Upperside: Dark brown; forewing with median band of gold spots. Underside: Hindwing with 3 *irregular dark bands; white submarginal patch on lower part of wing.* **SIMILAR SPECIES:** Zilpa Longtail has squared-off forewing apex and differently shaped, more central white patch on hindwing underside. **EARLY STAGES:** Not reported. **FOOD:** Tree legumes, including *Amerimnon* and *Ictyomenthia.* **FLIGHT:** June, Oct. in s. Tex.; April–Oct. in Mex. **RANGE:** Resident from Mex. south to Panama. Rare stray in lower Rio Grande Valley and w. Tex. **HABITAT:** Tropical woods.

DESERT MOTTLED SKIPPER *Codatractus mysie*   **PL. 37**
1 ½–1 ⅞ in. (38–48 mm). Wings broad and rounded. Fringes checkered with dark and light brown. Upperside: Dark reddish

brown with pattern of white spots on outer half of forewing. Usually a double or hourglass-shaped spot in the cell. Underside: Hindwing dark brown with 2 *darker wavy bands*. Outer portion of hindwing with series of *arched dark spots with a row of crescent-shaped light red buff spots* just inside dark spot row. **SIMILAR SPECIES:** Other dark brown skippers lack reddish brown appearance, have more pointed wings, lack transparent spot in cell, and have less complicated patterns below. **EARLY STAGES:** Not reported. **FOOD:** *Tephrosia.* **FLIGHT:** Late July–late Aug. (1 flight). **RANGE:** Se. Ariz. to s. Mex. (Oaxaca). **HABITAT:** Rocky canyons. **REMARKS:** Very rarely seen because of restricted range. Flies during the morning and visits flowers such as *Aloysia, Cnidiscolus*, and *Rhus*. Perches with wings closed.

LONG-TAILED SKIPPER

LONG-TAILED SKIPPER *Urbanus proteus* PL. 35

1¼–2 in. (38–52 mm). This and the 2 following very similar species have distinct but subtle pattern characters, as well as distinct genitalia. Upperside dark black-brown with *body* and *basal portion of wings iridescent blue-green*. Male with costal fold. **SIMILAR SPECIES:** Dorantes Longtail lacks green scaling on the upper wing surfaces and has shorter tails. **EARLY STAGES:** Caterpillar yellow-green; thin black dorsal line; yellow and red stripe and 2 green lines along each side; head black with brown top and 2 large yellow to orange spots low on front. **FOOD:** Many viny legumes, including beans. **FLIGHT:** All year in s. Fla. and s. Tex. (2–3 broods), usually late summer to the north. **RANGE:** Resident from peninsular Fla. and s. Tex. south through West Indies and mainland tropical Amer. to Argentina. Stray and occasional colonist north to cen. Calif., s. Ariz., sw. N.M. and w. Tex. More regular stray and temporary colonist in East. **HABITAT:** Tropical thorn forest and scrub, open disturbed situations, brushy fields, gardens. May appear in many situations as strays, especially at flowers.

DORANTES LONGTAIL *Urbanus dorantes* PL. 36

1⅜–1¾ in. (36–46 mm). *Tailed*. Brown body and wings. Fringes checkered. Upperside: Forewing with *conspicuous transparent spots*. **SIMILAR SPECIES:** Long-tailed Skipper has green body and green wing bases above. **EARLY STAGES:** Caterpillar green to pink-orange,

brown at rear; dark red-brown dorsal line; head brown to black.
FOOD: Viny legumes, especially beggar ticks. **FLIGHT:** All year in lowland tropics (3–4 flights), mid-July–late Nov. in s. Ariz. **RANGE:** Resident from se. Ariz., s. Tex., and peninsular Fla. south through
West Indies and mainland American tropics to Argentina. Strays
north to n. Calif. **HABITAT:** Low foothill canyons, overgrown fields,
wood edges in U.S. Open fields, scrub, second growth in lowland
tropics.

PLAIN LONGTAIL *Urbanus simplicius*   **PL. 36**
   1 ½–1 ¹⁵/₁₆ in. (37–50 mm). Tailed. Brown. Upperside: *Forewing
marks obscured or absent.* Male has costal fold. Underside: *Postbasal band joined to brown spot near costa.* **SIMILAR SPECIES:** Brown
Longtail is virtually identical and can be reliably separated only by
dissection and examination of genitalia. **EARLY STAGES:** Not reported.
FOOD: Viny legumes. **FLIGHT:** Oct.–July in Mex. and Cen. Amer. **RANGE:**
Mex. south through tropical Amer. to Argentina. Rare stray to s.
Calif. and s. Tex. **HABITAT:** Openings in lowland tropical forests and
second growth. **REMARKS:** S. Calif. record may represent an individ-
ual imported as caterpillar on nursery stock.

BROWN LONGTAIL *Urbanus procne*   **PL. 36**
   1 ⅝–1 ⅞ in. (42–48 mm). Tailed, brown. Fringes uncheckered. Upperside: Male has forewing *costal fold.* Underside: Hindwing *postbasal band is separated from brown spot* near costa. **SIMILAR SPECIES:**
Plain Longtail and Teleus Longtail can be reliably identified only
by genitalic dissection. **EARLY STAGES:** Not reported. **FOOD:** Grasses,
including Bermuda grass. **FLIGHT:** All year in s. Tex. and lowland
tropics (3 flights), Sept.–Oct. in se. Ariz. as rare stray. **RANGE:** Resident from s. Tex. south through tropical Amer. to Argentina. Rare
stray to s. Calif., s. Ariz., and s. N.M. **HABITAT:** Second-growth

scrub, beach dunes, plantations in lowland tropical Amer. **REMARKS:** Adults readily visit flowers. Records in our area should be documented by capture and dissection.

TWO-BARRED FLASHER
Astraptes fulgerator   **PL. 36**

1⅞–2⅜ in. (47–60 mm). Tailless. Unmistakable. *Head and thorax golden yellow.* Upperside: *Basal portion of wings iridescent blue.* Forewing with transverse white median band and tiny white spots near apex. Male has costal fold on forewing. Underside: Hindwing *costa white at base.* **EARLY STAGES:** Caterpillar black above, maroon below, with yellow hairs and yellow cross rings; maroon patch near head. Head black with white hairs. **FOOD:** Coyotillo and *Vitex.* **FLIGHT:** All year in s. Tex. and lowland tropics (several flights), 2 records from se. Ariz. in June and late Aug. **RANGE:** Resident from s. Tex. south through lowland tropics to Argentina. **HABITAT:** Tropical woods near streams or rivers. **REMARKS:** One of the more beautiful skippers. Avidly visits flowers such as bougainvillea, thevetia, and plumbago.

GOLDEN-BANDED SKIPPER *Autochton cellus*   **PL. 36**

1¼–1¾ in. (32–46 mm). Each *antenna has white ring below club.* Upperside: Black with *broad yellow band* crossing forewing. Small *coalesced white patch* near forewing apex. **SIMILAR SPECIES:** Sonoran Banded-Skipper, extirpated in U.S., has rounder wings, narrower gold band, and 2 dark bands on underside of hindwing. **EARLY STAGES:** Caterpillar bright yellow-green with scattered yellow points and yellow lateral lines; head red-brown with 2 large round yellow patches on front. **FOOD:** New Mexico locust and other legumes. **FLIGHT:** Mid-June–early Sept., mainly July (1 flight). **RANGE:** Resident from cen. Ariz., sw. N.M., and w. Tex. south to El Salvador. Also from Md. south to S.C., west to e. Okla. and ne. Tex. An isolated population in n. Fla. Older records north to N.J. **HABITAT:** Canyon bottoms with permanent water. **REMARKS:** Adults readily visit flowers and have a slow flight.

SONORAN BANDED-SKIPPER *Autochton pseudocellus* **PL. 36**

1¼–1⅝ in. (32–42 mm). Each *antenna has a white ring below club. Fringes distinctly checkered.* Wings relatively rounded. Upperside: *Slightly curved gold band* across forewing. Underside:

Two darker bands across hindwing. SIMILAR SPECIES: Golden Banded-Skipper is larger, has less distinctly checkered fringes and broader gold band, and lacks 2 darker bands on hindwing below. Genitalia are also distinctive. EARLY STAGES: Not reported. FOOD: Probably beggar ticks. FLIGHT: June–Sept. (1 flight). RANGE: Se. Ariz. (formerly) south to Oaxaca, Mex. HABITAT: Canyon bottoms in mountains. REMARKS: The Sonoran Banded-Skipper has not been found in the U.S. since 1936, although it is still common in adjacent portions of Mex.

CHISOS BANDED-SKIPPER *Autochton cinctus*   **PL. 36**
1⅜–1¾ in. (36–44 mm). Unmistakable. *Hindwing fringe white.* Upperside: Brown-black with *white translucent band across forewing.* SIMILAR SPECIES: No other skipper has combination of white band across forewing and white fringe on hindwing. EARLY STAGES: Not reported. FOOD: Beggar ticks. FLIGHT: Late March–late Nov. (several flights). RANGE: W. Tex. (Chisos Mts.) south through mountains to El Salvador. HABITAT: Oak-pine woodland. REMARKS: Adult perches on branches with wings closed. Visits a variety of flowers.

DESERT CLOUDYWING *Achalarus casica*   **PL. 36**
1½–1¹⁵⁄₁₆ in. (37–50 mm). Upperside: Forewing with separated, white transparent spots; hindwing with *white fringe.* Underside: Hindwing with 2 *dark bands and broad mottled white marginal band.* SIMILAR SPECIES: Drusius Cloudywing lacks broad white mottled submarginal band on underside of hindwing. EARLY STAGES: Not reported. FOOD: Beggar ticks and *Clitoria.* FLIGHT: Late March–Oct. (2 flights). RANGE: Resident se. Ariz., sw. N.M., and w. Tex. south through Mex. to Guatemala. HABITAT: Pinyon-juniper woodland, mountains at low and middle elevations.

SKINNER'S CLOUDYWING *Achalarus albociliatus* **PL. 36**
1¹¹⁄₁₆–1³⁄₁₆ in. (43–46 mm). Forewing pointed. Upperside: Dark
brown with faint pattern on forewing. Male lacks costal fold.
Hindwing has white fringe. Underside: Forewing has *pale outer
margin contrasting with adjacent darker inner area.* **SIMILAR SPECIES:**
Coyote Cloudywing male has costal fold, lacks distinct pale outer
margin on underside of forewing. **EARLY STAGES:** Not reported. **FOOD:**
Unknown. **FLIGHT:** Most of year in lowland tropics (several flights),
June, July in se. Ariz. **RANGE:** Lowland tropics south to Venezuela.
Rare stray to se. Ariz. and s. Tex. **HABITAT:** Tropical thorn scrub, sea-
sonally dry forest. **REMARKS:** Difficult to distinguish from Coyote
Skipper without seeing pale band on outer edge of forewing be-
low.

COYOTE CLOUDYWING *Achalarus toxeus* **PL. TK**
1⅝–1¹⁵⁄₁₆ in. (40–50 mm). Forewing pointed. Upperside: Dark
brown with *darker rectangular spots* in forewing. Male has *short
costal fold* on forewing. Hindwing usually with *white fringe.* **SIMILAR
SPECIES:** Skinner's Cloudywing has pale outer edge on lower surface
of forewing. Males lacks costal fold. **EARLY STAGES:** Not reported.
FOOD: Texas ebony. **FLIGHT:** Feb.–Nov. (3 broods). **RANGE:** Resident
from cen. Tex. south through Mex. and Cen. Amer. to Panama.
May stray north to s. Ariz. **HABITAT:** Tropical scrub, open areas. **RE-
MARKS:** Males may perch on hilltops to await receptive females.

NORTHERN CLOUDYWING *Thorybes pylades* **PL. 36**
1¼–1⁹⁄₁₆ in. (31–40 mm). This is the most broadly distributed
cloudywing. Upperside: Forewing with *transparent spots triangular, small, and not aligned.* Male is one of 2 cloudywings with a
costal fold. **SIMILAR SPECIES:** (1) Western cloudywing is smaller, male
lacks costal fold on forewing, transparent spots on forewing tend
to be elongate and aligned; spot below cell is the largest and
slightly curved; bands on un-
derside of hindwing much
more indistinct. (2) Drusius
Cloudywing has costal fold but
white fringe on outer edge of
hindwing. **EARLY STAGES:** Caterpillar dark green with brown or
maroon dorsal line; 2 pale or-
ange-pink lateral lines on each
side; covered with minute
bumps bearing short orange
hairs; head black to dark
brown. **FOOD:** Vetches, beggar

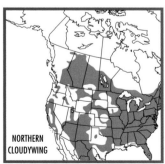

NORTHERN
CLOUDYWING

SOUTHERN CLOUDYWING

WESTERN CLOUDYWING

ticks, bush clovers, milk vetches, and other legumes. **FLIGHT:** May–July (1 flight) in north, flying earlier to the south. Late April–early Sept. in s. Ariz. (possibly 1 flight). **RANGE:** Resident through much of temperate N. Amer. from B.C. south along Pacific Coast to n. Baja Calif., thence east across s. Canada, most of w. U.S., and n. Mex. to Atlantic Coast. **HABITAT:** Open woodlands, prairie watercourses, and canyons. **REMARKS:** Adults nectar at white, pink, or purple flowers such as dame's rocket, mints, vetches, and thistles.

SOUTHERN CLOUDYWING *Thorybes bathyllus*   **PL. 36**

1¼–1⅝ in. (32–42 mm). Upperside: Forewing with *transparent spot band broad and aligned. Male lacks costal fold.* **SIMILAR SPECIES:** Northern Cloudywing has smaller scattered transparent spots that tend to be triangular. Male has costal fold. **EARLY STAGES:** Caterpillar dull red-brown with pale dorsal and lateral lines; head black with short golden brown hairs. **FOOD:** Beggar ticks, bush clover, wild bean, milk vetch, and other legumes. **FLIGHT:** Mid-June–mid-July in north (1 flight), June–early Oct. in most of range (2–3 flights). **RANGE:** Cen. Neb., se. Colo., w. Kans., w. Okla, and cen. Tex. east through most of e. U.S. and s. Ont. **HABITAT:** Open, scrubby areas such as dry meadows, and prairie hills. **REMARKS:** An infrequent, uncommon species in our area.

WESTERN CLOUDYWING *Thorybes diversus*   **PL. 36**

1⅛–1⅜ in. (29–36 mm). Forewing relatively pointed. Upperside: Blackish brown with *line of transparent elongate spots* crossing middle of forewing. The lowermost spot most elongate and curved. Male *lacks costal fold* on forewing. Underside: Hindwing *dark brown basally, grayer outwardly. Two black bands indistinct.* **SIMILAR SPECIES:** Northern Cloudywing is larger, has more scattered

MEXICAN CLOUDYWING

DRUSIUS CLOUDYWING

triangular transparent spots on forewing. Bands on underside of hindwing relatively distinct. Male has costal fold. Wings more rounded. **EARLY STAGES:** Caterpillar dark olive-brown with heavy sprinkling of pale dots. A darker line runs up middle of back and 2 pale stripes run along each side. First thoracic segment is red-brown and head is black. **FOOD:** Wormskjold's clover and others. **FLIGHT:** May–June (1 flight). **RANGE:** S. Ore. south to Klamath Mts., Trinity Mts., and west slope of Sierra Nevada, Calif. **HABITAT:** Ponderosa pine forest and associated moist glades and small streamsides. **REMARKS:** Colonies are very local and adults nectar at vetches, clovers, and other flowers. Males perch on the ground or dead branches near ground level to await prospective mate.

MEXICAN CLOUDYWING *Thorybes mexicanus*   PL. 37

1–1¼ in. (26–38 mm). Small. Wings relatively rounded. Fringes more or less checkered. Upperside: Pale brown to dark brown. Spots variable from relatively large to small. Male has *costal fold*. Underside: Hindwing with 2 *dark bands*. Outer portion with wide *pale gray band with short, fine striations*. **SIMILAR SPECIES:** Northern Cloudywing is larger, darker, and lacks striations on underside of hindwing. **EARLY STAGES:** Not reported. **FOOD:** Clovers, vetches. **FLIGHT:** Late April–Aug. (1 flight). **RANGE:** Cascades of Ore. south to Sierra Nevada of w. Nev. and Calif. (subspecies *nevada*). Main population from extreme se. Idaho and s. Wyo. south through Rocky Mts. and Sierra Madre to s. Mex. **HABITAT:** Open montane, often rocky, flats and hills; moist areas near streams. **REMARKS:** Adults nectar at flowers such as pussytoes, wild onion, and iris.

DRUSIUS CLOUDYWING *Thorybes drusius*   PL. 37

1½–1⁹⁄₁₆ in. (38–40 mm). Forewings somewhat pointed. Upperside: Dark brown with *scattered small transparent spots*. Hindwing

Drusius Cloudywing nectaring at milk-weed, Cochise Co., Ariz. Note pointed forewing and white fringe on hindwing. Similar Desert Cloudywing has 2 dark bands and pronounced white submarginal area on underside of hindwing.

with *prominent white fringe.* **SIMILAR SPECIES:** Northern Cloudywing lacks white fringes on hindwing. Desert Cloudywing tends to be larger and has 2 dark bands and pronounced marginal white band on underside of hindwing. **EARLY STAGES:** Not reported. **FOOD:** *Cologania* and possibly other legumes. **FLIGHT:** July–Aug. in s. Ariz., April–June in w. Tex. (1 flight). **RANGE:** Se. Ariz., sw. N.M., and w. Tex. south to s. Mex. **HABITAT:** Grassy oak and pine-oak woodland and desert grasslands. **REMARKS:** Adults nectar at flowers such as knapweeds, milkweeds, *Aloysia,* and *Guardiola.*

POTRILLO SKIPPER *Cabares potrillo*   PL. 37

1 1/16–1 1/2 in. (28–38 mm). Hindwing outer margin with shallow lobes. Upperside: Forewing with *double U-shaped transparent spot in cell.* Underside: Hindwing with 2 dark bands. **SIMILAR SPECIES:** Mimosa Skipper has only a few small apical white spots and lacks lobes on hindwing. **EARLY STAGES:** Caterpillar light brown with black line up back and orange line along each side. Head black. **FOOD:** *Priva lappulacea.* **FLIGHT:** All year in s. Tex., late May and early Sept. in se. Ariz. **RANGE:** Rare stray to se. Ariz. Resident from s. Tex. south through mainland tropical Amer. and West Indies to Venezuela and Colombia. **HABITAT:** Open fields, moist woods. **REMARKS:** Males perch with open wings on low plants.

FRITZGAERTNER'S FLAT *Celaenorrhinus fritzgaertneri*   PL. 37

1 5/8–1 15/16 in. (41–50 mm). *Fringes checkered.* Upperside: Forewing with *white band; hindwing mottled.* **EARLY STAGES:** Not reported. **FOOD:** Unknown. **FLIGHT:** Most of year in Mex. Early July and late Aug. in se. Ariz. (several flights). **RANGE:** Strays north to se. Ariz. and s. Tex. Resident from n. Mex. south to Costa Rica. **HABITAT:** Tropical de-

ciduous forests. **REMARKS:** The butterflies fly in early morning and at dusk. They rest on the ceilings of caves, culverts, and buildings during the day.

MIMOSA SKIPPER *Cogia calchas* PL. 37

1 ³⁄₁₆–1 ¾ in. (30–44 mm). Forewing apex extended, especially in males. Upperside: Dark brown. Forewing with 3 or 4 tiny white apical spots; sometimes a vague white costal spot halfway from base. Underside: Hindwing brown with *gray anal fold and pale wormlike markings.* **SIMILAR SPECIES:** No other dark skipper has combination of extended forewing apex and pale wormlike lines on underside of hindwing. **EARLY STAGES:** Caterpillar yellow with fine white dots. **FOOD:** *Mimosa pigra*, *Indigofera*—both mimosoid legumes. **FLIGHT:** March–Nov. (3 flights); flies all year in Mex. and Cen. Amer. **RANGE:** Resident from s. Tex. and Mex. south through mainland tropical Amer. to Argentina. One stray reported from s. Calif. **HABITAT:** City flower gardens, lakes formed from cut-off river oxbows, canals, fields. **REMARKS:** During hottest part of day these skippers perch in the open on dirt roads or dry riverbeds. This is a time when only a few other butterflies, for example, Common Buckeyes, remain active in open sunlight.

ACACIA SKIPPER *Cogia hippalus* PL. 37

1 ⁵⁄₁₆–1 ⅞ in. (34–47 mm). Upperside: Pale brown. Forewing with *prominent white spots.* Hindwing *fringe prominently white.* Underside: Hindwing with lavender or purplish cast. **SIMILAR SPECIES:** Desert Cloudywing has hindwing underside with more prominent white fringe. **EARLY STAGES:** Not reported. **FOOD:** *Acacia angustissima.* **FLIGHT:** Late March–mid-Oct. in se. Ariz. (2 flights). **RANGE:** Resident from cen. Ariz., sw. N.M., and w. Tex. south to Brazil. Rare

stray to lower Rio Grande Valley, Tex. **HABITAT:** Desert grassland, pinyon-juniper woodland. **REMARKS:** Adults perch with wings closed. Flowers such as seepwillow are visited for nectar.

OUTIS SKIPPER *Cogia outis* PL. 37

1 3/16–1 9/16 in. (30–40 mm). *Hindwing fringe brown*, sometimes checkered. Upperside: Forewing with *white transparent spots reduced in number and size.* **SIMILAR SPECIES:** Acacia Skipper is slightly larger, has more prominent white fringe on hindwing, and more prominent white spots on forewing. **EARLY STAGES:** Not reported. **FOOD:** Acacias. **FLIGHT:** March–Oct. (4 flights). **RANGE:** Resident in cen. Tex.; strays north to Okla., sw. Mo., and nw. Ark. as well as south to n. Chihuahua and Coahuila, Mex. **HABITAT:** Parks, roadsides, hedgerows. **REMARKS:** Rare resident at eastern edge of our territory.

CAICUS SKIPPER *Cogia caicus* PL. 37

1 1/16–1 5/8 in. (27–41 mm). Upperside: Dark brown. *Forewing costa gold.* Pattern of transparent white spots similar to Acacia Skipper. Underside: Hindwing with 2 *transverse bluish bands and broad whitish gray outer band* (similar to Desert Cloudywing). **SIMILAR SPECIES:** Desert Cloudywing lacks golden-edged forewing costa, has less conspicuous dark markings on hindwing below, a more prominent white outer area, and usually perches with open wings. **EARLY STAGES:** Not reported. **FOOD:** *Acacia angustissima.* **FLIGHT:** Mid-March–early September (2 flights). **RANGE:** Cen. Ariz. and s. N.M. south through Mex. to Guatemala. **HABITAT:** Rocky canyons in oak-pine woodland, especially in limestone formations. **REMARKS:** Adults perch on ground, often on rocks, with closed wings. They occasionally visit flowers.

WIND'S SKIPPER *Windia windi*

1 ¼–1 ½ in. (32–38 mm). Labial palpi long, directed forward. Male forewing pointed. Both sexes have hindwing outer margin with 1 or 2 *concave scallops.* Forewing fringes checkered black and dark brown. Upperside: Ground dark brown. Both sexes with series of *3 or 4 closely placed translucent white spots just in from wingtip and group of 5 large transparent patches* in middle of forewing. Additional ill-defined squarish patches on forewing. Male hindwing with scattered small gray spots. Female hindwing blotchy. **EARLY STAGES:** Not reported. **FOOD:** Unknown. **FLIGHT:** Aug.–Sept. (1 flight), May–June to south in Mex. **RANGE:** Cen. Sonora south along Pacific slope to s. Mex. (Guerrero). Strayed once to se. Ariz. **HABITAT:** Subtropical scrub and associated gullies. Males perch on tall shrubs in steep canyons.

MOTTLED BOLLA *Bolla clytius*

⅞–1 3/16 in. (23–30 mm). Upperside: Brown-black with *darker mottling.* Forewing with *tiny white transparent spots at wingtip.* Spring-emerging individuals are more heavily patterned than those found in the fall. **SIMILAR SPECIES:** Golden-headed Scallopwing has head and palps covered with golden orange scales. **EARLY STAGES:** Not reported. **FOOD:** Unknown. **FLIGHT:** Late Aug.–mid-Oct. in se. Ariz., most of year in Mex. (several flights). **RANGE:** Mex. south to Honduras. Strays north to se. Ariz. and s. Tex. **HABITAT:** Tropical scrub, weedy areas, canyons. **REMARKS:** A rare stray in our area. Perches with open wings.

GOLDEN-HEADED SCALLOPWING *Staphylus ceos*

13/16–1 1/16 in. (21–28 mm). Wings are less scalloped than other scallopwings. *Head and palpi covered with golden orange scales.* Females may lack orange scales, especially in spring flight. Upperside: Wings black with a few *tiny white points on costa near apex.*
SIMILAR SPECIES: Common Sootywing and other blackish skippers that perch with open wings lack golden-orange scales on head and palps. **EARLY STAGES:** Not reported. **FOOD:** Goosefoots. **FLIGHT:** Early Feb.–early Nov. in se. Ariz. (2–3 flights). **RANGE:** Resident from s. Ariz., s. N.M., and w. and s. Tex. south to Durango, Mex. Rarely strays to s. Calif. and s. Nev. **HABITAT:** Valleys, desert canyons, and

GOLDEN-HEADED SCALLOPWING

washes. **REMARKS:** Adults perch with open wings and frequent valley or canyon bottoms. On hot days when taking moisture along streams they may close their wings. These skippers often fly in shade beneath trees and shrubs. The Aztec Scallopwing (*Staphylus azteca*) was reported from w. Tex. but was a misidentified Golden-headed Scallopwing.

MAZANS SCALLOPWING *Staphylus mazans*   PL. 37

⅞–1 ¹⁄₁₆ in. (22–28 mm). Wing margins *distinctly scalloped. Fringes uncheckered* dark brown. Upperside: Blackish brown with scattered golden yellow scales and 1–2 tiny white points on costa near wingtip. *Two darker bands on each wing.* **SIMILAR SPECIES:** Hayhurst's Scallopwing has checkered fringes, and dark bands are more apparent. **EARLY STAGES:** Not reported. **FOOD:** Lamb's-quarters, amaranths. **FLIGHT:** All year in s. Tex. (several flights). **RANGE:** Cen. Tex. south to Veracruz, Mex. One record from w. Tex. **HABITAT:** Small clearing in subtropical or tropical woodlands; weedy areas in parks, woods edges.

HAYHURST'S SCALLOPWING   PL. 37
Staphylus hayhurstii

⅞–1 ¹⁄₁₆ in. (22–28 mm). Hindwing outer margin *scalloped. Fringes checkered* brown-black and tan. Upperside: Black-brown (males) or light brown (females) with *scattered golden yellow scales and darker bands.* **SIMILAR SPECIES:** Mazans Scallopwing (see above). **EARLY STAGES:** Caterpillar deep green, orangish toward rear, covered with fine white hairs. Head purplish brown. **FOOD:** Lamb's-quarters, chaff-flower. **FLIGHT:** May–Aug. (2 flights). **RANGE:** Resident of s. two-thirds of e. U.S. west to n. Tex., w. Kans., cen. Neb., and se. S.D. **HABITAT:** Vacant weedy lots, gardens, open woods. **REMARKS:** Perches with wings flat. Visits low flowers such as dogbane, marigold, and white clover.

GLASSY-WINGED SKIPPER

Xenophanes tryxus **PL. 37**

TEXAS POWDERED-SKIPPER

1 1/16–1 5/16 in. (27–34 mm). Forewing with outer margin irregular; hindwing slightly scalloped. Upperside: Gray-black with *irregular transparent patches* in middle of each wing. **SIMILAR SPECIES:** White-patched Skipper has narrower forewings, more extensive white on upperside, lacks transparent areas on wings, and is almost completely white below. Resident in s. Tex. and much more likely north of the Mexican border. **EARLY STAGES:** Caterpillar mottled green-white. Head brown. **FOOD:** Turk's-cap. **FLIGHT:** Feb.–Dec. in s. Tex. (3 flights). **RANGE:** Resident from n. Mex. south through mainland tropical Amer. to Argentina. Rare stray to sw. N.M. Periodic resident in lower Rio Grande Valley, Tex. **HABITAT:** Openings in tropical lowland forests or thorn scrub.

EMORSUS SKIPPER *Antigonus emorsus* **PL. 37**

1 1/2–1 5/8 in. (37–42 mm). Unique. Hindwing with irregular wavy outer margin. Upperside: *Largely white with black outer margins and blackish at wing bases.* **EARLY STAGES:** Not reported. **FOOD:** Unknown. **FLIGHT:** Mid-July–late Sept. in Ariz. Most of year in Mex. (several flights). **RANGE:** Rare stray to se. Ariz. and sw. N.M. Resident in Mex. south to Oaxaca. **HABITAT:** Found in dry canyons in Ariz. Seasonally dry forests in Mex. **REMARKS:** Found at wet spots in desert canyons. Perches with wings flat against ground. Adult markings vary between wet and dry seasons.

TEXAS POWDERED-SKIPPER *Systasea pulverulenta* **PL. 37**

15/16–1 1/4 in. (24–32 mm). Hindwing outer margin with 2 *lobed projections.* Upperside: Orange-brown with darker olive-brown areas. Forewing with transparent band across middle of wing. *Two spots in center of band aligned.* **SIMILAR SPECIES:** Arizona Powdered-Skipper is slightly larger, more olive-brown, has offset spots in transparent band, and more prominent scallops. **EARLY STAGES:** Not reported. **FOOD:** Mallows, especially *Abutilon, Sphaeralcea,* and *Wissadula.* **FLIGHT:** Feb.–Dec. in s. Tex. (several flights), mainly Aug.–Nov. in se. Ariz. **RANGE:** Regular stray or possibly temporary resident in se. Ariz. and s. N.M. Resident from s. and w. Tex. south through Mex. to Guatemala. **HABITAT:** Canyons, washes, open woods, parks, vicinity of rivers. **REMARKS:** This species is found in moister habitats than the Arizona Powdered-Skipper.

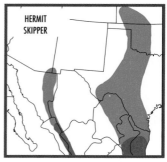

ARIZONA POWDERED-SKIPPER *Systasea zampa*   **PL. 37**

1–1½ in. (25–38 mm). Hindwing outer margin with 2 *lobed projections*. Upperside: Olive-brown with small orange-brown patches. Forewing with transparent band across middle of wing. *Two spots in center of band offset.* **SIMILAR SPECIES:** Texas Powdered-Skipper (see above). **EARLY STAGES:** Caterpillar pale green with orange-brown head. **FOOD:** Mallows, especially *Abutilon.* **FLIGHT:** All year in se. Ariz. (several overlapping flights). **RANGE:** W. Tex., s. N.M., s. Ariz., s. Nev., and s. Calif. south to nw. Mex. and Baja Calif. **HABITAT:** Dry canyons and arroyos at base of desert mountains. **REMARKS:** Adults patrol back and forth along the edges of streamcourses or dry washes and perch with wings flat and wingtips slightly downward. Adults visit flowers such as desert lavender, *Bidens,* and *Lagascea.*

HERMIT SKIPPER *Grais stigmaticus*   **PL. 37**

1¾–2³⁄₁₆ in. (45–55 mm). *Palpi bright orange-yellow below;* abdomen yellow-buff below with dark line up middle. Forewing extended at apex; *back half of hindwing extended.* Upperside: Dark brown with 2 *rows of black-brown squarish spots* on each wing. Male usually without hyaline white spots on forewing, but female with variable number—ranging from a few near costa at apex to a submarginal row and a few in or near cell. Underside: Noticeably light with scattered pale patches. **EARLY STAGES:** Not reported. **FOOD:** Unknown. **FLIGHT:** June–Dec. (2 or more flights). **RANGE:** Mex. south through Cen. Amer. and Jamaica to Argentina. Stray north to se. Ariz., sw. N.M., Kans., and Tex. **HABITAT:** Tropical and subtropical woodlands. **REMARKS:** Adults visit flowers and rest under leaves with wings flattened when inactive.

BROWN-BANDED SKIPPER *Timochares ruptifasciatus* **PL. 37**

1½–1¾ in. (37–44 mm). Upperside: Somewhat similar in size and pattern to a duskywing. Forewing lacks transparent spots and is *dark brown with broken bands of darker spots. Hindwing orange-brown with 3 dark bands*. Underside: Orange-brown with faint mottling. **EARLY STAGES:** Caterpillar with first segment light green; remainder blue-green with many fine yellow dots; orange-yellow lines on each side with orange spots on each segment; head dark brown, ivory, and olive green. **FOOD:** Bermuda cherry and related plants. **FLIGHT:** March–Nov. in s. Tex. and Mex. (several flights). **RANGE:** Resident from s. Tex. south through Mex., also occurs on Jamaica. Strays to s. Ariz. and sw. N.M. **HABITAT:** Openings in tropical lowland forests, wood edges, city flower gardens. **REMARKS:** Males perch on projecting low branches and occasionally fly back and forth only to return to the perch.

WHITE-PATCHED SKIPPER *Chiomara georgina* **PL. 37**

1⁵⁄₁₆–1⅜ in. (27–35 mm). Perches with wings wide open. Upperside: Brown-black variably invaded by *irregular white patches*. Underside: White except on outer and costal margins. **SIMILAR SPECIES:** Glassy-winged Skipper is much rarer north of the Mexican border, has less white and large transparent areas on both wings. **EARLY STAGES:** Caterpillars are greenish. **FOOD:** *Malpighia glabra* and other Malpighia family plants. **FLIGHT:** All year where resident (3–4 flights). **RANGE:** Resident from s. Tex. south through Baja Calif. Norte and mainland tropical Amer. to Argentina. Strays north to s. Nev., s. Ariz., sw. N.M., w. Tex., and w. Kans. **HABITAT:** Small clearings in tropical woodlands, city flower gardens, wood edges. **REMARKS:** Adults nectar at a variety of flowers including bonesets and waltheria. Males perch on bare projecting twigs and branches. Adults perch with wings out flat and tips curved downward.

MITHRAX SKIPPER
Chiomara mithrax **NOT SHOWN**

1⅜–1⁹⁄₁₆ in. (35–40 mm). Upperside: Male primarily dark brown with purplish gloss, female lighter. Submarginal band of *small dark spots outlined* with *outward-directed* scallops. Hindwing with 3 *concentric dark bands*. **SIMILAR SPECIES:** Most duskywings and other similar skippers in se.

WHITE-PATCHED SKIPPER

FALSE DUSKYWING

DREAMY DUSKYWING

Ariz. have translucent white spots on forewings and/or white hindwing fringes. **EARLY STAGES:** Not reported. **FOOD:** Unknown. **FLIGHT:** Probably all year in tropics (3–4 flights). **RANGE:** Resident from n. Mex. south through mainland tropical Amer. and West Indies to Argentina. Rare stray north to se. Ariz. **HABITAT:** Subtropical thorn scrub. **REMARKS:** Adults nectar at white flowers such as *Bidens* and *Cordia*. Adults perch with wings flat and forward edge of forewing at a slight downward curve.

FALSE DUSKYWING *Gesta invisus*   PL. 37

1 5/16–1 3/8 in. (24–35 mm). Upperside: Banded brown-black. Forewing with submarginal *blue-gray band* and irregular *brown or black patch overlapping discal cell*. **SIMILAR SPECIES:** Funereal Duskywing, the only true duskywing (*Erynnis*) likely in most of its range, is larger and has distinct white fringes on the outer margin of the hindwing. **EARLY STAGES:** Caterpillar gray or yellow-green, whitish toward rear; green dorsal stripe; yellow and orange lateral bands. Head white or orange, spotted red-brown or black. **FOOD:** *Indigofera*s. **FLIGHT:** April–Nov. in s. Tex. (4 flights); all year from Mex. southward. **RANGE:** Resident from s. Tex. south through mainland tropical Amer. to Argentina. Strays to Tex. **HABITAT:** Tropical thorn scrub, dry riverbeds, abandoned fields. **REMARKS:** This tropical skipper has been previously placed in the genus *Erynnis* (true duskywings) but is distinctive. It perches on low plants or other objects and visits flowers of yellow composites and waltheria.

DUSKYWINGS: GENUS *Erynnis* SCHRANK

The somber black duskywings are richest in North America, with two species (*E. funeralis* and *E. tristis*) ranging through Central America to South America. Adults are all very similar in a general

way, although many southwestern species often have white
hindwing fringes. Our several
groups of duskywings have
species that are difficult to
separate except by microscopic
examination of wing scales or
dissection of genitalia. Males
perch, either in openings or on
promontories, as their method
of locating receptive mates.
Freshly emerged males are often found visiting moist sand

SLEEPY
DUSKYWING

or mud, where they imbibe moisture. Adults are avid flower visitors. Adults perch with open wings most often, but will perch with
closed wings during hot conditions. Caterpillars of most species
feed on leaves of woody plants, but members of the Persius group
are exceptional in their choice of herbaceous legumes.

DREAMY DUSKYWING *Erynnis icelus* PL. 38
⅞–1 ¹⁄₁₆ in. (24–27 mm). Black. *Labial palpi project forward* more
than those of other duskywings. *Lacks* small *transparent spots* on
forewing. Upperside: Forewing grizzled gray with *darker median
and postmedian bands.* SIMILAR SPECIES: Sleepy Duskywing is larger,
less gray, has more distinct forewing bands. Other duskywings
have labial palpi not projected forward, small transparent spots
on forewing. EARLY STAGES: Caterpillar pale green with small white
hair-bearing bumps; head strongly angled, depressed, black with
reddish and yellowish spots. FOOD: Willows, poplars, aspen, occasionally birch. FLIGHT: April–early July (1 flight). RANGE: Widespread
in boreal N. Amer. from w. N.W. Terr. south through w. mountains south to s. Ariz. and s. N.M., east across s. Canada to N.S.,
and south in East to Ark., ne. Ala., and n. Ga. HABITAT: Open
woods, stream margins, or forest edges.

SLEEPY DUSKYWING *Erynnis brizo* PL. 38
1 ³⁄₁₆–1 ⅜ in. (30–35 mm). Upperside: *Forewing bands* usually *distinct and complete.* SIMILAR SPECIES: Dreamy Duskywing is smaller
and has long forward-directed palpi. The upperside of the
forewing is grizzled gray, and the 2 forewing bands are interrupted. EARLY STAGES: Caterpillar gray-green with purplish on front
and rear; a subdorsal faint white stripe on each side and a dark
middorsal stripe. Head is yellowish to dark brown with an orange
spot. FOOD: Oaks, usually shrubby species. FLIGHT: Early Feb.–June
(1 flight). RANGE: Resident in West from n. Calif., Utah, and s.

Wyo. south through mountains to n. Baja Calif. and cen. Mex., and in East from w.-cen. Man., Gaspé Peninsula, and Prince Edward Is. south through s. Ont. and e. U.S. to cen. Fla., Gulf Coast, and cen. Tex. **HABITAT:** Oak or oak-pine scrub, chaparral, often on sandy or rocky soils. **REMARKS:** Males perch on hilltops and ridges to await receptive females. Adults nectar at a variety of flowers including verbena, redbud, heaths, and dandelions.

JUVENAL'S DUSKYWING *Erynnis juvenalis*   **PL. 38**

1 5/16–1 1/2 in. (33–38 mm). Upperside: Male dark blackish brown with *scattered long whitish hairs* on forewing. Female paler brown with more definite pattern. Both sexes have *white semitransparent spots* on outer portion of forewing. Hindwing with white fringe in Southwest, dark fringe elsewhere. Underside: *2 round light subapical spots* on leading edge of hindwing. **SIMILAR SPECIES:** Most similar species do not overlap in range. (1) In places of overlap with Rocky Mountain Duskywing, the latter has a dark fringe. (2) Horace's Duskywing usually lacks spots on hindwing underside. **EARLY STAGES:** Caterpillar pale to blue-green or dark green; body covered with tiny yellow-white dots and a yellow subdorsal stripe. Head is tan or green-brown with 4 orange spots. **FOOD:** Oaks. **FLIGHT:** Mid-March–early Sept. in Southwest (several overlapping flights), May–June (1 flight) in Black Hills. **RANGE:** White-fringed individuals (subspecies *clitus*) south from w. Tex. and cen. Ariz. south to cen. Mex. Dark-fringed butterflies (subspecies *juvenalis*) in temperate e. N. Amer. from s. Sask. and Black Hills of S.D. east to N.S. south through most of area to s.-cen. and w. Tex., Gulf Coast, and s. Fla. **HABITAT:** Oak or oak-pine woodland and adjacent edges, in West usually in mountains. **REMARKS:** Males do not hilltop but perch along trails or streamcourses. Adults nectar at a wide variety of flowers.

ROCKY MOUNTAIN DUSKYWING

Erynnis telemachus   **PL. 38**

PROPERTIUS DUSKYWING

1 5/16–1 5/8 in. (33–41 mm). Very similar to Juvenal's Duskywing but differing chiefly in genitalic structures. **Upperside:** Pale brown-gray with dark patches and *hyaline spots* on forewing. Forewing has *long curved gray hairlike scales.* Hindwing fringes dark. **Underside:** 2 *small pale spots* along leading edge of hindwing. **SIMILAR SPECIES:** Most similar species do not overlap in range. Horace's Duskywing usually lacks spots on leading edge of hindwing below. **EARLY STAGES:** Not reported in detail. **FOOD:** Oaks, especially Gambel oak. **FLIGHT:** April–July (1 flight). **RANGE:** E. Nev., Utah, s. Wyo., Colo., and w. Okla. south to cen. Ariz., N.M., and w. Tex. **HABITAT:** Oak woodland and thickets, oak-juniper woodland, and oak-pine woodland. **REMARKS:** Males perch along paths, streambeds, and depressions, where they await receptive females.

PROPERTIUS DUSKYWING *Erynnis propertius*   **PL. 38**

1 1/8–1 3/4 in. (29–44 mm). Similar to Rocky Mountain Duskywing. **Upperside:** Gray-brown with *hyaline white spots* on outer portion of forewing. *Long curved white hairlike scales* on male forewing. Hindwing *fringes dark.* **Underside:** 2 pale brown spots on leading edge of hindwing. **SIMILAR SPECIES:** Within its Pacific Coast range it is the only large duskywing with dark hindwing fringes. **EARLY STAGES:** Not reported. **FOOD:** Oaks, including coast live oak and Garry oak. **FLIGHT:** Mid-March–early July (1 flight). **RANGE:** Pacific Coast from s. B.C. south to n. Baja Calif. **HABITAT:** Oak woodland, oak-pine woodland. **REMARKS:** Adults are fond of nectar of such flowers as blue dicks, yerba santa, ceanothus, vetches, and lilac. Males perch in openings on hilltops or along stream banks.

MERIDIAN DUSKYWING *Erynnis meridianus*   **PL. 38**

1 5/16–1 11/16 in. (33–43 mm). Black. **Upperside:** Forewing with *pattern* showing *little contrast.* Transparent spots of male small, those of female large. Hindwing *fringes* are *pale-tipped.* **Underside:** Hindwing is uniform in color; 2 *subapical pale spots* are much *reduced* in size or *absent.* **SIMILAR SPECIES:** (1) Juvenal's Duskywing has larger white spots on forewing, dark fringes on hindwing, and 2 large subapical spots on hindwing below. (2) Horace's

Duskywing has dark fringes on hindwing and usually lacks the 2 subapical pale spots on hindwing below. These 2 species are reliably separated from the Meridian Duskywing only by dissection and examination of the distinctive male genitalia. **EARLY STAGES:** Unreported. **FOOD:** Oaks. **FLIGHT:** March–Sept. (2 flights). **RANGE:** Se. Nev., sw. Utah, N.M., and n. and w. Tex. south to nw. Mex. **HABITAT:** Oak thickets in foothills. **REMARKS:** Males perch on hilltops to await receptive females for courtship and mating.

SCUDDER'S DUSKYWING *Erynnis scudderi*   **PL. 38**

1 $^{3}/_{16}$–1 $^{1}/_{2}$ in. (31–38 mm). Upperside: Black-brown with darker brown patches. Forewing with *translucent white spots* on outer half. Male forewing with dense covering of *long brown hairlike scales*. Hindwing with *white fringe*. Underside: *Lacks 2 pale spots* on leading edge of hindwing. **SIMILAR SPECIES:** Extremely similar to Juvenal's Duskywing and Pacuvius Duskywing, which can be reliably separated from Scudder's Duskywing only by dissection of male genitalia. **EARLY STAGES:** Not reported. **FOOD:** Probably oaks. **FLIGHT:** Late April–early Sept. (2 or more flights). **RANGE:** Se. Ariz., sw. N.M., and w. Tex. south through Mexican highlands (7,000–8,000 ft.) to Chiapas. **HABITAT:** Oak woodland. **REMARKS:** Males of this rarely observed skipper are usually found perching on hilltops.

HORACE'S DUSKYWING *Erynnis horatius*   **PL. 38**

1 $^{5}/_{16}$–1 $^{3}/_{4}$ in. (33–44 mm). Upperside: Dark brown. Male forewing *lacks white hairlike scales* and has *little pattern contrast*. Female forewing is pale brown with *contrasting pattern* and *large transparent spots* on outer portion of forewing. Underside: Hindwing *usually lacks 2 subapical spots*. **SIMILAR SPECIES:** (1) Rocky Mountain Duskywing and (2) Meridian Duskywing have pale hairlike scales on male forewing and almost always have 2 pale subapical spots

on hindwing below. **EARLY STAGES:** Not reported. **FOOD:** Oaks. **FLIGHT:** April–Aug. (2 flights). **RANGE:** E. S.D., se. Utah, and ne. Ariz. south to s. N.M. and s. Tex., thence east to extreme s. Ont. and e. U.S. from s. New England south to s. Fla. and Gulf Coast. **HABITAT:** Oak woodlands and brush. **REMARKS:** Males perch on hilltops in western part of its range.

MOURNFUL DUSKYWING *Erynnis tristis*   **PL. 38**
    1 ³⁄₁₆–1 ¹¹⁄₁₆ in. (30-43 mm). Dark brown-black with *white* hindwing *fringe.* Underside: Hindwing has marginal row of long *white spots adjacent* to *white fringe* (except in Calif.). **SIMILAR SPECIES:** (1) Where other white-fringed duskywings are found, especially in s. Ariz. and N.M., the other species lack marginal row of white spots on hindwing below. (2) In Calif. the Funereal Duskywing may be separated by its longer forewings and the pale patch on the forewing beyond the cell. **EARLY STAGES:** Caterpillar is pale gray-green with minute white points, yellowish subdorsal line, dark dorsal line, and an orange-brown head showing 3 pale orange spots on each side. **FOOD:** Oaks. **FLIGHT:** March–Nov., rarely Dec. (3 or more flights). **RANGE:** Resident from n. Calif., cen. Ariz., cen. N.M., and w. Tex. south to s. Baja Calif. and through mountains of Mex. and Cen. Amer. to Colombia. **HABITAT:** Oak woodlands. **REMARKS:** Males perch on hilltops. Adults drink nectar of flowers such as yellow star thistle and wild buckwheats.

MOTTLED DUSKYWING *Erynnis martialis*   **PL. 38**
    1 –1 ³⁄₁₆ in. (25–30 mm). Upperside: Both wings with *strong mottling.* Forewing often with a faint *iridescent violet sheen.* Hindwing *fringes dark.* **SIMILAR SPECIES:** Where they co-occur along the Rocky Mt. front, Pacuvius Duskywing has white fringes and is less mottled. **EARLY STAGES:** Caterpillar light green with dark red

MOTTLED DUSKYWING

PACUVIUS DUSKYWING

marks on black head. **FOOD:** *Ceanothus* species referred to as buckbrush, New Jersey tea, and other colloquial names. **FLIGHT:** Mid-May–June (1 flight). **RANGE:** Resident from s. Que. and s. Ont. west to se. Man., ne. Wyo., cen. Colo., prairie states, and cen. Tex., south to S.C. and the Gulf Coast. **HABITAT:** Open, brushy fields, barrens, prairie hills. **REMARKS:** Males are usually found patrolling and perching on ridgetops.

PACUVIUS DUSKYWING *Erynnis pacuvius*   **PL. 38**

1 ⅟₁₆–1 ⁵⁄₁₆ in. (28–33 mm). Variable. Upperside: Ranging from unicolored black often without forewing apical white spots (subspecies *pernigra*) to highly contrasting blackish gray with black patches and consistent white spots on outer half of forewing (subspecies *pacuvius* and *lilius*). Hindwing with *white fringe* (subspecies *pacuvius*) or *dark fringe* (other subspecies). Underside: Hindwing may show row of *submarginal pale spots.* **SIMILAR SPECIES:** (1) Dark-fringed subspecies are most similar to the Persius and Afranius Duskywings from which they may be separated by their less contrasting wing pattern, larger white apical forewing spots, and the presence on male of a tibial brush on the hindleg. (2) In the southern part of subspecies *pacuvius'* range, several other white-fringed duskywings (Juvenal's, Scudder's, Mournful, and Funereal) may be separated by their larger size, less contrasting forewing pattern, or presence of white marginal marks on the under surface of the hindwing. **EARLY STAGES:** Not reported in detail. **FOOD:** Various *Ceanothus* species (buckthorns and wild lilacs). **FLIGHT:** May–July (1 flight) in north, late March–Sept., rarely Oct. (2 flights) in south. **RANGE:** S. B.C. and w. Mont. south in Cascade-Sierra Nevada axis to n. Baja Calif. (dark-fringed populations) and Rocky Mts. through Sierra Madre of Mex. to Veracruz (white-fringed populations from cen. Colo. south. **HABITAT:** Chaparral,

conifer, mixed-conifer forests, pine-oak woodlands. **REMARKS:**
Males perch on hilltops or along ridges to await receptive females
for mating. Adults nectar at a variety of flowers, including buck-
brushes and yellow composites.

FUNEREAL DUSKYWING *Erynnis funeralis*   **PL. 38**
1 5⁄16–1 1⁄2 in. (33–38 mm). *Forewing narrow* and *pointed.* Hindwing
more or less triangular. Upperside: Black. Forewing with *brown
patch at end of cell. Hindwing* outer margin with *white fringe.* **SIMI-
LAR SPECIES:** (1) Mournful Duskywing has broader forewings and
submarginal white band on underside of hindwing. (2) Other
white-fringed duskywings also have broader forewings and most
lack reddish brown discal patch on forewing. **EARLY STAGES:** Caterpillar is pale green with yellow subdorsal stripe, dark mid-dorsal
stripe, blue below, and black head. **FOOD:** Legumes such as New
Mexican locust, bush lotis, alfalfa, and many other legumes.
FLIGHT: Feb.–Sept. in s. Calif., all year in se. Ariz. (3 or more
flights). **RANGE:** Resident from deep Southwest south through
mainland tropical Amer. to Argentina. Strays north to ne. Neb.,
cen. Colo., s. Nev., n. Calif., and n. Ill. **HABITAT:** Desert washes,
foothill ravines, gardens, alfalfa fields, and other open, generally
arid locales. **REMARKS:** Males perch along dry washes or adjacent
flats, periodically flying back and forth. Adults visit flowers avidly.
Some consider this skipper a subspecies of the more eastern
Zarucco Duskywing.

WILD INDIGO DUSKYWING *Erynnis baptisiae*   **PL. 38**
1 3⁄16–1 9⁄16 in. (31–40 mm). Upperside: Forewing with *distinct orange-brown patch at end of cell* and small white spots near apex.
Basal half is dark; distal half is lighter. Hindwing with series of
pale submarginal spots. **SIMILAR SPECIES:** Persius Duskywing is

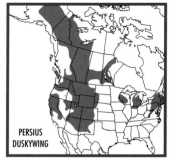

smaller, has indistinct gray patch at end of discal cell on forewing, and has numerous raised white scales on forewing above. Genitalia are distinctive. **EARLY STAGES:** Not reported. **FOOD:** Wild indigos, lupine, crown-vetch. **FLIGHT:** April–Sept. (2 flights). **RANGE:** Expanding. Resident from s. New England and extreme s. Ont. west to cen. Neb. and s.-cen. Tex., south to Gulf Coast. One report from Colo. indicates species is spreading westward. **HABITAT:** Barrens and open woods on native hosts, highway shoulders, railroad beds, and upland fields on crown-vetch. **REMARKS:** This butterfly has rapidly expanded its range and abundance by colonizing the plantings of crown-vetch along highways, interstates, and railroad beds.

AFRANIUS DUSKYWING *Erynnis afranius* PL. 38

⅞–1 ⁵⁄₁₆ in. (23–33 mm). Hindwing *fringes* on male *pale-tipped.* Upperside: Brownish black. Forewing of male with *scattered* covering of *flat white scales.* Genitalia are distinctive. **SIMILAR SPECIES:** Persius Duskywing male has long white hairlike scales on upper surface of forewing. Females must be dissected. Where the two occur together, Persius Duskywings have a single flight between Afranius' flights, and male Persius perches on hilltops. **EARLY STAGES:** Caterpillar pale green or yellow-green with white dots, a dark line up middle of back, a yellow line along each side. Head black or dark brown with extensive diffuse pale markings. **FOOD:** Lupines, golden banner, lotises, and possibly other legumes. **FLIGHT:** Mar.–Aug. (2 flights). **RANGE:** Cen. Alaska east to cen. Yukon, then main range from se. Wash., ne. Ore., s. Alta., Sask., and w. Man. south through mountains and plains generally east of Great Basin south through Sierra Madre Occidentale to Mex. City. Seemingly isolated cluster of populations in mountains of s. Calif. and n. Baja Calif. **HABITAT:** Prairie hills, woodland, tundra, streamcourse edges, and meadows. **REMARKS:** Males perch in depressions and streamcourse edges to await receptive females. Adults actively nectar at plants such as golden banner.

PERSIUS DUSKYWING *Erynnis persius* PL. 38

⅞–1⅜ in. (23–36 mm). Hindwing *fringes* on male *dark brown*. Upperside: Forewing with *patch at end of cell more gray* than brown. Male forewing with *numerous raised white hairs*. Genitalia distinctive. **SIMILAR SPECIES:** Afranius Duskywing (see p. 402). **EARLY STAGES:** Caterpillar pale green with minute white points, a dark green line up middle of back, cream or yellowish line on each side. Head black to dark red-brown or yellow-green with pale vertical streaks. **FOOD:** Lupines, golden banner, milk vetches, and other legumes. **FLIGHT:** April–June (1 flight). **RANGE:** Alaska and McKenzie R. delta south through western mountain archipelago to s. Calif., s. Ariz., and se. N.M., to se. Man. A second isolated group of populations on sand-pine-oak barrens in the ne. U.S. **HABITAT:** Mountain meadows, streamsides, meadows, tundra, sandy flats where various hosts grow. **REMARKS:** This is a group of populations with different habitats and hosts. The relationships are still poorly understood. Males perch on hilltops to await the arrival of mates.

CHECKERED-SKIPPERS: GENUS *Pyrgus* HÜBNER

The checkered-skippers occur in both the Old and New Worlds. There are eight species in western North America. One, the Grizzled Skipper, also occurs in Eurasia and belongs to a diverse group of small species that feeds mainly on rose family plants. Two others, the Two-banded and Mountain Checkered-Skippers, are also small species whose caterpillars feed on plants in the Rose family. The other five are mallow-feeders and are limited to the New World, extending southward to South America. Males of our species perch and patrol in open habitats with bare soil in their search for receptive females. Our species may wander and can colonize new areas. The Common Checkered-Skipper is an excellent colonizer and each summer probably invades areas north of the zone where it can survive the winter. The caterpillars live and feed under webbed leaf shelters.

GRIZZLED SKIPPER *Pyrgus centaureae* PL. 38

⅞–1¾₆ in. (22–31 mm). *Fringes checkered* white with black tufts at vein endings. Upperside: Gray-black with white checks. Forewing with *small bar* in *discal cell* and *blurred white spots* on hindwing. **SIMILAR SPECIES:** Two-banded Checkered-Skipper is smaller, blacker, has a square white spot in the forewing discal

cell and more clearly defined spots on hindwing. It usually flies earlier and at lower elevations. **EARLY STAGES:** Not reported. **FOOD:** Wild strawberry and cinquefoil. **FLIGHT:** Biennial, mainly in odd-numbered years, early May–early Aug., mainly late June and July (1 flight). **RANGE:** Holarctic. In N. Amer., from n. Alaska south in Rocky Mts. south to ne. Utah and n. N.M. and east to cen. Ont. and n. Mich. Isolated population, possibly a separate species, in cen. Appalachian shale barrens. **HABITAT:** Open moist tundra above timberline, clearings in black spruce bogs, and forest clearings.

TWO-BANDED CHECKERED-SKIPPER   PL. 38
Pyrgus ruralis

¾–1 ¹⁄₁₆ in. (20–28 mm). Fringes checkered. Upperside: Black with small white spots (subspecies *lagunae* has large white spots). Forewing of male with *costal fold. White spots form an apparent X.* Hindwing with a *very small white spot at base.* **SIMILAR SPECIES:** (1) Grizzled Skipper (see above). (2) Mountain Checkered-Skipper overlaps only slight in range, lacks a forewing costal fold on males, and does not have the appearance of an X on the forewing. **EARLY STAGES:** Not reported. **FOOD:** Cinquefoils and horkelias. **FLIGHT:** May–mid-July (1 flight), subspecies *lagunae* found in San Diego Co., Calif. has partial second flight in late June and July. **RANGE:** S. B.C. and sw. Alta. south in mountains to cen. Calif., s. Utah, and cen. Colo. **HABITAT:** Open meadows or hillsides in mountains. **RE-MARKS:** Laguna Mountains Checkered-Skipper (subspecies *lagunae*) is listed as an endangered species.

MOUNTAIN CHECKERED-SKIPPER *Pyrgus xanthus* PL. 38
¾–1 in. (20–25 mm). Upperside: Fringes checkered. Upperside: Black with small white spots. *Median band* on hindwing usually *prominent.* Forewing of male *lacks costal fold.* **SIMILAR SPECIES:** Two-

banded Checkered-Skipper has more northern range, and the male has costal fold. **EARLY STAGES:** Caterpillar green with upper half slightly reddish yellow, dark gray-green line up middle of back. Head and collar black. **FOOD:** Several cinquefoils. **FLIGHT:** Late April–mid-June (1 flight). **RANGE:** S. Utah and cen. Colo. south to e.-cen. Ariz. and s. N.M. **HABITAT:** Openings in forests, open grasslands, roadside ditches. **REMARKS:** Adults nectar at dandelions and other flowers.

SMALL CHECKERED-SKIPPER *Pyrgus scriptura*   PL. 39

⅝–⅞ in. (16–22 mm). *Fringe incompletely checkered,* mostly white. Black checks on edge of hindwing not reaching outer edge. Upperside: Dark gray with small white spots. Male lacks forewing *costal fold.* Usually with *prominent square white spot* in center of hindwing. **SIMILAR SPECIES:** Two-banded and Mountain Checkered-

Male Small Checkered-Skipper perching, Larimer Co., Colo. Note mostly white incompletely checkered wing fringes. These small butterflies are usually found in arid, often alakali or basic, flats or nearby gradual slopes.

Skippers fly at higher elevations. In rare instances, individuals in range of Mountain Checkered-Skipper could require capture and dissection for confident identification. **EARLY STAGES:** Caterpillar gray-green. Head black. **FOOD:** Various native mallows, including alkali mallow and copper mallow. **FLIGHT:** March–Nov. (several flights), possibly only one at northern limit of range. **RANGE:** N. Calif., cen. Nev., se. Alta, and w. N.D. south to cen. Mex. (Zacatecas) and w. Tex. **HABITAT:** Open habitats with bare patches including alkali flats, short-grass prairie, and disturbed fields. **REMARKS:** Nectars on low plants such as mints, milkweeds, and composites.

COMMON CHECKERED-SKIPPER *Pyrgus communis* PL. 39

⅞–1¼ in. (22–32 mm). Male genitalia with elongated double-toothed tip to each valve. *Top of head* on most males with *long white and black hairs.* Fringes checkered but *black checks often reach only halfway.* Upperside: Most males have a *blue-gray tone,* while females appear black with small white spots. Hindwing spots in marginal row are much smaller than those of sub-marginal row. Underside: Hindwing with *bands variable in width* and color from *gray-white* to *gray-brown.* **SIMILAR SPECIES:** White Checkered-Skipper is most easily separated by examination of male genitalia. Males tend to lack long white scales on top of head. Underside of hindwing with antemedian and postmedian bands more uniform and tending to yellow-brown. Females not easily separated. **EARLY STAGES:** Caterpillar yellow-white varying to brown with lateral brown and white lines, covered with small white bumps. Head and collar black, covered with yellow-brown hair. **FOOD:** Many mallows, hollyhock. **FLIGHT:** Feb.–Nov. (several flights). **RANGE:** Found in West from s. B.C. and cen. Alta. south to Calif., se. Ariz., w. Tex. south into mountains of n. Mex., and most of East from s. Ont., and s. New England southward. Northern-

Male White Checkered-Skipper perching, Sinaloa state, Mex. Note full-length black checks in fringe and gray-brown more or less equal-width bands on hindwing.

most portions of range may be the result of periodic colonization. **HABITAT:** Open sunny areas with at least some bare soil and low vegetation—prairies, landfills, highway shoulders, vacant lots, etc. **REMARKS:** The White Checkered-Skipper is treated as a separate species by most recent authors, but its precise relationships with the Common Checkered-Skipper and its distribution have not been treated in detail.

WHITE CHECKERED-SKIPPER *Pyrgus albescens*   **PL. 39**
1–1 ³⁄₁₆ in. (25–30 mm). Male genitalia has shortened single-toothed tip to each valve. *Top of head* (vertex) *shiny black,* often *without long hairlike scales. Fringes checkered* with black checks *usually* reach *full length.* Pattern elements similar to those of Common Checkered-Skipper but much less variable. Upperside: *Median white band* of male *prominent, clear-cut.* Males usually lack blue-gray appearance. Underside: Hindwing with antemedian and postmedian *bands uniform,* varying from *gray to yellow-brown.* **SIMILAR SPECIES:** (1) Common Checkered-Skipper tends to be larger and darker, especially in female. Can be reliably identified only by examination of male genitalia; tip of valve is elongate and has 2 teeth. (2) Tropical Checkered-Skipper has marginal and submarginal spot rows on hindwing with equal-sized spots, and there is a strong infusion of brown on hindwing below. Male has a mat of long blue-gray hairlike scales on upperside of forewing. (3) Desert Checkered-Skipper is smaller, has minute spots in marginal and submarginal rows on hindwing. **EARLY STAGES:** Caterpillar yellow-white with faint gray-green lines along middle of back and upper portion of each side. Head and collar black. **FOOD:** Various mallows including *Sida*s and globe mallows. **FLIGHT:** All

year (several flights). **RANGE:** S. Calif. east across low-lying areas of desert Southwest to s. Tex. and south in lowlands to cen. Mex. Related populations extend south through tropical Amer. to Argentina but may represent another species. **HABITAT:** Low deserts, foothills, suburbs, gardens, second-growth fields. **REMARKS:** One individual showing some features of the more southern *Pyrgus adepta* was found in w. Tex.

TROPICAL CHECKERED-SKIPPER *Pyrgus oileus*   **PL. 39**
1–1 3⁄16 in. (26–31 mm). Forewing fringes always checkered, hindwing fringes sometimes checkered. Upperside: Male forewing with *overlying mat of long blue-gray hairs.* Female has elongate white streaks at base of forewing and has *white spots in median band reduced and elongate.* Hindwing of both sexes has *marginal and submarginal* rows of *small equal-sized white spots.* Underside: Hindwing often with a strong infusion of brown. *Little contrast between bands and pale ground color.* **SIMILAR SPECIES:** Common and White Checkered-Skippers have hindwings with marginal spots much smaller than those of submarginal row. **EARLY STAGES:** Caterpillar green with faint dorsal line, small white bumps; head black. **FOOD:** Mallows including *Sidas,* and hollyhock. **FLIGHT:** Early March–mid-June, early Sept.–early Nov. in se. Ariz. All year where resident such as n. Sonora, Mex., Fla. and s. Tex. (several flights). **RANGE:** Stray north to n. Tex., Ark., and Ga. Resident from se. Ariz. (periodic), s. Tex. and Fla. south through West Indies and mainland tropical Amer. to Argentina. **HABITAT:** Pastures, brushy fields, roadsides, wooded trails.

DESERT CHECKERED-SKIPPER *Pyrgus philetas*   **PL. 39**
7⁄8–1 1⁄16 in. (22–28 mm). Forewing fringes always checkered, hindwing fringes sometimes checkered. Upperside: Forewing with re-

ERICHSON'S WHITE-SKIPPER

NORTHERN WHITE-SKIPPER

duced blue-gray hair cover. Hindwing with *marginal and sub-marginal spots minute*, especially the marginal series. Female with median series highly reduced. Underside: Hindwing *pale gray-white with pattern elements indistinct*. **SIMILAR SPECIES:** See White Checkered-Skipper on p. 407. **EARLY STAGES:** Not reported. **FOOD:** Mallows, especially *Sidas*. **FLIGHT:** All year where resident, such as lowland s. Ariz. and Mex. (several flights). **RANGE:** Resident from s. Tex., s. N.M., and s. Ariz. south to s. Mex., strays north to n. Ariz. and n. Tex. **HABITAT:** Hot desert canyons, moist areas near streams and washes, weedy fields.

ERICHSON'S WHITE-SKIPPER *Heliopetes domicella*   PL. 39

1 1/10–1 3/8 in. (26–34 mm). Fringes checkered. Upperside: Slate gray with a *broad white median band on each wing*. Underside: Whitish and dull yellow-brown. **SIMILAR SPECIES:** Female Northern White-Skipper is only similar species possible, but has barely overlapping range (see maps) and has irregular blurred white band across both wings. **EARLY STAGES:** Not reported. **FOOD:** Mallows, including *Abutilon* and *Herrisantia*. **FLIGHT:** All year in se. Ariz. and tropics, especially March and Sept.–Oct. (possibly 2 flights). **RANGE:** Resident from se. Calif., s. Ariz., s. N.M., and n. Mexico south through mainland tropical Amer. to Argentina. Regular stray north to s. Nev., cen. Ariz., and cen. Tex. **HABITAT:** Dry desert canyons, weedy areas along streams and rivers, subtropical scrub. **REMARKS:** Adults nectar at flowers of composites and other plants. Males perch on vegetation within a few inches of the ground.

NORTHERN WHITE-SKIPPER *Heliopetes ericetorum*   PL. 39

1 1/16–1 1/2 in. (27–37 mm). Upperside: Male is *white with narrow black marginal chevrons* on both wings. Female with *broad median white band with blurry gray pattern* on either side. **SIMILAR**

Male courting female of Northern White-Skipper, San Bernardino Mts., Calif. Difference between mainly white male (below) and grayish-banded female is obvious. The only white-skipper in most of its range.

SPECIES: Female could be confused with Erichson's White-Skipper in s. Ariz. but the latter has a more distinct pattern. **EARLY STAGES:** Caterpillar pale green-yellow with faint line up middle of back and along each side. Head black. **FOOD:** Bushmallow and other mallows. **FLIGHT:** April–Oct. (2 flights). **RANGE:** E. Wash., Idaho, and nw. Wyo. south to n. Baja Calif., s. Ariz. and nw. N.M. **HABITAT:** Chaparral, desert washes, canyons. **REMARKS:** Adults visit flowers such as yerba santa, yellow composites, and mints. Adults are strong, rapid fliers.

LAVIANA WHITE-SKIPPER *Heliopetes laviana*   PL. 39

1¼–1⅝ in. (32–41 mm). *Forewing apex truncated.* Upperside: Male largely white; female with more extensive black pattern on margins. Underside: *Hindwing with outer third olive-brown, sharply cut off from paler median area. Basal dark area with pale triangular patch.* **SIMILAR SPECIES:** Northern White-Skipper has irregular postmedian line on underside of hindwing. **EARLY STAGES:** Not reported. **FOOD:** Mallows. **FLIGHT:** Mid-April–mid-Nov. (several flights). All year where resident, such as in cen. Sonora, Mex., and s. Tex. **RANGE:** Resident from s. Tex. and n. Mex. south through mainland tropical Amer. to Argentina. Possibly a periodic temporary resident in se. Ariz. Strays regularly to s. Ariz., s. N.M. and

LAVIANA
WHITE-SKIPPER

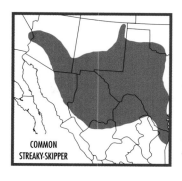

cen. Tex.—rarely to n. Tex. **HABITAT:** Edge of brushy areas, trails, roadsides.

COMMON STREAKY-SKIPPER *Celotes nessus*   PL. 39

⅞–1 in. (21–25 mm). Fringes conspicuously checkered. Upperside: Both wings orange-brown to dark brown with *inward-projecting dark brown streaks and irregular median series of small transparent spots.* **SIMILAR SPECIES:** The slightly larger Scarce Streaky-Skipper is identical in appearance, can be separated only by examination of genitalia and color of hairs on male hair pencil flaps. Limited to w. Tex., especially Davis Mts. (see below). **EARLY STAGES:** Not reported. **FOOD:** Mallows and *Ayenia* (Sterculia family). **FLIGHT:** Late Feb.–mid-Sept. in se. Ariz.; March–Nov. in Tex. (several flights). **RANGE:** Resident from se. Calif. and w. Ariz. east to western two-thirds of Tex. south to n. Mex. Rare stray to s. Okla. and n. La. **HABITAT:** Open thorn scrub, washes, gulches, flower gardens.

SCARCE STREAKY-SKIPPER *Celotes limpia*   NOT SHOWN

¾–¹⁵⁄₁₆ in. (20–24 mm). Male has *long prong on upper edge of valve* and also *cream hairlike scales* covering the flaps hiding hair pencils that project from rear of thorax underside. Female genitalia also differ. Wing pattern identical to that of Common Streaky-Skipper. **SIMILAR SPECIES:** Common Streaky-Skipper is slightly smaller on average, but can be separated only by examination of genitalia and male hair pencil flaps. Male has short prong on upper edge of valve. Male also has brown hairlike scales covering the hair pencil flaps. **EARLY STAGES:** Not reported. **FOOD:** Various mallows. **FLIGHT:** March– Sept. (several flights). **RANGE:** W. Tex. and ne. Mex. **HABITAT:** Washes and gullies in mountains. **REMARKS:** Since the Common Streaky-Skipper shares the same range, the two species cannot be reliably separated in the field.

SOOTYWINGS: GENUS *Pholisora* SCUDDER

COMMON SOOTYWING *Pholisora catullus*   PL. 39

⅞–1 in. (23–26 mm). Our commonest, most widespread small black skipper. Upperside: *Glossy black* with *white spots* on forewing. Female with more white spots, including submarginal row on hindwing. SIMILAR SPECIES: Mexican Sootywing has underside of hindwing iridescent blue-gray with contrasting black-lined veins. EARLY STAGES: Caterpillar green with pale dots. Head and collar black. FOOD: Lamb's-quarters, amaranths, cockscomb. FLIGHT: May–Aug. in most of range, mid-April–Oct. in s. Ariz. and s. Calif. (2 flights), 2–3 flights in Mex. RANGE: Resident at low elevations and plains in s. Canada and most of U.S. south to Colima, Mex. May be stray or temporary colonist in northern part of range. HABITAT: Landfills, roadsides, agricultural areas, vacant lots, gardens.

MEXICAN SOOTYWING *Pholisora mejicana*   PL. 39

⅞–1 1/16 in. (22–28 mm). Upperside: Identical to Common Sootywing. Underside: Hindwing *iridescent blue-gray contrasting with black-lined veins*. SIMILAR SPECIES: Common Sootywing has underside of hindwing plain black, without darker veins, but can shown iridescent sheen in certain light. EARLY STAGES: Caterpillar similar to Common Sootywing but body hairs twice as long. FOOD: Amaranths. FLIGHT: May–Aug. (2 flights); virtually year-round in Mex. RANGE: Resident from cen. Colo. south through Mex. to Oaxaca. Rare stray to s. and cen. Tex. HABITAT: Gulches, canyons, and weedy areas.

MOHAVE SOOTYWING *Hesperopsis libya*   PL. 39

15/16–1 5/16 in. (24–33 mm). Upperside: *Postmedian white bar on forewing costa.* Other white markings may be present or absent on

MOHAVE
SOOTYWING

SALTBUSH
SOOTYWING

forewing and include submarginal band on male, white cell spot, and postmedian band, the latter usually on females. Underside: *Forewing apex and hindwing gray, usually with white spotting.* **SIMILAR SPECIES:** Common Sootywing has smaller white spots above and has entirely black hindwing below. **EARLY STAGES:** Caterpillar blue-green covered with white points, each bearing a short white hair. Several rows of tiny black dots along each side. Black head covered with short orange hairs. **FOOD:** Saltbushes. **FLIGHT:** March–Oct. (2 flights). **RANGE:** Se. Ore., sw. Idaho, e. Mont., and w. N.D. south through intermountain w. U.S. and s. Calif. to cen Baja Calif., Sonora, Mex., and nw. N.M. **HABITAT:** Alkali flats, sagebrush desert, desert hills, shale barrens, watercourses, and ravines.

SALTBUSH SOOTYWING *Hesperopsis alpheus*   **PL. 39**
¾–1 ³⁄₁₆ in. (20–30 mm). Fringes checkered at least on forewing. Blackish. Upperside: Forewing with *series of darker discal dashes at the base of which are tiny whitish spots.* Adults from the Mojave Desert and Great Basin (subspecies *oricus*) have especially distinctly checkered fringes and grayish forewings. **SIMILAR SPECIES:** MacNeill's Sootywing is smaller and has buff and black checkered fringes, shorter discal dashes on forewings, and has buffy overscaling above. Limited to riparian habitats. **EARLY STAGES:** Not reported. **FOOD:** Four-winged saltbush. **FLIGHT:** March–Sept. (2 flights). **RANGE:** Arid w. U.S. from n. Nev. and se. Calif. east to cen. Colo., n. Tex., and lower Rio Grande Valley, Tex., and south to s. Ariz., s. N.M., and Chihuahua and Coahuila, Mex. **HABITAT:** Usually restricted to saltbush flats, arid canyons, dry washes, and ditches. **REMARKS:** This butterfly is considered by some to include MacNeill's Sootywing. I consider the species separate because the two occur in close proximity without intergradation and maintain their habitat preferences.

MACNEILL'S SOOTYWING *Hesperopsis gracielae*   **PL. 39**
$^{11}/_{16}$–$^{15}/_{16}$ in. (18–24 mm). Fringes checkered black and buff. Upperside: *Buffy overscaling on both wings. Forewing with short dark discal dashes.* **SIMILAR SPECIES:** Saltbush Sootywing (see above). **EARLY STAGES:** Caterpillar dark green with many white dots. Head black with short yellow hairs. **FOOD:** Primarily *Atriplex lentiformis,* occasionally *A. argentea,* and pigweed. **FLIGHT:** April–May and July–Oct. (2 flights). **RANGE:** Lower Colorado R. drainage from se. Utah to nw. Baja Calif. extending up Gila and Salt R. in Ariz. **HABITAT:** Tangles of *Atriplex* along flats adjacent to rivercourses. **REMARKS:** This species is a close relative of the Saltbush Sootywing. It seldom leaves the shelter of its host-plant shrubs and is difficult to view closely. It seldom visits flowers.

SKIPPERLINGS: SUBFAMILY HETEROPTERINAE

These small skippers are most closely related to the branded skippers, and they have similar biology. Their antennae lack an apiculus—the extension found at the antennal tips of other skippers. Adult males seek females by patrolling low over vegetation in suitable habitats. When perched or visiting flowers, they hold their wings up at a 45° angle. The caterpillars feed on grasses.

ARCTIC SKIPPER *Carterocephalus palaemon*   **PL. 40**
1–1¼ in. (26–31 mm). Upperside: Black *with checkerboard pattern of orange spots.* Underside: Hindwing yellow-orange to tan with *black-outlined cream spots.* **EARLY STAGES:** Caterpillar cream to blue-green, with a dark green dorsal line and pale yellow lateral stripes enclosed by black spots; head whitish. **FOOD:** Purple reedgrass, probably other grasses. **FLIGHT:** May–early Aug. (1 flight). **RANGE:** Holarctic. Boreal N. Amer. from cen. Alaska south to cen.

Calif., nw. Wyo. and east across Canada to the Maritime Provinces, south in East to Great Lakes states and N.Y. and New England. **HABITAT:** Openings and glades in boreal woodlands. **REMARKS:** Not found in the true Arctic, despite its common name. Adults patrol in glades and bask with open wings on low vegetation.

RUSSET SKIPPERLING *Piruna pirus* PL. 40

⅞–1 in. (22–26 mm). Fringe tan and uncheckered. Upperside: Dark brown *with 3–6 subapical white spots on forewing.* Underside: *Russet brown.* Hindwing unmarked. **SIMILAR SPECIES:** In Ariz. and N.M. mountains. Four-spotted Skipperling co-occurs and may be separated by its heavier spotting above and below. **EARLY STAGES:** Caterpillar green covered with tiny cream hairs, a white line edged with dark green along each side below back, and several darker and lighter green lines and bands. Head pale olive green with orange-brown stripes edged with cream. **FOOD:** Several wide-leaved grasses. **FLIGHT:** Late May–early Aug. (1 flight). **RANGE:** Se. Idaho and s. Wyo. south through Rocky Mts. of Utah, Colo., Ariz., N.M., and w. Tex. **HABITAT:** Moist, grassy streamsides. **REMARKS:** Adults fly in sun or shade and visit small flowers such as dogbanes, alfalfa, fleabanes, wild geranium, and Canada thistle.

FOUR-SPOTTED SKIPPERLING *Piruna polingi* PL. 40

¾–1 in. (20–26 mm). Fringe tan, uncheckered. Upperside: Blackish brown with *many pale cream spots, including a median series.* Underside: Hindwing *red-brown with median series of 3–4 large cream spots* and a somewhat smaller basal spot. **SIMILAR SPECIES:** Russet Skipperling (see above). **EARLY STAGES:** Not reported. **FOOD:** Unknown. **FLIGHT:** Mid-July–mid-Sept. (1 flight). **RANGE:** Mountains of Ariz. and sw. N.M. south to Guerrero, Mex. **HABITAT:** Moist

meadows and streamsides in mountains. **REMARKS:** Usually flies later than the Russet Skipperling and in somewhat different habitats. Adults visit flowers such as yellow composites.

MANY-SPOTTED SKIPPERLING *Piruna aea*   PL. 40
¹³⁄₁₆–⅞ in. (21–23 mm). Fringe pale tan, uncheckered. Upperside: Dark brown with a few scattered white spots. Underside: Hindwing with *distinctive pattern of off-white spots on golden brown background*, marginal series especially prominent. **SIMILAR SPECIES:** Several roadside-skippers co-occur but lack distinctive underside pattern and usually perch with wings closed. **EARLY STAGES:** Not reported. **FOOD:** Possibly side-oats grama grass. **FLIGHT:** Early Aug.–early Sept. (1 flight). **RANGE:** Se. Ariz. south to Guatemala. **HABITAT:** Grassy arroyos in oak woodland. **REMARKS:** Readily visits flowers.

CHISOS SKIPPERLING *Piruna haferniki*   PL. 40
¾–⅞ in. (19–22 mm). Upperside: Dark brown with postmedian series of *small white spots* on forewing. Underside: Hindwing unmarked *blackish brown with basal third grayish*. **SIMILAR SPECIES:** Roadside-skippers in area usually perch with closed wings. **EARLY STAGES:** Not reported. **FOOD:** Unknown. **FLIGHT:** March–Aug. (several fights). **RANGE:** Chisos Mts. of w. Tex. south in Sierra Madre of e. Mex. to Hidalgo. **HABITAT:** Pine-oak woodland.

GRASS SKIPPERS: SUBFAMILY HESPERIINAE

The grass skippers, comprising more than 2,000 species, occur worldwide, but most of their species are in the American tropics. The small to medium-sized adults usually have abruptly angled antennae with an apiculus at the tip. Male forewings usually have a brand or stigma with specialized scales. Males never have a forewing costal fold or specialized tufts of modified scales on the tibia as do the open-winged skippers (subfamily Pyrginae). Many temperate species are predominantly orange, while brown is the most common color among tropical species. Adult flight is rapid, and perching posture is unique: the hindwings are opened at a wider angle than the forewings. Males of most species perch as their principal mate-locating behavior. Most species have long proboscises and are avid flower-visitors. The caterpillars feed on monocotyledons (grasses and allied plants) and live in silken leaf nests that sometimes extend underground. Winter is usually passed by caterpillars within their shelters.

FACETED SKIPPER *Synapte syraces* **PL. 40**

1–1 ¼ in. (26–32 mm). Fringe checkered black and orange. Upperside: *Striking dark brown and orange.* Forewing of male with pale orange median band and darker orange narrow bars along costal and trailing margins. Underside: *Hindwing gray-white with grainy brown striations; a black triangle along costal margin and a small black patch at outer edge of cell.* **EARLY STAGES:** Not reported. **FOOD:** Unknown. **FLIGHT:** Aug. and Nov. in se. Ariz., more extended in Mex. (several flights). **RANGE:** Se. Ariz. (rare stray) south through mountains of Mex. and Cen. Amer. to El Salvador. **HABITAT:** Not reported.

JULIA'S SKIPPER *Nastra julia* **PL. 40**

¹⁵⁄₁₆–1 ⅛ in. (24–28 mm). Upperside: Dark brown. Forewing with 2–5 *pale yellowish spots.* Underside: Hindwing *yellow-brown without paler veins.* **SIMILAR SPECIES:** Eufala Skipper is more gray-brown with distinct white subapical spots and pale gray hindwings below. **EARLY STAGES:** Not reported. **FOOD:** Bermuda grass. **FLIGHT:** All year in s. Tex., shorter period elsewhere (several flights). **RANGE:** S. Calif., s. Nev., s. Ariz., and cen. Tex. south to Costa Rica. **HABITAT:** Open grassy areas, flower gardens, irrigation levees, usually in low, moist areas. **REMARKS:** Older records of the Neamathla Skipper (*Nastra neamathla*) from the West probably refer to Julia's Skipper. Males perch close to the ground in swales or open weedy areas.

JULIA'S SKIPPER

BANANA SKIPPER *Erionota torus* (Hawaii only)   **NOT SHOWN**
2⅜–2½ in. (60–64 mm). Forewing pointed. Upperside: Brown.
Forewing *with 2 large translucent yellow spots and a smaller sub-*
apical spot. Underside: *Mottled red-brown. Large yellow spots*
showing through on forewing. **SIMILAR SPECIES:** Only one other dissimilar skipper is found in Hawaii. **EARLY STAGES:** Not reported in detail. **FOOD:** Banana leaves. **FLIGHT:** All year (several flights). **RANGE:** Se.
Asia. Introduced on several Hawaiian Is. in 1973. **HABITAT:** Tropical
forests, banana groves, suburbs, gardens. **REMARKS:** Can be a pest in
banana plantations. Previously reported incorrectly as a different
species, *Erionota thrax.*

CLOUDED SKIPPER *Lerema accius*   **PL. 40**
1⅜–1¾ in. (34–44 mm). Upperside: Male with strong black
stigma; female forewing with white transparent spots. Underside:
hindwing variegated with violet-blue sheen. **SIMILAR SPECIES:** In se.
Ariz. Umber Skipper would usually be higher in mountains, has
different pattern on underside of hindwing and larger more yellowish spots on forewing. **EARLY STAGES:** Caterpillar white, mottled
with black; head black-margined with 3 vertical black streaks on
front. **FOOD:** Grasses. **FLIGHT:** Mid-April–early Dec. in se. Ariz., all
year in Fla. and s. Tex. (several flights). **RANGE:** Resident in se. Ariz.
near Mexican border, also in se. U.S. south through s. Tex. and
mainland tropical Amer. to Venezuela and Colombia. In West
strays north as far e. Colo., s. N.M., and w. Tex.; in East strays to
s. New England, s. Ill., and se. Kans. **HABITAT:** Woods edges and
clearings near swamps and rivers, suburban gardens. **REMARKS:**
Adults in search of nectar will disappear inside the corolla of
large flowers. They also favor lantana and a wide variety of other
flowers.

COMMON LEAST SKIPPER *Ancyloxypha numitor*   **PL. 40**

⅞–1⅛ in. (22–28 mm). *Antennae short. Wings rounded.* Upperside: *Forewing primarily black* (hidden in normal posture) except for orange apex and costa. *Hindwing yellow-orange with wide black margin.* Underside: *Forewing black except apex and costa.* **SIMILAR SPECIES:** Tropical Least Skipper is primarily orange on both wings above and has pale ray on underside of hindwing. **EARLY STAGES:** Caterpillar grass green. Head dark brown or black, ringed with a white line on front and several ocher marks. Collar white on front, black on back half. **FOOD:** Various tall broad-leaved grasses, including corn and other agricultural species. **FLIGHT:** May–Oct. (3 flights) in most of range, flies longer in southern part of range (4 flights). **RANGE:** Resident from se. Sask., cen. N.D., ne. Colo., ne. N.M. and possibly se. Ariz. east to N.S. south to s. Fla., Gulf Coast, and s. Tex. Strays are known west of residence area, for example, s. Alta. **HABITAT:** Wet open areas, ditches, marshes, sluggish streams. **REMARKS:** Weak, fluttering, patrolling flight. May be incredibly abundant in freshwater marshes and ditches. Adults usually nectar at tiny flowers close to ground.

TROPICAL LEAST SKIPPER *Ancyloxypha arene*   **PL. 40**

⅞–1 1/16 in. (22–27 mm). *Antennae short. Tiny, orange. Forewing rounded.* Upperside: *Black border, usually narrow, on both wings. Male lacks stigma.* Underside: Hindwing golden orange, with *paler ray extending from base through cell* to outer margin. **SIMILAR SPECIES:** Southern Skipperling has narrower black borders on forewing above, and a white ray (not pale orange) on hindwing below. **EARLY STAGES:** Not reported. **FOOD:** Grasses. **FLIGHT:** Feb.–Nov. (several flights). **RANGE:** Resident from se. Ariz., s. N.M., and w.-cen. Tex. south through mainland tropical Amer. to Costa Rica. Strays to s. Tex. and ne. N.M. **HABITAT:** Damp grassy areas in ciene-

gas (moist spring areas in Southwest) or near streams. **REMARKS:** Flight is weak, often over water or saturated soils.

GARITA SKIPPERLING *Oarisma garita*   **PL. 40**

¾–1³⁄₁₆ in. (20–30 mm). Fringe white. Upperside: Varies from black to orange. *Veins often darker than background.* Underside: Forewing largely orange; *hindwing light brown, often with veins distinctly lighter; anal fold clear orange.* **SIMILAR SPECIES:** Edwards' Skipperling has dark fringes, is always orange above, and lacks paler veins on underside of hindwing. **EARLY STAGES:** Caterpillar pale green with white, green-white, and darker green lines and bands. Head pale green-tan. **FOOD:** Grasses. **FLIGHT:** June–July (1 flight); as early as May in Mex. **RANGE:** Resident from ne. and se. B.C. east to cen. Ont. and thence south through Rocky Mt. region to se. Ariz. and s. N.M. **HABITAT:** Short-grass prairie knolls, moist prairies, stream edges, meadows, and limestone openings. **REMARKS:** Flutters with weak flight through grasses and stops frequently at flowers such as asters, wild geraniums, dogbane, and gaillardia.

EDWARDS' SKIPPERLING *Oarisma edwardsii*   **PL. 40**

⅞–1¹⁄₁₆ in. (22–28 mm). *Fringes black or black-tipped.* Upperside: *Orange-brown.* Underside: *Hindwing pale tan, dusky, or gray-orange with orange area* adjacent to abdomen (anal area). Veins are rarely lighter than background. **SIMILAR SPECIES:** Garita Skipperling (see above). **EARLY STAGES:** Not reported. **FOOD:** Unknown. **FLIGHT:** June–Aug. (1 flight). **RANGE:** Ariz., s. Colo., N.M., and w. Tex. south to Puebla, Mex. **HABITAT:** Bunchgrass habitat in open areas or mixed with shrubs in oak-pine or juniper woodland. **REMARKS:** Males patrol through low areas in search of mates. They visit a variety of flowers.

ORANGE SKIPPERLING *Copaeodes aurantiaca*   **PL. 40**
 $^{15}/_{16}$–1 $^{1}/_{8}$ in. (24–29 mm). *Antennae short. Underside of head, thorax, and abdomen white.* Wing *fringes dark-tipped.* Upperside: Bright orange; male with *narrow black stigma.* Base of wings with a *small black area.* Underside: *Hindwing pale yellow-orange.* **SIMILAR SPECIES:** Southern Skipperling has white ray running length of underside hindwing. **EARLY STAGES:** Caterpillar green or tan with 2 purplish stripes above converging on a rear hornlike projection; head multicolored, with 2 symmetrical horns. **FOOD:** Several grasses, including Bermuda grass and side-oats grama. Caterpillars are one of the few western species that do not make nests. **FLIGHT:** Year-round in se. Ariz. as weather permits, March–Sept. northward (several flights). **RANGE:** Resident in sw. U.S. south through mainland tropical Amer. to Panama. Strays to e. Colo., Kans., Okla., e. Tex., and cen. Ark. **HABITAT:** Usually along streamcourses, washes, or canyons, often near moist areas or pools. **REMARKS:** Males perch and seemingly protect small areas in their wait for prospective mates. Adults visit small flowers such as fogfruit and yellow composites.

SOUTHERN SKIPPERLING *Copaeodes minima*   **PL. 40**
 $^{9}/_{16}$–$^{3}/_{4}$ in. (14–20 mm). The smallest North American skipper. *Underside of head, thorax, and abdomen white. Wing fringes orange.* Upperside: Pale orange. Forewing with narrow black border. Male has *short narrow black stigma.* Underside: Hindwing with *white ray extending from base through cell* to outer margin. Veins of forewing tip and hindwing may be darkened in fall and winter individuals. **SIMILAR SPECIES:** Orange Skipperling lacks white ray on hindwing underside. Fringes not dark-tipped. **EARLY STAGES:** Not reported. **FOOD:** Bermuda grass and probably others. **FLIGHT:** March–Oct. (2 flights) in La.; all year in Fla. and lowland tropics.

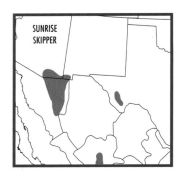

RANGE: Stray or temporary resident in se. Ariz. and w.-cen. Tex. Resident in se. U.S., especially near coast, south through mainland tropical Amer. to Costa Rica. **HABITAT:** Open sunny fields, flats. **REMARKS:** Males perch close to the ground and interact frequently with other passing insects. The tiny adults may be easily overlooked.

SUNRISE SKIPPER *Adopaeoides prittwitzi* **PL. 40**

⅞–1 1⁄16 in. (22–28 mm). *Wing fringes orange.* Upperside: Orange with *black margins and black veining,* only to center of wings in male. Male with short black stigma. Underside: Hindwing orange with *white ray extending from base to outer margin.* **SIMILAR SPECIES:** Southern Skipperling is smaller, lacks darkened veins. **EARLY STAGES:** Not reported. **FOOD:** Knotgrass. **FLIGHT:** May–Sept. (2 flights). **RANGE:** Se. Ariz., sw. N.M., and w. Tex. south to cen. Mex. **HABITAT:** Springs along river valleys in arid zones. **REMARKS:** The butterfly occurs in small isolated colonies. Its flight is weak and it visits small flowers, such as those of watercress.

EUROPEAN SKIPPER *Thymelicus lineola* **PL. 40**

1–1 1⁄8 in. (25–29 mm). *Underside of head and thorax white.* Wing fringes tan to light orange-brown. Upperside: Brassy shining orange. Both wings with *black borders and veins lined with black. Male has narrow black stigma.* Underside: Hindwing *orange-brown to tan, unmarked.* **SIMILAR SPECIES:** Garita Skipperling lacks black stigma in male, has lightened veins on underside of hindwing. **EARLY STAGES:** Caterpillar green with dark dorsal stripe; head light brown with white or yellow stripes on front. **FOOD:** Timothy grass. **FLIGHT:** Mid-May–mid-July (1 flight). **RANGE:** Holarctic. Introduced accidentally to N. Amer. at London, Ont. in 1910. Resident B.C. east to Nfld. south through Rockies to cen. Colo., mainly as

Male European Skipper basking with open wings, Ricketts Glen, Pa. Note short dark stigma on forewing. Males of similar Garita Skipperling lack black stigma on forewing.

isolated populations. Abundant in East south to s. Ill. and w. S.C. **HABITAT:** Open grassy fields, pastures, roadsides. **REMARKS:** This species is spreading in the West and will probably become more widespread and abundant. Adults visit flowers such as clovers, hawkweeds, and dogbane. A rare albino form occurs in parts of the East, notably N.J. Females lay eggs in rowlike clusters.

FIERY SKIPPER *Hylephila phyleus*   **PL. 40**
1 ¼–1 ½ in. (32–38 mm). Strong sexual dimorphism. *Antennae very short.* Male yellow-orange. Upperside: *Both wings with toothed black margins;* forewing with black stigma. Underside: Hindwing with *scattered small black spots.* Female upperside: *Black with irregular orange postmedian band.* Underside: Hindwing *pale brown*

Female Fiery Skipper nectaring at verbena, Callaway Gardens, Ga. Female is more brown below than the orange male (Plate 40). Also note white fringe.

FIERY SKIPPER

ALKALI SKIPPER

with paler checks. **SIMILAR SPECIES:** (1) Sachem female has forewing with transparent spot at end of cell; hindwing underside has pale spots or checks instead of black spots. Sachem male is not likely to be confused with either sex of the Fiery Skipper. (2) Male of Whirlabout, likely only in w. Tex., has upperside forewing with more even black margins. Underside hindwing is yellow-orange with fewer and larger dark smudges, not distinct spots. **EARLY STAGES:** Caterpillar gray-brown to yellow-brown with 3 dark longitudinal stripes; head black with red-brown frontal stripes. **FOOD:** Weedy grasses, especially crabgrass and Bermuda grass. **FLIGHT:** All year in s. Ariz. and lowland tropics, April–Dec. in s. Calif. (several flights). **RANGE:** Resident from coastal n. Calif. south along coast to Baja Calif. and from s. Ariz. w. Tex., and Deep South through West Indies and lowland tropical Amer. to Argentina. Strays north to n. Calif., n. Nev., s. Utah, se. Colo., e. Neb., s. Minn., s. Ont., and s. New England. **HABITAT:** Open sunny areas, including lawns, fields, levees, etc.

ALKALI SKIPPER *Pseudocopaeodes eunus*   **PL. 40**
⅞–1 ¹⁄₁₆ in. (22–28 mm). *Underside of head and thorax white. Wing fringes white, sometimes back-tipped.* Upperside: Orange with *narrow black border and blackened veins near wing margins.* Male has *narrow black stigma.* Underside: Yellow-orange to tan with 2 *cream white rays,* one through discal cell and the second along anal margin. In some areas the butterflies have very faint markings (subspecies *alinea*). **SIMILAR SPECIES:** Orange Skipperling is smaller, lacks white rays on underside of hindwing, and lacks black borders and blackened vein endings above. **EARLY STAGES:** Not reported. **FOOD:** Only desert saltgrass. **FLIGHT:** April–Sept. (several flights). **RANGE:** Ne. Calif., w.-cen. Nev., and se. Calif. **HABITAT:** Alkali flats in arid areas. **REMARKS:** This skipper occurs in highly localized colonies near its host grass.

MORRISON'S SKIPPER
Stinga morrisoni **PL. 40**

MORRISON'S SKIPPER

1–1¼ in. (26–32 mm). Very much like a species of *Hesperia*. Underside of hindwing unmistakable: brownish tan *edged all around with white*, postmedian shining white band, and *white arrowlike bar* from base of wing through discal cell. **SIMILAR SPECIES:** All *Hesperia* skippers lack white edging and median white bar on underside of hindwing. **EARLY STAGES:** Body translucent, tan with gray-tan bands along side. Head brown-black, collar translucent in front, black at rear. **FOOD:** *Stipa scribneri* and probably other grasses. **FLIGHT:** Early April–early July in most of range (1 flight), spring and Sept. in w. Tex. (2 flights). **RANGE:** Front Range of n. Colo. south through e. Ariz., N.M., and w. Tex. to cen. Mex. **HABITAT:** Ridges with open pine, pine-juniper, or oak-juniper woodland. **REMARKS:** Males perch on hilltops to await receptive mates. Males will occasionally fly to valley bottoms to seek moisture at wet spots.

GENUS *Hesperia* FABRICIUS

There are 20 species worldwide in this primarily temperate-zone genus. One species occurs widely in Eurasia. Western North America, with 15 species, is the "hot spot" for the genus. The adults are predominantly orange, medium-sized skippers, often with a pattern of white spots on the underside of the hindwing. The "normal" band configuration is a chevron-shaped band of spots with the lower half of the chevron canted basally and not parallel with the outer wing margin. The male stigma is narrow and slightly curved, with a central silver line. The species are difficult to identify, but the location and season can narrow the possibilities — usually to one or two, but occasionally to as many as four or five species. Some species, notably the Green and Pahaska Skippers, cannot be reliably separated without capture and microscopic examination of the stigma for "felt" color. Some females cannot be identified without examination of the genitalia. Males perch on hilltops or in glades in their quest for receptive mates. Females lay eggs singly on leaves of perennial grasses or sedges, their caterpillar hosts. The caterpillars live in and feed near a silken shelter at the base of their host grass clump and overwinter in partly underground shelters.

UNCAS SKIPPER *Hesperia uncas*   **PL. 40**

1 ¼–1 ⅝ in. (32–40 mm). Upperside: Forewing of male with *narrow stigma and black interior "felt."* Underside: Hindwing with white postmedian spot band "normal" and *usually extended along veins, contrasting with black submarginal patches.* Males of subspecies *macswaini* lack the light veins and black submarginal patches and may be separated by spot band and genitalia. **SIMILAR SPECIES:** Rhesus Skipper usually flies earlier, has contrasting white wing fringes, lacks orangish color and distinct forewing stigma on upper surface. **EARLY STAGES:** Caterpillar pale brown. Head dark brown with front marked with cream spots and streaks. **FOOD:** Primarily Blue Grama Grass, but also other grasses. **FLIGHT:** Late April–Sept. (2 flights), mid-June–July (1 flight) at high elevations in Colo. and e. Calif. to w. Nev. **RANGE:** Cen. Alta. east to s. Man., thence south to e.-cen. Calif. (subspecies *macswaini*), se. Ariz., and w. and n. Tex. Strays to sw. Iowa and e. Minn. **HABITAT:** Short-grass prairie.

JUBA SKIPPER *Hesperia juba*   **PL. 40**

1–1 ½ in. (26–38 mm). Antennal club relatively short. Upperside: Forewing *with black pattern extending between veins in inward-directed lobes.* Male stigma with black interior "felt." Female has 2 *elongate dark spots* below discal cell. Hindwing *slightly translucent so that underside pattern shows through.* Underside: Hindwing greenish or greenish brown with orange along anal margin. *Spots in band large, squarish, and white. White spot in chevron closest to abdomen offset basally.* **SIMILAR SPECIES:** Other *Hesperia*s lack black marginal lobes on forewing, translucent hindwing, and inwardly offset white spot at end of chevron. **EARLY STAGES:** Caterpillar tan. Head black with 2 short vertical streaks on face. **FOOD:** Various grasses, especially blue grama and smooth brome. **FLIGHT:** Late

April–June, Aug.–early Oct. (2 flights). **RANGE:** Cen. B.C. east to se. Mont., w. S.D., and Neb. south to n. Baja Calif., n. Ariz., and nw. N.M. **HABITAT:** Arid brushlands — especially with sagebrush, dunes, pine or pine-juniper woodland with grassy openings. **REMARKS:** How the skipper emerges in an early spring flight after such a late fall flight has sparked suggestions that some adults overwin-

COMMON
BRANDED SKIPPER

ter. This idea is unlikely; more likely the caterpillars are able to complete development during late fall and winter warm spells.

COMMON BRANDED SKIPPER *Hesperia comma*   **PL. 41**

1⅛–1¼ in. (22–30 mm). Hairs on head long, especially those around eyes. Antennae relatively short, club long. *Forewing "stubby" with apex relatively round.* Upperside: Forewing brownish orange with *broad black borders.* Male *stigma with black interior "felt"* (use hand lens). Underside: Hindwing *greenish to green-brown with chevron of distinct lustrous white spots, the closest to abdomen often offset inwardly* as in the Juba and Nevada Skippers. **SIMILAR SPECIES:** See Western Branded Skipper, Plains Skipper, Juba Skipper, and Leonard's Skipper. Other *Hesperia*s do not fly at same season. **EARLY STAGES:** Caterpillar olive green. Head black or brown. **FOOD:** Perennial grasses, sedges. **FLIGHT:** Early June–mid-Sept. (1 flight). Probably biennial at high elevations and in Arctic. For example, it flies only in odd-numbered years in the Alaskan interior. **RANGE:** N. Amer., Eurasia, and n. Africa. From n. Alaska south in mountains to B.C. and Alta. and east across n. Canada to Lab. and south to n. Mich. and Me. **HABITAT:** Open sunny areas: tundra, alpine meadows, taiga, forest openings in West. **REMARKS:** Previously considered a single species in N. Amer. Recent authors consider this to be a group of 3 slightly overlapping species. Further research must clarify this situation.

PLAINS SKIPPER *Hesperia assiniboia*   **PL. 41**

1³⁄₁₆–1¼ in. (21–30 mm). Antennae relatively long. Wing fringes long, white or pale. Upperside: Tawny areas reduced. Appearance dark. Male stigma with *black interior "felt."* Underside: Hindwing pale green or pale green-gray. *Chevron broken into 2 or 3 groups of spots. Spots of chevron white or pale yellow, often very small and sometimes absent.* **SIMILAR SPECIES:** Common Branded Skipper has

darker color on underside of hindwing, larger lustrous white spots in continuous chevron. Spot closest to abdomen not offset inwardly. **EARLY STAGES:** Not described. **FOOD:** Several native prairie grasses. **FLIGHT:** Mid-July, occasionally late June–early Sept. (1 flight). **RANGE:** W.-cen. B.C. east to cen. and se. Man. south to plains of Mont., N.D. and e. S.D. **HABITAT:** Native short-grass prairie, aspen parkland. **REMARKS:** Individuals in northern portion of range are darker. Blend zones with this skipper and the Western Branded Skipper suggest this may be a subspecies of the latter.

WESTERN BRANDED SKIPPER *Hesperia colorado*   **PL. 41**
⅞–1⅜ in. (22–36 mm). This is the most variable *Hesperia*. Antennae relatively long. Forewing often pointed, but sometimes rounded. Upperside: Dark border broad (moister or more mountainous areas) ranging to narrow in more low-lying arid situations. Most individuals with *orange or tawny background*, but some populations reddish (subspecies *susanae* in southwestern U.S. mountains). Male forewing stigma with *interior black "felt."* Underside: Variable in background color including *greenish, reddish, orange, gray-brown, and chocolate brown. Spots in chevron lustrous white, flat white, tan, or yellowish; spots full-sized or reduced in some populations.* Spot band even absent in some populations. **SIMILAR SPECIES:** (1) Common Branded Skipper, Plains Skipper, or Juba Skipper (see above). (2) Woodland Skipper is often found at same time but has different stigma, underside of hindwing either uniform orange or with pale scattered spots (not in form of chevron). **EARLY STAGES:** Caterpillar tan. Head dark brown with broad tan or light brown areas. **FOOD:** Several grasses or sedges. **FLIGHT:** July–Sept. in most areas, as early as late May in Calif. (1 flight). **RANGE:** S. B.C. east to sw. Sask. south to n. Baja Calif., se. Ariz., and sw.

Male Western Branded Skipper nectaring at rabbitbrush along Sanke River valley, Idaho. This individual has pointed forewing, dark outer forewing, and long narrow black stigma.

N.M. **HABITAT:** Wide variety of grasslands, open woodlands, alpine tundra, and brushlands. **REMARKS:** Adults avidly take nectar from many flowers, including asters, gayfeathers, thistles, and others.

APACHE SKIPPER *Hesperia woodgatei* **PL. 41**

1 ⅜–1 ⅝ in. (35–42 mm). *Antennae long with small club.* Upperside: Male forewing stigma with *black felt* (use hand lens). Underside: Hindwing dark brown to dark olive green, with *spots in chevron small, rounded, and usually separated.* **SIMILAR SPECIES:** Late individuals of the Western Branded Skipper, Juba Skipper, or Green Skipper might rarely co-occur with the Apache Skipper but are usually smaller and have a wider, more continuous chevron. **EARLY STAGES:** Not reported. **FOOD:** Grasses, sedges. **FLIGHT:** Mid-Sept.–early Nov. (1 flight). **RANGE:** Separate populations in (1) cen. Ariz. and s. cen.-Colo. south to nw. Mex., (2) w. Tex. and ne. Mex., and (3) cen. Tex. **HABITAT:** Open grassy slopes, mountain meadows, usually in open pine forests.

OTTOE SKIPPER

Hesperia ottoe **PL. 41**

1 ⅜–1 ¹¹⁄₁₆ in. (35–43 mm). Upperside: Upper surface with *extensive tawny orange.* Male forewing stigma with *black or gray felt.* Underside: Hindwing *yellow-orange, unmarked in males, occasionally with faint spot band in females.* **SIMILAR**

APACHE SKIPPER

SPECIES: Leonard's Skipper (subspecies *pawnee*) upperside forewing stigma has yellow interior felt, but flies at end of summer. **EARLY STAGES:** Caterpillar green-brown; head dark brown. **FOOD:** Big bluestem, little bluestem, fall witchgrass, and other grasses. **FLIGHT:** Late June–early Aug. (1 flight). **RANGE:** Se. Mont., w. N.D., and s. Man. south along high plains and foothills to cen. Colo. and n. Tex., east across Neb. and Kans. to cen. Ill. and sw. Mich. **HABITAT:** Tall-grass prairie. Populations of this skipper should be conserved wherever found.

LEONARD'S SKIPPER *Hesperia leonardus* **PL. 41**
1½–1¾ in. (37–45 mm). Upperside: Pale tawny orange. Male *stigma relatively long with yellow interior "felt."* Underside: *Pale yellow-orange, hindwing of female may have faint darker spot band.* The threatened Pawnee Montane Skipper (subspecies *montana*)

Male Leonard's Skipper (subspecies pawnee*) perching, Goshen Co., Wyo. The male is almost entirely orange below and is similar to the earlier flying Ottoe Skipper, found in the same prairie habitats.*

flies in the South Platte River Canyon above Denver, Colo., and is identified by its large amount of variability ranging from that described above to that of intermediates with the dark eastern subspecies *leonardus*. Such individuals are smaller and darker above with red-orange cream-spotted hindwings below. **SIMILAR SPECIES:** No similar species fly at the same season. **EARLY STAGES:** Caterpillar

PAHASKA SKIPPER

tan mottled with red-brown. Head dark brown with cream marks on face and cheeks. **FOOD:** Various perennial grasses, including little bluestem and blue grama grass, and probably sedges. **FLIGHT:** Late July–early Oct. (1 flight). **RANGE:** Cen. Mont. and se. Sask. south to cen. Colo., n. Ark., and n. Ga., and thence east to s. Que. and N.S. **HABITAT:** Short-grass prairie, grassy openings in Ponderosa pine forest. **REMARKS:** Adults nectar avidly at prairie gayfeather, asters, thistles, and a few other flowers. Adults have a powerful, swift flight. Most of our populations belong to subspecies *pawnee*.

PAHASKA SKIPPER *Hesperia pahaska* PL. 41

1 ⅟₁₆–1 ½ in. (28–38 mm). Upperside: Yellow-orange with broad black borders. Male forewing stigma *black with yellow interior felt* (use hand lens). Underside: Hindwing orange-brown with *white spots usually in complete chevron* (except separate spots in subspecies *martini* and *williamsi* of the Southwest). *Posterior arm usually*

Male Pahaska Skipper perching, Larimer Co., Colo. Note protruding yellow-orange felt from forewing stigma. Where it occurs with Green Skipper it can be difficult to distinguish.

straight and more or less parallel to wing margin, except in some females and subspecies *martini* where it is concave outwardly. *White bar at base of discal cell.* **SIMILAR SPECIES:** (1) Green Skipper is nearly identical. Males can be best separated by habitat and the presence of black felt in the forewing stigma. Females tend to have lighter forewing margins above but where the two species reside in the same area cannot be separated confidently except by dissection and examination of their genitalia. Where they co-occur the 2 butterflies fly at the same season. Males of Pahaska Skipper perch on hilltops, whereas those of the Green Skipper are usually found along gullies and streamcourses. (2) Some populations with butterflies similar to Columbian Skipper, but the two are never found together. **EARLY STAGES:** Caterpillar light brown; head dark brown with cream streaks and spots. **FOOD:** Blue grama grass and other grasses. **FLIGHT:** Late May–early Aug. (1 flight) in North, April–Oct. (2 flights) in se. Calif. and w. Tex., April–Oct. in se. Ariz. (3 or more flights). **RANGE:** Rocky Mt. foothills and prairies from cen. Mont., s. Sask., and sw. Man. south to w. Tex. and cen. Mex., west to se. Calif. **HABITAT:** Foothills with short-grass prairie, prairie hills, desert grassland, open pine forest. **REMARKS:** Adults nectar avidly, especially at thistles.

COLUMBIAN SKIPPER *Hesperia columbia*   **PL. 41**
⅞–1 ⁵⁄₁₆ in. (22–34 mm). Upperside: Bright or dark orange with surrounding dark dusky areas. Males *stigma seemingly broad with interior yellow "felt."* Underside: Yellow-orange varying to golden-green with *chevron usually limited to posterior arm composed of small bright white spots.* **SIMILAR SPECIES:** (1) Lindsey's Skipper flies between the 2 flights of the Columbian Skipper and (2) the similar Pahaska Skipper. Populations are not found where the Columbian Skipper occurs in the U.S. **EARLY STAGES:** Caterpillar tan.

Head dark brown with cream dashes and spots. **FOOD:** *Koeleria cristata.* **FLIGHT:** March–June (rarely July), Sept.–Oct. (2 flights). **RANGE:** Sw. Ore south through Coast Range and Sierra Nevada foothills of Calif. to n. Baja Calif. **HABITAT:** Edges of chaparral, hilltops in or near chaparral. **REMARKS:** Males perch on hilltops to await receptive mates.

DOTTED SKIPPER

GREEN SKIPPER *Hesperia viridis* PL. 41

1–1 ⁵⁄₁₆ in. (25–33 mm). Upperside: Bright golden orange, *black marginal scaling on forewing blends gradually with golden orange.* Stigma of male with *black interior felt.* Underside: Hindwing bright green-orange to yellow-orange with well-developed white spot pattern. Posterior *arm of spot band concave from outer margin.* **SIMILAR SPECIES:** Pahaska Skipper is nearly identical and can best be separated by behavior. Male Pahaska Skippers perch on hilltops or knolls and have yellow interior felt in the male forewing stigma (use hand lens). Females usually have darker, more distinct forewing margins above, but dissection may be necessary in areas where the two species overlap. **EARLY STAGES:** Caterpillar tan. Head dark brown with cream streaks and spots. **FOOD:** Various native grasses, especially blue grama. **FLIGHT:** Late May–Aug., rarely Sept. in north (1 flight), April–Oct. to the south (2 flights). **RANGE:** E. Wyo. and w. Neb. south in a broad band through high plains and foothills to cen. Ariz., cen. Tex. and n. Mex. **HABITAT:** Canyons, ravines, mesquite grassland, and dunes.

DOTTED SKIPPER *Hesperia attalus* NOT SHOWN

1 ¹⁄₁₆–1 ⁵⁄₁₆ in. (28–34 mm). Forewing strongly pointed, especially in male. Upperside: Male tawny to dark with broad dark borders. Female dark with a few light spots. Underside: Dull orange to green-brown with or without tiny pale spots. **SIMILAR SPECIES:** (1) Ottoe and (2) Pawnee Skippers are oranger above and below. **EARLY STAGES:** Not reported. **FOOD:** Grasses, including switchgrass and fall witchgrass. **FLIGHT:** May–Sept. (2 flights). **RANGE:** S.-cen. Kans. and e. edge of Tex. panhandle east to w. Mo. And south to e.-cen. Tex. Separate population on Atlantic coastal plain. **HABITAT:** Short-grass prairies. **REMARKS:** This skipper seems to be adapting to disturbed conditions. It is quite variable and difficult to characterize.

Female Lindsey's Skipper basking, Angelus National Forest, Calif. Forewing of female is bright orange with reduced black areas. Note yellow spots. Photo by Jack N. Levy.

LINDSEY'S SKIPPER *Hesperia lindseyi* PL. 41

$^1\!\%_6$–$1\%_6$ in. (24–34 mm). Upperside: Black borders blend to orange areas in males, may be clear-cut in females. Male stigma with *black interior "felt."* Underside: Hindwing yellow-brown to greenish with chevron of cream or yellow spots in male, white in female. *Pale spots are usually angulate and extended along the veins* (except in cen. Sierra Nevada foothills). *Narrow black marginal line along base of fringe.* **SIMILAR SPECIES:** In cen. Sierra Nevada foothills almost identical to the later-flying Western Branded Skipper (subspecies *yosemite*), but can be easily separated by flight date or genitalic dissection. **EARLY STAGES:** Caterpillar tan. Head dark brown with cream spots. **FOOD:** Several native grasses. **FLIGHT:** May–July (1 flight). **RANGE:** S. Ore south through Coast Ranges and Sierra Nevada foothills of Calif. and nw. Nev. to w. Riverside Co., Calif. Isolated records in desert mountains of s. Calif and sw. Ariz. **HABITAT:** Grassy openings in mixed chaparral or oak woodland. **REMARKS:** Adults do not orient to hilltops. Females lay eggs on tree trunks, lichens, or broadleaf plants; young caterpillars must find their host grasses.

SIERRA SKIPPER *Hesperia miriamae* PL. 41

$1\%_6$–$1\%_6$ in. (28–34 mm). Distinctive *iridescent bluish sheen* on both wing surfaces of fresh individuals. Upperside: Marking with *"washed out"* appearance. Apical spots relatively large. Male stigma with *black interior "felt."* Underside: *Bluish gray to golden. Chevron with large white to cream spots* **SIMILAR SPECIES:** None in this skipper's alpine and subalpine habitat. **EARLY STAGES:** Not reported. **FOOD:** Grasses. **FLIGHT:** Late July–Aug. (1 flight). **RANGE:** High elevations of Calif. Sierra Nevada from Alpine Co. south to Tulare Co.

LINDSEY'S SKIPPER

SIERRA SKIPPER

and White Mts. of e.-cen. Calif. and w.-cen. Nev. **HABITAT:** Alpine rockslides and meadows above 11,000 ft. **REMARKS:** Males perch on hilltops or ridges to await receptive mates. Their flight is so rapid that as the butterfly takes flight it seems to disappear before one's eyes.

DAKOTA SKIPPER *Hesperia dacotae*   SEE PHOTOGRAPH

1³/₁₆–1³/₈ in. (21–35 mm). *Forewings stubby,* not noticeably pointed. Upperside: Golden-orange; dark markings blurred; male forewing stigma with *black interior "felt."* Female forewing with *white transparent spot below end of cell.* Underside: *Male hindwing yellow-orange with or without faint macular band. Female hindwing brown-gray with or without faint chevron.* **SIMILAR SPECIES:** Ottoe Skipper is larger; forewings pointed. Male upperside hindwing usually immaculate; female hindwing yellow-orange, not gray.

Female Dakota Skipper nectaring at purple coneflower, Dickinson Co., Iowa. Note rounded wings and gray-brown hindwing with faint orange stigma.

EARLY STAGES: Caterpillar light brown, cervical shield black. Head dark brown. **FOOD:** Little bluestem and other native grasses. **FLIGHT:** Mid-June–early Aug. (1 flight). **RANGE:** S. Man., w. N.D., and e. S.D. to w. Minn. south to nw. Iowa, formerly e. Iowa and possibly ne. Ill. **HABITAT:** Native tall-grass prairies. **REMARKS:** A scarce prairie relative of the more eastern Indian Skipper. All populations should be protected. Adults nectar at purple coneflowers and other prairie composites.

INDIAN SKIPPER *Hesperia sassacus*   **SEE PHOTOGRAPH**
1–1 ⅜ in. (25–35 mm.). Upperside: Yellow-orange with *clear-cut black markings*. Hindwing with black border often with *toothlike inward projections*. Underside: *Yellow-orange with yellow chevron not contrasting with background.* **SIMILAR SPECIES:** Dakota Skipper, range to south, has blurred black markings above. Female has

Male Indian Skipper perching, Pendleton Co., W. Va. Note clear-cut black border. Hindwing has toothlike inward projections from black border.

Male Nevada Skipper perching, Rio Arriba Co., N.M. Dark borders gradually blend with inward orange. Stigma has black interior felt. Photo by Steve Cary.

brown-gray hindwing below. **EARLY STAGES:** Not reported. **FOOD:** Native grasses, including little bluestem. **FLIGHT:** May–July (1 flight). **RANGE:** S. Canada and ne. U.S. from w.-cen. Manitoba east to N.B. and cen. Me. south to n. Ind., s. Ohio, and w. N.C. **HABITAT:** Brushy old fields, pastures, clearings in forests, headlands.

NEVADA SKIPPER *Hesperia nevada*   **PL. 41**

1–1 ⁵⁄₁₆ in. (26–34 mm). Forewing apex relatively rounded or blunt. Upperside: *Tawny orange with dark borders blended.* Male forewing stigma with *black interior "felt."* Females vary from tawny orange to very dark. Underside: Hindwing greenish with *irregular white chevron—most basal spot often offset inward, giving posterior arm a 3-stepped appearance.* **SIMILAR SPECIES:** (1) Western Branded Skipper does not have spot in chevron closest to abdomen as off-set and usually flies later in summer. (2) Juba Skipper is larger with more pointed forewing. **EARLY STAGES:** Not reported. **FOOD:** Native grasses, including fescues, koeleria, and stipa. **FLIGHT:** Late May–early Aug. (1 flight). **RANGE:** Western mountains from s. B.C. east to sw. Man. and thence south to e.-cen. Calif., e.-cen. Ariz. and n. N.M. **HABITAT:** Sagebrush flats, prairies, aspen parkland, mountain summits.

NEVADA SKIPPER

Female Sachem nectaring at French marigold, Fairfax Co., Va. Note tranparent spot on forewing. Similar to Hesperia skippers. Often shows up as late-summer or fall immigrant.

SACHEM *Atalopedes campestris*

PL. 42

1 ⅜–1 ⅝ in. (35–41 mm). Upperside: Male forewing with *large 4-sided black stigma*. Females variable, light to very dark, but can always be identified by *square white transparent spot at end of forewing cell*. Underside: Female hindwing brown with *squarish white or cream spots*—similar to a *Hesperia*. **SIMILAR SPECIES:** Fiery Skipper females lack square transparent spot on forewing, and underside of hindwing has black spots instead of pale spots. **EARLY STAGES:** Caterpillar dark olive green with dark bumps. Head black. **FOOD:** Grasses, especially Bermuda Grass. **FLIGHT:** Jun–Oct. (1–2 flights) where colonist, March–Dec. (4–5 flights) in s. Calif. (rare) and s. Ariz. **RANGE:** Resident in s. U.S. south through lowland Mex. and mainland tropical Amer. to Brazil. Regular stray and colonist north as far as s. B.C., s. Nev., cen. Wyo., n. N.D., s. Man., s. Ont., and n. Pa. **HABITAT:** Open sunny areas including gardens, roadsides, short-grass prairie, open areas near streamcourses. **REMARKS:** This predictable colonist on the Great Plains is most often found at garden flowers such as marigolds and zinnias. In more native settings look for it on rabbitbrush flowers. It is a very close relative of *Hesperia* skippers.

GENUS *Polites* SCUDDER

This is a medium-sized genus of 14 species, all of which are North American. Eleven are found in the West, and often several are found in a local environment. Five of these have ranges that extend south into Mexico. Most are small orange species with short, stout-clubbed antennae. Males have a prominent sinuous (almost S-shaped) stigma. Often there is a patch of dark special-

SACHEM

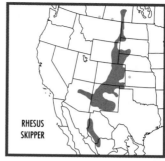

RHESUS SKIPPER

ized scales outside and below the stigma. Two of our species (*Polites origenes* and *P. themistocles*) are especially difficult to separate without close inspection, but the others are distinctive. Grasses, including those found in lawns such as bluegrasses, are the hosts. In the West a few species are limited to undisturbed prairie environments. The skippers are found in open sunlit grassy habitats, and males take up perches, usually in flats or depressions, but sometimes on hilltops or ridges, where they await receptive mates.

RHESUS SKIPPER *Polites rhesus*   PL. 41

1–1 ³⁄₁₆ in. (26–30 mm). *Fringes white.* Upperside: *Dark gray-brown with a few white spots* on forewing. Those of female larger and more prominent. Male stigma slender, not obvious. Underside: *Hindwing splotchy black and yellow-green with white post-basal mark and postmedian band. White band extended outward along veins.* **SIMILAR SPECIES:** Uncas Skipper is larger and has extensive orangish above with prominent stigma on male. **EARLY STAGES:** Caterpillar light gray-green to brown green (red-brown on top of last few segments) with various pale cream, red-brown, and tan marks and areas as well as darker line up middle of back. Head black with cream marks. Collar black with pale green streak. **FOOD:** Blue grama grass. **FLIGHT:** May -early June (1 flight). **RANGE:** S. Alta. and s. Sask. south along high plains and foothills of Rockies (w. N.D., w. S.D., e. Wyo., w. Neb., e. Colo., w. Kans., n. Tex., N.M., and n. Ariz.) south in mountains to Durango, Mex. **HABITAT:** Short-grass prairie. **REMARKS:** Males perch on flat open areas on low ridges or hilltops where they await receptive mates. The species is rare in most years, but can be locally common. They are found easiest at small yellow composites or white milk vetch flowers.

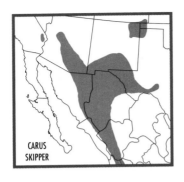

CARUS SKIPPER *Polites carus*   PL. 41
⅞–1 3/16 in. (22–30 mm). Upperside: Dark brown with pale yellowish spots. Male stigma black. Underside: *Hindwing yellow dusted with black. Chevron of buffy yellow spots. Veins pale buff.* SIMILAR SPECIES: Rhesus Skipper has prominent white fringe, white spots above, and is more blotchy below. Male has inconspicuous stigma. EARLY STAGES: Not reported. FOOD: Unknown. FLIGHT: Mid-March–Sept., rarely Nov. (2–3 flights). RANGE: Extreme se. Calif. east across Ariz. and N.M. to se. Colo. and n. Tex. thence south into the mountains of Mex. to Zacatecas. HABITAT: Grassy areas in oak woodland or brush. REMARKS: Adults readily visit flowers. Males may take up perches on hilltops to await receptive mates.

PECK'S SKIPPER *Polites peckius*   PL. 41
1–1¼ in. (25–31 mm). Upperside: Dark; yellow-orange areas restricted. Male has gray-brown patch below sinuous black stigma on forewing that extends almost to dark border. Male stigma has interior yellow "felt." Underside: Hindwing with *central patch of yellow spots surrounded by dark border.* SIMILAR SPECIES: No other skipper has central yellow patch with dark border on underside of hindwing. EARLY STAGES: Caterpillar dark maroon to dark brown with mottled light brown. Head black with white and/or brown streaks and patches. FOOD: Grasses including salt grass, Kentucky blue grass, and smooth brome. FLIGHT: May–Sept. (1–2 flights). RANGE: Temperate N. Amer. from B.C. east across s. Canada to s. Lab., Nfld., and N.S., thence south to ne. Ore., e.-cen Ariz., s. Colo., and n. Tex. In East south to nw. Ark., n. Ala., and n. Ga. HABITAT: Open grassy areas, including mountain meadows, edges of prairie marshes, and lawns. REMARKS: Populations in n. Rockies have only a single flight (July–Aug.), while those on prairie have two flights (May–June, Aug.–Sept.).

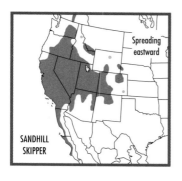

SANDHILL SKIPPER *Polites sabuleti*   **PL. 41**

¾–1 ¹⁄₁₆ in. (20–28 mm.) Upperside: Yellow-orange extends along veins giving border a "sawtooth" appearance. Male has stigma with interior brown "felt." Underside: In most populations hindwing has *cobweb appearance due to lighter yellow banding along veins.* In some low-lying populations the hindwing is unicolored pale yellow. In other areas the underside of the hindwing may vary from chocolate brown to gray. **SIMILAR SPECIES:** (1) Draco Skipper (see below). (2) Smaller than *Hesperia* species that might be found with it. **EARLY STAGES:** Caterpillar dull green or light gray mottled with brown. Head black with prominent white or cream lines. **FOOD:** Various grasses, including salt grass and Bermuda grass. **FLIGHT:** March–Nov. (2–3 flights) at lower elevations and more arid habitats, July–Aug. (1 flight) at high elevations. **RANGE:** S. B.C., n. Idaho, nw. Mont., Wyo., w. Neb., Colo., and n. N.M., south to w. and n. Ariz. and s. Baja Calif. **HABITAT:** Subalpine meadows, coastal dunes and saltmarshes, lawns and gardens, interior alkali flats, and roadsides. **REMARKS:** This extremely variable butterfly requires further study. Genetic differences of subalpine California populations (subspecies *tecumseh*) suggest more than a single biological species.

MARDON SKIPPER *Polites mardon*   **PL. 41**

¾–¹⁵⁄₁₆ in. (20–24 mm). Forewings rounded and stubby. Upperside: Yellow-orange with black borders with moderate *"sawtooth" border.* Male stigma small with outside gray-brown patch small. Underside: Red-tan, sometimes with green-gray overscaling. *Postmedian band of large squarish yellow spots.* **SIMILAR SPECIES:** (1) Sandhill Skipper has more extreme "sawtooth" border, cobweb appearance underneath. (2) Long Dash is larger, more yellowish, found much farther east. **EARLY STAGES:** Caterpillar light gray with

dark brown dots. Head black with 2 light stripes on top. **FOOD:** Grasses. **FLIGHT:** Mid-June–mid-July (1 flight). **RANGE:** Cascades of Wash. and Klamath Range of nw. Calif. **HABITAT:** Grassy areas in subalpine mountains or serpentine outcrops.

DRACO SKIPPER *Polites draco*   PL. 41

¹³⁄₁₆–1 ³⁄₁₆ in. (21–30 mm). Upperside: Dark with broad diffuse black borders on forewing. Tawny area of hindwing restricted. Male forewing *stigma black and S-shaped.* Gray-brown specialized patch large. Underside: Hindwing varying from orange-yellow to brown to green. *Spot band yellow or white, not extended along veins. Two spots in middle of band elongated into long dashes.* **SIMILAR SPECIES:** Sandhill Skipper has more distinct dentate black margin on forewing, cobweb pattern on hindwing below. **EARLY STAGES:** Caterpillar dark brown with brown-black bands. Head and collar black. **FOOD:** Grasses. **FLIGHT:** Early June–early Aug. (1 flight). **RANGE:** Sw. Yukon and n. B.C., then from w.-cen. Alta. and sw. Sask. south through Rocky Mts. to s. Nev., cen. Ariz., and cen. N.M. **HABITAT:** Dry mountain meadows, grassy hillsides, and alpine tundra. **REMARKS:** Adults nectar at flowers such as footsteps of spring and yellow composites.

TAWNY-EDGED SKIPPER *Polites themistocles*   PL. 41

⅞–1 ⅜ in. (23–36 mm). Forewings slightly rounded. Upperside: Forewing of both sexes with orange along costa invading end of cell. Male *stigma sinuous (in 3 segments)* with interior *tan "felt."* Specialized scale patch outside stigma connects with dark margin. Female completely dark, usually with fairly extensive orange on leading edge of forewing. Underside: Hindwing usually *brassy orange-brown or gray, occasionally with postmedian band of pale spots.* **SIMILAR SPECIES:** Crossline Skipper is larger; male with forewing more pointed, brown-tan straighter stigma and usually lacks specialized scale patch; female darker with upperside of forewing usually without orange along costa. **EARLY STAGES:** Caterpillar similar to that of the Crossline Skipper. Head with 2 white vertical stripes on front. **FOOD:** Kentucky bluegrass and other grasses. **FLIGHT:** July in north and mountains (1 flight); April–Sept. (2 flights) at lower

elevations and to the south. **RANGE:** Se. B.C. and ne. Wash. east to N.S., south to e.-cen. Ariz., s. N.M., se. Tex., Gulf Coast, and cen. Fla. Apparently isolated populations in n. Calif. and w. Ore. **HABITAT:** Mountain meadows, lawns, pastures, vacant lots, prairie swales.

CROSSLINE SKIPPER *Polites origenes* **PL. 41**

1 ³⁄₁₆–1 ½ in. (30–38 mm). Forewing pointed. Upperside: Male forewing with *stigma gray-brown, long, and relatively straight.* Male has extensive orange on forewing, and specialized scale patch is usually absent. Female dark, forewing usually without orange along costa. Large squarish spot below end of cell. Underside: *Hindwing usually brown or tan with postmedian band of distinct pale spots.* **SIMILAR SPECIES:** Tawny-edged Skipper is smaller and is brassy tan or gray on hindwing underside, without a spot row. Male stigma on upperside of forewing is sinuous; female has orange invading front area of forewing upperside. **EARLY STAGES:** Caterpillar dark brown to red-brown with dirty white mottling. Head and collar dull black. **FOOD:** Big bluestem and other grasses. **FLIGHT:** June–early Aug. (1 flight) along Rocky Mt. front and in north; May–Sept. (2 flights) elsewhere. **RANGE:** W. N.D. south along Rocky Mt. front to ne. N.M. thence east discontinuously to s. Ont. and se. Que., and cen. Me. south to ne. Tex., Gulf Coast, and n. Fla. **HABITAT:** Open grassy areas, including old fields, openings, prairie hills, barrens, and power-line cuts. **REMARKS:** Populations along Rocky Mt. front in Mont., Wyo., and Colo. (subspecies *rhena*) are closely associated with remnant patches of big bluestem. Adults in these areas nectar at native thistles.

LONG DASH *Polites mystic* **PL. 41**

1 ³⁄₁₆–1 ½ in. (30–38 mm). Upperside: Forewing with *male stigma long, slightly curved*—may or may not be connected to dash run-

ning to apex. Hindwing orange-brown with contrasting curved postmedian band of equal-sized yellow spots. Female has broad black basal patch on upperside of forewing. Underside: Hindwing ranging from yellow-orange to reddish brown with *postmedian band of large paler spots and postbasal pale spot.* **SIMILAR SPECIES:** Woodland Skipper usually flies later in year, is smaller, and has shorter stigma on male forewing. **EARLY STAGES:** Caterpillar dark brown with mottled dull white. Head dull black. **FOOD:** Various grasses. **FLIGHT:** Late May–early Aug. (1 flight). **RANGE:** S. B.C. and nw. Wash. east to e. Ont. and N.S., south to cen. Ariz. (isolated population), sw. Colo., s. Iowa, s. Ohio, and s. Va. (mountains). **HABITAT:** Moist open areas: prairie swales, streamsides, marshes.

SONORAN SKIPPER *Polites sonora*   PL. 41

¹¹⁄₁₆–1¼ in. (24–32 mm). Upperside: Reddish brown to orange. Dark areas usually invaded by heavy orange scaling. Male has *black stigma and broad adjacent black specialized scale patch.* Underside: Hindwing varying from gray-green (subspecies *utahensis*), orange-tan (subspecies *sonorensis*), to red-brown (subspecies *sirius*) with *narrow band of yellow-cream spots* (off-white in subspecies *utahensis*). Also a *pair of pale postbasal spots.* **SIMILAR SPECIES:** Draco Skipper (see p. 442). **EARLY STAGES:** Caterpillar gray-green to brown. Head and collar black. **FOOD:** Probably various grasses. **FLIGHT:** June–Sept. (1 flight), as early as late May in coastal Calif. **RANGE:** S. B.C. east to sw. Mont. south to s. Calif., n. Ariz., and Rocky Mts. Isolated population in n. Baja Calif. **HABITAT:** Moist meadows. **REMARKS:** Closely related to the Long Dash, but although their ranges overlap, the two skippers almost never fly at the same season.

WHIRLABOUT *Polites vibex*   PL. 41

1³⁄₁₆–1½ in. (30–38 mm). Sexes dissimilar. Male yellow-orange. Female dark brown. Upperside: Male forewing with *black stigma*

WHIRLABOUT

NORTHERN
BROKEN-DASH

and associated modified scales forming large 4-sided patch. Hindwing with black margins smooth inwardly. Underside: Male hindwing with *large smudged black spots.* Female hindwing *gray or sooty yellow with pale central patch outlined with dark scaling.* **SIMILAR SPECIES:** Male Fiery Skipper has narrower toothed outer margins on both wings above and more smaller black dots on hindwing below. Females are not similar. **EARLY STAGES:** Caterpillar pale with faint lateral stripes. Head black with yellow-white stripes and patches. **FOOD:** Grasses, including Bermuda grass and St. Augustine grass. **FLIGHT:** April–Sept. (2 flights) at northern limits of residence, all year in Fla. and s. Tex. **RANGE:** Se. U.S. and West Indies south through e. Mex. and mainland tropical Amer. to Argentina. Periodic strays north to w. Tex., ne. Iowa, n. Ohio, and Conn. **HABITAT:** Open areas: lowland tropics, fields, dunes, pinewoods, roadsides, etc. **REMARKS:** Unreliably reported from se. Ariz. Adults nectar at a wide variety of flowers, including lantana and Bougainvillea.

NORTHERN BROKEN-DASH *Wallengrenia egeremet*   **PL. 41**
1–1½ in. (25–37 mm). Upperside: Dark brown. Male forewing with *cream or yellow spot at end of cell;* female forewing with a few (usually 2) *elongated cream or yellow spots.* Underside: Hindwing *dark brown or purple-brown with distinctive paler spot band,* usually with reflective highlights when freshly emerged. **SIMILAR SPECIES:** (1) Female Dun Skipper has 2 tiny blurred white spots on forewing, and lacks pale spot band and purple-brown color on underside of hindwing. (2) Southern Broken-Dash (Pl. 41) (possible along Rio Grande Valley west to Val Verde Co., Tex., where Northern Broken-Dash does not occur) has underside of hindwing orange or red-orange with only a faint postmedian spot band. On upperside, male has orange or red-orange areas along costa and outer end of forewing discal cell. **EARLY STAGES:** Caterpillar pale,

mottled green; green and yellow side stripes; head dark brown with dark central and pale vertical stripes on front. **FOOD:** Panic grasses. **FLIGHT:** June–Aug. (1 flight), May–early Oct. (2 flights) in Deep South and e. Tex. **RANGE:** Se. N.D., w. Neb., cen. Kans, and cen. Tex. east across Great Lakes states, s. Ont. and s. Que. to se. Me., south to cen. Okla., se. Tex., Gulf Coast, and cen. Fla. **HABITAT:** Open areas near woods or scrub. **REMARKS:** Adults nectar avidly at milkweeds and dogbane.

LITTLE GLASSYWING *Pompeius verna*   PL. 41

1 1/16–1 1/2 in. (27–37 mm). Upperside: Black or black-brown. Male with *black stigma surrounded by several transparent white spots* above and below, including a large one below outer end of stigma. Female forewing with *square transparent white spot* at end of discal cell. Underside: Hindwing black, often with *postmedian band of small white spots.* **SIMILAR SPECIES:** Female Dun Skipper has small rounded opaque spots on forewing, lacks spot band on underside of hindwing. Some females must be captured and examined for reliable identification. Association with the more readily identified males is helpful. **EARLY STAGES:** Caterpillar yellow-green to yellow-brown, covered with dark brown bumps; dark line up middle of back and 3 dark lines along each side. Head red-brown edged with black. **FOOD:** Redtop, possibly other grasses. **FLIGHT:** Mid-June–early Aug. (1 flight) in most of range, April–Sept. (2 flights) in Southeast. **RANGE:** Cen. Neb. east to s. Ont., s. Que., and s. New England thence south to s. Tex., Gulf Coast, and s. Fla. **HABITAT:** Moist areas near shaded wood edges. **REMARKS:** Adults most easily observed when visiting flowers such as dogbane, French marigold, or zinnia.

AROGOS SKIPPER *Atrytone arogos*   PL. 42

1 1/8–1 7/16 in. (28–36 mm). Bright yellow-orange. Upperside: Wings with *broad black borders.* Underside: Hindwing *veins with pale scaling.* **SIMILAR SPECIES:** Delaware Skipper is brighter orange, lacks broad black borders. **EARLY STAGES:** Caterpillar pale yellow-green or green cream with pale yellow-green intersegmental folds. Head gray-white or pale tan with 4 vertical orange-brown stripes. **FOOD:** Big bluestem, probably other native grasses. **FLIGHT:** Late June–July (1 flight) in north and West, April–Sept. (2 flights) in Southeast. **RANGE:** Separate prairie populations: (1) Ne. Wyo., se. Mont., N.D., and cen. Minn. south to s. Tex., (2) Colo. Front Range, (3) N.J. (formerly N.Y.) south to ne. Ga., (4) peninsular Fla., and (5) Gulf Coast. Also Atlantic Coast and Gulf Coast marshes. Strays to Ill., n. Ark., and w. Va. **HABITAT:** Undisturbed prairies, serpentine barrens. **REMARKS:** Unlike most other prairie butterflies, Arogos

Skippers court and mate in overcast conditions. During sunny periods they nectar at flowers such as thistles, milkweeds, and alfalfa.

DELAWARE SKIPPER *Anatrytone logan* PL. 42

1–1⅝ in. (25–42 mm). Bright yellow-orange. Upperside: Outer margins black; *veins with black in submarginal area*; forewing with *black bar at end of discal cell*. Underside: *Hindwing yellow-orange, unmarked*. **SIMILAR SPECIES:** Arogos Skipper is limited to native prairies; has broader black borders on both wings above and lacks any black markings inside borders. **EARLY STAGES:** Caterpillar pale blue-green or blue-white with minute black bumps. Head black with 3 cream or white frontal stripes. **FOOD:** Grasses. **FLIGHT:** July–Aug. (1 flight) in north; May–Sept. (2 flights) in Southeast. **RANGE:** S. Alta. and Sask. south in Rocky Mts. to s.-cen. Ariz. and w. Tex. thence east across Great Plains to extreme s. Ont. to s. New England, south through most of e. U.S., and Mexican highlands to El Salvador. **HABITAT:** Damp or wet fields, marshes, prairies. **REMARKS:** The perching males are obvious along streamcourses and ravines. As in many butterfly species, the females are less easily discovered.

WOODLAND SKIPPER *Ochlodes sylvanoides* PL. 42

¾–1⅛ in. (20–29 mm). Forewing apex rounded. Upperside: Orange to orange-yellow with *blackish-brown dentate border with inward dark projections between veins*. Male forewing with *prominent black stigma* containing a central thin gray line with a dark more or less rectangular patch between stigma and apex. Female more variable but forewing has dark patch in place of male stigma and a second dark, rectangular patch outwardly. Females may have extensive dark markings that make the dark patches less ob-

vious. Underside: Hindwing variable, but usually yellow-orange with *postmedian band of squarish yellow or yellow-cream spots, often merged as a band.* Hindwing color varies from almost yellow (spot band not apparent) to purplish or chocolate brown (cream spot band prominent). **SIMILAR SPECIES:** (1) Long Dash is similar below but is larger, has diffuse dark border, and flies earlier in year. (2) Fall-flying *Hesperia* skippers have more pointed forewings, lack the dark patch beyond the discal cell, usually have white spots on forewing apex below, and do not have hindwing spot bands composed of squarish spots. **EARLY STAGES:** Caterpillar pale green or buff yellow with 7 dark longitudinal lines or bands. Head black or tan-cream with black central stripe and margins. Collar white in front, black at rear. **FOOD:** Tall broad-leaved grasses. **FLIGHT:** July–Oct. (1 flight) in most of range, June–Oct. (2 flights) in lowland Calif., as early as April on Santa Cruz Is. off s. Calif. **RANGE:** N.-cen. B.C., s. Alta., sw. Sask., w. N.D., and w. S.D. south through much of the mountainous w. U.S. to n. Baja Calif., n. Ariz., and n.-cen. N.M. **HABITAT:** Hillsides, chaparral openings, swales, and grassy areas near streamcourses. **REMARKS:** The adults are slow-flying and sedentary, spending much of their adult lives at flowers such as asters and thistles.

RURAL SKIPPER *Ochlodes agricola*   **PL. 42**
¾–1 in. (20–26 mm). Upperside: Orange with diffuse black border. *Male stigma black and relatively broad with thin central gray line. A narrow transparent white patch lies just outside the stigma.* Female has *dark patch in cell and 2 transparent spots* just outside it. Underside: Hindwing orange in male, orange-brown to purplish in female. Male may have postmedian band of small yellow spots; female usually has postmedian band of larger yellow spots. **SIMILAR SPECIES:** (1) Usually flies before Woodland Skipper, which

lacks transparent white spots on forewing. (2) *Hesperia* skippers in range all have more prominent spot bands on hindwing below. **EARLY STAGES:** Not reported. **FOOD:** Probably grasses. **FLIGHT:** Mid-May–July, rarely early Aug. (1 flight). **RANGE:** Southwest Ore. south through foothills and coast ranges of Calif. to n. Baja Calif. **HABITAT:** Forest edges and clearings, usually along streamcourses or north-facing slopes. **REMARKS:** Adults are most frequent near flowering California buckeye trees at which they nectar and under which they court and mate.

YUMA SKIPPER *Ochlodes yuma* PL. 42

1 1/16–1 3/8 in. (28–36 mm). *Forewings pointed.* Upperside: Tawny orange with diffuse narrow black borders. Male has *long narrow black stigma.* Female has diagonal series of pale cream translucent spots. Underside: *Immaculate yellow-orange in male, orange-tan with faint postmedian spot band in females.* Subspecies *anasazi* in n. N.M. is darker and has gray-yellow hindwing with faint spot band. **SIMILAR SPECIES:** Ottoe Skipper and subspecies *pawnee* of Leonard's Skipper are similar but have ranges that do not approach Yuma Skippers. **EARLY STAGES:** Caterpillar pale green. Head cream with vague brown lines. **FOOD:** Common reed. **FLIGHT:** June–Sept. (1–2 flights). **RANGE:** E. Wash., e. Ore., s. Idaho, Nev., cen. and e. Calif., Utah, n. Ariz., w. Colo., and n. N.M. **HABITAT:** Colonies of common reed, usually in arid environments. **REMARKS:** A strong-flying butterfly found in isolated colonies. Adults visit a variety of flowers, especially thistles.

HOBOMOK SKIPPER *Poanes hobomok* PL. 42

1 3/8–1 5/8 in. (34–42 mm). *Forewings rounded.* Upperside: *Male yellow-orange with irregular black borders; lacks stigma. Female with 2 forms:* (1) normal form is similar to male, but orange is less ex-

tensive and duller. (2) Pocahontas form is purple-black with a few clouded white spots on forewing. Underside: hindwing with yellow-orange (male) or orange (normal female) *outer postmedian area and inner margin purple-gray*. Pocahontas form purple-black, pattern obscured. **SIMILAR SPECIES:** (1) Male Taxiles Skipper has more extensive yellow-orange above, lacks dark base and anal margin on hindwing below. Female is similar to normal female of Hobomok but is browner with smaller yellow spots on forewing apex and has postmedian spots (not band) and yellow-orange anal margin. (2) Zabulon Skipper has somewhat more pointed forewings. Male is similar but has underside of hindwing with more extensive yellow-orange and base dark brown. Female is most similar to Pocahontas form of Hobomok Skipper, but underside of hindwing is 2-toned brown and purple-gray, and costal margin is white-edged. **EARLY STAGES:** Not fully reported. **FOOD:** Panic grasses, bluegrasses. **FLIGHT:** April–July (1 flight). **RANGE:** Isolated population from cen. Colo. to cen. N.M. Temperate e. N. Amer. from e.-cen. Alta. across s. Canada to N.S. south to e. Wyo., cen. Kans., e. Okla., and n. Ga. **HABITAT:** Edges of damp woods or bogs, openings along streams, city parks. **REMARKS:** The isolated population found along the Rocky Mt. front (subspecies *wetona*) lacks the Pocahontas female form.

ZABULON SKIPPER *Poanes zabulon*   **PL. 42**

1 ⅜–1 ¹⁵⁄₁₆ in. (34–49 mm). Sexes dissimilar. Forewings pointed. Upperside: Male bright yellow-orange. Female purple-brown. Underside: *Male hindwing mainly yellow; base and outer margin dark brown. Female hindwing 2-toned brown and purple-gray; costal margin white-edged.* **SIMILAR SPECIES:** Male Taxiles Skipper has more rounded forewing, narrower black margins, and differently patterned hindwing below. Females are not similar. **EARLY STAGES:** Not

reported. **FOOD:** Grasses. **FLIGHT:** May–Sept. (2 flights) in North, all year in tropics. **RANGE:** E. U.S. from cen. Kans. east through s. Mich. to Mass., south to ne. Tex., s. La., and cen. Fla. Strays to N.M. and S.D. Also Mex. south to Panama. **HABITAT:** Brushy areas and openings near moist woods or streams, city parks.

TAXILES SKIPPER *Poanes taxiles* **PL. 42**

1 ⅜–1 ¹¹⁄₁₆ in. (36–43 mm). Forewings somewhat rounded. Upperside: Male is yellow-orange with very narrow black borders; female, unlike male, is dark orange-brown with patches of pale orange in forewing and central hindwing. Underside: Forewing of male has slightly darkened apex and outer margin. *Hindwing yellow-orange with darkened base and outer margin. Anal margin orange-brown. Hindwing of female violet-brown with patch of gray scales near outer margin and paler postmedian spot band.* **SIMILAR SPECIES:** Zabulon Skipper has wings less rounded, orange less extensive. **EARLY STAGES:** Caterpillar orange-tan with several brown lateral lines. Head red-brown with orange on front. Collar black. **FOOD:** Tall broad-leaved grasses. **FLIGHT:** Mid-June–Aug. (1 flight). **RANGE:** Se. Idaho, Utah, e. Wyo., w. S.D. , and n.-cen. Neb. south through Colo., Ariz., N.M. and w. Tex. to cen. Mex. **HABITAT:** Openings in forests along stream and river valleys, ravines. **REMARKS:** Perching and nectaring males are hard to miss, but the duller females are much less obvious. Taxiles Skippers nectar at a wide variety of white, pink, and purple flowers.

BROAD-WINGED SKIPPER *Poanes viator* **SEE PHOTOGRAPH**

1 ¹⁄₁₆–1 ⁵⁄₁₆ in. (27–34 mm). Forewings rounded. Upperside: Dark brown. Forewing primarily dark with small cream spots and small

Broad-winged Skipper resting, New Kent Co., Va. The inland subspecies zizaniae, associated with wild rice, is resident in western Nebr. Look for the characteristic pattern on the underside of the hindwings.

yellow-orange area. Hindwing primarily orange with black border. Veins black-lined. Underside: *Hindwing orange-brown with yellow-orange streak running outward from base and postmedian band of yellow-orange squarish spots.* **SIMILAR SPECIES:** No other similar skipper is found in freshwater marshes in our region. **EARLY STAGES:** Not reported. **FOOD:** Common reed. **FLIGHT:** Late June–early Aug. (1 flight). East and Gulf Coast populations have several flights. **RANGE:** W. Neb. and e. Dakotas east to s. Que. and e. N.Y. Coastal populations from Mass. south to n. Fla. and west along Gulf Coast to cen Tex. **HABITAT:** Freshwater and brackish marshes with tall grasses. **REMARKS:** In our area found at edges of freshwater lakes in Neb. sandhills.

UMBER SKIPPER *Poanes melane*   **PL. 42**

1 1/16–1 5/16 in. (28–34 mm). Upperside: Dark orange-brown above. Three or four yellow (male) or yellow-orange (female) spots diagonally on forewing. Hindwing flushed with orange. Underside: *Purplish brown with postmedian band of yellow-orange spots* (vague in Calif., sharply defined in se. Ariz. and w. Tex.). **SIMILAR SPECIES:** None in Calif. Female Taxiles Skipper in Ariz. and w. Tex. has extensive orange above. **EARLY STAGES:** Caterpillar yellow-green with tiny black spots and stripes. Head yellow-brown. **FOOD:** Various grasses. **FLIGHT:** Feb.–Oct. (2 flights). **RANGE:** Calif. lowlands and foothills west of mts. south to n. Baja Calif. (subspecies *melane*); se. Ariz., sw. N.M., and w. Tex. south to Costa Rica. **HABITAT:** Shady gardens, openings along streams, foothill canyons. **REMARKS:** This species once occurred no farther north than s. Calif. but invaded most of Calif. during the twentieth century. Adults nectar at flowers such as thistles, abelia, and red valerian.

SNOW'S
SKIPPER

TWO-SPOTTED
SKIPPER

SNOW'S SKIPPER *Paratrytone snowi*   **PL. 42**

1 ¹⁄₁₆–1 ⅜ in. (28–36 mm). Forewing fringe brown, that of hindwing light yellow. Upperside: Dark brown with large square black stigma (male) or patch (female). Hourglass-shaped pale spot in discal cell, other pale spots beyond cell and near apex. Underside: *Hindwing red-brown, usually with postmedian band of discrete small yellow spots.* **SIMILAR SPECIES:** Female Taxiles Skipper is dark orange above and has gray marginal patch below. **EARLY STAGES:** Not reported. **FOOD:** Grasses, especially pine dropseed. **FLIGHT:** Late June–Sept. (1 flight). **RANGE:** Se. Wyo., Colo., n. and w. N.M., and e. Ariz. south to cen. Mex. **HABITAT:** Foothill streamcourses and ravines. **REMARKS:** Adults nectar at blue and purple flowers, often with long corolla tubes into which they may crawl. Their flight is extremely rapid.

TWO-SPOTTED SKIPPER *Euphyes bimacula*   **PL. 42**

1 ⅜–1 ⅝ in. (35–41 mm). *Underside of head and body white. Fringes white.* Forewings pointed. Upperside: Male forewing with limited tawny patch; female dark, forewing with 2 pale spots. Underside: *Hindwing orange-brown. Veins paler. Anal margin white.* **SIMILAR SPECIES:** No other large skipper in our area has combination of white fringes, white underside of body, and golden-orange on underside of hindwing. **EARLY STAGES:** Caterpillar light green with many black points each bearing a white hair. Head cream with redbrown vertical bands. Collar black. **FOOD:** Sedges. **FLIGHT:** June–July (1 flight). **RANGE:** Three populations: (1) a western one in ne. Colo., nw. Kans., and w. Neb., and (2) an eastern one from e. Neb. east in an expanding band to s. Que., and from N.B. and s. Me. south to cen. Va. and (3) a third on coastal plain from s. Va.

DUN SKIPPER

DUSTED SKIPPER

south to Ga. and on Gulf Coast. **HABITAT:** Wet sedge meadows, marshes, bogs. **REMARKS:** Colonies are highly localized. Adults perch close to the ground.

DUN SKIPPER *Euphyes vestris*   PL. 42

1 1/16–1 3/8 in. (28–35 mm). *Face and top of thorax golden orange.* Underside of head, front legs, and thorax often white. Upperside: Male brown-black with black stigma. Female forewing with up to 2 tiny diffuse white spots. Underside: *Gray-black with veins blacker.* **SIMILAR SPECIES:** (1) Orange-headed Roadside-Skipper is smaller and has striking golden-white fringes. (2) Female Little Glassywing's forewing has eyes rimmed with white and relatively large transparent white spot on forewing. (3) Female Northern Broken-Dash has 1 or 2 elongate yellow or cream forewing spots and red-purple sheen on underside of hindwing. **EARLY STAGES:** Caterpillar pale green with a white overcast, many white dashes. Head tricolored black, caramel brown, and cream. Collar black. **FOOD:** Sedges. **FLIGHT:** June–early Aug. (1 flight), more flights in East. **RANGE:** S. B.C. south to n. Calif. (subspecies *vestris*), coastal s. Calif. (subspecies *harbisoni*), from e.-cen. Alta., Idaho, and s. Mont. south through e. Wyo., Colo., and sw. Utah, to e. Ariz., N.M., w. Tex., and Nuevo León, Mex. The species occurs eastward across s. Canada to N.S. and south to s. Tex., Gulf Coast, and peninsular Fla. Absent from high elevations of Rockies, much of the intermountain West, and much of lowland Calif. **HABITAT:** Moist areas near streams, marshes, swales.

DUSTED SKIPPER *Atrytonopsis hianna*   PL. 42

1 3/8–1 5/8 in. (35–42 mm). *White facial area.* Fringes gray-brown. Upperside: Dark gray. A few white spots. Male with a tiny stigma. Underside: *Hindwing gray, lighter outwardly.* **SIMILAR SPECIES:** (1)

Viereck's Skipper has slightly checkered fringes, larger forewing spots, and 2 dark bars crossing underside of hindwing. (2) Deva Skipper is larger, has lighter fringes, does not overlap in distribution. (3) Cloudywings (genus *Thorybes*) have broader wings and usually hold their wings open instead of closed. **EARLY STAGES:** Caterpillar pale lavender above with prothorax and sides pale gray; cervical shield dark brown; head deep red-purple. **FOOD:** Big bluestem and little bluestem. **FLIGHT:** May–June (1 flight). **RANGE:** Se. Sask., s. Man., e. Mont., and N.D. south through Great Plains to e. Wyo., cen. Colo., n. N.M., and cen. Tex., thence east to s. Ont., N.H., and Mass. south to Gulf Coast. **HABITAT:** Mid-grass and tall-grass prairies, foothills. **REMARKS:** An uncommon, highly localized skipper. Adults often nectar at beardtongues (*Penstemon* species) and readily enter the long corolla tubes to reach nectar.

DEVA SKIPPER *Atrytonopsis deva* PL. 42

1 ½–1 ⅝ in. (38–42 mm). *Fringes light, those of hindwing almost white.* Upperside: Dark gray. Similar to Dusted Skipper. Lacks white spot in discal cell. Underside: *Brown dusted with gray.* May have a *few white spots along hindwing costa* or a faint dark bar on hindwing. **SIMILAR SPECIES:** Viereck's Skipper has larger white spots on forewing, including an hourglass-shaped spot in discal cell. **EARLY STAGES:** Not reported. **FOOD:** Unknown. **FLIGHT:** April–July (1 flight). **RANGE:** S. two-thirds of Ariz. and sw. N.M. south to cen. Mex. **HABITAT:** Clearings in oak and oak-pine woodland with open grassy areas, roadsides. **REMARKS:** Very cyclical in abundance.

MOON-MARKED SKIPPER *Atrytonopsis lunus* PL. 42

1 ⁹⁄₁₆–1 ¾ in. (40–44 mm). Forewing fringes pale tan, *white fringes encircling most of hindwing.* Upperside: *Forewing with large white translucent spots including discal cell.* Underside: brown with or

without darker marks. SIMILAR SPECIES: Viereck's Skipper lacks strong white fringes. Other *Atrytonopsis* in its range have white marks on hindwing. EARLY STAGES: Not reported. FOOD: Unknown. FLIGHT: Late June–early Sept. (1 flight). RANGE: Se. two-thirds of Ariz. and sw. N.M. south to mts. of Sonora, Mex. HABITAT: Openings in oak woodland. REMARKS: Adults, especially females, most often seen at flowers such as thistles.

VIERECK'S SKIPPER *Atrytonopsis vierecki* PL. 42

1 5/16–1 1/2 in. (34–38 mm). Fringes weakly brown and tan-checkered. Upperside: Several translucent white spots on forewing including *hourglass-shaped spot in discal cell*. Underside: Hindwing *dark brown with 2 narrow darker bars*. SIMILAR SPECIES: Dusted Skipper lacks hourglass-shaped spot in discal cell and lacks bars on underside of hindwing. EARLY STAGES: Not reported. FOOD: Unknown. FLIGHT: Late April–early June (1 flight). RANGE: S. Utah and cen. Colo. south to s. Ariz., s. N.M., and w. Tex. HABITAT: Ravines or gulches in juniper woodland or oak-juniper woodland. REMARKS: Males perch in or near gulch bottoms or washes and await receptive females. They visit white and blue flowers, including verbena and legumes.

WHITE-BARRED SKIPPER *Atrytonopsis pittacus* PL. 42

1 1/4–1 5/16 in. (32–34 mm). Fringes tan. Upperside: Large white hyaline spots on forewing. Hindwing with straight postmedian band of connected white hyaline spots. Underside: Hindwing with *white postmedian band as on upperside*. SIMILAR SPECIES: (1) Viereck's Skipper lacks white band on hindwing. (2) Python Skipper has checkered fringes and irregular hindwing band of yellowish spots. EARLY STAGES: Not reported. FOOD: Unknown. FLIGHT: Late Feb.–early June, late Aug.–Oct. (2 flights). RANGE: S. and cen. Ariz., sw. N.M.,

nw. Mex., and w. Tex. south to Oaxaca, Mex. **HABITAT:** Open oak woodland and grasslands. **REMARKS:** Males seen in w. Tex. and s. Ariz. perching on hilltops awaiting the arrival of receptive females.

PYTHON SKIPPER *Atrytonopsis python*   **PL. 42**

1¼–1½ in. (32–38 mm). *Fringes checkered* black and white. Upperside: Both wings with large white or yellowish translucent spots. Underside: Hindwing *purple-gray with very irregular yellowish spots or band.* **SIMILAR SPECIES:** (1) White-barred Skipper has uncheckered fringes and very narrow straight white bar on hindwing above and below. (2) Cestus Skipper has larger white irregular band on forewing as well as white postbasal spot in most individuals. **EARLY STAGES:** Caterpillar pink to blue-green. Head pale brown. **FOOD:** Unknown. **FLIGHT:** Late April–mid July (1 flight). **RANGE:** S. Nev., Ariz., N.M., and w. Tex. **HABITAT:** Open oak woodland.

CESTUS SKIPPER *Atrytonopsis cestus*   **PL. 43**

1³⁄₁₆–1⅜ in. (31–36 mm). *Fringes checkered* black and white. Upperside: Forewing with large white spots including *hourglass-shaped spot in discal cell. Hindwing has jagged irregular postmedian translucent white band and postbasal white spot.* Underside: Hindwing has white markings as above, outlined in black. **SIMILAR SPECIES:** Python Skipper does not have hourglass-shaped spot in discal cell and lacks postbasal white spot on hindwing. **EARLY STAGES:** Not reported. **FOOD:** Unknown. **FLIGHT:** Late March–late May, mid-Aug.–Sept. (2 flights). **RANGE:** S. Ariz., and nw. Mex. **HABITAT:** Gullies and canyons in thorn scrub grassland. **REMARKS:** Males perch on sunlit rocks and cliffs in the morning to await the arrival of possible mates.

SHEEP SKIPPER

SIMIUS ROADSIDE-SKIPPER

SHEEP SKIPPER *Atrytonopsis edwardsi*   **PL. 43**

1 ⁵⁄₁₆–1 ⁹⁄₁₆ in. (34–40 mm). Forewing slightly more rounded that other *Atrytonopsis*. Fringes weakly checkered black and pale tan. Upperside: Gray-brown. Forewing with *large white translucent spots, including large spot in discal cell*. Male with *prominent black stigma*. Hindwing with *postmedian series of 3 or 4 separated small white translucent spots*. Underside: Powdered gray with postmedian spots and occasionally 1 or 2 postbasal white spots. **SIMILAR SPECIES:** Pittacus Skipper lacks checkered fringes, and white spots on hindwing are usually equal-sized and lined up in straight line. Hindwing appears browner. **EARLY STAGES:** Not reported. **FOOD:** Unknown. **FLIGHT:** Early April–Oct., rarely to Jan. (2 or more flights). **RANGE:** S. Ariz., sw. N.M., and w. Tex. south into Mex. **HABITAT:** Canyons with steep cliffs in arid mountains. **REMARKS:** Males perch on sunlit rocks and cliffs. Adults visit deep-throated flowers, such as morning glories, for nectar.

SIMIUS ROADSIDE-SKIPPER *"Amblyscirtes" simius*   **PL. 43**

⅞–1 ⅟₁₆ in. (22–28 mm). Fringes white, uncheckered. Upperside: Orangish to blackish with *postmedian V-shaped band of small cream or orangish spots*. An additional pale spot at end of discal cell. Male has short stigma. Underside: Forewing with *large orange area on basal two-thirds. Hindwing pale whitish gray, covered with a sheen in freshly emerged individuals.* **SIMILAR SPECIES:** (1) Bronze Roadside-Skipper has checkered fringes and is darker on underside of hindwing. (2) See also Uncas Skipper (p. TK). **EARLY STAGES:** Caterpillar pale blue-green with darker midline. Head tan and brown-tan. Collar green. **FOOD:** Blue grama grass. **FLIGHT:** Late May–June in north, April–May in w. Tex., July–Aug. in Ariz. (1 flight). **RANGE:** S. Sask. south along high plains and Rocky Mt. front through e. Mont., w. Neb., e. Wyo., Colo., Ariz., N.M., and

n. Tex. to n. Mex. **HABITAT:** Short-grass prairie, mixed grasslands, grassy areas in open woodland. **REMARKS:** The Simius Roadside-Skipper is not a true *Amblyscirtes*, but no alternate genus name is available. In Colorado, Simius is found on many of the same hilltops occupied by the Rhesus Skipper a month earlier.

LARGE ROADSIDE-SKIPPER *Amblyscirtes exoteria*   **PL. 43**
1–1¼ in. (26–32 mm). Forewing pointed. Fringes checkered dark brown and white. Upperside: Dark brown with short series of small white or yellowish spots toward apex of forewing. Male with short stigma. Underside: *Hindwing gray-brown with distinct small white spots in a postmedian band as well as toward base.* **SIMILAR SPECIES:** (1) Dotted Roadside-Skipper is smaller, blacker above, and has white spots underneath outlined with black. (2) Celia's Roadside-Skipper is similar but its range is well separated. **EARLY STAGES:** Not reported. **FOOD:** Bullgrass. **FLIGHT:** Mid-June–Sept. (1 flight). **RANGE:** Se. two-thirds of Ariz. and sw. N.M. south to s. Mex. **HABITAT:** Oak woodland, coniferous forest, etc. **REMARKS:** This is the largest of our roadside-skippers. It is often seen at flowers, including red thistles, red penstemon, mints, and knapweed.

CASSUS ROADSIDE-SKIPPER *Amblyscirtes cassus*   **PL. 43**
¹⁵⁄₁₆–1¹⁄₁₆ in. (24–28 mm). Fringes checkered dark brown and tan. Upperside: Orange-brown with yellow-orange spots on forewing. Male with short distinct stigma. Underside: *Forewing very orange with obvious paler spots. Hindwing mottled gray.* **SIMILAR SPECIES:** Simius Roadside-Skipper has uncheckered fringes and pale unmottled hindwing underside. Usually in different habitats. **EARLY STAGES:** Not reported. **FOOD:** Panic grass. **FLIGHT:** May–Sept., mainly mid-June–early Aug. (1 flight). **RANGE:** Cen. Ariz., w. two-thirds of N.M. and w. Tex. south to Jalisco, Mex. **HABITAT:** Open oak wood-

BRONZE ROADSIDE-SKIPPER

OSLAR'S ROADSIDE-SKIPPER

land and mixed woodland near ravines and watercourses. **REMARKS:** Often seen at flowers, including milkweed, dandelion, and pink legumes.

BRONZE ROADSIDE-SKIPPER *Amblyscirtes aenus* **PL. 43**

1 1/16–1 1/4 in. (27–32 mm). Fringes checkered brown and tan or cream. Upperside: Brown with slight orange sheen. Few indistinct obscure pale spots on forewing. Male stigma indistinct. Underside: *Forewing red-brown basally.* Form erna, formerly considered a separate species, is an unspotted variety. **SIMILAR SPECIES:** (1) Oslar's Roadside-Skipper has more pointed forewing, less distinctly checkered fringes, always has muted pattern, and is darker on underside of forewing; (2) Texas Roadside-Skipper always has more distinct forewing spots, including a small one in the discal cell, and the underside of the forewing is brown; (3) Cassus Roadside-Skipper is more orange with a more mottled gray hindwing below. **EARLY STAGES:** Caterpillar pale blue-white. Head cream with orange-brown bands. Collar brown in front, black at rear. **FOOD:** Grasses. **FLIGHT:** April–July (1 flight) in Colo., April–Sept. (2 flights) in southern part of range. **RANGE:** S. Utah and n.-cen. Colo. east to s. Kans., w. Okla., and cen. Tex. south to Ariz., N.M., and w. Tex. south to cen. Mex. **HABITAT:** Gullies and stream bottoms, foothills in a wide variety of brushy and wooded habitats. **REMARKS:** Confusing because the species has both spotted and unspotted forms. May be difficult to identify when worn.

OSLAR'S ROADSIDE-SKIPPER *Amblyscirtes oslari* **PL. 43**

1 1/8–1 3/8 in. (29–34 mm). Forewings pointed. Fringes gray, slightly checkered. Upperside: Orange-brown, unspotted. Underside: *Forewing with discal area red-brown. Hindwing light gray with paler postmedian band.* **SIMILAR SPECIES:** See (1) Bronze Roadside-Skipper and (2) Texas Roadside-Skipper. **EARLY STAGES:** Pale yellow-

green or blue-green with darker midline. Head cream with orange-brown bands. Collar black. **FOOD:** Side-oats grama and a few other grasses. **FLIGHT:** May–July in north and east, July–Sept. in Ariz. (1 flight). **RANGE:** Se. Alta. and s. Sask. south along high plains and Rocky Mts. to Ariz., N.M., cen. Tex., Nuevo León, Mex. **HABITAT:** Prairie ravines and canyon bottoms in a wide variety of brushy or wooded habitats. **REMARKS:** Ariz. adults often fly in late afternoon when roadside-skippers are usually inactive.

ELISSA ROADSIDE-SKIPPER *Amblyscirtes elissa*   **PL. 43**

¹³/₁₆–⁷/₈ in. (21–23 mm). Fringes white, somewhat checkered. Upperside: Dark brown. Forewing with bent postmedian row of white spots and *small white spot in discal cell.* Underside: Forewing with pattern as above. *Hindwing brown with postmedian and posthasal small white spots.* **SIMILAR SPECIES:** (1) Dotted Roadside-Skipper lacks discal cell spot, has more distinctly checkered fringe, and underside of hindwing is grayer. (2) Toltec Roadside-Skipper is very similar but has postmedian series of white forewing spots offset with apical series, and upperside of male hindwing may be spotted. **EARLY STAGES:** Not reported. **FOOD:** Side-oats grama grass. **FLIGHT:** Mid-July–late Aug. (1 flight). **RANGE:** Se. Ariz. and sw. N.M. south to s. Mex. **HABITAT:** Open woodland.

PEPPER AND SALT SKIPPER *Amblyscirtes hegon*   **PL. 43**

1–1³/₁₆ in. (25–30 mm). Fringes pale, checkered. Upperside: Forewing lightly spotted, including *discal cell.* Underside: *Hindwing light gray-green with paler postmedian band.* **SIMILAR SPECIES:** Likely to be confused only with Common Roadside-Skipper (see below). **EARLY STAGES:** Caterpillar pale green-white with 3 dark green dorsal stripes and 2 white lateral stripes. Head dark brown with pale brown vertical stripes and bands. **FOOD:** Grasses. **FLIGHT:** April–July, rarely early Aug. (1 flight), earliest in south. **RANGE:** E. N. Amer. from e.-cen. Sask. and Man. east to N.S., south to se. Tex. and n. Fla.; largely absent from coastal plain. **HABITAT:** Glades, wood edges, and by streams.

TEXAS ROADSIDE-SKIPPER

Amblyscirtes texanae   **PL. 43**

¹⁵/₁₆–1¹/₁₆ in. (24–28 mm). Fringe tan checkered with brown. Upperside: Forewing with discrete yellowish postbasal band and *small yellow*

ELISSA
ROADSIDE-SKIPPER

PEPPER AND SALT SKIPPER

TEXAS ROADSIDE-SKIPPER

spot in discal cell (occasionally absent). Underside: Forewing brown. *Hindwing gray with vague postmedian band of whitish spots.* **SIMILAR SPECIES:** Oslar's and Bronze Roadside-Skippers (see p. 460). **EARLY STAGES:** Not reported. **FOOD:** Panic grass. **FLIGHT:** May and mid-July–early Sept. in Ariz. (1 or more flights); April–Aug. in w. Tex. (2 flights). **RANGE:** Se. Ariz., s. N.M., n. and w. Tex. **HABITAT:** Ravines, open limestone canyons, dry washes in a variety of low-elevation habitats.

TOLTEC ROADSIDE-SKIPPER *Amblyscirtes tolteca*   PL. 43

⅞–1 in. (22–26 mm). Fringes white, checked with brown. Upperside: Blackish brown with well-developed white spots on forewing, including *single or double spot in discal cell.* Subapical spot series well separated from rest of postmedian band. Males usually have pattern of white spots on hindwing as well. Underside: *Hindwing dark brown with postmedian band and postbasal white spots.* **SIMILAR SPECIES:** (1) Dotted Roadside-Skipper lacks spot in forewing discal cell and has gray background on underside of hindwing. (2) Elissa Roadside-Skipper has subapical spots on forewing more or less continuous with bent postmedian band and never has white spots on upper surface of hindwing. **EARLY STAGES:** Not reported. **FOOD:** Unknown. **FLIGHT:** May–Sept. (probably 2 flights). **RANGE:** S. Ariz. and nw. Mex. **HABITAT:** Open woodland and desert grassland. **REMARKS:** Previously called the Prenda Roadside-Skipper, but *prenda* is our subspecies of the Toltec Roadside-Skipper whose range extends into Mex.

SLATY ROADSIDE-SKIPPER *Amblyscirtes nereus*   PL. 43

¹⁵⁄₁₆–1 ¹⁄₁₆ in. (24–28 mm). Fringes whitish, slightly checkered. Upperside: Blackish above with well-developed pattern of white

TOLTEC
ROADSIDE-SKIPPER

SLATY
ROADSIDE-SKIPPER

spots on forewing but not including discal cell; hindwing with *postmedian series of equal-sized white spots*. Underside: Apex and costal margin of forewing gray-green or yellow-green. Hindwing *gray-green or yellow-green with postmedian series on white spots,* but not in high contrast with background. **SIMILAR SPECIES:** Other roadside-skippers lack the combination of white spotting on the upper surface of the hindwing and the pale greenish color below. **EARLY STAGES:** Not reported. **FLIGHT:** May–June in w. Tex., May (rare), mainly July–Aug. in Ariz. (1 flight). **RANGE:** Se. Ariz., s. N.M., and w. Tex. south into n. Mex. **HABITAT:** Open grassy slopes, watercourses, and ravines in oak and mixed foothill woodlands. **REMARKS:** Adults are seldom common and most often seen at flowers or visiting moist spots.

NYSA ROADSIDE-SKIPPER *Amblyscirtes nysa*   PL. 43

¹⁵⁄₁₆–1 ³⁄₁₆ in. (24–30 mm). Fringes checkered black and white. Upperside: Black with 3–5 tiny white spots on forewing apex. Underside: *Hindwing variegated with irregular black, gray, and brown patches.* **SIMILAR SPECIES:** No other small skipper in our area has combination of colored patches on underside of hindwing. **EARLY STAGES:** Caterpillar pale green with dark green dorsal stripe. Head cream white with vertical orange-brown streaks and bands. **FOOD:** Grasses. **FLIGHT:** March–Nov. (several flights). **RANGE:** Se. Neb., Kans., and w. Mo. west to s. Ariz. and south to n. Mex. **HABITAT:** Dry, rocky

NYSA
ROADSIDE-SKIPPER

ravines, wood edges, yards, gardens. **REMARKS:** Males perch in gully bottoms to await likely mates. Cannot be confused with other roadside-skippers in its range.

DOTTED ROADSIDE-SKIPPER *Amblyscirtes eos*   **PL. 43**
1 1/16–1 1/4 in. (27–32 mm). *Fringes checkered* white and black. Upperside: Black with tiny white spots. Underside: *Hindwing gray-brown with basal and postmedian round white spots narrowly edged with black.* **SIMILAR SPECIES:** (1) Elissa and Toltec Roadside-Skippers have spot in forewing discal cell, while (2) Large Roadside-Skipper is larger, has more pointed forewing, and lacks gray background on underside of hindwing. **EARLY STAGES:** Not reported. **FOOD:** Vine mesquite (a panic grass). **FLIGHT:** March–Oct. (2 or more flights). **RANGE:** Southwest from se. Colo., s. Kans., w. Okla., N.M., and ne. Tex. south to cen. Ariz., s. Tex., and Durango, Mex. **HABITAT:** Ravines, canyons, roadsides in juniper or oak-juniper woodland.

COMMON ROADSIDE-SKIPPER *Amblyscirtes vialis*   **PL. 43**
1–1 3/16 in. (25–30 mm). Our most widespread roadside-skipper. *Fringes checkered* buff and black. Upperside: Black with tiny white spots on forewing apex. Underside: *Forewing apex and outer half of hindwing dusted with violet-gray.* **SIMILAR SPECIES:** Pepper and Salt Skipper has light spots in center of forewing above and gray-green dusted hindwing with postmedian row of paler spots. **EARLY STAGES:** Caterpillar pale blue-green, covered with small green bumps. Head dull white with vertical red-brown stripes on front. Collar black. **FOOD:** Tall broad-leaved grasses. **FLIGHT:** March–July (1 flight), partial second brood to Sept. in Southeast. **RANGE:** Much of temperate N. Amer. from B.C. east across Canada to the Gaspé

Peninsula and N.S., south to cen. Calif., n. N.M., ne. Tex., and peninsular Fla. **HABITAT:** Open areas in or near deciduous woods, often near streams and small rivers. **REMARKS:** Absent from Great Basin and other areas of intermountain West.

CELIA'S ROADSIDE-SKIPPER *Amblyscirtes celia*   PL. 43

⅞–1 ¹⁄₁₆ in. (23–27 mm). *Fringes* cream to tan, *checkered.* Upperside: Dark brown. Forewing usually with light spot at end of discal cell. Underside: *Hindwing gray with white basal and postmedian spot series.* **SIMILAR SPECIES:** Dotted Roadside-Skipper lacks spot at end of forewing cell and has gray background on hindwing below. **EARLY STAGES:** Not reported. **FOOD:** *Paspalum.* **FLIGHT:** May–Sept. in cen. Tex.; all year in s. Tex. (2 or more flights). **RANGE:** Tex. south to ne. Mex., stray to sw. La. **HABITAT:** Openings in woods.

ORANGE-HEADED ROADSIDE-SKIPPER   PL. 43
Amblyscirtes phylace (W. H. Edwards)

1–1 ¹⁄₁₆ in. (26–28 mm). *Top of head* with *orange* scales. Forewing *apex somewhat squared off. Fringes cream or buff, uncheckered.* Upperside: Gray-brown. Unmarked. Male has *large oval stigma* on forewing. Underside: *Blackish, unmarked.* **SIMILAR SPECIES:** (1) Orange-edged Roadside-Skipper has bright orange rather than cream or buff fringes and stigma on male is 3-parted. (2) Dun Skipper has dark fringes. **EARLY STAGES:** Caterpillar pale green. Head cream with reddish brown vertical bands. Collar black. **FOOD:** Big bluestem, rarely other grasses. **FLIGHT:** June–Aug. (1 flight). **RANGE:** Cen. Colo. south through N.M., e. Ariz., and w. Tex. to cen. Mex. **HABITAT:** Gulches and small ravines in open woodlands and grasslands.

ORANGE-EDGED ROADSIDE-SKIPPER PL. 43

Amblyscirtes fimbriata

    ¹⁵/₁₆–1 ¼ in. (24–32 mm). Top of *head* with orange *scales. Fringes bright orange.* Upperside: Gray-brown. Stigma on male forewing is in 3 aligned parts. Underside: *Blackish.* **SIMILAR SPECIES:** Orange-headed Roadside-Skipper (see p. 465). **EARLY STAGES:** Caterpillar grass-green. Head creamy yellow with orange-brown vertical stripes. **FOOD:** Several grasses. **FLIGHT:** Late May–late Aug. (1 flight). **RANGE:** Se. Ariz. (Cochise Co.) and sw. N.M. (Hidalgo Co.) south to Guerrero, Mexico. **HABITAT:** Coniferous forests, oak-juniper woodlands, and roadsides.

EUFALA SKIPPER *Lerodea eufala* PL. 43

    1 ⅛–1 ⅜ in. (27–34 mm). Upperside: Gray-brown. Forewing with 3-5 *small translucent white spots.* Stigma lacking. Underside: *Hindwing brown with gray overscaling,* rarely with faint spots. **SIMILAR SPECIES:** (1) Julia's Skipper has underside hindwing yellow-brown with paler veins. (2) Roadside-skippers have stubbier wings, and if gray below have distinct spot pattern as well, as in Dotted Roadside-Skipper, for example. **EARLY STAGES:** Caterpillar bright green with dark dorsal stripe and faint white lateral lines; head dull white with orange-brown blotches. **FOOD:** Grasses. **FLIGHT:** Virtually year-round in s. Ariz. (several flights), July–Oct. in Calif. (1 or 2 flights). **RANGE:** Resident in Cuba and s. U.S. from s. Calif., s. Nev., s. Ariz., s. N.M., and cen. Tex. south through mainland tropical Amer. to Patagonia. Vagrant and occasional colonist north to cen. Calif., s. Utah, se. Colo., N.D., s. Wisc., n. Mich., and Wash., D.C. **HABITAT:** Open sunny areas: road edges, vacant lots, agricultural areas. **REMARKS:** This small skipper occasionally expands its range northward in the summer but dies out during the succeeding cold winter. Adults readily visit an array of flowers, often pink, purple, or white.

OLIVE-CLOUDED SKIPPER *Lerodea arabus*   **PL. 43**

⅞–1 1/16 in. (22–28 mm). Upperside: Gray-brown. Forewing with several small translucent white spots, often including spot at end of discal cell. Underside: Hindwing with *central dark brown patch that may not be well defined outwardly.* **SIMILAR SPECIES:** Eufala Skipper lacks white spot in forewing discal cell and central dark patch on underside of hindwing. **EARLY STAGES:** Not reported. **FOOD:** Probably grasses. **FLIGHT:** Feb.–Dec. in s. Ariz. (2 or more flights). **RANGE:** S. Ariz. and s. Tex. south to El Salvador. **HABITAT:** Lowland thorn forest and scrub, urban yards and gardens. **REMARKS:** Adults readily nectar at a variety of flowers including vinca, lantana, and bougainvillea. Males perch in gully bottoms during late afternoon.

BRAZILIAN SKIPPER *Calpodes ethlius*   **PL. 43**

2–2⅜ in. (50–61 mm). Also known as the Canna Leafroller. Large and robust. *Proboscis notably long.* Upperside: Brown-black with large translucent spots, forewing pointed. Underside: *Red-brown with postmedian series of squarish cream spots.* **EARLY STAGES:** Caterpillar pale green with white subdorsal lines; head dark orange with black spots. **FOOD:** Cannas. **FLIGHT:** July–Nov. in s. Ariz.; April–Dec. in s. Tex.; all year in Fla. and tropics. **RANGE:** S. Fla. and s. Tex. south through the West Indies and mainland tropical Amer. to Argentina. Not resident in West. Strays and temporary colonist north to s. Calif., s. Nev., Ariz., N.M., n. Tex., Ill., and Mass. **HABITAT:** Residential areas and gardens with cannas. **REMARKS:** Colonizes garden plantings of cannas and is known to colonize far to the north of its natural range.

WANDERING SKIPPER *Panoquina errans*   **PL. 43**

15/16–1¼ in. (24–32 mm). Upperside: Dark brown with several translucent yellow spots on forewing. Underside: *Dark brown*

with postmedian series of several yellow spots. Wing veins some-times lined with yellow (most noticeable in freshly emerged indi-viduals). **SIMILAR SPECIES:** Eufala Skipper has white spots on forewing and is gray below. **EARLY STAGES:** Caterpillar green with 4 green-white stripes running up back and a thin yellow stripe along each side. Head bright green. **FOOD:** Salt grass. **FLIGHT:** July–Sept. in Calif. (2 flights), year-round in s. Baja Calif. and mainland Mex. **RANGE:** Coastal s. Calif. (Santa Barbara Co. south), Baja Calif., and the Pacific coast of mainland Mex. south to Col-ima. **HABITAT:** Upper edges of coastal salt marshes in Calif., weedy fields near coastline in coastal Mex. **REMARKS:** The species has dis-appeared from much of its range in coastal s. Calif. because of habitat destruction, but is still widespread and common in its Mexican range.

OCOLA SKIPPER *Panoquina ocola*   PL. 43

1 5/16–1 5/8 in. (34–42 mm). *Forewings elongate, project far beyond hindwings when perching.* Hindwing with slightly pronounced lobe at rear. Upperside: Forewing with a few white or yellowish translucent spots. Underside: *Dark brown. Unmarked or with veins lighter* than background. Some individuals have a post-median band of small pale blurred spots. Hindwing with blue-purple iridescent sheen in some females. **SIMILAR SPECIES:** Brazilian Skipper is much larger with distinct cream spots on underside of hindwing. **EARLY STAGES:** Caterpillar gray-green with first 2 segments blue-green, dark line up middle of back and a green-white stripe running along each side. Head pale green. **FOOD:** Grasses. **FLIGHT:** All year in Fla., s. Tex., and lowland tropical Amer. (several flights). Late Aug.–Oct. in s. Ariz. **RANGE:** Resident from s. Tex. and Fla. south through West Indies and lowland tropics to Paraguay. In

West rare strays found in w. Tex. and se. Ariz. **HABITAT:** Lowland tropics, thorn forest, scrub, gardens, disturbed areas. **REMARKS:** Most likely near Mexican border during years with good late summer–fall monsoons.

PURPLE-WASHED SKIP-PER *Panoquina leucas* **PL. 43**

1 ³⁄₁₆–1 ½ in. (30–37 mm). Upperside: Forewing of males with *elongated spot in discall cell.* Underside: *Hindwing with straight line of white or blue spots.* Female with blue or purple wash. **SIMILAR SPECIES:** Ocola Skipper lacks white spot in forewing discal cell. **EARLY STAGES:** Caterpillar gray-green with dorsal lines and a white lateral stripe on each side; head green with black marks on front. **FOOD:** Coarse grasses, including Sugar Cane. **FLIGHT:** Aug.–Dec. in s. Tex.; all year in Mex. **RANGE:** N.M. south through West Indies and mainland tropical Amer. to Argentina. Regular stray north to lower Rio Grande Valley, rarely to se. Ariz. and cen. Tex. **HABITAT:** Openings in subtropical scrub, forest edges, and adjacent fields. **REMARKS:** Easily confused with Ocola Skipper. Previously known as *Panoquina sylvicola.*

VIOLET-BANDED SKIPPER **PL. 43**
Nyctelius nyctelius

1 ¹⁄₁₆–1 ½ in. (27–37 mm). Upperside: Brownish black with white double spot in forewing discal cell. Underside: Hindwing pale brown often with *violet cast* (especially in freshly emerged individuals), 2 *darker bands and a small round spot along forward* edge. **SIMILAR SPECIES:** Ocola Skipper lacks complex hindwing pattern below. **EARLY STAGES:** Caterpillar blue-gray with faint pale gray bands; black shield behind head. Head yellowish with vertical black stripes. **FOOD:** Sugar cane and other coarse grasses. **FLIGHT:** All year in lowland tropics (several flights), Sept.–Nov. in s. Ariz. and s. Calif. **RANGE:** Resident in lowland tropical Amer. south to Argentina. Regular stray to s. Tex. Rare stray to s. Calif. and se. Ariz. **HABITAT:** Disturbed areas and second growth. Tropical gardens. **REMARKS:** Males perch a foot or two from the ground, often near nectar sources, where they await the arrival of receptive mates. Adults nectar at flowers such as boneset, bougainvillea, and vinca.

The giant-skippers comprise four genera. These large robust insects are limited to the United States and Mexico. Most species occur in the Southwest and adjacent desert portions of Mexico. Outside of s. and w. Tex., where *Stallingsia* occurs, the reader will encounter species of *Agathymus* (whose caterpillars bore in agaves) and *Megathymus* (whose caterpillars bore in yuccas). The antennae are not hooked, and some species have a short apiculus—others none at all. The males have long hairlike scales on the upper surface of the hindwings, and they lack brands or costal folds. Males visit wet sand, where they imbibe moisture. Giant-skippers rarely feed as adults. Eggs are glued to host leaves (*Megathymus* and *Stallingsia*) or dropped into host plant clumps (*Agathymus*). Caterpillars burrow into host leaves and stems and feed within their silk-lined tunnels. The pupae, which are flexible, are formed in the larval tunnels and are capable of moving up and down. Most captive adults are obtained by raising them from immature stages collected from host plants; they are rarely observed in nature.

ORANGE GIANT-SKIPPER
PL. 44
Agathymus neumoegeni

2–2⅜ in. (50–60 mm). Fringes checkered black and white. Upperside: Both wings *suffused extensively with orange,* especially on basal half. *Broad black margins* on both wings. Remainder of wings largely orange and orange-yellow. Underside: Hindwing gray with incomplete postbasal and postmedian paler bands. Two indistinct white spots along upper margin. **SIMILAR SPECIES:** Adults of most *Agathymus* are seen only while resting with wings closed. They are best identified by location and season, since most wing characters used to separate these butterflies are seen only in

ORANGE
GIANT-SKIPPER

ARIZONA
GIANT-SKIPPER

Arizona Giant-Skipper, Hidalgo Co., N.M. Underside is dark gray with obscure pale spots. The Agathymus Giant-Skippers usually perch with wings closed but the best identifying marks are on the upperside. Photo by Steve Cary.

pinned specimens. The Orange Giant-Skipper co-occurs with the similar Arizona Giant-Skipper only in sw. N.M. and with Poling's Giant-Skipper only in cen. Ariz. Its range does not overlap that of the Huachuca Giant-Skipper. **EARLY STAGES:** Caterpillar white with blue or green tinge. Head and collar dark brown. **FOOD:** Parry's and scabrous agaves. Also hybrids with *Agave lecheguilla*. **FLIGHT:** Sept.–Oct. (1 flight). **RANGE:** Cen. Ariz., s. N.M., and w. Tex. **HABITAT:** Mountainous terrain with host agaves. **REMARKS:** The agave-feeding giant-skippers rest with wings closed, covering the best potential identification marks. Only more subtle features can be seen on the underside of the resting butterflies.

ARIZONA GIANT-SKIPPER *Agathymus aryxna*   **PL. 44**
2–2⅜ in. (50–61 mm). Upperside: *Both wings suffused with orange,* especially basally. Postmedian *band of orange-yellow spots on both wings. Underside dark gray with obscure pale gray postmedian spots.* **SIMILAR SPECIES:** (1) Range barely overlaps that of Orange Giant-Skipper in sw. N.M.; (2) also co-occurs with the Huachuca and Poling's Giant-Skippers (see accounts for those species). **EARLY STAGES:** Caterpillar similar to that of Orange Giant-Skipper. **FOOD:** Palmer's agave. **FLIGHT:** Late Aug.–mid-Nov., rarely July (1 flight). **RANGE:** Se. Ariz. and sw. N.M. south into nw. Mex. **HABITAT:** Canyons with good stands of hosts and intermittent water. **REMARKS:** Adults sip moisture at wet places along streams and cliff faces.

BAUER'S GIANT-SKIPPER *Agathymus baueri*   **NOT SHOWN**
2¹⁄₁₆–2¼ in. (53–58 mm). Upperside: *Both wings suffused with orange, especially basally. Postmedian band of orange-yellow spots on*

both wings. Spot band narrow in subspecies *baueri* and wider in subspecies *freemani.* Underside: *Dark gray with postbasal and postmedian bands of gray-white spots.* **SIMILAR SPECIES:** (1) Some apparent intermediates with the Arizona Giant-Skipper occur in s.-cen. Ariz. (2) The Mojave Giant-Skipper occurs just to the north and is found with Utah agave. **EARLY STAGES:** Caterpillar similar to that of Orange Giant-Skipper. **FOOD:** Desert agave, chrysantha agave, and hybrids with Parry's agave. **FLIGHT:** Sept.–Nov. (1 flight). **RANGE:** E. Calif., cen. and ne. Ariz. **HABITAT:** Canyons and rocky slopes in desert mountain ranges.

HUACHUCA GIANT-SKIPPER *Agathymus evansi*   **PL. 44**
1¾–2¼ in. (45–58 mm). *Forewing relatively rounded.* Upperside: Orange overscaling on basal half of hindwing, that of forewing absent or limited. Forewing with broad postmedian band of orange-yellow spots. *Spot band of female often touching spot in discal cell. Hindwing spot band narrower,* but broader than that of the Arizona Giant-Skipper. **SIMILAR SPECIES:** (1) Arizona Giant-Skipper has more pointed forewings, narrower postmedian spot bands, and more extensive orange overscaling. (2) Poling's Giant-Skipper is smaller, has broader spot bands and extensive orange-yellow suffusion at base of both wings. **EARLY STAGES:** Caterpillar green with red or blue tinge, last segment black-brown. Head red-brown. Divided collar black. **FOOD:** Parry's agave. **FLIGHT:** Aug.–Nov. (1 flight). **RANGE:** Se. Ariz. and adjacent Sonora, Mex. **HABITAT:** Open oak woodland in canyons with stands of Parry's agave. **REMARKS:** Adults sip moisture from mud or sand along streamcourses.

MARY'S GIANT-SKIPPER *Agathymus mariae*   **PL. 44**
1¾–2 in. (45–50 mm). Upperside: *Postmedian spot bands narrow, orange-yellow. Spot band on hindwing becomes broader toward ab-*

domen. Underside: *Pale gray with postmedian and postbasal rows of large whitish spots.* **SIMILAR SPECIES:** Occurs only with (1) Coahuila and (2) Orange Giant-Skippers. The former tends to fly earlier, has narrower postmedian spot bands, and spots in its hindwing band become smaller toward the abdomen. The latter has extensive orange suffusion and more extensive pale areas. **EARLY STAGES:** Caterpillar pale blue. Head and collar black. **FOOD:** Lecheguilla agave and hybrids. **FLIGHT:** Late Sept.–Nov. (1 flight). **RANGE:** S. N.M. and w. Tex. south into ne. Mex. **HABITAT:** Chihuahuan Desert scrub.

COAHUILA GIANT-SKIPPER *Agathymus remingtoni*   PL. 44

2–2¼ in. (50–55 mm). Upperside: *Postmedian spot bands very narrow, cream in males, wider and orangish yellow in females. Spot band on hindwing becomes narrow toward abdomen.* Hindwing with basal pale spots usually absent. Underside: Hindwing *dark gray with straight row of pale postmedian spots. Postbasal spots absent.* **SIMILAR SPECIES:** Mary's Giant-Skipper (see above). **EARLY STAGES:** Caterpillar light tan. Head red-brown. Collar black. **FOOD:** Lecheguilla agave. **FLIGHT:** Mid-Sept.–Oct., possible rarely in April (1 flight). **RANGE:** Sw. Tex. along Rio Grande south into ne. Mex. **HABITAT:** Chihuahuan Desert scrub.

CALIFORNIA GIANT-SKIPPER *Agathymus stephensi*   PL. 44

2–2³⁄₁₆ in. (51–56 mm). Upperside: *Wings with narrow postmedian spot bands, cream in males, slightly yellower in females.* Some orange suffusion and hint of pale spots at wing bases. Underside: Hindwing *dark gray with large postmedian and basal cream spots.* **SIMILAR SPECIES:** No other agave-feeders overlap in range. **EARLY STAGES:** Caterpillar white with blue-green tinge. Head and collar brown. **FOOD:** Desert agave. **FLIGHT:** Late Sept.–early Nov. (1 flight). **RANGE:** S.

California Giant-Skipper, Colorado Desert, Calif. Note dark gray hindwing with large cream spot. This is the only giant-skipper found in its relatively small range. Photo by Jim Brock.

Calif. south into n. Baja Calif. **HABITAT:** Desert and foothills with rich array of cacti and agave host plants.

POLING'S GIANT SKIPPER *Agathymus polingi*   **PL. 44**
1 ⅝–1 ¾ in. (41–44 mm). Upperside: Wing bases suffused with or-ange-yellow. Wide postmedian spot band yellow-orange, often touching large spot in discal cell in female. Underside: Dark gray, postmedian row and postbasal spots large and prominent. **SIMILAR SPECIES:** (1) Orange Giant-Skipper is larger and brighter orange. (2) Huachuca Giant-Skipper is also larger, has more rounded forewings, and tends to lack orange suffusion on base of forewing. **EARLY STAGES:** Caterpillar not reported. **FOOD:** Schott's agave. **FLIGHT:** Oct.–Nov. (1 flight). **RANGE:** S. Ariz. and sw. N.M. south into nw. Mex. **HABITAT:** Hillsides with dense stands of host plant and other spine-bearing plants. **REMARKS:** Males perch over dense stands of Schott's agave to await likely mates. Adults do not visit watercourses.

CALIFORNIA GIANT-SKIPPER

POLING'S GIANT-SKIPPER

MOJAVE GIANT-SKIPPER *Agathymus alliae*   **PL. 44**
2³⁄₁₆–2⅜ in. (56–61 mm). Upperside: *Basal portion of both wings with orange-yellow suffusion. Postmedian spot band of yellow-orange spots, separate on male forewing*, otherwise continuous. Underside: *Dark gray with pale postmedian and postbasal spots varying from small to large.* **SIMILAR SPECIES:** Arizona Giant-Skipper is the only agave-feeder whose range overlaps, but not in the same localities. This species has more-orange spots above and tends to have larger pale spots on the underside of the hindwing. **EARLY STAGES:** Caterpillar white with green or blue tinge. **FOOD:** Utah agave. **FLIGHT:** Sept.–Oct. (1 flight). **RANGE:** Se. Calif., s. Nev., sw. Utah, and nw. Ariz. **HABITAT:** Canyons with open pine woodland and desert.

YUCCA GIANT-SKIPPER *Megathymus yuccae*   **PL. 44**
1⅞–3⅛ in. (48–79 mm). Black. Upperside: Forewing with small white spots near apex and costa; *yellow submarginal band on outer margin*. Hindwing with *yellow band on outer margin*. Females with additional spots on hindwing. Underside: Hindwing *gray with white marks on costa.* **SIMILAR SPECIES:** Strecker's Giant Skipper is usually larger, flies later where the two species are found together, and has a series of larger postmedian white spots on the hindwing below. **EARLY STAGES:** Caterpillar white with black shield behind head and black head. **FOOD:** Yuccas. **FLIGHT:** Mid-Feb.–mid-May (1 flight). **RANGE:** Southeast from se. Va. south to s. peninsular Fla., west to Ark. and La. In West from s. Calif. and cen. Nev. east to Neb. and e. Tex., south to n. Mex. **HABITAT:** Deserts, including high deserts, pinyon-juniper hills, canyons, dunes, and foothills. **REMARKS:** The populations west of the Mississippi R. are sometimes called a separate species, the Southwestern Yucca Skipper (*Megathymus coloradensis*). I consider the group to be one species.

STRECKER'S GIANT-SKIPPER
STRECKER'S GIANT-SKIPPER *Megathymus streckeri*   **PL. 44**
2½–3¹⁄₁₆ in. (64–78 mm). A large western plains relative of the southeastern Cofaqui Skipper. Upperside: Hindwing with *long erect hairlike scales*. Underside: *Hindwing with several large white postmedian spots*. **SIMILAR SPECIES:** Yucca Giant-Skipper is usually smaller, flies earlier, has more-pointed forewings, and lacks postmedian white spots on underside of hindwing. **EARLY STAGES:** Caterpillar yellow-white with brown hairs; shield behind head and plate on rear are both yellow-white. Head dark red-brown. **FOOD:** Small soapweed and other small yuccas. **FLIGHT:** May–July (1 flight). **RANGE:** Se. Mont. and sw. N.D. south to s. Tex. and west to nw. Ariz. and sw. Utah. **HABITAT:** Short-grass prairie, sand hills, rocky bluffs.

URSINE GIANT-SKIPPER
URSINE GIANT-SKIPPER *Megathymus ursus*   **PL. 44**
2½–3¼ in. (63–83 mm). *Antennae white*. Fringes predominantly white, faintly black checked. Upperside: Forewing with *broad yellow or yellow-orange postmedian band*. Hindwing *black except for narrow white strip along leading edge*. Underside: Hindwing *primarily gray-white with small black area at base. Two small white spots just along leading edge*. **SIMILAR SPECIES:** Yucca Giant-Skipper has black antennae and more pointed forewings; on upperside it has narrower band on forewing and yellow marginal band on hindwing. Below, hindwing has less extensive gray. **EARLY STAGES:** Caterpillar white. Head, collar, and anal plate black. **FOOD:** Schott's yucca, banana yucca, and Arizona yucca. **FLIGHT:** May–Sept., mainly July–Aug. (1 flight). **RANGE:** S. Ariz., s. N.M., and w. Tex. (subspecies *violae*) south into n. Mex. **HABITAT:** Canyon bottoms with large yuccas near lower edge of oak belt in southwestern mountains. **REMARKS:** Despite its being the largest, bulkiest western skipper, adults are rarely observed.

MANFREDA GIANT-SKIPPER

Stallingsia maculosa   **PL. 44**

1⅞–2 in. (47–50 mm). Brown-black. Upperside: Forewing has *postmedian series of small oval cream spots.* Underside: Hindwing *brown-black with gray dusting* outwardly. **SIMILAR SPECIES:** No similar skippers, such as *Agathymus* giant-skippers, are found in this butterfly's former range. **EARLY STAGES:** Caterpillar white with tan hairs; shield behind head brown; plate on rear whitish; head pale tan. **FOOD:** Manfreda. **FLIGHT:** April–May, Sept.–Oct. (2 flights). **RANGE:** S. Tex. west possibly to Dimmit Co. and ne. Mex. **HABITAT:** Subtropical thorn forest and pine forest. **REMARKS:** This species may now be extinct because of destruction of its habitat—stands of *Manfreda.*

LIFE LIST

GLOSSARY

REFERENCES

INDEX TO PLANTS

INDEX TO BUTTERFLIES

LIFE LIST
BUTTERFLIES OF WESTERN NORTH AMERICA AND HAWAII

Keep a life list, checking the butterflies you have seen. Or keep a checklist of the butterflies in your collection.

This list covers those species that have been found in western North America west of the 100th meridian and those few additional species found in the Hawaiian Islands. It includes all of the species mentioned in the text, but does not include undocumented species.

This list follows the order found in the Miller and Brown 1981 *Catalogue/Checklist of the Butterflies of North America* and the supplement to the list by Ferris (1989), both published as *Memoirs of the Lepidopterists' Society,* except that skippers are placed after the true butterflies. Generic name usage is conservative and follows that used in the *Peterson Field Guide to Butterflies of Eastern North America* and other recent works. The English (common) names conform to the North American Butterfly Association's *Common Names of North American Butterflies.*

The list that follows lists superfamily, family, and subfamily categories. Species within genera are numbered, and those names representing taxa not found in western North America are indicated by an asterisk. Those persons interested in subspecies names should refer to regional handbooks. So many populations of western butterflies have been given subspecies names that space prevents their being listed here. Some relatively distinct subspecies are mentioned in the text.

PARNASSIANS AND SWALLOWTAILS: PAPILIONIDAE

PARNASSIANS: SUBFAMILY PARNASSINAE
____Eversmann's Parnassian *Parnassius eversmanni* Ménétriés

____Clodius Parnassian *Parnassius clodius* Ménétriés
____Phoebus Parnassian *Parnassius phoebus* (Fabricius)
____Sierra Nevada Parnassian *Parnassius behrii* W. H. Edwards
____Rocky Mountain Parnassian *Parnassius smintheus* Doubleday

SWALLOWTAILS: SUBFAMILY PAPILIONINAE
____White-dotted Cattleheart *Parides alopius* Godman and Salvin
____Pipevine Swallowtail *Battus philenor* (Linnaeus)
____Polydamas Swallowtail *Battus polydamas* (Linnaeus)
____Zebra Swallowtail *Eurytides marcellus* (Cramer)
____Black Swallowtail *Papilio polyxenes* Fabricius
____Old World Swallowtail *Papilio machaon* Linnaeus
____Anise Swallowtail *Papilio zelicaon* Lucas
____Indra Swallowtail *Papilio indra* Reakirt
____Xuthus Swallowtail *Papilio xuthus* Linnaeus
____Giant Swallowtail *Papilio cresphontes* (Cramer)
____Thoas Swallowtail *Papilio thoas* (Linnaeus)
____Ornythion Swallowtail *Papilio ornythion* Boisduval
____Broad-banded Swallowtail *Papilio astyalus* Godart
____Ruby-spotted Swallowtail *Papilio anchisiades* Esper
____Eastern Tiger Swallowtail *Papilio glaucus* Linnaeus
____Canadian Tiger Swallowtail *Papilio canadensis* Rothschild
     and Jordan
____Western Tiger Swallowtail *Papilio rutulus* Lucas
____Pale Swallowtail *Papilio eurymedon* Lucas
____Two-tailed Swallowtail *Papilio mutlicaudatus* W. F. Kirby
____Three-tailed Swallowtail *Papilio pilumnus* Boisduval
____Spicebush Swallowtail *Papilio troilus* Linnaeus
____Palamedes Swallowtail *Papilio palamedes* Drury

WHITES AND SULPHURS: PIERIDAE

WHITES: SUBFAMILY PIERINAE
____Mexican Dartwhite *Catasticta nimbice* (Boisduval)
____Pine White *Neophasia menapia* (C. and R. Felder)
____Chiricahua White *Neophasia terlootii* Behr
____Florida White *Appias drusilla* (Cramer)
____Becker's White *Pontia beckerii* (W. H. Edwards)
____Spring White *Pontia sisymbrii* (Boisduval)
____Checkered White *Pontia protodice* (Boisduval and Leconte)
____Western White *Pontia occidentalis* (Reakirt)
____Arctic White *Pieris angelika* Eitschberger
____Mecky's White *Pieris meckyae* Eitschberger
____Margined White *Pieris marginalis* Scudder
____Mustard White *Pieris oleracea* Harris

____Cabbage White *Pieris rapae* Linnaeus
____Great Southern White *Ascia monuste* Linnaeus
____Giant White *Ganyra josephina* (Godart)
____Howarth's White *Ganyra howarthi* (Dixey)
____Large Marble *Euchloe ausonides* Lucas
____Green Marble *Euchloe naina* Kozhantshikov
____Northern Marble *Euchloe creusa* Doubleday
____Sonoran Marble *Euchloe guaymasensis* Opler
____Olympia Marble *Euchloe olympia* W. H. Edwards
____California Marble *Euchloe hyantis* (W. H. Edwards)
____Desert Marble *Euchloe lotta* Beutenmüller
____Desert Orangetip *Anthocharis cethura* C. and R. Felder
____Pacific Orangetip *Anthocharis sara* Lucas
____Southern Rocky Mountain Orangetip *Anthocharis julia* W. H. Edwards
____Stella Orangetip *Anthocharis stella* W. H. Edwards
____Southwestern Orangetip *Anthocharis thoosa* (Scudder)
____Gray Marble *Anthocharis lanceolata* (Lucas)
____Falcate Orangetip *Anthocharis midea* (Hübner)

SULPHURS AND YELLOWS: SUBFAMILY COLIADINAE
____Clouded Sulphur *Colias philodice* Godart
____Orange Sulphur *Colias eurytheme* Boisduval
____Western Sulphur *Colias occidentalis* Scudder
____Christina Sulphur *Colias christina* W. H. Edwards
____Queen Alexandra's Sulphur *Colias alexandra* W. H. Edwards
____Harford's Sulphur *Colias harfordii* Hy. Edwards
____Mead's Sulphur *Colias meadii* W. H. Edwards
____Johansen's Sulphur *Colias johanseni* Troubridge and Philip
____Hecla Sulphur *Colias hecla* Lefébvre
____Canada Sulphur *Colias canadensis* Ferris
____Booth's Sulphur *Colias tyche* de Böber
____Labrador Sulphur *Colias nastes* Boisduval
____Scudder's Sulphur *Colias scudderii* Reakirt
____Giant Sulphur *Colias gigantea* Strecker
____Pelidne Sulphur *Colias pelidne* Boisduval and Leconte
____Pink-edged Sulphur *Colias interior* Scudder
____Palaeno Sulphur *Colias palaeno* Linnaeus
____Sierra Sulphur *Colias behrii* W. H. Edwards
____California Dogface *Zerene eurydice* Boiduval
____Southern Dogface *Zerene cesonia* (Stoll)
____White Angled-Sulphur *Anteos clorinde* (Godart)
____Yellow Angled-Sulphur *Anteos maerula* (Fabricius)
____Cloudless Sulphur *Phoebis sennae* (Linnaeus)
____Orange-barred Sulphur *Phoebis philea* (Linnaeus)

____Large Orange Sulphur *Phoebis agarithe* (Boisduval)
____Apricot Sulphur *Phoebis argante* (Fabricius)
____Statira Sulphur *Phoebis statira* (Cramer)
____Tailed Sulphur *Phoebis neocypris* Hübner
____Lyside Sulphur *Kricogonia lyside* (Godart)
____Barred Yellow *Eurema daira* (Godart)
____Boisduval's Yellow *Eurema boisduvaliana* (C. & R. Felder)
____Mexican Yellow *Eurema mexicana* (Boisduval)
____Tailed Orange *Eurema proterpia* (Fabricius)
____Little Yellow *Eurema lisa* (Boisduval and Leconte)
____Mimosa Yellow *Eurema nise* (Cramer)
____Dina Yellow *Eurema dina* (Poey)
____Sleepy Orange *Eurema nicippe* (Cramer)
____Dainty Sulphur *Nathalis iole* Boisduval

HARVESTERS, COPPERS, HAIRSTREAKS, AND BLUES: LYCAENIDAE:

HARVESTERS: SUBFAMILY MILETINAE
____Harvester *Feniseca tarquinius* (Fabricius)

COPPERS: SUBFAMILY LYCAENINAE
____Tailed Copper *Lycaena arota* (Boisduval)
____American Copper *Lycaena phlaeas* (Linnaeus)
____Lustrous Copper *Lycaena cupreus* (W. H. Edwards)
____Great Copper *Lycaena xanthoides* (Boisduval)
____Gray Copper *Lycaena dione* (Scudder)
____Bronze Copper *Lycaena hyllus* (Cramer)
____Edith's Copper *Lycaena editha* (Mead)
____Gorgon Copper *Lycaena gorgon* (Boisduval)
____Ruddy Copper *Lycaena rubidus* (Behr)
____Ferris' Copper *Lycaena ferrisi* K. Johnson and Balogh
____Blue Copper *Lycaena heteronea* Boisduval
____Dorcas Copper *Lycaena dorcas* W. Kirby
____Purplish Copper *Lycaena helloides* (Boisduval)
____Lilac-bordered Copper *Lycaena nivalis* (Boisduval)
____Mariposa Copper *Lycaena mariposa* (Reakirt)
____Hermes Copper *Lycaena hermes* (W. H. Edwards)

HAIRSTREAKS: SUBFAMILY THECLINAE
____Colorado Hairstreak *Hypaurotis crysalus* (W. H. Edwards)
____Golden Hairstreak *Habrodais grunus* (Boisduval)
____Great Purple Hairstreak *Atlides halesus* (Cramer)
____Silver-banded Hairstreak *Chlorostrymon simaethis* (Drury)
____White M Hairstreak *Parrhasius malbum* (Boisduval and Leconte)

____Red-spotted Hairstreak *Tmolus echion* (Linnaeus)

____Leda Ministreak *Ministrymon leda* (W. H. Edwards)

____Gray Ministreak *Ministrymon azia* (Hewitson)

____Arizona Hairstreak *Erora quaderna* (Hewitson)

____Sonoran Hairstreak *Hypostrymon critola* (Hewitson)

____Red-banded Hairstreak *Calycopis cecrops* (Fabricius)

____Dusky-blue Groundstreak *Calycopis isobeon* (Butler and H. Druce)

____Creamy Stripe-streak *Arawacus jada* (Hewitson)

____Marius Hairstreak *Rekoa marius* Lucas

____Soapberry Hairstreak *Phaeostrymon alcestis* (W. H. Edwards)

____Southern Hairstreak *Fixsenia favonius* (J.E. Smith)

____Ilavia Hairstreak *Fixsenia ilavia* (Beutenmüller)

____Poling's Hairstreak *Fixsenia polingi* (Barnes and Benjamin)

____Behr's Hairstreak *Satyrium behrii* (W. H. Edwards)

____Sooty Hairstreak *Satyrium fuliginosum* (W. H. Edwards)

____Acadian Hairstreak *Satyrium acadica* (W. H. Edwards)

____California Hairstreak *Satyrium californica* (W. H. Edwards)

____Sylvan Hairstreak *Satyrium sylvinus* (Boisduval)

____Coral Hairstreak *Satyrium titus* (Fabricius)

____Edwards' Hairstreak *Satyrium edwardsii* (Grote and Robinson)

____Banded Hairstreak *Satyrium calanus* (Hübner)

____Striped Hairstreak *Satyrium liparops* (Leconte)

____Gold-hunter's Hairstreak *Satyrium auretorum* (Boisduval)

____Mountain-Mahogany Hairstreak *Satyrium tetra* (W. H. Edwards)

____Hedgerow Hairstreak *Satyrium saepium* (Boisduval)

____Amyntor Greenstreak *Cyanophrys amyntor* (Cramer)

____Long-winged Greenstreak *Cyanophrys longula* (Hewitson)

____Western Green Hairstreak *Callophrys affinis* (W. H. Edwards)

____Coastal Green Hairstreak *Callophrys dumetorum* (Boisduval)

____Desert Green Hairstreak *Callophrys comstocki* Henne

____Sheridan's Hairstreak *Callophrys sheridanii* (W. H. Edwards)

____Thicket Hairstreak *Callophrys spinetorum* (Hewitson)

____Johnson's Hairstreak *Callophrys johnsoni* (Skinner)

____Nelson's Hairstreak *Callophrys nelsoni* (Boisduval)

____Muir's Hairstreak *Callophrys muiri* (Hy. Edwards)

____Juniper Hairstreak *Callophrys gryneus* (Hübner)

____Thorne's Hairstreak *Callophrys thornei* (J.W. Brown)

____Xami Hairstreak *Callophrys xami* (Reakirt)

____Sandia Hairstreak *Callophrys mcfarlandi* (P. Ehrlich and Clench)

____Brown Elfin *Callophrys augustinus* (W. Kirby)

____Desert Elfin *Callophrys fotis* (Strecker)

____Moss' Elfin *Callophrys mossii* (Hy. Edwards)

____Hoary Elfin *Callophrys polios* (Cook and Watson)

____Henry's Elfin *Callophrys henrici* (Grote and Robinson)

_____Eastern Pine Elfin *Callophrys niphon* Hübner
_____Western Pine Elfin *Callophrys eryphon* (Boisduval)
_____Gray Hairstreak *Strymon melinus* Hübner
_____Avalon Scrub-Hairstreak *Strymon avalona* (W.G. Wright)
_____Red-lined Scrub-Hairstreak *Strymon bebrycia* (Hewitson)
_____Yojoa Scrub-Hairstreak *Strymon yojoa* (Reakirt)
_____Lacey's Scrub-Hairstreak *Strymon alea* (Godman and Salvin)
_____Mallow Scrub-Hairstreak *Strymon istapa* (Reakirt)
_____Tailless Scrub-Hairstreak *Strymon cestri* (Reakirt)
_____Lantana Scrub-Hairstreak *Strymon bazochii* (Godart)
_____Bromeliad Scrub-Hairstreak *Strymon serapio* (Godman and Salvin)

BLUES: SUBFAMILY POLYOMMATINAE
_____Western Pygmy-Blue *Brephidium exile* Scudder
_____Cassius Blue *Leptotes cassius* (Cramer)
_____Marine Blue *Leptotes marina* (Reakirt)
_____Pea Blue *Lampides boeticus* (Linnaeus)
_____Cyna Blue *Zizula cyna* (W. H. Edwards)
_____Ceraunus Blue *Hemiargus ceraunus* (Fabricius)
_____Reakirt's Blue *Hemiargus isola* (Reakirt)
_____Eastern Tailed-Blue *Everes comyntas* (Godart)
_____Western Tailed-Blue *Everes amyntula* (Boisduval)
_____Spring Azure *Celastrina ladon* (Cramer)
_____Summer Azure *Celastrina neglecta* (W. H. Edwards)
_____Hops Azure *Celastrina humulus* Scott and D. Wright
_____Sonoran Blue *Philotes sonorensis* (C. Felder and R. Felder)
_____Western Square-dotted Blue *Euphilotes battoides* (Behr)
_____Bernardino Dotted-Blue *Euphilotes bernardino* (Barnes and McDunnough)
_____Ellis' Dotted-Blue *Euphilotes ellisi* (Shields)
_____Bauer's Dotted-Blue *Euphilotes baueri* (Shields)
_____Intermediate Dotted-Blue *Euphilotes intermedia* (Barnes and McDunnough)
_____Pacific Dotted-Blue *Euphilotes enoptes* (Boisduval)
_____Mojave Dotted-Blue *Euphilotes mojave* (Watson and W.P. Comstock)
_____Rocky Mountain Dotted-Blue *Euphilotes ancilla* (Barnes and McDunnough)
_____Pallid Dotted-Blue *Euphilotes pallescens* (Tilden and Downey)
_____Rita Dotted-Blue *Euphilotes rita* (Barnes and McDunnough)
_____Spalding's Dotted-Blue *Euphilotes spaldingi* (Barnes and McDunnough)
_____Small Dotted-Blue *Philotiella speciosa* (Hy. Edwards)
_____Arrowhead Blue *Glaucopsyche piasus* (Boisduval)
_____Silvery Blue *Glaucopsyche lygdamus* (Doubleday)

____Cranberry Blue *Vacciniina optilete* (Knoch)
____Hawaiian Blue *Vaga blackburni* (Tuely)
____Arctic Blue *Agriades glandon* (de Prunner)
____Sierra Nevada Blue *Agriades podarce* (C. Felder and R. Felder)
____Cassiope Blue *Agriades cassiope* Emmel and Emmel
____Northern Blue *Lycaeides idas* (Linnaeus)
____Melissa Blue *Lycaeides melissa* (W. H. Edwards)
____Greenish Blue *Plebejus saepiolus* (Boisduval)
____San Emigdio Blue *Plebulina emigdionis* (F. Grinnell)
____Boisduval's Blue *Icaricia icarioides* (Boisduval)
____Shasta Blue *Icaricia shasta* (W. H. Edwards)
____Acmon Blue *Icaricia acmon* (Westwood and Hewitson)
____Lupine Blue *Icaricia lupini* (Boisduval)
____Veined Blue *Icaricia neurona* (Skinner)

METALMARKS: FAMILY RIODINIDAE

____Fatal Metalmark *Calephelis nemesis* (W. H. Edwards)
____Wright's Metalmark *Calephelis wrighti* Holland
____Rounded Metalmark *Calephelis nilus* (C. Felder & R. Felder)
____Rawson's Metalmark *Calephelis rawsoni* McAlpine
____Zela Metalmark *Emesis zela* Butler
____Ares Metalmark *Emesis ares* (W. H. Edwards)
____Maria's Metalmark *Lasaia maria* Clench
____Mormon Metalmark *Apodemia mormo* (C. Felder & R. Felder)
____Behr's Metalmark *Apodemia virgulti* (Behr)
____Sonoran Metalmark *Apodemia mejicanus* (Behr)
____Mexican Metalmark *Apodemia duryi* (W. H. Edwards)
____Hepburn's Metalmark *Apodemia hepburni* Godman and Salvin
____Palmer's Metalmark *Apodemia palmeri* (W. H. Edwards)
____Crescent Metalmark *Apodemia phyciodoides* Barnes and Benjamin
____Nais Metalmark *Apodemia nais* (W. H. Edwards)
____Chisos Metalmark *Apodemia chisosensis* H.A. Freeman

BRUSHFOOT BUTTERFLIES: FAMILY NYMPHALIDAE

SNOUT BUTTERLIES: SUBFAMILY LIBYTHEINAE
____American Snout *Libytheana carinenta* (Cramer)

LONGWINGS AND FRITILLARIES: SUBFAMILY HELICONIINAE
____Gulf Fritillary *Agraulis vanillae* Linnaeus
____Mexican Silverspot *Dione moneta* Hübner
____Julia *Dryas julia* (Fabricius)

_____Isabella's Heliconian *Eueides isabella* (Stoll)
_____Zebra *Heliconius charithonius* (Linnaeus)
_____Variegated Fritillary *Euptoieta claudia* (Cramer)
_____Mexican Fritillary *Euptoieta hegesia* (Cramer)
_____Great Spangled Fritillary *Speyeria cybele* (Fabricius)
_____Aphrodite Fritillary *Speyeria aphrodite* (Fabricius)
_____Regal Fritillary *Speyeria idalia* (Drury)
_____Nokomis Fritillary *Speyeria nokomis* (W. H. Edwards)
_____Edwards' Fritillary *Speyeria edwardsii* (Reakirt)
_____Coronis Fritillary *Speyeria coronis* (Behr)
_____Carol's Fritillary *Speyeria carolae* (dos Passos and Grey)
_____Zerene Fritillary *Speyeria zerene* (Boisduval)
_____Callippe Fritillary *Speyeria callippe* (Boisduval)
_____Great Basin Fritillary *Speyeria egleis* (Behr)
_____Unsilvered Fritillary *Speyeria adiaste* (W. H. Edwards)
_____Atlantis Fritllary *Speyeria atlantis* (W. H. Edwards)
_____Northwestern Fritillary *Speyeria hesperis* (W. H. Edwards)
_____Hydaspe Fritillary *Speyeria hydaspe* (Boisduval)
_____Mormon Fritillary *Speyeria mormonia* (Boisduval)
_____Mountain Fritillary *Boloria napaea* (Hoffmansegg)
_____Bog Fritillary *Boloria eunomia* (Esper)
_____Silver-bordered Fritillary *Boloria selene* (Holland)
_____Meadow Fritillary *Boloria bellona* (Fabricius)
_____Pacific Fritillary *Boloria epithore* (W. H. Edwards)
_____Frigga Fritillary *Boloria frigga* (Thunberg)
_____Dingy Fritillary *Boloria improba* (Butler)
_____Relict Fritillary *Boloria kriemhild* (Strecker)
_____Polaris Fritillary *Boloria polaris* (Boisduval)
_____Freija Fritllary *Boloria freija* (Thunberg)
_____Beringian Fritillary *Boloria natazhati* (Gibson)
_____Alberta Fritillary *Boloria alberta* (W. H. Edwards)
_____Astarte Fritillary *Boloria astarte* (Doubleday and Hewitson)
_____Arctic Fritillary *Boloria chariclea* (Schneider)

BRUSHFOOTS: SUBFAMILY NYMPHALINAE
_____Dotted Checkerspot *Poladryas minuta* (W. H. Edwards)
_____Theona Checkerspot *Thessalia theona* (Ménétriés)
_____Black Checkerspot *Thessalia cyneas* (Godman and Salvin)
_____Fulvia Checkerspot *Thessalia fulvia* (W. H. Edwards)
_____Leanira Checkerspot *Thessalia leanira* (C. and R. Felder)
_____California Patch *Chlosyne californica* Butler
_____Bordered Patch *Chlosyne lacinia* (Geyer)
_____Definite Patch *Chlosyne definita* (Aaron)
_____Banded Patch *Chlosyne endeis* (Godman and Salvin)
_____Red-spotted Patch *Chlosyne marina* (Hübner)
_____Crimson Patch *Chlosyne janais* (Drury)

____Rosita Patch *Chlosyne rosita* Hall
____Gorgone Checkerspot *Chlosyne gorgone* (Hübner)
____Silvery Checkerspot *Chlosyne nycteis* (Doubleday and Hewitson)
____Harris' Checkerspot *Chlosyne harrisii* (Scudder)
____Northern Checkerspot *Chlosyne palla* (Boisduval)
____Sagebrush Checkerspot *Chlosyne acastus* (W. H. Edwards)
____Gabb's Checkerspot *Chlosyne gabbii* (Behr)
____Rockslide Checkerspot *Chlosyne whitneyi* (Behr)
____Hoffmann's Checkerspot *Chlosyne hoffmanni* (Behr)
____Elf *Microtia elva* H.W. Bates
____Tiny Checkerspot *Dymasia dymas* (W. H. Edwards)
____Elada Checkerspot *Texola elada* (Hewitson)
____Texan Crescent *Phyciodes texana* (W. H. Edwards)
____Tulcis Crescent *Phyciodes tulcis* (H.W. Bates)
____Vesta Crescent *Phyciodes vesta* (W. H. Edwards)
____Phaon Crescent *Phyciodes phaon* (W. H. Edwards)
____Pearl Crescent *Phyciodes tharos* (Drury)
____Northern Crescent *Phyciodes cocyta* (Cramer)
____Tawny Crescent *Phyciodes batesii* (Reakirt)
____Field Crescent *Phyciodes pratensis* (Behr)
____Painted Crescent *Phyciodes picta* (W. H. Edwards)
____California Crescent *Phyciodes orseis* W. H. Edwards
____Pale Crescent *Phyciodes pallida* (W. H. Edwards)
____Mylitta Crescent *Phyciodes mylitta* (W. H. Edwards)
____Gillette's Checkerspot *Euphydryas gillettii* (Barnes)
____Variable Checkerspot *Euphydryas chalcedona* (Doubleday)
____Edith's Checkerspot *Euphydryas editha* (Boisduval)
____Baltimore Checkerspot *Euphydryas phaeton* (Drury)
____Question Mark *Polygonia interrogationis* (Fabricius)
____Eastern Comma *Polygonia comma* (Harris)
____Satyr Comma *Polygonia satyrus* (W. H. Edwards)
____Green Comma *Polygonia faunus* (W. H. Edwards)
____Hoary Comma *Polygonia gracilis* (Grote and Robinson)
____Gray Comma *Polygonia progne* (Cramer)
____Compton Tortoiseshell *Nymphalis vaualbum* (Denis and Schiffer-
       müller)
____California Tortoiseshell *Nymphalis californica* (Boisduval)
____Mourning Cloak *Nymphalis antiopa* (Linnaeus)
____Milbert's Tortoiseshell *Nymphalis milberti* (Godart)
____Red Admiral *Vanessa atalanta* (Linnaeus)
____American Lady *Vanessa virginiensis* (Drury)
____Painted Lady *Vanessa cardui* (Linnaeus)
____Kamehameha Lady *Vanessa tameamea* Eschscholtz
____West Coast Lady *Vanessa annabella* (Field)
____Common Buckeye *Junonia coenia* Hübner
____Tropical Buckeye *Junonia genoveva* (Stoll)

_____White Peacock *Anartia jatrophae* (Johansson)
_____Banded Peacock *Anartia fatima* (Fabricius)
_____Malachite *Siproeta stelenes* (Linnaeus)
_____Rusty-tipped Page *Siproeta epaphus* (Latreille)

ADMIRALS AND RELATIVES: SUBFAMILY LIMENITIDINAE
_____White Admiral *Limenitis arthemis* (Drury)
_____Viceroy *Limenitis archippus* (Cramer)
_____Weidemeyer's Admiral *Limenitis weidemeyerii* (W. H. Edwards)
_____Lorquin's Admiral *Limenitis lorquini* (Boisduval)
_____California Sister *Adelpha bredowii* Geyer
_____Mexican Bluewing *Myscelia ethusa* (Boisduval)
_____Blackened Bluewing *Myscelia cyananthe* C. and R. Felder
_____Dingy Purplewing *Eunica monima* (Stoll)
_____Florida Purplewing *Eunica tatila* (Herrich-Schäffer)
_____Tithian Sailor *Dynamine tithia* (Hübner)
_____Anna's Eighty-eight *Diaethria anna* (Guérin-Méneville)
_____Common Mestra *Mestra amymone* (Ménétriés)
_____Red Rim *Biblis hyperia* (Cramer)
_____Gray Cracker *Hamadryas februa* Hübner
_____Black-patched Cracker *Hamadryas atlantis* (Bates)
_____Glaucous Cracker *Hamadryas glauconome* (Bates)
_____Blomfild's Beauty *Smyrna blomfildia* (Hübner)
_____Acheronta *Historis acheronta* (Fabricius)
_____Waiter *Marpesia zerynthia* Hübner
_____Many-banded Daggerwing *Marpesia chiron* (Fabricius)
_____Ruddy Daggerwing *Marpesia petreus* (Cramer)

LEAFWINGS AND RELATIVES: SUBFAMILY CHARAXINAE
_____Tropical Leafwing *Anaea troglodyta* (Fabricius)
_____Goatweed Leafwing *Anaea andria* Scudder
_____Angled Leafwing *Memphis glycerium* (Doubleday)

EMPERORS: SUBFAMILY APATURINAE
_____Hackberry Emperor *Asterocampa celtis* (Boisduval and Leconte)
_____Empress Leilia *Asterocampa leilia* (W. H. Edwards)
_____Tawny Emperor *Asterocampa clyton* (Boisduval and Leconte)
_____Dusky Emperor *Asterocampa idyja* (Hübner)

MORPHOS AND RELATIVES: SUBFAMILY MORPHINAE
_____White Morpho *Morpho polyphemus* Doubleday and Hewitson

SATYRS AND WOOD-NYMPHS: SUBFAMILY SATYRINAE
_____Northern Pearly-eye *Enodia anthedon* A.H. Clark
_____Eyed Brown *Satyrodes eurydice* (Johannson)

_____Nabokov's Satyr *Cyllopsis pyracmon* (Butler)
_____Canyonland Satyr *Cyllopsis pertepida* (Dyar)
_____Little Wood-Satyr *Megisto cymela* (Cramer)
_____Red Satyr *Megisto rubricata* (W. H. Edwards)
_____Pine Satyr *Paramacera allyni* L. Miller
_____Hayden's Ringlet *Coenonympha haydenii* (W. H. Edwards)
_____Common Ringlet *Coenonympha tullia* (Müller)
_____Common Wood-Nymph *Cercyonis pegala* (Fabricius)
_____Great Basin Wood-Nymph *Cercyonis sthenele* (Boisduval)
_____Mead's Wood-Nymph *Cercyonis meadii* (W. H. Edwards)
_____Small Wood-Nymph *Cercyonis oetus* (Boisduval)
_____Vidler's Alpine *Erebia vidleri* Elwes
_____Ross' Alpine *Erebia rossii* (Curtis)
_____Disa Alpine *Erebia disa* (Thunberg)
_____Taiga Alpine *Erebia mancinus* Doubleday and Hewitson
_____Magdalena Alpine *Erebia magdalena* Strecker
_____Mt. McKinley Alpine *Erebia mackinleyensis* Gunder
_____Banded Alpine *Erebia fasciata* Butler
_____Red-disked Alpine *Erebia discoidalis* (W. Kirby)
_____Theano Alpine *Erebia theano* (Tauscher)
_____Four-dotted Alpine *Erebia youngi* Holland
_____Scree Alpine *Erebia anyuica* Kurentzov
_____Reddish Alpine *Erebia lafontainei* Troubridge and Philip
_____Colorado Alpine *Erebia callias* W. H. Edwards
_____Common Alpine *Erebia epipsodea* Butler
_____Red-bordered Satyr *Gyrocheilus patrobas* (Hewitson)
_____Ridings' Satyr *Neominois ridingsii* (W. H. Edwards)
_____Swale Satyr *Neominois wyomingo* Scott
_____Great Arctic *Oeneis nevadensis* (C. and R. Felder)
_____Macoun's Arctic *Oeneis macounii* (W. H. Edwards)
_____Chryxus Arctic *Oeneis chryxus* (Doubleday and Hewitson)
_____Uhler's Arctic *Oeneis uhleri* (Reakirt)
_____Alberta Arctic *Oeneis alberta* Elwes
_____White-veined Arctic *Oeneis bore* (Schneider)
_____Jutta Arctic *Oeneis jutta* (Hübner)
_____Melissa Arctic *Oeneis melissa* (Fabricius)
_____Polixenes Arctic *Oeneis polixenes* (Fabricius)
_____Philip's Arctic *Oeneis rosovi* Kurentzov
_____Sentinel Arctic *Oeneis alpina* Kurentzov

MILKWEED BUTTERFLIES: SUBFAMILY DANAINAE
_____Monarch *Danaus plexippus* (Linnaeus)
_____Queen *Danaus gilippus* (Cramer)
_____Soldier *Danaus eresimus* (Cramer)
_____Tiger Mimic-Queen *Lycorea cleobaea* (Godart)

THE SKIPPERS: SUPERFAMILY HESPERIOIDEA

FAMILY HESPERIIDAE

FIRETIPS: SUBFAMILY PYRRHOPYGINAE
____Dull Firetip *Pyrrhopyge araxes* (Hewitson)

SPREAD-WING SKIPPERS, PYRGINES: SUBFAMILY PYRGINAE
____Mercurial Skipper *Proteides mercurius* (Fabricius)
____Silver-spotted Skipper *Epargyreus clarus* (Cramer)
____Wind's Silverdrop *Epargyreus windi* H.A. Freeman
____Hammock Skipper *Polygonus leo* (Gmelin)
____White-striped Longtail *Chioides catillus* (Cramer)
____Zilpa Longtail *Chioides zilpa* (Butler)
____Gold-spotted Aguna *Aguna asander* (Hewitson)
____Mexican Longtail *Polythrix mexicana* H.A. Freeman
____Short-tailed Skipper *Zestusa dorus* (W. H. Edwards)
____Arizona Skipper *Codatractus arizonensis* (Skinner)
____White-crescent Longtail *Codatractus alcaeus* (Hewitson)
____Desert Mottled Skipper *Codatractus mysie* (Dyar)
____Long-tailed Skipper *Urbanus proteus* (Linnaeus)
____Dorantes Longtail *Urbanus dorantes* (Stoll)
____Plain Longtail *Urbanus simplicius* (Stoll)
____Brown Longtail *Urbanus procne* (Plötz)
____Two-barred Flasher *Astraptes fulgerator* (Walch)
____Golden-Banded Skipper *Autochton cellus* (Boisduval and Leconte)
____Sonoran Banded-Skipper *Autochton pseudocellus* (Coolidge and Clemence)
____Chisos Banded-Skipper *Autochton cinctus* (Plötz)
____Desert Cloudywing *Achalarus casica* (Herrich-Schäffer)
____Skinner's Cloudywing *Achalarus albociliatus* (Mabille)
____Coyote Cloudywing *Achalarus toxeus* (Plötz)
____Northern Cloudywing *Thorybes pylades* (Scudder)
____Southern Cloudywing *Thorybes bathyllus* (J.E. Smith)
____Western Cloudywing *Thorybes diversus* Bell
____Mexican Cloudywing *Thorybes mexicanus* (Herrich-Schäffer)
____Drusius Cloudywing *Thorybes drusius* (W. H. Edwards)
____Potrillo Skipper *Cabares potrillo* (Lucas)
____Fritzgaertner's Flat *Celaenorrhinus fritzgaertneri* (Bailey)
____Mimosa Skipper *Cogia calchas* (Herrich-Schäffer)
____Acacia Skipper *Cogia hippalus* (W. H. Edwards)
____Outis Skipper *Cogia outis* (Skinner)
____Caicus Skipper *Cogia caicus* (Herrich-Schäffer)
____Wind's Skipper *Windia windi* H.A. Freeman
____Mottled Bolla *Bolla clytius* (Godman and Salvin)

____Golden-headed Scallopwing *Staphylus ceos* (W. H. Edwards)
____Mazans Scallopwing *Staphylus mazans* (Reakirt)
____Hayhurst's Scallopwing *Staphylus hayhurstii* (W. H. Edwards)
____Glassy-winged Skipper *Xenophanes tryxus* (Stoll)
____Emorsus Skipper *Antigonus emorsus* (R. Felder)
____Texas Powdered-Skipper *Systasea pulverulenta* (R. Felder)
____Arizona Powdered-Skipper *Systasea zampa* (W. H. Edwards)
____Hermit Skipper *Grais stigmaticus* (Mabille)
____Brown-banded Skipper *Timochares ruptifasciatus* (Plötz)
____White-patched Skipper *Chiomara georgina* (Reakirt)
____Mithrax Skipper *Chiomara mithrax* Möschler
____False Duskywing *Gesta invisus* (Butler and Druce)
____Dreamy Duskywing *Erynnis icelus* (Scudder and Burgess)
____Sleepy Duskywing *Erynnis brizo* (Boisduval and Leconte)
____Juvenal's Duskywing *Erynnis juvenalis* (Fabricius)
____Rocky Mountain Duskywing *Erynnis telemachus* Burns
____Propertius Duskywing *Erynnis propertius* (Scudder and Burgess)
____Meridian Duskywing *Erynnis meridianus* Bell
____Scudder's Duskywing *Erynnis scudderi* (Skinner)
____Horace's Duskywing *Erynnis horatius* (Scudder and Burgess)
____Mournful Duskywing *Erynnis tristis* (Boisduval)
____Mottled Duskywing *Erynnis martialis* (Scudder)
____Pacuvius Duskywing *Erynnis pacuvius* (Lintner)
____Funereal Duskywing *Erynnis funeralis* (Scudder and Burgess)
____Wild Indigo Duskywing *Erynnis baptisiae* (Forbes)
____Afranius Duskywing *Erynnis afranius* (Lintner)
____Persius Duskywing *Erynnis persius* (Scudder)
____Grizzled Skipper *Pyrgus centaureae* (Rambur)
____Two-banded Checkered-Skipper *Pyrgus ruralis* (Boisduval)
____Mountain Checkered-Skipper *Pyrgus xanthus* W. H. Edwards
____Small Checkered-Skipper *Pyrgus scriptura* (Boisduval)
____Common Checkered-Skipper *Pyrgus communis* (Grote)
____White Checkered-Skipper *Pyrgus albescens* (Plötz)
____Tropical Checkered-Skipper *Pyrgus oileus* (Linnaeus)
____Desert Checkered-Skipper *Pyrgus philetas* W. H. Edwards
____Erichson's White-Skipper *Heliopetes domicella* (Erichson)
____Northern White-Skipper *Heliopetes ericetorum* (Boisduval)
____Laviana White-Skipper *Heliopetes lavianus* (Hewitson)
____Common Streaky-Skipper *Celotes nessus* (W. H. Edwards)
____Scarce Streaky-Skipper *Celotes limpia* Burns
____Common Sootywing *Pholisora catullus* (Fabricius)
____Mexican Sootywing *Pholisora mejicanus* (Reakirt)
____Mohave Sootywing *Hesperopsis libya* (Scudder)
____Saltbush Sootywing *Hesperopsis alpheus* (W. H. Edwards)
____MacNeill's Saltbush Sootywing *Hesperopsis gracielae* (MacNeill)

Skipperlings: Subfamily Heteropterinae

____Arctic Skipper *Carterocephalus palaemon* (Pallas)
____Russet Skipperling *Piruna pirus* (W. H. Edwards)
____Four-spotted Skipperling *Piruna polingi* (Barnes)
____Many-spotted Skipperling *Piruna aea* Dyar
____Chisos Skipperling *Piruna haferniki* H.A. Freeman

Grass Skippers: Subfamily Hesperiinae

____Faceted Skipper *Synaptes syraces* (Godman)
____Julia's Skipper *Nastra julia* (H.A. Freeman)
____Banana Skipper *Erionota torus* Evans
____Clouded Skipper *Lerema accius* (J.E. Smith)
____Common Least Skipper *Ancyloxypha numitor* (Fabricius)
____Tropical Least Skipper *Ancyloxypha arene* (W. H. Edwards)
____Garita Skipperling *Oarisma garita* (Reakirt)
____Edwards' Skipperling *Oarisma edwardsii* (Barnes)
____Orange Skipperling *Copaeodes aurantiaca* (Hewitson)
____Southern Skipperling *Copaeodes minima* (W. H. Edwards)
____Sunrise Skipper *Adopaeoides prittwitzi* (Plötz)
____European Skipper *Thymelicus lineola* (Ochsenheimer)
____Fiery Skipper *Hylephila phyleus* (Drury)
____Alkali Skipper *Pseudocopaeodes eunus* (W. H. Edwards)
____Morrison's Skipper *Stinga morrisoni* (W. H. Edwards)
____Uncas Skipper *Hesperia uncas* W. H. Edwards
____Juba Skipper *Hesperia juba* (Scudder)
____Common Branded Skipper *Hesperia comma* (Linnaeus)
____Plains Skipper *Hesperia assiniboia* (Lyman)
____Western Branded Skipper *Hesperia colorado* (Scudder)
____Apache Skipper *Hesperia woodgatei* R.C. Williams
____Ottoe Skipper *Hesperia ottoe* W. H. Edwards
____Leonard's Skipper *Hesperia leonardus* Harris
____Pahaska Skipper *Hesperia pahaska* (Leussler)
____Columbian Skipper *Hesperia columbia* (Scudder)
____Green Skipper *Hesperia viridis* (W. H. Edwards)
____Dotted Skipper *Hesperia attalus* (W. H. Edwards)
____Lindsey's Skipper *Hesperia lindseyi* (Holland)
____Sierra Skipper *Hesperia miriamae* MacNeill
____Dakota Skipper *Hesperia dacotae* (Skinner)
____Indian Skipper *Hesperia sassacus* (Harris)
____Nevada Skipper *Hesperia nevada* (Scudder)
____Sachem *Atalopedes campestris* (Boisduval)
____Rhesus Skipper *Polites rhesus* (W. H. Edwards)
____Carus Skipper *Polites carus* (W. H. Edwards)
____Peck's Skipper *Polites peckius* (W. Kirby)
____Sandhill Skipper *Polites sabuleti* (Boisduval)

_____Mardon Skipper *Polites mardon* (W. H. Edwards)
_____Draco Skipper *Polites draco* (W. H. Edwards)
_____Tawny-edged Skipper *Polites themistocles* (Latreille)
_____Crossline Skipper *Polites origenes* (Fabricius)
_____Long Dash *Polites mystic* (W. H. Edwards)
_____Sonoran Skipper *Polites sonora* (Scudder)
_____Whirlabout *Polites vibex* (Geyer)
_____Northern Broken-dash *Wallengrenia egeremet* (Scudder)
_____Southern Broken-Dash *Wallengrenia otho* (J.E. Smith)
_____Little Glassywing *Pompeius verna* (W. H. Edwards)
_____Arogos Skipper *Atrytone arogos* (Boisduval and Leconte)
_____Delaware Skipper *Anatrytone logan* (W. H. Edwards)
_____Woodland Skipper *Ochlodes sylvanoides* (Boisduval)
_____Rural Skipper *Ochlodes agricola* (Boisduval)
_____Yuma Skipper *Ochlodes yuma* (W. H. Edwards)
_____Hobomok Skipper *Poanes hobomok* (Harris)
_____Zabulon Skipper *Poanes zabulon* (Boisduval and Leconte)
_____Taxiles Skipper *Poanes taxiles* (W. H. Edwards)
_____Broad-winged Skipper *Poanes viator* (W. H. Edwards)
_____Umber Skipper *Poanes melane* (W. H. Edwards)
_____Snow's Skipper *Paratrytone snowi* (W. H. Edwards)
_____Two-spotted Skipper *Euphyes bimacula* (Grote and Robinson)
_____Dun Skipper *Euphyes vestris* (Boisduval)
_____Dusted Skipper *Atrytonopsis hianna* (Scudder)
_____Deva Skipper *Atrytonopsis deva* (W. H. Edwards)
_____Moon-marked Skipper *Atrytonopsis lunus* (W. H. Edwards)
_____Viereck's Skipper *Atrytonopsis vierecki* (Skinner)
_____White-barred Skipper *Atrytonopsis pittacus* (W. H. Edwards)
_____Python Skipper *Atrytonopsis python* (W. H. Edwards)
_____Cestus Skipper *Atrytonopsis cestus* (W. H. Edwards)
_____Sheep Skipper *Atrytonopsis edwardsi* Barnes and McDunnough
_____Simius Roadside-Skipper *"Amblyscirtes" simius* W. H. Edwards
_____Large Roadside-Skipper *Amblyscirtes exoteria* (Herrich-Schäffer)
_____Cassus Roadside-Skipper *Amblyscirtes cassus* W. H. Edwards
_____Bronze Roadside-Skipper *Amblyscirtes aenus* W. H. Edwards
_____Oslar's Roadside-Skipper *Amblyscirtes oslari* (Skinner)
_____Elissa Roadside-Skipper *Amblyscirtes elissa* Godman
_____Pepper and Salt Skipper *Amblyscirtes hegon* (Scudder)
_____Texas Roadside-Skipper *Amblyscirtes texanae* Bell
_____Toltec Roadside-Skipper *Amblyscirtes tolteca* Scudder
_____Slaty Roadside-Skipper *Amblyscirtes nereus* (W. H. Edwards)
_____Nysa Roadside-Skipper *Amblyscirtes nysa* W. H. Edwards
_____Dotted Roadside-Skipper *Amblyscirtes eos* (W. H. Edwards)
_____Common Roadside-Skipper *Amblyscirtes vialis* (W. H. Edwards)
_____Celia's Roadside-Skipper *Amblyscirtes celia* Skinner

____Orange-headed Roadside-Skipper *Amblyscirtes phylace* (W.H. Edwards)
____Orange-edged Roadside-Skipper *Amblyscirtes fimbriata* (Plötz)
____Eufala Skipper *Lerodea eufala* (W. H. Edwards)
____Olive-clouded Skipper *Lerodea arabus* (W. H. Edwards)
____Brazilian Skipper *Calpodes ethlius* (Stoll)
____Wandering Skipper *Panoquina errans* (Skinner)
____Ocola Skipper *Panoquina ocola* (W. H. Edwards)
____Purple-washed Skipper *Panoquina leucas* (Fabricius)
____Violet-banded Skipper *Nyctelius nyctelius* (Latreille)

GIANT-SKIPPERS: SUBFAMILY MEGATHYMINAE
____Orange Giant-Skipper *Agathymus neumoegeni* (W. H. Edwards)
____Arizona Giant-Skipper *Agathymus aryxna* (Dyar)
____Bauer's Giant-Skipper *Agathymus baueri* (Stallings and Turner)
____Huachuca Giant-Skipper *Agathymus evansi* (H.A. Freeman)
____Mary's Giant-Skipper *Agathymus mariae* (Barnes and Benjamin)
____Coahuila Giant-Skipper *Agathymus remingtoni* Stallings and Turner
____California Giant-Skipper *Agathymus stephensi* (Skinner)
____Poling's Giant-Skipper *Agathymus polingi* (Skinner)
____Mojave Giant-Skipper *Agathymus alliae* (D. Stallings and Turner)
____Yucca Giant-Skipper *Megathymus yuccae* (Boisduval and Leconte)
____Strecker's Giant-Skipper *Megathymus streckeri* (Skinner)
____Ursine Giant-Skipper *Agathymus ursus* Poling
____Manfreda Giant-Skipper *Stallingsia maculosus* H.A. Freeman

GLOSSARY

ABDOMEN. The terminal (third) body region of an adult insect.

ALKALINE. Basic, not acidic—as of habitats with soils dominated by alkaline salts.

ALPINE. The area above timberline in mountainous regions.

ANAL. The vein along the inner margin of a butterfly's hindwing (see Figure 3, p. 7).

ANDROCONIA. Specialized wing scales, usually of males, believed to produce odors involved in courtship.

ANGLE. The angle of a butterfly's wing where 2 margins are joined.

ANTENNA(AE). One of two long clubbed filamentous sensory structures on the insect head.

APEX. The tip, referring here to the outer tip of a butterfly's forewing (See Figure 2, p. 6).

APICAL. The area near the apex (see Figure 2, p. 6).

APICULUS. An extension of the antennal club in skippers.

ARCHIPELAGO. A group of islands.

ARCTIC. Found above the Arctic Circle or in arcticlike habitats.

AURORA. The submarginal pink, red, or orange band on the hindwing of certain blues.

BASAL. The wing area closest to the thorax (see Figure 2, p. 6).

BASKER. A butterfly that exposes its wings to sunlight in order to attain flight temperature.

BIOGEOGRAPHER. A person who studies the distribution of animals, plants, and their habitats.

BIOSPHERE. The thin layer of the Earth where life abounds.

BIOTIC PROVINCE. A geographic region within which similar habitats are likely to be occupied by the same sets of animal and plant species.

BOREAL. Pertaining to cooler environments, especially the Canadian, Hudsonian, and Arctic life zones.

BRACKISH. The slightly salty transitional area between saltwater and freshwater environments.

BROAD-LEAF. Non-coniferous woody trees, shrubs, or vines.

CELL. An area of a butterfly wing bounded on all sides by veins.

CHEVRON. The more or less V-shaped postmedian band of pale spots, usually white or silvery.

CHITINOUS. Characteristic of the hard exoskeleton of an insect; made with chitin.

CHRYSALIS (CHRYSALID). The resting stage of development during which a caterpillar, enclosed in a firm, hard case, transforms to an adult.

COLONIST. A butterfly that establishes a temporary or permanent population in a new area.

CONIFER. A needle-bearing tree or shrub, usually but not always evergreen.

CONIFEROUS. A habitat dominated or characterized by conifers.

COSTA. The front or forward edge of a butterfly's wing (see Figure 2, p. 6).

COSTAL MARGIN. The wing area adjacent to the costa (see Figure 2, p. 6).

COXA. The segment of an insect's leg closest to the body.

CREMASTER. The hooklike structures at the terminal end of a chrysalis.

CUBITAL. Pertaining to wing veins.

DECIDUOUS. Capable of detaching; descriptive of trees that lose their leaves and remain bare for at least a brief period.

DIAPAUSE. A state of developmental arrest in insects in which they may pass seasons unfavorable for growth or activity.

DIMORPHIC. Having different forms for the two sexes, or two forms of one sex, as in the yellow and white female forms of most sulphurs.

DIPHENIC. Having two seasonal forms, e.g., summer and winter or dry-season and wet-season forms.

DISCAL CELL. A cell in the center of a butterfly's wing.

DISTAL. That portion which is farthest away from the origin or point of attachment.

DIURNAL. Active during daylight.

DORSAL. The upper portion or surface.

ECOLOGY. The study of animals, plants, and their environments.

ECOREGION. A geographic region characterized by similar ecological features.

EMBRYO. The dividing mass of cells inside the egg destined to become a caterpillar.

EMIGRANT. A butterfly that leaves an area, usually embarking on a long-distance flight.

ESTIVATE. To spend the summer in an inactive state.

ETHYL ACETATE. A chemical used to kill butterflies.

EVAPOTRANSPIRATION. The loss of moisture to the atmosphere due to evaporation.

EVERGREEN. A tree or shrub that keeps its leaves year-round, often a conifer.

EXCRETORY. Pertaining to structures that rid a caterpillar's body of waste products.

EXOSKELETON. The hard outer covering of an insect's body, composed of chitin.

EXTRALIMITAL. Outside of a species' usual distribution.

FAT BODY. Globular structures in an insect's abdomen used to store energy-rich fats and oils.

FEMUR. The second segment of an insect's leg. (Plural: femora.)

FOLD. (as in costal fold or anal fold). A folded-over portion of a butterfly's wing, thought to house scales or hairs that emit chemicals employed during courtship.

FOREWING. The forward wing of each pair.

FRASS. The solid excretory product of caterpillars.

FRENULUM. A series of hooks that holds a moth's forewing and hindwing together in flight.

FUMIGANT. A chemical, usually naphthalene or paradichlorbenzene, used to protect insect collections from "museum pests."

GENITALIA. The structures used in mating.

GLASSINE. A translucent material used to store unmounted butterfly specimens.

GRAVID. Pertaining to female butterflies when carrying eggs.

HABITAT. The place where a butterfly may find all of its necessary resources—its home.

HAIR PENCIL. A packet of hairlike scales on the legs or abdomens of some butterflies and moths—thought to be used in discriminating chemicals during courtship.

HAMMOCK. Groves of trees, usually evergreen, surrounded by brush or marsh habitat.

HEMIMETABOLA. Insects that have an incomplete life cycle, i.e., egg, nymph, adult. See Holometabola.

HEMOLYMPH. The circulatory fluid of insects.

HERBACEOUS. Plants that lack woody stems, often but not always annual.

HERBICIDE. A chemical used to kill plants.

HIBERNATION. The process of overwintering in an inactive or torpid condition.

HINDWING. The rear wing of each pair.

HOLARCTIC. Native to both North America and Eurasia.

HOLOMETABOLA. Insects that have a complete life cycle, i.e., egg, larva, pupa, adult. See Hemimetabola.

IMMIGRANT. A butterfly that enters an area, often after a long-distance flight.

INNER MARGIN. The trailing, or hind, edge of the forewing (see Figure 2, p. 6).

INSECTICIDE. A chemical used to kill insects.

INSTAR. A caterpillar stage between molts.

INTERVEIN. An area between veins on a butterfly wing.

INVERTEBRATE. An animal that lacks a backbone.

LABIAL PALPUS. The mouth part that lies outside the coiled proboscis of adult butterflies. (Plural: palpi.)

LARVA. The eating and growth stage of butterflies, i.e., the caterpillar. (Plural: larvae.)

MARGINAL. Pertaining to the outer margin of the wing (see Figure 2, p. 6).

MEDIAL. Pertaining to the fourth wing vein and its three branches (see Figure 3, p. 7).

MEDIAN. The area of a butterfly's wing halfway between the base and apex.

MESOTHORAX. The central portion of the thorax, with which the forewings and middle pair of legs articulate.

METATHORAX. The rear portion of the thorax with which the hindwings and rear pair of legs move.

MIGRANT. An insect that makes regular two-way long-distance flights.

MOLTING. The process by which a caterpillar sheds its exoskeleton; also termed ecdysis.

NAPHTHALENE. A chemical fumigant.

NECTAR. The sugar fluid secreted by flowers of many plants. The principal food of many kinds of adult butterflies.

NOCTURNAL. Active at night.

NUDUM. The inner part of the antennal club, bare or sparsely covered with scales.

OMMATIDIUM. One of the visual elements that make up an insect's compound eye. (Plural: ommatidia.)

OUTER MARGIN. The outer edge of a butterfly's wing (see Figure 2, p. 6).

OVIPOSIT. To deposit one or more eggs.

OVIPOSITION. The process of depositing eggs.

PALPUS. An insect mouthpart; herein usually a labial palp.

PARADICHLORBENZENE (PDB). A chemical fumigant.

PARASITE. A small animal that lives on and feeds on a larger animal.

PARASITOIDISM. Feeding by insect parasites on another insect's immature stages.

PATROLLING. A mate-locating behavior of butterflies characterized by males flying through likely habitat in search of receptive females.

PERCHING. A mate-locating behavior of butterflies characterized by males perching on objects or spaces by which receptive females are likely to pass.

PERENNIAL. Plants that live two or more years.

PESTICIDE. A chemical agent used to kill pest organisms.

POSTBASAL. That part of the wing that lies just beyond the base (see Figure 2, p. 6).

POSTMEDIAN. That part of the wing that lies just beyond the central, or median, portion (see Figure 2, p. 6).

PROBOSCIS. The coiled tube through which adult butterflies imbibe nectar and other fluids.

PROLEG. One of the front pair of legs.

PROTEINACEOUS. Composed of proteins.

PULVILLUS. The pad between the tarsal claws of an adult butterfly's legs.

PUPA. The resting stage within which a caterpillar transforms to an adult. (Plural: pupae.)

PUPATE. To form a pupa or chrysalis; to pass through a pupal stage.

RADIAL VEINS. Butterfly wing veins that terminate in the apical area (see Figure 3, p. 7).

REHYDRATE. To restore the former moisture content.

SEGMENT. One of the ringlike units of a caterpillar or an adult butterfly's abdomen.

SETA. The hair or scale of a caterpillar or adult butterfly. (Plural: setae.)

SPIRACLE. A circular or oval breathing hole along the side of a caterpillar or adult butterfly.

STIGMA. A group of specialized scales on the forewing of most male branded skippers.

SUBAPICAL. Just inward from the apical part of the wing (see Figure 2, p. 6).

SUBARCTIC. Those habitats or environments that lie just below the Arctic Circle.

SUBCOSTAL VEIN. The second wing vein, unbranched (see Figure 3, p. 7).

SUBDORSAL. Referring to marks or stripes on a caterpillar just below the dorsal area.

SUBMARGINAL. That part of the wing that lies between the median and postbasal areas (see Figure 2, p. 6).

SUCTORIAL. Capable of sucking.

TAIGA. A broad zone of stunted trees, lakes, and bogs lying south of the tundra.

TARSAL CLAW. The claw at the end of an insect's leg.

TARSOMERES. The five separate segments of the tarsus, the most distal portion of an insect leg.

TARSUS. The last portion of an insect's leg, composed of several segments.

TEGULA (ae). The scale-covered flaplike structure found at the outer edge of the thorax on butterflies and moths. Color of this structure is important in identification of some swallowtails.

TERMINAL LINE. A line of scales on the margin of a butterfly wing. Often a black line on the underside of blues.

TERRITORIALITY. A behavior by which a male protects and occupies a specific piece of landscape.

THERMOREGULATION. The process of regulating body temperature.

THORAX. The central portion of an insect's body.

TIBIA. That part of an insect's leg lying between the femur and tarsus. (Plural: tibiae.)

TIMBERLINE. The line above which trees cannot grow.

TORNUS. The wing angle between the outer and inner margins (see Figure 2, p. 6).

TRANSLUCENT. Capable of transmitting light, but not a clear image.

TROPICAL. Occurring between the tropic of Cancer and tropic of Capricorn; occurring in tropical environments.

TUBERCLE. A small rounded projection on the body surface.

TUNDRA. An arctic or alpine environment with dense growths of short herbaceous vegetation.

ULTRAVIOLET. Light characterized by short wavelengths, some of which are beyond the visible range.

REFERENCES

GENERAL

Brewer, Jo, and Dave Winter. 1986. *Butterflies and Moths—A Companion to Your Field Guide*. New York: Phalarope Books.

Douglas, M. M. 1986. *The Lives of Butterflies*. Ann Arbor: University of Michigan Press.

Edwards, William Henry. 1868-1897. *The Butterflies of North America*. 3 vols. Philadelphia: American Entomological Society, vol. 1; Boston: Houghton Mifflin Co., vols. 2 & 3.

Ferris, C. D., ed. 1989. *Supplement to: A Catalogue/Checklist of the Butterflies of America North of Mexico*. Lepidopterists' Memoir no. 3.

Glassberg, J. 1995. *Common Names of North American Butterflies Occurring North of Mexico*. Morristown, N.J.: North American Butterfly Association.

Howe, W. H. 1975. *The Butterflies of North America*. Garden City, N.Y.: Doubleday and Co.

Klots, A. B. 1951. *A Field Guide to the Butterflies of Eastern North America*. Boston: Houghton Mifflin Co.

Layberry, R. A., P. W. Hall, and J. D. Lafontaine. 1998. *The Butterflies of Canada*. Toronto: University of Toronto Press.

Miller, J. Y., ed. 1991. *The Common Names of North American Butterflies*. Washington, D.C.: Smithsonian Institution Press.

Miller, L. D., and Brown, F. M. 1981. *Catalog/Checklist of the Butterflies of North America*. Lepidopterists' Society Memoir no. 2.

Mitchell, Robert T., and Herbert S. Zim. 1962. *Butterflies and Moths*. New York: Golden Press.

Opler, P. A. 1994. *First Guide to Butterflies and Moths*. Boston: Houghton Mifflin Co.

Opler, P. A., and J. A. Ebner. 1996. *Butterflies for Beginners*. Videotape. New York: MasterVision.

Opler, P. A., and G. O. Krizek. 1984. *Butterflies East of the Plains*. Baltimore: Johns Hopkins University Press.

Pyle, R. M. 1981. *The Audubon Society Field Guide to North American Butterflies*. New York: Chanticleer Press.

_____. 1995. *The Audubon Society Handbook for Butterfly Watchers*. Boston: Houghton Mifflin Co.

Scott, J. A. 1986. *The Butterflies of North America*. Stanford, Calif.: Stanford University Press.

Scudder, Samuel H. 1989. *The Butterflies of the Eastern United States and Canada with Special Reference to New England*. Cambridge, Mass.: Samuel Scudder.

Wright, A. B. 1993. *First Guide to Caterpillars*. Boston: Houghton Mifflin Co.

STATE AND REGIONAL

Bailowitz, R. A., and J. P. Brock. 1991. *Butterflies of Southeastern Arizona*. Tucson, Ariz.: Sonoran Arthropod Studies, Inc.

Bird, C. D., C. J. Hilchie, N. G. Kondla, E. M. Pike, and F. A. H. Sperling. 1995. *Alberta Butterflies*. Edmonton, Alta.: The Provincial Museum of Alberta.

Brown, F. M., J. D. Eff, and B. Rotger. 1957. *Colorado Butterflies*. Denver: Denver Museum of Natural History.

Brown, J. W., H. G. Real, and D. K. Faulkner. 1992. *Butterflies of Baja California*. Beverly Hills, Calif.: Lepidoptera Research Foundation.

Comstock, J. A. 1927. *Butterflies of California*. Los Angeles, Calif.: Privately published. (Facsimile available from Entomological Reprint Specialists, Los Angeles, Calif.)

Dameron, W. 1997. *Searching for Butterflies in Southern California*. Los Angeles: Flutterby Press.

Dankert, N., H. Nagel, and T. Nightengale. 1993. *Butterfly Distribution Maps—Nebraska*. Kearney: University of Nebraska.

Dornfeld, E. J. 1980. *The Butterflies of Oregon*. Forest Grove, Ore.: Timber Press.

Elrod, M. J. 1906. *The Butterflies of Montana*. Bulletin of the University of Montana 30: 1–174.

Ely, C., M. D. Schwilling, and M. E. Rolfs. 1986. *An Annotated List of the Butterflies of Kansas*. Fort Hays Studies (Science) 7. Fort Hays, Kans.: Fort Hays State University.

Emmel, T. C., and J. F. Emmel. 1973. *The Butterflies of Southern California*. Natural History Museum of Los Angeles County, Science Series no. 26.

Ferris, C. D. 1971. *An Annotated Checklist of the Rhopalocera (Butterflies) of Wyoming.* University of Wyoming Agriculture Experiment Station Science Monograph 23: 1–75.

Ferris, C. D., and F. M. Brown. 1980. *Butterflies of the Rocky Mountain States.* Norman: University of Oklahoma Press.

Garth, J. S. 1950. *Butterflies of Grand Canyon National Park.* Grand Canyon, Ariz.: Grand Canyon Natural History Association.

Garth, J. S., and J. W. Tilden. 1986. *California Butterflies.* California Natural History Guide 51. Berkeley: University of California Press.

Hinchliff, J. 1994. *The Distribution of the Butterflies of Oregon.* Corvallis: Oregon State University Bookstore.

――――――. 1996. *The Distribution of the Butterflies of Washington.* Corvallis: Oregon State University Bookstore.

Hooper, R. R. 1973. *The Butterflies of Saskatchewan: a Field Guide.* Regina: Saskatchewan Museum of Natural History.

Klassen, P., A. R. Westwood, W. B. Preston, and W. B. McKillop. 1989. *The Butterflies of Manitoba.* Winnipeg: The Manitoba Museum of Man and Nature.

Neck, R. W. 1996. *A Field Guide to Butterflies of Texas.* Houston, Texas: Gulf Publishing Co.

Orsak, L. J. 1977. *The Butterflies of Orange County, California.* University of California, Irvine: Museum of Systematic Biology.

Pyle, R. M. 1974. *Watching Washington Butterflies.* Seattle: Seattle Audubon Society.

――――――. 1999. *Butterflies of Cascadia.* Seattle: Seattle Audubon Society.

Royer, R. A. 1988. *Butterflies of North Dakota.* Science Monograph 1, Minot, N. D.: Minot State Univeristy.

Stanford, R. E., and P. A. Opler. 1993. *Atlas of Western USA Butterflies.* Denver: Privately published.

Steiner, J. 1990. *Bay Area Butterflies: The Distribution and Natural History of San Francisco Region Rhopalocera.* Masters Thesis. Hayward, Calif.: Hayward State University.

Tilden, J. W. 1965. *Butterflies of the San Francisco Bay Region.* California Natural History Guide 12. Berkeley: University of California Press.

Tilden, J. W., and A. C. Smith. 1986. *A Field Guide to Western Butterflies.* Boston: Houghton Mifflin Co.

Toliver, M. E., and R. Holland. 1991. *Distribution of Butterflies in New Mexico (Lepidoptera: Hesperioidea and Papilionoidea).* Albuquerque: Privately published.

Ajilvsgi, G. 1990. *Butterfly Gardening for the South*. Dallas: Taylor Publishing Co.

Dennis, J. V., and M. Tekulsky. 1991. *How to Attract Hummingbirds and Butterflies*. San Ramon, Calif.: Ortho Books.

Ebner, J. A., and P. A. Opler. 1996. *Butterfly Gardening*. Videotape. New York: MasterVision.

Lewis, A., ed. 1995. *Butterfly Gardens*. Brooklyn: Brooklyn Botanical Garden.

Malcolm, S. B., and M. P. Zalucki, eds. 1993. *Biology and Conservation of the Monarch Butterfly*. Los Angeles: Natural History Museum of Los Angeles County.

Mikula, R. 1997. *Garden Butterflies of North America*. Minocqua, Wisc.: Willow Creek Press.

Sedenko, J. 1991. *The Butterfly Garden*. New York: Villard Books.

Tekulsky, M. 1985. *The Butterfly Garden*. Boston: The Harvard Common Press.

Xerces Society and Smithsonian Institution. 1998. *Butterfly Gardening*. San Francisco: Sierra Club Books.

WORLD WIDE WEB SITES

Butterflies of North America. U.S. Geological Survey, Northern Prairie Wildlife Research Center, Jamestown, N.D.
www.npwrc.usgs.gov/resource/distr/lepid/bflyusa/bflyusa.htm

A virtual handbook about U.S. butterflies that features images, species accounts, and county-level maps.

Children's Butterfly Site. U.S. Geological Survey, Midcontinent Ecological Science Center, Ft. Collins, Colo.
www.mesc.usgs.gov/butterfly/butterfly.html

An educational site for children and others interested in butterflies. Features answers to frequently asked questions, coloring pages, an image gallery, lists of organizations, books and videos, as well as hot links to dozen of other sites about butterflies.

Electronic Resources on Lepidoptera
www.chebucto.ns.ca/environment/NHR/lepidoptera.htm

Provides information about butterflies and moths as well as a comprehensive set of links to other Lepidoptera web sites.

BUTTERFLY HOUSES

Butterfly House, Western Colorado Botanical Gardens, 605 Struthers Avenue, Grand Junction, CO. 81501

Butterfly Pavilion and Insect Center, 6252 West 104th Street, Westminster, CO. 80020

Okanagan Butterfly World, 1190 Stevens Road, Kelowna, BC V1Z 1G1

Hidden Jungle, San Diego Wild Animal Park, 15500 San Pasqual Valley Road, Escondido, CA. 92027-9614

Victoria Butterfly Gardens, 1461 Benvenuto Avenue, Brentwood Bay, BC V8M 1R3

ORGANIZATIONS DEVOTED TO LEPIDOPTERA

High Country Lepidopterists, c/o Paul A. Opler, P.O. Box 2662, Loveland, CO. 80539-2662. Devoted to the study and conservation of Lepidoptera of the high plains and Rocky Mountain states. Annual meeting.

Holarctic Lepidoptera, c/o J. B. Heppner, P.O. Box 141210, Gainesville, FL 32614.

Idalia Society of Mid-American Lepidopterists, c/o Suzette Slocomb, 219 W. 68th Street, Kansas City, MO. 64113. Publishes a newsletter.

Monarch Watch, c/o Dr. O. R. Taylor, Department of Entomology, University of Kansas, Lawrence, KS 66045.

Nebraska Lepidopterist Newsletter, c/o Steve Spomer, 1235 N. 50th Street, Lincoln, NE. 68504.

North American Butterfly Association, 4 Delaware Road, Morristown, NJ 07960.

The Lepidoptera Research Foundation, c/o Santa Barbara Museum of Natural History, 2559 Puesta Del Sol Road, Santa Barbara, CA 93105. Publishes *Journal of Research on the Lepidoptera.*

The Lepidopterists' Society. Publishes *Journal of the Lepidopterists' Society, News of the Lepidopterists' Society,* and *Memoirs,* M. J. Smith, 1608 Presidio Way, Roseville, CA 95661.

INDEX TO HOST AND
NECTAR PLANTS

abelia, 21, 452
Abelia species, 21
Abutilon, 391-392, 409
acacia, 246, 388
Acacia angustissima, 181, 388
Acanthaceae, 229
Acanthus family, 294-296, 303-304,
    330-331
Agave lecheguilla, 471
agaves, 470
Alcea rosea, 22
alder, 140, 186, 319
alfalfa, 22, 162-164, 229, 232, 249,
    401, 415, 447
alkali mallow, 406
Aloysia, 379, 386
alpine clover, 167
alpine forget-me-nots, 357
alpine milk-vetch, 169
alpine sorrel, 188, 192
amaranths, 390, 412
American plum, 210
Amerimnon, 377-378
Anacardium family, 201
anise, 134
Apiaceae, 22
Arceuthobium, 216-217
arctic bilberry, 172
arctic wormwood, 133
Aristolochia species, 22
Arizona oak, 335, 373, 377
Arizona yucca, 476
Asclepias tuberosa, 21
ash, 44, 140-141
aspen, 272, 319, 321, 332-334, 395
Aster family, 184, 213, 371
asters, 187, 281, 291, 297-299, 301,
    305-307, 309-310, 312, 333,
    420, 431, 448

Atamisquea, 154
Atriplex argentea, 414
Atriplex lentiformis, 414
Ayenia, 411

Baccharis, 256
Baccharis glutinosa, 21
Bacopa, 330
balloon cine, 198, 224
bamboos, 346
banana, 418
banana yucca, 476
beach cabbage, 153
beans, 379
bearberry, 221
beardtongues, 22, 291, 315, 455
Bebbea juncea, 257
bee balm, 21
beeplant, 313
beggar's-ticks, 181, 380, 382-384
Beloperone, 302
Bermuda cherry, 393
Bermuda grass, 22, 380, 417, 421, 424,
    438, 441, 445
Bernardia, 225
Besseya, 313
Bidens, 392, 394
big bluestem, 430, 443, 446, 455, 465
bilberry, 171, 282, 287
bindweed, 309
birch, 42, 139, 319, 321-322, 395
Bishop pine, 223
bistorts, 282
black cherry, 42, 139
black mustard, 149
black oaks, 332
black-eyed susans, 291, 297
Blackthorn family, 196
bladderpod, 147

Blechum, 330
bleeding heart, 34, 126, 127
bloodflower, 371
blue dicks, 397
blue grama, 362, 426, 431-433, 439, 458
blue jasmine, 229
blueberry, 171, 287, 319
bluegrasses, 358, 361, 439, 450
Boehmeria, 327
boneset, 257, 375-376, 393, 469
bottlebrush, 347
bougainvillea, 21, 375, 381, 445, 469
Bougainvillea, 21
Brassica species, 22
Brassicaceae, 145
broad dock, 189
broad-leaved grasses, 415, 419, 448, 451, 464
broad-leaved uniola, 347
broccoli, 21, 22, 152-153
buckbrush, 21, 212, 292, 400
Buckthorn family, 44, 140
buckthorns, 44, 140, 400
buckwheats, 186, 236, 252, 260, 262, 354
Buddleia, 21
buddleias, vii
bullgrass, 459
bunchgrass, 366, 420
bur marigold, 184
bur oak, 209-210
bush clovers, 384
bush lotis, 401
bushmallow, 410
butterflybush, 21
butterfly milkweed, 21

cabbage, 21, 22, 152-153
cacti, 204
cafetin, 330
California buckeye, 211, 233, 334-335, 353, 449
California false indigo, 56, 173
Calliandra, 174
Canada thistle, 25, 333, 415
cannas, 467
canyon live oak, 197, 335
Caper family, 46, 145, 147, 149, 152-154
capers, 145, 147
Cardiospermum, 224
Carduus, 312
carrot, 21, 22, 132, 134
Casimiroa, 138
Cassia, 22, 175-176, 178, 182-183

Cassia leptocarpa, 181
Cassia spectabilis, 174
cassias, 22, 56, 178
Cassiope mertensiana, 248
ceanothus, 397
Ceanothus, 21, 322, 400
cecropia, 340
celery, 132
Celtis, 22
ceniza blanca, 292
Cesalpinia family, 230
chaff flower, 390
Chinese houses, 233
chinquapin, 197, 335
chokecherry, 44, 141, 208, 210, 333
chrysantha agave, 472
Chrysopsis, 301
Chrysothamnus nauseosus, 21
cinereous buckwheat, 237
cinquefoil, 186, 194, 246, 404-405
Cirsium, 310-312
Citrus family, 40, 42, 132, 135-137
citrus trees, 136-138
Clematis, 256, 264
cliff rose, 221
Clitoria, 382
clover, 21, 162-163, 167, 229, 232, 249, 251, 385, 423
club mosses, 346
Cnidiscolus, 379
coast live oak, 335
coastal buckwheat, 236
cockscomb, 412
coffeeberry, 44
collards, 153
Collinsia, 233
Cologania, 386
common lilac, 21
common milkweed, 138, 322
common reed, 449, 452
Compositae, 325
composites, 406, 409, 436
conifer mistletoe, 216-217
coppermallow, 406
Cordia, 394
cordias, 341
Corethrogyne, 300
corn, 419
corydalis, 126
corymbose buckwheat, 238, 260
cottongrass, 358, 367-368
cottonwood, 44, 140, 322, 333
cow parsnip, 334
coyotillo, 381
crab apple, 42, 139
crabgrass, 424

cranberries, 245
crosswort, 296
crotons, 342-343
crown vetch, 402
crown-beard, 295, 297
crucifers, 144
curled dock, 187, 190
currants, 186, 319-320
Cymopterus, 135
Cynodon dactylon, 22

Dalbergia, 178
Dalechampia, 338-339
Dalechampia scandens, 340
dame's-rocket, 21, 384
dandelion, 21, 152, 396, 460
Danthonia spicata, 365
deerbrush, 205, 207
deerweed, 166, 214
desert agave, 472-473
desert lavender, 392
desert saltgrass, 424
desert sunflower, 294
dill, 21, 22, 132, 134
Diphysia, 181
docks, 186, 188-189, 191-192, 194-195
dogbane, 210-212, 235, 264, 369, 390, 415, 420, 423, 446
dogwoods, 233
Douglas-fir, 46, 145-146
*Draba*s, 156
Dudleya, 235
dwarf bilberry, 170
Dyschoriste, 304

eastern redcedar, 218-219
Echeveria, 219
effuse buckwheat, 242
Elm family, 212
elms, 316-317, 321-322
elongate buckwheat, 191
Emory oak, 205, 258, 335, 373, 377
Encelia, 256
Engelmann spruce, 146
English plantain, 315
Eriogonum, 21
Eriogonum pusillum, 240
Eriogonum reniforme, 240
Eupatorium greggii, 257
Eupatorium havanense, 257
Eupatorium odoratum, 257
Euphorbia family, 336, 338
everlastings, 325
Eysenhardtia orthocarpa, 378

fall witchgrass, 430, 433
false foxglove, 315, 328
false indigo, 174
false nettle, 316-317, 324
fasciculate buckwheat, 190, 237, 261
Fendler's buckbrush, 213
fennel, 22
fescue, 366, 437
fetid marigold, 184
fig, 341, 371
Figwort family, 315
firs, 145
flat-topped white aster, 297
fleabane, 292, 298, 301, 306, 309, 314, 415
Foeniculum vulgare, 22
fogfruit, 304-305, 309, 312, 421
four-winged saltbush, 413
French lavender, 21
French marigold, 21, 446

gaillardia, 420
Gambel oak, 196, 209-210, 243, 335, 377, 397
Gaultheria, 171
globe-mallows, 407
goatweed, 342
golden banner, 163, 165, 402-403
goldenglow, 297
goldenrod, 209, 333
gooseberry, 186, 319-320
goosefoots, 389
grasses, 346-355, 357-358, 361-366, 368, 380, 414, 417-421, 424-434, 436-447, 449, 452-453, 460-461, 463, 465-469
gray oak, 205
green ash, 142
Guardiola, 386
gumbo limbo, 337
gumweed, 308

hackberry, 22, 267, 316, 322, 344-346
hairy milk pea, 228
hairy tubetongue, 304, 309
Havard's plum, 265
hawkweed, 423
hawthorns, 210
Heath family, 220, 222, 287
heaths, 162, 396
Heerman buckwheat, 238
Herrisantia, 409
Hesperis matronalis, 21
Heterotheca, 300
hibiscus, 225
hollyhock, 22, 328, 406, 408

honey mesquite, 263
Honeysuckle family, 315
hop-tree, 44, 136, 140-141
hops, 234, 317, 324
horehound, 211-212
horkelias, 404
huckleberry oak, 197

Ictyomenthia, 377-378
incense-cedar, 217
Indian paintbrushes, 313
indigo bush, 174
Indigofera, 387, 394
inflated buckwheat, 239, 262
Inga, 177, 346
iris, 385

jacaratia, 371
Jack pine, 222, 364
Jamaican dogwood, 375
Japanese hops, 316
jewelflowers, 148, 157, 161
joe-pye weed, 333
joint vetch, 179
juneberries, 207
junipers, 204, 218-219, 294, 350, 382,
    420, 425, 427, 464, 466, 475

kale, 21, 153
Karum tree, 375
Kearney's buckwheat, 241
Kennedy buckwheat, 238
Kentucky blue grass, 440, 443
knapweed, 25, 386, 459
knotgrass, 422
knotweed, 186, 191-192, 194-195
Koa, 246
koeleria, 437
Koeleria cristata, 432
Kramerias, 262

Lagascea, 392
lamb's quarters, 390, 412
lantana, 21, 199, 226, 267, 418, 445
Lantana camara, 21, 267
laurel, 44, 142
Lavandula dentata, 21
lead plant, 174
leadwort, 228-229
leafy spurge, 25
Lechuguilla agave, 473
legumes, 56, 144, 162-165, 169, 173-
    174, 178-179, 203, 213, 229,
    245, 249, 251, 253, 263, 326,
    346, 373-374, 376-381, 386-387,
    401-403, 456

lichen, 357, 434
lignum vitae, 179
lilac, 140, 397
Lima bean, 228
Lippia, 329
lippias, 226, 330
little bluestem, 430-431, 437, 455
Lobb's buckwheat, 239
locoweed, 65, 251
locusts, 374
lodgepole pine, 223
Lomatium, 135
lotis, 164, 224, 232, 245, 248, 252-
    253, 402
low blueberry, 172, 195, 245
lupines, 22, 165, 206, 244, 245, 248-
    249, 251-252, 402-403
Lupinus argenteus, 234
Lupinus species, 22

Machaeranthera, 299
Mallow family, 224
mallows, 225, 326, 328, 373, 391-392,
    403, 406-411
Malpighia family, 393
Malpighia glabra, 393
malpighias, 203
manfreda, 477
maple, 44, 140
marigold, 390, 438
mat grass, 283, 304
Maytenus phyllanthoides, 200
meadow rue, 282
Medicago sativa, 22
mesquite, 181, 199, 229, 350, 433
Mexican alvaradoa, 183
milk maids, 159
milk-vetches, 163, 165, 229, 232, 244-
    245, 248-249, 251-252, 384,
    403, 439
milkweed vines, 369-371
milkweeds, 142, 208, 259, 271, 369-
    371, 386, 406, 446-447, 460
Mimosa family, 177, 200, 230
Mimosa malacophylla, 200
Mimosa pigra, 387
mimosoid legumes, 387
mints, 226, 271, 280, 384, 406, 410,
    459
mistletoes, 46, 145, 197
Monarda, 273
Monarda didyma, 21
monkeyflowers, 313, 328-329
monocotyledons, 417
Monterey pine, 223
morning glory, 258, 271, 458

moss campion, 288
mountain avens, 287, 288
mountain snowbush, 264
mountain-mahogany, 205, 207, 211
Muhlenbergia, 348, 362
Mustard family, 46, 144-145, 147-152, 155-156, 162
mustards, 149, 152, 155, 159, 161

nasturtium, 152
netleaf hackberry, 344-345
nettle, 316-317, 324, 328
Nettle family, 327, 340
New Jersey tea, 234, 400
New Mexico locust, 381, 401
northern black oak, 209
noseburn, 336, 338-339
nude buckwheat, 191, 239

oaks, 197-198, 200-201, 204, 207, 211, 264, 294, 299, 350, 373, 377, 395-399, 401, 416, 420, 457, 459, 463, 466, 472
oblong-leafed oak, 258
ocean spray, 333
orange milkweed, 264
osier dogwood, 234
oval-leafed buckwheat, 238
owl's clover, 328
*Oxytheca*s, 243
Oxytropis, 165

paintbrush, 292-293
Palmer's agave, 471
panic grasses, 450, 459, 462, 464
papaya, 371
Parry's agave, 471-472
parsley, 21, 22, 134
Parsley family, 132, 134, 135
Paspalum, 465
Passiflora lutea, 269
passion-vine, 22, 268-269, 271
Paullinia, 346
paw-paw, 36, 131
Pea family, 224, 230, 248
pellitory, 324
pencil flower, 179
penstemon, 313
Penstemon species, 22, 455
Pentaclethra, 177
Pepper family, 40
peppergrasses, 149, 152
phlox, 288, 357
Picramnia, 183
pigweeds, 228, 414
pine dropseed, 453

pines, 46, 145-146, 222, 396-397, 401, 420, 425, 427, 475
pinyon, 218, 382, 475
pipers, 137
pipevines, 22, 36, 131
Pipterus, 327
Pithecellobium, 177
Plantago family, 315
plantain, 328
plum, 44, 140, 207, 334
plumate buckwheat, 241
plumbago, 381
Poa, 358
Polygonum bistortoides, 282
Polygonum viviparum, 282
ponderosa pine, 145-146, 223, 243
poplars, 332, 395
Porliera, 179
porterweed, 329
prairie clovers, 174
prairie gayfeather, 431
prairie tea, 342
Prince's plume, 46, 147, 158
Priva lappulacea, 386
privet, 334
Pteryxia, 135
purple coneflower, 435-436
purple reedgrass, 414
pussytoes, 302, 325, 385
pussypaws, 281

quaking aspen, 42, 44, 139, 140, 334
Quercus species, 22

rabbitbrush, 21, 267, 271, 273, 298-299, 324, 326-327, 334-335, 354, 363, 429, 438
racemose buckwheat, 214, 243
ragweed, 295
rattlebox, 228
rattleweed, 166
red bay, 143
redberry, 186, 195
redbud, 396
red penstemon, 459
red thistles, 459
red valerian, 452
redbud, 169
redtop, 446
reniforme buckwheat, 243
Reseda family, 46, 149
Rhamnus crocea, 195
rhododendron, 319
Rhus, 379
rock cresses, 46, 148-149, 151-152, 155-156, 158-159, 161

rock-primroses, 246
roses, vii
Rose family, 44, 140, 403
Rudbeckia, 297
ruellia, 329
Ruellia, 330
rushes, 346
Russian-thistle, 228

sagebrush, 166, 251, 427, 437
salicornia, 228
Salix species, 22
saltbush, 228, 250, 413
saltgrass, 440-441, 468
saltwort, 153
sandbar willow, 206
Sapindaceae, 338, 346
Sargeant's cypress, 217
sassafras, 143
saxifrage, 288
scabrous agave, 471
Schott's agave, 474
Schott's yucca, 476
Scrub oak, 204, 209
sedges, 346, 348, 356-358, 361, 364-368, 425, 427-429, 453-454
Sedum, 128,
seepwillow, 21, 242, 256, 259, 263, 267, 292, 302, 335, 341, 388
sensitive plant, 182
serviceberry, 333
sheep sorrel, 187
shepherd's-needle, 305
shepherd's-purse, 162
Shockley buckwheat, 237
shooting stars, 247
showy locoweed, 169
shrub willow, 170, 172, 285, 290
Sidas, 407-409
side-oats grama, 416, 421, 461
Silybium, 312
Simarouba family, 183
small soapweed, 476
smartweeds, 190, 195
smooth brome, 25, 426, 440
snapdragon, 328
snow willow, 286
snowberry, 210, 313, 334
Solanum umbellatum, 202
Spanish-moss, 227
speedwell, 312, 329
Sphaeralcea, 391
spicebush, 143
spiny hackberry, 344
spotted saxifrage, 289
spreading dogbane, 208

St. Augustine grass, 445
stemodia, 329
Stenandrium barbatum, 295
Sterculia family, 411
sticky monkey-flower, 313
stipa, 437
Stipa scribneri, 425
stonecrop, 34, 127-129, 221, 244
strict buckwheat, 238
succulents, 219
sugar cane, 469
sugarberry, 267, 344
sulphur-flower, 215, 236, 239-241,
sumacs, 201, 235
sunflower, 273, 295-298
Sunflower family, 294-296, 300
sweet bay, 42, 139
sweet bush, 257
sweet clover, 25, 249
sweet coltsfoot, 133
sweet fennel, 134
sweet-vetch, 165
switchgrass, 433
sycamore, 44, 140
Syringa vulgaris, 21

Tagetes patula, 21
tan oak, 197, 335
tansy asters, 309
tansy mustard, 148-149, 155-156, 158, 161
Tecate cypress, 219
Tephrosia, 379
Tetramerium, 302
Texas croton, 342
Texas ebony, 383
Texas nolina, 219
thevetia, 381
thistles, 132, 136, 271-273, 279, 310-311, 326, 352, 376, 384, 431, 447, 448-449, 452, 456
Tillandsia, 227
Timothy, 422
toadflax, 328
toothworts, 151-152
tower mustard, 155, 159
Tragia, 339
trailing arbutus, 221
Tridax, 256
tube-tongue, 302
tulips, vii
tumble mustard, 148-149
Turk's-cap, 391
Turneras, 271
turnips, 21
turpentine broom, 132

turtlehead, 315
twinberry, 312

Ungnadia, 222
Urera, 340
Utah agave, 475

Vaccinium uliginosum, 287
Valerian family, 315
verbena, 21, 292, 396, 423, 456
Verbena, 21
Verbena family, 212-213
vetches, 165, 232, 248, 383-385, 397
Viguera deltoidea, 294
vinca, 250, 469
vine mesquite, 464
violets, 270-273, 275-281, 282-285, 290
Vitex, 381

waltheria, 376, 393-394
walnuts, 197
water cress, 151-152, 422
water dock, 190
water hyssop, 330
wax myrtle, 201
waxflower, 233, 235
western redcedar, 217
western soapberry, 203
wheatgrasses, 363
white clover, 163-164, 306, 390
white sweet-clover, 163-164, 353
whitegrass, 347
whitetop, 25
wild bean, 384
wild buckwheats, 21, 193, 206, 211-215, 224, 235, 240-241, 253, 260, 312, 399

wild cherry, 139, 208, 332
wild flax, 270
wild geranium, 352, 415, 420
wild licorice, 374
wild lilacs, 21, 44, 140, 200, 212, 321, 400
wild oats, 25
wild onion, 385
wild plums, 44, 140, 208
wild strawberry, 231, 404
wild tarragon, 133
willows, 22, 44, 140, 162, 170, 206-207, 282, 286, 319, 321-322, 333-334, 395
winter cress, 162
Wissadula, 391
wisteria, 374
wood nettle, 324
Wormskjold's clover, 385
Wright's buckwheat, 214, 239, 242, 254, 261-262,

yellow composites, 187, 206, 260, 262, 280, 291-292, 294, 298, 302, 306, 311-312, 352, 354, 394, 410, 416, 421, 439
yellow star-thistle, 312, 399
yellow-poplar, 42, 139
yerba santa, 334, 397, 410
yuccas, 470, 475-476

Zanthoxylum, 138
Zinnia, 21
zinnias, vii, 21, 438

INDEX TO BUTTERFLIES

Acacia Skipper, Pl. 37, 387
Acadian Hairstreak, Pl. 16, 206
acadica (Satyrium), Pl. 16, 206
acastus (Chlosyne), Pl. 27, 299
accius (Lerema), Pl. 40, 418
Achalarus, Pl. 36, 382-383
    albociliatus, Pl. 36, 383
    casica, Pl. 36, 382
    toxeus, Pl. 36, 383
Acheronta, Pl. 31, 340
acheronta (Historis), Pl. 31, 340
Acmon Blue, Pl. 21, 252
acmon (Icaricia), Pl. 21, 252
acrocnema (Boloria improba), Pl. 25, 25-26, 286
Adelpha bredowii, Pl. 30, 334
adepta (Pyrgus), 408
adiaste (Speyeria), Pl. 24, 278
Admirals, Pl. 30, 324, 331
    Lorquin's, Pl. 30, 32, 334
    Red, Pl. 29, 324
    Weidemeyer's, Pl. 30, 28, 32, 333
    White, 331
Adopaeoides prittwitzi, Pl. 40, 422
aea (Piruna), Pl. 40, 416
aenus (Amblyscirtes), Pl. 43, 460
affinis (Callophrys), Pl. 17, 213
afranius (Erynnis), Pl. 38, 402
Afranius Duskywing, Pl. 38, 402
agarithe (Phoebis), Pl. 13, 176
Agathymus, Pl. 44, 470-475
    alliae, Pl. 44, 475
    aryxna, Pl. 44, 471
    baueri, 471
    evansi, Pl. 44, 472
    mariae, Pl. 44, 27, 472
    neumoegeni, Pl. 44, 470
    polingi, Pl. 44, 474
    remingtoni, Pl. 44, 473

    stephensi, Pl. 44, 474
Agraulis vanillae, Pl. 23, 268
Agriades, Pl. 21, 246-248
    cassiope, Pl. 21, 247
    franklinii (glandon), Pl. 21
    glandon, Pl. 21, 246
    megalo (glandon), Pl. 21
    podarce, Pl. 21, 28, 247
    rustica (glandon), Pl. 21
agricola (Ochlodes), Pl. 42, 28, 448
Aguna asander, Pl. 35, 376
Aguna, Gold-spotted, Pl. 35, 376
aidea (Anaea), 342
alberta (Boloria), Pl. 25, 28, 288
Alberta Arctic, Pl. 34, 366
Alberta Fritillary, Pl. 25, 28, 288
alberta (Oeneis), Pl. 34, 366
albescens (Pyrgus), Pl. 39, 407
albociliatus (Achalarus), Pl. 36, 383
alcaeus (Codatractus), Pl. 35, 378
alcestis (Phaeostrymon), Pl. 16, 203
alea (Strymon), Pl. 18, 225
alexandra (Colias), Pl. 10, 28, 165
aliaska (Papilio machaon), Pl. 3, 38
Alkali Skipper, Pl. 40, 424
alliae (Agathymus), Pl. 44, 475
alma (Thessalia leanira), Pl. 26, 294
allyni (Euphilotes battoides), 25-26
allyni,(Paramacera), Pl. 32, 350
alopius (Parides), Pl. 2, 129
Alpines, Pls. 32-33, 355-361
    Banded, Pl. 33, 358
    Colorado, Pl. 33, 28, 361
    Common, Pl. 33, 361
    Disa, Pl. 32, 356
    Four-dotted, Pl. 33, 359
    Magdalena, Pl. 32, 357
alpheus (Hesperopsis), Pl. 39, 413
alpina (Oeneis), Pl. 34, 369

Alpines, (cont.)
  Mt. McKinley, Pl. 32, 357
  Red-disked, Pl. 33, 358
  Reddish, Pl. 33, 360
  Reddish Four-dotted, 360
  Ross', Pl. 32, 355
  Scree, Pl. 33, 359
  Taiga, Pl. 32, 356
  Theano, Pl. 33, 358
  Vidler's, Pl. 32, 355
Amblyscirtes, Pl. 43, 458-466
  aenus, Pl. 43, 460
  cassus, Pl. 43, 459
  celia, Pl. 43, 465
  elissa, Pl. 43, 461
  eos, Pl. 43, 464
  exoteria, Pl. 43, 459
  fimbriata, Pl. 43, 466
  hegon, Pl. 43, 461
  nereus, Pl. 43, 462
  nysa, Pl. 43, 463
  oslari, Pl. 43, 460
  phylace, Pl. 43, 465
  prenda (tolteca), 462
  texanae, Pl. 43, 461
  tolteca, Pl. 43, 462
  vialis, Pl. 43, 464
"Amblyscirtes" simius, Pl. 43, 458
American Copper, Pl. 14, 187
American Lady, Pl. 29, 325
American Snout, Pl. 22, 267
amymone (Mestra), Pl. 31, 338
amyntor (Cyanophrys), Pl. 17, 212
Amyntor Greenstreak, Pl. 17, 212
amyntula (Everes), Pl. 19, 232
Anaea, Pl. 31, 341-343
  aidea, 342
  andria, Pl. 31, 342
  troglodyta, Pl. 31, 342
Anartia, Pl. 30, 330
  fatima, Pl. 30, 330
  jatrophae, Pl. 30, 330
anasazi (Phyciodes batesii), Pl. 28
Anatrytone delaware, Pl. 42, 447
anchisiades (Papilio), Pl. 5, 137
ancilla (Euphilotes), Pl. 20, 240
Ancyloxypha, Pl. 40, 419
  arene, Pl. 40, 419
  numitor, Pl. 40, 419
andria (Anaea), Pl. 31, 342
angelika (Pieris), Pl. 8, 30, 150
Angled Leafwing, 343
Angled-Sulphurs, Pl. 12, 174-175
  White, Pl. 12, 174
  Yellow, Pl. 12, 175
anicia (Euphydryas chalcedona), 31, 313

Anise Swallowtail, Pl. 3, 134
Anna's Eighty-eight, 338
annabella (Vanessa), Pl. 29, 327
Anteos, Pl. 12, 174-175
  clorinde, Pl. 12, 174
  maerula, Pl. 12, 175
anthedon (Enodia), Pl. 32, 347
Anthocharis, Pl. 9, 158-162
  cethura, Pl. 9, 27, 32, 158
  julia, Pl. 9, 159
  lanceolata, Pl. 9, 161
  midea, Pl. 9, 161
  pima (cethura), Pl. 9, 158
  sara, Pl. 9, 159
  stella, Pl. 9, 160
  thoosa, Pl. 9, 28, 160
Antigonus emorsus, Pl. 37, 391
antiopa (Nymphalis), Pl. 29, 12, 322
antonia (Asterocampa celtis), 344
anyuica (Erebia), Pl. 33, 359
Apache Skipper, Pl. 41, 429
Apaturinae, 343-345
aphrodite (Speyeria), Pl. 23, 272
Aphrodite Fritillary, Pl. 23, 272
Apodemia, Pl. 22, 260-265
  chisosensis, 27, 265
  cythera (mormo), 260
  deserti (mejicanus), Pl. 22, 261
  dialeuca (virgulti), Pl. 22
  duryi , Pl. 22, 262
  hepburni, Pl. 22, 262
  langei (mormo), Pl. 22, 261
  mejicanus, Pl. 22, 261
  mormo, Pl. 22, 260
  nais, Pl. 22, 264
  palmeri, Pl. 22, 263
  phyciodoides, 263
  tuolumnensis (mormo), 260
  virgulti, Pl. 22, 28, 261
Appias drusilla, Pl. 7, 147
Apricot Sulphur, 177
arabus (Lerodea), Pl. 43, 467
arachne (Poladryas minuta), Pl. 26, 291
Arawacus jada, Pl. 18, 202
araxes (Pyrrhopyge), Pl. 35, 373
archippus (Limentis), Pl. 30, 332
Arctic Blue, Pl. 20, 246
Arctic Fritillary, Pl. 25, 289
Arctic Skipper, Pl. 40, 414
Arctic White, Pl. 8, 30, 150
Arctics, Pl. 33, 363-369
  Alberta, Pl. 34, 366
  Chryxus, Pl. 33, 364
  Great, Pl. 33, 363
  Jutta, Pl. 34, 367
  Macoun's, Pl. 33, 364
  Melissa, Pl. 34, 367

Philip's, **Pl. 34**, 368
Polixenes, **Pl. 34**, 368
Sentinel, **Pl. 34**, 369
Uhler's, **Pl. 33**, 28, 365
arene (Ancyloxipha), **Pl. 40**, 419
ares (Emesis), **Pl. 22**, 258
Ares Metalmark, **Pl. 22**, 258
argante (Phoebis), 177
Arizona Giant-Skipper, **Pl. 44**, 475
Arizona Hairstreak, **Pl. 18**, 27, 200
Arizona Metalmark, **Pl. 22**, 258
Arizona Powdered-Skipper, **Pl. 37**, 392
Arizona Skipper, **Pl. 35**, 378
arizonensis (Calephelis rawsoni), **Pl. 22**, 258
arizonensis (Codatractus), **Pl. 35**, 378
arizonensis (Limenitis arthemis), 332
arogos (Atrytone), **Pl. 42**, 446
Arogos Skipper, **Pl. 42**, 446
arota (Lycaena), **Pl. 14**, 186
Arrowhead Blue, **Pl. 20**, 243
arthemis (Limenitis), **Pl. 30**, 331
aryxna (Agathymus), **Pl. 44**, 471
asander, Aguna, **Pl. 35**, 376
Ascia monuste, **Pl. 8**, 153
assiniboia (Hesperia), **Pl. 41**, 427
astarte (Boloria), **Pl. 25**, 288
Astarte Fritillary, **Pl. 25**, 288
asterias (Papilio polyxenes), **Pl. 3**, 38
Asterocampa, **Pl. 31**, 344-345
    antonia (celtis), 344
    celtis, **Pl. 31**, 344
    clyton, **Pl. 31**, 345
    idyja, 345
    leilia, **Pl. 31**, 344
Astraptes fulgerator, **Pl. 36**, 381
astyalus (Papilio), **Pl. 4**, 137
atalanta (Vanessa), **Pl. 29**, 324
Atalopedes campestris, **Pl. 42**, 438
Atlantis Fritillary, **Pl. 24**, 279
atlantis (Hamadryas), **Pl. 31**, 339
atlantis (Speyeria), **Pl. 24**, 279
Atlides halesus, **Pl. 15**, 197
Atrytone arogos, **Pl. 42**, 446
Atrytonopsis, **Pl. 42-43**, 454-458
    cestus, **Pl. 43**, 457
    deva, **Pl. 42**, 455
    edwardsi, **Pl. 43**, 458
    hianna, **Pl. 42**, 454
    lunus, **Pl. 42**, 455
    pittacus, **Pl. 42**, 456
    python, **Pl. 42**, 457
    vierecki, **Pl. 42**, 456
attalus (Hesperia), 433
augustinus (Callophrys), **Pl. 17**, 220
aurantiaca (Copaeodes), **Pl. 40**, 421
auretorum (Satyrium), **Pl. 16**, 28, 210

ausonides (Euchloe), **Pl. 8**, 154
Autochton, **Pl. 36**, 381-382
    cellus, **Pl. 36**, 10, 381
    cinctus, **Pl. 36**, 382
    pseudocellus, **Pl. 36**, 381
Avalon Scrub-Hairstreak, **Pl. 18**, 28, 224
avalona (Strymon), **Pl. 18**, 28, 224
azia (Ministrymmon), **Pl. 18**, 199
Aztec Scallopwing, 390
azteca (Staphylus), 390
Azures, **Pl. 19**, 232-234
    Hops, **Pl. 19**, 234
    Spring, **Pl. 19**, 232
    Summer, **Pl. 19**, 233

bachmanii (Libytheana carinenta), 267
bairdii (Papilio machaon), **Pl. 3**, 130
Baltimore Checkerspot, 315
Banana Skipper, 418
Banded Alpine, **Pl. 33**, 358
Banded Hairstreak, **Pl. 16**, 209
Banded Patch, **Pl. 26**, 295
Banded Peacock, **Pl. 30**, 330
Banded-Skipper, **Pl. 36**, 381-382
    Chisos, **Pl. 36**, 382
    Sonoran, **Pl. 36**, 381
baptisiae (Erynnis), **Pl. 38**, 401
Barred Yellow, **Pl. 13**, 11, 179
barryi (Callophrys gryneus), **Pl. 17**
batesii (Phyciodes), **Pl. 28**, 307
bathyllus (Thorybes), **Pl. 36**, 384
battoides (Euphilotes), **Pl. 19**, **Pl. 20**, 25-26, 236
Battus, **Pl. 2**, 130
    philenor, **Pl. 2**, 130
    philenor hirsuta, 130
    polydamas, **Pl. 2**, 131
Bauer's Dotted-Blue, **Pl. 20**, 28, 238
Bauer's Giant-Skipper, 471
baueri (Agathymus), 471
baueri (Euphilotes), **Pl. 20**, 28, 238
Bay Checkerspot, **Pl. 28**, 25, 26, 315
bayensis (Callophrys mossii), 25, 26
bayensis (Euphydryas editha), **Pl. 44**, 25, 26, 315
bazochii (Styrmon), **Pl. 18**, 226
Beauty, Blomfild's, **Pl. 31**, 340
bebrycia (Strymon), **Pl. 18**, 224
beckerii (Pontia), **Pl. 7**, 28, 145, 147
Becker's White, **Pl. 7**, 28, 145, 147
Behren's Silverspot, 25, 26, 277
behrensii (Speyeria zerene), 25, 26, 277
Behr's Hairstreak, **Pl. 16**, 205
Behr's Metalmark, **Pl. 22**, 261
behrii (Colias), **Pl. 11**, 28, 172
behrii (Parnassius), **Pl. 1**, 28, 128

behrii, (Satyrium), Pl. 16, 205
Behr's Hairstreak, Pl. 16, 205
bellona (Boloria), Pl. 25, 284
Beringian Fritillary, Pl. 25, 30, 287
bernadetta (Euphydryas chalcedona), Pl. 28
bernardino (Euphilotes), Pl. 19, 28, 236
Bernardino Dotted-Blue, Pl. 19, 28, 236
Biblis hyperia, Pl. 31, 338
bimacula, (Euphyes) , Pl. 42, 453
Black Checkerspot, Pl. 26, 27, 292
Black Swallowtail, Pl. 3, 130
blackburni (Vaga), Pl. 21, 245
Blackened Bluewing, 336
Black-patched Cracker, Pl. 31, 339
blomfildia (Smyrna), Pl. 31, 340
Blomfild's Beauty, Pl. 31, 340
Blue Copper, Pl. 15, 193
Blues, Pls. 19-21, 25-26, 227-254
    Acmon, Pl. 21, 252
    Arctic, Pl. 21, 246
    Arrowhead, Pl. 20, 243
    Boisduval's, Pl. 21, 25-26, 250
    Cassiope, Pl. 21, 247
    Cassius, Pl. 19, 228
    Ceraunus, Pl. 19, 230
    Cranberry, Pl. 21, 245
    Cyna, Pl. 19, 229
    El Segundo, 25-26
    Greenish, P. 20, 249
    Hawaiian, Pl. 21, 245
    Karner, 249
    Lotis, 25
    Lupine, Pl. 21, 252
    Marine, Pl. 19, 228
    Melissa, Pl. 20, 249
    Mission, 25-26, 251
    Northern, Pl. 20, 25, 248
    Palos Verdes, 25
    Pea, Pl. 19, 229
    Reakirt's, Pl. 19, 230
    San Emigdio, Pl. 20, 28, 249
    Shasta, Pl. 21, 251
    Sierra Nevada, Pl. 21, 28, 247
    Silvery, Pl. 20, 25, 245
    Smith's, 25
    Sonoran, Pl. 19, 235
    Veined, Pl. 21, 253
    Western Square-dotted, Pls. 19, 20, 236
    Xerces, P. 20, 245
boeticus (Lampides), Pl. 19, 229
Bog Fritillary, Pl. 25, 282
boisduvaliana (Eurema), Pl. 13, 180
Boisduval's Blue, Pl. 21, 250

Boisduval's Yellow, Pl. 13, 180
Bolla, Mottled, Pl. 37, 389
Bolla clytius, Pl. 37, 389
Boloria, Pl. 25, 282-290
    acrocnema (improba), Pl. 25, 25-26, 286
    alberta, Pl. 25, 28, 288
    astarte, Pl. 25, 288
    bellona, Pl. 25,284
    chariclea, Pl. 25, 289
    distincta (astarte), Pl. 25, 289
    epithore, Pl. 25, 284
    eunomia, Pl. 25, 282
    freija, Pl. 25, 287
    frigga, Pl. 25,285
    harryi (improba), 286
    improba , Pl. 25,25-26, 285
    kriemhild, Pl. 25, 286
    napaea, Pl. 25, 282
    natazhati, Pl. 25, 30, 287
    polaris, Pl. 25, 287
    selene, Pl. 25, 283
    titania, 290
Booth's Sulphur, Pl. 11, 30, 168
Bordered Patch, Pl. 26, 295
bore (Oeneis), Pl. 34, 366
Brazilian Skipper, Pl. 43, 467
bredowii (Adelpha), Pl. 30, 334
Brephidium exile, Pl. 19, 227
brizo (Erynnis), Pl. 38, 395
Broad-banded Swallowtail, Pl. 4, 137
Broad-winged Skipper, 451
Broken-Dash, Pl. 41, 445-446
    Northerrn, Pl. 41, 445
    Southern, Pl. 41, 445
Bromeliad Scrub-Hairstreak, Pl. 18, 226
Bronze Copper, Pl. 14, 190
Bronze Roadside-Skipper, Pl. 43, 460
Brown, Eyed, Pl. 32, 347
Brown Elfin, Pl. 17, 220
Brown Longtail, Pl. 36, 380
Brown-banded Skipper, Pl. 37, 393
Brushfoots, 290-371
Buckeyes, Pl. 30, 328-329
    Common, Pl. 30, 328
    Dark, Pl. 30, 329
    Tropical, Pl. 30, 329

Cabares potrillo, Pl. 37, 386
Cabbage White, Pl. 8, 9, 152
caicus (Cogia), Pl. 37, 388
Caicus Skipper, Pl. 37, 388
calanus (Satyrium), Pl. 16, 209
calchas (Cogia), Pl. 37, 387
Calephelis, Pl. 22, 255-258

arizonensis (rawsoni), Pl. 22, 258
freemani (rawsoni), 258
nemesis, Pl. 22, 255
nilus, Pl. 22, 257
rawsoni, Pl. 22, 257
wrighti, Pl. 22, 28, 256
california (*Coenonympha tullia*), Pl. 32
California Crescent, Pl. 28, 28, 309
California Dogface, Pl. 12, 173
California Giant-Skipper, Pl. 44, 473
California Hairstreak, Pl. 16, 207
California Marble, Pl. 9, 28, 157
California Patch, Pl. 26, 28, 294
California Sister, Pl. 30, 334
California Tortoiseshell, Pl. 29, 321
californica (Chlosyne), Pl. 26, 294
californica (Nymphalis), Pl. 29, 321
californica (Satyrium) , Pl. 16, 207
callias (Erebia), Pl. 33, 28, 361
callidice (Pontia), 150
callippe (Speyeria), Pl. 24, 277
callippe callippe (Speyeria), 25, 26
Callippe Fritillary, Pl. 24, 277
Callippe Silverspot, 25, 26
Callophrys, Pl. 17, 25-26, 213-223
   affinis, Pl. 17, 213
   augustinus, Pl. 17, 220
   barryi (gryneus), Pl. 17, 218
   bayensis (mossii), 25-26
   comstocki, Pl. 17, 28, 214
   dumetorum, Pl. 17, 213
   eryphon, Pl. 18, 223
   fotis, Pl. 17, 220
   gryneus, Pl. 17, 32, 217
   henrici, Pl. 18, 222
   homoperplexa (affinis), Pl. 17,
   johnsoni, Pl. 17, 216
   mcfarlandi, Pl. 17, 28, 219
   mossii, Pl. 18, 25-26, 221
   muiri, Pl. 17, 28, 217
   nelsoni, Pl. 17, 217
   niphon, Pl. 18, 222
   perplexa (affinis), Pl. 17
   polios, Pl. 18, 221
   schryveri (mossii), Pl. 18
   sheridanii, Pl. 17, 214
   siva (gryneus), Pl. 17, 218
   spinetorum, Pl. 17, 215
   thornei, Pl. 17, 219
   xami, Pl. 17, 219
Calpodes ethlius, Pl. 43, 467
Calycopis, Pl. 18, 201
   cecrops, Pl. 18, 201
   isobeon, Pl. 18, 201
campestris (Atalopedes), Pl. 42, 438
Canada Sulphur, Pl. 11, 28, 168

canadensis (Colias), Pl. 11, 28, 168
canadensis (Papilio), Pl. 5, 139
Canadian Tiger Swallowtail, Pl. 5, 139
Canyonland Satyr, Pl. 32, 348
cardui (Vanessa), Pl. 29, 325
carinenta (Libytheana), Pl. 22, 267
Carol's Fritillary, 276
carolae (Speyeria), 276
Carterocephalus palaemon, Pl. 40, 414
carus (Polites), Pl. 41, 440
Carus Skipper, Pl. 41, 440
caryae (Vanessa), 328
casica (Achalarus), Pl. 36, 382
cassiope (Agriades), Pl. 21, 247
Cassiope Blue, Pl. 21, 247
cassius (Leptotes), Pl. 19, 228
Cassius Blue, Pl. 19, 228
cassus (Amblyscirtes), Pl. 43, 459
Cassus Roadside-Skipper, Pl. 43, 459
Catasticta nimbice, Pl. 7, 145
catillus (Chioides), Pl. 35, 375
Cattleheart, White-dotted, Pl. 2, 129
catullus (Pholisora), Pl. 39, 412
cecrops (Calycopis), Pl. 18, 201
Celaenorrhinus fritzgaertneri, Pl. 37,
   386
Celastrina, Pl. 19, 232-234
   echo (ladon), 233
   humulus,Pl. 19, 234
   ladon,Pl. 19, 232
   neglecta, Pl. 19, 233
celia (Amblyscirtes), Pl. 43, 465
Celia's Roadside-Skipper, Pl. 43, 465
cellus (Autochton), Pl. 36, 10, 381
Celotes, Pl. 39, 411
   limpia, 411
   nessus, Pl. 39, 411
celtis (Asterocampa), Pl. 31, 344
centaureae (Pyrgus), Pl. 38, 403
centralis (Euphilotes battoides), Pl. 20
ceos (Staphylus), Pl. 37, 389
ceraunus (Hemiargus),Pl. 19, 230
Ceraunus Blue, Pl. 19, 230
Cercyonis, Pl. 32, 11, 352-354
   meadii, Pl. 32, 28, 353
   oetus, Pl. 32, 354
   pegala, Pl. 32, 352
   sthenele, Pl. 32, 352
cerrita (Thessalia leanira), Pl. 26
cesonia (Zerene), Pl. 12, 173
cestri (Strymon), Pl. 18, 225
cestus (Atrytonopsis), Pl. 43, 457
Cestus Skipper, Pl. 43, 457
cethura (Anthocharis), Pl. 9, 27, 32,
   158
Chalcedon Checkerspot, 313

chalcedona (Euphydryas), Pl. 28, 313
Charaxinae, 341-343
chariclea (Boloria), Pl. 25, 289
charithonius (Heliconius), Pl. 23, 11,
13, 269
charlottei (Speyeria cybele), 272
Checkered-Skippers, Pl. 38-39, 403-
409
  Common, Pl. 39, 406
  Desert, Pl. 39, 408
  Mountain, Pl. 38, 404
  Small, Pl. 39, 405
  Tropical, Pl. 39, 408
  Two-banded, Pl. 38, 25, 404
  White, Pl. 39, 407
Checkered White, Pl. 7, 148
Checkerspots, Pl. 26-28, 290-293
  Anicia, Pl. 28, 31, 313
  Baltimore, 315
  Bay, Pl. 28, 25, 26, 315
  Black, Pl. 26, 27, 292
  Chalcedona, Pl. 28, 313
  Colon, 313
  Dotted, Pl. 26, 290
  Edith's, Pl. 28, 314
  Elada, Pl. 27, 302
  Fulvia, Pl. 26, 293
  Gabb's, Pl. 27, 300
  Gillette's, Pl. 28, 28, 286, 312
  Gorgone, Pl. 27, 296
  Harris', Pl. 27, 297
  Hoffmann's, Pl. 27, 301
  Leanira, Pl. 26, 293
  Neumoegen's, 299
  Northern, Pl. 27, 298
  Quino, 25, 26, 315
  Rockslide, Pl. 27, 301
  Sagebrush, Pl. 27, 299
  Silvery, Pl. 27, 297
  Theona, Pl. 26, 291
  Tiny, Pl. 27, 302
  Variable, Pl. 28, 313
chinatiensis (Thessalia theona), Pl. 26,
292
Chioides, Pl. 35, 375-376
  catillus, Pl. 35, 375
  zilpa, Pl. 35, 376
Chiomara, Pl. 37, 393-394
  georgina, Pl. 37, 393
  mithrax, 393
Chiricahua White, Pl. 7, 27, 145
chiron (Marpesia), Pl. 31, 341
Chisos Banded-Skipper, Pl. 36, 382
Chisos Metalmark, 27, 265
Chisos Skipperling, Pl. 40, 416
chisosensis (Apodemia), 27, 265
chloridice (Pontia), 149

Chlorostrymon simaethis, Pl. 15, 198
Chlosyne, Pl. 27, 294-302
  acastus, Pl. 27, 299
  californica, Pl. 26, 28, 294
  definita, Pl. 26, 27, 295
  drusius (nycteis), Pl. 27
  endeis, Pl. 26, 295
  gabbii, Pl. 27, 300
  gorgone, Pl. 27, 296
  harrissii, Pl. 27, 297
  hoffmanni, Pl. 27, 301
  janais, Pl. 26, 296
  lacinia, Pl. 26, 295
  manchada (hoffmannii), Pl. 27
  marina, 296
  neumoegeni, 299
  nycteis, Pl. 27, 297
  palla, Pl. 27, 298
  rosita, Pl. 26, 296
  whitneyi, Pl. 27, 301
christina (Colias), Pl. 10, 165
Christina Sulphur, Pl. 10, 165
chrysomelas (Colias occidentalis), Pl. 10,
164
chryxus (Oeneis), Pl. 33, 364
Chryxus Arctic, Pl. 33, 364
cinctus (Autochton), Pl. 36, 382
clarus (Epargyreus), Pl. 35, 374
claudia (Euptoieta), Pl. 23, 270
cleobaea, Lycorea, 371
clodius (Parnassius), Pl. 1, 126
Clodius Parnassian, Pl. 1, 126
clorinde (Anteos), Pl. 12, 174
Clouded Skipper, Pl. 40, 418
Clouded Sulphur, Pl. 10, 162
Cloudless Sulphur, Pl. 12, 175
Cloudywings, Pl. 36-37, 382-385
  Coyote, Pl. 36, 383
  Desert, Pl. 36, 382
  Drusius, Pl. 37, 385
  Mexican, Pl. 37, 385
  Northern, Pl. 36, 383
  Skinner's, Pl. 36, 383
  Southern, Pl. 36, 384
  Western, Pl. 36, 384
clytius (Bolla), Pl. 37, 389
clyton (Asterocampa), Pl. 31, 345
Coahuila Giant-Skipper, Pl. 44, 473
Coastal Green Hairstreak, Pl. 17, 213
cocyta (Phyciodes), Pl. 28, 306
Codatractus, Pl. 35, 378-379
  alcaeus, Pl. 35, 378
  arizonensis, Pl. 35, 378
  mysie, Pl. 37, 378
coenia (Junonia), Pl. 30, 328
Coenonympha, Pl. 32, 350-351
  california (tullia), Pl. 32

haydenii, Pl. **32**, 2 86, 3 50
inornata (tullia), Pl. **32**
ochracea (tullia), Pl. **32**
oedippus, 350
tullia, Pl. **32**, 3 50
Cogia, Pl. **37**, 387-388
caicus, Pl. **37**, 388
calchas, Pl. **37**, 3 87
hippalus, Pl. **37**, 3 87
outis, Pl. **37**, 388
Colias, Pl. **10-11**, 1 3, 1 62-173
alexandra, Pl. **10**, 28, 1 65
behrii, Pl. **11**, 28, 1 72
canadensis, Pl. **11**, 28, 1 68
christina, Pl. **10**, 1 65
chrysomelas (occidentalis), Pl. **10**,
   1 64
eurytheme, Pl. **10**, 1 63
gigantea, Pl. **11**, 1 70
harfordi, Pl. **10**, 28, 1 66
hecla, Pl. **11**, 1 67
interior, Pl. **11**, 1 71
johanseni, Pl. **10**, 1 67
meadii, Pl. **10**, 28, 1 66
nastes, Pl. **11**, 1 69
occidentalis, Pl. **10**, 1 64
palaeno, Pl. **11**, 1 72
pelidne, Pl. **11**, 1 71
philodice, Pl. **10**, 1 62
scudderii, Pl. **11**, 28, 1 69
tyche, Pl. **11**, 30, 1 68
Colon Checkerspot, 3 1 3
coloradensis (Megathymus yuccae), 475
colorado (Hesperia), Pl. **41**, 4 28
Colorado Alpine, Pl. **33**, 28, 3 61
Colorado Hairstreak, Pl. **15**, 1 96
coloro (Papilio polyxenes), Pl. **3**, 38
columbia (Hesperia), Pl. **41**, 28, 4 32
Columbian Skipper, Pl. **41**, 28, 4 32
comma (Hesperia), Pl. **41**, 4 27
comma (Polygonia), Pl. **29**, 3 16
Commas, Pl. **29**, 3 16-320
   Eastern, Pl. **29**, 3 16,
   Gray, Pl. **29**, 3 19
   Green, Pl. **29**, 3 18
   Hoary, Pl. **29**, 3 19
   Satyr, Pl. **29**, 3 17
Common Alpine, Pl. **33**, 3 61
Common Branded Skipper, Pl. **41**, 4 27
Common Buckeye, Pl. **30**, 3 28
Common Checkered-Skipper, Pl. **39**,
   406
Common Least Skipper, Pl. **40**, 4 19
Common Mestra, Pl. **31**, 3 38
Common Ringlet, Pl. **32**, 3 50
Common Roadside-Skipper, Pl. **43**, 4 64
Common Sootywing, Pl. **39**, 4 1 2

Common Streaky-Skipper, Pl. **39**, 4 1 1
Common Wood-Nymph, Pl. **32**, 3 52
communis (Pyrgus), Pl. **39**, 4 06
Compton Tortoiseshell, Pl. **29**, 1 1, 3 20
comstocki (Callophrys), Pl. **17**, 28, 2 14
comyntas (Everes), Pl. **19**, 2 31
Copaeodes, Pl. **40**, 4 21-422
   aurantiaca, Pl. **40**, 4 21
   minima, Pl. **40**, 4 21
Coppers, Pl. **14**, Pl. **15**, 1 86-196
   American, Pl. **14**, 1 87
   Blue, Pl. **15**, 1 93
   Bronze, Pl. **14**, 1 90
   Dorcas, Pl. **15**, 1 93
   Edith's, Pl. **14**, 1 91
   Gorgon, Pl. **14**, 28, 1 91
   Gray, Pl. **14**, 1 89
   Great, Pl. **14**, 28, 1 88
   Hermes, Pl. **15**, 28, 1 95
   Lilac-bordered, Pl. **15**, 1 95
   Lustrous, Pl. **14**, 1 87
   Mariposa, Pl. **15**, 1 95
   Purplish, Pl. **15**, 1 94
   Ruddy, Pl. **15**, 1 92
   Tailed, Pl. **14**, 1 86
Coral Hairstreak, Pl. **16**, 2 08
coronis (Speyeria), Pl. **24**, 2 76
Coronis Fritillary, Pl. **24**, 2 76
Coyote Cloudywing, Pl. **36**, 3 83
Crackers, Pl. **31**, 3 39
   Black-patched, Pl. **31**, 3 39
   Glaucous, Pl. **31**, 3 39
   Gray, Pl. **31**, 3 39
Cranberry Blue, Pl. **21**, 2 45
Creamy Stripe-streak, Pl. **18**, 2 02
Crescent Metalmark, 2 63
Crescents, Pl. **27**, 3 03-312
   California, Pl. **28**, 28, 3 09
   Field, Pl. **28**, 3 08
   Northern, Pl. **28**, 3 06
   Mylitta, Pl. **28**, 3 1 1
   Painted, Pl. **28**, 3 09
   Pale, Pl. **28**, 3 1 0
   Pearl, Pl. **28**, 3 04
   Phaon, Pl. **28**, 3 04
   Tawny, Pl. **28**, 3 07
   Texan, Pl. **27**, 3 03
   Tulcis, Pl. **27**, 3 03
   Vesta, Pl. **27**, 3 04
cresphontes (Papilio), Pl. **4**, 1 36
creusa (Euchloe), Pl. **9**, 1 55
Crimson Patch, Pl. **26**, 2 96
critola, Hypostrymon, Pl. **18**, 2 00
Crossline Skipper, Pl. **41**, 4 43
crysalus (Hypaurotis), Pl. **15**, 1 96
cupreus (Lycaena), Pl. **14**, 1 87
cyananthe (Myscelia), 3 36

Cyanophrys, **Pl. 17** , 212-213
   amyntor, **Pl. 17**, 212
   longula, **Pl. 17**, 212
cybele (*Speyeria*), **Pl. 23**, 271
Cyllopsis, **Pl. 32**, 348-349
   henshawi (=*pyracmon*), 348
   pertepida, **Pl. 32**, 348
   pyracmon, **Pl. 32**, 27, 348
cymela (*Megisto*), **Pl. 32**, 349
Cyna Blue, **Pl. 19**, 229
cyna (*Zizula*), **Pl. 19**, 229
cyneas (*Thessalia*), **Pl. 26**, 27, 292
cythera (*Apodemia mormo*), 260

dacotae (*Hesperia*), 435
Daggerwings, **Pl. 31**, 341
   Many-banded, **Pl. 31**, 341
   Ruddy, **Pl. 31**, 341
   Waiter, 340
Dainty Sulphur, **Pl. 13**, 184
daira (*Eurema*), **Pl. 13**, 11, 179
Dakota Skipper, 435
Danainae, 369-371
Danaus, **Pl. 34**, 369-371
   eresimus, **Pl. 34**, 371
   gilippus, **Pl. 34**, 370
   plexippus, **Pl. 34**, 10, 11, 369
Dark Buckeye, 329
Dartwhite, Mexican, **Pl. 7**, 145
Dash, Long, **Pl. 41**, 443
definita, *Chlosyne*, **Pl. 26**, 27, 295
Definite Patch, **Pl. 26**, 27, 295
Delaware Skipper, **Pl. 42**, 447
Desert Checkered-Skipper, **Pl. 39**, 408
Desert Cloudywing, **Pl. 36**, 382
Desert Elfin, **Pl. 17**, 220
Desert Green Hairstreak, **Pl. 17**, 28, 214
Desert Marble, **Pl. 9**, 28, 157
Desert Mottled Skipper, **Pl. 37**, 378
Desert Orangetip, **Pl. 9**, 27, 32, 158
deserti (*Apodemia mejicanus*), **Pl. 22**, 260
deva (*Atrytonopsis*), **Pl. 42**, 455
Deva Skipper, **Pl. 42**, 455
Diaethria anna, 338
Diana Fritillary, 130
dina (*Eurema*), **Pl. 13**, 182
Dina Yellow, **Pl. 13**, 182
Dingy Fritillary, **Pl. 25**, 285
Dingy Purplewing, **Pl. 30**, 336
dione (*Lycaena*), **Pl. 14**, 189
Dione moneta, **Pl. 23**, 268
disa (*Erebia*), **Pl. 32**, 356
Disa Alpine, **Pl. 32**, 356
discoidalis (*Erebia*), **Pl. 33**, 358

distincta (*Boloria astarte*), **Pl. 25**, 288
diversus (*Thorybes*), **Pl. 36**, 384
domicella (*Heliopetes*), **Pl. 39**, 409
dorantes (*Urbanus*), **Pl. 36**, 379
Dorantes Longtail, **Pl. 36**, 379
dorcas (*Lycaena*), **Pl. 15**, 193
Dorcas Copper, **Pl. 15**, 193
dorus (*Zestusa*), **Pl. 35**, 377
Dotted-Blues, **Pls. 19-20**, 235—243
   Bauer's, **Pl. 20**, 28, 238
   Bernardino, **Pl. 19**, 28, 236
   Ellis', **Pl. 20**, 238
   Intermediate, 239
   Mojave, **Pl. 20**, 28, 240
   Pacific, **Pls. 19-20**, 25, 239
   Pallid, **Pl. 20**, 28, 241
   Rita, **Pl. 20**, 241
   Rocky Mountain, **Pl. 20**, 240
   Small, **Pl. 20**, 243
   Spalding's, **Pl. 20**, 242
Dotted Checkerspot, **Pl. 26**, 290
Dotted Roadside-Skipper, **Pl. 43**, 464
Dotted Skipper, 433
draco (*Polites*), **Pl. 41**, 442
Draco Skipper, **Pl. 41**, 442
Dreamy Duskywing, **Pl. 38**, 395
drusilla (*Appias*), **Pl. 7**, 146
drusius (*Chlosyne nycteis*), **Pl. 27**
drusius (*Thorybes*), **Pl. 37**, 385
Drusius Cloudywing, **Pl. 37**, 385
Dryas julia, **Pl. 23**, 269
dryope (*Satyrium sylvinus*), 207
Dull Firetip, **Pl. 35**, 373
dumetorum (*Callophrys*), **Pl. 17**, 213
Dun Skipper, **Pl. 42**, 454
duryi (*Apodemia*), **Pl. 22**, 262
Dusky Emperor, 345
Dusky-blue Groundstreak, **Pl. 18**, 201
Duskywings, **Pl. 37-38**, 13, 394-403
   Afranius, **Pl. 38**, 402
   Dreamy, **Pl. 38**, 395
   False, **Pl. 37**, 394
   Funereal, **Pl. 38**, 401
   Horace's, **Pl. 38**, 398
   Juvenal's, **Pl. 38**, 396
   Meridian, **Pl. 38**, 397,
   Mottled, **Pl. 38**, 399
   Mournful, **Pl. 38**, 399
   Pacuvius, **Pl. 38**, 400
   Persius, **Pl. 38**, 403
   Propertius, **Pl. 38**, 397
   Rocky Mountain, **Pl. 38**, 397
   Scudder's, **Pl. 38**, 398
   Sleepy, **Pl. 38**, 395
   Wild Indigo, **Pl. 38**, 401
Dusted Skipper, **Pl. 42**, 454

dymas (Dymasia), Pl. 27, 302
Dymasia dymas, Pl. 27, 302
Dynamine tithia, 337

Eastern Comma, Pl. 29, 316
Eastern Pine Elfin, Pl. 18, 220
Eastern Tailed-Blue, Pl. 19, 231
Eastern Tiger Swallowtail, Pl. 5, 138
echion, Tmolus, Pl. 18, 199
echo (Celastrina ladon), 233
Edith's Checkerspot, Pl. 28, 314
Edith's Copper, Pl. 14, 191
editha (Euphydryas), Pl. 28, 314
editha (Lycaena), Pl. 14, 191
Edwards' Fritillary, Pl. 24, 275
Edwards' Hairstreak, Pl. 16, 209
Edwards' Skipperling, Pl. 40, 420
edwardsi (Atrytonopsis), Pl. 43, 458
edwardsii (Oarisma), Pl. 40, 420
edwardsii (Satyrium), Pl. 16, 209
edwardsii (Speyeria), Pl. 24, 275
egeremet (Wallengrenia), Pl. 41, 445
egleis, Speyeria, Pl. 24, 278
El Segundo Blue, 25-26
Elada Checkerspot, Pl. 27, 302
elada (Texola), Pl. 27, 302
Elf, Pl. 27, 302
Elfins, Pl. 17, 220-223
    Brown, Pl. 17, 220
    Desert, Pl. 17, 220
    Eastern Pine Pl. 18, 222
    Henry's, Pl. 18, 222
    Hoary, Pl. 18, 221
    Moss', Pl. 18, 25-26, 221
    San Bruno, 25-26
    Western Pine, Pl. 18, 223
Ellis' Dotted-Blue, Pl. 20, 238
elissa (Amblyscirtes), Pl. 43, 461
Elissa Roadside-Skipper, Pl. 43, 461
ellisi (Euphilotes), Pl. 20, 238
elva (Microtia), Pl. 27, 302
Emesis, Pl. 22, 258-259
    ares, Pl. 22, 258
    zela, Pl. 22, 258
emigdionis (Plebulina), Pl. 20, 28, 249
emorsus (Antigonus), Pl. 37, 391
Emorsus Skipper, Pl. 37, 391
Emperors, Pl. 31, 344-345
    Dusky, 345
    Hackberry, Pl. 31, 344
    Tawny, Pl. 31, 345
Empress Leilia, Pl. 31, 344
endeis (Chlosyne), Pl. 26, 295
Enodia anthedon, Pl. 32, 347
enoptes (Euphilotes), Pls. 19-20, 25, 239

eos (Amblyscirtes), Pl. 43, 464
epaphus (Siproeta), Pl. 30, 330
Epargyreus, Pl. 35, 374
    clarus, Pl. 35, 374
    windi, Pl. 35, 374
epipsodea (Erebia), Pl. 33, 361
epithore (Boloria), Pl. 25, 284
Erebia, Pl. 32, 355-361
    anyuica, Pl. 33, 359
    callias, Pl. 33, 28, 361
    disa, Pl. 32, 356
    discoidalis, Pl. 33, 358
    epipsodea, Pl. 33, 361
    fasciata, Pl. 33, 358
    kozhantikovi, 360
    lafontainei, Pl. 33, 360
    mackinleyensis, Pl. 32, 357
    magdalena, Pl. 32, 357
    mancinus, Pl. 32, 356
    rossii, Pl. 32, 355
    theano, Pl. 33, 358
    vidleri, Pl. 32, 355
    youngi, Pl. 33, 359
eresimus (Danaus), Pl. 34, 371
ericetorum (Heliopetes), Pl. 39, 409
Erichson's White-Skipper, Pl. 39, 409
Erionota, 418
    thrax, 418
    torus, 418
Erora quaderna, Pl. 18, 27, 200
errans (Panoquina), Pl. 43, 467
Erynnis, Pl. 38, 13, 394-403
    afranius, Pl. 38, 402
    baptiseae, Pl. 38, 401
    brizo, Pl. 38, 395
    funeralis, Pl. 38, 401
    horatius, Pl. 38, 398
    icelus, Pl. 38, 395
    juvenalis, Pl. 38, 396
    martialis, Pl. 38, 399
    meridianus, Pl. 38, 397,
    pacuvius, Pl. 38, 400
    persius, Pl. 38, 403
    propertius, Pl. 38, 397
    scudderi, Pl. 38, 398
    telemachus, Pl. 38, 397
    tristis, Pl. 38, 399
eryphon (Callophrys), Pl. 18, 223
ethlius (Calpodes), Pl. 43, 467
ethusa (Myscelia), 335
Euchloe, Pl. 8, Pl. 9, 154-58
    ausonides, Pl. 8, 154
    creusa, Pl. 9, 155
    hyantis, Pl. 9, 28, 157
    guaymasensis, Pl. 9, 156
    lotta, Pl. 9, 28, 157

Euchloe, (cont.)
  naina, Pl. 9, 30, 155
  olympia, Pl. 9, 156
Eueides isabella, Pl. 23, 269
eufala (Lerodea), Pl. 43, 466
Eufala Skipper, Pl. 43, 466
Eunica, Pl. 30, 336
  monima, Pl. 30, 336
  tatila, Pl. 30, 337
eunomia (Boloria), Pl. 25, 282
eunus (Pseudocopaeodes), Pl. 40, 424
Euphilotes, Pl. 19-20, 235-243
  allyni (battoides), 25-26
  ancilla, Pl. 20, 240
  battoides, Pl. 19, 236
  baueri, Pl. 20, 28, 238
  bernardino, Pl. 19, 28, 236
  centralis (battoides), Pl. 20
  ellisi, Pl. 20, 238
  enoptes Pls. 19-20, 239
  intermedia, 239
  mojave, Pl. 20, 28, 240
  pallescens, Pl. 20, 28, 241
  rita, Pl. 20, 241
  smithi (enoptes), 25
  spaldingi, Pl. 20, 242
Euphydryas, Pl. 28, 32, 312-315
  bayensis (editha), Pl. 28, 25, 26, 315
  bernadetta (chalcedona), Pl. 28
  chalcedona, Pl. 28, 31, 313
  editha, Pl. 28, 314
  gillettei, Pl. 28, 28, 286, 312
  phaeton, 315
  quino, 25, 26, 315
Euphyes, Pl. 42, 453-454
  bimacula, Pl. 42, 453
  harbisoni (vestris), 454
  vestris, Pl. 42, 454
Euptoieta, Pl. 23, 270-271,
  claudia, Pl. 23, 270
  hegesia, Pl. 23, 270
Eurema, Pl. 13, 179-184
  boisduvaliana, Pl. 13, 180
  daira, Pl. 13, 11, 179
  dina, Pl. 13, 182
  lisa, Pl. 13, 182
  mexicana, Pl. 13, 181
  nicippe, Pl. 13, 183
  nise, Pl. 13, 182
  proterpia, Pl. 13, 181
European Skipper, Pl. 40, 422
eurydice (Satyrodes), Pl. 32, 347
eurydice (Zerene), Pl. 12, 173
eurymedon (Papilio), Pl. 6, 140
eurytheme (Colias), Pl. 10, 163
Eurytides marcellus, Pl. 2, 131

evansi (Agathymus), Pl. 44, 472
Everes, Pl. 19, 231-232
  amyntula, Pl. 19, 232
  comyntas, Pl. 19, 231
eversmanni (Parnassius), Pl. 1, 30, 126
Eversmann's Parnassian, Pl. 1, 30, 126
exilis (Brephidium), Pl. 19, 227
exoteria (Amblyscirtes), Pl. 43, 459
Eyed Brown, Pl. 32, 347

Faceted Skipper, Pl. 40, 417
Falcate Orangetip, Pl. 9, 161
False Duskywing, Pl. 37, 394
False Ringlet, 350
fasciata (Erebia), Pl. 33, 358
Fatal Metalmark, Pl. 22, 255
fatima (Anartia), Pl. 30, 330
faunus (Polygonia), Pl. 29, 318
favonius (Fixsenia), Pl. 16, 203
februa (Hamadryas), Pl. 31, 339
Feniseca tarquinius, Pl. 14, 186
Ferris' Copper, 192
ferrisi (Lycaena), 192
Field Crescent, Pl. 28, 308
Fiery Skipper, Pl. 40, 423
fimbriata (Amblyscirtes), Pl. 43, 466
Firetips, Pl. 35, 373
  Dull, Pl. 35, 373
Fixsenia, Pl. 16-17, 203-205
  favonius, Pl. 16, 203
  ilavia, Pl. 16, 204
  polingi, Pl. 17, 27, 204
  violae (favonius), Pl. 16
Flasher, Two-barred, Pl. 36, 381
Flat, Fritzgaertner's, Pl. 37, 386
Florida Purplewing, Pl. 30, 337
Florida White, Pl. 7, 145, 146
fordi (Papilio indra), Pl. 4, 40
fotis (Callophrys), Pl. 17, 220
Four-dotted Alpine, Pl. 33, 359
Four-spotted Skipperling, Pl. 40, 415
freemani (Calephelis rawsoni), 258
Freeman's Metalmark, 258
freija (Boloria), Pl. 25, 287
Freija Fritllary, Pl. 25, 287
frigga (Boloria), Pl. 25, 285
Frigga Fritillary, Pl. 25, 285
Fritillaries, Pls. 23- 25, 9, 11, 31, 268,
       270-289
  Alberta, Pl. 25, 28, 288
  Aphrodite, Pl. 23, 272
  Arctic, Pl. 25, 289
  Astarte, Pl. 25, 288
  Atlantis, Pl. 24, 279
  Beringian, Pl. 25, 30, 287
  Bog, Pl. 25, 282

Callippe, Pl. 24, 25, 26, 277
Coronis, Pl. 24, 276
Dingy, Pl. 25, 25-26, 285
Edwards', Pl. 24, 275
Freija, Pl. 25, 287
Frigga, Pl. 25, 285
Great Basin, Pl. 24, 278
Great Spangled, Pl. 23, 271
Gulf, Pl. 23, 268
Hydaspe, Pl. 24, 281
Meadow, Pl. 25, 284
Mexican, Pl. 23, 270
Mormon, Pl. 24, 281
Mountain, Pl. 25, 282
Nokomis, Pl. 23, 274
Northwestern, Pl. 24, 28, 279
Pacific, Pl. 25, 284
Polaris, Pl. 25, 287
Purple, 290
Regal, Pl. 23, 273
Relict, Pl. 25, 286
Silver-bordered, Pl. 25,283
Uncompahgre, Pl. 25, 25-26, 286
Unsilvered, Pl. 24, 28, 278
Variegated, Pl. 23, 270
Zerene, Pl. 24, 276
fritzgaertneri (Celaenorrhinus), Pl. 37, 386
Fritzgaertner's Flat, Pl. 37, 386
fulgerator (Astraptes), Pl. 36, 381
fuliginosum (Satyrium), Pl. 16, 205
fulvia (Thessalia), Pl. 26, 27, 293
Fulvia Checkerspot, Pl. 26, 27, 293
funeralis (Erynnis), Pl. 38, 401
Funereal Duskywing, Pl. 38, 401

gabbii (Chlosyne), Pl. 27, 300
Gabb's Checkerspot, Pl. 27, 300
Ganyra, Pl. 8, 153
  howarthi, Pl. 8, 27, 154
  josephina, Pl. 8, 153
garita (Oarisma), Pl. 40, 420
Garita Skipperling, Pl. 40, 420
genoveva (Junonia), Pl. 30, 329
georgina (Chiomara), Pl. 37, 393
Gesta invisus, Pl. 37, 394
Giant-Skippers, Pl. 44, 476
  Arizona, Pl. 44, 471
  Bauer's, 471
  California, Pl. 44, 473
  Coahuila, Pl. 44, 473
  Huachuca, Pl. 44, 472
  Manfreda, Pl. 44, 477
  Mary's, Pl. 44, 27, 472
  Mojave, Pl. 44, 475
  Orange, Pl. 44, 470

Poling's, Pl. 44, 474
Southwestern, Pl. 44, 475
Strecker's, Pl. 44, 476
Ursine, Pl. 44, 476
Yucca, Pl. 44, 475
Giant Sulphur, Pl. 11, 170
Giant Swallowtail, Pl. 4, 136
Giant White, Pl. 8, 153
gigantea (Colias), Pl. 11, 170
gilippus (Danaus), Pl. 34, 370
Gillette's Checkerspot, Pl. 28, 28, 286, 312
gillettii (Euphydryas), Pl. 28, 28, 286, 312
glandon (Agriades), Pl. 21, 246
Glassywing, Little, Pl. 41, 446
Glassy-winged Skipper, Pl. 37, 391
glauconome (Hamadryas), Pl. 31, 339
Glaucopsyche, Pl. 20,243-245
  lygdamus, Pl. 20, 245
  palosverdesensis (lygdamus), 25
  piasus, Pl. 20, 243
  xerces (lygdamus), Pl. 20, 245
Glaucous Cracker, Pl. 31, 339
glaucus (Papilio), Pl. 5, 138
Goatweed Leafwing, Pl. 31, 342
Golden Hairstreak, Pl. 15, 197
Golden-banded Skipper, Pl. 36, 10, 381
Golden-headed Scallopwing, Pl. 37, 389
Gold-hunter's Hairstreak, Pl. 16, 28, 210
Gold-spotted Aguna, Pl. 35, 376
gorgon (Lycaena), Pl. 14, 28, 191
Gorgon Copper, Pl. 14, 28, 191
gorgone (Chlosyne), Pl. 27, 296
Gorgone Checkerspot, Pl. 27, 296
graciela (Hesperopsis), Pl. 39, 414
gracilis (Polygonia), Pl. 29, 319
Grais stigmaticus, Pl. 37, 392
Grass Skippers, 416-469
Gray Comma, Pl. 29, 319
Gray Copper, Pl. 14, 189
Gray Cracker, Pl. 31, 339
Gray Hairstreak, Pl. 18, 223
Gray Marble, Pl. 9, 28, 161
Gray Ministreak, Pl. 18, 199
Great Arctic, Pl. 33, 363
Great Basin Fritillary, Pl. 24, 278
Great Basin Wood-Nymph, Pl. 32, 352
Great Copper, Pl. 14, 28, 188
Great Purple Hairstreak, Pl. 15, 197
Great Southern White, Pl. 8, 153
Great Spangled Fritillary, Pl. 23, 271
Green Comma, Pl. 29, 318
Green Marble, Pl. 9, 30, 155

Green Skipper, Pl. 41, 433
Greenish Blue, Pl. 20, 249
Greenstreaks, Pl. 17, 212-213
  Amyntor, Pl. 17, 212
  Long-winged, Pl. 17, 212
Grizzled Skipper, Pl. 38, 403
Groundstreak, Dusky-Blue, Pl. 18, 201
grunus (Hhabrodais), Pl. 15, 197
gryneus (Callophrys), Pl. 17, 32, 217
guaymasensis (Euchloe), Pl. 9, 156
Gulf Fritillary, Pl. 23, 268
Gyrocheilus patrobas, Pl. 33, 27, 362

Habrodais grunus, Pl. 15, 197
Hackberry Emperor, Pl. 31, 344
haferniki (Piruna), Pl. 40, 416
Hairstreaks, Pl. 14-18, 196-227
  Acadian, Pl. 16, 206
  Arizona, Pl. 18, 27, 200
  Banded, Pl. 16, 209
  Behr's, Pl. 16, 205
  California, Pl. 16, 207
  Coastal Green, Pl. 17, 213
  Colorado, Pl. 14, 196
  Coral, Pl. 16, 208
  Desert Green, Pl. 17, 28, 214
  Edwards', Pl. 16, 209
  Golden, Pl. 14, 197
  Gold-hunter's, Pl. 16, 28, 210
  Great Purple, Pl. 14, 197
  Hedgerow, Pl. 16, 28, 211
  Ilavia, Pl. 16, 204
  Johnson's, Pl. 17, 216
  Juniper, Pl. 17, 32, 217
  Marius, Pl. 18, 202
  Mountain-Mahogany, Pl. 16, 211
  Muir's, Pl. 17, 28, 217
  Nelson's, Pl. 17, 217
  Poling's, Pl. 17, 27, 204
  Red-banded, Pl. 18, 201
  Red-spotted, Pl. 18, 199
  Sandia, Pl. 17, 28, 219
  Silver-banded, Pl. 14, 198
  Soapberry, Pl. 16, 203
  Sonoran, Pl. 18, 200
  Sooty, Pl. 16, 205
  Southern, Pl. 16, 203
  Striped, Pl. 16, 210
  Sylvan, Pl. 16, 207
  Thicket, Pl. 17, 215
  Thorne's, Pl. 17, 219
  Western Green, Pl. 17, 213
  White M, Pl. 18, 198
  Xami, Pl. 17, 219
halesus (Atlides), Pl. 15, 197
Hamadryas, Pl. 31, 339-340

atlantis, Pl. 31, 339
februa, Pl. 31, 339
glauconome, Pl. 31, 339
Hammock Skipper, Pl. 35, 374
harbisoni (Euphyes vestris), 454
harfordii (Colias), Pl. 10, 28, 166
Harford's Sulphur, Pl. 10, 28, 166
harrisii (Chlosyne), Pl. 27, 297
Harris's Checkerspot, Pl. 27, 297
Harvester, Pl. 14, 186
Hawaiian Blue, Pl. 21, 245
haydenii (Coenonympha), Pl. 32, 286, 350
Hayden's Ringlet, Pl. 32, 286, 350
hayhurstii (Staphylus), Pl. 37, 390
Hayhurst's Scallopwing, Pl. 37, 390
hecla (Colias), Pl. 11, 167
Hecla Sulphur, Pl. 11, 167
Hedgerow Hairstreak, Pl. 16, 28, 211
Hedyliidae, 4
hegesia (Euptoieta), Pl. 23, 270
hegon (Amblyscirtes), Pl. 43, 461
Heliconian, Isabella's, Pl. 23, 269
Heliconiinae, 267-290
Heliconius charithonius, Pl. 23, 11, 13, 269
Heliopetes, Pl. 39, 409-410
  domicella, Pl. 39, 409
  ericetorum, Pl. 39, 409
  laviana, Pl. 39, 410
helloides (Lycaena), Pl. 15, 194
Hemiargus, Pl. 19, 230
  ceraunus, Pl. 19, 230
  isola, Pl. 19, 230
henrici (Callophrys), Pl. 18, 222
Henry's Elfin, Pl. 18, 222
Henshaw's Satyr, 348
Hepburn's Metalmark, Pl. 22, 262
hepburni (Apodemia), Pl. 22, 262
herlani (Phyciodes orseis), 310
Hermes Copper, Pl. 15, 28, 195
hermes (Lycaena), Pl. 15, 28, 195
Hermit Skipper, Pl. 37, 392
Hesperia, Pls. 40-41, 425-437
  assiniboia, Pl. 41, 427
  attalus, 433
  colorado, Pl. 41, 428
  columbia, Pl. 41, 28, 432
  comma, Pl. 41, 427
  dacotae, 435
  juba, Pl. 40, 426
  leonardus, Pl. 41, 430
  lindseyi, Pl. 41, 28, 434
  macswaini (uncas), 426
  martini (pahaska), 431-432
  miriamae, Pl. 41, 28, 434

montana (leonardus), Pl. **41**, 25, 430
nevada, Pl. **41**, 437
ottoe, Pl. **41**, 429
pahaska, Pl. **41**, 431
pawnee (leonardus), 430
sassacus, 436
uncas, Pl. **40**, 426
viridis, Pl. **41**, 433
williamsi (pahaska), 431
woodgatei, Pl. **41**, 429
yosemite (colorado), 434
Hesperiidae, 372-477
Hesperiinae, 416-469
Hesperioidea, 1, 372-477
hesperis (Speyeria), Pl. **24**, 28, 279
Hesperopsis, Pl. **39**, 412-414
   alpheus, Pl. **39**, 413
   gracielae, Pl. **39**, 414
   libya, Pl. **39**, 412
heteronea (Lycaena), Pl. **15**, 193
Heteropterinae, 414-416
hianna (Atrytonopsis), Pl. **42**, 454
hippalus (Cogia), Pl. **37**, 387
hippolyta (Speyeria zerene), 277
hirsuta (Battus philenor), 130
Historis acheronta, Pl. **31**, 340
Hoary Comma, Pl. **29**, 319
Hoary Elfin, Pl. **18**, 221
hobomok (Poanes), Pl. **42**, 449
Hobomok Skipper, Pl. **42**, 449
hoffmannii (Chlosyne), Pl. **27**, 301
Hoffmann's Checkerspot, Pl. **27**, 301
homoperplexa (Callophrys affinis),
   Pl. **17**
Hops Azure, Pl. **19**, 234
Horace's Duskywing, Pl. **38**, 398
horatius (Erynnis), Pl. **38**, 398
howarthi (Ganyra), Pl. **8**, 27, 154
Howarth's White, Pl. **8**, 27, 154
Huachuca Giant-Skipper, Pl. **44**, 472
humulus (Celastrina), Pl. **19**, 234
hyantis (Euchloe), Pl. **9**, 28, 157
hydaspe (Speyeria), Pl. **24**, 281
Hydaspe Fritillary, Pl. **24**, 281
Hylephila phylaeus, Pl. **40**, 423
hylas (Polygonia faunus), 318
hyllus (Lycaena), Pl. **14**, 190
Hypaurotis crysalus, Pl. **15**, 196
hyperia (Biblis), Pl. **31**, 338
Hypostrymon critola, Pl. **18**, 200

Icaricia, Pl. **21**, 250-
   acmon, Pl. **21**, 252
   icarioides, Pl. **21**, 25-26, 250
   lupini, Pl. **21**, 252
   missionensis (icarioides), 25-26, 251

neurona, Pl. **21**, 253
   shasta, Pl. **21**, 251
icarioides, Pl. **21**, 25-26, 250
icelus (Erynnis), Pl. **38**, 395
idalia (Speyeria), Pl. **23**, 273
idas (Lycaeides), Pl. **20**, 25, 248
idyja (Asterocampa), 345
ilavia (Fixsenia), Pl. **16**, 204
Ilavia Hairstreak, Pl. **16**, 204
improba (Boloria), Pl. **25**, 25, 285
Indian Skipper, 436
indra (Papilio), Pl. **4**, 27, 130
Indra Swallowtail, Pl. **4**, 27, 130
interior (Colias), Pl. **11**, 171
intermedia (Euphilotes), 239
Intermediate Dotted-Blue, 239
interrogationis (Polygonia), Pl. **29**, 316
invisus (Gesta), Pl. **37**, 394
iole (Nathalis), Pl. **13**, 184
isabella, Eueides, Pl. **23**, 269
Isabella's Heliconian, Pl. **23**, 269
isobeon (Calycopis), Pl. **18**, 201
isola (Hemiargus), Pl. **19**, 230
istapa (Strymon), Pl. **18**, 225
ivallda (Oeneis chryxus), Pl. **33**,

jada (Arawacus), Pl. **18**, 202
janais (Chlosyne), Pl. **26**, 296
jatrophae (Anartia), Pl. **30**, 330
johanseni (Colias), Pl. **10**, 167
Johansen's Sulphur, Pl. **10**, 167
johnsoni (Callophrys), Pl. **17**, 216
Johnson's Hairstreak, Pl. **17**, 216
josephina (Ganyra), Pl. **8**, 153
juba (Hesperia), Pl. **40**, 426
Juba Skipper, Pl. **40**, 426
Julia, Pl. **23**, 269
julia (Anthocharis), Pl. **9**, 159
julia (Dryas), Pl. **23**, 269
julia (Nastra), Pl. **40**, 417
Julia's Skipper, Pl. **40**, 417
Juniper Hairstreak, Pl. **17**, 32, 217
Junonia, Pl. **30**, 328-329
   coenia, Pl. **30**, 328
   genoveva, Pl. **30**, 329
   nigrosuffusa (genoveva), 329
jutta (Oeneis), Pl. **34**, 367
Jutta Arctic, Pl. **34**, 367
juvenalis (Erynnis), Pl. **38**, 396
Juvenal's Duskywing, Pl. **38**, 396

kahli (Papilio polyxenes), 132
kaibabensis (Papilio indra), 130
Kamehameha Lady, Pl. **29**, 326
karwinskii (Smyrna), 340
kozhantikovi (Erebia), 360

Kricogonia lyside, Pl. 13, 179
kriemhild (*Boloria*), Pl. 25, 286

Labrador Sulphur, Pl. 11, 169
Lacey's Scrub-Hairstreak, Pl. 18, 225
lacinia (*Chlosyne*), Pl. 26, 295
ladon (*Celastrina*), Pl. 19, 232
Lady, Pl. 29, 325-328
    American, Pl. 29, 325
    Kamehameha, Pl. 29, 326
    Painted, Pl. 29, 325
    West Coast, Pl. 29, 327
lafontainei (*Erebia*), Pl. 33, 360
Laguna Mountain Skipper, Pl. 38, 25, 404
lagunae (*Pyrgus ruralis*), Pl. 38, 25, 404
Lampides boeticus, Pl. 19, 229
lanceolata (*Anthocharis*), Pl. 9, 28, 161
langei (*Apodemia mormo*), Pl. 22, 25, 261
Lange's *Metalmark*, Pl. 22, 25, 261
Lantana Scrub-Hairstreak, Pl. 18, 226
Large Marble, Pl. 8, 154
Large Orange Sulphur, Pl. 13, 176
Large Roadside-Skipper, Pl. 43, 459
Lasaia maria, 259
Lavinia White-Skipper, Pl. 39, 410
laviana (*Heliopetes*), Pl. 39, 410
Leafwings, Pl. 31, 341-343
    Angled, 342
    Goatweed, Pl. 31, 341
    Tropical, Pl. 31, 342
leanira (*Thessalia*), Pl. 26, 293
Leanira Checkerspot, Pl. 26, 293
leda (*Ministrymon*), Pl. 18, 27, 199
Leda Ministreak, Pl. 18, 27, 199
leilia (*Asterocampa*), Pl. 31, 344
leo, *Polygonus*, Pl. 35, 374
Leonard's Skipper, Pl. 41, 25, 430
leonardus (*Hesperia*), Pl. 41, 25, 430
Leptotes, Pl. 19, 228
    cassius, Pl. 19, 228
    marina, Pl. 19, 228
Lerema accius, Pl. 40, 418
Lerodea, Pl. 43, 466-467
    arabus, Pl. 43, 467
    eufala, Pl. 43, 466
leto (*Speyeria cybele*), Pl. 23, 271
leucas (*Panoquina*), Pl. 43, 469
libya (*Hesperopsis*), Pl. 39, 412
Libytheana, Pl. 22, 267
    bachmanii (*carinenta*), 267
    carinenta, Pl. 22, 267
Libytheinae, 266-267
Lilac-bordered Copper, Pl. 15, 195
Limenitidinae, 331-341

Limenitis, Pl. 30, 331-334
    archippus, Pl. 30, 332
    arizonensis (*arthemis*), 332
    arthemis, Pl. 30, 331
    astyanax (*arthemis*), Pl. 30, 332
    lorquini, Pl. 30, 334
    obsoleta (*archippus*), 333
    proserpina (form of *arthemis*), 331
    weidemeyerii, Pl. 30, 333
limpia (*Celotes*), 411
lindseyi (*Hesperia*), Pl. 41, 28, 434
Lindsey's Skipper, Pl. 41, 28, 434
lineola (*Thymelicus*), Pl. 40, 422
liparops (*Satyrium*), Pl. 16, 210
lisa (*Eurema*), Pl. 13, 182
Little Glassywing, Pl. 41, 446
Little Wood-Satyr, Pl. 32, 349
Little Yellow, Pl. 13, 182
logan (*Anatrytone*), Pl. 42, 447
Long Dash, Pl. 41, 443
Longtails, Pl. 36, 375
    Brown, Pl. 36, 380
    Dorantes, Pl. 36, 379
    Mexican, Pl. 35, 376
    Plain, Pl. 36, 380
    White-crescent, Pl. 35, 378
    White-striped, Pl. 35, 375
    Zilpa, Pl. 35, 376
Long-tailed Skipper, Pl. 35, 379
longula (*Cyanophrys*), Pl. 17, 212
Long-winged Greenstreak, Pl. 17, 212
Longwings, 267-290
Lorquin's Admiral, Pl. 30, 32, 334
lorquini (*Limenitis*), Pl. 30, 32, 334
lotis (*Lycaeides idas*), 25, 248
Lotis Blue, 25, 248
lotta (*Euchloe*), Pl. 9, 28, 157
lunus (*Atrytonopsis*), Pl. 42, 455
Lupine Blue, Pl. 21, 252
lupini (*Icaricia*), Pl. 21, 252
luski (*Speyeria mormonia*), 281
Lustrous Copper, Pl. 14, 187
Lycaeides, Pl. 20, 248-249
    idas, Pl. 20, 248
    lotis (*idas*), 25, 248
    melissa, Pl. 20, 249
Lycaena, Pl. 14, 186-196
    arota, Pl. 14, 186
    cupreus, Pl. 14, 187
    dione, Pl. 14, 189
    dorcas, Pl. 15, 193
    editha, Pl. 14, 191
    ferrisi, 192
    gorgon, Pl. 14, 28, 191
    helloides, Pl. 15, 194
    hermes, Pl. 15, 28, 195

heteronea, Pl. 15, 193
hyllus, Pl. 14, 190
mariposa, Pl. 15, 195
nivalis, Pl. 15, 195
phlaeas, Pl. 14, 187
pyrrhias, 186
rubidus, Pl. 14, 192
snowi (cupreus), Pl. 14, 188
xanthoides, Pl. 14, 28, 188
Lycaenidae, Pl. 14, 185
Lycaeninae, Pl. 14, 186-196
Lycorea cleobaea, 371
lygdamus (Glaucopsyche), Pl. 20, 25, 245
lyside (Kricogonia), Pl. 13, 179
Lyside Sulphur, Pl. 13, 179

machaon (Papilio), Pl. 3, 132
mackinleyensis (Erebia), Pl. 32, 357
MacNeill's Sootywing, Pl. 39, 414
macounii (Oeneis), Pl. 33, 364
Macoun's Arctic, Pl. 33, 364
macswaini (Hesperia uncas), 426
maculosa (Stallingsia), Pl. 44, 477
maerula (Anteos), Pl. 12, 175
magdalena (Erebia), Pl. 32, 357
Magdalena Alpine, Pl. 32, 357
Malachite, Pl. 30, 330
m-album, Parrhasius, Pl. 18, 198
Mallow Scrub-Hairstreak, Pl. 18, 225
manchada (Chlosyne hoffmannii), Pl. 27
mancinus (Erebia), Pl. 32, 356
Manfreda Giant-Skipper, Pl. 44, 477
Many-banded Daggerwing, Pl. 31, 341
Many-spotted Skipperling, Pl. 40, 416
Marbles, Pls. 8-9, 154-58, 161
    California, Pl. 9, 28, 157
    Desert, Pl. 9, 28, 157
    Gray, Pl. 9, 28, 161
    Green, Pl. 9, 30, 155
    Large, Pl. 8, 154
    Northern, Pl. 9, 155
    Olympia, Pl. 9, 156
    Sonoran, Pl. 9, 156
marcellus (Eurytides), Pl. 2, 131
mardon (Polites), Pl. 41, 441
Mardon Skipper, Pl. 41, 441
marginalis (Pieris), Pl. 8, 151
Margined White, Pl. 8, 151
Maria's Metalmark, 259
mariae (Agathymus), Pl. 44, 27, 472
marina (Chlosyne), 296
marina (Leptotes), Pl. 19, 228
Marine Blue, Pl. 19, 228
mariposa (Lycaena), Pl. 15, 195

Mariposa Copper, Pl. 15, 195
marius (Rekoa), Pl. 18, 202
Marius Hairstreak, Pl. 18, 202
Marpesia, Pl. 31, 340-341
    chiron, Pl. 31, 341
    petreus, Pl. 31, 341
    zerynthia, 340
martialis (Erynnis), Pl. 38, 399
martini (Hesperia pahaska), 431-432
martini (Papilio indra), Pl. 4, 40
Mary's Giant-Skipper, Pl. 44, 27, 472
mazans (Staphylus), Pl. 37, 390
Mazans Scallopwing, Pl. 37, 390
mcfarlandi (Callophrys), Pl. 17, 27, 219
meadii (Cercyonis), Pl. 32, 28, 353
meadii (Colias), Pl. 10, 28, 166
meadii (Speyeria callippe), Pl. 24
Meadow Fritillary, Pl. 25, 284
Mead's Sulphur, Pl. 10, 28, 166
Mead's Wood-Nymph, Pl. 32, 28, 353
meckyae (Pieris), 150
Mecky's White, 150
Megathyminae, 470-477
Megathymus, Pl. 44, 475-477
    coloradensis (yuccae), 475
    streckeri, Pl. 44, 476
    ursus, Pl. 44, 476
    violae (ursus), 476
    yuccae, Pl. 44, 475
Megisto, Pl. 32, 349-350
    cymela, Pl. 32, 349
    rubricata, Pl. 32, 349
mejicana (Pholisora), Pl. 39, 412
mejicanus (Apodemia), Pl. 22, 261
melane (Poanes), Pl. 42, 452
melinus (Strymon), Pl. 18, 223
melissa (Lycaeides), Pl. 20, 249
melissa (Oeneis), Pl. 34, 367
Melissa Arctic, Pl. 34, 367
Melissa Blue, Pl. 20, 249
Memphis, 341, 343
    glycerium, 343
menapia (Neophasia), Pl. 7, 145
Mercurial Skipper, 373
mercurius, Proteides, 373
Meridian Duskywing, Pl. 38, 397
meridianus (Erynnis), Pl. 38, 397
Mestra amymone, Pl. 31, 338
Metalmarks, Pl. 22, 6, 255-265
    Ares, Pl. 22, 258
    Arizona, Pl. 22, 258
    Behr's, Pl. 22, 28, 261
    Chisos, 27, 265
    Crescent, 263
    Fatal, Pl. 22, 255
    Freeman's, 258

Metalmarks, *(cont.)*
  Hepburn's, **Pl. 22**, 262
  Lange's, **Pl. 22**, 25, 261
  Maria's, 259
  Mexican, **Pl. 22**, 262
  Mormon, **Pl. 22**, 260
  Nais, **Pl. 22**, 264
  Palmer's, **Pl. 22**, 263
  Rawson's, **Pl. 22**, 257
  Rounded, **Pl. 22**, 257
  Sonoran, **Pl. 22**, 261
  Wright's, **Pl. 22**, 28, 256
  Zela, **Pl. 22**, 258
Mexican Bluewing, 335
Mexican Cloudywing, **Pl. 37**, 385
Mexican Dartwhite, **Pl. 7**, 145
Mexican Fritillary, **Pl. 23**, 270
Mexican Longtail, **Pl. 35**, 376
Mexican Metalmark, **Pl. 22**, 262
Mexican Silverspot, **Pl. 23**, 268
Mexican Sootywing, **Pl. 39**, 412
Mexican Yellow, **Pl. 13**, 181
mexicana (Eurema), **Pl. 13**, 181
mexicanus (Polythrix), **Pl. 35**, 376
mexicanus (Thorybes), **Pl. 37**, 385
Microtia elva, **Pl. 27**, 302
midea (Anthocharis), **Pl. 9**, 161
milberti (Nymphalis), **Pl. 29**, 11, 323
Milbert's Tortoiseshell, **Pl. 29**, 11, 323
Miletinae, 186
Mimic-Queen, Tiger, 371
Mimosa Skipper, **Pl. 37**, 387
Mimosa Yellow, **Pl. 13**, 182
minima (Copaeodes), **Pl. 40**, 421
Ministreaks, **Pl. 18**, 199-200
  Gray, **Pl. 18**, 199
  Leda, **Pl. 18**, 27, 199
Ministrymon, **Pl. 18**, 199-200
  azia, **Pl. 18**, 199
  leda, **Pl. 18**, 27, 199
minori (Papilio indra), **Pl. 4**, 40
minuta (Poladryas), **Pl. 26**, 290
miriamae (Hesperia), **Pl. 41**, 28, 434
Mission Blue, 25-26, 251
mithrax (Chiomara), 393
Mithrax Skipper, 393
Mohave Sootywing, **Pl. 39**, 412
mojave (Euphilotes), **Pl. 20**, 28, 240
Mojave Dotted-Blue, **Pl. 20**, 28, 240
Mojave Giant-Skipper, **Pl. 44**, 475
Monarch, **Pl. 34**, 10, 11, 369
moneta (Dione), **Pl. 23**, 268
monima (Eunica), **Pl. 30**, 336
montana (Hesperia leonardus), **Pl. 41**, 25, 430
montana (Phyciodes pratensis), 309

monuste (Ascia), **Pl. 8**, 153
Moon-marked Skipper, **Pl. 42**, 455
mormo (Apodemia), **Pl. 22**, 260
Mormon Fritillary, **Pl. 24**, 281
Mormon Metalmark, **Pl. 22**, 260
mormonia (Speyeria), **Pl. 24**, 281
Morphinae, 346
Morpho polyphemus, **Pl. 32**, 346
Morphos, **Pl. 32**, 346
  White, **Pl. 32**, 346
morrisoni (Stinga), **Pl. 40**, 425
Morrison's Skipper, **Pl. 40**, 425
Moss' Elfin, **Pl. 18**, 25-26, 221
mossii (Callophrys), **Pl. 18**, 25-26, 221
Mottled Bolla, **Pl. 37**, 389
Mottled Duskywing, **Pl. 38**, 399
Mountain Checkered-Skipper, **Pl. 38**, 404
Mountain Fritillary, **Pl. 25**, 282
Mountain-Mahogany Hairstreak, **Pl. 16**, 211
Mournful Duskywing, **Pl. 38**, 399
Mourning Cloak, **Pl. 29**, 12, 322
Mt. McKinley Alpine, **Pl. 32**, 357
Muir's Hairstreak, **Pl. 17**, 28, 217
muiri (Callophrys), **Pl. 17**, 28, 217
Mustard White, **Pl. 8**, 151
multicaudatus (Papilio), **Pl. 6**, 141
mylitta (Phyciodes), **Pl. 28**, 311
Mylitta Crescent, **Pl. 28**, 311
myrtleae (Speyeria zerene), 25, 277
Myrtle's Silverspot, 25, 277
Myscelia, 335-336
  cyananthe, 336
  ethusa, 335
mysie (Codatractus), **Pl. 37**, 378
mystic (Polites), **Pl. 41**, 443

Nabokov's Satyr, **Pl. 32**, 27, 348
naina (Euchloe), **Pl. 9**, 30, 155
nais (Apodemia), **Pl. 22**, 264
Nais Metalmark, **Pl. 22**, 264
napaea (Boloria), **Pl. 25**, 282
nastes (Colias), **Pl. 11**, 169
Nastra, 417
  julia, **Pl. 40**, 417
  neamathla, 417
natazhati (Boloria), **Pl. 25**, 30, 287
Nathalis iole, **Pl. 13**, 184
nausicaa, (Speyeria hesperis), 280
neamathla (Nastra), 417
neglecta (Celastrina), **Pl. 19**, 233
nelsoni (Callophrys), **Pl. 17**, 217
Nelson's Hairstreak, **Pl. 17**, 217
nemesis (Calephelis), **Pl. 22**, 255
neocypris (Phoebis), 178

Neominois, Pl. 33, 362-363
  ridingsii, Pl. 33, 362
  wyomingo, 32, 363
Neophasia, Pl. 7, 145
  menapia, Pl. 7, 145
  terlootii, Pl. 7, 27, 145
nereus (Amblyscirtes), Pl. 43, 462
nessus (Celotes), Pl. 39, 411
neumoegeni (Agathymus), Pl. 44, 470
neumoegeni (Chlosyne acastus), 299
neurona (Icaricia), Pl. 21, 253
nevada (Hesperia), Pl. 41, 437
Nevada Skipper, Pl. 41, 437
nevadensis (Oeneis), Pl. 33, 363
nicippe (Eurema), Pl. 13, 183
nigrosuffusa (Junonia genoveva), 329
nilus (Calephelis), Pl. 22, 257
nimbice (Catasticta), Pl. 7, 145
niphon (Callophrys), Pl. 18, 222
nise (Eurema), Pl. 13, 182
nitra (Papilio zelicaon), 134
nivalis (Lycaena), Pl. 15, 195
nokomis (Speyeria), Pl. 23, 28, 274
Nokomis Fritillary, Pl. 23, 28, 274
Northern Blue, Pl. 20, 248
Northern Broken-dash, Pl. 41, 445
Northern Checkerspot, Pl. 27, 298
Northern Cloudywing, Pl. 36, 383
Northern Crescent, Pl. 28, 306
Northern Marble, Pl. 9, 155
Northern Pearly-eye, Pl. 32, 347
Northern White-Skipper, Pl. 39, 409
Northwestern Fritillary, Pl. 24, 28, 279
numitor (Ancyloxypha), Pl. 40, 419
nycteis (Chlosyne), Pl. 27, 297
Nyctelius nyctelius, Pl. 43, 469
Nymphalidae, 6, 266-371
Nymphalinae, 290-331
Nymphalis, Pl. 29, 320-324
  antiopa, Pl. 29, 12, 322
  californica, Pl. 29, 320
  milberti, Pl. 29, 11, 323
  vaualbum, Pl. 29, 11, 320
nysa (Amblyscirtes), Pl. 43, 463
Nysa Roadside-Skipper, Pl. 43, 463

Oarisma, Pl. 40, 420
  edwardsii, Pl. 40, 420
  garita, Pl. 40, 420
obsoleta (Limenitis archippus), 333
occidentalis (Colias), Pl. 10, 164
occidentalis (Pontia), Pl. 8, 149
Ochlodes, Pl. 42, 447-449
  agricola, Pl. 42, 28, 448
  sylvanoides, Pl. 42, 447
  yuma, Pl. 42, 449

ocola (Panoquina), Pl. 43, 468
Ocola Skipper, Pl. 43, 468
oedippus (Coenonympha), 350
Oenius, Pls. 33-34, 363-369
  alberta, Pl. 34, 366
  alpina, Pl. 34, 369
  bore, Pl. 34, 366
  chryxus, Pl. 33, 364
  ivallda (chryxus), Pl. 33, 364
  jutta, Pl. 34, 367
  macouni, Pl. 33, 364
  melissa, Pl. 34, 367
  nevadensis, Pl. 33, 363
  philipi, 369
  polixenes, Pl. 34, 368
  rosovi, Pl. 34, 368
  taygete, Pl. 34, 367
  uhleri, Pl. 33, 28, 365
oetus (Cercyonis), Pl. 32, 354
oileus (Pyrgus), Pl. 39, 408
Old World Swallowtail, Pl. 3, 130, 132
oleracea (Pieris), Pl. 8, 151
Olive-clouded Skipper, Pl. 43, 467
olympia (Euchloe), Pl. 9, 156
Olympia Marble, Pl. 9, 156
optilete (Vacciniina), Pl. 21, 245
Oranges, Pl. 13, 181, 183
  Sleepy, Pl. 13, 183
  Tailed, Pl. 13, 181
Orange Giant-Skipper, Pl. 44, 470
Orange Skipperling, Pl. 40, 421
Orange Sulphur, Pl. 10, 163
Orange-barred Sulphur, Pl. 12, 176
Orange-edged Roadside-Skipper,
  Pl. 43, 466
Orange-headed Roadside-Skipper,
  Pl. 43, 465
Orangetips, Pl. 9, 158-162
  Desert, Pl. 9, 27, 32, 158
  Falcate, Pl. 9, 161
  Pacific, Pl. 9, 159
  Southern Rocky Mountain, Pl. 9,
    159
  Southwestern, Pl. 9, 28, 160
  Stella, Pl. 9, 160
oreas (Polygonia progne), Pl. 29, 320
Oregon Silverspot, 25, 26, 277
oregonius (Papilio machaon), Pl. 3, 38,
  133
origenes (Polites), Pl. 41, 443
ornythion (Papilio), Pl. 4, 137
Ornythion Swallowtail, Pl. 4, 137
orseis (Phyciodes), Pl. 28, 28, 309
oslari (Amblyscirtes), Pl. 43, 460
Oslar's Roadside-Skipper, Pl. 43, 460
otho (Wallengrenia), Pl. 41, 445

ottoe (Hesperia), Pl. 41, 429
Ottoe Skipper, Pl. 41, 429
outis (Cogia), Pl. 37, 388
Outis Skipper, Pl. 37, 388

Pacific Dotted-Blue, Pls. 19-20, 239
Pacific Fritillary, Pl. 25, 284
Pacific Orangetip, Pl. 9, 159
pacuvius (Erynnis), Pl. 38, 400
Pacuvius Duskywing, Pl. 38, 400
Page, Rusty-tipped, Pl. 30,
pahaska (Hesperia), Pl. 41, 431
Pahaska Skipper, Pl. 41, 431
Painted Crescent, Pl. 28, 309
Painted Lady, Pl. 29, 325
palaemon (Carterocephalus), Pl. 40,
    414
palaeno (Colias), Pl. 11, 172
Palaeno Sulphur, Pl. 11, 172
palamedes (Papilio), Pl. 6, 143
Palamedes Swallowtail, Pl. 6, 143
Pale Crescent, Pl. 28, 310
Pale Swallowtail, Pl. 6, 140
palla (Chlosyne), Pl. 27, 298
pallescens (Euphilotes), Pl. 20, 28, 241
Pallid Dotted-Blue, Pl. 20, 28, 241
pallida (Phyciodes), Pl. 28, 310
palmerii (Apodemia), Pl. 22, 28, 263
Palmer's Metalmark, Pl. 22, 28, 263
Palos Verdes Blue, 25
palosverdesensis (Glaucopsyche lyg-
    damus), 25
Panoquina, Pl. 43, 467-469
    errans, Pl. 43, 467
    leucas, Pl. 43, 469
    ocola, Pl. 43, 468
    sylvicola, 469
Papilio, Pls. 2-6, 136-142
    aliaska (machaon), Pl. 3
    anchisiades, Pl. 5, 137
    asterias (polyxenes), Pl. 3
    astyalus , Pl. 4, 137
    bairdii (machaon), Pl. 3
    canadensis, Pl. 5, 139
    cresphontes, Pl. 4, 136
    eurymedon, Pl. 6, 140
    fordi (indra), Pl. 4
    glaucus, Pl. 5, 138
    indra, Pl. 4, 27, 135
    machaon, Pl. 3, 132
    martini (indra), Pl. 4
    minori (indra), Pl. 4
    oregonius (machaon), Pl. 3, 133
    ornythion, Pl. 4, 137
    palamedes, Pl. 6, 143
    pikei (machaon), Pl. 3

pilumnus, Pl. 6, 142
polyxenes, Pl. 3, 131
rutulus, Pl. 6, 139
thoas, Pl. 4, 136
troilus, 142
xuthus, Pl. 4, 135
zelicaon, Pl. 3, 134
Papilionidae, 125-143
Papilioninae, 129-143
Paramacera allyni, Pl. 32, 350
Paratrytone snowi, Pl. 42, 453
Parrhasius m-album, Pl. 18, 198
Parides alopius, Pl. 2, 129
Parnassians, Pl. 1, 125-129
    Clodius, Pl. 1, 126
    Eversmann's, Pl. 1, 30, 126
    Phoebus, Pl. 1, 30, 127
    Rocky Mountain, Pl. 1, 28, 128
    Sierra Nevada, Pl. 1, 28, 128
Parnassiinae, 126-129
Parnassius, Pl. 1, 126-129
    behrii, Pl. 1, 28, 128
    clodius, Pl. 1, 126
    eversmanni, Pl. 1, 30, 126
    phoebus, Pl. 1, 30, 127
    smintheus, Pl. 1, 28, 128
Patches, Pl. 26, 294-296
    Banded, Pl. 26, 295
    Bordered, Pl. 26, 295
    California, Pl. 26, 27, 294
    Crimson, Pl. 26, 296
    Definite, Pl. 26, 27, 295
    Red-spotted, 296
    Rosita, Pl. 26, 296
patrobas (Gyrocheilus), Pl. 33, 27, 362
pawnee (Hesperia leonardus), 430
Pea Blue, Pl. 19, 229
Peacocks, Pl. 30, 330
    Banded, Pl. 30, 330
    White, Pl. 30, 330
Pearl Crescent, Pl. 28, 305
Pearly-Eye, Northern, Pl. 32, 347
peckius (Polites), Pl. 41, 440
Peck's Skipper, Pl. 41, 440
pegala (Cercyonis), Pl. 32, 352
pelidne (Colias),Pl. 11, 171
Pelidne Sulphur, Pl. 11, 171
Pepper and Salt Skipper, Pl. 43, 461
perplexa (Callophrys affinis), Pl. 17
persius (Erynnis), Pl. 38, 403
Persius Duskywing, Pl. 38, 403
pertepida (Cyllopsis), Pl. 32, 348
petreus (Marpesia), Pl. 31, 341
Phaeostrymon alcestis, Pl. 16, 203
phaeton (Euphydryas), 315
phaon (Phyciodes), Pl. 28, 304

Phaon Crescent, **Pl. 28**, 304
philea (Phoebis), **Pl. 12**, 176
philenor (Battus), **Pl. 2**, 130
philetas (Pyrgus), **Pl. 39**, 408
philipi (Oeneis), 369
Philip's Arctic, **Pl. 34**, 368
philodice (Colias), **Pl. 10**, 162
Philotes sonorensis, **Pl. 19**, 235
Philotiella speciosa, **Pl. 20**, 243
phlaeas (Lycaena), **Pl. 14**, 187
Phoebis, **Pl. 12**, 175-178
   agarithe, **Pl. 13**, 176
   argante, 177
   neocypris, 178
   philea, **Pl. 12**, 176
   sennae, **Pl. 12**, 175
   statira, **Pl. 13**, 178
phoebus (Parnassius), **Pl. 1**, 30, 127
Phoebus Parnassian, **Pl. 1**, 30, 127
Pholisora, **Pl. 39**, 412
   catullus, **Pl. 39**, 412
   mejicana, **Pl. 39**, 412
Phyciodes, **Pl. 27-28**, 303-312
   anasazi (batesii), **Pl. 28**
   batesii, **Pl. 28**, 307
   cocyta, **Pl. 28**, 306
   herlani (orseis), 310
   mylitta, **Pl. 28**, 311
   pallida, **Pl. 28**, 310
   phaon, **Pl. 28**, 304
   picta, **Pl. 28**, 309
   pratensis, **Pl. 28**, 308
   orseis, **Pl. 28**, 28, 309
   texana, **Pl. 27**, 303
   tharos, **Pl. 28**, 305
   tulcis, **Pl. 28**, 303
   vesta, **Pl. 28**, 304
phyciodoides (Apodemia), 263
phylace (Amblyscirtes), **Pl. 43**, 465
phyleus (Hylephila), **Pl. 40**, 423
piasus (Glaucopsyche), **Pl. 20**, 243
picta (Phyciodes), **Pl. 28**, 309
Pieridae, 144-184
Pierinae, 145-162
Pieris, **Pl. 8**, 150-153
   angelika, **Pl. 8**, 30, 150
   marginalis, **Pl. 8**, 151
   meckyae, 150
   oleracea, **Pl. 8**, 151
   rapae, **Pl. 8, 9**, 152
pikei (Papilio machaon), **Pl. 3**
pilumnus (Papilio) , **Pl. 6**, 142
pima (Anthocharis cethura), **Pl. 9**, 158
Pine Satyr, **Pl. 32**, 350
Pine White, **Pl. 7**, 145
Pink-edged Sulphur, **Pl. 11**, 171

Pipevine Swallowtail, **Pl. 12**, 130
Piruna, **Pl. 40**, 415-416
   aea, **Pl. 40**, 416
   haferniki, **Pl. 40**, 416
   pirus, **Pl. 40**, 28, 415
   polingi, **Pl. 40**, 415
pirus (Piruna) , **Pl. 40**, 28, 415
pittacus (Atrytonopsis), **Pl. 42**, 456
Plain Longtail, **Pl. 36**, 380
Plains Skipper, **Pl. 41**, 427
Plebejus saepiolus, **Pl. 20**, 249
Plebulina emigdionis, **Pl. 20**, 28, 249
plexippus (Danaus) , **Pl. 34**, 10, 11, 369
Poanes, **Pl. 42**, 449-452
   hobomok, **Pl. 42**, 449
   melane, **Pl. 42**, 452
   taxiles, **Pl. 42**, 28, 451
   viator, 451
   wetona (hobomok), 451
   zabulon, **Pl. 42**, 450
   zizaniae (viator), 451
podarce (Agriades), **Pl. 21**, 28, 247
Poladryas minuta, **Pl. 26**, 290
polaris (Boloria), **Pl. 25**, 287
Polaris Fritillary, **Pl. 25**, 287
Poling's Giant-Skipper, **Pl. 44**, 474
Poling's Hairstreak, **Pl. 17**, 27, 204
polingi (Agathymus), **Pl. 44**, 474
polingi (Fixsenia), **Pl. 17**, 27, 204
polingi (Piruna), **Pl. 40**, 415
polios (Callophrys), **Pl. 18**, 221
Polites, **Pl. 41**, 438-445
   carus, **Pl. 41**, 440
   draco, **Pl. 41**, 442
   mardon, **Pl. 41**, 441
   mystic, **Pl. 41**, 443
   origenes, **Pl. 41**, 443
   peckius, **Pl. 41**, 440
   rhesus, **Pl. 41**, 439
   sabuleti, **Pl. 41**, 441
   sonora, **Pl. 41**, 444
   tecumseh (sabuleti), 441
   themistocles, **Pl. 41**, 442
   vibex, **Pl. 41**, 444
polixenes (Oeneis), **Pl. 34**, 368
Polixenes Arctic, **Pl. 34**, 368
polydamas (Battus), **Pl. 2**, 131
Polydamas Swallowtail, **Pl. 2**, 131
Polygonia, **Pl. 29**, 11, 316-320
   comma, **Pl. 29**, 316
   faunus, **Pl. 29**, 318
   gracilis, **Pl. 29**, 319
   hylas (faunus), 318
   interrogationis, **Pl. 29**, 316
   oreas (progne), **Pl. 29**, 320
   progne, **Pl. 29**, 319

Polygonia, (cont.)
  satyrus, **Pl. 29**, 317
  zephyrus (gracilis), **Pl. 29**, 319
Polygonus leo, **Pl. 35**, 374
Polyommatinae, 227
polyphemus, *Morpho*, **Pl. 32**, 346
Polythrix mexicana, **Pl. 35**, 376
polyxenes (Papilio), **Pl. 3**, 130
Pompeius verna, **Pl. 41**, 446
Pontia, **Pl. 7- 8**, 147-150
  beckerii, **Pl. 7**, 28, 145, 147
  callidice, 150
  chloridice, 147
  occidentalis, **Pl. 8**, 149
  protodice, **Pl. 7**, 148
  sisymbrii, **Pl. 7**, 147
  transversa (sisymbrii), 148
potrillo (Cabares), **Pl. 37**, 386
Potrillo Skipper, **Pl. 37**, 386
Powdered-Skippers, **Pl. 37**, 391
  Arizona, **Pl. 37**, 392
  Texas, **Pl. 37**, 391
pratensis (Phyciodes), **Pl. 28**, 308
prenda (Amblyscirtes tolteca), 462
prittwitzi (Adopaeoides), **Pl. 40**, 422
procne (Urbanus), **Pl. 36**, 380
progne (Polygonia), **Pl. 29**, 319
propertius (Erynnis), **Pl. 38**, 397
Propertius Duskywing, **Pl. 38**, 397
proserpina (form of *Limenitis arthemis*), 331
Proteides mercurius, 373
proterpia (Eurema), **Pl. 13**, 181
proteus (Urbanus), **Pl. 35**, 379
protodice (Pontia), **Pl. 7**, 148
pseudocellus (Autochton), **Pl. 36**, 381
Pseudocopaeodes eunus, **Pl. 40**, 424
pulverulenta (Systasea), **Pl. 37**, 391
Purple, Red-spotted, **Pl. 30**,
Purple Fritillary, 290
Purple-washed Skipper, **Pl. 43**, 469
Purplewing, **Pl. 30**, 337
  Dingy, **Pl. 30**, 337
  Florida, **Pl. 30**, 337
Purplish Copper, **Pl. 15**, 194
Pygmy-Blue, Western, **Pl. 19**, 227
pylades (Thorybes), **Pl. 36**, 383
pyracmon (Cyllopsis) , **Pl. 32**, 27, 348
Pyrginae, 373-414
Pyrgines, 373-414
Pyrgus, **Pl. 38-39**, 403-409
  adepta, 408
  albsecens, **Pl. 39**, 406
  centaureae, **Pl. 38**, 403
  communis, **Pl. 39**, 406
  oileus, **Pl. 39**, 408

  lagunae (ruralis), **Pl. 38**, 25, 404
  philetas, **Pl. 39**, 408
  ruralis, **Pl. 38**, 25, 404
  scriptura, **Pl. 39**, 405
  xanthus, **Pl. 38**, 404
pyrrhias (Lycaena), 186
Pyrrhopyge araxes, **Pl. 35**, 373
Pyrrhopyginae, 372-373
python (Atrytonopsis) , **Pl. 42**, 457
Python Skipper, **Pl. 42**, 457

quaderna (Erora), **Pl. 18**, 27, 200
Queen, **Pl. 34**, 370
Queen Alexandra's Sulphur, **Pl. 10**, 28, 165
Question Mark, **Pl. 29**, 316
quino (Euphydryas editha), 25, 26, 315
Quino Checkerspot, 25, 26, 315

rapae (Pieris), **Pl. 8**, 9, 152
rawsoni (Calephelis), **Pl. 22**, 257
Rawson's Metalmark, **Pl. 22**, 257
Reakirt's Blue, **Pl. 19**, 230
Red Admiral, **Pl. 29**, 324
Red Rim, **Pl. 31**, 338
Red Satyr, **Pl. 32**, 349
Red-banded Hairstreak, **Pl. 18**, 201
Red-bordered Satyr, **Pl. 33**, 27, 362
Reddish Alpine, **Pl. 33**, 360
Reddish Four-dotted Alpine, 360
Red-disked Alpine, **Pl. 33**, 358
Red-lined Scrub-Hairstreak, **Pl. 18**, 224
Red-spotted Hairstreak, **Pl. 18**, 199
Red-spotted Patch, 296
Red-spotted Purple, **Pl. 30**, 130
Regal Fritillary, **Pl. 23**, 273
Rekoa marius, **Pl. 18**, 202
Relict Fritillary, **Pl. 25**, 286
remingtoni (Agathymus), **Pl. 44**, 473
rhesus (Polites), **Pl. 41**, 439
Rhesus Skipper, **Pl. 41**, 439
Ridings' Satyr, **Pl. 33**, 362
ridingsii (Neominois) , **Pl. 33**, 362
Ringlets, **Pl. 32**, 350-351
  Common, **Pl. 32**, 350
  False, 350
  Hayden's, **Pl. 32**, 286, 350
Riodinidae, **Pl. 22**, 255-265
rita (Euphilotes), **Pl. 20**, 241
Rita Dotted-Blue, **Pl. 20**, 241
Roadside-Skippers, **Pl. 43**, 459-466
  Bronze, **Pl. 43**, 460
  Cassus, **Pl. 43**, 459
  Celia's, **Pl. 43**, 465
  Common, **Pl. 43**, 464
  Dotted, **Pl. 43**, 464

Elissa, **Pl. 43,** 461
Large, **Pl. 43,** 459
Nysa, **Pl. 43,** 463
Orange-edged, **Pl. 43,** 466
Orange-headed, **Pl. 43,** 465
Oslar's, **Pl. 43,** 460
Slaty, **Pl. 43,** 462
Texas, **Pl. 43,** 461
Toltec, **Pl. 43,** 462
Rockslide Checkerspot, **Pl. 27,** 301
Rocky Mountain Dotted-Blue, **Pl. 20,** 240
Rocky Mountain Duskywing, **Pl. 38,** 397
Rocky Mountain Parnassian, **Pl. 1, 28,** 127
rosita (Chlosyne), **Pl. 26,** 296
Rosita Patch, **Pl. 26,** 296
rosovi (Oeneis), **Pl. 34,** 368
Ross' Alpine, **Pl. 32,** 355
rossii (Erebia), **Pl. 32,** 355
Rounded Metalmark, **Pl. 22,** 257
Royalty, **Pl. 34,**
rubidus (Lycaena), **Pl. 14,** 192
rubricata (Megisto), **Pl. 32,** 349
Ruby-spotted Swallowtail, **Pl. 5,** 137
Ruddy Copper, **Pl. 14,** 192
Ruddy Daggerwing, **Pl. 31,** 341
ruptifasciatus (Timochares), **Pl. 37,** 393
Rural Skipper, **Pl. 42, 28,** 449
ruralis (Pyrgus), **Pl. 38, 25,** 404
Russet Skipperling, **Pl. 40, 28,** 415
Rusty-tipped Page, **Pl. 30,** 330
rutulus (Papilio), **Pl. 6,** 139

sabuleti (Polites), **Pl. 41,** 441
Sachem, **Pl. 42,** 438
saepiolus (Plebejus), **Pl. 20,** 249
saepium (Satyrium), **Pl. 16, 28,** 211
Sagebrush Checkerspot, **Pl. 27,** 299
Saltbush Sootywing, **Pl. 39,** 413
San Bruno Elfin, 25-26
San Emigdio Blue, **Pl. 20, 28,** 249
Sandhill Skipper, **Pl. 41,** 441
Sandia Hairstreak, **Pl. 17, 27,** 219
sara (Anthocharis), **Pl. 9,** 159
sassacus (Hesperia), 436
Satyr Comma, **Pl. 29,** 317
Satyrinae, 346-369
Satyrium, **Pl. 16,** 205-212
    acadica, **Pl. 16,** 206
    auretorum, **Pl. 16, 28,** 210
    behrii, **Pl. 16,** 205
    calanus, **Pl. 16,** 209
    californica, **Pl. 16,** 207
    dryope (sylvinus), 207

edwardsii, **Pl. 16,** 209
fuliginosum, **Pl. 16,** 205
liparops, **Pl. 16,** 210
saepium, **Pl. 16, 28,** 211
sylvinus, **Pl. 16,** 207
tetra, **Pl. 16,** 211
titus, **Pl. 16,** 208
Satyrodes eurydice, **Pl. 32,** 347
Satyrs, **Pl. 32,** 346-369
    Canyonland, **Pl. 32,** 348
    Henshaw's, 348
    Nabokov's, **Pl. 32, 27,** 348
    Red, **Pl. 32,** 349
    Ridings', **Pl. 33,** 362
    Swale, 32, 363
satyrus (Polygonia), **Pl. 29,** 317
Scallopwings, **Pl. 37,** 389-390
    Aztec, 390
    Golden-headed, **Pl. 37,** 389
    Hayhurst's, **Pl. 37,** 390
    Mazans, **Pl. 37** 390
Scarce Streaky-Skipper, 411
schryveri (Callophrys mossii), **Pl. 18**
Scree Alpine, **Pl. 33,** 359
scriptura (Pyrgus), **Pl. 39,** 405
scudderi (Erynnis), **Pl. 38,** 398
scudderii (Colias), **Pl. 11, 28,** 169
Scudder's Duskywing, **Pl. 38,** 398
Scudder's Sulphur, **Pl. 11, 28,** 169
selene (Boloria), **Pl. 25,** 283
sennae (Phoebis), **Pl. 12,** 175
Sentinel Arctic, **Pl. 34,** 369
serapio (Strymon), **Pl. 18,** 226
shasta (Icaricia), **Pl. 21,** 251
Shasta Blue, **Pl. 21,** 251
Sheep Skipper, **Pl. 43,** 458
sheridanii (Callophrys), **Pl. 17,** 214
Sheridan's Hairstreak, **Pl. 17,** 214
Short-tailed Skipper, **Pl. 35,** 377
Sierra Nevada Blue, **Pl. 21, 28,** 247
Sierra Nevada Parnassian, **Pl. 1, 28,** 128
Sierra Skipper, **Pl. 41, 28,** 434
Sierra Sulphur, **Pl. 11, 28,** 172
Silver-banded Hairstreak, **Pl. 15,** 198
Silver-bordered Fritillary, **Pl. 25,** 283
Silverdrops, 374

Scrub-Hairstreak, **Pl. 18,** 224-227
    Avalon, **Pl. 18, 28,** 224
    Bromeliad, **Pl. 18,** 226
    Lacey's, **Pl. 18,** 225
    Lantana, **Pl. 18,** 226
    Mallow, **Pl. 18,** 225
    Red-lined, **Pl. 18,** 224
    Tailless, **Pl. 18,** 225
    Yojoa, 225

Exadeus, 374
  Wind's, **Pl. 35**, 374
Silvered fritillaries, 271
Silverspots, 25-26, 268, 277
  Behren's, 25, 277
  Callippe, 25, 26
  Mexican, **Pl. 23**, 268
  Myrtle's, 25, 277
  Oregon, 25, 26, 277
Silver-spotted Skipper, **Pl. 35**, 374
Silvery Blue, **Pl. 20**, 245
Silvery Checkerspot, **Pl. 27**, 297
simaethis (Chlorostrymon), **Pl. 15**, 198
simius, "Amblyscirtes", **Pl. 43**, 458
Simius Roadside-Skipper, **Pl. 43**, 458
simplicius (Urbanus), **Pl. 36**, 380
Siproeta, **Pl. 30**, 330-331
  epaphus, **Pl. 30**, 330
  stelenes, **Pl. 30**, 330
Sister, California, **Pl. 30**,
sisymbrii (Pontia), **Pl. 7**, 147
siva (Callophrys gryneus), **Pl. 17**
Skinner's Cloudywing, **Pl. 36**, 383
Skipperlings, **Pl. 40**, 414-416, 420-421
  Chisos, **Pl. 40**, 415
  Edwards', **Pl. 40**, 420
  Four-spotted, **Pl. 40**, 415
  Garita, **Pl. 40**, 420
  Many-spotted, **Pl. 40**, 416
  Orange, **Pl. 40**, 421
  Russet, **Pl. 40**, 28, 415
  Southern, **Pl. 40**, 421
Skippers, **Pls. 35-44**, 8, 372-477
  Acacia, **Pl. 37**, 387
  Alkali, **Pl. 40**, 424
  Apache, **Pl. 41**, 429
  Arctic, **Pl. 40**, 414
  Arizona, **Pl. 35**, 378
  Arogos, **Pl. 42**, 446
  Banana, 418
  Brazilian, **Pl. 43**, 467
  Broad-winged, 451
  Brown-banded, **Pl. 37**, 393
  Caicus, **Pl. 37**, 388
  Carus, **Pl. 41**, 440
  Cestus, **Pl. 43**, 457
  Clouded, **Pl. 40**, 418
  Columbian, **Pl. 41**, 28, 432
  Common Branded, **Pl. 41**, 427
  Common Least, **Pl. 40**, 419
  Crossline, **Pl. 41**, 443
  Dakota, 435
  Delaware, **Pl. 42**, 447
  Desert Mottled, **Pl. 37**, 378
  Deva, **Pl. 42**, 455
  Dotted, 433

Draco, **Pl. 41**, 442
Dun, **Pl. 42**, 454
Dusted, **Pl. 42**, 454
Emorsus, **Pl. 37**, 391
Eufala, **Pl. 43**, 466
European, **Pl. 40**, 422
Faceted, **Pl. 40**, 417
Fiery, **Pl. 40**, 423
Glassy-winged, **Pl. 37**, 391
Golden-banded, **Pl. 36**, 381
Grass, 416-469
Green, **Pl. 41**, 433
Grizzled, **Pl. 38**, 403
Hammock, **Pl. 35**, 374
Hobomok, **Pl. 42**, 449
Indian, 436
Juba, **Pl. 40**, 426
Julia's, **Pl. 40**, 417
Leonard's, **Pl. 41**, 25, 430
Laguna Mountain, **Pl. 38**, 25, 404
Mardon, **Pl. 41**, 441
Mithrax, 393
Lindsey's, **Pl. 41**, 28, 434
Long-tailed, **Pl. 35**, 379
Mercurial, 373
Mimosa, **Pl. 37**, 387
Moon-marked, **Pl. 42**, 455
Morrison's, **Pl. 40**, 425
Nevada, **Pl. 41**, 437
Ocola, **Pl. 43**, 468
Olive-clouded, **Pl. 43**, 466
Ottoe, **Pl. 41**, 429
Outis, **Pl. 37**, 388
Pahaska, **Pl. 41**, 431
Pawnee Montane, **Pl. 41**, 25, 430
Peck's, **Pl. 41**, 440
Pepper and Salt, **Pl. 43**, 461
Plains, **Pl. 41**, 427
Potrillo, **Pl. 37**, 386
Purple-washed, **Pl. 43**, 469
Python, **Pl. 42**, 457
Rhesus, **Pl. 41**, 439
Rural, **Pl. 42**, 28, 448
Sandhill, **Pl. 41**, 441
Sheep, **Pl. 43**, 458
Short-tailed , **Pl. 35**, 377
Sierra, **Pl. 41**, 28, 434
Silver-spotted, **Pl. 35**, 374
Snow's, **Pl. 42**, 453
Sonoran, **Pl. 41**, 444
Sunrise, **Pl. 40**, 422
Tawny-edged, **Pl. 41**, 442
Taxiles, **Pl. 42**, 28, 451
Tropical Least, **Pl. 40**, 419
Two-spotted, **Pl. 42**, 453
Umber, **Pl. 42**, 452

Uncas, **Pl. 40**, 426
Viereck's, **Pl. 42**, 456
Violet-banded, **Pl. 43**, 469
Wandering, **Pl. 43**, 467
Western Branded, **Pl. 41**, 428
White-barred, **Pl. 42**, 456
White-patched, **Pl. 37**, 393
Wind's, **Pl. 37**, 389
Woodland, **Pl. 42**, 447
Yuma, **Pl. 42**, 449
Zabulon, **Pl. 42**, 450
Slaty Roadside-Skipper, **Pl. 43**, 462
Sleepy Duskywing, **Pl. 38**, 395
Sleepy Orange, **Pl. 13**, 183
Small Checkered-Skipper, **Pl. 39**, 405
Small Dotted-Blue, **Pl. 20**, 243
Small Wood-Nymph, **Pl. 32**, 354
smintheus (Parnassius) , **Pl. 1**, 28, 127
smithi (Euphilotes enoptes), 25
Smith's Blue, 25
Smyrna, 340
  blomfildia, **Pl. 31**, 340
  karwinskii, 340
Snout, American, **Pl. 22**, 267
Snout butterflies, 6, 266
snowi (Paratrytone), **Pl. 42**, 453
Snow's Skipper, **Pl. 42**, 453
Soapberry Hairstreak, **Pl. 16**, 203
Soldier, **Pl. 34**, 371
sonora (Polites), **Pl. 41**, 444
Sonoran Banded-Skipper, **Pl. 36**, 381
Sonoran Blue, **Pl. 19**, 235
Sonoran Hairstreak, **Pl. 18**, 200
Sonoran Marble, **Pl. 9**, 156
Sonoran Metalmark, **Pl. 22**, 261
Sonoran Skipper, **Pl. 41**, 444
sonorensis (Philotes), **Pl. 19**, 235
Sooty Hairstreak, **Pl. 16**, 205
Sootywings, **Pl. 39**, 412-414
  Common, **Pl. 39**, 412
  MacNeill's, **Pl. 39**, 414
  Mexican, **Pl. 39**, 412
  Mohave, **Pl. 39**, 412
  Saltbush, **Pl. 39**, 413
Southern Broken-Dash, **Pl. 41**, 445
Southern Cloudywing, **Pl. 36**, 384
Southern Dogface, **Pl. 12**, 173
Southern Hairstreak, **Pl. 16**, 203
Southern Rocky Mountain Orangetip,
  Pl. 9, 159
Southern Skipperling, **Pl. 40**, 421
Southwestern Orangetip, **Pl. 9**, 28, 160
spaldingi (Euphilotes), **Pl. 20**, 242
Spalding's Dotted-Blue, **Pl. 20**, 242
speciosa (Philotiella), **Pl. 20**, 243
Speyeria, **Pl. 23- 24**, 9, 11, 31, 271 -282

adiaste, **Pl. 24**, 28, 278
aphrodite, **Pl. 23**, 272
atlantis, **Pl. 24**, 279
behrensii (zerene), 25, 277
callippe, **Pl. 24**, 25, 277
carolae, 276
charlottei (cybele), 272
coronis, **Pl. 24**, 276
cybele, **Pl. 23**, 271
edwardsii, **Pl. 24**, 275
egleis, **Pl. 24**, 278
hesperis, **Pl. 24**, 28, 279
hippolyta (zerene), 25-26, 277
hydaspe, **Pl. 24**, 281
idalia, **Pl. 23**, 273
leto (cybele), **Pl. 23**, 272
luski (mormonia), 281
meadii (callippe), **Pl. 24**
mormonia, **Pl. 24**, 281
nausicaa (hesperis), 280
nokomis, **Pl. 23**, 28, 274
zerene, **Pl. 24**, 276
Spicebush Swallowtail, 130, 142
spinetorum (Callophrys), **Pl. 17**, 215
Spread-wing Skippers, 373-414
Spring Azure, **Pl. 19**, 232
Spring White, **Pl. 7**, 147
Stallingsia maculosus, **Pl. 44**, 477
Staphylus, **Pl. 37**, 389-390
  azteca, 390
  ceos, **Pl. 37**, 389
  hayhurstii, **Pl. 37**, 390
  mazans, **Pl. 37**, 390
statira (Phoebis), **Pl. 13**, 178
Statira Sulphur, **Pl. 13**, 178
stelenes (Siproeta), **Pl. 30**, 330
stella (Anthocharis), **Pl. 9**, 160
Stella Orangetip, **Pl. 9**, 160
stephensi (Agathymus), **Pl. 44**, 473
sthenele (Cercyonis), **Pl. 32**, 352
stigmaticus (Grais), **Pl. 37**, 392
Stinga morrisoni, **Pl. 40**, 425
Streaky-Skippers, **Pl. 39**, 411
  Common, **Pl. 39**, 411
  Scarce, 411
Strecker's Giant-Skipper, **Pl. 44**, 476
streckeri (Agathymus), **Pl. 44**, 476
Striped Hairstreak, **Pl. 16**, 210
Stripe-streak, Creamy, **Pl. 18**, 202
Strymon, **Pl. 18**, 223-227
  alea, **Pl. 18**, 225
  avalona, **Pl. 18**, 28, 224
  bazochii, **Pl. 18**, 226
  bebrycia, **Pl. 18**, 224
  cestri, **Pl. 18**, 225
  istapa, **Pl. 18**, 225

Strymon, (cont.)
    melinus, Pl. 18, 223
    serapio, Pl. 18, 226
    yojoa, 225
Sulphurs, Pl. 13, 13, 144, 162-184
    Apricot, 177
    Booth's, Pl. 11, 30, 168
    Canada, Pl. 11, 28, 168
    Christina, Pl. 10, 165
    Clouded, Pl. 10, 162
    Cloudless, Pl. 12, 175
    Dainty, Pl. 13, 184
    Giant, Pl. 11, 170
    Harford's, Pl. 10, 28, 166
    Hecla, Pl. 11, 167
    Johansen's, Pl. 10, 167
    Labrador, Pl. 11, 169
    Large Orange, Pl. 13, 176
    Lyside, Pl. 13, 179
    Mead's, Pl. 10, 28, 166
    Orange, Pl. 10, 163
    Orange-barred, Pl. 12, 176
    Palaeno, Pl. 11, 172
    Pelidne, Pl. 11, 171
    Pink-edged, Pl. 11, 171
    Queen Alexandra's, Pl. 10, 28, 165
    Scudder's, Pl. 11, 28, 169
    Sierra, Pl. 11, 28, 172
    Statira, Pl. 13, 178
    Tailed, 178
    Western, Pl. 10, 164
Summer Azure, Pl. 19, 233
Sunrise Skipper, Pl. 40, 422
Swale Satyr, 363
Swallowtails, Pls. 2-6, 8, 125-143
    Anise, Pl. 3, 134
    Black, Pl. 3, 130
    Broad-banded, Pl. 4, 137
    Canadian Tiger, Pl. 5, 139
    Eastern Tiger, Pl. 5, 138
    Giant, Pl. 4, 136
    Indra, Pl. 4, 27, 130, 135
    Old World, Pl. 3, 132
    Ornython, Pl. 4, 137
    Palamedes, Pl. 6, 143
    Pale, Pl. 6, 140
    Pipevine, Pl. 2, 130
    Polydamas, Pl. 2, 131
    Ruby-spotted, Pl. 5, 137
    Spicebush, 142
    Thoas, Pl. 4, 136
    Three-tailed, Pl. 6, 142
    Two-tailed, Pl. 6, 141
    Western Tiger, Pl. 6, 139
    Xuthus, Pl. 4, 135
    Zebra, Pl. 2, 131

Sylvan Hairstreak, Pl. 16, 207
sylvanoides (Ochlodes), Pl. 42, 447
sylvicola (Panoquina), 469
sylvinus (Satyrium), Pl. 16, 207
Synapte syraces, Pl. 40, 417
syraces (Synapte), Pl. 40, 417
Systasea, Pl. 37, 391-392
    pulverulenta, Pl. 37, 391
    zampa, Pl. 37, 392

Taiga Alpine, Pl. 32, 356
Tailed-Blues, Pl. 19, 231-232
    Eastern, Pl. 19, 231
    Western, Pl. 19, 232
Tailed Copper, Pl. 14, 186
Tailed Orange, Pl. 13, 181
Tailed Sulphur, Pl. 13, 178
Tailless Scrub-Hairstreak, Pl. 18, 225
tameamea (Vanessa), Pl. 29, 326
tarquinius (Feniseca), Pl. 14, 186
tatila (Eunica), Pl. 30, 337
Tawny Crescent, Pl. 28, 307
Tawny Emperor, Pl. 31, 345
Tawny-edged Skipper, Pl. 41, 442
taxiles (Poanes), Pl. 42, 28, 451
Taxiles Skipper, Pl. 42, 28, 451
taygete (Oeneis), 367
tecumseh (Polites sabuleti), 441
telemachus (Erynnis), Pl. 38, 397
terlootii (Neophasia), Pl. 7, 27, 145
tetra (Satyrium), Pl. 16, 211
Texan Crescent, Pl. 27, 303
texana (Phyciodes), Pl. 27, 303
texanae (Amblyscirtes), Pl. 43, 461
Texas Powdered-Skipper, Pl. 37, 391
Texas Roadside-Skipper, Pl. 43, 461
Texola elada, Pl. 27, 302
tharos (Phyciodes), Pl. 28, 305
theano (Erebia), Pl. 33, 358
Theano Alpine, Pl. 33, 358
Theclinae, 196
themistocles (Polites), Pl. 41, 442
theona (Thessalia), Pl. 26, 291
Theona Checkerspot, Pl. 26, 291
Thessalia, Pl. 26, 291-294
    alma (leanira), Pl. 26, 294
    cerrita (leanira), Pl. 26
    chinatiensis (fulvia), 292
    cyneas, Pl. 26, 27, 292
    fulvia, Pl. 26, 293
    leanira, Pl. 26, 293
    theona, Pl. 26, 291
Thicket Hairstreak, Pl. 17, 215
thoas (Papilio), Pl. 4, 136
Thoas Swallowtail, Pl. 4, 136
thoosa (Anthocharis), Pl. 9, 160

thornei (Callophrys), Pl. 17, 219
Thorne's Hairstreak, Pl. 17, 219
Thorybes, Pl. 36-37, 383-386
  bathyllus, Pl. 36, 384
  diversus, Pl. 36, 384
  drusius, Pl. 37, 385
  mexicanus, Pl. 37, 385
  pylades, Pl. 36, 383
thrax (Erionota), 418
Three-tailed Swallowtail, Pl. 6, 142
Thymelicus lineola, Pl. 40, 422
Tiger Mimic-Queen, 371
Timochares ruptifasciatus, Pl. 37, 393
Tiny Checkerspot, Pl. 27, 302
titania (Boloria), 290
Tithian Sailor, 337
titus (Satyrium), Pl. 16, 208
Tmolus echion, Pl. 18, 199
Toltec Roadside-Skipper, Pl. 43, 462
tolteca (Amblyscirtes), Pl. 43, 462
Tortoiseshells, Pl. 29, 320-324
  California, Pl. 29, 321
  Compton, Pl. 29, 11, 320
  Milbert's, Pl. 29, 11, 323
torus (Erionota), 418
toxeus (Achalarus), Pl. 36, 383
transversa (Pontia sisymbrii), 148
tristis (Erynnis), Pl. 38, 399
troglodyta (Anaea), Pl. 31, 342
troilus (Papilio), 142
Tropical Buckeye, Pl. 30, 329
Tropical Checkered-Skipper, Pl. 39,
  408
Tropical Leafwing, Pl. 31, 342
Tropical Least Skipper, Pl. 40, 419
True Butterflies, 4, 125
tryxus, Xenophanes, Pl. 37, 391
tulcis (Phyciodes), Pl. 27, 303
Tulcis Crescent, Pl. 27, 303
tullia (Coenonympha), Pl. 32, 350
tuolumnensis (Apodemia mormo), 260
Two-banded Checkered-Skipper, Pl. 38,
  25, 404
Two-barred Flasher, Pl. 36, 381
Two-spotted Skipper, Pl. 42, 453
Two-tailed Swallowtail, Pl. 6, 141
tyche (Colias), Pl. 11, 30, 168

uhleri (Oeneis), Pl. 33, 28, 365
Uhler's Arctic, Pl. 33, 28, 365
Umber Skipper, Pl. 42, 452
uncas (Hesperia), Pl. 40, 426
Uncas Skipper, Pl. 40, 426
Uncompahgre Fritillary, Pl. 25, 25-26,
  286
Unsilvered Fritllary, Pl. 24, 28, 278

Urbanus, Pl. 35-36, 379-381
  dorantes, Pl. 36, 379
  procne, Pl. 36, 380
  proteus, Pl. 35, 379
  simplicius, Pl. 36, 380
Ursine Giant-Skipper, Pl. 44, 476
ursus (Megathymus), Pl. 44, 476

Vacciniina optilete, Pl. 21, 245
Vaga blackburni, Pl. 21, 245
Vanessa, Pl. 29, 324-328
  annabella, Pl. 29, 327
  atalanta Pl. 29, 324
  cardui, Pl. 29, 325
  caryae, 328
  tameamea, Pl. 29, 326
  virginiensis, Pl. 29, 325
vanillae, Agraulis, Pl. 23, 268
Variable Checkerspot, Pl. 28, 31, 313
Variegated Fritillary, Pl. 23, 270
vaualbum (Nymphalis), Pl. 29, 11, 320
Veined Blue, Pl. 21, 253
verna (Pompeius), Pl. 41,
vesta (Phyciodes), Pl. 27, 304
Vesta Crescent, Pl. 27, 304
vestris (Euphyes), Pl. 42, 454
vialis (Amblyscirtes), Pl. 43, 464
viator (Poanes), 451
vibex (Polites), Pl. 41, 444
Viceroy, Pl. 30, 332
Vidler's Alpine, Pl. 32, 355
vidleri (Erebia), Pl. 32, 355
Viereck's Skipper, Pl. 42, 456
vierecki (Atrytonopsis), Pl. 42, 456
violae (Fixsenia favonius), Pl. 16
violae (Megathymus ursus), 476
Violet-banded Skipper, Pl. 43, 469
virginiensis (Vanessa), Pl. 29, 325
virgulti (Apodemia), Pl. 22, 28, 261
viridis (Hesperia), Pl. 41, 433

Waiter Daggerwing, 340
Wallengrenia, Pl. 41, 445-446
  egeremet, Pl. 41, 445
  otho, Pl. 41, 446
Wandering Skipper, Pl. 43, 467
weidemeyerii, (Limenitis), Pl. 30, 28,
  32, 333
Weidemeyer's Admiral, Pl. 30, 28, 32,
  333
West Coast Lady, Pl. 29, 327
Western Branded Skipper, Pl. 41, 428
Western Cloudywing, Pl. 36, 384
Western Green Hairstreak, Pl. 17, 213
Western Pine Elfin, Pl. 18, 223
Western Pygmy-Blue, Pl. 19, 227

Western Square-dotted Blue, Pl. 19, Pl. 20, 236
Western Sulphur, Pl. 10, 164
Western Tailed-Blue, Pl. 19, 232
Western Tiger Swallowtail, Pl. 6, 139
Western White, Pl. 8, 149
wetona (Poanes hobomok), 450
Whirlabout, Pl. 41, 444
White Admiral, 331
White Angled-Sulphur, Pl. 12, 174
White Checkered-Skipper, Pl. 39, 407
White M Hairstreak, Pl. 18, 198
White Morpho, Pl. 32, 346
White Peacock, Pl. 30, 330
White-barred Skipper, Pl. 42, 456
White-crescent Longtail, Pl. 35, 378
White-dotted Cattleheart, Pl. 2, 129
White-patched Skipper, Pl. 37, 393
Whites, Pl. 7, Pl. 8, 144-162
   Arctic, Pl. 8, 30, 150
   Becker's, Pl. 7, 28, 145, 147
   Cabbage, Pl. 8, 9, 152
   Chiricahua, Pl. 7, 27, 145
   Eurasian Peak, 150
   Florida, Pl. 7, 145, 147
   Giant, Pl. 8, 153
   Great Southern, Pl. 8, 153
   Howarth's, Pl. 8, 27, 154
   Margined, Pl. 8, 151
   Mecky's, 150
   Mustard, Pl. 8, 151
   Pine, Pl. 7, 145
   Small Bath, 147
   Spring, Pl. 7, 147
White-Skippers, Pl. 39, 409-410
   Erichson's, Pl. 39, 409
   Laviana, Pl. 39, 410
   Northern, Pl. 39, 409
White-striped Longtail, Pl. 35, 375
White-veined Arctic, Pl. 34, 366
whitneyi (Chlosyne), Pl. 27, 301
Wild Indigo Duskywing, Pl. 38, 401
williamsi (Hesperia pahaska), 431
windi (Epargyreus), Pl. 35, 374
Windia windi, Pl. 37, 389
Wind's Silverdrop, Pl. 35, 374
Wind's Skipper, Pl. 37, 389
windi (Windia), Pl. 37, 389
woodgatei (Hesperia), Pl. 41, 429
Woodland Skipper, Pl. 42, 447
Wood-nymphs, Pl. 32, 11, 352-354
   Common, Pl. 32, 352
   Great Basin, Pl. 32, 352

   Mead's, Pl. 32, 28, 353
   Small, Pl. 32, 354
wrightii (Calephelis), Pl. 22, 28, 256
Wright's Metalmark, Pl. 22, 28, 256
wyomingo (Neominois), 32, 363

xami (Callophrys), Pl. 17, 219
Xami Hairstreak, Pl. 17, 219
xanthoides (Lycaena), Pl. 14, 28, 188
xanthus (Pyrgus), Pl. 38, 404
Xenophanes tryxus, Pl. 37, 391
xuthus (Papilio), Pl. 4, 135
Xuthus Swallowtail, Pl. 4, 135

Yellow Angled-Sulphur, Pl. 12, 175
Yellows, Pl. 13, 179-182
   Barred, Pl. 13, 11, 179
   Boisduval's, Pl. 13, 180
   Dina, Pl. 13, 182
   Little, Pl. 13, 182
   Mexican, Pl. 13, 181
   Mimosa, Pl. 13, 182
yojoa (Strymon) , 225
Yojoa Scrub-Hairstreak, 225
yosemite (Hesperia colorado), 434
youngi (Erebia), Pl. 33, 359
Yucca Giant-Skipper, Pl. 44, 475
yuccae (Megathymus), Pl. 44, 475
yuma (Ocxhlodes), Pl. 42, 449
Yuma Skipper, Pl. 42, 449

zabulon (Poanes), Pl. 42, 450
Zabulon Skipper, Pl. 42, 450
zampa (Systasea), Pl. 37, 392
Zebra, Pl. 23, 11, 13, 269
Zebra Swallowtail, Pl. 2, 131
zela (Emesis), Pl. 22, 258
Zela Metalmark, Pl. 22, 258
zelicaon (Papilio), Pl. 3, 134
Zephyr, Pl. 29, 319
zephyrus (Polygonia gracilis), Pl. 29, 319
Zerene, Pl. 12, 173
   cesonia, Pl. 12, 173
   eurydice, Pl. 12, 173
Zerene Fritillary, Pl. 24, 276
zerene (Speyeria), Pl. 24, 276
zerynthia (Marpesia), 340
Zestusa dorus, Pl. 35, 377
zilpa (Chioides), Pl. 35, 376
Zilpa Longtail, Pl. 35, 376
zizaniae (Poanes viator), 451
Zizula cyna, Pl. 19, 229

THE PETERSON SERIES®

PETERSON FIELD GUIDES®

BIRDS

ADVANCED BIRDING (39) North America 53376-7
BIRDS OF BRITAIN AND EUROPE (8) 66922-7
BIRDS OF TEXAS (13) Texas and adjacent states 92138-4
BIRDS OF THE WEST INDIES (18) 67669-X
EASTERN BIRDS (1) Eastern and central North America
    91176-1
EASTERN BIRDS' NESTS (21) U.S. east of Mississippi River 48366-2
    HAWKS (35) North America 44112-9

        WESTERN BIRDS (2) North America west of 100th meridian
          and north of Mexico 91173-7
          WESTERN BIRDS' NESTS (25) U.S. west of Mississippi River 47863-4
            MEXICAN BIRDS (20) Mexico, Guatemala, Belize, El
            Salvador 48354-9
           WARBLERS (49) North America 78321-6

FISH

PACIFIC COAST FISHES (28) Gulf of Alaska to Baja California 33188-9
ATLANTIC COAST FISHES (32) North American Atlantic coast 39198-9
FRESHWATER FISHES (42) North America north of Mexico 91091-9

INSECTS

INSECTS (19) North America north of Mexico
    91170-2
BEETLES (29) North America 91089-7
EASTERN BUTTERFLIES (4) Eastern and central North
    America 90453-6
WESTERN BUTTERFLIES (33) U.S. and Canada west of 100th meridian, part of
    northern Mexico 79151-0
EASTERN MOTHS North America east of 100th meridian 36100-1

MAMMALS

MAMMALS (5) North America north of Mexico 91098-6
ANIMAL TRACKS (9) North America 91094-3

ECOLOGY

EASTERN FORESTS (37) Eastern North America 9289-5
CALIFORNIA AND PACIFIC NORTHWEST FORESTS (50) 92896-6
ROCKY MOUNTAIN AND SOUTHWEST FORESTS (51) 92897-4
VENOMOUS ANIMALS AND POISONOUS PLANTS (46) North America north of
    Mexico 35292-4

PLANTS

EDIBLE WILD PLANTS (23) Eastern and central North America 31870-X
EASTERN TREES (11) North America east of 100th meridian 90455-2
FERNS (10) Northeastern and central North America, British Isles and Western Europe 19431-8
MEDICINAL PLANTS (40) Eastern and central North America 92066-3
MUSHROOMS (34) North America 91090-0
PACIFIC STATES WILDFLOWERS (22) Washington, Oregon, California, and adjacent areas 91095-1
ROCKY MOUNTAIN WILDFLOWERS (14) Northern Arizona and New Mexico to British Columbia 18324-3
TREES AND SHRUBS (11A) Northeastern and north-central U.S. and southeastern and south-central Canada 35370-X
WESTERN TREES (44) Western U.S. and Canada 90454-4
WILDFLOWERS OF NORTHEASTERN AND NORTH-CENTRAL NORTH AMERICA (17) 91172-9
SOUTHWEST AND TEXAS WILDFLOWERS (31) 36640-2

EARTH AND SKY

GEOLOGY (48) Eastern North America 66326-1
ROCKS AND MINERALS (7) North America 91096-X
STARS AND PLANETS (15) 91099-4
ATMOSPHERE (26) 33033-5

REPTILES AND AMPHIBIANS

EASTERN REPTILES AND AMPHIBIANS (12) Eastern and central North America 90452-8
WESTERN REPTILES AND AMPHIBIANS (16) Western North America, including Baja California 38253-X

SEASHORE

SHELLS OF THE ATLANTIC (3) Atlantic and Gulf coasts and the West Indies 69779-4
PACIFIC COAST SHELLS (6) North American Pacific coast, including Hawaii and the Gulf of California 18322-7
ATLANTIC SEASHORE (24) Bay of Fundy to Cape Hatteras 31828-9
CORAL REEFS (27) Caribbean and Florida 46939-2
SOUTHEAST AND CARIBBEAN SEASHORES (36) Cape Hatteras to the Gulf Coast, Florida, and the Caribbean 46811-6

PETERSON FIRST GUIDES®

ASTRONOMY	93542-3
BIRDS	90666-0
BUTTERFLIES AND MOTHS	90665-2
CATERPILLARS	91184-2
CLOUDS AND WEATHER	90993-6
DINOSAURS	52440-7
FISHES	91179-6
INSECTS	90664-4
MAMMALS	91181-8
REPTILES AND AMPHIBIANS	62232-8
ROCKS AND MINERALS	93543-1
SEASHORES	91180-X
SHELLS	91182-6
SOLAR SYSTEM	52451-2
TREES	91183-4
URBAN WILDLIFE	93544-X
WILDFLOWERS	90667-9
FORESTS	71760-4

PETERSON FIELD GUIDE COLORING BOOKS

BIRDS	32521-8
BUTTERFLIES	34675-4
DESERTS	67086-1
DINOSAURS	49323-4
ENDANGERED WILDLIFE	57324-6
FISHES	44095-5
FORESTS	34676-2
INSECTS	67088-8
MAMMALS	44091-2
REPTILES	37704-8
SEASHORES	49324-2
SHELLS	37703-X
TROPICAL FORESTS	57321-1
WILDFLOWERS	32522-6

PETERSON NATURAL HISTORY COMPANIONS

LIVES OF NORTH AMERICAN BIRDS	77017-3

AUDIO AND VIDEO

EASTERN BIRDING BY EAR
cassettes 97523-9
CD 97524-7

WESTERN BIRDING BY EAR
cassettes 97526-3
CD 97525-5

EASTERN BIRD SONGS, Revised
cassettes 53150-0
CD 97522-0

WESTERN BIRD SONGS, Revised
cassettes 51746-X
CD 975190

BACKYARD BIRDSONG
cassettes 97527-1
CD 97528-X

MORE BIRDING BY EAR
cassettes 71260-2
CD 71259-9

WATCHING BIRDS
Beta 34418-2
VHS 34417-4

PETERSON'S MULTIMEDIA GUIDES: NORTH AMERICAN BIRDS
(CD-ROM for Windows) 73056-2

PETERSON FLASHGUIDES™

ATLANTIC COASTAL BIRDS	79286-X
PACIFIC COASTAL BIRDS	79287-8
EASTERN TRAILSIDE BIRDS	79288-6
WESTERN TRAILSIDE BIRDS	79289-4
HAWKS	79291-6
BACKYARD BIRDS	79290-8
TREES	82998-4
MUSHROOMS	82999-2
ANIMAL TRACKS	82997-6
BUTTERFLIES	82996-8
ROADSIDE WILDFLOWERS	82995-X
BIRDS OF THE MIDWEST	86733-9
WATERFOWL	86734-7
FRESHWATER FISHES	86713-4

WORLD WIDE WEB: http://www.petersononline.com

PETERSON FIELD GUIDES can be purchased at your local bookstore or by calling our toll-free number, (800) 225-3362.

When referring to title by corresponding ISBN number, preface with 0-395.